The Original Scots Colonists of Early America, 1612-1783

S The Original
Scots
Colonists
of
Early America

1612-1783

By David Dobson

REFERENCE

Genealogical Publishing Co., Inc.

Introduction

he Scottish participation in the settlement of America dates from the early seventeenth century, and from that time until the American Revolution probably around 150,000 Scots emigrated to the New World. During the seventeenth century many Scots settled within the English, Dutch and French colonies, while others attempted to establish independent Scots colonies in Nova Scotia, New Jersey, South Carolina and at Darien. After the political union of Scotland and England in 1707 the Scots had unrestricted access to the English plantations in America. Emigration expanded slowly but steadily until 1763 when a combination of factors in Scotland and in America stimulated emigration, especially from the Highlands. Although Scots could be found throughout the American colonies, from Barbados to Rupert's Land, areas such as Georgia, the Carolinas, upper New York, Nova Scotia and Jamaica had the greatest concentration of Scottish immigrants. This then was the general pattern of Scottish immigration and settlement in colonial America. Family historians, however, require quite specific data regarding their immigrant ancestors, the absence of which has presented insuperable problems for researchers of the colonial era. Nevertheless, it has been clear for some time that in archival holdings scattered throughout Great Britain, as well as in published material, especially official records, there is a wealth of information on a minority of these early Scottish emigrants.

This work is the culmination of several years of research in archives and libraries throughout Great Britain for information pertaining to these original Scottish emigrants to the American colonies. The data has been extracted from a wide miscellany of primary sources including family and estate papers, testamentary and probate records, burgh muniments, registers of sasines, registers of deeds, Sheriffs' Court records, Court of Session and High Court of Justiciary records, port books and customs registers, contemporary diaries and journals, contemporary newspapers and magazines, professional and university records, Privy Council and colonial records, records of the Episcopalian and the Presbyterian churches, monumental inscription lists, and the 1774-75 Register of Emigrants. On occasion it has been possible to enhance the basic source material with supplementary data obtained from one or more of the above sources and a few secondary sources.

The record for each individual contains a maximum of twenty-three points of information in the following order: name, date of birth or baptism, place of birth, occupation, place of education, cause of banishment (where applicable), residence, names of parents, date of emigration and whether voluntarily shipped ("sh") or involuntarily transported ("tr"), port of embarkation, destination, name of ship, place of arrival, date of arrival, place of settlement, name of spouse, names of children, date of death, place of death, where buried, probate record, and source citation. Every known or potential source of information has been investigated, with the notable exception of the Loyalist Claims—a major project in its own right and one which should be tackled on an independent basis. Thus, from primary source material in Great Britain, this book attempts to bring together, in concise form, data pertaining to Scots who settled in America prior to 1783. In order to achieve a greater degree of completeness—as far as British records will allow—it has been necessary to include material published in earlier books (my own as well as others); however, this data now appears, in most cases, in an enhanced form. Wherever possible, for example, parish registers were consulted to establish date and place of birth as well as names of parents; similarly, university and apprenticeship records were examined; and in a number of cases it was possible to identify the ship and the destination of the emigrant. With these refinements, plus the fact that the entries have been fully documented, this work is as near to being complete as British sources will allow.

Note to the reader:

With regard to the text, the reader is asked to note that on a number of occasions, with a view to aesthetics, commas were omitted from the entries, specifically in references to the emigrant's place of residence and the names of his children. Typically, the place name consists of up to three elements—the name of the house or farm, the name of the village or parish, and the name of the county or shire (many of which can still be identified through the use of highly detailed maps, such as Ordnance Survey maps). With regard to the names of the children, except where a hyphen is used, each forename signifies a distinct child.

Note also that owing to a program fault, there are several duplicate entries in the work. The text is unaffected, however.

David Dobson
St. Andrews, Scotland
Martinmas, 1988

Acknowledgement

I should like to acknowledge Dr. John Henderson of the University of St. Andrews for his advice and assistance in the preparation of this book.

ADDENDA

Brown, Gustavus, born 1744, ed. Edinburgh University, M.D. 1770 Emigrated from Scotland to Maryland 1770. Died in 1801. (SA). From *Scottish Settlers in North America, Volume II.*

Brown, Gustavus, Dr. Gustavus Brown of Mainside, residing in Maryland, eldest son and heir of Richard Brown, Charles Co., Maryland, landowner in Roxburghshire, appointed James Home, Writer to the Signet, as his attorney in Scotland. Subscribed in Leonardtown, St. Mary's Co., Maryland, on 6 May 1771. Witnesses Gabriel Wood, merchant, and his assistant Archibald Henderson, both in Leonardtown, Md. (RD3.253.804). From *Scottish Settlers in North America, Volume VI.*

Sources and Abbreviations

Record Sources and Repositories

ABR	Aberdeen Burgh Records
APB	Aberdeen Propinquity Books
BritMus	British Museum, London
BRO	Bristol Record Office
CLRO	City of London Record Office
EBR	Edinburgh Burgh Records
LRO	Liverpool Record Office
NLS	National Library of Scotland, Edinburgh
PCC	Prerogative Court of Canterbury (PRO)
PerthMAGA	Perth Museum and Art Gallery Archives
PRO	Public Record Office, London
RAWL	Rawlinson Manuscripts, Bodleian Library, Oxford
SRA	Strathclyde Regional Archives, Glasgow
SRO	Scottish Record Office, Edinburgh
TRA	Tayside Regional Archives, Dundee
WCF	Worshipful Company of Fishmongers, London

Newspapers and Journals

AJ	Aberdeen Journal (Aberdeen, 1748-)
AnHib	Analecta Hibernica (Dublin, 1930-)
CAR	Caribbeana (London, 1909-)
EA	Edinburgh Advertiser (Edinburgh, 1764-)
GC	Glasgow Courier (Glasgow, 1791-)
GM	Gentleman's Magazine (London, 1731-)
NNQ	Northern Notes and Queries (Edinburgh, 1886-)
SCHR	Scottish Church History Records (Edinburgh, 1926-)

SHR	Scottish Historical Review (Edinburgh, 1904-)
SM	Scots Magazine (Edinburgh, 1739-)
SNQ	Scottish Notes and Queries (Aberdeen, 1887-)
TGI	Transactions of the Gaelic Society of Inverness (Inverness, 1872-)
UJA	Ulster Journal of Archaeology (Belfast, 1853-)

Published Transcripts of Official Records

AOB	Annals of Banff, by W. Cramond. Aberdeen, 1843.
BGBG	The Burgesses and Guild Brethren of Glasgow, by J. R. Anderson. Edinburgh, 1935.
CalHOpp	Calendar of Home Office Papers. London, 1878. *Series*
CBK	The Court Book of Kirkintilloch 1658-1694, by G. S. Pryde. Edinburgh, 1963.
CPD	Consistorial Processes and Decreets, by F. J. Grant. Edinburgh, 1909.
CTB	Calendar of Treasury Books. London, 1904. *Series*
CTP	Calendar of Treasury Papers. London, 1868. *Series*
DBR	Records of the Burgh of Dunbarton 1627-1746. Dunbarton, 1860.
DP	The Darien Papers, by J. H. Burton. Edinburgh, 1849.
DSP	Darien Shipping Papers 1696-1707, by G. P. Insh. Edinburgh, 1924.
EBE	Extracts from the Records of the Burgh of Edinburgh, by M. Wood. Edinburgh, 1938.
ECJ	Erskine of Carnock's Journal 1683-1687, by W. McLeod. Edinburgh, 1893.
EMR	Register of Marriages in the City of Edinburgh, by F. J. Grant. Edinburgh, 1922.
ETR	Extracts from Edinburgh Tolbooth Records 1657-1686, by J. A. Fairley. Edinburgh, 1923.
F	Fasti Ecclesiae Scoticanae, by J. Scott. Edinburgh, 1915.
FAB	Fasti Aberdonensis 1494-1854, by C. Innes. Aberdeen, 1854.
FAS	The Faculty of Advocates in Scotland 1532-1943, by F. J. Grant. Edinburgh, 1944.

FPA	The Fulham Papers in the Lambeth Palace Library, by W. W. Manross. Oxford, 1965.
GR	Extracts from the Records of the Burgh of Glasgow, by R. Renwick. Glasgow, 1908.
HBRS	Hudson Bay Record Society. London, 1938. *Series*
JAB.1	Jacobites of Aberdeen and Banff in the Rising of 1715, by A. Tayler and H. Tayler. Edinburgh, 1934.
JAB.2	Jacobites of Aberdeen and Banff in the '45, by A. Tayler and H. Tayler. Aberdeen, 1928.
JRA	Justiciary Records of Argyll, by J. Imrie. Edinburgh, 1969.
KCA	Officers and Graduates of King's College, by P. J. Anderson. Aberdeen, 1893.
LJ	Letters and Journals 1663-1887, by J. G. Dunlop. London, 1953.
MAGU	Matriculation Albums of Glasgow University 1727-1858, by W. I. Addison. Glasgow, 1913.
MCA	Records of Marischal College, by P. J. Anderson. Aberdeen, 1898.
MR	The Muster Roll of Prince Charles Edward Stuart's Army 1745-1746, by A. Livingstone. Aberdeen, 1984.
OR	The Forfarshire or Lord Ogilvie's Regiment, by A. Mackintosh. Forfar, 1914.
P	Prisoners of the '45, by B. Seton. Edinburgh, 1929.
PC	Register of the Privy Council of Scotland. 3rd Series. Edinburgh, 1908-.
PCCol	Calendar of the Privy Council, Colonial. London, 1908. *Series*
RBS	Extracts from the Burgh of Stirling 1667-1752, by R. Renwick. Glasgow, 1889.
REB	Roll of Edinburgh Burgesses, by C. B. Watson. Edinburgh, 1930.
RSC	Records of the Scots Colleges. Aberdeen, 1906.
RSM	Records of the Synod of Moray, by W. Cramond. Elgin, 1906.
SAA	Society of Advocates in Aberdeen, by J. Henderson. Aberdeen, 1912.

SGB	Extracts from the Guildry Records of Stirling 1592-1846, by W. B. Cook. Stirling, 1916.
SPC	Calendar of State Papers, America and the West Indies. London, 1880. *Series*
SPG	Calendar of Letters of the Society for the Propagation of the Gospel 1721-1793. London, 1972.
UPC	Annals and Statistics of the United Presbyterian Church, by W. MacKelvie. Edinburgh, 1873.
VI	Viri Illustrates Universitas Aberdonensis. Aberdeen, 1923.

Secondary Sources

AP	American Presbyterianism, by C. A. Briggs. Edinburgh, 1885.
BLG	Burke's Landed Gentry. London, 1939.
CC	Clan Campbell. Edinburgh, 1912.
EMA	A List of Emigrant Ministers to America 1690-1811, by G. Fothergill. London, 1904.
HAF	History of Ayrshire and its Families, by J. Paterson. Ayr, 1847.
Insh	Scottish Colonial Schemes, by G. P. Insh. Glasgow, 1922.
MdArch	Maryland Archives. *Series*
MIBWI	Monumental Inscriptions in the British West Indies, by J. H. Lawrence-Archer. London, 1875.
MWI	Monumental Inscriptions of the British West Indies, by V. L. Oliver. Dorchester, 1927.
NC	Nisbet of Carfin, by J. A. Nisbet. London, 1916.
NEHGS	New England Historical and Genealogical Register. Scots Charitable Society Papers.
OD	Scots in the Old Dominion, by C. Haws. Edinburgh, 1980.
RTI	Rutherford of that Ilk, by T. C. Hood. Edinburgh, 1884.
SA	Scotus Americanus, by W. R. Brock. Edinburgh, 1982.
SCM	Spalding Club Miscellany, by J. Stuart. Aberdeen, 1852.
SO	The Scots Overseas, by G. Donaldson. London, 1966.

The Original Scots Colonists of Early America, 1612-1783

1. Abbott, Frederick, Jacobite, tr. 29 June 1716, fr. Liverpool to Jamaica or Va, in *Elizabeth & Anne*. (SPC.1716.310)
2. Abercrombie, Bobby, b. 1753, servant, res. Dysart Fife, sh. May 1775, fr. Leith to Philadelphia, in *Friendship*. (PRO.T47.12)
3. Abercromby, John, Jacobite, res. Skeith Banffshire, tr. 29 June 1716, fr. Liverpool to Jamaica or Va, in *Elizabeth & Anne*. (SPC.1716.310)
4. Abernethy, Janet, thief, res. Foveran Aberdeenshire, pts. William Abernethy, tr. 1772, in *Betsy*, arr. James River Va 29 Apr 1772. (SRO.JC27.10.3)
5. Adair, John, b. 1730, laborer, res. Beak, sh. 31 May 1775, fr. Stranraer to N.Y., in *Jackie*, m. Janet McNillie, ch. Janet Jean Agnes John. (PRO.T47.12)
6. Adair, Margaret, whore, res. Edinburgh, tr. 19 Mar 1695. (SRO.PC2.25.216)
7. Adair, Patrick, b. 1724, farmer, res. Glenluce Wigtonshire, sh. May 1774, fr. Stranraer to N.Y., in *Gale*, ch. Agnes Jean William. (PRO.T47.12)
8. Adam, Agnes, robber & murderer, tr. Mar 1774. (SRO.RH2.4.255)
9. Adam, Jean, b. 1752, spinner, res. Paisley Renfrewshire, sh. Feb 1774, fr. Greenock to N.Y., in *Commerce*. (PRO.T47.12)
10. Adam, John, Covenanter, res. Ormidale Argyll, tr. 7 Aug 1685, fr. Leith to Jamaica. (PC.2.329)
11. Adam, Patrick, b. 13 Sept 1722, Arbroath Angus, res. Arbroath, pts. John Adam & Christian Alexander, d. pre 1761 Kingston Jamaica, Edin pr1761 CC8.8.118
12. Adam, Robert, b. 1729, Jacobite, res. Stirling, tr. 5 May 1747, fr. Liverpool to Leeward Islands, in *Veteran*, arr. Martinique June 1747. (PRO.SP36.102)
13. Adam, Robert, b. 1759, res. Stirling, sh. May 1775, fr. Greenock to N.Y., in *Monimia*. (PRO.T47.12)
14. Adam, William, foremastman, res. Bridgeness Aberdeen, pts. James Adam, sh. 14 July 1698, fr. Leith to Darien, in *Caledonia*, Edin pr1707 CC8.8.83
15. Adam, William, merchant, Covenanter, res. Culross Fife, tr. 1670. (PC.3.204)

1

16. Adams, James, clerk, res. Aberdeen, d. pre 1711 N.C., PCC pr1711
17. Adamson, David, b. 1661, sh. Mar 1684, fr. London to Jamaica, in
    Providence. (CLRO\AIA)
18. Adamson, John, b. 1705, res. Largo Fife, sh. Aug 1723, fr. London to
    Md. (CLRO\AIA)
19. Adamson, Thomas, b. 1754, tanner, sh. July 1775, fr. Bristol to Md, in
    Fortune. (PRO.T47.9\11)
20. Adamson, William, smith, Covenanter, res. Williamston, tr. Sept 1668,
    fr. Leith to Va, in *Convertin.* (PC.2.534)
21. Adamson, William, sh. c1684, fr. London to Barbados. (WCF6679)
22. Addison, John, b. 1748, clergyman, res. Glasgow, sh. May 1774, fr.
    Greenock to N.Y., in *George.* (PRO.T47.12)
23. Aedie, Patrick, horsethief, tr. May 1755. (SM.17.265)
24. Aggie, Catherine, b. 1759, spinner, res. Paisley Renfrewshire, sh. Feb
    1774, fr. Greenock to N.Y., in *Commerce.* (PRO.T47.12)
25. Aggie, Janet, b. 1739, spinner, res. Paisley Renfrewshire, sh. Feb 1774,
    fr. Greenock to N.Y., in *Commerce.* (PRO.T47.12)
26. Aggie, Margaret, b. 1738, spinner, res. Paisley Renfrewshire, sh. Feb
    1774, fr. Greenock to N.Y., in *Commerce.* (PRO.T47.12)
27. Agnew, Agnes, b. 1755, spinner, res. Paisley Renfrewshire, sh. Feb
    1774, fr. Greenock to N.Y., in *Commerce.* (PRO.T47.12)
28. Agnew, Alexander, b. 1734, husbandman, res. Galloway, sh. May 1774,
    fr. Stranraer to N.Y., in *Gale,* m. Janet .., ch. Forbes William.
    (PRO.T47.12)
29. Agnew, Andrew, clergyman, sh. 1706, to Jamaica, sett. Va. (EMA10)
30. Agnew, George, overseer, sh. 1699, to Darien, Edin pr1707 CC8.8.84
31. Agnew, John, res. Sheuchan Wigtonshire, sh. 1774, sett. Newfoundland.
    (PCCol.5.368)
32. Agnew, John, b. 1727, Wigtonshire, clergyman, sh. 1753, sett. Suffolk
    Va, d. 1812 N.B. (EMA10)
33. Agnew, William, d. 7 Feb 1779 Mornsedue Grenada. (SM.41.286)
34. Aiken, Alexander, sailor, res. Bo'ness West Lothian, pts. ... Aiken &
    Susanna Hardy, sh. 18 Aug 1699, fr. Clyde to Darien, in *Rising
    Sun,* Edin pr1707 CC8.8.83
35. Aiken, Charles, b. 1753, clerk, res. Colvend Kirkcudbrightshire, sh. May
    1775, fr. Dumfries to P.E.I., in *Lovely Nelly.* (PRO.T47.12)
36. Aiken, John, sh. pre 1773, sett. Pincader Mulinghouse Newcastle Del.
    (SRO.CS.Dal.ICS\136)
37. Aikin, James, b. 1733, millwright, sh. June 1774, fr. Whitehaven to
    N.Y., in *Golden Rule.* (PRO.T47.9\11)
38. Aikman, Alexander, b. 23 June 1755, Bo'ness West Lothian, printer &
    publisher, res. Bo'ness, pts. Andrew Aikman & Ann Hunter, sh.
    1771, sett. S.C. & Jamaica, d. 6 July 1838 Prospect Pen St
    Andrews Jamaica. (GM.NS10.556)

2

39. Aikman, Francis, merchant, res. Edinburgh, sh. pre 1669, sett. Va. (EBR.3.63)
40. Ainsley, John, b. 1728, sailcloth weaver, sh. Feb 1774, fr. London to Md, in *Mermaid*. (PRO.T47.9\11)
41. Ainsley, Thomas, b. 1701, carpenter, res. Jedburgh Roxburghshire, sh. Aug 1720, fr. London to Md. (CLRO\AIA)
42. Ainslie, Thomas, customs collector, res. Roxburghshire(?), sh. pre 1722, sett. Boston Mass & Quebec, m. Elizabeth Martin. (SRO.RD4.275.447\RD4.239.11)
43. Ainslie, Walter, soldier, thief, tr. June 1766. (SM.28.388)
44. Aird, James, carpenter, res. Ayrshire, sh. pre 1777, sett. Orangefield Plantation North Side Bay of Pensacola WFla. (PRO.CO5.613.536)
45. Airey, Thomas, clergyman, sh. 1726, sett. Dorchester Co Md, ch. Louisa. (EMA10)
46. Aitcheson, Samuel, merchant, sh. pre 1773, sett. Northampton Va. (SRA.T76.6.3)
47. Aitchison, John, merchant, pts. John Aitchison of Rosalloch, sett. Grenada, d. 25 Aug 1770 New London Ct. (SM.32.630)
48. Aitchison, Peter, physician & surgeon, res. Glasgow, pts. Walter Aitchison of Rosehalloch, d. 1752 St Elizabeth's Jamaica, Edin pr1758 CC8.8.117
49. Aitken, Alexander, b. 1757, weaver, res. Paisley Renfrewshire, sh. Feb 1774, fr. Greenock to N.Y., in *Commerce*. (PRO.T47.12)
50. Aitken, James, clergyman, res. Islay Argyll, pts. John Aitken of Rashiehill sr, d. pre 1783 America, Edin pr1783 CC8.8.126
51. Aitken, John, b. 1725, laborer, res. Caerlaverock Dumfries-shire, sh. May 1775, fr. Dumfries to P.E.I., in *Lovely Nelly*, m. Margaret Lowden, ch. James Gordon Margaret Agnes. (PRO.T47.12)
52. Aitken, Robert, b. 1756, nailer, res. Paisley Renfrewshire, sh. Feb 1774, fr. Greenock to N.Y., in *Commerce*. (PRO.T47.12)
53. Aitken, Samuel, b. 1750, farmer, res. Inverness, sh. May 1774, fr. Greenock to N.Y., in *George*. (PRO.T47.12)
54. Aitken, Thomas, pickpocket, res. Glasgow, pts. James Aitken, tr. 1766. (SRO.JC27.10.3)
55. Aitken, William, b. 1727, impost waiter, Jacobite, res. Edinburgh, tr. 24 Feb 1747, fr. Liverpool to Va, in *Gildart*, arr. Port North Potomac Md 5 Aug 1747. (PRO.T1.328)(MR50)
56. Aitken, William, b. 1744, farmer, res. Perth, sh. May 1774, fr. Greenock to N.Y., in *Commerce*. (PRO.T47.12)
57. Aitkenhead, William, d. pre 1768 St Thomas in the Vale Jamaica, Edin pr1768 CC8.8.121
58. Aiton, John, Covenanter, res. Heuchhead Avondale Lanarkshire, tr. 1684. (PC.10.258)

3

59. Aldcorn, Adam, clergyman, Covenanter, tr. 12 Dec 1678, fr. Leith to
    West Indies, in *St Michael of Scarborough*. (PC.6.76)
60. Alexander, Andrew, sh. 1684, to East N.J., sett. Perth Amboy N.J.
    (Insh273)
61. Alexander, Boyd, storekeeper, pts. Claud Alexander of Newton, sh. pre
    1775, sett. Baltimore. (SRA.CFI)
62. Alexander, Cosmos, painter, pts. John Alexander, sh. pre 1772, sett. N.E.
    (SRO.RD4.212.837)
63. Alexander, David, tr. 1775, fr. Greenock to Port Hampton Va, in
    Rainbow, arr. 3 May 1775. (SRO.JC27.10.3)
64. Alexander, David, res. Glasgow, d. pre 1757 Md, PCC pr1757
65. Alexander, David, b. 1756, merchant, res. Maybole Ayrshire, sh. July
    1775, fr. Greenock to Jamaica, in *Isabella*. (PRO.T47.12)
66. Alexander, Duncan, Covenanter, res. Argyll, tr. 7 Aug 1685, fr. Leith to
    Jamaica. (PC.11.329)
67. Alexander, George, Covenanter, res. Newburgh Fife, tr. 12 Dec 1678, fr.
    Leith to West Indies, in *St Michael of Scarborough*. (PC.6.76)
68. Alexander, Hugh, b. 1729, carpenter, res. Galloway, sh. May 1774, fr.
    Stranraer to N.Y., in *Gale*, m. Agnes .., ch. John Ann Hugh
    Alexander James Robert. (PRO.T47.12)
69. Alexander, Janet, b. 1751, servant, res. Egilsay Orkney Islands, sh. Sept
    1774, fr. Kirkwall to Savannah Ga, in *Marlborough*, sett.
    Richmond Co Ga. (PRO.T47.12)
70. Alexander, John, Covenanter, res. Mauchline Ayrshire, tr. June 1684, fr.
    Port Glasgow, in *Pelican*. (PC.9.208)
71. Alexander, John, merchant, pts. Robert Alexander of Blackhouse, d. 8 Oct
    1699 Carolina, Edin pr1707 CC8.8.83
72. Alexander, Robert, b. 1749, house carpenter, res. Dailly Ayrshire, sh.
    May 1774, fr. Stranraer to N.Y., in *Gale*. (PRO.T47.12)
73. Alexander, William, b. 1750, shoemaker, res. Dunfermline Fife, sh. May
    1775, fr. Greenock to N.Y. or Ga, in *Christy*. (PRO.T47.12)
74. Alison, Colin, tr. Aug 1685, fr. Leith to East N.J., in *Henry & Francis*.
    (PC.11.155)
75. Alison, Patrick, Covenanter, res. Carnwath Lanarkshire, tr. Aug 1684, fr.
    Leith to Carolina. (PC.9.28)(ETR271)
76. Allan, Adam, Covenanter, res. Dalmellington Ayrshire, tr. June 1684, fr.
    Port Glasgow, in *Pelican*. (PC.9.208)
77. Allan, Alexander, b. 1723, shoemaker, Jacobite, res. Edinburgh, tr. 24
    Feb 1747. (P.2.6)(MR69)
78. Allan, Charles, b. 1728, cooper's servant, Jacobite, res. Leith Midlothian,
    pts. Harry Allan, tr. 31 Mar 1747, fr. Tilbury to Jamaica, in *St
    George or Carteret*, arr. Jamaica 1747.
    (P.2.8)(MR50)(PRO.CO137.58)

79. Allan, David, mason & bricklayer, res. Berwickshire(?), sett. St
Catherine's Middlesex Co Jamaica, m. Katherine Drummond, ch.
David, d. 1783 Jamaica. (SRO.RD2.235.215)
80. Allan, David, b. 9 Aug 1718, New Machar Aberdeenshire, res. New
Machar, pts. Peter Allan, sh. 1749, to Antigua, d. June 1759 St
John Antigua. (APB.3.200)
81. Allan, Helen, whore & thief, res. Edinburgh, tr. 28 Nov 1704, fr. Leith
to Md. (SRO.PC2.28.307)
82. Allan, James, b. 1747, laborer, res. Greenock Renfrewshire, sh. Aug
1774, fr. Greenock to Philadelphia, in *Magdalene*. (PRO.T47.12)
83. Allan, John, Covenanter, res. Cumnock Ayrshire, tr. 7 Aug 1685, fr.
Leith to Jamaica. (PC.11.330)
84. Allan, John, journeyman wright, housebreaker & thief, res. Pollockshaws
Glasgow, tr. Jan 1774. (SM.36.174)
85. Allan, John, Jacobite, res. Manchester, tr. 1747. (MR196)
86. Allan, Margaret, b. 1745, res. Strathspey, sh. May 1774, fr. Greenock to
N.Y., in *George*. (PRO.T47.12)
87. Allan, Robert, thief, tr. July 1749. (SRO.HCR.I.79)
88. Allan, Robert, merchant, res. Alyth Perthshire, sh. pre 1759, sett. Chaple
Plantation Barbados, ch. Henry. (SRO.RS35.20.197)
89. Allason, David, b. 16 May 1736, Govan Glasgow, storekeeper, res.
Gorbals, pts. Zachariah Allason & Isabel Hall, sh. 1760, sett.
Rappahannock & Winchester Va, d. post 1815. (SRA.CFI)
90. Allason, John, res. Glasgow, pts. John Allason, sh. pre 1774, sett. Va.
(SRO.CS.GMB235)
91. Allason, Robert, b. 19 Nov 1721, Glasgow, merchant, res. Gorbals, pts.
Zachariah Allason & Janet Grahame, sh. 1761, sett. Va.
(SRA.CFI)
92. Allason, William, merchant, res. Gorbals Glasgow, pts. Zachariah
Allason & Isabel Hall, sh. 1737, sett. Falmouth Va, m. Anne
Hume. (SRA.CFI)
93. Allason, William, b. 16 Mar 1712, Glasgow, surgeon, res. Glasgow, pts.
John Allason & Mary Maxwell, sett. Port Royal Va, d. 1768 Va.
(SRA.B10.15.7345)(SRO.SH.12.10.1770)
94. Allen, David, seaman, res. Fisherrow Musselburgh Midlothian, sh. 14
July 1698, fr. Leith to Darien, in *Unicorn*, ch. Bessie, Edin pr1707
CC8.8.83
95. Allen, David, b. 1751, wright, res. Breadalbane Perthshire, sh. June 1775,
fr. Greenock to N.Y., in *Commerce*. (PRO.T47.12)
96. Allen, George, res. Queensferry West Lothian, d. pre 1673 Va, PCC
pr1673
97. Allen, James, Jacobite, tr. 24 May 1716, fr. Liverpool to Md, in
Friendship, arr. Md Aug 1716. (SPC.1716.311)(HM387)

5

98. Allen, James, b. 1687, town caddy or laborer, Jacobite, tr. 24 Feb 1747, fr. Liverpool to Va, in *Johnson*, arr. Port Oxford Md 5 Aug 1747. (P.2.8)(MR210)(PRO.T1.328)
99. Allen, James, b. 1709, res. Glasgow, sh. July 1728, fr. London to Pa. (CLRO\AIA)
100. Allen, Margaret, b. pre 1682, res. Leith Midlothian, pts. James Carlisle & Margaret Allen, sett. Elizabethtown N.J., m. Eliphet Frazie. (SRO.EQR.15.336)
101. Allen, Robert, merchant, sh. pre 1755, sett. Barbados. (SRO.SH.15.2.1755)
102. Allerdyce, George, b. 1752, carpenter, sh. Sept 1774, fr. London to Jamaica, in *Standlinch*. (PRO.T47.9\11)
103. Allison, James, b. 1758, weaver, res. Paisley Renfrewshire, sh. Feb 1774, fr. Greenock to N.Y., in *Commerce*. (PRO.T47.12)
104. Alston, Mary, thief & vagabond, res. Roxburghshire, tr. May 1732. (SRO.JC.12.4) (alias 7125)
105. Alton, John, b. 1725, servant, Jacobite, tr. 24 Feb 1747. (P.2.10)
106. Anderson, Agnes, tr. Feb 1667, to Barbados or Va. (PC.2.263)
107. Anderson, Alexander, sailor, sh. 18 Aug 1699, fr. Clyde to Darien, m. Jean Edgar, Edin pr1707 CC8.8.83
108. Anderson, Alexander, forger, res. Burntbrae Aberdeenshire, tr. Sept 1754. (SM.16.449)
109. Anderson, Alexander, forger, res. Old Deer Aberdeenshire, tr. Feb 1768. (AJ1051)
110. Anderson, Alexander, servant, Covenanter, res. Kirkliston West Lothian, tr. 12 Dec 1678, fr. Leith to West Indies, in *St Michael of Scarborough*. (PC.6.76)
111. Anderson, Alexander, Jacobite, res. Upper Dalachie Banffshire, tr. 21 Sept 1748. (P.2.10)
112. Anderson, Andrew, merchant, res. Lanark, sh. pre 1757. (SRO.RS42.16.343)
113. Anderson, Andrew, merchant, sett. Grenades & Antigua, d. pre 1784, Edin pr1784 CC8.8.126
114. Anderson, Andrew, merchant, res. Edinburgh, sh. pre 1755, sett. Jappahannock Va, d. 1760 Va. (SRO.RD4.198.558)
115. Anderson, Andrew, b. 1664, laborer, res. Selkirk, sh. 5 Aug 1685, fr. London to Md. (CLRO\AIA)
116. Anderson, Catherine, thief, res. Glasston Galloway, pts. John Logan, tr. 1762. (EBR.BC.3.110) (alias 3305)
117. Anderson, Charles, b. 1752, gentleman, sh. Feb 1774, fr. London to N.Y., in *Earl Dunmore*. (PRO.T47.9\11)
118. Anderson, David, sailor, housebreaker, res. Leith Midlothian, tr. Apr 1774. (AJ1374)

6

119. Anderson, David, wright, ch. Margaret, d. pre 1777 Antigua.
(SRO.SH.20.11.1777)
120. Anderson, George, clergyman, res. St Andrews Fife, pts. Rev John
Anderson, sh. 1698, to Darien, Edin pr1707 CC8.8.83
121. Anderson, George, b. 1727, res. Canongate Edinburgh, sh. Aug 1745.
(SRO.B59.29.82)
122. Anderson, Harry, res. Glasgow, pts. Harry Anderson, sh. 1665, to
Barbados. (GR67)
123. Anderson, Hugh, gentleman, res. Bridgecastle Cromarty, sh. 1737, fr.
Inverness to Ga, in *Two Brothers.*
(SPC.43.226)(PRO.CO5.670.287)
124. Anderson, James, physician edu. Marischal Col Aberdeen 1737, sett.
Jamaica. (MCA.2.118)
125. Anderson, James, merchant, res. Glasgow, sh. pre 1772, sett. Brokesbank
Rappahannock Va. (SRO.RD3.231.708)
126. Anderson, James, Covenanter, tr. Sept 1668, fr. Leith to Va, in
Convertin. (PC.2.534)
127. Anderson, James, Jacobite, res. Bellie Morayshire, tr. Apr 1747.
(P.2.12)(MR94)
128. Anderson, James, servant, res. Boghead Aberdeenshire, tr. Sept 1775.
(AJ1446) (alias 5437)
129. Anderson, James, laborer, res. Lanarkshire, sh. Nov 1684, fr. London to
Jamaica. (CLRO\AIA)
130. Anderson, James, clergyman edu. Glasgow Uni 1703, sh. 1710, fr.
Glasgow to Philadelphia, sett. Newcastle Del. (AP164)
131. Anderson, James, b. 17 Nov 1678, clergyman edu. Glasgow Uni, sh.
1709, sett. N.Y. Del Va, m. Suit Garland, d. 16 July 1740.
(F.7.662)(SA102)
132. Anderson, James, b. 1722, tailor, Jacobite, res. Ross-shire, tr. 5 May
1747, fr. Liverpool to Leeward Islands, in *Veteran*, arr. Martinique
June 1747. (P.2.12)(PRO.SP36.102)
133. Anderson, James, b. 11 June 1743, Drainie Morayshire, housewright, res.
Elgin Morayshire, pts. Robert Anderson, d. Mar 1775 Jamaica,
Edin pr1776 CC8.8.123
134. Anderson, James, b. 1748, wright, res. Alloa Clackmannanshire, sh. May
1775, fr. Greenock to N.Y. or Ga, in *Christy.* (PRO.T47.12)
135. Anderson, James, b. 1753, wright, res. Glasgow, sh. Aug 1774, fr.
Greenock to Philadelphia, in *Magdalene.* (PRO.T47.12)
136. Anderson, Janet, res. Ormiston, pts. James Anderson, tr. June 1754, fr.
Leith. (SRO.JC3.29.574)
137. Anderson, Janet, b. 1757, res. Alloa Clackmannanshire, sh. May 1775,
fr. Greenock to N.Y. or Ga, in *Christy.* (PRO.T47.12)
138. Anderson, John, clergyman, sh. 1717, to Leeward Islands. (EMA11)

7

139. Anderson, John, merchant, res. Glasgow, sh. pre 1748, sett. Jamaica. (SRO.SC36.63.2)
140. Anderson, John, clergyman, d. pre 1771 Antigua. (SRO.RD4.209.146)
141. Anderson, John, maltman's servant, Covenanter, res. Glasgow, tr. 12 Dec 1678, fr. Leith to West Indies, in *St Michael of Scarborough*. (PC.6.76)
142. Anderson, John, Covenanter, tr. 11 Oct 1681, fr. Leith to West Indies. (PC.7.219)
143. Anderson, John, Covenanter, res. Lanark, tr. 17 Dec 1685, fr. Leith to Barbados, in *John & Nicholas*. (PC.11.384)(ETR389)
144. Anderson, John, physician edu. Marischal Col Aberdeen, res. Boharine Banffshire, pts. William Anderson & Lillias Strathdee, sh. 1700, fr. London to Barbados, d. 1718. (APB.2.139)
145. Anderson, John, clergyman, d. 1734 St Kitts. (SRO.RD3.251.201)
146. Anderson, John, b. 1703, scholar, res. Glasgow, sh. Oct 1722, fr. London to Va. (CLRO\AIA)
147. Anderson, John, b. 1729, gardener, Jacobite, res. Aberdeenshire, tr. 8 May 1747, to Antigua. (P.2.12)
148. Anderson, John, b. 1729, gardener, Jacobite, tr. 5 May 1747, fr. Liverpool to Leeward Islands, in *Veteran*, arr. Martinique June 1747. (P.2.12)(JAB.2.419)(MR69)(PRO.SP36.102)
149. Anderson, John, b. 1750, wright, res. Alloa Clackmannanshire, sh. May 1775, fr. Greenock to N.Y. or Ga, in *Christy*. (PRO.T47.12)
150. Anderson, Lauchlan, res. Fife, pts. Mrs Margaret Moncrieff or Anderson, sett. Detroit, d. pre 1785, PCC pr1785
151. Anderson, Margaret, whore, res. Edinburgh, tr. 19 Mar 1695. (SRO.PC2.25.216)
152. Anderson, Margaret, thief, res. Mains of Allardyce Arbuthnott Kincardineshire, tr. Sept 1770, m. John Copland. (AJ1183)
153. Anderson, Margaret, b. 1754, res. Alloa Clackmannanshire, sh. May 1775, fr. Greenock to N.Y. or Ga, in *Christy*. (PRO.T47.12)
154. Anderson, Mary, b. 1749, sh. Feb 1774, fr. London to Ga. (PRO.T47.9\11)
155. Anderson, Nathaniel, b. 1758, clerk, res. Alloa Clackmannanshire, sh. July 1775, fr. Greenock to Jamaica, in *Isabella*. (PRO.T47.12)
156. Anderson, Robert, Jacobite, tr. 29 June 1716, fr. Liverpool to Jamaica or Va, in *Elizabeth & Anne*, arr. Va. (SPC.1716.310)(CTB31.208)(VSP.1.186)
157. Anderson, Robert, b. 1749, farmer, res. Stirling, sh. May 1774, fr. Greenock to N.Y., in *Matty*. (PRO.T47.12)
158. Anderson, Robert, b. 1758, clerk, res. Edinburgh, sh. Nov 1774, fr. London to Antigua, in *Warnees*. (PRO.T47.9\11)

159. Anderson, Thomas, servant, Jacobite, res. Balmaduthie Ross-shire, tr. 31
     Mar 1747, fr. Tilbury to Jamaica, in *St George or Carteret*, arr.
     Jamaica 1747. (P.2.12)(MR80)(PRO.CO137.58)
160. Anderson, Thomas, naval architect, sh. pre 1769, to Antigua.
     (SRO.SH.28.7.1769)
161. Anderson, Walter, weaver, thief, res. Portsoy Banffshire, tr. Sept 1770.
     (AJ1184)
162. Anderson, Walter, b. 1746, laborer, res. Kippen Stirlingshire, sh. May
     1775, fr. Greenock to N.Y., in *Lilly*. (PRO.T47.12)
163. Anderson, William, cordiner, res. Portsburgh Edinburgh, sh. 14 July
     1698, fr. Leith to Darien, in *St Andrew*, Edin pr1707 CC8.8.83
164. Anderson, William, sailor, res. Arbroath Angus, sh. 14 July 1698, fr.
     Leith to Darien, in *St Andrew*, Edin pr1707 CC8.8.83
165. Anderson, William, bosun, res. Linktown of Abbotshall Fife, sh. 14 July
     1698, fr. Leith to Darien, in *Endeavour*, Edin pr1707 CC8.8.83
166. Anderson, William, brewer, res. Leith Midlothian, sh. 14 July 1698, fr.
     Leith to Darien, in *Endeavour*, Edin pr1708 CC8.8.84
167. Anderson, William, b. 1700, res. Orkney Islands, sh. Aug 1718, fr.
     London to Md. (CLRO\AIA)
168. Anderson, William, b. 1741, husbandman, sh. Jan 1775, fr. London to
     Md, in *Diana*. (PRO.T47.9\11)
169. Anderson, William, b. 1752, servant, res. Anass , sh. July 1775, fr.
     Stornaway to Philadelphia, in *Clementina*. (PRO.T47.12)
170. Andrew, David, thief, tr. 1653, fr. Ayr to Barbados. (SRO.JC27.10.3)
171. Andrew, David, b. 1751, ship's carpenter, res. Ayrshire, sh. Mar 1775, fr.
     Glasgow to Quebec, in *Friendship*. (PRO.T47.12)
172. Andrew, James, sailor, res. Edinburgh, sh. 14 July 1698, fr. Leith to
     Darien, in *St Andrew*, Edin pr1707 CC8.8.83
173. Andrew, William, Covenanter, res. Linlithgow West Lothian, tr. Aug
     1684, fr. Leith to Carolina. (PC.8.526)
174. Andrews, John, clergyman, sh. 1749, sett. King William Co & Fairfax
     Co Va. (SNQ.I.153)(EMA11)
175. Andrews, William, clergyman, sh. 1700, sett. Mohawk Castle N.Y., d.
     1728. (SCHR.14.143)
176. Angus, Andrew, sh. pre 1754, sett. St Kitts. (SRO.SH.18.12.1754)
177. Angus, Anne, res. Dunbartonshire, sh. pre 1775, sett. Princeton N.J., m.
     James Finlay. (SRO.RS .7.172)
178. Angus, Gilbert, sailor, res. Burntisland Fife, sh. 14 July 1698, fr. Leith
     to Darien, in *Unicorn*, Edin pr1707 CC8.8.83
179. Angus, John, foremastman, sh. 14 July 1698, fr. Leith to Darien, in
     Unicorn, Edin pr1707 CC8.8.83
180. Angus, John, b. 1744, farmer, res. Forfar Angus, sh. Apr 1775, fr.
     Greenock to N.Y., in *Lilly*. (PRO.T47.12)

181. Angus, Joseph, merchant, res. Glasgow, sh. pre 1763, sett. St Kitts. (SRA.B10.12.2)
182. Angus, Mary, spirits thief, res. Torryburn Fife, tr. 1772. (SM.34.579)
183. Angus, Mary, infanticide, res. Glasgow, tr. 1753. (SM.15.468)
184. Angus, William, Covenanter, res. Abercorn West Lothian, tr. 12 Dec 1678, fr. Leith to West Indies, in *St Michael of Scarborough*. (PC.6.76)
185. Angus, William, b. 1750, laborer, res. Galloway, sh. May 1774, fr. Stranraer to N.Y., in *Gale*. (PRO.T47.12)
186. Annan, Alexander, b. 1728, butcher, Jacobite, res. Aberdeen, tr. 24 Feb 1747, fr. Liverpool to Va, in *Gildart*, arr. Port North Potomac Md 5 Aug 1747. (P.2.14)(JAB.2.419)(MR210)(PRO.T1.328)
187. Annan, Robert, clergyman, res. Ceres Fife, sh. 1761, sett. Philadelphia. (AP338)(UPC654)
188. Annand, Isabel, thief, tr. July 1763. (AJ809)
189. Annand, Walter, tr. Aug 1685, fr. Leith to East N.J., in *Henry & Francis*. (PC.11.137)
190. Anton, Jean, infanticide, res. Perthshire, tr. May 1728. (SRO.JC27.10.3)
191. Arbuckle, John, Covenanter, tr. 17 Dec 1685, fr. Leith to Barbados, in *John & Nicholas*. (PC.11.386)(ETR389)
192. Arbuckle, William, merchant, sh. 24 Apr 1683, fr. Port Glasgow to N.E., in *Good Hope of Preston*. (SRO.E72.19.8)
193. Arbuthnott, Alexander, merchant, res. Inverbervie Kincardineshire, sh. pre 1720, sett. Philadelphia. (SRO.B51.12.1)
194. Arbuthnott, James, clergyman, sh. 1705, to Leeward Islands. (EMA11)
195. Arbuthnott, John, b. 1684, tailor, Jacobite, res. Aberdeen, tr. 22 Apr 1747, fr. Liverpool to Va, in *Johnson*, arr. Port North Potomac Md 5 Aug 1747. (P.2.14)(MR69)(JAB.2.419)(PRO.T1.328)
196. Arbuthnott, Sir John, Jacobite, res. Paris, pts. Robert Arbuthnott, tr. 1747. (P.2.14)
197. Arbuthnott, Thomas, surgeon, res. Peterhead Aberdeenshire, d. 10 Nov 1742 Va, Edin pr1745 CC8.8.109
198. Archibald, John, sailor, res. Burntisland Fife, sh. 14 July 1698, fr. Leith to Darien, in *Endeavour*, Edin pr1707 CC8.8.83
199. Armand, Isabel, thief, res. Aberdeenshire, tr. June 1763. (SRO.RH2.4.255)
200. Armor, James, merchant, sh. Sept 1685, fr. Leith to N.J., in *Henry & Francis*. (SRO.E72.15.32)
201. Armstrong, Christian, b. 1765, res. Nethermiln Glencairn Dumfries-shire, sh. May 1775, fr. Dumfries to P.E.I., in *Lovely Nelly*. (PRO.T47.12)
202. Armstrong, David, b. 1760, laborer, res. Nethermiln Glencairn Dumfries-shire, sh. May 1775, fr. Dumfries to P.E.I., in *Lovely Nelly*. (PRO.T47.12)

10

203. Armstrong, Edward, drummer, thief, tr. 1772, fr. Port Glasgow to Md, in *Matty*, arr. Port Oxford Md 16 May 1772. (SRO.JC27.10.3)
204. Armstrong, John, writer, res. Edinburgh, sh. pre 1778, sett. Jamaica. (SRO.CS.GMB56)
205. Armstrong, Richard, laborer, horsethief, res. Falstain Northumberland, tr. Oct 1769. (SM.31.500)
206. Armstrong, Robert, res. Jedburgh Roxburghshire, tr. 17 Apr 1666, fr. Leith to Barbados. (ETR106) (alias 2698)
207. Armstrong, Thomas, b. 1758, laborer, res. Nethermiln Glencairn Dumfries-shire, sh. May 1775, fr. Dumfries to P.E.I., in *Lovely Nelly*. (PRO.T47.12)
208. Arnot, Andrew, clergyman, sh. 1753, to Pa. (AP278)
209. Arnot, James, sh. 29 Nov 1773, fr. Greenock to Jamaica, in *Mary of Glasgow*. (SRO.CE60.1.7)
210. Arnot, John, Covenanter, res. Balgedie Milnathort Kinross-shire, tr. 12 Dec 1678, fr. Leith to West Indies, in *St Michael of Scarborough*. (PC.6.76)
211. Arnott, David, Jacobite, tr. 29 June 1716, fr. Liverpool to Jamaica or Va, in *Elizabeth & Anne*, arr. Va. (SPC.1716.310)(CTB31.208)(VSP.1.186)
212. Arnott, David, b. 1755, smith, sh. Sept 1775, fr. Newcastle to Ga, in *Georgia Packet*, sett. Friendsborough Ga. (PRO.T47.9\11)
213. Arthur, Helen, b. 1753, servant, res. Edinburgh, sh. May 1775, fr. Leith to Philadelphia, in *Friendship*. (PRO.T47.12)
214. Arthur, Isabel, b. 1748, servant, res. Edinburgh, sh. May 1775, fr. Leith to Philadelphia, in *Friendship*. (PRO.T47.12)
215. Asher, John, b. 1745, gardener, res. Edinburgh, sh. Dec 1773, fr. London to Va, in *Elizabeth*. (PRO.T47.9\11)
216. Asking, Joseph, Jacobite, tr. 30 Mar 1716, fr. Liverpool to Antigua, in *Scipio*. (SPC.1716.310)(CTB31.204)
217. Astine, Isobel, b. 1757, servant, res. Nairn, sh. July 1775, fr. Stornaway to Philadelphia, in *Clementina*. (PRO.T47.12)
218. Atcheson, William, b. 1746, laborer, res. Dunbarton, sh. Apr 1775, fr. Greenock to N.Y., in *Lilly*. (PRO.T47.12)
219. Auchenleck, Joseph, Jacobite, tr. 30 Mar 1716, fr. Liverpool to Antigua, in *Scipio*. (SPC.1716.310)(CTB31.204)
220. Auchmuty, Robert, Admiralty judge, d. 1750 N.E. (SM.7.349)
221. Auld, John, b. 1733, drummerboy, Jacobite, res. Falkirk Stirlingshire, tr. 1747. (P.2.16)(MR43)
222. Austie, Robert, thief, res. Forres Morayshire, tr. 1771, fr. Port Glasgow to Md, in *Crawford*, arr. Port Oxford Md 23 July 1771. (SRO.JC27.10.3)(AJ1167)
223. Austin, Adam, merchant, res. Kilspindie Perthshire, pts. Joseph Austin, sh. pre 1782, sett. Charleston S.C. (SRO.SH.3.7.1782)

11

224. Austin, William, surgeon's mate, res. Kilspindie Perthshire, pts. Joseph Austin, d. 1764 Albany N.Y., PCC pr1764
225. Aven, Archibald, clergyman, res. Banff, sh. pre 1774, sett. Norfolk Va. (SRO.CS.GMB354)
226. Ayre, William, Jacobite, tr. 24 May 1716, fr. Liverpool to Md, in *Friendship*, arr. Md Aug 1716. (SPC.1716.311)(HM387)
227. Ayston, James, Jacobite, tr. 29 June 1716, fr. Liverpool to Jamaica or Va, in *Elizabeth & Anne*. (SPC.1716.310)(CTB31.208)
228. Babie, Kenneth, b. 1761, servant, res. Stornaway Isle of Lewis, sh. May 1774, fr. Stornaway to Philadelphia, in *Friendship*. (PRO.T47.12)
229. Badenoch, George, cattlethief, res. Moulin Perthshire, tr. Feb 1772. (SRO.HCR.I.107) (alias 3624)
230. Bagby, John, Jacobite, tr. 21 Apr 1716, fr. Liverpool to S.C., in *Wakefield*. (CTB31.205)
231. Baillie, Andrew, clergyman edu. Edinburgh Uni 1695, sh. 1709, to Barbados. (EMA12)
232. Baillie, Anne, b. 1750, servant, res. Inverness, sh. July 1775, fr. Stornaway to Philadelphia, in *Clementina*. (PRO.T47.12)
233. Baillie, Ewan, res. Inverness, sh. pre 1775, sett. St Vincent. (SRO.RS38.13.261\293)
234. Baillie, Geills, whore & thief, res. Edinburgh, tr. 28 Nov 1704, fr. Leith to Md. (SRO.PC2.28.307)
235. Baillie, George, b. 1703, bonnetmaker, Jacobite, res. Dundee Angus, tr. 24 Feb 1747, fr. Liverpool to Va, in *Gildart*, arr. Port North Potomac Md 5 Aug 1747. (P.2.18)(PRO.T1.328)
236. Baillie, Gilbert, gypsy, tr. 21 Oct 1682, fr. Greenock to N.Y. (ETR221)
237. Baillie, Hugh, gypsy, tr. 21 Oct 1682, fr. Greenock to N.Y. (ETR221)
238. Baillie, James, tr. Jan 1773. (AJ1306)
239. Baillie, James, schoolmaster, forger, res. Dundee Angus, tr. Feb 1766, fr. Glasgow. (AJ915\946)
240. Baillie, James, murderer, tr. Feb 1774. (SRO.RH2.4.255)
241. Baillie, James jr, gypsy, tr. 21 Oct 1682, fr. Greenock to N.Y. (ETR221)
242. Baillie, Jean, tr. 1772, fr. Glasgow to Va, in *Brilliant*, arr. Port Hampton Va 7 Oct 1772. (SRO.JC27.10.3) (alias 3637)
243. Baillie, John, gypsy, tr. 21 Oct 1682, fr. Greenock to N.Y. (ETR221)
244. Baillie, John, surgeon, res. Peebles-shire, pts. Alexander Baillie of Callends, sh. 18 Aug 1699, fr. Clyde to Darien, in *Rising Sun*, d. Darien, Edin pr1707 CC8.8.83
245. Baillie, John, merchant, res. Edinburgh, pts. Michael Baillie, sh. 1733, to Ga. (PRO.CO5.670.106)
246. Baillie, Margaret, gypsy, tr. 21 Oct 1682, fr. Greenock to N.Y. (ETR221)
247. Baillie, Robert, gypsy & thief, res. Dumfries-shire, tr. May 1739. (SRO.JC12.5)

248. Baillie, Thomas, gentleman, res. Orkney Islands, sh. 1735, to Ga. (PRO.CO5.670.219)
249. Baillie, William, soldier, res. Backbie, d. Darien 1699, Edin pr1707 CC8.8.83
250. Baillie, William, soldier, res. Inverness-shire, sh. 1756, PCC pr1759. (SRO.SC29.55.10.27)
251. Bain, Alexander, b. 1747, sawyer, sh. Jan 1774, fr. London to Md, in *Peggy*. (PRO.T47.9\11)
252. Bain, Andrew, b. 1751, farmer, res. Strathspey, sh. May 1774, fr. Greenock to N.Y., in *George*. (PRO.T47.12)
253. Bain, Donald, servant, housebreaker & thief, res. Borrowstoun Caithness, tr. 1772, fr. Glasgow. (AJ1292\8) (alias 4463)
254. Bain, Donald, Jacobite, res. Corrimony Glen Urquhart Inverness-shire, tr. 1747, fr. Tilbury. (P.2.18)
255. Bain, Duncan, b. 1717, farmer, Jacobite, res. Glastollaigh Ross-shire, tr. 31 Mar 1747, fr. London to Jamaica, in *St George or Carteret*, arr. Jamaica 1747. (P.2.17)(MR80)(PRO.CO137.58)
256. Bain, George, b. 21 June 1722, Kemnay Aberdeenshire, laborer, Jacobite, res. Aberdeenshire, pts. Alexander Bain, tr. 5 May 1747, fr. Liverpool to Leeward Islands, in *Veteran*, arr. Martinique June 1747. (P.2.20)(JAB.2.419)(PRO.SP36.102)
257. Bain, Isobel, b. 1757, res. Strathspey, sh. May 1774, fr. Greenock to N.Y., in *George*. (PRO.T47.12)
258. Bain, James, b. 1742, farmer, res. Strathspey, sh. May 1774, fr. Greenock to N.Y., in *George*, m. Christian .., ch. Ann William Alexander Isobel. (PRO.T47.12)
259. Bain, John, thief, res. Shurrive Caithnesss, tr. June 1767. (AJ1018) (alias 4986)
260. Bain, John, Jacobite, res. Corrimony Glen Urquhart Inverness-shire, tr. 1747, fr. Tilbury. (P.2.20)
261. Bain, Kenneth, b. 1723, servant, Jacobite, res. Ross-shire, tr. 31 Mar 1747, fr. London to Jamaica, in *St George or Carteret*, arr. Jamaica 1747. (P.2.20)(MR80)(PRO.CO137.58)
262. Bain, Margaret, b. 1738, servant, res. Stornaway Isle of Lewis, sh. Nov 1774, fr. Stornaway to N.Y., in *Peace & Plenty*. (PRO.T47.12)
263. Bain, Matthew, b. 1749, wright, res. Glasgow, sh. May 1774, fr. Greenock to N.Y., in *Matty*. (PRO.T47.12)
264. Bain, Robert, b. 1745, wright, res. Stirling, sh. May 1775, fr. Greenock to N.Y., in *Monimia*. (PRO.T47.12)
265. Bain, William, sheep stealer, res. Elgin Morayshire, tr. 1752. (SM.14.461)
266. Bain, William, sailor, res. Abbotshall Fife, pts. John Bain, sh. 18 Aug 1699, fr. Clyde to Darien, in *Rising Sun*, Edin pr1707 CC8.8.83

13

267. Bain, William, Jacobite, tr. 24 May 1716, fr. Liverpool to Md, in
     Friendship. (SPC.1716.311)
268. Bain, William, b. 1737, shopkeeper, res. Wick Caithness, sh. Apr 1774,
     to Wilmington N.C., in *Bachelor of Leith*. (PRO.T47.12)
269. Bain, William, b. 1749, weaver, res. Wick Caithness, sh. Sept 1775, fr.
     Kirkwall to Savannah Ga, in *Marlborough*, sett. Richmond Co Ga.
     (PRO.T47.12)
270. Baine, John, Jacobite, tr. 21 Apr 1716, fr. Liverpool to S.C., in
     Wakefield. (SPC.1716.309)(CTB31.205)
271. Baine, Lauchlan, physician, sh. pre 1697, sett. Barbados. (EBR.4.217)
272. Baird, Eliza, b. 1754, spinner, res. Paisley Renfrewshire, sh. Feb 1774,
     fr. Greenock to N.Y., in *Commerce*. (PRO.T47.12)
273. Baird, James, Covenanter, res. Calderwater Lanarkshire, tr. Aug 1685, fr.
     Leith to Jamaica. (PC.11.330)
274. Baird, James, physician, pts. Dr Baird, sh. pre 1717, sett. Jamaica.
     (SRA.TPM.115.68)
275. Baird, James, merchant, sh. pre 1772, sett. Va. (SRA.T.MJ.79)
276. Baird, James, b. 1731, res. Banff, sh. Aug 1749, fr. London to Jamaica.
     (CLRO\AIA)
277. Baird, Robert, merchant, sh. pre 1689, sett. Surinam.
     (SRO.RH1.2.772\3)
278. Baird, Thomas, thief, tr. Mar 1774. (AJ1367)
279. Baird, William, sailor, d. 24 Nov 1698 Darien. (NLS.RY2b8\19)
280. Baird, William, b. 6 June 1729, St Nicholas Aberdeen, wool merchant &
     silk dyer, Jacobite, res. Aberdeen, pts. William Baird & Janet
     Brown, tr. 24 Feb 1747, fr. Liverpool to Va, in *Gildart*, arr. Port
     North Potomac Md 5 Aug 1747.
     (P.2.20)(JAB.2.129)(MR219)(PRO.T1.328)
281. Baird, William, b. 1753, laborer, res. Linlithgow West Lothian, sh. Apr
     1775, fr. Greenock to N.Y., in *Lilly*. (PRO.T47.12)
282. Bald, William, b. 1745, wright, res. Glasgow, sh. May 1775, fr.
     Greenock to N.Y., in *Monimia*. (PRO.T47.12)
283. Baldie, .., sh. 29 Nov 1773, fr. Greenock to Jamaica, in *Mary of
     Glasgow*. (SRO.CE60.1.7)
284. Balfour, Alexander, Covenanter, res. Fife, tr. June 1684. (PC.8.516)
285. Balfour, David, sailor, housebreaker, res. Leith Midlothian, tr. Apr 1774.
     (AJ1374)
286. Balfour, Henry, soldier, sh. pre 1765, sett. N.Y. (PCCol.4.818)
287. Balfour, James, Covenanter, res. Fife, tr. June, fr. 1684. (PC.8.516)
288. Balfour, James, res. Wick Caithness, pts. Andrew Balfour, sh. pre 1743,
     sett. Charles City Va. (SRO.RS21.2.341\2)
289. Balfour, James, b. 15 Aug 1731, Banchory Tiernan Kincardineshire,
     clergyman edu. Marischal Col Aberdeen 1756, res. Banchory, pts.

14

Alexander Balfour, sh. 1764, sett. Trinity Bay Newfoundland. (EMA12)(FPA.21.299)

290. Balfour, Janet, b. 1757, servant, res. Edinburgh, sh. May 1775, fr. Leith to Philadelphia, in *Friendship*. (PRO.T47.12)

291. Balfour, John, merchant, res. Glasgow, sett. Black River Jamaica, d. pre 1750 Jamaica, Edin pr1750 CC8.8.113

292. Balfour, John, merchant & planter, pts. Andrew Balfour of Braidwood, sett. Peedee River S.C., m. Mary Ann Gray, ch. Isabella, d. 15 Nov 1781 S.C., Edin pr1783 CC8.8.126

293. Balfour, William, foremastman, res. Fife, sh. 14 July 1698, fr. Leith to Darien, in *Caledonia*, Edin pr1707 CC8.8.83

294. Balfour, William, clergyman edu. Marischal Col Aberdeen 1730, sh. 1738, sett. Va. (EMA12)

295. Balfour, William, d. pre 1686 Va, PCC pr1686

296. Ballantine, Thomas, b. 1758, weaver, res. Dundee Angus, sh. May 1775, fr. Leith to Philadelphia, in *Friendship*. (PRO.T47.12)

297. Ballantyne, John, seaman, res. Leith Midlothian, sh. 14 July 1698, fr. Leith to Darien, in *St Andrew*, Edin pr1707 CC8.8.83

298. Ballantyne, Joseph, Jacobite, tr. 30 Mar 1716, fr. Liverpool to Antigua, in *Scipio*. (CTB31.204)

299. Ballentyne, George, sailor, pts. James Ballentyne of Kellie & Margaret Stewart, sh. 18 Aug 1699, fr. Clyde to Darien, in *Rising Sun*, Edin pr1708 CC8.8.84

300. Ballintyne, William, Jacobite, tr. 30 Mar 1716, fr. Liverpool to Antigua, in *Scipio*. (SPC.1716.310)

301. Ballon, Angello, sailor, sh. 14 July 1698, fr. Leith to Darien, in *Unicorn*, Edin pr1707 CC8.8.83

302. Balmaine, Alexander, b. 1740, Edinburgh, clergyman edu. St Andrews & Edinburgh Unis 1757-60, sh. 1772, sett. Copley Va, d. 1820 Fredericksburg Va. (EMA12)(FPA.310)

303. Balnaves, Robert, steward's mate, sh. 14 July 1698, fr. Leith to Darien, in *Caledonia*, Edin pr1707 CC8.8.83

304. Balneavis, William, clergyman edu. Marischal Col Aberdeen 1688, sh. 1712, to Antigua. (EMA12)

305. Banks, Joseph, b. 1701, carpenter, res. Edinburgh, sh. Jan 1721, fr. London to Jamaica. (CLRO\AIA)

306. Bannatyne, George, res. Craigmuir, tr. Dec 1684. (PC.10.77)

307. Bannatyne, John, Covenanter, res. Craigmuir, tr. Dec 1684. (PC.10.77)

308. Bannatyne, Thomas, res. Edinburgh, sh. pre 1684, sett. Charlton Island Hudson Bay. (SRO.RH15.14.41)

309. Bannatyne, William, sailor, res. Canongate Edinburgh, pts. Captain John Bannatyne & Elizabeth Trotter, sh. 14 July 1698, fr. Leith to Darien, in *Caledonia*, Edin pr1708 CC8.8.84

310. Bannerman, Mark, Jacobite, tr. 26 June 1716, fr. Liverpool to St Kitts, in *Hockenhill*. (CTB31.209)
311. Baptie, John, steward, sh. 14 July 1698, fr. Leith to Darien, in *Unicorn*, Edin pr1707 CC8.8.83
312. Baptista, Joannes, sailor, sh. 14 July 1698, fr. Leith to Darien, in *Unicorn*, Edin pr1707 CC8.8.83
313. Barclay, Alexander, soldier, robber, tr. Sept 1758. (AJ557)
314. Barclay, Alexander, customs controller, d. Jan 1770 Philadelphia. (SM.33.109)
315. Barclay, David, Covenanter, res. Courquhally, tr. 12 Dec 1678, fr. Leith to West Indies, in *St Michael of Scarborough*. (PC.6.76)
316. Barclay, David, merchant, sh. 6 Aug 1683, fr. Leith to N.J., in *Exchange of Stockton*. (SRO>E72.15.26)
317. Barclay, George, sailor, res. Inverkeithing Fife, pts. Alexander Barclay, sh. 1698, to Darien, in *Olive Branch*, Edin pr1707 CC8.8.83
318. Barclay, Hugh, steward's mate, sh. 14 July 1698, fr. Leith to Darien, in *St Andrew*, d. 1699 Darien, Edin pr1707 CC8.8.83
319. Barclay, Hugh, sailor, d. 5 Nov 1698 Darien. (NLS.RY2b8\19)
320. Barclay, James, merchant, sett. Jamaica, d. pre 1750. (SRO.SH.15.11.1750)
321. Barclay, James, b. 1750, farmer, res. Stewarton Ayrshire, sh. May 1775, fr. Greenock to N.Y., in *Christy*. (PRO.T47.12)
322. Barclay, Janet, rioter, res. Dundee Angus, tr. June 1773, m. William Craighead. (SRO.B59.26.11.16.18)
323. Barclay, John, b. 1659, res. Stonehaven Kincardineshire, pts. David Barclay of Urie & Katherine Gordon, sh. 1684, sett. Plainfields Perth Amboy N.J., m. Catherine .., ch. John, d. 1731. (Insh264)
324. Barclay, Patrick, merchant, res. Edinburgh, pts. Andrew Barclay & Helen Lyon, sh. pre 1745, to Va. (SRO.SH.24.8.1745)
325. Barclay, Robert, b. 1751, farmer, res. Stirling, sh. May 1774, fr. Greenock to N.Y., in *Matty*. (PRO.T47.12)
326. Barclay, Thomas, b. 1664, Collairney Castle Fife, clergyman edu. St Andrews Uni 1688, sh. 1707, sett. St Peter's Albany N.Y., m. Anne Dorothea Drauyer, ch. Thomas Henry Andrew John, d. 1734 Albany. (EMA12)(BLG2547)(SCHR.14.144)
327. Barclay, Thomas, b. 1746, farmer, res. Stewarton Ayrshire, sh. May 1775, fr. Greenock to N.Y., in *Christy*. (PRO.T47.12)
328. Barclay, William, apprentice barber, res. Huntly Aberdeenshire, tr. Mar 1770. (AJ1157)
329. Barclay, William, sailor, res. Edinburgh, sh. 18 Aug 1699, fr. Clyde to Darien, in *Rising Sun*, Edin pr1707 CC8.8.83
330. Barclay, William, clergyman, sh. 1703, to N.E. (EMA12)
331. Barnet, John, servant, rapist, res. Muirfold Aberdeenshire, tr. Sept 1764. (AJ872)

16

332. Barnett, Thomas, Jacobite, tr. 21 Apr 1716, fr. Liverpool to S.C., in *Wakefield*. (SPC.1716.309)(CTB31.205)
333. Baron, Robert, clergyman, sh. 1700, to Bermuda, sett. Md. (EMA13)
334. Barr, Agnes, b. 1752, spinner, res. Paisley Renfrewshire, sh. Feb 1774, fr. Greenock to N.Y., in *Commerce*. (PRO.T47.12)
335. Barr, Andrew, b. 1755, gardener, res. Dalkeith Midlothian, sh. May 1775, fr. Leith to Philadelphia, in *Friendship*. (PRO.T47.12)
336. Barron, Janet, thief, res. Aberdeenshire, tr. 1753. (SM.15.468)
337. Barron, Robert, tailor, Jacobite, res. Gartmore Perthshire, tr. 1747. (P.3.88) (alias 3777)
338. Barron, William, planter, d. 17 Dec 1698 Darien. (NLS.RY2b8\19)
339. Barry, Thomas, Jacobite, tr. 28 July 1716, fr. Liverpool to Va, in *Godspeed*, arr. Md Oct 1716. (SPC.1716.310)(CTB31.209)(HM389)
340. Barry, William, Jacobite, tr. 21 Apr 1716, fr. Liverpool to S.C., in *Wakefield*. (SPC.1716.309)(CTB31.205)
341. Barton, Lewis, Jacobite, res. Lancashire, tr. 1747. (P.2.29)(MR196)
342. Bartram, Alexander, merchant, res. Biggar Lanarkshire, pts. George Bartram, sh. pre 1777, sett. Philadelphia. (SRO.RS42.20.426)
343. Bartram, Christian, seaman, res. Burntisland Fife, sh. 14 July 1698, fr. Leith to Darien, in *St Andrew*, Edin pr1707 CC8.8.83
344. Bartram, James, brazier, res. Biggar Lanarkshire, sh. pre 1777, sett. St George's Grenada. (SRO.RS42.20.426)
345. Bathgate, William, writer, res. Edinburgh, sh. 3 Sept 1736, to Jamaica. (SRO.RH9.17.316)
346. Baxter, Agnes, infanticide, res. Cardean Airlie Angus, pts. William Baxter, tr. 1760. (SM.22.501)
347. Baxter, Alexander, b. 1741, butcher, res. Glasgow, sh. Feb 1774, fr. Greenock to N.Y., in *Commerce*. (PRO.T47.12)
348. Baxter, David, weaver, Jacobite, res. Crieff Perthshire, tr. 20 Mar 1747, fr. Tilbury. (P.2.30)(MR69)
349. Baxter, Isabel, infanticide, res. Dumfries, tr. June 1758. (SM.20.327)
350. Bayn, John, sheepstealer, res. Glasgow, tr. Oct 1752. (AJ248)
351. Bayne, Agnes, res. Edinburgh, tr. 8 May 1663, fr. Leith to Barbados, in *Mary*. (EBR.186.13.4)
352. Bayne, Alexander, d. 1683 Hudson Bay. (HBRS.20.166)
353. Bayne, Alexander, thief, res. Perthshire, tr. 18 Dec 1720, fr. Leith. (SRO.HH.11) (alias 1993)
354. Bayne, William, thief, res. Rieneclash Ross-shire, tr. 1755. (SM.17.266) (alias 3910)
355. Bean, Alexander, b. 1752, shoemaker, sh. Sept 1775, fr. Newcastle to Ga, in *Georgia Packet*, sett. Friendsborough Ga, m. Christianna .. (PRO.T47.9\11)

356. Bean, Duncan, Jacobite, tr. 26 Apr 1716, fr. Liverpool to Jamaica, in
Two Brothers, arr. Montserrat June 1716.
(SPC.1716.313)(CTB31.205)(CTP.CC.43)
357. Bean, Duncan, Jacobite, tr. 20 Mar 1747, fr. Tilbury. (P.2.30)
358. Bean, George, Jacobite, tr. 8 May 1747, to Antigua. (P.2.30)
359. Bean, Kennedy, Jacobite, tr. 25 June 1716, fr. Liverpool to St Kitts, in
Hockenhill. (SPC.1716.312)(CTB31.207)
360. Bean, Kenneth, Jacobite, res. Cromarty, tr. 20 Mar 1747, fr. London to
Barbados , in *Frere*. (P.2.30)(MR81)
361. Beaton, Alan, Jacobite, tr. 7 May 1716, fr. Liverpool to S.C., in
Susannah. (SPC.1716.309)(CTB31/206)
362. Beaton, Alison, whore, res. Edinburgh, tr. 19 Mar 1695.
(SRO.PC2.25.216)
363. Beaton, Allan, b. 1756, butcher, res. Dundee Angus, sh. May 1774, fr.
Greenock to N.Y., in *George*. (PRO.T47.9\11)
364. Beaton, Angus, b. 1699, miller, Jacobite, res. Ardglogh Little Laids
Caithness, tr. 31 Mar 1747, fr. London to Barbados, in *Frere*.
(P.2.32)(MR81)
365. Beaton, David, b. 1756, farmer, res. Kintyre Argyll, sh. Aug 1774, fr.
Greenock to Wilmington N.C., in *Ulysses*, m. Flora Bride.
(PRO.T47.12)
366. Beaton, John, Jacobite, res. Inverness, tr. 1751(?). (P.2.32)(MR68)
367. Beattie, Francis, b. 1752, farmer, res. Dumfries-shire, sh. Oct 1774, fr.
Greenock to Charleston S.C., in *Countess*. (PRO.T47.12)
368. Beattie, James, Covenanter, res. Crossdykes, tr. Dec 1670, in *Merchant of
Glasgow*. (PC.3.679)
369. Beatty, Francis, Jacobite, tr. 29 June 1716, fr. Liverpool to Jamaica or
Va, in *Elizabeth & Anne*, arr. Va.
(SPC.1716.310)(CTB31.208)(VSP.1.185)
370. Beatty, John, clergyman edu. Glasgow Uni 1729, sh. 1732, sett. Va.
(EMA14)
371. Beatty, William, b. 1734, laborer, res. Galloway, sh. May 1774, fr.
Stranraer to N.Y., in *Gale*, m. Agnes .., ch. Mary. (PRO.T47.12)
372. Begg, Miles, Jacobite, tr. 28 July 1716, fr. Liverpool to Va, in *Godspeed*,
arr. Md Oct 1716. (SPC.1716.310)(CTB31.209)(HM388)
373. Belches, Alison, servant, infanticide, res. Lintlaw Berwickshire, tr. July
1744. (SRO.HCR.I.72)
374. Belinda, Bengal, servant, infanticide, res. Balgonie Fife, tr. Sept 1771.
(AJ1237) (alias 375)
375. Bell, Bengal, servant, infanticide, res. Balgonie Fife, tr. Sept 1771.
(AJ1237) (alias 374)
376. Bell, Alexander, merchant, res. Glasgow, sh. pre 1777, sett. WFla(?).
(PRO.CO5.613.414)
377. Bell, Alison, tr. 21 Oct 1682, fr. Greenock to N.Y. (ETR221)

18

378. Bell, David, merchant & planter, res. Glasgow, sh. pre 1745, sett. Va. (SRA.B10.15.5959\60)
379. Bell, James, b. 1749, stonecutter, sh. Dec 1773, fr. London to Jamaica, in *Britannia*. (PRO.T47.9\11)
380. Bell, John, ropemaker, thief, res. Stirling, tr. 1770. (SM.32.516)
381. Bell, John, res. Glasgow, d. 1773 Jamaica, Edin pr1773 CC8.8.122
382. Bell, John, b. 1749, farmer, res. Paisley Renfrewshire, sh. May 1774, fr. Greenock to N.Y., in *Matty*. (PRO.T47.12)
383. Bell, John, b. 1753, surgeon, res. Edinburgh, sh. Jan 1774, fr. Greenock to Nevis, in *Aurora*. (SRO.CE60.1.7)
384. Bell, Mary, b. 1751, spinner, res. Paisley Renfrewshire, sh. Feb 1774, fr. Greenock to N.Y., in *Commerce*. (PRO.T47.12)
385. Bell, Mrs, b. 1744, res. Paisley Renfrewshire, sh. May 1774, fr. Greenock to N.Y., in *Matty*. (PRO.T47.12)
386. Bell, William, b. 1701, bookseller, Jacobite, res. Berwickshire, tr. 5 May 1747, fr. Liverpool to Leeward Islands, in *Veteran*, arr. Martinique June 1747. (P.2.32)(PRO.SP36.102)
387. Bell, William, b. 1745, farmer, res. Glasgow, sh. May 1774, fr. Greenock to N.Y., in *Matty*. (PRO.T47.12)
388. Bell, William, b. 1749, farmer, res. Paisley Renfrewshire, sh. May 1774, fr. Greenock to N.Y., in *Matty*. (PRO.T47.12)
389. Bembs, Mary, whore, res. Edinburgh, tr. 19 Mar 1695. (SRO.PC2.25.216)
390. Bennet, George, res. Polmont Stirlingshire, pts. Rev Patrick Bennet, sh. pre 1783, sett. Charleston S.C. (SRO.RD4.236.795)
391. Bennet, William, b. pre 1671, forger, res. Roxburghshire, tr. 1751. (SM.13.501)
392. Bennett, Henry, carpenter, res. Elie Fife, sh. 1698, to Darien, in *Dolphin*, d. North America, Edin pr1707 CC8.8.83
393. Berry, Francis, foremastman, res. Leith Midlothian, sh. 14 July 1698, fr. Leith to Darien, in *Caledonia*, Edin pr1707 CC8.8.83
394. Berry, James, b. 1757, clockmaker, res. Queensferry West Lothian, sh. May 1775, fr. Leith to Philadelphia, in *Friendship*. (PRO.T47.12)
395. Berry, John, b. 1711, schoolmaster, res. Aberdeen, sh. Sept 1735, fr. London to Md. (CLRO\AIA)
396. Berwick, Andrew, b. 1714, res. Falkland Fife, sh. July 1730, fr. London to Jamaica. (CLRO\AIA)
397. Bethune, John, b. 1751, Skye Inverness-shire, clergyman edu. King's Col Aberdeen, sh. pre 1776, sett. S.C. & Canada, d. 23 Sept 1815 Williamstown Upper Canada. (F.7.626)(GM.85.635)
398. Beveridge, John, Covenanter, res. Islay Argyll, tr. Aug 1685, fr. Leith to East N.J., in *Henry & Francis*. (PC.11.330)
399. Beveridge, Thomas, clergyman, res. Alloa Clackmannanshire, sh. 1783, sett. Cambridge N.Y., d. 1798. (UPC656)

19

400. Beverley, John, Jacobite, res. Aberdeen, tr. 22 Apr 1747, fr. Liverpool to Va, in *Johnson*, arr. Port Oxford Md 5 Aug 1747. (P.2.34)(MR210)(PRO.T1.328) (alias 401)

401. Beverley, William, Jacobite, res. Aberdeen, tr. 22 Apr 1747, fr. Liverpool to Va, in *Johnson*, arr. Port Oxford Md 5 Aug 1747. (P.2.34)(MR210)(PRO.T1.328) (alias 400)

402. Bews, John, b. 1742, laborer, res. Stromness Orkney Islands, sh. Sept 1774, fr. Kirkwall to Savannah Ga, in *Marlborough*, sett. Richmond Co Ga, m. Isabel .. (PRO.T47.12)

403. Bews, William, b. 1736, farmer, res. Evie Orkney Islands, sh. Sept 1775, fr. Kirkwall to Savannah Ga, in *Marlborough*, sett. Richmond Co Ga, m. Christian Smith. (PRO.T47.12)

404. Bibby, Henry, weaver, Jacobite, res. Wigan Lancashire, tr. 1747. (MR196)

405. Biggam, Thomas, b. 1734, weaver, res. Galloway, sh. May 1774, fr. Stranraer to N.Y., in *Gale*, m. Mary .., ch. Andrew Jean. (PRO.T47.12)

406. Biggam, William, b. 1734, farmer, res. Galloway, sh. May 1774, fr. Stranraer to N.Y., in *Gale*. (PRO.T47.12)

407. Biggar, John, b. 1754, tailor, res. Paisley Renfrewshire, sh. Feb 1774, fr. Greenock to N.Y., in *Commerce*. (PRO.T47.12)

408. Bill, Dr, physician, sh. pre 1705, sett. Va. (SPC.1705.431)

409. Bird, George, Jacobite, tr. 30 Mar 1716, fr. Liverpool to Antigua, in *Scipio*. (SPC.1716.310)(CTB31.204)

410. Birrell, James, sailor, res. Kinghorn Fife, sh. 14 July 1698, fr. Leith to Darien, in *Caledonia*, m. Bessie Lily, Edin pr1707 CC8.8.83

411. Bishop, Peter, hosier, reset, res. Paisley Renfrewshire, tr. 1767. (AJ1002)

412. Bishop, Robert, surgeon's mate, d. 8 Dec 1698 Darien. (NLS.RY2b8\19)

413. Bitack, John, housebreaker, res. Inverness-shire, tr. Sept 1756. (AJ453) (alias 2425)

414. Bittleston, ..., thief, res. Stirling, tr. Oct 1773. (AJ1347) (alias 5731)

415. Black, Andrew, merchant, res. Glasgow, pts. Archibald Black, sh. pre 1782, sett. Westmoreland Jamaica. (SRA.B10.15.8403)

416. Black, Archibald Ray, servant, res. Kiles Jura Argyll, sh. 1754, to Cape Fear N.C. (SRO.GD64\5.21)

417. Black, David, merchant, res. Glasgow, sh. pre 1775, sett. Boston, m. Janet Greenlaw, ch. Margaret. (GlasgowOPR)

418. Black, David, b. 1755, bookbinder, sh. Aug 1774, fr. Whitby to Savannah Ga, in *Marlborough*. (PRO.T47.9\11)

419. Black, Donald, res. Feolin Jura Argyll, sh. 1754, to Cape Fear N.C. (SRO.GD64\5.21)

420. Black, Donald, b. 1730, laborer, res. Lismore Argyll, sh. Sept 1775, to Wilmington N.C., in *Jupiter*, m. Janet .., ch. Christian Ann Ewan Duncan. (PRO.T47.12)

421. Black, Duncan, res. Sannaig Jura Argyll, sh. 1754, to Cape Fear N.C. (SRO.GD64\5.21)
422. Black, Elizabeth, grocer's servant, infanticide, res. Edinburgh, tr. Dec 1774. (SRO.HCR.I.112)
423. Black, Gavin, res. Monkland Lanarkshire, tr. June 1684, fr. Port Glasgow, in *Pelican.* (PC.9.208)
424. Black, Henry, sailor, sh. 1698, to Darien, in *Dolphin,* Edin pr1707 CC8.8.83
425. Black, Hugh, b. 1733, farmer, res. Perthshire, sh. May 1775, fr. Greenock to N.Y., in *Monimia,* m. Janet .. (PRO.T47.12)
426. Black, James, sailor, res. Edinburgh, sh. 1698, to Darien, in *Dolphin,* Edin pr1707 CC8.8.83
427. Black, James, b. 1729, laborer, Jacobite, tr. 24 Feb 1747, fr. Liverpool to Va, in *Gildart,* arr. Port North Potomac Md 5 Aug 1747. (P.2.36)(PRO.T1.328)
428. Black, Janet, servant, infanticide, res. Airth Stirlingshire, tr. 1771, fr. Port Glasgow to Md, in *Crawford,* arr. Port Oxford Md 23 July 1771. (SRO.JC27.10.3)
429. Black, John, Covenanter, res. Water of Orr, tr. Aug 1685, fr. Leith to East N.J., in *Henry & Francis.* (PC.11.154)
430. Black, John, b. 1750, farmer, res. Kilsyth Stirlingshire, sh. May 1775, fr. Greenock to N.Y., in *Christy.* (PRO.T47.12)
431. Black, John, b. 1761, servant, res. Breadalbane Perthshire, sh. Sept 1775, to Wilmington N.C., in *Jupiter.* (PRO.T47.12)
432. Black, Malcolm, farmer, Covenanter, res. Achahoish Argyll, tr. Aug 1685, fr. Leith to Jamaica. (PC.11.136)
433. Black, Mary, b. 1759, servant, res. Breaalbane Perthshire, sh. Sept 1775, to Wilmington N.C., in *Jupiter.* (PRO.T47.12)
434. Black, Neil, Covenanter, res. Melford Glenbeg Argyll, tr. Aug 1685, fr. Leith to Jamaica. (PC.11.329)
435. Black, Peter, assault, res. Portavaidue, pts. Hugh Black, tr. 13 July 1765, to Grenada. (LC311)(SRO.E173.J2.3.339)
436. Black, Thomas, vagabond & robber, tr. 3 Sept 1668, fr. Leith or Burntisland to Va, in *Convertin.* (PC.2.534)
437. Black, William, b. 19 Jan 1724, St Nicholas Aberdeen, surgeon, res. Aberdeen, pts. James Black, sett. Gray's Inn Kingston Jamaica, d. 1747 Jamaica. (APB.3.147)
438. Blackburn, George, b. 1743, mason, res. Perthshire, sh. May 1775, fr. Greenock to N.Y., in *Monimia.* (PRO.T47.12)
439. Blackburn, John, merchant, res. Glasgow, sh. pre 1752, sett. Norfolk Va. (SRA.B10.15.6183)
440. Blackhall, Agnes, b. 1748, spinner, res. Paisley Renfrewshire, sh. Feb 1774, fr. Greenock to N.Y., in *Commerce.* (PRO.T47.12)

441. Blackie, Charles, b. 1745, farmer, res. Milnbank Southwick
Kirkcudbrightshire, sh. 1775, fr. Kirkcudbright to P.E.I., in
Lovely Nelly, m. Janet Herries, ch. John William James Ann.
(PRO.T47.12)
442. Blackie, David, sailor, res. Grangepans West Lothian, pts. John Blackie
& Margaret Japp, sh. 14 July 1698, fr. Leith to Darien, in
Caledonia, Edin pr1707 CC8.8.83
443. Blackie, Helen, b. 1750, servant, res. Gifford East Lothian, sh. May
1775, fr. Leith to Philadelphia, in *Friendship*. (PRO.T47.12)
444. Blackie, James, b. 1729, farmer, res. Stirling, sh. May 1774, fr.
Greenock to N.Y., in *Monimia*, m. Margaret Davie. (PRO.T47.12)
445. Blacklock, William, b. 1751, farmer, res. Dumfries-shire, sh. Oct 1774,
fr. Greenock to Charleston S.C., in *Countess*. (PRO.T47.12)
446. Blackly, Robert, passenger, sh. Feb 1681, fr. Ayr to West Indies, in
James of Ayr. (SRO.E72.3.6)
447. Blackswik, James, b. 1753, clerk, sh. Feb 1774, fr. London to N.C., in
Margaret & Mary. (PRO.T47.9\11)
448. Blackton, Hannah, b. 1754, servant, res. Edinburgh, sh. May 1775, fr.
Leith to Philadelphia, in *Friendship*. (PRO.T47.12)
449. Blackwood, James, Covenanter, res. Carmunnock Lanarkshire, tr. 12 Dec
1678, fr. Leith to West Indies, in *St Michael of Scarborough*.
(PC.6.76)
450. Blackwood, James, Jacobite, tr. 29 June 1716, fr. Liverpool to Jamaica or
Va, in *Elizabeth & Anne*, arr. Va.
(SPC.1716.310)(CTB31.208)(VSP.1.185)
451. Blackwood, James, thief, res. Glasgow, tr. 1753. (SM.15.437)
452. Blackwood, John, res. Airdsgreen Lanarkshire, pts. John Blackwood, sh.
1780, sett. Canada. (SRO.NRAS.0097\1)
453. Blaikie, James, thief, res. Galashiels Selkirkshire, pts. James Blaikie, tr.
Oct 1752. (AJ250)
454. Blain, Patrick, b. 1740, farmer, res. Galloway, sh. May 1774, fr.
Stranraer to N.Y., in *Gale*, m. Eliza .., ch. Jean Jenny.
(PRO.T47.12)
455. Blair, Archibald, tr. 1728, fr. Glasgow to Md, in *Concord*, arr. Charles
Co Md May 1728. (SRO.JC27.10.3)
456. Blair, David, res. Giffordland Ayrshire, sh. 1736, to Ga.
(PRO.CO5.670.286)(SPC.43.148)
457. Blair, James, Jacobite, tr. 30 Mar 1716, fr. Liverpool to Antigua, in
Scipio. (SPC.1716.310)(CTB31.204)
458. Blair, James, Crombie Banffshire, clergyman edu. King's Col Aberdeen
1670, res. Alvah Banffshire, pts. Rev Robert Blair, sett. Va.
(KCA.2.234)(SRO.RD2.59.439)
459. Blair, John, soldier, thief, tr. June 1766. (SM.28.388)
460. Blair, John, thief, tr. 1653, fr. Ayr to Barbados. (SRO.JC27.10.3)

461. Blair, John, physician, res. Angus, sh. pre 1700, sett. Port Royal
      Jamaica. (DP313)
462. Blair, John, clergyman, sh. 1702, to West Indies, sett. N.C. (EMA15)
463. Blair, John, physician, res. Perthshire, pts. Alexander Blair of Inchyra, d.
      July 1736 Jamaica, Edin pr1738 CC8.8.101
464. Blair, John, b. 1668, sh. 1699, to Darien, sett. St Catherine's Jamaica,
      m. (1)Nidime ..(2)Elizabeth, ch. John Thomas Christian Mary, d.
      27 June 1728. (MIBWI28)
465. Blair, Robert, b. 1725, sailor, res. Drum New Abbey Kirkcudbrightshire,
      sh. 1775, fr. Kirkcudbright to P.E.I., in Lovely Nelly.
      (PRO.T47.12)
466. Blair, Thomas, farmer, Jacobite, res. Gartmore Perthshire, tr. 21 Mar
      1747. (P.2.38)
467. Blair, William, clergyman, sh. 1750, sett. Montserrat. (EMA15)
468. Blair, William, b. 1745, mariner, res. Colvend Kirkcudbrightshire, sh.
      May 1775, fr. Dumfries to P.E.I., in Lovely Nelly. (PRO.T47.12)
469. Blenshall, Thomas, planter, d. 9 June 1768 Jamaica. (SM.30.503)
470. Blyth, Henry, merchant's clerk, res. Newburgh Fife, d. pre 1763 Jamaica.
      (SRO.B54.10.33)
471. Boag, John, b. 1715, res. Kirkwall Orkney Islands, sh. July 1733, fr.
      London to Jamaica. (CLRO\AIA)
472. Boath, Elizabeth, b. 1753, spinner, res. Paisley Renfrewshire, sh. Feb
      1774, fr. Greenock to N.Y., in Commerce. (PRO.T47.12)
473. Bogie, Robert, tr. 15 Nov 1679, fr. Leith. (ETR162)
474. Bogle, Robert, sh. 16 Dec 1773, fr. Greenock to Jamaica, in Ross.
      (SRO.CE60.1.7)
475. Bogle, Robert sr, merchant, sett. Grenada, d. 1 June 1777. (SM.39.455)
476. Bogle, William, merchant, sh. 9 Oct 1685, fr. Port Glasgow to Va, in
      Mayflower of Preston. (SRO.E72.19.8)
477. Boigs, John, sailor, res. Crawforddykes Renfrewshire, sh. 1699, fr.
      Greenock to Darien, in Speedy Return, m. Agnes Dougall, Edin
      pr1707 CC8.8.83
478. Bold, Thomas, Jacobite, res. Wigan Lancashire, tr. 1747. (MR196)
479. Bone, Janet, infanticide, res. Ayrshire, tr. Oct 1751. (AJ199)
480. Bontein, Archibald, engineer, res. Balglass Dunbartonshire, pts. Robert
      Bontein of Mildorran , sh. pre 1751, sett. Jamaica & Dominica, m.
      Margaret .., ch. James Margaret Isobel Grizell Thomas, d. pre
      1774. (SRO.RD2.169.88\RD4.216.299)
481. Bontein, Thomas, gentleman, sh. pre 1749, sett. Port Royal Jamaica.
      (SRO.RD2.169.499)
482. Bonthron, James, bosun, res. Brigton of Inverteil Kimghorn Fife, pts.
      James Bonthron, sh. 14 July 1698, fr. Leith to Darien, in
      Caledonia, Edin pr1707 CC8.8.83

23

483. Boo, George, b. 1716, weaver, res. Earkups, sh. Oct 1736, fr. London to Jamaica. (CLRO\AIA)
484. Boog, John, b. 1749, weaver, res. Paisley Renfrewshire, sh. Feb 1774, fr. Greenock to N.Y., in *Commerce*. (PRO.T47.12)
485. Boreland, John, storekeeper, res. Newmills Ayrshire, d. Sept 1728 Jamaica, Edin pr1789 CC8.8.128
486. Boreland, Robert, physician, res. Kilmarnock Ayrshire, pts. Robert & Euphan Boreland, sh. pre 1770, sett. St James Cornwall Co Jamaica. (SRO.RD4.209.836)
487. Borland, Francis, b. 1666, clergyman edu. Glasgow Uni , res. East Kilbride Lanarkshire, pts. John Borland, sh. pre 1685, sett. Surinam Barbados Darien, d. 1722 Lesmahagow Lanarkshire. (F.7.662)(HMC.Laing I.331)
488. Borthwick, James, tr. pre 1733, sett. Rappahannock Va. (SRO.GD24.1.464)
489. Borthwick, James, sailor, d. 3 Dec 1698 Darien. (NLS.RY2b8\19)
490. Boss, James, b. 1701, smith, res. Kinglassie Fife, sh. July 1729, fr. London to Jamaica. (CLRO\AIA)
491. Boswell, James, physician, d. Dec 1767 Montserrat. (SM.30.110)
492. Bourman, James, b. 1754, surgeon, sh. Jan 1775, fr. London to Md, in *Baltimore*. (PRO.T47.9\11)
493. Bow, James, Jacobite, tr. 28 July 1716, fr. Liverpool to Va, in *Godspeed*, arr. Md Oct 1716. (SPC.1716.310)(CTB31.209)(HM388)
494. Bower, James, merchant, res. Dundee Angus, sh. 1699, to Darien, in *Hope*, m. Elizabeth Blair, ch. Thomas Andrew Grisell James Janet John, Edin pr1708 CC8.8.84
495. Bower, John, tailor, Jacobite, res. Glasgow, tr. 24 Feb 1747, fr. Liverpool to Va, in *Gildart*, arr. Port North Potomac Md 5 Aug 1747. (P.2.44)(PRO.T1.328)
496. Bowie, Angus, Jacobite, res. Craskie Glenmoriston Inverness-shire, tr. 1747, fr. London. (P.2.60)
497. Bowie, John, Covenanter, res. Glasgow, tr. 12 Dec 1678, fr. Leith to West Indies, in *St Michael of Scarborough*. (PC.6.76)
498. Bowie, John, sailor, res. Newcastle, sh. 14 July 1698, fr. Leith to Darien, in *St Andrew*, Edin pr1707 CC8.8.83
499. Bowie, John, clergyman edu. Marischal Col Aberdeen 1770, sh. 1771, sett. St George Md. (FPA.21.302)
500. Bowie, John, b. 1733, servant, Jacobite, res. Aberdeen, tr. 5 May 1747, fr. Liverpool to Leeward Islands, in *Veteran*, arr. Martinique June 1747. (P.2.44)(JAB.2.420)(PRO.SP36.102)
501. Bowie, Margaret, cottar, res. Knocknafeolin Jura Argyll, sh. 1754, to Cape Fear N.C. (SRO.GD64\5.21)

502. Bowie, Robert, b. 1733, servant, Jacobite, res. Strathbogie Aberdeenshire, tr. 22 Apr 1747, fr. Liverpool to Va, in *Johnson*, arr. Port Oxford Md 5 Aug 1747. (P.2.46)(MR127)(PRO.T1.328)

503. Bowie, William, Jacobite, res. Ballindrum Glenmoriston Inverness-shire, tr. 1747, fr. Tilbury. (P.2.62)(MR150)

504. Bowman, Christian, whore, res. Edinburgh, tr. 19 Mar 1695. (SRO.PC2.25.216)

505. Bowman, James, thief, res. Ayrshire, tr. May 1775. (SM.37.406)

506. Bowman, William, sh. pre 1656, sett. Barbados. (AnHib.4.234)

507. Bowyer, Francis, b. 1683, schoolmaster, Jacobite, res. Morar Inverness-shire, tr. 20 Mar 1747, fr. Tilbury. (P.2.44)

508. Boy, George, Jacobite, tr. 8 May 1747, to Antigua. (P.2.44)

509. Boyce, Janet, b. 1758, spinner, res. Paisley Renfrewshire, sh. Feb 1774, fr. Greenock to N.Y., in *Commerce*. (PRO.T47.12)

510. Boyd, Andrew, clergyman, sh. 1709, to Va. (EMA16)

511. Boyd, Hugh, b. 4 May 1746, Glasgow, pickpocket, res. Glasgow, pts. Robert Boyd & Janet Grindlay, tr. Aug 1766. (SRO.HCR.I.98)

512. Boyd, James, b. 1742, merchant, res. Galloway, sh. May 1774, fr. Stranraer to N.Y., in *Gale*. (PRO.T47.12)

513. Boyd, Jean, b. 1752, res. Galloway, sh. May 1774, fr. Stranraer to N.Y., in *Gale*. (PRO.T47.12)

514. Boyd, John, clergyman edu. Glasgow Uni 1701, res. Borland, pts. George Boyd, sh. pre 1706, sett. Tennant Freehold N.J., d. 30 Aug 1708 Tennant, Edin pr1710 CC8.8.84. (F.7.662)

515. Boyd, Robert, merchant, res. Twynholm Kirkcudbrightshire, pts. Rev Andrew Boyd, d. pre 1783 Va, Edin pr1783 CC8.8.126

516. Boyd, Robert, b. 17 Jan 1748, pickpocket, res. Glasgow, pts. Robert Boyd & Janet Grindlay, tr. Aug 1766. (SRO.HCR.I.98)

517. Boyd, Robert, b. 1750, ship's carpenter, res. Ayrshire, sh. Mar 1775, fr. Glasgow to Quebec, in *Friendship*. (PRO.T47.12)

518. Boyd, Spencer, merchant, pts. Dr James Boyd, sh. pre 1770, sett. King & Queen Co Va. (SRO.RD2.233.108)(SRO.GD1.26.60)

519. Boyd, Thomas, res. Pitcon Ayrshire, sh. 1736, sett. Ga. (PRO.CO5.670.286)(SPC.43.148)

520. Boyle, Alexander, Jacobite, tr. 31 July 1716, fr. Liverpool to Va, in *Anne*. (SPC.1716.310)(CTB31.209)

521. Boyle, Andrew, executioner, thief, res. Edinburgh, tr. May 1768. (AJ1063)

522. Boyle, John, sh. pre 1777, sett. St Croix, ch. James. (SRO.SH.12.2.1777)

523. Boyle, Stair, merchant, res. Inverkip Renfrewshire, sh. pre 1761, sett. St Kitts. (SRA.B10.12.2)

524. Boyne, Margaret, infanticide, res. Elgin Morayshire, tr. May 1768. (AJ1064)

525. Brace, William, b. 1755, musician, res. Dumfries, sh. May 1775, fr. Whitehaven to Jamaica, in *Tyger*. (PRO.T47.9\11)
526. Brachader, John, horsethief, res. Rictian Inverness-shire, tr. May 1768. (AJ1064\1080) (alias 2426)
527. Bradley, Charles, sailor, rioter, res. Greenock Renfrewshire, tr. May 1773. (AJ1324)
528. Bradley, Peter, b. 1717, weaver, Jacobite, res. Monaghan, tr. 21 Feb 1747. (P.2.46)
529. Bradner, John, clergyman edu. Edinburgh Uni, sh. pre 1715, sett. Cape May & Orange Co N.Y., ch. Benoni, d. 1733. (F.7.662)
530. Bradshaw, Thomas, counterfeiter, tr. July 1749. (SRO.HCR.I.79)
531. Braiden, Robert, b. 1737, laborer, res. Dumfries, sh. May 1775, fr. Dumfries to P.E.I., in *Lovely Nelly*, m. Jean Kirkpatrick, ch. James William David Edward. (PRO.T47.12)
532. Braidfoot, John, clergyman, sh. 1772, sett. Va, d. 1785 Portsmouth Va. (EMA16)
533. Braidie, Elspeth, res. Edinburgh, tr. 8 May 1663, fr. Leith to Barbados, in *Mary*. (EBR186.13.4)
534. Braidwood, James, Covenanter, res. Carmunnock Lanarkshire, tr. 12 Dec 1678, fr. Leith to West Indies, in *St Michael of Scarborough*. (PC.6.76)
535. Brand, James, Jacobite, tr. 24 Feb 1747, fr. Liverpool to Va, in *Gildart*, arr. Port North Potomac Md 5 Aug 1747. (PRO.T1.328)
536. Brander, Adam, b. 1749, carpenter, sh. Mar 1774, fr. London to Jamaica, in *Jamaica Planter*, sett. Portland Surry Co Jamaica. (PRO.T47.9\11)(SRO.RD2.236.612)
537. Brass, Thomas, b. 1749, weaver, res. Birsay Orkney Islands, sh. Sept 1774, fr. Kirkwall to Savannah Ga, in *Marlborough*, sett. Richmond Co Ga. (PRO.T47.12)
538. Brebner, Alexander, merchant, res. Peterhead Aberdeenshire, pts. John Brebner & May Davidson, sett. Christianstad St Croix, d. pre 1775 St Croix. (APB.4.65)
539. Brebner, James, judge edu. King's Col Aberdeen 1722, sett. Grenada. (KCA.2.298)
540. Brebner, James, judge, res. Aberdeenshire, sh. pre 1768, sett. Grenada. (SRO.SH.7.3.1770) (alias 2274)
541. Brechin, James, clergyman, sh. 1702, sett. Va. (EMA16)(SNQ.I.153)
542. Breeding, Andrew, b. 1664, pts. Thomas Breeding, sh. June 1684, fr. London to Md, in *Brothers Adventure*. (CLRO\AIA)
543. Bremner, Helen, servant, res. Mill of Dunadeer Aberdeenshire, tr. Sept 1779. (SM.40.613)
544. Bremner, William, b. 1754, house carpenter, res. Kirkwall Orkney Islands, sh. Sept 1775, fr. Kirkwall to Savannah Ga, in *Marlborough*. (PRO.T47.12)

545. Brendan, John, Jacobite, tr. 24 May 1716, fr. Liverpool to Md, in
    Friendship, arr. Md Aug 1716.
    (SPC.1716.311)(CTB31.207)(HM387)
546. Breymer, Thomas, b. 1760, groomboy, res. Dundee Angus, sh. May
    1775, fr. Leith to Philadelphia, in *Friendship*. (PRO.T47.12)
547. Brice, John, Jacobite, tr. 1747. (P.2.150)
548. Bridson, John, b. 1700, laborer, res. Kirkcudbright, sh. Feb 1719, fr.
    London to Jamaica. (CLRO\AIA)
549. Briggs, Andrew, b. 1745, blacksmith, res. Kirkbean Galloway, sh. May
    1775, fr. Dumfries to P.E.I., in *Lovely Nelly*. (PRO.T47.12)
550. Briggs, Daniel, Jacobite, tr. 30 Mar 1716, fr. Liverpool to Antigua, in
    Scipio. (CTB31.204)
551. Briggs, Paul, Jacobite, tr. 30 Mar 1716, fr. Liverpool to Antigua, in
    Scipio. (SPC.1716.310)(CTB31.204)
552. Briggs, Samuel, b. 1747, dyer, sh. Sept 1775, fr. Newcastle to Ga, in
    Georgia Packet, sett. Friendsborough Ga. (PRO.T47.12)
553. Brisbane, Matthew, assault, res. Rosland, tr. 1 May 1674, fr. Leith to
    Barbados, in *St John of Leith*. (PC.4.144)
554. Britter, William, lawyer's clerk, Jacobite, res. London, tr. 21 July 1748.
    (P.2.50)
555. Broa, Margaret, b. 1750, spinner, res. Paisley Renfrewshire, sh. Feb
    1774, fr. Greenock to N.Y., in *Commerce*. (PRO.T47.12)
556. Brock, Andrew, gunner, res. Glasgow, sh. 14 July 1698, fr. Leith to
    Darien, in *St Andrew*, Edin pr1707 CC8.8.83
557. Brock, James, b. 1754, porter, sh. Sept 1775, fr. Kirkwall to Savannah
    Ga, in *Marlborough*, sett. Richmond Co Ga. (PRO.T47.12)
558. Brock, Walter, b. 1746, merchant, res. Glasgow, sh. Apr 1775, fr.
    Greenock to N.Y., in *Lilly*. (PRO.T47.12)
559. Brodie, Francis, sailor, res. Windyhills Morayshire, pts. John Brodie, sh.
    14 July 1698, fr. Leith to Darien, in *Unicorn*, Edin pr1707
    CC8.8.83
560. Brodie, George, b. 1713, saddler, res. Elgin Morayshire, sh. 1734, fr.
    London. (CLRO\AIA)
561. Brodie, James, professor of physics, res. Elgin Morayshire, sh. pre 1780,
    sett. Barbados. (SRO.RS 6.635)
562. Brodie, John, sh. Nov 1737, fr. Inverness to Savannah Ga, in *Two
    Brothers*. (SPC.44.6)
563. Brodie, John, b. 1727, servant, tr. 24 Feb 1747, fr. Liverpool to Va, in
    Gildart, arr. Port North Potomac Md 5 Aug 1747. (PRO.T1.328)
564. Brodie, Robert, b. 1738, wright, res. Perthshire, sh. May 1775, fr.
    Greenock to N.Y., in *Monimia*, m. Katherine Black.
    (PRO.T47.12)
565. Brody, .., clergyman, sh. 1709, to Va. (EMA16)

27

566. Brody, John, sh. 1737, fr. Inverness to Ga, in *Two Brothers*, 16 Nov 1737. (PRO.CO5.640.39)
567. Brokey, Charles, b. 1750, gardener, sh. Sept 1775, fr. Newcastle to Ga, in *Georgia Packet*, sett. Friendsborough Ga. (PRO.T47.9\11)
568. Brough, George, b. 1739, farmer, res. Evie Orkney Islands, sh. Sept 1774, fr. Kirkwall to Savannah Ga, in *Marlborough*, sett. Richmond Co Ga, m. Barbara .., ch. Thomas Christian James Helen. (PRO.T47.12)
569. Browester, John, b. 1753, weaver, res. Paisley Renfrewshire, sh. Feb 1774, fr. Greenock to N.Y., in *Commerce*. (PRO.T47.12)
570. Brown, Alexander, tr. 21 Oct 1682, fr. Greenock to N.Y. (ETR221)
571. Brown, Alexander, surgeon, res. Glasgow, sh. pre 1749, sett. Jamaica, m. Ann Boyd, ch. Alexander, Glasgow pr1749 CC9.7.60
572. Brown, Alexander, res. Old Crag Daviot Aberdeenshire, pts. ... Brown & Janet Stevens, sh. pre 1756, sett. St Kitts. (ABR.Deeds1757)
573. Brown, Alexander, deputy receiver general, d. 10 Oct 1770 Jamaica, Edin pr1779 CC8.8.124. (SRO.SH.16.8.1771)(SM.33.53)
574. Brown, Alexander, b. 1763, servant, res. Wester Leys Isle of Lewis, sh. July 1775, fr. Stornaway to Philadelphia, in *Clementina*. (PRO.T47.12)
575. Brown, Andrew, sailor, res. Strichen Aberdeenshire, sh. 14 July 1698, fr. Leith to Darien, in *St Andrew*, Edin pr1708 CC8.8.84
576. Brown, Andrew, tr. June 1753. (SRO.B59.26.11.5.4)
577. Brown, Andrew, d. 24 Dec 1698 Darien. (NLS.RY2.8\19)
578. Brown, Andrew, b. 1727, farmer, Jacobite, res. Dunnichen Angus, tr. 24 Feb 1747, fr. Liverpool to Va, in *Gildart*, arr. Port North Potomac Md 5 Aug 1747. (P.2.52)(PRO.T1.328)
579. Brown, Andrew, b. 1729, gentleman, res. Dumfries, sh. Aug 1774, fr. Greenock to Philadelphia, in *Magdalene*. (PRO.T47.12)
580. Brown, Anna, whore, res. Edinburgh, tr. 19 Mar 1695. (SRO.PC2.25.216)
581. Brown, Archibald, Covenanter, res. Argyll, tr. Aug 1685, fr. Leith to Jamaica. (PC.11.330)
582. Brown, Charles, tr. 1775, fr. Greenock to Va, in *Rainbow*, arr. Port Hampton Va 3 May 1775. (SRO.JC.27.10.3)
583. Brown, David, d. 1697 Somerset Co Md. (SRO.RH1.2.488)
584. Brown, David, b. 1695, Glasgow, clergyman edu. Glasgow Uni 1719, res. Belhelvie Aberdeenshire, sh. pre 1748, sett. Philadelphia, d. 10 Mar 1751 Scotland. (F.7.662)
585. Brown, Francis, Jacobite, res. Lancashire, tr. 1747. (P.2.52)(MR196)
586. Brown, George, Covenanter, tr. Aug 1685, fr. Leith to East N.J. (PC.11.154)
587. Brown, George, vagabond & robber, res. Annandale Dumfries-shire, tr. 1671(?). (PC.3.428)

28

588. Brown, Hugh, b. 1737, farmer, res. Inverness, sh. July 1775, fr. Stornaway to Philadelphia, in *Clementina*. (PRO.T47.12)
589. Brown, James, Covenanter, res. Frosk, tr. 12 Dec 1678, fr. Leith to West Indies, in *St Michael of Scarborough*. (PC.6.76)
590. Brown, James, carter, horsethief, res. Glasgow, tr. Feb 1774. (SRO.RH2.4.255)(CalHOpp.1774.847)
591. Brown, James, clergyman edu. Glasgow Uni, res. Newmilns Ayrshire, pts. Nicol Brown, sh. pre 1687, sett. Swansea Mass. (F.7.662)
592. Brown, James, thief, res. Edinburgh, tr. Feb 1697. (SRO.PC2.26)
593. Brown, Janet, vagabond, res. Aberdeenshire, tr. May 1717. (SRO.JC.11.4)
594. Brown, Janet, infanticide, res. Banffshire, tr. July 1740. (SRO.HCR.I.68)
595. Brown, Janet, vagrant & thief, res. Banffshire, tr. June 1773, fr. Glasgow. (AJ1323\8)
596. Brown, Jean, tr. May 1672, fr. Leith, in *Ewe & Lamb*. (PC.3.523)
597. Brown, Jean, gypsy, thief, res. Dumfries-shire, tr. May 1739. (SRO.JC.12.5)
598. Brown, Jean, thief, res. Aberdeen, tr. 1753. (SM.15.468)
599. Brown, Jean, res. Midmar Aberdeenshire, pts. John Brown & Jean Westland, sh. 1743, to Philadelphia, sett. Barbados & St Croix, m. Daniel Aspinall, d. 1758 St Croix. (APB.3.202)
600. Brown, Joan, res. Edinburgh, tr. 1696, fr. Newhaven to Va. (SRO.RH15.14.58)
601. Brown, John, Covenanter, res. Buchlyvie Stirlingshire, tr. 12 Dec 1678, fr. Leith to West Indies, in *St Michael of Scarborough*. (PC.6.76)
602. Brown, John, tailor edu. Kirkcudbright, tr. Oct 1684. (PC.10.258)
603. Brown, John, Jacobite, tr. 29 June 1716, fr. Liverpool to Jamaica or Va, in *Elizabeth & Anne*. (SPC.1716.310)(CTB31.208)(VSP.1.186)
604. Brown, John, vagabond & robber, res. Annandale Dumfries-shire, tr. 1671(?). (PC.3.428)
605. Brown, John, physician, res. Roxburghshire, sett. Williamsburg Va, ch. Charles, d. 1727 Va, Edin pr1730 CC8.8.93
606. Brown, John, b. 1703, res. Kirkbean Galloway, sh. Aug 1718, fr. London to Md. (CLRO\AIA)
607. Brown, John, b. 1756, joiner, res. Dumfries-shire, sh. Oct 1774, fr. Greenock to Charleston S.C., in *Countess*. (PRO.T47.12)
608. Brown, Joseph, b. 1731, tailor, Jacobite, res. Banff, tr. 5 May 1747, fr. Liverpool to Leeward Islands, in *Veteran*, arr. Martinique June 1747. (P.2.54)(JAB.2.420)(PRO.SP36.102)
609. Brown, Lilleas, infanticide, res. Kilmarnock Ayrshire, pts. Robert Brown, tr. Aug 1741. (SRO.JC27)
610. Brown, Magnus, seaman, sh. Apr 1683, to Hudson Bay. (HBRS.9.95)
611. Brown, Marion, infanticide, res. Lochrutten Kirkcudbrightshire, pts. John Brown, tr. Mar 1767. (SM.29.221)(SRO.JC27.D35)

612. Brown, Ninian, Jacobite, tr. 28 July 1716, fr. Liverpool to Va, in
     Godspeed, arr. Md Oct 1716.
     (SPC.1716.310)(CTB31.209)(HM389)
613. Brown, Patrick, robber, res. Annandale Dumfries-shire, tr. 1671(?).
     (PC.3.428)
614. Brown, Peter, carpenter, res. Dundee Angus, sh. Oct 1752, fr. Leith to
     Cape Fear N.C. (SRO.RD4.178.2)
615. Brown, Peter, b. 1752, barber, res. Glasgow, sh. May 1775, fr. Greenock
     to N.Y., in *Monimia*. (PRO.T47.12)
616. Brown, Robert, vagabond, res. Aberdeenshire, tr. May 1717.
     (SRO.JC.11.4)
617. Brown, Thomas, tr. July 1751. (AJ187)
618. Brown, Thomas, Covenanter, tr. July 1685. (PC.11.114)
619. Brown, Thomas, merchant, res. Glasgow, sh. 1770, sett. King & Queen
     Co Va. (SRO.RD2.233.108)
620. Brown, William, tr. 15 Nov 1679, fr. Leith. (ETR162)
621. Brown, William, soldier, fraudster, res. Aberdeen, tr. 1772, in *Betsy*, arr.
     Port of James River Va 29 Apr 1772. (SRO.JC27.10.3)(AJ1238)
622. Brown, William, sailor, sh. 14 July 1698, fr. Leith to Darien, in
     Unicorn, Edin pr1707 CC8.8.83
623. Brown, William, merchant & planter, res. Glasgow(?), sett. St Kitts &
     Tobago, d. 1767. (SRA.B10.15.7493)
624. Brown, William, sh. 16 Dec 1773, fr. Greenock to Jamaica, in *Ross*.
     (SRO.CE60.1.7)
625. Brown, William, res. Airdrie Lanarkshire, pts. Alexander Brown, sh. pre
     1773, sett. Jamaica. (SRO.CS.GMB7.73)
626. Brown, William, b. 1733, cooper, res. Edinburgh, sh. Apr 1751, fr.
     London to Va. (CLRO\AIA)
627. Brown, William, b. 1763, blacksmith, sh. Sept 1774, fr. London to
     Jamaica, in *Standlinch*. (PRO.T47.9\11)
628. Browne, John, Jacobite, tr. 31 July 1716, fr. Liverpool to Va, in *Anne*.
     (SPC.1716.310)(CTB31.209)
629. Browne, Mark, Jacobite, tr. 31 July 1716, fr. Liverpool to Va, in *Anne*.
     (SPC.1716.310)(CTB31.209)
630. Brownhills, Thomas, b. 1725, laborer, Jacobite, res. Kinnaird Inchture
     Perthshire, tr. 5 May 1747, fr. Liverpool to Leeward Islands, in
     Veteran, arr. Martinique June 1747. (P.2.52)(PRO.SP36.102)
631. Brownlee, Alexander, b. 1727, Edinburgh, watchmaker, Jacobite, res.
     Edinburgh, pts. Archibald Brownlee, tr. 5 May 1747, fr. Liverpool
     to Leeward Islands, in *Veteran*, arr. Martinique June 1747.
     (P.2.54)(MR132)(PRO.SP36.102)
632. Brownlie, Robert, b. 1739, laborer, res. Perthshire, sh. May 1775, fr.
     Greenock to N.Y., in *Monimia*. (PRO.T47.12)

633. Bruce, .., mason's servant, rioter, res. Edinburgh, tr. Sept 1666, fr. Leith to Barbados. (P.2.195)
634. Bruce, Alexander, Jacobite, tr. 29 June 1716, fr. Liverpool to Jamaica or Va, in *Elizabeth & Anne*, arr. Va. (SPC.1716.310)(CTB31.208)(VSP.1.185)
635. Bruce, Andrew, pts. David Bruce of Kinnaird, d. 25 Aug 1773 St Vincent. (SM.35.616)
636. Bruce, Ann, b. 1759, servant, res. Edinburgh, sh. May 1775, fr. Leith to Philadelphia, in *Friendship*. (PRO.T47.12)
637. Bruce, David, housebreaker, res. Brechin Angus, tr. June 1753. (AJ286)(SRO.B59.26.11.5.4)
638. Bruce, James, thief, res. Ellon Aberdeenshire, tr. Feb 1766. (AJ947)
639. Bruce, James, Jacobite, tr. 7 May 1716, fr. Liverpool to S.C., in *Susannah*. (SPC.1716.309)(CTB31.206)
640. Bruce, James, pts. Alexander Bruce of Garland, sh. pre 1728, sett. Jamaica. (SRO.SH.9.1.1728)
641. Bruce, James, b. 1727, farmer, sh. May 1775, fr. Greenock to N.Y., in *Monimia*, m. Janet Black. (PRO.T47.12)
642. Bruce, Janet, b. 1757, servant, res. Edinburgh, sh. May 1775, fr. Leith to Philadelphia, in *Friendship*. (PRO.T47.12)
643. Bruce, John, tr. 16 Dec 1774. (SRO.HCR.I.112)
644. Bruce, John, clergyman, sh. 1775, to Va. (EMA17)
645. Bruce, John, gardener, res. Tyrie Aberdenshire, fr. London to Barbados, sett. St Thomas Jamaica, d. 10 Aug 1763 Jamaica. (APB.3.220)
646. Bruce, Michael, tr. July 1668, to Barbados or Va. (PC.2.478)
647. Bruce, Robert, Jacobite, tr. 29 June 1716, fr. Liverpool to Jamaica or Va, in *Elizabeth & Anne*, arr. Va. (SPC.1716.310)(CTB31.208)(VSP.1.185)
648. Bruce, Robert, Jacobite, tr. 31 July 1716, fr. Liverpool to Va, in *Anne*. (SPC.1716.310)(CTB31.209)
649. Bruce, Robert, b. 1740, carpenter, sh. Mar 1774, fr. London to N.E., in *Amherst*. (PRO.T47.9\11)
650. Bruce, Robert, b. 1752, gardener, res. Galloway, sh. May 1774, fr. Stranraer to N.Y., in *Gale*. (PRO.T47.12)
651. Bruce, William, sailor, res. Peterhead Aberdeenshire, sh. 14 July 1698, fr. Leith to Darien, in *St Andrew*, d. July 1700, Edin pr1707 CC8.8.83
652. Bruce, William, b. 1727, husbandman, Jacobite, res. Dunbeath Caithness, tr. 31 Mar 1747, fr. London to Jamaica, in *St George or Carteret*, arr. Jamaica 1747. (P.2.56)(PRO.CO137.58)
653. Brunton, Grizel, b. 1750, res. Perth, sh. Apr 1775, fr. Greenock to Salem, in *Glasgow Packet*. (PRO.T47.12)
654. Bruntoun, Janet, tr. 21 Oct 1682, fr. Greenock to N.Y. (ETR221)
655. Bryan, William, Jacobite, tr. 21 Mar 1747. (P.2.58)

656. Bryce, Alexander, b. 1728, husbandman, res. Kirkbride Anwoth
     Kirkcudbrightshire, sh. May 1774, fr. Kirkcudbright to N.Y., in
     Gale , m. Mary .., ch. Jane. (PRO.T47.12)
657. Bryce, Archibald, factor, res. Glasgow, sh. pre 1776, sett. Richmond Va.
     (SRA.B10.12.4)
658. Bryce, Charles, b. 1759, res. Glasgow, sh. Sept 1774, fr. Greenock to
     Jamaica, in *Jamaica*. (PRO.T47.12)
659. Bryce, John, mealmaker, Covenanter, res. Cambusnethan Lanarkshire, tr.
     18 June 1668, fr. Leith to Va, in *Convertin*. (PC.2.534)
660. Bryce, Malcolm, Covenanter, tr. Aug 1685. (PC.11.330)
661. Bryce, Thomas, maltman, Covenanter, res. Irvine Ayrshire, tr. June 1684,
     fr. Port Glasgow, in *Pelican*. (PC.9.208)
662. Brydie, Charles jr, thief, res. New Deer Aberdeenshire, tr. 22 May 1752,
     fr. Aberdeen to Va, in *Jean & Elizabeth of Aberdeen*. (AJ227)
663. Bryson, James, b. 1756, farmer, res. Glasgow, sh. May 1774, fr.
     Greenock to N.Y., in *Matty*. (PRO.T47.12)
664. Buchan, James, b. 1764, res. Paisley Renfrewshire, sh. Feb 1774, fr.
     Greenock to N.Y., in *Commerce*. (PRO.T47.12)
665. Buchan, Robert, clergyman edu. Edinburgh Uni 1770, sh. 1772, to Va.
     (EMA17)(FPA.310)
666. Buchan, Thomas, b. 1745, farmer, res. Stirling, sh. May 1775, fr.
     Greenock to N.Y., in *Monimia*. (PRO.T47.12)
667. Buchanan of Drumhead, Archibald, merchant, res. Dunbartonshire, sh. pre
     1751, sett. Williamsburg & Norfolk Va. (SRO.RS10.8.250)
668. Buchanan, Alexander, Covenanter, res. Buchlyvie Stirlingshire, tr. 12 Dec
     1678, fr. Leith to West Indies, in *St Michael of Scarborough*.
     (PC.6.76)
669. Buchanan, Alexander, b. 1728, Jacobite, res. Auchleishie Callender
     Stirlingshire, tr. 22 Apr 1747, fr. Liverpool to Va, in *Johnson*, arr.
     Port Oxford Md 5 Aug 1747. (P.2.58)(MR67)(PRO.T1.328)
670. Buchanan, Andrew, res. Kippen Stirlingshire, tr. June 1684, fr. Glasgow.
     (PC.8.710)
671. Buchanan, Andrew, Covenanter, res. Shirgarton, tr. 12 Dec 1678, fr.
     Leith to West Indies, in *St Michael of Scarborough*. (PC.6.76)
672. Buchanan, Archibald, merchant, res. Glasgow, pts. Archibald Buchanan of
     Drumhead & Janet Buchanan, sh. pre 1757, sett. Silverbank Prince
     Edward Co Va. (SRO.RS10.9.84)
673. Buchanan, Archibald, b. 1740, pewterer, res. Edinburgh, sh. May 1775,
     fr. Greenock to N.Y. or Ga, in *Christy*. (PRO.T47.12)
674. Buchanan, Charles, b. 1728, Killearn Stirlingshire, surgeon edu. Glasgow
     Uni 1743, res. Killearn, pts. William Buchanan of Carbeth, sett.
     Jamaica, d. 1752 Jamaica. (MAGU30)

675. Buchanan, David, b. 10 Dec 1760, Glasgow, merchant edu. Glasgow Uni 1772, res. Glasgow, pts. George Buchanan & Lillias Dunlop, sett. Va, d. 20 May 1827 Glasgow. (MAGU100)
676. Buchanan, Duncan, b. 1756, res. Glasgow, sh. Sept 1774, fr. Greenock to Jamaica, in *Jamaica*. (PRO.T47.12)
677. Buchanan, George, physician, res. Dunbartonshire, sh. pre 1739, sett. Baltimore Co Md. (SRO.RS10.7.275)
678. Buchanan, George, Covenanter, res. Kippen Stirlingshire, tr. 21 July 1684, fr. Gourock to Port Royal S.C., in *Carolina Merchant*. (ECJ72)(PC.8.710)
679. Buchanan, Gilbert, baker, Covenanter, res. Glasgow, pts. Walter Buchanan, tr. June 1678, to West Indies. (PC.5.474)
680. Buchanan, Grisel, thief, res. Westfield of Cathcart Glasgow, tr. Sept 1766. (AJ978)
681. Buchanan, Henry, b. 1751, wright, res. Glasgow, sh. Apr 1775, fr. Greenock to Salem, in *Glasgow Packet*. (PRO.T47.12)
682. Buchanan, James, merchant, res. Dunbartonshire, pts. James Buchanan of Gyleston, sh. pre 1756, sett. Falmouth Va. (SRO.RS10.9.40)
683. Buchanan, James, merchant, res. Dunbartonshire, sh. pre 1771, sett. Jamaica. (SRO.RS10.10.361)
684. Buchanan, James, merchant, pts. Archibald Buchanan of Drumhead, sh. pre 1759, sett. Va. (SRO.SH.16.3.1759)
685. Buchanan, Jean, b. 1738, res. Glasgow, sh. Apr 1775, fr. Greenock to Salem, in *Glasgow Packet*. (PRO.T47.12)
686. Buchanan, John, cooper, res. Glasgow, pts. John Buchanan, tr. June 1684, fr. Port Glasgow, in *Pelican*. (PC.9.208)
687. Buchanan, John, b. 1716, farmer, res. Galloway, sh. May 1774, fr. Stranraer to N.Y., in *Gale*. (PRO.T47.12)
688. Buchanan, John, b. 1725, servant, Jacobite, res. Auchterarder Perthshire, tr. 24 Feb 1747, fr. Liverpool to Va, in *Gildart*, arr. Port North Potomac Md 5 Aug 1747. (P.2.60)(MR69)(PRO.T1.328)
689. Buchanan, John, b. 1743, Dumfries-shire, clergyman edu. Edinburgh Uni 1774, sh. 1774, sett. Henrico Co Va, d. 19 Dec 1822 Richmond Va. (FPA311)
690. Buchanan, John, b. 1748, Dumfries, clergyman, sh. Sept 1775, sett. Lexington & Henrico Va, d. 1822 Henrico. (EMA17)(OD20)
691. Buchanan, Margaret, pts. John Buchanan of Glens, sh. pre 1768, sett. Va, m. Thomas Peters. (CPD540)
692. Buchanan, Margaret, b. 1740, res. Glasgow, sh. May 1775, fr. Greenock to N.Y., in *Lilly*. (PRO.T47.12)
693. Buchanan, Marion, tr. 21 Oct 1682, fr. Greenock to N.Y. (ETR221)
694. Buchanan, Matthew, clergyman, sh. 1704, to N.Y., sett. Carolina. (EMA17)

695. Buchanan, Robert, sailor, res. Craigward of Alloway, pts. Robert
     Buchanan, sh. 14 July 1698, fr. Leith to Darien, in *Unicorn*, Edin
     pr1707 CC8.8.83)
696. Buchanan, Walter, thief, res. Balquhan Stirlingshire, tr. May 1729.
     (SRO.JC.13.6)
697. Buchanan, Walter, sailor, res. Kilmarnock Ayrshire, sh. 14 July 1698, fr.
     Leith to Darien, in *St Andrew*, d. Jamaica, Edin pr1707 CC8.8.83
698. Buchanan, William, b. 1750, weaver, res. Paisley Renfrewshire, sh. May
     1775, fr. Greenock to N.Y., in *Lilly*. (PRO.T47.12)
699. Budge, William, b. 1753, joiner, sh. Sept 1775, fr. Newcastle to Ga, in
     Georgia Packet, sett. Friendsborough Ga. (PRO.T47.12)
700. Buges, James, b. 1748, merchant, res. Edinburgh, sh. May 1775, fr.
     Greenock to N.C., in *Ulysses*. (PRO.T47.12)
701. Buie, Donald, smith, res. Jura Argyll, sh. 1754, to Cape Fear N.C.
     (SRO.GD64\5.21)
702. Buist, John, sailor, res. Auchterderran Fife, sh. 14 July 1698, fr. Leith to
     Darien, in *Caledonia*, Edin pr1707 CC8.8.83
703. Bulman, George, b. 1729, carpenter, sh. Sept 1775, fr. Newcastle to Ga,
     in *Georgia Packet*, sett. Friendsborough Ga, m. Elizabeth .., ch.
     George Diana. (PRO.T47.10)
704. Buntine, James, sh. 16 Dec 1773, fr. Greenock to Jamaica, in *Mary of
     Glasgow*. (SRO.CE60.1.7)
705. Buntine, Robert, sailor, res. Bo'ness West Lothian, sh. 1698, to Darien,
     in *Olive Branch*, Edin pr1707 CC8.8.83
706. Burbaux, Thomas, coxswain, sh. 14 July 1698, fr. Leith to Darien, in
     Unicorn, Edin pr1707 CC8.8.83
707. Burch, Richard, Jacobite, tr. 28 July 1716, fr. Liverpool to Va, in
     Godspeed, arr. Md Oct 1716.
     (SPC.1716.310)(CTB31.209)(HM389)
708. Burd, James, pts. Erward Burd of Ormiston & Jean Haliburton, sh. pre
     1771, sett. Lancaster Pa. (SRO.RD2.212.867)
709. Burn, Henry, merchant, res. Edinburgh, pts. Henry Burn, sh. Feb 1714.
     (EBR.4.242)
710. Burn, James, res. Edinburgh, pts. William Burn & Janet Scotland, sh. pre
     1782, sett. Baltimore. (SRO.RD3.294.274)
711. Burn, John, Jacobite, res. Northumberland, tr. 1747. (MR196)
712. Burn, John, Jacobite, tr. 21 Apr 1716, fr. Liverpool to S.C., in
     Wakefield. (SPC.1716.309)(CTB31.205)
713. Burne, John, Jacobite, tr. 29 June 1716, fr. Liverpool to Jamaica or Va,
     in *Elizabeth & Anne*, arr. Va.
     (SPC.1716.310)(CTB31.208)(VSP.1.186)
714. Burnet, Alexander, res. Edinburgh, sh. 7 Feb 1774, fr. London to Va, in
     Planter, arr. Fredericksburg Va 10 May 1774. (PRO.T47.9\11)

715. Burnet, Anna, whore, res. Edinburgh, tr. 19 Mar 1695. (SRO.PC2.25.216)
716. Burnet, George, tr. Aug 1751, fr. Aberdeen to Va. (AJ193)
717. Burnet, Janet, whore, res. Edinburgh, tr. 19 Mar 1695. (SRO.PC2.25.216)
718. Burnet, Margaret, infanticide, tr. 22 Nov 1755. (SRO.HCR.I.89)
719. Burnet, William, physician, res. Dumfries-shire, sh. pre 1776, sett. WFla. (SRO.RS23.21.335)
720. Burnet, William, sh. 1684, to East N.J. (Insh242)
721. Burnett, .., clergyman, sh. 1700, to Va. (EMA18)
722. Burnett, Alexander, court clerk, sh. pre 1705, sett. Barbados. (SPC.1705.409)
723. Burnett, John, b. 1611, Aberdeen, merchant, sh. 24 Oct 1635, fr. London to Va, in *Abraham of London*. (SPC.1638.277)(PRO.E157.20)
724. Burnett, John, b. 1719, miller, Jacobite, res. Ballandarg Kirriemuir Angus, tr. 22 Apr 1747, fr. Liverpool to Va, in *Johnson*, arr. Port Oxford Md 5 Aug 1747. (P.2.64)(MR96)(PRO.T1.328)
725. Burns, George, sailor, res. Dysart Fife, sh. 14 July 1698, fr. Leith to Darien, in *St Andrew*, m. Margaret Watson, Edin pr1707 CC8.8.83
726. Burns, John, b. 1739, weaver, res. Paisley Renfrewshire, sh. Feb 1774, fr. Greenock to N.Y., in *Commerce*. (PRO.T47.12)
727. Burnside, Harry, b. 1735, laborer, res. Perthshire, sh. May 1775, fr. Greenock to N.Y., in *Monimia*. (PRO.T47.12)
728. Burrol, John, sailor, d. 29 Nov 1698 Darien. (NLS.RY2b8\19)
729. Bursick, George, Jacobite, tr. 21 Apr 1716, fr. Liverpool to S.C., in *Wakefield*. (SPC.1716.309)(CTB31.205)
730. Burt, Charles, b. 1748, wright, res. Glasgow, sh. May 1774, fr. Greenock to N.Y., in *Matty*. (PRO.T47.12)
731. Burt, Patrick, res. Perth, pts. James Burt & Marjory Donaldson, sett. St Michael's S.C., d. pre 1775, Edin pr1775 CC8.8.123
732. Burt, Thomas, cook, res. Burntisland Fife, sh. 14 July 1698, fr. Leith to Darien, in *Unicorn*, m. Margaret Gray, Edin pr1707 CC8.8.83
733. Burt, Thomas, clerk, sh. 14 July 1698, fr. Leith to Darien, in *Unicorn*, Edin pr1707 CC8.8.83
734. Burton, Joseph, Jacobite, tr. 30 Mar 1716, fr. Liverpool to Antigua, in *Scipio*. (SPC.1716.310)(CTB31.204)
735. Butter, Thomas, Jacobite, tr. 24 May 1716, fr. Liverpool to Md, in *Friendship*, arr. Md Aug 1716. (SPC.1716.311)(HM387)
736. Butter, William, b. 1745, coppersmith, res. Perth, sh. May 1775, fr. Leith to Philadelphia, in *Friendship*. (PRO.T47.12)
737. Byres, William, thief, tr. Mar 1774. (AJ1367)
738. Caddell, Christian, res. Edinburgh, tr. 8 May 1663, fr. Leith to Barbados, in *Mary*. (EBR.186.13.4)

739. Caddell, John, b. 1749, mason, res. Perth, sh. May 1774, fr. Greenock to N.Y., in *George*. (PRO.T47.12)
740. Caddie, James, b. 1742, farmer, res. Montrose Angus, sh. May 1775, fr. Greenock to N.Y., in *Lilly*. (PRO.T47.12)
741. Caigow, Janet, infanticide, res. Ayrshire, tr. 1749. (SM.11.462)
742. Cairg, John, b. 1722, pedlar, Jacobite, tr. 1747. (P.2.66)
743. Cairns, David, b. 1753, attorney, sh. Apr 1774, fr. London to Quebec, in *Amity's Desire*. (PRO.T47.9\11)
744. Cairns, Jane, b. 1756, spinner, sh. Apr 1774, fr. London to Quebec, in *Amity's Desire*. (PRO.T47.9\11)
745. Cairns, John, b. 1751, wright, res. Fife, sh. May 1775, fr. Leith to Philadelphia, in *Friendship*. (PRO.T47.12)
746. Calder, Alexander, b. 1733, wright, res. Wick Caithness, sh. Sept 1775, fr. Kirkwall Orkney to Savannah Ga, in *Marlborough*, sett. Richmond Co Ga, m. Henrietta Bain, ch. Katherine Robert John James Christian Peggy. (PRO.T47.12)
747. Calder, James, b. 1756, farmer, res. Strathspey, sh. May 1774, fr. Greenock to N.Y., in *George*. (PRO.T47.12)
748. Calder, Margaret, b. 1750, res. Strathspey, sh. May 1774, fr. Greenock to N.Y., in *George*. (PRO.T47.12)
749. Calder, Ninian, b. 1756, weaver, res. Paisley Renfrewshire, sh. Feb 1774, fr. Greenock to N.Y., in *Commerce*. (PRO.T47.12)
750. Calder, William, b. 1739, weaver, res. Paisley Renfrewshire, sh. Feb 1774, fr. Greenock to N.Y., in *Commerce*, m. Agnes Roddan, ch. James Agnes Margaret Elizabeth Robert. (PRO.T47.12)
751. Calderwood, George, quartermaster, sh. 14 July 1698, fr. Leith to Darien, in *St Andrew*, Edin pr 1707 CC8.8.83
752. Calderwood, John, thief, res. Edinburgh, tr. 7 Nov 1667. (PC.2.385)
753. Caldwell, Donald, b. 1756, shoemaker, res. Kintyre Argyll, sh. Aug 1774, fr. Greenock to Wilmington N.C., in *Ulysses*. (PRO.T47.12)
754. Caldwell, James, seaman, res. Falkirk Stirlingshire, m. Agnes .., d. 1774 Boston Mass, PCC pr1774
755. Caldwell, John, sailor, res. Burntisland Fife, sh. 14 July 1698, fr. Leith to Darien, in *Caledonia*, m. Marion Orrock, Edin pr1707 CC8.8.83
756. Caldwell, John, sailor, fr. Leith to Darien, in *Caledonia*, Edin pr 1707 CC8.8.83
757. Caldwell, Robert, sailor, res. Glasgow, sh. 18 Aug 1699, fr. Clyde to Darien, in *Rising Sun*, Edin pr 1707 CC8.8.83
758. Callan, Alexander, b. 1752, workman, sh. Aug 1774, fr. Greenock to Wilmington N.C., in *Ulysses*. (PRO.T47.12)
759. Callander, John, res. Craigforth Stirlingshire, sh. 1767, sett. EFla. (PRO.CO5.542)

760. Callander, John, res. Craigforth Stirlingshire, sh. 1767, sett. E Fla. (PRO.CO5.542)
761. Callend, James, glover, Covenanter, tr. May 1685, fr. Glasgow. (PC.8.516)
762. Callum, James, glover, Covenanter, res. Dumfries, tr. 1666, d. Carolina. (HD443)
763. Camby, Jacob, sailor, sh. 14 July 1698, fr. Leith to Darien, in *Unicorn*, Edin pr1708 CC8.8.84
764. Cameron, Alexander, sh. 1737, sett. Darien Ga. (SPC.43.172)
765. Cameron, Alexander, thief, tr. Apr 1755. (SRO.HCR.I.89)
766. Cameron, Alexander, 1727, Jacobite, res. Nairn, tr. 31 Mar 1747, fr. Tilbury to Barbados, in *Frere*. (P.2.70)(MR174)
767. Cameron, Alexander, cattlethief, res. Inverness-shire, tr. May 1765, fr. Glasgow. (AJ908) (alias 3738)
768. Cameron, Alexander, b. 1728, laborer, Jacobite, res. Lochaber Inverness-shire, tr. 31 Mar 1747. (P.2.70)(MR33)
769. Cameron, Alexander, b. 1728, cartwright, Jacobite, res. Dunmaglass Inverness-shire, tr. 5 May 1747, fr. Liverpool to Leeward Islands, in *Veteran*, arr. Martinique June 1747. (PRO.SP36.102)(MR174)(P.2.70)
770. Cameron, Alexander, b. 1731, laborer, Jacobite, res. Lochaber, tr. 8 May 1747, to Antigua. (P.2.70)(MR30)
771. Cameron, Alexander, b. 1742, farmer, res. Strathspey, sh. May 1774, fr. Greenock to N.Y., in *George*, m. Jean ..., ch. Janet Elspa Jean. (PRO.T47.12)
772. Cameron, Alexander, b. 1744, servant, res. Auchhall, sh. Nov 1774, fr. Stornaway to N.Y., in *Peace and Plenty*. (PRO.T47.12)
773. Cameron, Alexander, b. 1761, servant, res. Garboost, sh. May 1774, fr. Stornaway to Philadelphia, in *Friendship*. (PRO.T47.12)
774. Cameron, Allan, sheepstealer, tr. Sept 1752. (SM.14.461)
775. Cameron, Allan, res. Camqheron Rannoch Perthshire, pts. Angus Cameron & Christian Menzies, pre 1771, sett. Jamaica. (SRO.RD2.218.744)
776. Cameron, Allan, b. 1746, farmer, res. Kintyre Argyll, sh. Aug 1774, fr. Greenock to Wilmington N.C., in *Ulysses*. (PRO.T47.12)
777. Cameron, Angus, inn-servant, thief, res. Strontian Argyll, tr. May 1767. (AJ1009)
778. Cameron, Angus, b. 1728, farmer, res. Breadalbane Perthshire, sh. June 1775, fr. Greenock to N.Y., in *Commerce*, m. Katherine McDonald, ch. Mary John Alexander. (PRO.T47.12)
779. Cameron, Angus, b. 1755, farmer, res. Kintyre Argyll, sh. Aug 1774, fr. Greenock to Wilmington N.C., in *Ulysses*, m. Katrine ... (PRO.T47.12)

780. Cameron, Anne, b. 1729, spinner, Jacobite, res. Lochaber Inverness-shire, tr. 5 May 1747, fr. Liverpool to Leeward Islands, in *Veteran*, arr. Martinique June 1747. (PRO.SP36.102)(P.2.72)
781. Cameron, Catherine, b. 1775, res. Beauly Inverness-shire, sh. July 1775, fr. Stornaway to Philadelphia, in *Clementina*. (PRO.T47.12)
782. Cameron, Charles, b. 1770, res. Beauly Inverness-shire, sh. July 1775, fr. Stornaway to Philadelphia, in *Clementina*. (PRO.T47.12)
783. Cameron, Daniel, b. 1707, Jacobite, res. Ardnamurchan Argyll, tr. 31 Mar 1747. (MR34)(P.2.74)
784. Cameron, Donald, Jacobite, tr. 22 Apr 1747, fr. Liverpool to Va, in *Johnson*, arr. Port Oxford Md 5 Aug 1747. (PRO.T1.328)
785. Cameron, Donald, thief, res. Inverness-shire, tr. May 1753. (SM.15.260)
786. Cameron, Donald, res. Highlands, sh. 1737, to Ga. (SPC.43.189)
787. Cameron, Donald, Jacobite, tr. 22 Apr 1747, fr. Liverpool, in *Johnson*, arr. Port Oxford Md 5 Aug 1747. (PRO.TI.328)
788. Cameron, Donald, Jacobite, tr. 7 May 1716, fr. Liverpool to S.C., in *Susannah*. (SPC.1716.309)(CTB31.206)
789. Cameron, Donald, b. 1699, husbandman, Jacobite, res. Fort William Inverness-shire, tr. 31 Mar 1747, to Barbados, in *Frere*. (P.2.76)(MR34)(PRO.CO137.58)
790. Cameron, Donald, b. 1710, res. Beauly Inverness-shire, sh. July 1775, fr. Stornaway to Philadelphia, in *Clementina*. (PRO.T47.12)
791. Cameron, Donald, b. 1717, farmer, Jacobite, res. Glen Urquhart Inverness-shire, tr. 31 Mar 1747, fr. Tilbury. (P.2.74)(MR150)
792. Cameron, Donald, b. 1727, pedlar, Jacobite, res. Rahoy Morvern Argyll , tr. 31 Mar 1747, fr. Tilbury, in *St George or Carteret*, arr. Jamaica 1747. (P.2.76)(MR34)(PRO.CO137.58)
793. Cameron, Donald, b. 1751, servant, res. Fort Augustus Inverness-shire, sh. July 1775, fr. Stornaway to Philadelphia, in *Clementina*. (PRO.T47.12)
794. Cameron, Donald Dow Oig, thief, res. Westermains Braes of Aird Inverness-shire, tr. June 1754. (SM.16.203) (alias 4514)
795. Cameron, Dougall, Jacobite, res. Inverness, tr. 24 Feb 1747, fr. Liverpool, in *Gildart*, arr. Port North Potomac Md 1747. (P.2.76)(MR34)(PRO.T1.328)
796. Cameron, Duncan, Jacobite, tr. 25 June 1716, fr. Liverpool to St Kitts, in *Hockenhill*. (CTB31.207)
797. Cameron, Duncan, Jacobite, tr. 22 Apr 1747, fr. Liverpool to Va, in *Johnson*, arr. Port Oxford Md 5 Aug 1747. (PRO.T1.328)
798. Cameron, Duncan, servant, thief, res. Aberdeenshire, tr. May 1726. (SRO.JC11.6)
799. Cameron, Duncan, Jacobite, tr. 25 June 1716, fr. Liverpool to St Kitts, in *Hockenhill*. (CTB31.207)

38

800. Cameron, Duncan, b. 1677, servant, Jacobite, res. Moidart Inverness-shire, tr. 21 Mar 1747, fr. London to Barbados, in *Frere*. (P.2.78)(MR9)

801. Cameron, Duncan, b. 1715, husbandman, Jacobite, res. Glenmoriston Inverness-shire, tr. 31 Mar 1747, fr. Tilbury to Barbados, in *Frere*. (P.2.78)(MR150)

802. Cameron, Duncan Donald, Jacobite, tr. 25 June 1716, fr. Liverpool to St Kitts, in *Hockenhill*. (SPC.1716.312)(CTB31.207)

803. Cameron, Effie, b. 1719, spinner, Jacobite, res. Lochaber Inverness-shire, tr. 5 May 1747, fr. Liverpool to Leeward Islands, in *Veteran*, arr. Martinique 1747. (P.2.80)(PRO.SP.36.102)

804. Cameron, Ewan, thief, tr. 25 Apr 1755. (SRO.HCR.I.89)

805. Cameron, Ewan, b. 1717, husbandman, Jacobite, res. Hillhouses Ross-shire, tr. 19 Mar 1747, fr. Tilbury to Jamaica , in *St George or Carteret*, arr. Jamaica 1747. (P.2.80)(MR117)(PRO.CO137.58)

806. Cameron, Ewan More, b. 1695, aleseller, Jacobite, res. Maryburgh Fort William Inverness-shire, tr. 19 Mar 1747, fr. Tilbury to Jamaica , in *St George or Carteret*, arr. Jamaica 1747. (MR34)(P.2.80)(PRO.CO137.58)

807. Cameron, Finlay, Jacobite, tr. 24 May 1716, fr. Liverpool, in *Friendship*, arr. Md Aug 1716. (SPC.1716.311)(HM387)

808. Cameron, Flora, b. 1707, spinner, Jacobite, res. Lochaber Inverness-shire, tr. 5 May 1747, fr. Liverpool to Leeward Islands, in *Veteran*, arr. Martinique June 1747. (P.2.80)(PRO.SP36.102)

809. Cameron, James, edu. Glasgow Uni 1767, res. Barony Glasgow, pts. John Cameron of Carntyn, d. 1794 Jamaica. (MAGU84)

810. Cameron, James, b. 1742, farmer, res. Strathspey, sh. May 1774, fr. Greenock to N.Y., in *George*. (PRO.T47.12)

811. Cameron, James, b. 1750, wright, res. Stirling, sh. May 1775, fr. Greenock to N.Y., in *Monimia*, m. Janet ... (PRO.T47.12)

812. Cameron, James, b. 1753, farmer, res. Blair Atholl Perthshire, sh. May 1775, fr. Greenock to N.Y., in *Monimia*. (PRO.T47.12)

813. Cameron, Janet, b. 1757, servant, res. Loch Broom Ross-shire, sh. July 1775, fr. Stornaway to Philadelphia, in *Clementina*. (PRO.T47.12)

814. Cameron, Jean, b. 1755, res. Strathspey, sh. May 1774, fr. Greenock to N.Y., in *George*. (PRO.T47.12)

815. Cameron, John, Jacobite, tr. 22 Apr 1747, fr. Liverpool to Va, in *Johnson*, arr. Port Oxford Md 5 Aug 1747. (PRO.T1.328)

816. Cameron, John, Jacobite, tr. 28 July 1716, fr. Liverpool to Va, in *Godspeed*, arr. Md Oct 1716. (SPC.1716.310)(HM388)

817. Cameron, John, herdsman, thief, res. Kinlochleven Inverness-shire, tr. June 1754. (SM.16.203)

818. Cameron, John, horsethief, res. Inverness-shire, tr. May 1775. (AJ1432)

819. Cameron, John, Jacobite, tr. 22 Apr 1747, fr. Liverpool to Va, in
    Johnson, arr. Port Oxford Md 5 Aug 1747. (PRO.T1.328)
820. Cameron, John, Jacobite, tr. 22 Apr 1747, fr. Liverpool to Va, in
    Johnson, arr. Port Oxford Md 5 Aug 1747. (PRO.T1.328)
821. Cameron, John, horsethief, res. Suinart Argyll, tr. 1732. (JRA.2.451)
    (alias 3733)
822. Cameron, John, Jacobite, tr. 7 May 1716, fr. Liverpool to S.C., in
    Susannah. (SPC.1716.309)(CTB31.206)
823. Cameron, John, b. 1677, laborer, Jacobite, tr. 1747, fr. London to
    Barbados, in *Frere*. (P.2.82)(MR35)
824. Cameron, John, b. 1687, laborer, Jacobite, tr. 31 Mar 1747, to Jamaica ,
    in *St George or Carteret*, arr. Jamaica 1747.
    (PRO.CO137.58)(MR35)(P.2.82)
825. Cameron, John, b. 1714, laborer, Jacobite, res. Lochaber Inverness-shire,
    tr. 31 Mar 1747. (MR35)(P.2.84)
826. Cameron, John, b. 1714, Highlands, husbandman, sh. Aug 1734, fr.
    London to Jamaica. (CLRO\AIA)
827. Cameron, John, b. 1725, weaver, Jacobite, res. Aigus Ross-shire, tr. 31
    Mar 1747, fr. Tilbury to Barbados, in *Frere*. (P.2.82)(MR117)
828. Cameron, John, b. 1741, farmer, res. Beauly Inverness-shire, sh. July
    1775, fr. Stornaway to Philadelphia, in *Clementina*. (PRO.T47.12)
829. Cameron, John, b. 1753, farmer, res. Strathspey, sh. May 1774, fr.
    Greenock to N.Y., in *George*. (PRO.T47.12)
830. Cameron, John Ban, cattle thief, res. Strowan Argyll, tr. Sept 1765.
    (AJ925)
831. Cameron, Kenneth, b. 1726, husbandman, Jacobite, res. Lochmallin
    Ross-shire, tr. 31 Mar 1747, to Jamaica , in *St George or Carteret*,
    arr. Jamaica 1747. (P.2.84)(PRO.CO137.58)
832. Cameron, Malcolm, Jacobite, res. Fort William Inverness-shire, tr. 24
    Feb 1747, fr. Liverpool, in *Gildart*, arr. Port North Potomac Md 5
    Aug 1747. (P.2.84)(MR35)(PRO.T1.328)
833. Cameron, Mary, b. 1772, res. Beauly Inverness-shire, sh. July 1775, fr.
    Stornaway to Philadelphia, in *Clementina*. (PRO.T47.12)
834. Cameron, Murdo, b. 1727, farmer, res. Auchhall, sh. Nov 1774, fr.
    Stornaway to N.Y., in *Peace and Plenty*, m. Mary ..., ch. Ann Bell
    Jean Mary Ann Kenneth Murdoch Hector. (PRO.T47.12)
835. Cameron, Robert, Covenanter, res. West Teviotdale, tr. Aug 1685, fr.
    Leith to Jamaica, d. 1685 at sea. (PC.11.329)(LJ15)
836. Cameron, Simon, b. 1746, farmer, res. Beauly Inverness-shire, sh. July
    1775, fr. Stornaway to Philadelphia, in *Clementina*. (PRO.T47.12)
837. Cameron, William, b. 1697, farmer, Jacobite, res. Glenmoriston
    Inverness-shire, tr. 31 Mar 1747, fr. Tilbury. (P.2.88)

838. Cameron, William, b. 1712, farmer, Jacobite, res. Glen Urquhart Inverness-shire, tr. 31 Mar 1747, fr. Tilbury to Barbados, in *Frere*. (P.2.88)(PRO.SP36.102)

839. Campbell, Alexander, physician, m. Elizabeth .., ch. John Louisa, d. 1751 Jamaica, Edin pr1753 CC8.8.114

840. Campbell, Alexander, d. 20 Dec 1699 Fort St Andrew Darien. (DP209)

841. Campbell, Alexander, Jacobite, tr. 22 Apr 1747, fr. Liverpool to Va, in *Johnson*, arr. Port Oxford Md 5 Aug 1747. (PRO.T1.328)

842. Campbell, Alexander, physician, sett. Jamaica, m. Elizabeth ..., ch. John & Louisa, d. pre Nov 1753 Jamaica, Edin pr 1753 CC8.8.114\2

843. Campbell, Alexander, sett. Darien, d. 20 Dec 1699 Fort St Andrew Darien. (DP209)

844. Campbell, Alexander, laborer, Jacobite, res. Claddie Aberdeenshire, tr. 22 Apr 1747, fr. Liverpool to Va, in *Johnson*, arr. Port Oxford Md 5 Aug 1747. (PRO.T1.328)(MR96)

845. Campbell, Alexander, sailor, sh. 18 Aug 1699, fr. Clyde to Darien, in *Rising Sun*, Edin pr 1707 CC8.8.83

846. Campbell, Alexander, pre 1757, sett. Prince George Co Md, m. Ann Arthur. (SRO.RD3.224.480)

847. Campbell, Alexander, b. 1707, weaver, Jacobite, res. Argyll, tr. 5 May 1747, fr. Liverpool to Leeward Islands, in *Veteran*, arr. Martinique June 1747. (P.2.88)(PRO.SP36.102)

848. Campbell, Alexander, b. 1717, drover, Jacobite, res. Lochaber Inverness-shire, tr. 22 Apr 1747. (P.2.88)

849. Campbell, Alexander, b. 1720, laborer, Jacobite, res. Argyll, tr. 5 May 1747, fr. Liverpool to Leeward islands, in *Veteran*, arr. Martinique June 1747. (PRO.SP36.102)

850. Campbell, Alexander, b. 1738, farmer, res. Natiskir, sh. May 1774, fr. Stornaway to Philadelphia, in *Friendship*, m. Margaret Morrison, ch. Neil Isobel. (PRO.T47.12)

851. Campbell, Alexander, b. 1762, res. Langwell Rogart Sutherland, sh. Apr 1774, to Wilmington N.C., in *Bachelor of Leith*. (PRO.T47.12)

852. Campbell, Allan, Jacobite, tr. 21 Feb 1747. (P.2.88)

853. Campbell, Andrew, merchant, res. Glasgow, pre 1744, sett. Jamaica. (SRO.RD2.169.74)

854. Campbell, Andrew, b. 1740, shoemaker, res. Galloway, sh. May 1774, fr. Stranraer to N.Y., in *Gale*, m. Agnes ..., ch. Jean Mary-Ann. (PRO.T47.12)

855. Campbell, Angus, Jacobite, res. Lochaber Inverness-shire, tr. 4 Sept 1748. (P.2.88)

856. Campbell, Archibald, marine, res. Roseneath Dunbartonshire, pts. Colin Campbell, d. 1775 Boston Mass, PCC pr1775

857. Campbell, Archibald, Covenanter, res. Mondrige Kintyre Argyll, tr. Aug 1685. (PC.11.329)

858. Campbell, Archibald, pts. Lord Neil Campbell, tr. 1685. (ETR377)
859. Campbell, Archibald, Kirnan, clergyman, sh. 1730, to Va. (EMA18)
860. Campbell, Archibald, b. 1736, farmer, res. Kintyre Argyll, sh. Sept
     1774, fr. Greenock to Wilmington N.C., in *Diana*, m. Jean
     McNeil, ch. Mary Girzie Lachlan. (PRO.T47.12)
861. Campbell, Archibald, b. 1755, res. Campbelltown Argyll, sh. Sept 1774,
     fr. Greenock to Jamaica, in *Jamaica*. (PRO.T47.12)
862. Campbell, Barbara, b. 1728, spinner, Jacobite, res. Perthshire, tr. 5 May
     1747, fr. Liverpool to Leeward Islands, in *Veteran*, arr. Martinique
     June1747. (P.2.90)(PRO.SP36.102)
863. Campbell, Barbara, b. 1757, servant, res. Ross-shire, sh. May 1775, fr.
     Leith to Philadelphia, in *Friendship*. (PRO.T47.12)
864. Campbell, Charles, Covenanter, res. Airth Stirlingshire, tr. Aug 1670.
     (PC.3.207)
865. Campbell, Colin, soldier, res. Kenmore Perthshire, pts. Rev Patrick
     Campbell, sh. 1698, to Darien, d. 1699 Jamaica, Edin pr1707
     CC8.8.83
866. Campbell, Colin, Covenanter, res. Argyll, tr. July 1685, fr. Leith to East
     N.J. (PC.11.329)
867. Campbell, Colin, mate, sh. 14 July 1698, fr. Leith to Darien, in *St
     Andrew*, Edin pr 1707 CC8.8.83
868. Campbell, Colin, soldier, res. Kenmore Perthshire, pts. Rev Patrick
     Campbell, sh. 1698, fr. Leith to Darien, d. 1699 Jamaica, Edin pr
     1707 CC8.8.83
869. Campbell, Colin, merchant, res. Greenock, sett. Holland Estate St
     Elizabeth Cornwall Jamaica, m. Henrietta Campbell 1776.
     (CPD73)
870. Campbell, Colin, b. 1707, Earnhill Nairn, clergyman edu. Aberdeen Uni
     1729, pts. Colin Campbell, sh. 1737, to Nevis, sett. Nevis Pa
     N.J., d. 9 Aug 1766 Burlington N.J. (EMA18)
871. Campbell, Colin, b. 1748, smith, res. Breadalbane Perthshire, sh. June
     1775, fr. Greenock to N.Y., in *Commerce*. (PRO.T47.12)
872. Campbell, Colin, b. 1751, merchant, res. Perthshire, sh. May 1775, fr.
     Greenock to N.Y., in *Monimia*. (PRO.T47.12)
873. Campbell, Colin, b. 1753, student, res. Inverness, sh. Jan 1774, fr.
     Greenock to Nevis, in *Aurora*. (SRO.CE60.1.7)
874. Campbell, Daniel, res. Kilbride, pts. Alexander Campbell, sh. Sept 1769,
     fr. Glasgow to Md, sett. Portobacco Md. (SRA.TD180.20)
875. Campbell, Daniel, planter, pre 1772, sett. St Elizabeth Cornwall Co
     Jamaica. (SRO.RD2.215.143)
876. Campbell, Daniel, b. 1702, res. Dunrobin Sutherland, sh. Aug 1720, fr.
     London to Md. (CLROIAIA)
877. Campbell, Daniel, b. 1727, Jacobite, tr. 31 Mar 1747, fr. Tilbury to
     Barbados, in *Frere*. (P.2.90)(MR151)

878. Campbell, Daniel, b. 1728, Jacobite, tr. 1747, fr. Tilbury. (P.2.90)(MR22)
879. Campbell, Daniel, b. 1749, farmer, res. Kintyre Argyll, sh. Aug 1774, fr. Greenock to Wilmington N.C., in *Ulysses*. (PRO.T47.12)
880. Campbell, David, Covenanter, res. Falkirk Stirlingshire, tr. 11 Aug 1685, fr. Leith to East N.J., in *Henry & Francis*. (PC.11.145)
881. Campbell, David, b. 1735, writer, res. Edinburgh, sh. July 1775, fr. Greenock to Ga, in *Georgia*, ch. David Ann Jean Mary Susie Betty. (PRO.T47.12)
882. Campbell, David, b. 1744, tailor, res. Perthshire, sh. Oct 1774, fr. Greenock to Charleston S.C., in *Countess*. (PRO.T47.12)
883. Campbell, Donald, thief, res. Upper Rudill Argyll, pts. Charles Dow Campbell or McIver, tr. Apr 1729. (JRA.2.403) (alias 4023)
884. Campbell, Donald, Jacobite, in *St George or Carteret*, arr. Jamaica 1747. (PRO.CO137.58)
885. Campbell, Donald, Covenanter, tr. Aug 1685, fr. Leith to Jamaica. (PC.11.330)
886. Campbell, Donald, b. 1719, cattleherd, Jacobite, res. Dalchosnie Perthshire, tr. 31 Mar 1747, fr. Tilbury to Jamaica , in *St George or Carteret*, arr. Jamaica 1747. (MR22)(PRO.CO137.58)
887. Campbell, Donald, b. 1722, Jacobite, res. Ross-shire, tr. 31 Mar 1747, fr. Tilbury to Jamaica, in *St George or Carteret*, arr. Jamaica 1747. (P.2.90)(MR81)(PRO.CO137.58)
888. Campbell, Donald, b. 1724, farmer, res. Adrahoolish Sutherland, sh. April 1774, to Wilmington N.C., in *Bachelor of Leith*. (PRO.T47.12)
889. Campbell, Donald, b. 1726, husbandman, Jacobite, res. Lentiarm Ross-shire, tr. 31 Mar 1747, fr. Tilbury to Jamaica, in *St George or Carteret*, arr. Jamaica 1747. (P.2.90)(PRO.CO137.58)
890. Campbell, Donald, b. 1757, res. Campbelltown Argyll, sh. Sept 1774, fr. Greenock to Jamaica, in *Jamaica*. (PRO.T47.12)
891. Campbell, Dougald, res. Kintyre Argyll, pre 1745, sett. Glencaradale St Andrew's Jamaica. (SRO.RD2.169.250)
892. Campbell, Dougald, surgeon, pts. George Campbell, pre 1774, sett. Jamaica. (SRO.RD4.217.5)
893. Campbell, Dougall, b. 1729, servant, Jacobite, res. Lochaber Inverness-shire, tr. 5 May 1747, fr. Liverpool to Leeward Islands, in *Veteran*, arr. Martinique June 1747. (P.2.90)(PRO.SP36.102)
894. Campbell, Dougall, b. 1729, servant, Jacobite, res. Argyll, tr. 8 May 1747, to Antigua. (P.2.90)
895. Campbell, Duncan, soldier, d. 1699 Darien, Edin pr1707 CC8.8.83
896. Campbell, Duncan, merchant, res. Kilbrandon Argyll, pts. Rev James Campbell, sh. pre 1771, sett. Jamaica. (SRO.RS10.10.327)
897. Campbell, Duncan, soldier, sett. Darien, Edin pr 1707 CC8.8.83

43

898. Campbell, Duncan, merchant, res. Kilbrandon Argyll, pts. Rev James Campbell, pre 1770, sett. Jamaica. (SRO.RD2.215.143)
899. Campbell, Duncan, b. 1723, Jacobite, res. Ross-shire, tr. 20 Mar 1747, fr. Tilbury to Jamaica, in *St George or Carteret*, arr. Jamaica 1747. (P.2.90)(MR81)(PRO.CO137.58)
900. Campbell, Duncan, b. 1731, laborer, Jacobite, res. Argyll, tr. 5 May 1747, fr. Liverpool to Leeward Islands, in *Veteran*, arr. Martinique June 1747. (P.2.92)(PRO.SP36.102)
901. Campbell, Duncan, b. 1750, farmer, res. Perthshire, sh. May 1775, fr. Greenock to N.Y., in *Monimia*. (PRO.T47.12)
902. Campbell, Elisabeth, pickpocket, tr. Sept 1763, m. Robert Campbell. (AJ815)
903. Campbell, Elspia, b. 1745, servant, res. Beauly Inverness-shire, sh. July 1775, fr. Stornaway to Philadelphia, in *Clementina*. (PRO.T47.12)
904. Campbell, Ewan, b. 1727, Jacobite, res. Ross-shire, tr. 31 Mar 1747, fr. Tilbury to Jamaica or Barbados. (P.2.92)(MR81)
905. Campbell, George, Covenanter, res. Irvine Ayrshire, tr. 1679. (Irvine Gs)
906. Campbell, George, soldier, sh. pre 1765, sett. N.Y. (PCCol.4.818)
907. Campbell, Gilbert, b. 1729, servant, Jacobite, res. Sutherland, tr. 31 Mar 1747, fr. Tilbury to Barbados, in *Frere*. (P.2.92)(MR127)
908. Campbell, Hector, b. 1758, res. Langwell Rogart Sutherland, sh. Apr 1774, to Wilmington N.C., in *Bachelor of Leith*. (PRO.T47.12)
909. Campbell, Hew, merchant, res. Glasgow, pre 1744, sett. Jamaica. (SRO.RD2.169.74)
910. Campbell, Hew, sh. Feb 1683, fr. Port Glasgow to West Indies, in *Walter of Glasgow*. (SRO.E72.19.8)
911. Campbell, Hugh, merchant, pre1679, sett. Boston Mass. (Insh191)
912. Campbell, Hugh, b. 1730, laborer, res. Perthshire, sh. May 1775, fr. Greenock to N.Y., in *Monimia*. (PRO.T47.12)
913. Campbell, Isaac, b. 1720, clergyman edu. Glasgow Uni 1734, res. Kilsyth Stirlingshire, pts. William Campbell, sh. 1747, sett. Trinity Newport Charles Co Md, m. Jean Brown, ch. William Jean Gustavus James John Cecilia, d. 30 July 1784 Trinity. (EMA18)
914. Campbell, Ivor, Jacobite, tr. 1746. (SRO.GD103)
915. Campbell, James, sailor, sh. 18 Aug 1699, fr. Clyde to Darien, in *Rising Sun*, Edin pr1707 CC8.8.83
916. Campbell, James, Jacobite, tr. 30 Mar 1716, fr. Liverpool to Antigua, in *Scipio*. (SPC.1716.310)(CTB31.204)
917. Campbell, James, piper, Jacobite, res. Crieff Perthshire, tr. 21 Nov 1748. (P.2.94)(MR167) (alias 3870)
918. Campbell, James, sailor, sh. 169, fr. Leith to Darien, in *Hope & Rising Sun*, Edin pr 1707 CC8.8.83
919. Campbell, James, Jacobite, tr. 30 Mar 1716, fr. Liverpool to Antigua, in *Scipio*. (CTB31.204)

920. Campbell, James, clergyman, sh. 1721, to Va. (EMA18)
921. Campbell, James, res. Burnbank, tr. 1725. (EBR158.6045)
922. Campbell, James, b. 1734, farmer, res. Perthshire, sh. May 1775, fr.
     Greenock to N.Y., in *Monimia*, m. Jane Campbell. (PRO.T47.12)
923. Campbell, James, b. 1739, farmer, res. Perthshire, sh. May 1775, fr.
     Greenock to N.Y., in *Monimia*. (PRO.T47.12)
924. Campbell, Janet, tr. 21 Oct 1682, fr. Greenock to N.Y. (ETR221)
925. Campbell, Janet, whore, res. Edinburgh, tr. 2 Feb 1697. (SRO.PC2.26)
926. Campbell, Jean, infanticide, res. Ayrshire, tr. Oct 1764. (AJ878)
927. Campbell, Jean, b. 1754, res. Galloway, sh. May 1774, fr. Stranraer to
     N.Y., in *Gale*. (PRO.T47.12)
928. Campbell, Jenny, b. 1759, servant, res. Edinburgh, sh. May 1775, fr.
     Leith to Philadelphia, in *Friendship*. (PRO.T47.12)
929. Campbell, John, Jacobite, res. Inverness, tr. 8 May 1747, to Antigua.
     (P.2.94)
930. Campbell, John, res. Dunbartonshire, sh. pre 1771, sett. Saltspring
     Hanover Co Jamaica. (SRO.RS10.10.327)
931. Campbell, John, clergyman edu. King's Col Aberdeen 1771, sh. 1773, to
     Va, sett. Jamaica. (EMA18)
932. Campbell, John, Covenanter, res. Dunalter Kintyre Argyll, pts. Walter
     Campbell, tr. Aug 1685, fr. Leith to Jamaica. (PC.11.329)
933. Campbell, John, Covenanter, res. Auchenchrydie Cowal Argyll, pts.
     Donald Campbell, tr. Aug 1685, fr. Leith to Jamaica. (PC.11.329)
934. Campbell, John, Covenanter, res. Lochwoar Lorne Argyll, pts. Robert
     Campbell, tr. Aug 1685, fr. Leith to Jamaica. (PC.11.136)
935. Campbell, John, Covenanter, res. Carrisk Lochfyneside Argyll, tr. July
     1685. (PC.11.329)
936. Campbell, John, tr. July 1685, fr. Leith to East N.J. (PC.11.329)
937. Campbell, John, Jacobite, tr. 24 Feb 1747, fr. Liverpool, in *Gildart*, arr.
     Port North Potomac Md 5 Aug 1747. (PRO.T1.328)
938. Campbell, John, fisherman, Jacobite, res. Mull Argyllshire, tr. 21 Mar
     1747. (P.2.96)
939. Campbell, John, Jacobite, tr. 9 Nov 1748. (P.2.96)
940. Campbell, John, 1684, sett. Perth Amboy N.J. (Insh249)
941. Campbell, John, Jacobite, res. Inverness, tr. 8 May 1747, to Antigua.
     (P.2.94)
942. Campbell, John, res. Dunbartonshire, pre 1771, sett. Saltspring Hanover
     Jamaica. (SRO.RS10.10.327)
943. Campbell, John, clergyman edu. King's Coll Aberdeen 1771, sh. 1773,
     to Va, sett. Jamaica 1780. (EMA18)
944. Campbell, John, merchant, res. Glasgow, sh. 1760, fr. Glasgow to Va,
     sett. Occoquan & Bladensburg Va. (SRA.CFI)
945. Campbell, John, res. Argyll, pts. Colin Campbell, pre 1769, sett.
     Jamaica. (SRO.RD4.223.303)

946. Campbell, John, Jacobite, tr. 7 May 1716, fr. Liverpool to S.C., in *Susannah*. (SPC.1716.309)(CTB31.206)
947. Campbell, John, b. 1674, Inveraray Argyll, planter, sh. 1699, fr. Leith to Darien, sett. Jamaica, m. (1)Katherine Clayborn (2)Elizabeth Gaines, ch. Colin, d. 29 Jan 1740 St Elizabeth Jamaica, bd. Black River Church. (MIBWI340)
948. Campbell, John, b. 1726, blacksmith, Jacobite, res. Skerhiese, tr. 21 Sept 1748. (P.2.96)
949. Campbell, John, b. 1727, laborer, Jacobite, res. Inverness, tr. 5 May 1747, fr. Liverpool to Leeward Islands, in *Veteran*, arr. Martinique June 1747. (P.2.94)(PRO.SP36.102)
950. Campbell, John, b. 1732, servant, Jacobite, res. Rannoch Argyll, tr. 5 May 1747, fr. Liverpool to Leeward Islands, in *Veteran*, arr. Martinique June 1747. (P.2.96)(MR151)(PRO.SP36.102)
951. Campbell, John, b. 1752, tailor, res. Galloway, sh. May 1774, fr. Stranraer to N.Y., in *Gale*. (PRO.T47.12)
952. Campbell, John, b. 1753, student, res. Inverness, sh. Jan 1774, fr. Greenock to Nevis, in *Aurora*. (SRO.CE60.1.7)
953. Campbell, John, b. 1762, servant, res. Stornaway Isle of Lewis, sh. May 1774, fr. Stornaway to Philadelphia, in *Friendship*. (PRO.T47.12)
954. Campbell, Lachlan, merchant, res. Glasgow, sh. 1764, fr. Glasgow to Va, sett. Fredericksburg Va. (SRA.AO13.28)
955. Campbell, Lillias, b. 1758, spinner, res. Paisley Renfrewshire, sh. Feb 1774, fr. Greenock to N.Y., in *Commerce*. (PRO.T47.12)
956. Campbell, Malcolm, horsethief, tr. Sept 1775, to West Indies. (SM.37.523) (alias 4622)
957. Campbell, Margaret, b. 1749, res. Galloway, sh. 1775, to P.E.I., in *Lovely Nelly*. (PRO.T47.12)
958. Campbell, Neil, Covenanter, res. Argyll, tr. Aug 1685, fr. Leith. (PC.11.136)
959. Campbell, Patrick, thief, res. Meikletoun of Edinaple Perthshire, pts. Duncan Campbell, tr. May 1726. (SRO.JC13.6)
960. Campbell, Patrick, b. 1704, husbandman, res. Edinburgh, sh. July 1722, fr. London to St Kitts. (CLRO\AIA)
961. Campbell, Peter, tobacco factor, res. Glasgow, sh. pre 1775, fr. Glasgow to Va, sett. Prince George Co Va. (SRA.CFI)
962. Campbell, Peter, b. 1755, merchant, res. Glasgow, sh. July 1775, fr. Greenock to Jamaica, in *Isabella*. (PRO.T47.12)
963. Campbell, Robert, Covenanter, tr. Aug 1685, fr. Leith to East N.J., in *Henry & Francis*. (PC.11.145)
964. Campbell, Robert, merchant, res. Glasgow, pre 1744, sett. Jamaica. (SRO.RD2.169.74)
965. Campbell, Ronald, b. 1739, farmer, res. Perthshire, sh. May 1775, fr. Greenock to N.Y., in *Monimia*. (PRO.T47.12)

966. Campbell, Sarah, b. 1754, maid-servant, res. Perthshire, sh. May 1775, fr. Greenock to N.Y., in *Monimia*. (PRO.T47.12)
967. Campbell, Sarah, b. 1759, spinner, res. Paisley Renfrewshire, sh. Feb 1774, fr. Greenock to N.Y., in *Commerce*. (PRO.T47.12)
968. Campbell, Saunders, Jacobite, tr. 22 Apr 1747, fr. Liverpool to Va, in *Johnson*, arr. Port Oxford Md 5 Aug 1747. (PRO.T1.328)
969. Campbell, Thomas, assault, res. Girvan Ayrshire, tr. Oct 1751. (AJ199)
970. Campbell, William, res. Dunbarton, sh. Nov 1667, to Barbados. (DBR9)
971. Campbell, William, sh. 1699, to Darien, Edin pr1707 CC8.8.83
972. Campbell, William, undershipman, res. Kildallogs Argyll, pts. John Campbell & Elizabeth McNeill, sh. 18 Aug 1699, fr. Clyde to Darien , in *Rising Sun*, Edin pr1708 CC8.8.84
973. Campbell, William, Covenanter, tr. Aug 1685, fr. Leith to East N.J., in *Henry & Francis*. (PC.11.154)
974. Campbell, William, horsethief, res. Kilmichael, pts. Gillian Campbell, tr. 1775, fr. Greenock, in *Rainbow*, arr. Port Hampton Va 3 May 1775. (SRO.JC27.10.3) (alias 4412)
975. Campbell, William, res. Argyll, pts. Hugh Campbell, sh. Jan 1737, fr. Leith to Carolina. (SRO.GD170)
976. Campbell, William, soldier, d. 1699 Darien, Edin pr 1707 CC8.8.83
977. Campbell, William, undershipman, res. Argyll, pts. John Campbell of Kildallogs & Elizabeth McNeill, sh. 1698, fr. Leith to Darien, Edin pr 1708 CC8.8.84
978. Campbell, William, merchant, res. Montrose Angus, sh. 1737, fr. Gravesend to Ga, in *Mary Anne*. (SPC.1737.107)
979. Campbell, William, b. 1726, weaver, Jacobite, res. Grandtully Perthshire, tr. 5 May 1747, fr. Liverpool to Leeward Islands, in *Veteran*, arr. Martinique June 1747. (P.2.98)(MR206)(PRO.SP36.102)
980. Campbell, William, b. 1729, tailor, Jacobite, res. Reay Caithness, tr. 31 Mar 1747, fr. Tilbury to Jamaica , in *St George or Carteret*, arr. Jamaica 1747. (P.2.98)(MR81)(PRO.CO137.58)
981. Campbell, William, b. 1747, laborer, res. Glen Orchy Argyll, sh. Sept 1775, to Wilmington N.C., in *Jupiter*. (PRO.T47.12)
982. Campbell, William, b. 1751, res. Galloway, sh. 1775, to P.E.I., in *Lovely Nelly*. (PRO.T47.12)
983. Campbell, William, b. 1758, weaver, res. Paisley Renfrewshire, sh. Feb 1774, fr. Greenock to N.Y., in *Commerce*. (PRO.T47.12)
984. Campbell, Zachariah, b. 9 Oct 1740, Glasgow, merchant, res. Glasgow, pts. James Campbell & Mary Murdoch, pre 1763, sett. Fredericksburg Va. (SRA.B10.15.6863)
985. Candow, Donald, Jacobite, tr. 1746. (SRO.GD103)
986. Cane, Hugh, Jacobite, tr. 29 June 1716, fr. Liverpool to Jamaica or Va, in *Elizabeth & Anne*, arr. Va. (SPC.1716.310)(CTB31.208)(VSP.1.186)

987. Cannie, John, sailor, d. 16 Nov 1698 Darien. (NLS.2b8\19)
988. Cannon, John, Jacobite, tr. 26 Apr 1716, fr. Liverpool to Jamaica, in
     Two Brothers, arr. Montserrat June 1716.
     (SPC.1716.313)(CTP.CC43)
989. Cannon, Samuel, Covenanter, res. Banscalloch Kirkcudbright, tr. 1685.
     (PC.10.258)
990. Cant, Catherine, b. 1756, servant, res. Edinburgh, sh. May 1775, fr.
     Leith to Philadelphia, in *Friendship*. (PRO.T47.12)
991. Cant, James, fireraiser, tr. Mar 1774. (SM.36.164)
992. Cant, John, Jacobite, tr. 30 Mar 1716, fr. Liverpool to Antigua, in
     Scipio. (CTB31.204)
993. Cantlie, Alexander, b. 1687, carpenter, res. Montrose Angus, sh. Feb
     1730, fr. London to Jamaica. (CLRO\AIA)
994. Cargill, Donald, res. Knockcrainie Jura Argyll, sh. 1754, to Cape Fear
     N.C. (SRO.GD64\5.21)
995. Cargill, John, clergyman, sh. 1708, to Leeward Islands. (EMA19)
996. Cargill, John, res. Knockcrainie Jura Argyll, sh. 1754, to Cape Fear N.C.
     (SRO.GD64\5.21)
997. Cargill, John, b. 1744, merchant, sett. Jamaica, d. Sept 1780 Jamaica,
     bd. Kingston Cathedral. (MIBWI89)
998. Cargill, Richard, b. 1744, sett. St Thomas in the East Jamaica, d. March
     1781 Jamaica, bd. Kingston Cathedral. (MIBWI89)
999. Cargill, William, b. 13 May 1726, Montrose Angus, tobacconist,
     Jacobite, res. Montrose, pts. James Cargill & Elizabeth Ramsay,
     tr. 24 Feb 1747, fr. Liverpool, in *Gildart*, arr. Port North Potomac
     Md 5 Aug 1747. (P.2.324/98)(MR96)(PRO.T1.328)
1000. Carlyle, Adam, merchant planter, res. Lymekills Lanarkshire, pts.
      Alexander Carlyle, pre 1750, sett. Va. (SRO.RS23.16.31)
1001. Carlyle, Alexander, merchant planter, res. Lymekills Lanarkshire, sh. pre
      1739, sett. Va. (SRO.RS23.13.197)
1002. Carlyle, John, merchant, res. Glasgow, pts. Alexander Carlyle, pre 1748,
      sett. Va. (SRO.SC36.63.1)
1003. Carmell, James, Jacobite, tr. 26 Apr 1716, fr. Liverpool to Jamaica, in
      Two Brothers, arr. Montserrat June 1716.
      (SPC.1716.313)(CTB31.206)(CTP.CC43)
1004. Carmichael, Alexander, surgeon, res. Greenock, sett. St Croix, d. 5 Jan
      1782 St Croix, Edin pr 1782 CC8.8.152\2
1005. Carmichael, Archibald, b. 1749, laborer, res. Lismore Argyll, sh. Sept
      1775, to Wilmington N.C., in *Jupiter*, m. Mary ..., ch. Catherine.
      (PRO.T47.12)
1006. Carmichael, Christian, b. 1751, servant, res. Breadalbane Perthshire, sh.
      Sept 1775, to Wilmington N.C., in *Jupiter*. (PRO.T47.12)
1007. Carmichael, Donald, servant, res. Breadalbane Perthshire, sh. Sept 1775,
      to Wilmington N.C., in *Jupiter*, ch. Lilly. (PRO.T47.12)

1008. Carmichael, Dugald, b. 1720, farmer, res. Breadalbane Perthshire, sh. Sept 1775, to Wilmington N.C., in *Jupiter*, m. Mary ..., ch. Archibald Ann. (PRO.T47.12)
1009. Carmichael, Ewan, b. 1735, laborer, res. Breadalbane Perthshire, sh. Sept 1775, to Wilmington N.C., in *Jupiter*, m. Margaret ..., ch. Archibald Allan Katherine. (PRO.T47.12)
1010. Carmichael, James, workman, assault, res. Leadhills Lanarkshire, tr. Apr 1725. (SRO.HH11)
1011. Carmichael, Jean, whore, res. Edinburgh, tr. 19 Mar 1695. (SRO.PC2.25.216)
1012. Carmichael, Marion, res. Edinburgh, tr. 1696, fr. Newhaven to Va. (SRO.RH15.14.58)
1013. Carmichael, Robert, merchant, res. Dunbartonshire, sh. pre 1770, sett. Va. (SRO.RS10.10.295)
1014. Carmichael, Walter, merchant, pre 1767, sett. Md, m. Mary Dick. (EMR.21.6.1767)
1015. Carmichael, William, merchant, pts. Archibald Carmichael, sh. pre 1695, sett. Barbados. (SRO.RD2.80.10\RD4.78.1253)
1016. Carmichael, William, cook's mate, sh. 14 July 1698, fr. Leith to Darien, in *Unicorn*, m. Jean Herd, Edin pr1707 CC8.8.83
1017. Carnegie, Alexander, b. 16 Oct 1705, Arbroath Angus, laborer, Jacobite, res. Brechin Angus, pts. Robert Carnegie & Janet Blair, tr. 22 Apr 1747, fr. Liverpool to Va, in *Johnson*, arr. Port Oxford Md 5 Aug 1747. (P.2.100)(MR96)(PRO.T1.328)
1018. Carnegie, John, res. Aberdeen, sh. Aug 1698, fr. Liverpool to Va, in *Loyalty*. (LRO.HQ325.2FRE)
1019. Carnegie, John, clergyman edu. Glasgow Uni, sh. 1702, sett. St Stephen's Va, d. 1709. (SCHR.14.142)
1020. Carnegie, John, bosun's yeoman, res. Edinburgh, pts. William Carnegie, sh. 1699, d. 22 Oct 1699 Darien, Edin pr 1707 CC8.8.83
1021. Carnegy, John, cook, res. Edinburgh, sh. 14 July 1698, fr. Leith to Darien, in *Caledonia*, m. Margaret Wilson, Edin pr 1707 CC8.8.83
1022. Carnochan, Edmond, tr. 17 Dec 1685, fr. Leith to Barbados, in *John & Nicholas*. (PC.11.389)(ETR389)
1023. Carr, Alexander, Jacobite, tr. 29 June 1716, fr. Liverpool to Jamaica or Va, in *Elizabeth & Anne*, arr. Va. (SPC.1716.310)(CTB31.208)(VSP.1.186)
1024. Carr, Alexander, thief, tr. 1764, in *Boyd*, arr. Norfolk Va 24 Aug 1764. (SRO.JC27.10.3)
1025. Carrick, James, merchant, res. Balveardmill Abernethy Fife, pts. James Carrick, sh. pre 1754, sett. Boston Mass. (SRO.SH.5.4.1754)
1026. Carrie, John, pedlar, Jacobite, res. Arbroath Angus, tr. 24 Feb 1747, fr. Liverpool to Va, in *Gildart*, arr. Port North Potomac Md 5 Aug 1747. (P.2.102)(MR96)(PRO.T1.328)

1027. Carron, Richard, Jacobite, tr. 8 May 1747, to Antigua. (P.2.102)
1028. Carry, John, b. 1749, stonemason, res. Fife, sh. Dec 1773, fr. London to
Va, in *Elizabeth*. (PRO.T47.9\11)
1029. Carson, Charles, b. 1757, laborer, res. Colvend Kirkcudbright, sh. May
1775, fr. Dumfries to P.E.I., in *Lovely Nelly*. (PRO.T47.12)
1030. Carson, James, b. 1755, husbandman, res. Queenshill, sh. May 1774, to
N.Y., in *Gale*. (PRO.T47.12)
1031. Carson, James, b. 1762, res. Dumfries, sh. Oct 1774, fr. Greenock to
Charleston S.C., in *Countess*. (PRO.T47.12)
1032. Carson, John, b. 1755, laborer, res. Colvend Kirkcudbrightshire, sh. May
1775, fr. Dumfries to P.E.I., in *Lovely Nelly*. (PRO.T47.12)
1033. Carson, John, b. 1756, laborer, res. Gatehouse Kirkcudbrightshire, sh.
May 1774, to N.Y., in *Gale*. (PRO.T47.12)
1034. Carson, Thomas, b. 1738, brewer, res. Gatehouse Kirkcudbrightshire, sh.
May 1774, to N.Y., in *Gale*. (PRO.T47.12)
1035. Carus, Christopher, Jacobite, tr. 29 June 1716, fr. Liverpool to Jamaica
or Va, in *Elizabeth & Anne*, arr. Va.
(SPC.1716.310)(CTB31.208)(VSP.1.185)
1036. Caskie, William, quartermaster, sh. 14 July 1698, fr. Leith to Darien, in
Unicorn, Edin pr1707 CC8.8.83
1037. Cassels, Isobel, b. 1756, servant, res. Edinburgh, sh. May 1775, fr. Leith
to Philadelphia, in *Friendship*. (PRO.T47.12)
1038. Cassels, John, b. 1759, servant, res. Edinburgh, sh. May 1775, fr. Leith
to Philadelphia, in *Friendship*. (PRO.T47.12)
1039. Cassie, Andrew, physician, d. 1759 St Katherine's Jamaica. (AJ612)
1040. Cassie, Andrew, physician, res. Aberdeen, sett. St Katherine's Jamaica, d.
1759. (AJ612)
1041. Cassills, Jean, servant, Covenanter, res. Easter Lenzie Dunbartonshire, tr.
1685. (PC.11.292)
1042. Cassills, John sr, mariner, res. Bo'ness West Lothian, sh. 14 July 1698,
fr. Leith to Darien, in *St Andrew*, d. Darien, Edin pr1707
CC8.8.83
1043. Cathcart, Allan, soldier, d. 1699 Darien, Edin pr 1707 CC8.8.83
1044. Cathcart, Andrew, passenger, sh. Feb 1681, fr. Ayr to West Indies, in
James of Ayr. (SRO.E72.3.6)
1045. Cathcart, Andrew, merchant, sh. Mar 1683, fr. Ayr to Caribee Islands, in
James of Ayr. (SRO.E72.3.12)
1046. Cathcart, Hugh, b. 6 Jan 1706, Glasgow, merchant, res. Glasgow, pts.
Andrew Cathcart & Janet Nisbet, sett. Kingston Jamaica, m. Helen
Woodrop, ch. William, d. pre 1772. (SRA.CFI)
1047. Cathcart, Robert, merchant, sh. pre 1769, sett. King's Co P.E.I.
(SRO.GD293.2.71)
1048. Cathcart, William, physician, sh. 1737, to S.C., ch. Gabriel.
(SRO.GD180)

1049. Cathcart, William, b. 1 Oct 1732, Glasgow, merchant edu. Glasgow Uni 1746, res. Glasgow, pts. Hugh Cathcart & Helen Woodrop, sh. pre 1768, sett. Kingston Jamaica. (SRO.SC36.63.12.51)(MAGU35)

1050. Cattenach, Alexander, b. 1730, miller, Jacobite, res. Badenoch Inverness-shire, tr. 5 May 1747, fr. Liverpool to Leeward Islands, in *Veteran*, arr. Martinique June 1747. (P.2.104)(PRO.SP36.102)

1051. Cattenach, John, b. 1724, farmer, res. Chabster Reay Caithness, sh. Apr 1774, to Wilmington N.C., in *Bachelor of Leith*. (PRO.T47.12)

1052. Cavers, John, Covenanter, tr. 12 Dec 1678, fr. Leith to West Indies, in *St Michael of Scarborough*. (PC.6.76)

1053. Cavie, Christian, Covenanter, tr. Aug 1685, fr. Leith to East N.J., in *Henry & Francis*. (PC.11.155)

1054. Caw, John, writer, Jacobite, res. Edinburgh, tr. 1747, fr. Tilbury. (P.2.106)

1055. Cawson, William, Jacobite, tr. 21 Apr 1716, fr. Liverpool to S.C., in *Wakefield*. (CTB31.205)

1056. Cearl, John, b. 1734, farmer, res. Dumfries-shire, sh. Oct 1774, fr. Greenock to Charleston S.C., in *Countess*. (PRO.T47.12)

1057. Chalmers, Anne, infanticide, res. Ayrshire, tr. 1752. (AJ228)

1058. Chalmers, Charles, b. 1717, merchant, Jacobite, res. Edinburgh, tr. 31 Mar 1747, fr. London to Barbados, in *Frere*. (P.2.106)(MR48)

1059. Chalmers, Isabel, b. 1722, knitter, Jacobite, res. Mearns, tr. 5 May 1747, fr. Liverpool to Leeward Islands, in *Veteran*, arr. Martinique June 1747. (P.2.108)(PRO.SP36.102)

1060. Chalmers, James, planter, res. Boharm Banffshire, pts. James Chalmers of Balnellan, pre 1766, sett. St Thomas in the Vale Jamaica. (CPD517)

1061. Chalmers, John, soldier, Jacobite, res. Kinneil, tr. 21 Mar 1747. (P.2.108)(MR137)

1062. Chalmers, John, b. 1726, laborer, Jacobite, res. Perthshire, tr. 5 May 1747, fr. Liverpool to Leeward Islands, in *Veteran*, arr. Martinique June1747. (P.2.110)(PRO.SP36.102)

1063. Chalmers, John, b. 1750, laborer, res. Partick Glasgow, sh. Apr 1775, fr. Greenock to N.Y., in *Lilly*. (PRO.T47.12)

1064. Chalmers, Patrick, Jacobite, tr. 31 July 1716, fr. Liverpool to Va, in *Anne*. (SPC.1716.310)(CTB31.209)

1065. Chalmers, William, gardener, Jacobite, res. Mearns, tr. 22 Apr 1747, fr. Liverpool to Va, in *Johnson*, arr. Port Oxford Md 5 Aug 1747. (P.2.110)(MR70)(PRO.T1.328)

1066. Chambers, John, Jacobite, tr. 28 July 1716, fr. Liverpool to Va, in *Godspeed*, arr. Md Oct 1716. (SPC.1716.310)(CTB31.209)(HM388)(MdArch25.347)

1067. Chambers, Joseph, Jacobite, tr. 7 May 1716, fr. Liverpool to S.C, in *Susannah*. (SPC.1716.309)(CTB31.206)

51

1068. Chandler, Thomas, Jacobite, tr. 21 Feb 1747. (P.2.110)
1069. Chaplin, George, merchant, res. Colliston Arbroath Angus, pts. John
Chaplin, sett. Kingston Jamaica, d. May 1723, Edin pr 1724
CC8.8.89
1070. Chaplin, Robert, res. Arbuthnott Kincardineshire, pts. William Chaplin
& Margaret Middleton, sh. 1723, to Jamaica, d. 1747 Jamaica.
(APB.3.206)
1071. Chapman, David, thief, res. Perthshire, tr. 12 Sept 1699.
(SRO.B59.26.1.1.6\12)
1072. Chapman, James, gardener, Jacobite, res. Durn Banffshire, tr. 22 Apr
1747, fr. Liverpool to Va, in *Johnson*, arr. Port Oxford Md 5 Aug
1747. (P.2.110)(MR122)(PRO.SP136.102)
1073. Chapp, James, b. 1726, smith, Jacobite, res. St Marnoch's Banffshire, tr.
24 Feb 1747, fr. Liverpool, in *Gildart*, arr. Port North Potomac
Md 5 Aug 1747. (P.2.110)(MR206)(PRO.T1.328)
1074. Chappell, Alexander, b. 1754, res. Renfrew, sh. Sept 1774, fr. Greenock
to Jamaica, in *Jamaica*. (PRO.T47.12)
1075. Charity, James, merchant, sh. pre 1765, sett. Boston Mass.
(SRO.SC36.63.8.168)
1076. Charnley, Thomas, b. 1728, weaver, Jacobite, res. Walton, tr. 8 May
1747, to Antigua. (P.2.112)
1077. Charteris, Lawrence, Jacobite, tr. 25 June 1716, fr. Liverpool to St Kitts,
in *Hockenhill*. (SPC.1716.312)(CTB31.207)
1078. Chatto, William, saddler, attempted murder, res. Kelso Roxburghshire, tr.
1769. (SM.31.333)
1079. Cheisley, John, Jacobite, tr. 1747. (MR196)
1080. Chesterfield, John, Jacobite, res. Lancashire, tr. 21 Feb 1747. (P.2.112)
1081. Childs, Robert, b. 1747, farmer, res. Sutherland, sh. Oct 1774, fr.
Greenock to Philadelphia, in *Sally*. (PRO.T47.12)
1082. Chisholm, Adam, Jacobite, tr. 29 June 1716, fr. Liverpool to Jamaica or
Va, in *Elizabeth & Anne*.
(SPC.1716.310)(CTB31.208)(VSP.1.186)
1083. Chisholm, Donald, b. 1720, farmer, Jacobite, res. Glenmoriston
Inverness-shire, tr. 21 Mar 1747, fr. Tilbury. (P.2.112)(MR151)
1084. Chisholm, Donald, b. 1721, Jacobite, res. Blairy Glen Urquhart
Inverness-shire, tr. 21 Mar 1747, fr. Tilbury to Jamaica, in *St
George or Carteret*, arr. Jamaica 1747.
(P.2.112)(MR151)(PRO.CO137.58)
1085. Chisholm, James, b. 1733, farmer, res. Beauly Inverness-shire, sh. July
1775, fr. Stornaway to Philadelphia, in *Clementina*. (PRO.T47.12)
1086. Chisholm, John, b. 1707, weaver, Jacobite, res. Invercannich Inverness-
shire, tr. 31 Mar 1747, fr. London to Jamaica, in *St George or
Carteret*, arr. Jamaica 1747. (P.2.114)(PRO.CO137.58)

1087. Chisholm, Thomas, b. 1739, farmer, res. Kirkbean Kirkcudbrightshire, sh. May 1775, fr. Dumfries to P.E.I., in *Lovely Nelly*. (PRO.T47.12)

1088. Chisholm, William, physician, m. Jean ..., d. 1745 Port Royal Jamaica. (SRO.RD2.171.182)

1089. Chrisley, James, b. 1712, clerk, res. Selkirk, sh. Nov 1736, fr. London to Jamaica. (CLRO\AIA)

1090. Christie, Adam, tr. Feb 1721, to Va. (SRO.HH11)

1091. Christie, Alexander, adultery, res. Howmill Aberdeenshire, tr. May 1775. (SM.37.405)

1092. Christie, Archibald, Jacobite, tr. 25 June 1716, fr. Liverpool to St Kitts, in *Hockenhill*. (SPC.1716.312)(CTB31.207)

1093. Christie, Donald, b. 1762, servant, res. Shather, sh. May 1774, fr. Stornaway to Philadelphia, in *Friendship*. (PRO.T47.12)

1094. Christie, George, apprentice musician, forger, res. Edinburgh, tr. Jan 1765. (SRO.HCR.I.96)

1095. Christie, James, b. 1714, linen weaver, Jacobite, tr. 24 Feb 1747, fr. Liverpool to Va, in *Gildart*, arr. Port North Potomac Md 5 Aug 1747. (P.2.114)(MR70)(PRO.T1.328)

1096. Christie, John, res. Edinburgh, tr. Nov 1734. (SRO.JC3.19.173)

1097. Christie, John, b. 1752, smith, res. Glasgow, sh. Apr 1775, fr. Greenock to N.Y., in *Lilly*. (PRO.T47.12)

1098. Christie, John, b. 1754, wright, res. Glasgow, sh. Apr 1775, fr. Greenock to N.Y., in *Lilly*. (PRO.T47.12)

1099. Christie, Murdo, b. 1765, res. Bregair Isle of Lewis, sh. May 1774, fr. Stornaway to Philadelphia, in *Friendship*. (PRO.T47.12)

1100. Christie, Patrick, merchant, sh. July 1682, fr. Aberdeen to West N.J., in *Golden Hynd of London*. (SRO.E72.1.7)

1101. Christie, Robert, merchant, res. Culross Fife, sh. 1667, sett. Fla Mexico, m. Margaret Sands. (PC.4.297)

1102. Christie, Robert, wharfinger, res. Glass Aberdeenshire, pre 1782, sett. St Catherine Middlesex Jamaica, m. Margaret Napier. (CPD758)

1103. Christie, William, b. 1763, wright, res. Glasgow, sh. Oct 1774, fr. Greenock to Philadelphia, in *Sally*. (PRO.T47.12)

1104. Christy, James, b. 1715, weaver, res. Dunbarton, sh. Aug 1774, fr. Greenock to Philadelphia, in *Magdalene*. (PRO.T47.12)

1105. Clanny, Hugh, tr. May 1717. (SRO.JC12.3)

1106. Claperton, Thomas, weaver, Jacobite, res. Fochabers Banffshire, tr. 22 Apr 1747, fr. Liverpool to Va, in *Johnson*, arr. Port Oxford Md 5 Aug 1747. (P.2.116)(MR122)(PRO.T1.328)

1107. Claperton, William, b. 1734, ploughboy, Jacobite, res. Fochabers Banffshire, pts. Thomas Claperton, tr. 5 May 1747, fr. Liverpool to Leeward Islands, in *Veteran*, arr. Martinique June 1747. (P.2.116)(JAB.2.135)(MR122)(PRO.SP36.102)

1108. Clark, Andrew, gentleman, res. Leith Midlothian, sh. pre 1770, sett. Port Royal Jamaica. (SRO.RD4.211.55)
1109. Clark, Archibald, res. Kiles Jura Argyll, sh. 1754, to Cape Fear N.C. (SRO.GD64\5.21)
1110. Clark, Benjamin, sh. 1684, to East N.J. (Insh171)
1111. Clark, Daniel, res. Perth, sett. Augusta Ga, d. pre 1757, PCC pr1757
1112. Clark, Donald, res. Kiles Jura Argyll, sh. 1754, to Cape Fear N.C. (SRO.GD64\5.21)
1113. Clark, Duncan, Jacobite, tr. 29 June 1716, fr. Liverpool to Jamaica or Va, in *Elizabeth & Anne*, arr. York Va. (SPC.1716.310)(CTB31.208)(VSP.1.185)
1114. Clark, George, res. Aberdeen, sett. Hanover Jamaica, m. Isabell Gall, d. pre 1781, Edin pr 1781 CC8.8.125\1
1115. Clark, Gilbert, m. Isabel Gall, d. pre 1780 Hanover Jamaica, Edin pr1780 CC8.8.125
1116. Clark, Gilbert, sh. 29 Nov 1773, fr. Greenock to Jamaica, in *Mary of Glasgow*. (SRO.CE60.1.7)
1117. Clark, Gilbert, res. Kiles Jura Argyll, sh. 1754, to Cape Fear N.C. (SRO.GD64\5.21)
1118. Clark, Hugh, Jacobite, tr. 7 May 1716, fr. Liverpool to S.C., in *Susannah*. (SPC.1716.309)(CTB31.206)
1119. Clark, James, waiter, res. Galloway, sh. May 1774, fr. Stranraer to N.Y., in *Gale*. (PRO.T47.12)
1120. Clark, James, planter, d. 7 Nov 1698 Darien. (NLS
1121. Clark, James, merchant, res. Glasgow, pre 1754, sett. Va. (SRA.B10.15.6653)
1122. Clark, James, Jacobite, tr. 21 Apr 1716, fr. Liverpool to S.C., in *Wakefield*. (SPC.1716.309)(CTB31.205)
1123. Clark, John, rioter, res. Alloa Clackmannanshire, tr. 1751. (AJ160)
1124. Clark, John, writer, res. Edinburgh, tr. 12 Dec 1678, fr. Leith to West Indies, in *St Michael of Scarborough*. (PC.6.76)
1125. Clark, John, woolcomber, murderer, res. Aberdeen, tr. 1772, fr. Glasgow, in *Brilliant*, arr. Port Hampton Va 7 Oct 1772. (AJ1272)(SRO.JC27.10.3)
1126. Clark, John, res. Greenock, pts. John Clark, sett. Jamaica, d. pre 1783. (SRO.SH.8.8.1783)
1127. Clark, John, b. 1746, farmer, res. Inverness, sh. July 1775, fr. Stornaway to Philadelphia, in *Clementina*, m. Betty ..., ch. Margaret. (PRO.T47.12)
1128. Clark, John, b. 1749, farmer, res. Stirling, sh. May 1774, fr. Greenock to N.Y., in *Matty*, 22 July 1774, sett. Barnet N.H. (PRO.T47.12)
1129. Clark, John jr, sailor, res. Bo'ness West Lothian, sh. 18 Aug 1699, fr. Clyde to Darien, in *Rising Sun*, Edin pr1707 CC8.8.83

1130. Clark, Joseph, b. 1730, joiner, res. Sanquhar Dumfries-shire, sh. May 1775, fr. Dumfries to P.E.I., in *Lovely Nelly*, m. Ann Wilkie, ch. Ann Joseph. (PRO.T47.12)
1131. Clark, Mary, b. 1752, servant, res. Aberdeen, sh. May 1775, fr. Leith to Philadelphia, in *Friendship*. (PRO.T47.12)
1132. Clark, Thomas, thief, res. Newcastle, pts. Thomas Clark, tr. 28 Nov 1704, fr. Leith to Md. (SRO.PC2.28.307)
1133. Clark, Thomas, botanist, res. Kirkgunzeon, pts. Rev William Clark & Janet McVunnel, pre 1778, sett. Kingston Jamaica. (SRO.RD2.226.1)
1134. Clark, Thomas, Jacobite, tr. 21 Apr 1716, fr. Liverpool to S.C., in *Wakefield*. (SPC.1716.309)(CTB31.205)
1135. Clark, William, rioter, res. Alloa Clackmannanshire, tr. 1751. (AJ160)
1136. Clark, William, sh. 1684, to East N.J., d. 1684 at sea. (Insh262)
1137. Clark, William, b. 1745, gardener, res. Caerlaverock Dumfriesshire, sh. May 1775, fr. Dumfries to P.E.I., in *Lovely Nelly*, m. Grizzel Kissock, ch. John. (PRO.T47.12)
1138. Clark, William, b. 1754, shoemaker, res. Glasgow, sh. Feb 1774, fr. Greenock to N.Y., in *Commerce*. (PRO.T47.12)
1139. Clarkson, James, merchant, Covenanter, res. Linlithgow West Lothian, tr. June 1684, fr. Leith to Carolina, m. Agnes Collin. (PC.8.527)
1140. Clarkson, James, clergyman, sh. 1772. (UPC656)
1141. Clarkson, Thomas, merchant, res. Langrig Lanarkshire, sh. pre 1766, sett. Barbados, m. Anne Russell. (SRO.RS32.18.33)
1142. Clavering, Elizabeth, b. 1725, seamstress, Jacobite, res. Banff, tr. 5 May 1747, fr. Liverpool to Leeward Islands, in *Veteran*, arr. Martinique June 1747, m. Edward Clavering. (P.2.118)(JAB.2.422)(PRO.SP36.102) (alias 2604)
1143. Cleghorn, Adam, sh. 1699, sett. N.Y. (DP147)
1144. Cleland, James, merchant, res. Edinburgh, sh. 18 Aug 1699, fr. Clyde to Darien, in *Rising Sun*, Edin pr1707 CC8.8.83
1145. Cleland, James, b. 1712, surgeon apothecary, res. Kirk O'Shotts Lanarkshire, sh. Mar 1735, fr. London to Jamaica. (CLRO\AIA)
1146. Cleland, William, merchant, res. Edinburgh, pts. Mary Cleland, pre 1705, sett. Barbados, m. Sarah ..., d. 1719 Barbados, Barbados 1719 RB6\4.519. (SPC.1705.409)
1147. Clelone, Robert, sailor, sh. 14 July 1699, fr. Leith to Darien, in *Caledonia*, Edin pr 1707 CC8.8.83
1148. Cleney, David, servant, res. Prestonpans East Lothian, sh. Feb 1684, to Hudson Bay. (HBRS.9.203)
1149. Clephane, David, clergyman edu. St Andrews Uni 1694-1703, sh. 1710, to Va. (EMA20)
1150. Clerk, Andrew, schoolmaster, sh. 1705, to N.Y. (EMA20)

1151. Clerk, Andrew, gentleman, pre 1771, sett. Port Royal Jamaica. (SRO.RD4.208.945)
1152. Clerk, Dougal, farmer, Covenanter, res. Otter Gallachie Argyll, tr. 12 Aug 1685, fr. Leith to Jamaica. (PC.2.330)(ETR.373)
1153. Clerk, James, merchant, res. Penicuik Midlothian, pts. Sir John Clerk, sh. pre 1716, sett. Boston Mass. (SRO.GD158)
1154. Clerk, John, Covenanter, res. Argyll, tr. 9 July 1685, fr. Leith to N.E. (PC.11.94)
1155. Clerk, John, b. 1738, servant, res. Findhorn Morayshire, sh. July 1775, fr. Stornaway to Philadelphia, in *Clementina*, m. Margaret ..., ch. John Margaret Janet Jean. (PRO.T47.12)
1156. Clerk, John, b. 1749, farmer, res. Stirling, sh. May 1774, fr. Greenock to N.Y., in *Matty*. (PRO.T47.12)
1157. Clerk, Mary, Covenanter, res. Kirkcudbright, tr. Aug 1685, fr. Leith to Jamaica, arr. Port Royal Jamaica Nov 1685. (PC.11.329)(LJ30)
1158. Clerk, Thomas, b. 1746, farmer, res. Stirling, sh. May 1774, fr. Greenock to N.Y., in *Matty*. (PRO.T47.12)
1159. Clintrie, Archibald, sailor, sh. 14 July 1698, fr. Leith to Darien, in *Unicorn*, Edin pr 1707 CC8.8.83
1160. Clydesdale, Richard, chapman, Covenanter, tr. 12 Dec 1678, fr. Leith to West Indies, in *St Michael of Scarborough*. (PC.6.76)
1161. Clydesdale, Robert, sh. Feb 1683, fr. Port Glasgow to West Indies, in *Walter of Glasgow*. (SRO.E72.19.8)
1162. Coats, William, b. 1692, laborer, Jacobite, res. Aberdeenshire, tr. 5 May 1747, fr. Liverpool to Leeward Islands, in *Veteran*, arr. Martinique June 1747. (P.2.120)(JAB.2.422)(PRO.SP36.102)
1163. Cobb, John, b. 1744, butcher, sh. Sept 1775, fr. Newcastle to Ga, in *Georgia Packet*. (PRO.T47.9\11)
1164. Cobin, Robert, Jacobite, tr. 29 June 1716, fr. Liverpool to Va or Jamaica, in *Elizabeth & Anne*. (CTB31.208)
1165. Cochran, John, physician edu. St Andrews Uni, sh. pre 1744, sett. Kingston Jamaica. (SRO.NRAS726.5)
1166. Cochran, Mungo, merchant burgess, Covenanter, res. Glasgow, tr. 12 Dec 1678, fr. Leith to West Indies, in *St Michael of Scarborough*, m. Christine Rattoun. (PC.6.76)
1167. Cochrane, David, merchant, res. Glasgow, pts. David Cochrane, pre 1776, sett. Richmond Va. (SRO.RD3.242.127)
1168. Cochrane, David, merchant, res. Ayr, sh. pre 1777, fr. Va, in *Friendship of Ayr*. (SRO.CS.GMB56)
1169. Cochrane, James, cook, sh. 14 July 1698, fr. Leith to Darien, in *Unicorn*, Edin pr 1707 CC8.8.83
1170, Cochrane, James, soldier, pre 1737, sett. Ga, ch. Maryann Betty Caroline. (PRO.CO5.670.334)

1171. Cochrane, John, physician, res. Edinburgh, pre 1714, sett. Kingston Jamaica. (SRO.GD237)
1172. Cock, Daniel, b. 1718, Roberton Lanarkshire, clergyman edu. Glasgow Uni 1744, res. Cartsdyke Greenock Renfrewshire, pts. James Cock, sh. 1771, sett. Truro N.S., d. 17 Mar 1805 Truro. (MAGU31)
1173. Cock, James, dyer, rioter, res. Huntly Aberdeenshire, tr. May 1767. (AJ1011)
1174. Cock, Ralph, b. 1749, linen weaver, sh. Aug 1774, fr. Whitby to Savannah Ga, in *Marlborough*. (PRO.T47.9\11)
1175. Cockburn, Alexander, clergyman, sh. 1710, sett. Leeward Islands. (EMA20)
1176. Cockburn, Alexander, b. 1739, physician, sett. Grenada, ch. George Walter, d. 8 Nov 1815, Grenada pr1817. (MWI202)
1177. Cockburn, Christine, res. Edinburgh, tr. 1696, fr. Newhaven to Va. (SRO.RH15.14.58)
1178. Cockburn, James, thief, res. Greenfaulds, tr. May 1766, fr. Glasgow. (AJ958)
1179. Cockburn, James, sailor, res. Lasswade Midlothian, sh. 14 July 1698, fr. Leith to Darien, in *St Andrew*, Edin pr 1707 CC8.8.83
1180. Cockburn, John, mason, res. Kelso Roxburghshire, sh. 1684, fr. Leith to East N.J., sett. Perth Amboy N.J. (Insh276)
1181. Coffie, James, tr. 1772, fr. Glasgow, in *Brilliant*, arr. Port Hampton Va 7 Oct 1772. (SRO.JC27.10.3)
1182. Cogle, David, sailor, res. Gallowhill Wick Caithness, sh. 14 July 1698, fr. Leith to Darien, in *Unicorn*, Edin pr 1708 CC8.8.84
1183. Colford, Margaret, tr. 1728, fr. Glasgow, in *Concord*, arr. Charles Co Md 24 May 1728. (SRO.JC27.10.3)
1184. Colley, James, horsehirer, rapist, res. Aberdeen, tr. July 1764, fr. Glasgow. (AJ819/861)
1185. Colquhoun, Alexander, surgeon, res. Edinburgh, pts. Alexander Colquhoun, sh. pre 1749, to N.Y. (REB.1750.42)
1186. Colquhoun, Archibald, b. 1715, farmer, Jacobite, res. Appin Argyll, tr. 20 Mar 1747, fr. Tilbury to Jamaica or Barbados, in *St George or Carteret*, arr. Jamaica 1747. (P.2.122)(MR14)(PRO.CO137.58)
1187. Colquhoun, Walter, b. 1750, res. Camstraddan Dunbartonshire, sh. Aug 1775, fr. Greenock to Antigua, in *The Chance*, sett. Dominica & Antigua, m. Elizabeth McAlister, d. 12 Feb 1802 St John's Antigua. (GM.66.435\72.374)(PRO.T47.12)
1188. Colt, Andrew, mariner, res. Quarrell Stirlingshire, sh. 14 July 1698, fr. Leith to Darien, in *Unicorn*, d. Darien, Edin pr 1707 CC8.8.83
1189. Colthred, John, sh. 1737, fr. Inverness to Ga, in *Two Brothers*. (SPC.43.161)
1190. Colven, Catherine, b. 1745, res. Galloway, sh. 1775, fr. Dumfries to P.E.I., in *Lovely Nelly*. (PRO.T47.12)

57

1191. Colvill, Archibald, planter, sett. Barbados, ch. Mary, d. 1647.
(EBR.1659.136)
1192. Colvill, John, midshipman, pts. John Colvill, sh. 18 Aug 1699, fr.
Clyde to Darien, in *Rising Sun*, Edin pr 1707 CC8.8.83
1193. Comin, James, schoolmaster, sh. 1695, to Leeward Islands. (EMA21)
1194. Comry, Alexander, b. 1750, farmer, res. Stirling, sh. May 1774, fr.
Greenock to N.Y., in *Matty*. (PRO.T47.12)
1195. Conaher, John, Jacobite, tr. 24 May 1716, fr. Liverpool, in *Friendship*,
arr. Md Aug 1716. (SPC.1716.311)(HM387)
1196. Congilton, John, res. Edinburgh, tr. 8 May 1663, fr. Leith to Barbados,
in *Mary*. (EBR.186.13.4)
1197. Congleton, James, Jacobite, tr. 25 June 1716, fr. Liverpool to St Kitts,
in *Hockenhill*. (SPC.1716.312)(CTB31.207)
1198. Conn, Hugh, clergyman, d. 28 June 1752 Bladensburg Prince George Co
Md. (SM.14.510)
1199. Connel, John, b. 1735, weaver, res. Paisley Renfrewshire, sh. Feb 1774,
fr. Greenock to N.Y., in *Commerce*, m. Barbara ..., ch. Robert
Margaret Jean John James. (PRO.T47.12)
1200. Connell, Robert, b. 1736, laborer, sh. Feb 1774, fr. Greenock to N.Y., in
Commerce, m. Elizabeth ... (PRO.T47.12)
1201. Connell, William, Jacobite, tr. 22 Apr 1747, fr. Liverpool to Va, in
Johnson, arr. Port Oxford Md 5 Aug 1747.
(P.2.124)(PRO.T1.328)
1202. Connelly, John, b. 1716, tailor, res. Edinburgh, sh. Aug 1736, fr.
London to Jamaica. (CLRO\AIA)
1203. Conow, John, Jacobite, tr. 26 Apr 1716, fr. Liverpool to Jamaica, in
Two Brothers. (CTB31.205)
1204. Conrodsmeyer, Daniel, trumpeter, sh. 14 July 1698, fr. Leith to Darien,
in *St Andrew*, Edin pr 1707 CC8.8.83
1205. Cook, Alexander, sailor, sh. 14 July 1698, fr. Leith to Darien, in
Unicorn, d. Darien, Edin pr 1707 CC8.8.83
1206. Cook, Isabel, whore, res. Edinburgh, tr. 19 Mar 1695.
(SRO.PC2.25.216)
1207. Cook, John, England, Jacobite, tr. 1747. (P.2.126)
1208. Cook, John, rapist, res. Dumfries, tr. Nov 1774. (SRO.RH2.4.255)
1209. Cook, John sr, sailor, res. Kirkcaldy Fife, sh. 14 July 1698, fr. Leith to
Darien, in *Caledonia*, ch. James, d. 1699 West Indies, Edin pr 1707
CC8.8.83
1210. Cook, Thomas, farmer, Jacobite, res. Cushnie Aberdeenshire, tr. 1716, fr.
Liverpool to Va. (JAB.1.150)
1211. Cooper, Ann, b. 1753, spinner, res. Wick Caithness, sh. Feb 1774, fr.
Greenock to N.Y., in *Commerce*. (PRO.T47.12)
1212. Cooper, George, res. Cairnbrogie Aberdeenshire, pts. Alexander Cooper &
Elspet Low, sh. 1725, sett. Jamaica, d. pre Oct 1734. (APB.3.6)

1213. Cooper, James, b. 1772, res. New Luce Wigtonshire, sh. 31 May 1775, fr. Stranraer to N.Y., in *Jackie*. (PRO.T47.12)

1214. Cooper, Patrick, Jacobite, tr. 24 May 1716, fr. Liverpool, in *Friendship*, arr. Md Aug 1716. (SPC.1716.311)(HM386)

1215. Cooper, Thomas, b. 1771, res. New Luce Wigtonshire, sh. 31 May 1775, fr. Stranraer to N.Y., in *Jackie*. (PRO.T47.12)

1216. Copland, Robert, Jacobite, tr. 29 June 1716, fr. Liverpool to Jamaica or Va, in *Elizabeth & Anne*, arr. Va. (SPC.1716.310)(VSP.1.185)

1217. Copland, William, gardener, thief, res. Aberdeen, tr. May 1775. (AJ1427)

1218. Corbet, Alexander, thief, res. Hamilton Lanarkshire, tr. Sept 1768, fr. Glasgow. (AJ1083)

1219. Corbett, Andrew, Covenanter, tr. Aug 1685, fr. Leith to East N.J., in *Henry & Francis*. (PC.11.154)

1220. Corbett, Edward, b. 1754, merchant, res. Edinburgh, sh. Oct 1774, fr. Greenock to Charleston S.C., in *Countess*. (PRO.T47.12)

1221. Corbett, John, Covenanter, tr. Aug 1685, fr. Leith to East N.J., in *Henry & Francis*. (PC.11.155)

1222. Corbett, William, merchant, res. Glasgow, pts. James Corbett, sett. Boston Mass, d. 1767. (SRA.B10.15.7234\7137)

1223. Cordiner, James, merchant, res. Paisley, pts. James Cordiner, sett. Rappahannock Va, d. pre Mar 1724 Rappahannock, Edin pr 1724 CC8.8.89

1224. Cordiner, John, merchant, res. Glasgow, pts. John Cordiner, sett. Boston Mass, ch. Christina, d. pre Oct 1712 Boston. (SRO.SH.17.10.1712)

1225. Corhead, Agnes, Covenanter, tr. Aug 1685, fr. Leith to East N.J., in *Henry & Francis*. (PC.11.154)

1226. Cormack, William, husbandman, res. Wick Caithness, sh. 17, fr. London. (CLRO\AIA)

1227. Cornell, George, Jacobite, tr. 7 May 1716, fr. Liverpool to S.C., in *Susannah*. (SPC.1716.309)(CTB31.206)

1228. Corrie, Archibald, forger, tr. 10 Aug 1747. (SRO.HCR.I.76)

1229. Corrie, Joseph, merchant, sh. pre 1783, sett. St Thomas West Indies. (SRO.SH.12.2.1783)

1230. Corrigil, Adam, b. 1742, farmer, res. Evie Orkney Islands, sh. Sept 1774, fr. Kirkwall to Savannah Ga, in *Marlborough*, sett. Richmond Co Ga, m. Janet ..., ch. Katherine William Robert. (PRO.T47.12)

1231. Corrigil, Elizabeth, b. 1755, servant, res. Kirkwall Orkney Islands, sh. Sept 1775, fr. Kirkwall to Savannah Ga, in *Marlborough*, sett. Richmond Co Ga. (PRO.T47.12)

1232. Corrigil, James, b. 1753, farm servant, res. Wick Caithness, sh. Sept 1775, fr. Kirkwall Orkney Islands to Savannah Ga, in *Marlborough*, sett. Richmond Co Ga. (PRO.T47.12)

1233. Corry, James, sh. Dec 1698, fr. Liverpool to Va. (LRO.HQ325.2FRE)

1234. Corsan, James, tr. Nov 1679, fr. Leith. (ETR162)
1235. Corsan, John, Covenanter, tr. Aug 1685, fr. Leith to East N.J., in *Henry & Francis.* (PC.11.154)
1236. Corsbie, James, Covenanter, tr. Aug 1685, fr. Leith to Jamaica. (PC.11.329)
1237. Corse, Elizabeth, Covenanter, tr. Aug 1685, fr. Leith to East N.J., in *Henry & Francis.* (PC.11.166)
1238. Corson, Laurence, Covenanter, res. Glencairn Dumfries-shire, tr. Oct 1684. (PC.10.311)
1239. Cossie, James, soldier, thief, tr. May 1772. (AJ1270)
1240. Cotton, John, b. 1730, laborer, Jacobite, res. Clifton Lancashire, tr. 8 May 1747, to Antigua. (P.2.128)
1241. Coughtry, Mary, b. 1759, res. Gatehouse Kirkcudbrightshire, sh. May 1774, fr. Stranraer to N.Y., in *Gale.* (PRO.T47.12)
1242. Coull, James, b. 21 June 1748, Cullen Aberdeenshire, clergyman edu. Marischal Col Aberdeen 1763, res. Cullen, pts. John Coull, sh. 1772, to Antigua. (FPA317)(EMA22)
1243. Coultart, Robert, b. 1755, laborer, res. Kirkgunzeon Kirkcudbrightshire, sh. 1775, fr. Dumfries to P.E.I., in *Lovely Nelly.* (PRO.T47.12)
1244. Coulter, Hugh, merchant, pts. Michael Coulter, sett. Md, d. Oct 1763 Md, Edin pr 1766 CC8.8.120\1
1245. Coupar, James, carpenter's mate, res. Park of Erskine, sh. 14 July 1698, fr. Leith to Darien, in *Rising Sun,* Edin pr 1707 CC8.8.83
1246. Coupar, Robert, b. 2 Sept 1750, Balseir Sorbie Wigtonshire, schoolmaster edu. Glasgow Uni 1770, res. Sorbie, pts. George Coupar, sh. pre 1776, sett. Va, d. 18 Jan 1818 Wigton. (MAGU92)
1247. Couper, John, b. 1759, clerk, res. Lochwinnoch Renfrewshire, sh. July 1775, fr. Greenock to Ga, in *Christy.* (PRO.T47.12)
1248. Coupland, Alexander, b. 1757, laborer, res. Galloway, sh. 1775, fr. Dumfries to P.E.I., in *Lovely Nelly.* (PRO.T47.12)
1249. Cousins, John, Jacobite, tr. 7 May 1716, fr. Liverpool to S.C., in *Susannah.* (SPC.1716.309)(CTB31.206)
1250. Coustoun, Robert, sailor, res. St Ninian's Stirlingshire, sh. 14 July 1698, to Darien, in *Caledonia,* Edin pr 1707 CC8.8.83
1251. Coute, Joseph, Jacobite, tr. 30 Mar 1716, fr. Liverpool to Antigua, in *Scipio.* (SPC.1716.310)
1252. Couter, John, tradesman, res. Edinburgh, sh. Mar 1683, to Hudson Bay. (HBRS.9.86)
1253. Coutts, Hercules, merchant, res. Montrose Angus, pre 1751, sett. Md, ch. James & Margaret. (SRO.RD4.177.298)
1254. Coutts, James, blackmailer, res. Aberdeen, tr. 25 May 1749, fr. Aberdeen to Va, in *Dispatch of Newcastle.* (AJ69)

1255. Coutts, James, clergyman, res. Aberdeen, pts. James Coutts, sh. 1767, to
Va, sett. Richmond Falls James River 1776, d. 1787.
(APB.4.106)
1256. Coutts, Patrick, res. Aberdeen, pts. James Coutts, sh. 1747, to Va, sett.
Richmond Falls James River, d. 1776. (APB.4.106)
1257. Coutts, Patrick, merchant, pre 1768, sett. Port Royal Va.
(SRO.RD4.212.846)
1258. Coventry, Anne, thief, res. Edinburgh, tr. Dec 1743. (EBR.BC.3.74)
(alias 2980, 3806)
1259. Cowan, Alexander, b. 1754, weaver, res. Glasgow, sh. May 1774, fr.
Greenock to N.Y., in *Matty*. (PRO.T47.12)
1260. Cowan, Barbara, Covenanter, tr. Aug 1685, fr. Leith to East N.J., in
Henry & Francis. (PC.11.154)
1261. Cowan, John, b. 1756, laborer, res. Breadalbane Perthshire, sh. May
1775, fr. Greenock to N.Y., in *Lilly*. (PRO.T47.12)
1262. Cowan, Marjory, Covenanter, tr. Aug 1685, fr. Leith to East N.J., in
Henry & Francis. (PC.11.154)
1263. Cowan, William, b. 1695, tailor, Jacobite, res. Prestonpans East Lothian,
tr. 22 Apr 1747, fr. Liverpool to Va, in *Johnson*, arr. Port Oxford
Md 5 Aug 1747. (P.2.130)(MR70)(PRO.T1.328)
1264. Cowson, William, Jacobite, tr. 21 Apr 1716, fr. Liverpool to S.C., in
Wakefield. (SPC.1716.309)
1265. Cowtie, David, Jacobite, tr. 30 Mar 1716, fr. Liverpool to Antigua, in
Scipio. (SPC.1716.310)(CTB31.204)
1266. Crab, James, housebreaker, res. Old Deer Aberdeenshire, tr. Apr 1754.
(AJ328)
1267. Crachter, John, sailor, res. Newcastle, pts. James Crachter, sh. 14 July
1698, fr. Leith to Darien, in *St Andrew*, Edin pr 1707 CC8.8.83
1268. Craich, John, weaver, res. Peebles, sh. 14 July 1698, fr. Leith to Darien,
in *Dolphin*, ch. Thomas, Edin pr 1707 CC8.8.83
1269. Craig, Ann, b. 1756, servant, res. Anstruther Fife, sh. May 1775, fr.
Leith to Philadelphia, in *Friendship*. (PRO.T47.12)
1270. Craig, George, Elgin Morayshire, clergyman edu. King's Col Aberdeen
1750, sh. 1751, to Philadelphia, sett. Pa, d. post 1783 Marcus
Hook Pa. (EMA22)
1271. Craig, James, b. 1 Nov 1748, Elgin Morayshire, clergyman edu.
Marischal Col 1763-1767, pts. Archibald Craig, sh. 1772, sett. St
John's Baltimore Co Md. (FPA.21.302)
1272. Craig, John, thief, res. Aberdeenshire, tr. Aug 1753, fr. Aberdeen to Va,
in *St Andrew*. (AJ294)
1273. Craig, John, b. 1755, weaver, res. Stoneykirk Wigtonshire, sh. 31 May
1775, fr. Stranraer to N.Y., in *Jackie*. (PRO.T47.12)
1274. Craig, Margaret, b. 1755, spinner, res. Paisley Renfrewshire, sh. Feb
1774, fr. Greenock to N.Y., in *Commerce*. (PRO.T47.12)

1275. Craig, Patrick, seaman, res. Kirkwall Orkney Islands, sh. 14 July 1698, fr. Leith to Darien, in *St Andrew*, Edin pr 1708 CC8.8.84

1276. Craig, Thomas, b. 1752, mason, sh. Sept 1774, fr. London to Jamaica, in *Standlinch*. (PRO.T47.9\11)

1277. Craighead, George, clandestine marriage, tr. Feb 1750. (SRO.HCR.I.79)

1278. Craigie, Margaret, b. 1745, farm servant, res. Rousay Orkney Islands, sh. Sept 1774, fr. Kirkwall to Savannah Ga, in *Marlborough*, sett. Richmond Co Ga. (PRO.T47.12)

1279. Craigin, Robert, b. 1726, tailor, Jacobite, tr. 22 Apr 1747, fr. Liverpool to Va, in *Johnson*, arr. Port Oxford Md 5 Aug 1747. (P.2.132)(PRO.T1.328)

1280. Crampton, James, Jacobite, tr. 28 July 1716, fr. Liverpool to Va, in *Godspeed*, arr. Md Oct 1716. (SPC.1716.310)(CTB31.209)(HM388)

1281. Crane, Peter, b. 1728, hardwareman, Jacobite, res. Perthshire, tr. 21 Feb 1747. (P.2.132)

1282. Craster, William, Jacobite, tr. 29 June 1716, fr. Liverpool to Jamaica or Va, in *Elizabeth & Anne*, arr. Va. (SPC.1716.310)(VSP.1.186)(CTB31.208)

1283. Crauford, John, b. 1728, surgeon, res. Irvine Ayrshire, sh. Sept 1750, fr. London to Jamaica. (CLRO\AIA)

1284. Crawford, Alexander, res. Drumgair, sh. 1736. (SRO.GD10.1421.12\489)

1285. Crawford, David, merchant, res. Dublin, pts. David Crawford, pre 1773, sett. St Eustatia. (SRO.RD4.213.1232)

1286. Crawford, Gideon, Covenanter, res. Lanark, tr. Aug 1684, fr. Leith to Carolina. (PC.9.28)(ETR271)

1287. Crawford, Henry, b. 1749, weaver, res. Paisley Renfrewshire, sh. May 1774, fr. Greenock to N.Y., in *Matty*. (PRO.T47.12)

1288. Crawford, James, sailor, res. Grangepans West Lothian, pts. Jean Gordon or Crawford, sh. 18 Aug 1699, fr. Clyde to Darien, in *Rising Sun*, d. Darien, Edin pr 1707 CC8.8.83

1289. Crawford, James, clergyman, sh. 1711, to Md. (EMA22)

1290. Crawford, James, sh. 16 Dec 1773, fr. Greenock to Jamaica, in *Ross*. (SRO.CE60.1.7)

1291. Crawford, James, merchant, sh. Sept 1684, fr. Port Glasgow to Va, in *Catherine of Glasgow*. (SRO.E72.19.9)

1292. Crawford, James, merchant, sh. Oct 1685, fr. Port Glasgow to Va, in *Katherine of London*. (SRO.E72.19.9)

1293. Crawford, Jean, b. 1747, spinner, res. Paisley Renfrewshire, sh. Feb 1774, fr. Greenock to N.Y., in *Commerce*, ch. John. (PRO.T47.12) (alias 5422)

1294. Crawford, John, Covenanter, res. Otter Argyll, tr. 12 Aug 1685, fr. Leith to Jamaica. (PC.11.136)(ETR373)

1295. Crawford, John, sailor, res. Kirkcaldy Fife, pts. Thomas Crawford, sh. 18 Aug 1699, fr. Clyde to Darien, in *Rising Sun*, Edin pr 1707 CC8.8.83

1296. Crawford, John, merchant, sh. Oct 1684, fr. Port Glasgow to West Indies, in *Mayflower of Glasgow*. (SRO.E72.19.9)

1297. Crawford, John, b. 1739, weaver, sh. Feb 1774, fr. Greenock to N.Y., in *Commerce*, m. Margaret ..., ch. Lawrence Margaret John. (PRO.T47.12)

1298. Crawford, Patrick, merchant, sh. pre 1699, fr. London to N.Y. (DP153)

1299. Crawford, Richard, sh. 29 Nov 1773, fr. Greenock to Jamaica, in *Mary of Glasgow*. (SRO.CE60.1.7)

1300. Crawford, Robert, b. 1759, yeoman, sh. Sept 1775, fr. Newcastle to Ga, in *Georgia Packet*, sett. Friendsborough Ga. (PRO.T47.9\11)

1301. Crawford, Thomas, clergyman, sh. 1703, sett. Md Va. (EMA22)(SPG.11.153)

1302. Crawford, Thomas, clergyman, 1709, sett. Dover Del. (SCHR.14.144)

1303. Crawford, Thomas, merchant, sh. June 1684, fr. Port Glasgow to Carolina, in *Charles of Glasgow*. (SRO.E72.19.9)

1304. Crawford, William, tr. 12 Dec 1685, fr. Leith to Jamaica. (PC.11.148)(ETR373)

1305. Crawford, William, merchant, sh. Feb 1685, fr. Port Glasgow to N.E., in *Goodhope of Boston*. (SRO.E72.19.9)

1306. Creighton, Alexander, b. 1753, merchant, res. Glasgow, sh. Jan 1774, fr. Greenock to Nevis, in *Aurora*. (SRO.CE60.1.7)

1307. Creighton, James, Jacobite, tr. 7 May 1716, fr. Liverpool to S.C., in *Susannah*. (SPC.1716.309)(CTB31.206)

1308. Creighton, William, b. 1757, merchant, res. Edinburgh, sh. July 1775, fr. Greenock to Jamaica, in *Isabella*. (PRO.T47.12)

1309. Cresswell, Robert, Jacobite, tr. 25 June 1716, fr. Liverpool to St Kitts, in *Hockenhill*. (SPC.1716.312)(CTB31.207)

1310. Crichton, David, Jacobite, res. Dundee, tr. 21 Mar 1747. (P.2.134)

1311. Crichton, James, b. 1704, res. Glen Isla Angus, sh. Aug 1721, fr. London to Va. (CLRO\AIA)

1312. Crichton, John, Covenanter, res. Kilpatrick-on-the-Muir Dunbartonshire, tr. Aug 1684, fr. Leith to Carolina. (PC.9.15)

1313. Crichton, John, Covenanter, res. Dalry Ayrshire, tr. Aug 1685, fr. Leith to East N.J., in *Henry & Francis*. (PC.11.154)

1314. Crichton, John, res. Sanquhar, d. pre 1728 Dumfries Va, PCC pr1728

1315. Crichtoun, Elizabeth, whore, res. Edinburgh, tr. 2 Feb 1697. (SRO.PC2.26)

1316. Crighton, Ann, b. 1746, servant, res. Stornaway Isle of Lewis, sh. May 1774, fr. Stornaway to Philadelphia, in *Friendship*. (PRO.T47.12)

63

1317. Crighton, James, Jacobite, res. Arbroath Angus, tr. 24 Feb 1747, fr. Liverpool to Va, in *Gildart*, arr. Port North Potomac Md 5 Aug 1747. (P.2.134)(MR97)(PRO.T1.328)
1318. Crighton, John, laborer, Jacobite, res. Cablen Perthshire, tr. 24 Feb 1747, fr. Liverpool to Va, in *Gildart*, arr. Port North Potomac Md 5 Aug 1747. (P.2.134)(PRO.T1.328)
1319. Crighton, Thomas, tr. Nov 1679, fr. Leith. (ETR162)
1320. Croaker, Robert, seaman, sh. 14 July 1698, fr. Leith to Darien, in *St Andrew*, Edin pr 1707 CC8.8.83
1321. Crocker, Hugh, b. 1754, laborer, res. Lochwinnoch Renfrewshire, sh. Oct 1774, fr. Greenock to Philadelphia, in *Sally*. (PRO.T47.12)
1322. Crocket, John, b. 1744, farmer, res. Thornyhills Colvend Kirkcudbrightshire, sh. 1775, fr. Dumfries to P.E.I., in *Lovely Nelly*, m. Margaret Young, ch. James William James. (PRO.T47.12)
1323. Crockett, James, merchant, sh. pre 1752, sett. Charleston S.C., ch. Charles. (SRO.RD4.178.252)
1324. Crockett, James, physician, res. Coupar Angus Perthshire, pts. George Crockett, pre 1752, sett. S.C., ch. Charles, d. 16 Apr 1765 S.C. (SRO.SH.18.5.1763)(SRO.RD4.178.252)
1325. Crockett, John, Jacobite, tr. 7 May 1716, fr. Liverpool to S.C., in *Susannah*. (SPC.1716.309)(CTB31.206)
1326. Crockett, John, merchant, sh. Nov 1737, to Charleston S.C., in *Georgia*. (PRO.CO5.667)
1327. Croft, David, Jacobite, tr. 21 Apr 1716, fr. Liverpool to S.C., in *Wakefield*. (SPC.1716.309)(CTB31.205)
1328. Cromar, James, schoolmaster, res. Aberdeenshire, sh. 1729, sett. Va, d. 1758. (APB.4.29)
1329. Cromar, James, res. Alford Aberdeenshire, sett. America, d. 1765. (APB.3.214)
1330. Crombie, William, saddler, res. Elgin Morayshire, pts. William Crombie, arr. pre 1764 Boston Mass. (SRO.SH.22.2.1764)
1331. Cromery, James, b. 1747, shoemaker, res. Breadalbane Perthshire, sh. June 1775, fr. Greenock to N.Y., in *Commerce*. (PRO.T47.12)
1332. Cromery, Patrick, b. 1752, wright, res. Breadalbane Perthshire, sh. June 1775, fr. Greenock to N.Y., in *Commerce*. (PRO.T47.12)
1333. Crooks, James, soldier, res. Garturk, d. 1699 Darien, Edin pr1707 CC8.8.83
1334. Crooks, John, res. Prestonpans East Lothian, sh. Feb 1684, to Hudson Bay. (HBRS.9.203)
1335. Crookshanks, William, overseer, res. Banff, pts. James Crookshanks of Monely, sett. St Kitts, d. 1740 St Kitts, Edin pr 1743 CC8.8.106

1336. Crosbie, David, Covenanter, res. Carmunnock Lanarkshire, tr. 12 Dec 1678, fr. Leith to West Indies, in *St Michael of Scarborough*. (PC.6.76)
1337. Crosbie, John, b. 1717, surgeon, Jacobite, res. West Meath, tr. 21 Feb 1747. (P.2.128)
1338. Crosby, William, weaver, Jacobite, res. Ballycrydaff Meath, tr. July 1748. (P.2.136)
1339. Crosby, William, weaver, Jacobite, res. Whitchurch, tr. 1747. (MR196)
1340. Cross, John, sea-captain edu. Glasgow Uni 1753, res. Lanarkshire, pts. William Cross, d. 10 Aug 1773 Cape Fear N.C. (MAGU49)
1341. Cross, John, clergyman, sh. 1732, sett. Philadelphia, d. 9 Aug 1766 Philadelphia. (APC274)(SM.28.558)
1342. Cruden, Alexander, b. 11 Dec 1721, Aberdeen, clergyman edu. King's Col Aberdeen 1736-1740, res. Aberdeen, pts. Alexander Cruden & Giles Walker, sett. South Farnham Va, PCC pr1792. (KCA.2.312)
1343. Cruden, John, res. Aberdeen, pts. William Cruden & Isobel Pyper, sett. Jamaica, d. pre 1748. (APB.3.145)
1344. Cruickshank, Elizabeth, infanticide, res. Aberdeen, tr. Aug 1751, fr. Aberdeen to Va. (AJ193)
1345. Cruickshank, Elizabeth, whore, res. Edinburgh, tr. 19 Mar 1695. (SRO.PC2.25.216)
1346. Cruikshank, Alexander, merchant, res. Aberdeen, sett. Antigua, d. 1713. (APB.2.111)
1347. Cruikshank, John, b. 1733, herdsman, Jacobite, res. Aberdeen, tr. 5 May 1747, fr. Liverpool to Leeward Islands, in *Veteran*, arr. Martinique June 1747. (P.2.138)(PRO.SP36.102)
1348. Cullen, Walter, b. 1755, merchant, res. Edinburgh, sh. July 1775, fr. Greenock to Jamaica, in *Isabella*. (PRO.T47.12)
1349. Cullens, David, b. 1754, laborer, res. Dundee, sh. May 1775, fr. Greenock to N.Y., in *Lilly*. (PRO.T47.11)
1350. Culton, Anthony, b. 1745, laborer, res. Traquair Peeblesshire, sh. May 1775, fr. Dumfries to P.E.I., in *Lovely Nelly*, m. Janet McCaughter, ch. Marion Robert Grizel Janet John Ann. (PRO.T47.12)
1351. Cumin, John, weaver, Covenanter, res. Bridgend of Glasgow, tr. 12 Dec 1678, fr. Leith to West Indies, in *St Michael of Scarborough*. (PC.6.76)
1352. Cuming, John, clergyman, sh. 1770, to Grenades. (EMA22)
1353. Cuming, Thomas, sailor, res. Valleyfield Culross Fife, pts. John Cuming, sh. 14 July 1698, fr. Leith to Darien, in *Endeavour*, Edin pr 1707 CC8.8.83
1354. Cummin, Alexander, Jacobite, tr. 31 July 1716, fr. Liverpool to Va, in *Anne*. (SPC.1716.310)(CTB31.209)

65

1355. Cummin, Patrick, Jacobite, tr. 30 Mar 1716, fr. Liverpool to Antigua, in *Scipio*. (CTB31.204)

1356. Cummin, Peter, Jacobite, tr. 30 Mar 1716, fr. Liverpool to Antigua, in *Scipio*. (SPC.1716.310.)(CTB31.204)

1357. Cumming, .., trumpeter, sh. 21 July 1684, fr. Gourock to Port Royal S.C., in *Carolina Merchant*. (ECJ72)

1358. Cumming, Alexander, clergyman edu. Marischal Col Aberdeen 1731, sett. Kingston Jamaica. (MCA.2.86)

1359. Cumming, Alexander, thief, res. Aberdeen, tr. Sept 1756. (AJ453)

1360. Cumming, Alexander, b. 1745, farmer, res. Strathspey, sh. May 1774, fr. Greenock to N.Y., in *George*. (PRO.T47.12)

1361. Cumming, Daniel, sailor, res. Edinburgh, sh. 14 July 1698, fr. Leith to Darien, in *Unicorn*, Edin pr 1707 CC8.8.83

1362. Cumming, Donald, b. 1729, farmer, res. Strathspey, sh. May 1774, fr. Greenock to N.Y., in *George*, m. Elspa ..., ch. Mary Alexander Peter John Margery. (PRO.T47.12)

1363. Cumming, Duncan, b. 1682, Jacobite, res. Auchtuie Glen Urquhart Inverness-shire, tr. 21 Mar 1747. (P.2.140)(MR151)

1364. Cumming, Elizabeth, res. Dunbarton, pre 1755, sett. N.Y., m. Andrew McFarlane. (SRO.RS10.9.3)

1365. Cumming, Helen, res. Aberdeenshire, pts. Sir Alexander Cumming of Culter, sh. pre 1725, sett. Concord Mass, m. Robert Cumming. (SRO.GD105.338\48)

1366. Cumming, James, b. 1755, farmer, res. Strathspey, sh. May 1774, fr. Greenock to N.Y. (PRO.T47.12)

1367. Cumming, Jane, Jacobite, res. Alvie Morayshire, tr. 22 Apr 1747, fr. Liverpool to Va, in *Johnson*, arr. Port Oxford Md 5 Aug 1747. (P.2.140)(PRO.T1.328)

1368. Cumming, John, clergyman, sh. 1770, to Grenades. (EMA22)

1369. Cumming, John, b. 1740, farmer, res. Strathspey, sh. May 1774, fr. Greenock to N.Y., in *George*. (PRO.T47.12)

1370. Cumming, John, b. 1748, tailor, res. Ayr, sh. May 1774, fr. Stranraer to N.Y., in *Gale*. (PRO.T47.12)

1371. Cumming, John, b. 1758, farmer, res. Strathspey, sh. May 1774, fr. Greenock to N.Y., in *George*. (PRO.T47.12)

1372. Cumming, Katherine, b. 1764, res. Strathspey, sh. May 1774, fr. Greenock to N.Y., in *George*. (PRO.T47.12)

1373. Cumming, Mary, b. 1768, res. Strathspey, sh. May 1774, fr. Greenock to N.Y., in *George*. (PRO.T47.12)

1374. Cumming, Thomas, skipper, res. Irvine Ayrshire, sh. 12 Oct 1699, fr. Clyde to Darien, in *Speedy Return*, Edin pr 1708 CC8.8.84

1375. Cumming, William, b. 1722, farmer, res. Strathspey, sh. May 1774, fr. Greenock to N.Y., in *George*, m. Isobel ..., ch. Barbara Margery Isobel Alexander Katherine John. (PRO.T47.12)

1376. Cummings, Archibald, clergyman edu. King's Col Aberdeen 1710, sh. 1725, PCC pr1741. (EMA22)
1377. Cummings, George, clergyman edu. King's Col Aberdeen 1701, sh. 1709, to Leeward Islands. (EMA22)
1378. Cummins, William, b. 1690, Forres Morayshire, Jacobite, pts. David Cummins, tr. 24 May 1716, fr. Liverpool, in *Friendship*, arr. Md Aug 1716. (SPC.1716.311)(HM386)
1379. Cunningham, Agnes, b. 1750, farmer, res. Inverness, sh. May 1774, fr. Greenock to N.Y., in *George*. (PRO.T47.12)
1380. Cunningham, Alexander, cook, fireraiser, res. Angus, tr. 10 Aug 1677, fr. Glasgow to Va, in *Swallow of Westchester*. (PC.5.277)
1381. Cunningham, Alexander, sailor, res. Dysart Fife, sh. 14 July 1698, fr. Leith to Darien, in *Unicorn*, Edin pr 1707 CC8.8.83
1382. Cunningham, Archibald, thief, tr. 23 Dec 1680, fr. Leith, in *The Blossom*. (ETR178)
1383. Cunningham, Arthur, res. Paisley Renfrewshire, tr. June 1684, fr. Glasgow, in *Pelican*. (PC.9.208)
1384. Cunningham, Charles, clergyman, sh. 1707, to Jamaica. (EMA22)
1385. Cunningham, David, tr. Nov 1679, fr. Leith. (ETR162)
1386. Cunningham, Edward, sh. pre 1676, sett. Barbados. (PC.4.671)
1387. Cunningham, George, Covenanter, tr. July 1685. (PC.11.114)
1388. Cunningham, George, Jacobite, tr. 21 Apr 1716, fr. Liverpool to S.C., in *Wakefield*. (SPC.1716.309)(CTB31.205)
1389. Cunningham, Henry, Governor, sett. Jamaica, d. 173- Jamaica, Edin pr 1739 CC8.8.102
1390. Cunningham, Henry, physician, res. Edinburgh, pts. John Cunningham of Balbougie, sett. St Augustine E Fla, m. Margaret ..., d. 23 Feb 1771 St Augustine, Edin pr 1792 CC8.8.129\1. (SM.33.331)
1391. Cunningham, James, tr. 17 Dec 1685, fr. Leith to Jamaica, arr. Port Royal Jamaica Nov 1685, d. 1685 Jamaica. (ETR390)(LJ35)
1392. Cunningham, James, clerk, res. Glengarnock Ayrshire, pts. Richard Cunningham, sh. pre 1730, sett. Port Mahon St Kitts. (SRO.CS230.3097)
1393. Cunningham, James, tr. 12 Dec 1685, fr. Leith to Barbados, in *John & Nicholas*. (ETR390)
1394. Cunningham, James, b. 1732, weaver, res. Paisley Renfrewshire, sh. Feb 1774, fr. Greenock to N.Y., in *Commerce*, m. Elizabeth ..., ch. Elizabeth Catherine Donald James Sarah. (PRO.T47.12)
1395. Cunningham, Jean, b. 1749, res. Stirling, sh. Apr 1775, fr. Greenock to Salem, in *Glasgow Packet*. (PRO.T47.12)
1396. Cunningham, John, tr. 11 Aug 1685, fr. Leith to Jamaica. (PC.11.329)(ETR369)
1397. Cunningham, John, physician, res. Baidland Ayrshire, pre 1740, sett. St Kitts. (SRO.SH.6.5.1740)

1398. Cunningham, John, b. 1715, Jacobite, res. Argyll, tr. 5 May 1747, fr. Liverpool to Leeward islands, in *Veteran*, arr. Martinique June 1747. (P.2.140)(MR70)(PRO.SP36.102)
1399. Cunningham, Patrick, Covenanter, tr. Aug 1685, fr. Leith to East N.J., in *Henry & Francis*. (PC.11.289)
1400. Cunningham, Robert, res. Cunningham's Rest Ayrshire, sett. Cayon St Kitts, m. Mary Gainer, ch. Susanna, d. 13 Nov 1743, Glasgow pr1745 CC9.7.59
1401. Cunningham, Robert, soldier & planter, res. Glengarnock Ayrshire, pts. Richard Cunningham, sh. ca1700, sett. St Kitts, m. Judith Bonnefaut, ch. Richard Elizabeth Daniel Robert, d. post 1727. (SRO.CS230.15.7)(CAR.1.101)
1402. Cunningham, Robert, soldier, sh. pre 1703, sett. Carolina. (SPC.1703.615)
1403. Cunningham, William, Covenanter, res. Ashinyards Ayrshire, tr. Aug 1685, fr. Leith to East N.J., in *Henry & Francis*. (PC.11.159)(ETR376)
1404. Cunningham, William, sailor, sh. 18 Aug 1699, fr. Clyde to Darien, in *Hope*. Edin pr 1707 CC8.8.83
1405. Cunningham, William, b. 1740, farmer, res. Dunblane Perthshire, sh. May 1775, fr. Greenock to N.Y. or Ga, in *Christy*. (PRO.T47.12)
1406. Cunnison, Alexander, carpenter, res. Hamilton Lanarkshire, pts. Thomas Cunnison, pre 1767, sett. Kingston Jamaica. (SRO.RS42.18.233)
1407. Cunnison, William, millwright & house carpenter, res. East Miln Lanarkshire, pts. James Cunnison of Jerviston, pre 1779, sett. St Thomas in the East Jamaica. (SRO.RS42.21.32\110)
1408. Currie, Alexander, merchant, res. Linlithgow West Lothian, pts. John Currie & Isabel Guthrie, pre 1728, sett. Curacao, d. 15 Apr 1728 Curacao, Edin pr 1741 CC8.8.104
1409. Currie, James, Jacobite, tr. 25 June 1716, fr. Liverpool to St Kitts, in *Hockenhill*. (SPC.1716.312)(CTB31.207)
1410. Currie, Janet, whore, res. Edinburgh, tr. 19 Mar 1695. (SRO.PC2.25.216)
1411. Currie, Joan, res. Edinburgh, tr. 8 May 1663, fr. Leith to Barbados, in *Mary*. (EBR.186.134)
1412. Currie, John, merchant, res. Haddington East Lothian, pts. Rev John Currie & Sarah Riddel, sett. Jamaica, d. 1747 Jamaica, Edin pr 1785 CC8.8.126\2
1413. Currie, Walter, res. Linlithgow West Lothian, sh. pre 1739, sett. Providence R.I. (SRO.GD119.140)
1414. Currie, William, b. 1710, clergyman edu. Glasgow Uni, sh. 1736, to Pa, sett. Pa, d. 1803 Radnor Pa. (EMA23)
1415. Curry, Robert, b. 1749, weaver, res. Kilsyth Stirlingshire, sh. May 1775, fr. Greenock to N.Y., in *Monimia*. (PRO.T47.12)

1416. Cussins, John, sailor, sh. 14 July 1698, fr. Leith to Darien, in *St Andrew*, Edin pr 1707 CC8.8.83
1417. Cuthbert of Drackies, John, gentleman, res. Inverness, 1735, sett. Ga. (PRO.CO5.670.219)
1418. Cuthbert, James, physician, res. Castlehill Inverness, pts. George Cuthbert & Mary Mackintosh, pre 1775, sett. Savannah Ga. (SRO.RD4.210.774)
1419. Cuthbert, James, b. 1755, blacksmith, res. Lanark, sh. Aug 1774, fr. Greenock to Philadelphia, in *Magdalene*, m. Margaret ... (PRO.T47.12)
1420. Cuthbert, John, gentleman, res. Drakies Inverness-shire, sh. 1735, sett. Ga. (PRO.CO5.670.219)
1421. Cuthbert, Mary, b. 1756, servant, res. Edinburgh, sh. May 1775, fr. Leith to Philadelphia, in *Friendship*. (PRO.T47.12)
1422. Cuthbertson, William, Covenanter, tr. June 1669. (PC.3.22)
1423. Dabrall, Wilson, b. 1749, jeweller, sh. Oct 1774, fr. London to Carolina, in *James*. (PRO.T47.9\11)
1424. Dalgetty, Alexander, Jacobite, tr. 7 May 1716, fr. Liverpool to S.C., in *Susannah*. (SPC.1716.309)(CTB31.206)
1425. Dalgetty, John, Jacobite, tr. 24 May 1716, fr. Liverpool to Md, in *Friendship*. (SPC.1716.311)
1426. Dalgleish, Alexander, Covenanter, res. Kilbride, tr. Aug 1685, fr. Leith to East N.J., in *Henry & Francis*. (PC.11.154)
1427. Dalgleish, Alexander, clergyman edu. Edinburgh Uni, sh. July 1698, fr. Leith to Darien, d. Nov 1698 Montserrat. (F.7.663)
1428. Dalgleish, Elizabeth, infanticide, tr. Mar 1768. (SRO.JC27.D35)
1429. Dallas, Alexander, b. 1757, merchant, res. Aberdeen, sh. July 1775, fr. Greenock to Jamaica, in *Isabella*. (PRO.T47.9\11)
1430. Dallas, Walter, b. 1690s, Edinburgh, merchant, res. Edinburgh, pts. James Dallas of St Martin & Elizabeth Riddell, sett. Annapolis Royal Baltimore Co Md, ch. Nathan Ann Rachel Keith, d. pre Aug 1772. (FD344)(SRO.CS.GMB282)
1431. Dalmahoy, Thomas, Jacobite, tr. 25 June 1716, fr. Liverpool to St Kitts, in *Hockenhill*. (SPC.1716.312)(CTB31.207)
1432. Dalrymple, David, sh. pre 1774, sett. St Kitts. (SRO.CS.GMB289)
1433. Dalrymple, Hew, attorney general, d. 8 Mar 1773 Grenada. (SM.36.222)
1434. Dalrymple, John, b. 1726, farmer, res. New Luce Wigtonshire, sh. May 1775, fr. Stranraer to N.C., in *Jackie*, m. Margaret Gordon, ch. Mary John Archibald James Ann Janet Jean William. (PRO.T47.12)
1435. Dalyell, George, merchant, res. Lanark, sh. pre 1765, sett. Antigua. (SRO.RS42.17.79)
1436. Dalyell, John, res. Whitehaven, pts. James Dalyell, sh. pre 1765, sett. Frederick Co Md. (SRO.RS23.19.339)

1437. Dalziel, John, Jacobite, tr. 1716, to Carolina or Va. (SPC.1716.128)
1438. Dalziel, Rev, clergyman, res. Edinburgh, sh. 1779, sett. Warwick
       Bermuda. (F.7.660)
1439. Dalziel, William, Jacobite, tr. 7 May 1716, fr. Liverpool to S.C., in
       Susannah. (SPC.1716.309)(CTB31.206)
1440. Dalziell, Charles, soldier, pts. Earl of Carnwath, d. 1699 Darien, Edin pr
       1707 CC8.8.83
1441. Darling, John, b. 1663, cordwainer, pts. John Darling, sh. Sept 1684, fr.
       London to Md, in *Hound*. (CLRO\AIA)
1442. Dason, James, res. Aberdeen, pts. John Dason, d. 1770 St Thomas
       Jamaica. (APB.4.43)
1443. Davidson, Abraham, b. 14 Feb 1725, Kincardine O'Neil Aberdeenshire,
       res. Aberdeenshire, pts. Alexander Davidson & Jean Strachan, sh.
       July 1741, fr. Aberdeen or Peterhead to Va or Md, in *Charming
       Peggy*. (Perth MAGA86)
1444. Davidson, Alexander, shoemaker, Jacobite, res. Canongate Edinburgh,
       pts. Alexander Davidson, tr. Mar 1747. (P.2.144)
1445. Davidson, Alexander, clergyman edu. King's Col Aberdeen 1693, sh.
       1710, to Md. (EMA23)
1446. Davidson, Alexander, b. 1720, Jacobite, res. Charlton Aberdeenshire, tr.
       31 Mar 1747, fr. London to Barbados, in *Frere*. (P.2.144)(MR202)
1447. Davidson, Alexander, b. 1730, herdsman, Jacobite, res. Badenoch
       Inverness-shire, tr. 5 May 1747, fr. Liverpool to Leeward Islands,
       in *Veteran*, arr. Martinique June 1747. (P.2.144)(PRO.SP36.102)
1448. Davidson, Andrew, Jacobite, tr. 24 May 1716, fr. Liverpool to Md, in
       Friendship, Aug 1716. (SPC.1716.311)(HM387)
1449. Davidson, Anne, infanticide, tr. Aug 1762. (SRO.RH2.4.255)
1450. Davidson, Barbara, infanticide, res. Kincardine O'Neil Aberdeenshire, pts.
       William Davidson, tr. June 1772. (AJ1280)(SRO.RH2.4.255)
1451. Davidson, Benjamin, soldier, thief, res. Perth, tr. Sept 1751, fr.
       Montrose(?). (SRO.B59.26.11.1520)(AJ145)
1452. Davidson, Charles, thief, res. Edinburgh, tr. 4 May 1666, fr. Leith to Va,
       in *Phoenix of Leith*. (ETR107)
1453. Davidson, Charles, servant, Jacobite, res. Aberzeldie, tr. 22 Apr 1747, fr.
       Liverpool to Va, in *Johnson*, arr. Port Oxford Md 5 Aug 1747.
       (P.2.144)(MR219)(PRO.T1.328)
1454. Davidson, Donald, Jacobite, tr. 7 May 1716, fr. Liverpool to S.C., in
       Susannah. (SPC.1716.309)(CTB31.206)
1455. Davidson, James, shoemaker, cattlethief, res. Cairngressie
       Kincardineshire, tr. Sept 1763. (AJ819) (alias 1674)
1456. Davidson, James, b. 1755, sailor, res. Kirkholm, sh. May 1775, fr.
       Stranraer to N.Y., in *Jackie*. (PRO.T47.12)
1457. Davidson, Jean, b. 1753, res. Kirkholm, sh. May 1775, fr. Stranraer to
       N.Y., in *Jackie*. (PRO.T47.12)

1458. Davidson, John, thief, res. Upper Old Garth Dumfries-shire, tr. May
1720. (SRO.JC12.3)
1459. Davidson, John, Jacobite, tr. 1747. (P.2.146)(MR70)
1460. Davidson, John, miller, wifebeater, res. Gordon's Mill Aberdeen, tr. Sept
1765, fr. Glasgow. (AJ924\7)
1461. Davidson, John, accountant, res. Inverness, sh. Jan 1755, fr. London to
Md. (CLRO\AIA)
1462. Davidson, John, res. Aberdeen, tr. pre 1666, sett. Barbados. (ABR
1463. Davidson, John, res. Aberdeenshire, sh. July 1741, fr. Aberdeen or
Peterhead to Va or Md, in Charming Peggy. (Perth MAGA150)
1464. Davidson, Joseph, gunner, res. Ayr, pts. Patrick Davidson & Katherine
Cathcart, sh. 14 July 1698, fr. Leith to Darien, in Dolphin, Edin
pr 1708 CC8.8.84
1465. Davidson, Peter, tr. Nov 1750. (AJ152)
1466. Davidson, Peter, thief, res. Strathmiglo Fife, tr. 1769. (SM.31.73)
1467. Davidson, Robert, sailor, res. Edinburgh, sh. 14 July 1698, fr. Leith to
Darien, in Dolphin, Edin pr 1707 CC8.8.83
1468. Davidson, Thomas, b. 1706, distiller, res. Berwick, sh. Apr 1731, fr.
London to Jamaica. (CLRO\AIA)
1469. Davidson, William, farmer, Jacobite, res. Cushnie Aberdeenshire, tr. 24
May 1716, fr. Liverpool to Va, in Friendship, arr. Md Aug 1716.
(SPC.1716.311)(JAB.1.151)(HM387)
1470. Davidson, William, robber, res. Perthshire, tr. 1773. (SM.35.334)
1471. Davidson, William, bosun, sh. 14 July 1698, fr. Leith to Darien, in St
Andrew, Edin pr 1707 CC8.8.83
1472. Davidson, William, robber, res. Inverness-shire, tr. June 1773.
(CalHOp312.847)
1473. Davidson, William, passenger, sh. Feb 1681, fr. Ayr to West Indies, in
James of Ayr. (SRO.E72.3.6)
1474. Davidson, William, b. 1707, tailor, res. Perth, sh. Nov 1727, fr. London
to Va. (CLRO\AIA)
1475. Davie, Marion, servant, infanticide, res. Wester Grange, tr. Dec 1766.
(SRO.HCR.I.98)
1476. Davie, Robert, Jacobite, tr. 22 Apr 1747, fr. Liverpool to Va, in
Johnson, arr. Port Oxford Md 5 Aug 1747. (PRO.T1.328)
1477. Davies, John, surgeon, res. Glassrie, pts. J Davies, pre 1772, sett.
Jamaica. (SRO.SH.14.7.1772)
1478. Davison, William, soldier, res. Peebles-shire, d. pre 1776 Boston Mass,
PCC pr 1776
1479. Daw, Andrew, Jacobite, tr. 24 May 1716, fr. Liverpool to Va, in
Friendship, arr. Md 20 Aug 1716. (SPC.1716.311)(HM387)
1480. Dawson, James, sh. 29 Nov 1773, fr. Greenock to Jamaica, in Mary of
Glasgow. (SRO.CE60.1.7)

1481. Dawson, William, clergyman, res. Perth, sett. Pensacola W Fla, d. pre 1770, Edin pr 1770 CC8.8.121
1482. Deacon, Charles Clement, b. 1730, Jacobite, res. Manchester, pts. Dr Thomas Deacon, tr. July 1748. (MR195)(P.2.148)
1483. Dean, John, clergyman, sh. 1723, to Carolina, d. 1726. (F.7.663)
1484. Dean, John, merchant, res. Glasgow?, sh. pre 1757, sett. Tapahannock Va. (SRA.B10.15.7036)
1485. Deas, David, merchant, res. Leith Midlothian, pts. David Deas, pre 1757, sett. Charleston S.C., d. 29 Aug 1775 Charleston. (SRO.RD3.224.627\30)(SM.37.637)
1486. Debeare, James, tailor, res. Berwick, sh. Nov 1685. (CLRO\AIA)
1487. Dempster, Alexander, b. 1757, gardener, res. Perthshire, sh. May 1775, fr. Leith to Philadelphia, in *Friendship*. (PRO.T47.12)
1488. Dempster, Lilly, b. 1759, servant, res. Edinburgh, sh. May 1775, fr. Leith to Philadelphia, in *Friendship*. (PRO.T47.12)
1489. Denham, James, Jacobite, tr. 24 May 1716, fr. Liverpool to Va, in *Friendship*, arr. Md Aug 1747. (SPC.1716.311)(HM387)
1490. Denham, Thomas, merchant, sh. 1774, sett. Charleston S.C. & Shelburne N.S. (PRO.AO13.25.138.141)
1491. Denholm, Elizabeth, res. Edinburgh, sh. pre 1753, sett. Hanover Jamaica, m. George Gordon. (SRO.SH.8.2.1753)
1492. Deniston, Margaret, b. 1738, res. Kirkcudbright, sh. May 1774, fr. Dumfries to N.Y., in *Gale*. (PRO.T47.12)
1493. Denistoun, Alison, res. Edinburgh, tr. 1696, fr. Newhaven to Va. (SRO.RH15.14.58)
1494. Denniston, Samuel, b. 1749, tailor, res. Auchincairn, sh. May 1774, fr. Kirkcudbright to N.Y., in *Adventure*. (PRO.T47.12)
1495. Denovan, James, horsethief, res. Foulshiels Whitburn Linlithgow West Lothian, tr. Mar 1763. (SRO.HCR.I.94)
1496. Denson, John, b. 1725, Jacobite, tr. 1747, fr. Tilbury. (P.2.152)
1497. Derritt, Peter, Jacobite, tr. 30 Mar 1716, fr. Liverpool to Antigua, in *Scipio*. (SPC.1716.310)(CTB31.204)
1498. Deuchar, Alexander, clergyman, res. Kemnay Aberdeenshire, pts. William Deuchar, sett. St Thomas Barbados, d. 3 Feb 1732 Barbados, Edin pr1738 CC8.8.100. (APB.3.28)
1499. Dewar, Andrew, customs collector, sh. pre1767, sett. Dominica, d. 19 July 1771 Dominica. (SM.33.503)(SRO.SH.16.1.1767)
1500. Dewar, Robert, merchant, res. Edinburgh, pts. Wiliam Dewar, sh. pre 1768, sett. Antigua & St Eustatia. (SRO.SH.14.1.1772)
1501. Dewar, William, b. 1744, blacksmith, res. Burntisland Fife, sh. Oct 1774, fr. Kirkcaldy to Antigua, in *Jamaica Packet*, m. Jane ... (PRO.T47.12)
1502. Dewars, Alexander, tr. 1730, fr. Glasgow to S.C., in *John & Robert*, 22 July 1730. (SRO.JC27.10.3)

1503. Dick, Alexander, res. Airth Stirlingshire, pts. George Dick, sett. S.C., d. pre 1742 S.C., PCC pr 1742
1504. Dick, Archibald, clergyman, sh. 1762, to Va. (EMA24)
1505. Dick, Catherine, b. 1754, servant, res. Breton, sh. May 1775, fr. Leith to Philadelphia, in *Friendship*. (PRO.T47.12)
1506. Dick, David, b. 1725, shoemaker, Jacobite, tr. 24 Feb 1747, fr. Liverpool to Va, in *Gildart*, arr. Port North Potomac Md 5 Aug 1747. (P.2.152)(PRO.T1.328)
1507. Dick, Edward, sailor, res. Airth Stirlingshire, sh. 14 July 1698, fr. Leith to Darien, in *Caledonia*, Edin pr 1707 CC8.8.83
1508. Dick, Jean, whore, tr. 19 Mar 1695. (SRO.PC2.25.216)
1509. Dick, John, Covenanter, res. Livingstone West Lothian, tr. June 1684, fr. Clyde to Carolina, in *Pelican*. (PC.9.208) (alias 3109)
1510. Dick, John, cook, res. Airth Stirlingshire, pts. George Dick, sh. 14 July 1698, fr. Leith to Darien, in *Caledonia*, Edin pr 1707 CC8.8.83
1511. Dick, John, b. 1751, ships carpenter, res. Ayrshire, sh. Mar 1775, fr. Glasgow to Quebec, in *Friendship*. (PRO.T47.12)
1512. Dick, John, b. 1761, laborer, sh. Sept 1775, fr. Newcastle to Ga, in *Georgia Packet*, sett. Friendsborough Ga. (PRO.T47.10)
1513. Dick, Quentin, Covenanter, tr. May 1685. (PC.11.289)
1514. Dick, Thomas, merchant, res. Edinburgh, pts. Robert Dick, sh. pre 1758, sett. Annapolis. (SRO.SH.21.3.1758)
1515. Dick, Thomas, b. 1747, wright, res. Stirling, sh. May 1775, fr. Greenock to N.Y. or Ga, in *Christy*. (PRO.T47.12)
1516. Dickenson, George, Jacobite, tr. 29 June 1716, fr. Liverpool to Jamaica or Va, in *Elizabeth & Anne*, arr. Va. (SPC.1716.310)(CTB31.208)(VSP.1.185)
1517. Dickinson, William, b. 1707, weaver, Jacobite, res. Lancashire, tr. 8 May 1747, fr. Liverpool to Antigua. (MR197)(P.2.154)
1518. Dickman, James, b. 1749, farmer, res. Perth, sh. Apr 1775, fr. Greenock to Salem, in *Glasgow Packet*. (PRO.T47.12)
1519. Dicks, Robert, res. Edinburgh, tr. 12 Dec 1678, fr. Leith to West Indies, in *St Michael of Scarborough*. (PC.6.76)
1520. Dickson, Alexander, soldier, res. Hartree Peeblesshire, pts. David Dickson, pre 1774, sett. Houma Chita W Fla. (PRO.CO5.613.257)
1521. Dickson, Andrew, b. 1746, laborer, res. Edinburgh, sh. Apr 1775, fr. Greenock to N.Y., in *Lilly*. (PRO.T47.12)
1522. Dickson, David, b. 1754, laborer, res. Glasgow, sh. May 1774, fr. Greenock to N.Y., in *Matty*. (PRO.T47.12)
1523. Dickson, James, ropemaker, thief, res. Stirling, tr. 1770. (SM.32.516)
1524. Dickson, Thomas, servant, rapist, res. Meadowhope, tr. Aug 1744. (SRO.JC27)

73

1525. Dickson, William, carpenter, res. Whitstead Glenholm Peebles-shire, pts. John Dickson, pre 1765, sett. Kingston Jamaica. (SRO.RD2.197.377)(SRO.RD2.222.203)
1526. Din, John, thief, res. Branshog Stirlingshire, tr. May 1729. (SRO.JC27) (alias 3019)
1527. Dingwall, Daniel, b. 1716, glover, Jacobite, res. Inverness, tr. 5 May 1747, fr. Liverpool to Leeward Islands, in *Veteran*, arr. Martinique June 1747. (P.2.154)(PRO.SP36.102)
1528. Dingwall, Donald, b. 1723, servant, Jacobite, res. Ross-shire, tr. 31 Mar 1747, fr. Tilbury to Barbados, in *Frere*. (MR81)(P.2.154)
1529. Dinwiddie, John, res. Glasgow, sett. Hanover King George Co Va, m. Rose Masson, ch. Elizabeth & Jean, Glasgow pr 1725 CC9.7.52
1530. Dixon, .., sh. 29 Nov 1773, fr. Greenock to Jamaica, in *Mary of Glasgow*. (SRO.CE60.1.7)
1531. Dixon, James, Jacobite, tr. 28 July 1716, fr. Liverpool to Va, in *Godspeed*, arr. Md. (SPC.1716.310)(CTB31.209)(HM387)
1532. Dobie, James, sh. 1684, to East N.J. (Insh249)
1533. Doctor, David, Jacobite, tr. 7 May 1716, fr. Liverpool to S.C., in *Susannah*. (SPC.1716.309)(CTB31.206)
1534. Dod, Ralph, soldier, sh. 1659, in *Grantham*, sett. Jamaica. (SPC.1659.126)
1535. Dodds, James, b. 1718, farmer, Jacobite, res. Setonhill Mains Belton Haddington East Lothian, tr. 31 Mar 1747, fr. London to Jamaica , in *St George or Carteret*, arr. Jamaica 1747. (P.2.156)(PRO.CO137.58)
1536. Doig, Charles, b. 1754, weaver, res. Perthshire, sh. May 1775, fr. Leith to Philadelphia, in *Friendship*. (PRO.T47.12)
1537. Doig, James, res. Montrose Angus, d. 14 July 1759 Antigua. (SM.21.557)
1538. Donald, Alexander, res. Glasgow, pts. James Donald, sh. Mar 1760, fr. Glasgow to Va. (SRA.CFI)
1539. Donald, Alexander, b. 1738, laborer, res. Killearn Stirlingshire, sh. May 1775, fr. Greenock to N.Y. or Ga, in *Christy*. (PRO.T47.12)
1540. Donald, Andrew, attorney, res. Broom Ayrshire, sett. Bedford Co Va, ch. Ann & Christian. (SRA.CFI)
1541. Donald, Bessie, whore & thief, res. Edinburgh, tr. 28 Nov 1704. (SRO.PC2.28.307)
1542. Donald, David, sailor, res. Kincardine on Forth, sh. 18 Aug 1699, fr. Greenock to Darien, in *Rising Sun*, Edin pr 1707 CC8.8.83
1543. Donald, David, res. Lochbank, pts. David Donald or McDonald of Shangzie, sh. 1699, to Darien, Edin pr 1709 CC8.8.84 (alias 3597)
1544. Donald, James, merchant, res. Cairnie Aberdeenshire, pts. James Donald, sett. Jamaica, d. Sept 1758 Jamaica. (APB.3.197)

1545. Donald, James, b. 1727, tailor, Jacobite, res. Mearns, tr. 5 May 1747, fr. Liverpool to Leeward Islands, in *Veteran*, arr. Martinique June 1747. (P.2.156)(MR23)(PRO.SP36.102)
1546. Donald, Robert, merchant, res. Dunbartonshire, pts. Thomas Donald of Lyleston & Janet Cumming, sh. pre 1757, sett. Va. (SRO.RS10.9.97)
1547. Donald, William, stampmaster, forger, res. Greenock Renfrewshire, tr. Feb 1744. (SRO.HCR.I.71)
1548. Donaldson, Alexander, b. 1707, laborer, Jacobite, res. Banff, tr. 1747. (P.2.156)
1549. Donaldson, Barbara, whore, res. Edinburgh, tr. Feb 1697. (SRO.PC2.26)
1550. Donaldson, Charles, Jacobite, tr. 24 May 1716, fr. Liverpool to Va, in *Friendship*, arr. Md Aug 1716. (SPC.1716.311)(HM387)
1551. Donaldson, James, b. 1697, wright, Jacobite, res. Edinburgh, tr. 24 Feb 1747, fr. Liverpool to Va, in *Gildart*, arr. Port North Potomac Md 5 Aug 1747. (P.2.158)(MR98)(PRO.T1.328)
1552. Donaldson, James, b. 1722, servant, Jacobite, res. Ranass Banffshire, tr. 1747, fr. Tilbury. (P.2.158)(MR58)
1553. Donaldson, John, Jacobite, tr. 29 June 1716, fr. Liverpool to Va, in *Elizabeth & Anne*, arr. Va. (SPC.1716.310)(CTB31.208)(VSP.1.186)
1554. Donaldson, John, clergyman edu. King's Col Aberdeen 1700, sh. 1711, sett. King & Queen Co Md, d. 1747 Md. (EMA24)
1555. Donaldson, John, horsehirer, counterfeiter, res. Hamilton Lanarkshire, tr. Aug 1753. (SRO.JC3.29.271)(SM.15.420)
1556. Donaldson, John, b. 1700, res. Kemnay Aberdeenshire, sh. Aug 1718, fr. London to Md. (CLRO\AIA)
1557. Donaldson, Mary, b. 1758, servant, res. Alloa Clackmannanshire, sh. May 1775, fr. Leith to Philadelphia, in *Friendship*. (PRO.T47.12)
1558. Donaldson, Peter, b. 1740, mason, res. Edinburgh, sh. Dec 1773, fr. London to Dominica, in *Greyhound*. (PRO.T47.9\11)
1559. Donaldson, Robert, merchant, res. Aberdeen, pts. Robert Donaldson & Isobel Irvine, sett. St Kitts, d. 1725. (APB.3.38)
1560. Donaldson, Thomas, Jacobite, tr. 24 May 1716, fr. Liverpool to Va, in *Friendship*, arr. Md Aug 1716. (SPC.1716.311)(HM387)
1561. Donaldson, William, Jacobite, tr. 29 June 1716, fr. Liverpool to Va, in *Elizabeth & Anne*, arr. Va. (SPC.1716.310)(CTB31.208)(VSP.1.185)
1562. Dorie, Daniel, Jacobite, tr. 30 Mar 1716, fr. Liverpool to Antigua, in *Scipio*. (CTB31.204)
1563. Dorwaite, James, b. 1701, cordwainer, res. Edinburgh, sh. Dec 1721, fr. London to Md. (CLRO\AIA)
1564. Dougal, James, b. 1755, weaver, res. Paisley Renfrewshire, sh. Feb 1774, fr. Greenock to N.Y., in *Commerce*. (PRO.T47.12)

1565. Dougall, Arthur, wright, Covenanter, res. Glasgow, tr. 13 June 1678, fr. Leith to West Indies, in *St Michael of Scarborough*, m. Katherine Hall. (PC.6.76)
1566. Dougall, John, sailor, res. Crawforddykes Renfrewshire, sh. 1699, to Darien, in *Speedy Return*. Edin pr 1707 CC8.8.83
1567. Dougall, Robert, carpenter's mate, res. Crawforddykes Renfrewshire, sh. 14 July 1698, fr. Leith to Darien, in *Rising Sun*, Edin pr 1707 CC8.8.83
1568. Dougall, Walter, b. 1757, weaver, res. Paisley Renfrewshire, sh. Feb 1774, fr. Greenock to N.Y., in *Commerce*. (PRO.T47.12)
1569. Dougherty, John, b. 1717, Ireland, laborer, Jacobite, tr. 1747. (P.2.160)
1570. Douglas, Alexander, clergyman edu. Edinburgh Uni, sh. 1750, sett. St James S.C. (EMA24)(FPA306)
1571. Douglas, Alexander, b. 1723, laborer, res. Perth, sh. May 1775, fr. Leith to Philadelphia, in *Friendship*. (PRO.T47.12)
1572. Douglas, Alexander, b. 1752, husbandman, sh. Nov 1774, fr. London to Carolina, in *Briton*. (PRO.T47.9\11)
1573. Douglas, Charles, Covenanter, tr. Aug 1685, fr. Leith to East N.J., in *Henry & Francis*. (PC.11.154)
1574. Douglas, Charles, pre 1782, sett. St Kitts. (EBR.171.6728)
1575. Douglas, Charles, b. 1714, res. Orkney Islands, sh. Dec 1731, fr. London to Jamaica. (CLRO\AIA)
1576. Douglas, George, soldier, d. 1699 Darien, Edin pr 1707 CC8.8.83
1577. Douglas, George, b. 1703, scholar, res. Linton Peebles-shire, sh. Feb 1721, fr. London to Va. (CLRO\AIA)
1578. Douglas, James, merchant, res. Carlisle Cumberland, pts. Dr James Douglas, pre 1781, sett. St John Middlesex Jamaica. (SRO.RD2.231.242)
1579. Douglas, James, surgeon, res. Whiterigs Aberdeenshire, pts. George Douglas, 1754, sett. St Mary Jamaica, d. 1763. (APB.3.224)
1580. Douglas, James, carpenter, res. Edinburgh, sh. 14 July 1698, fr. Leith to Darien, in *St Andrew*, m. Katherine Waterstone, ch. James & Christian, Edin pr 1707 CC8.8.83
1581. Douglas, James, edu. Glasgow Uni 1737, res. Dunbartonshire, pts. James Douglas of Mains, d. 18 Nov 1766 Dumfries Prince William Co Va. (MAGU19)
1582. Douglas, James, sh. Dec 1698, fr. Liverpool to Va, in *Globe*. (LRO.HQ325.2FRE)
1583. Douglas, James, b. 1718, laborer, res. New Abbey Galloway, sh. May 1775, fr. Dumfries to P.E.I., in *Lovely Nelly*, m. Janet Neish, ch. James. (PRO.T47.12)
1584. Douglas, James, b. 1732, customs collector edu. Glasgow & Oxford Unis, pts. John Douglas of Kellhead, sh. pre 1762, sett. Jamaica. (MAGU33)

1585. Douglas, John, laborer, res. Dundee Angus, sh. June 1775, fr. Kirkcaldy to Brunswick N.C., in *Jamaica Packet*. (PRO.T47.12)
1586. Douglas, John, clergyman, sh. 1732, to Antigua. (EMA24)
1587. Douglas, John, b. 1750, laborer, res. Kirkbean Galloway, sh. May 1775, fr. Dumfries to P.E.I., in *Lovely Nelly*. (PRO.T47.12)
1588. Douglas, John, b. 1755, gardener, sh. Sept 1775, fr. Newcastle to Ga, in *Georgia Packet*, sett. Friendsborough Ga. (PRO.T47.9\11)
1589. Douglas, Margaret, servant, res. Netherthornwhat Dumfriesshire, tr. May 1767. (AJ104)
1590. Douglas, Patrick, schoolmaster, clandestine marriage, res. Mortlach Banff, tr. July 1750. (AJ135)
1591. Douglas, Patrick, b. 1740, mason, res. Perthshire, sh. May 1775, fr. Greenock to N.Y., in *Monimia*. (PRO.T47.12)
1592. Douglas, Peter, pts. Archibald Douglas of Dornick, sh. pre 1771, sett. St Thomas in the Vale Middlesex Jamaica. (SRO.RD4.211.263)
1593. Douglas, Robert, res. Dumfries, sh. May 1775, fr. Whitehaven to P.E.I., in *Lovely Nelly*. (PRO.T47.12)
1594. Douglas, Robert, d. 24 Oct 1779 St Kitts. (SM.42.54)
1595. Douglas, Robert, b. 1706, res. Aberdeen, sh. June 1721, fr. London to Jamaica. (CLRO\AIA)
1596. Douglas, Thomas, tr. 17 Dec 1685, fr. Leith. (ETR390)
1597. Douglas, Thomas, tinker, thief, res. Bannockburn Stirlingshire, tr. 1754. (SM.16.258)
1598. Douglas, William, Covenanter, res. Bridge of Ken, tr. Aug 1685, fr. Leith to East N.J., in *Henry & Francis*. (PC.11.154)
1599. Douglas, William, clergyman, pre 1749, sett. St James Northam Goochland Co Va, m. Nicholas Hunter. (SNQ.1.154)(EMA25)
1600. Douglas, William, b. 1754, laborer, res. Kirkbean Galloway, sh. May 1775, fr. Dumfries to P.E.I., in *Lovely Nelly*. (PRO.T47.12)
1601. Doull, James, surgeon, res. Edinburgh, pts. James Doull, sh. pre 1751, sett. Md. (SRO.RD4.172.158\525)
1602. Dow, James, coxswain, sh. 14 July 1698, fr. Leith to Darien, in *Caledonia*, d. West Indies, Edin pr 1707 CC8.8.83
1603. Dow, John, clergyman edu. King's Col Aberdeen 1727, sh. 1728, to Jamaica. (EMA25)
1604. Dow, John, b. 1717, servant, Jacobite, res. Stanly Auchtergavin, tr. 24 Feb 1747, fr. Liverpool to Va, in *Gildart*, arr. Port North Potomac Md 5 Aug 1747. (P.2.162)(MR23)(PRO.T1.328)
1605. Dowie, Wiliam, clergyman, sh. 1762, to Md. (EMA25)
1606. Downie, James, sailor, res. Peterhead Aberdeenshire, sh. 14 July 1698, fr. Leith to Darien, in *Unicorn*, Edin pr 1707 CC8.8.83
1607. Downie, John, Covenanter, tr. Aug 1685, fr. Leith to Jamaica. (PC.11.130)
1608. Downie, John, murderer, tr. Dec 1774. (SRO.RH2.4.255)

77

1609. Downie, Katherine, b. 1745, spinner, res. Glen Orchy Argyll, sh. Sept 1775, to Wilmington N.C., in *Jupiter*, ch. Mary Joseph. (PRO.T47.12) (alias 4731)
1610. Downie, Robert, b. 1704, res. Glasgow, sh. Dec 1724, fr. London to Jamaica. (CLRO\AIA)
1611. Downy, Christian, b. 1750, spinner, res. Glen Orchy Argyll, sh. Sept 1775, to Wilmington N.C., in *Jupiter*. (PRO.T47.12)
1612. Drenan, William, Covenanter, tr. 11 Aug 1685, fr. Leith to Jamaica. (PC.11.329)(ETR369)
1613. Drummond, George, tinker, horsethief, res. Pathhead Fife, tr. Apr 1773. (AJ1321)
1614. Drummond, Gilbert, b. 1714, servant, Jacobite, res. Meiklour Caputh Perthshire, tr. 1747, fr. Liverpool, d. 7 June 1747 at sea. (P.2.162)(PRO.T1.328)
1615. Drummond, John, Jacobite, res. Balnacuik Balquhidder Perthshire, tr. 1747. (P.2.164)(MR167) (alias 3871)
1616. Drummond, John, cooper, res. Leith Midlothian, sh. June 1775, fr. Kirkcaldy to Brunswick N.C., in *Jamaica Packet*. (PRO.T47.12)
1617. Drummond, John, physician, d. 20 June 1754 Savanna la Mar Jamaica. (SM.16.503)
1618. Drummond, John, physician, sh. 1764, sett. Jamaica, d. 14 Apr 1804 Westmoreland Jamaica. (SM.66.566)
1619. Drummond, John, sh. 29 Nov 1773, fr. Greenock to Jamaica, in *Mary of Glasgow*. (SRO.CE60.1.7)
1620. Drummond, John, b. 1755, weaver, res. Paisley Renfrewshire, sh. Feb 1774, fr. Greenock to N.Y., in *Commerce*. (PRO.T47.12)
1621. Drummond, Mr, res. Edinburgh, sh. 1684, to East N.J. (Insh263)
1622. Drummond, Thomas, soldier, res. Edinburgh, sh. 169, to Darien, Edin pr 1707 CC8.8.83
1623. Drummond, William, sett. Va, m. Sarah .., d. pre1677, PCC pr1677
1624. Drummond, William, b. 1749, laborer, res. Renfrew, sh. Oct 1774, fr. Greenock to Philadelphia, in *Sally*. (PRO.T47.12)
1625. Dryden, Adam, b. 1746, gardener, sh. Aug 1774, fr. Whitby to Savannah Ga, in *Marlborough*. (PRO.T47.9\11)
1626. Drysdale, David, sailor, res. Culross Fife, sh. 18 Aug 1699, fr. Clyde to Darien, in *Rising Sun*, m. Jean Archibald, Edin pr 1707 CC8.8.83
1627. Drysdale, John, Covenanter, tr. Oct 1681, to West Indies. (PC.7.219)
1628. Duff, Alexander, Jacobite, tr. 30 Mar 1716, fr. Liverpool to Antigua, in *Scipio*. (SPC.1716.310)(CTB31.204)
1629. Duff, Alexander, b. 1732, Jacobite, res. Dundee Angus, tr. 1747. (MR98)
1630. Duff, Daniel, Jacobite, res. Atholl Perthshire, tr. 21 Apr 1747, fr. London to Barbados, in *Frere*. (P.2.168)

1631. Duff, Daniel, b. 1721, laborer, Jacobite, res. Perthshire, tr. 5 May 1747, fr. Liverpool to Leeward Islands, in *Veteran*, arr. Martinique June 1747. (P.2.168)(MR206)(PRO.SP36.102)

1632. Duff, David, tutor, sh. 1772, sett. Portobacco Md. (SRO.GD248)

1633. Duff, Donald, Jacobite, tr. 7 May 1716, fr. Liverpool to S.C., in *Susannah*. (SPC.1716.309)(CTB31.206)

1634. Duff, James, Jacobite, res. Strathbraan Perthshire, tr. 1747, fr. Liverpool. (P.2.168)(MR206)

1635. Duff, John, laborer, Jacobite, res. Kirkton Perthshire, tr. 22 Apr 1747, fr. Liverpool to Va, in *Johnson*, arr. Port Oxford Md 5 Aug 1747. (P.2.168)(MR206)(PRO.T1.328)

1636. Duff, John, b. 1755, herdsman, res. New Luce Wigtonshire, sh. May 1775, fr. Stranraer to N.C., in *Jackie*. (PRO.T47.12)

1637. Duff, Robert, b. 1722, painter, Jacobite, res. Glasgow, tr. 24 Apr 1747, fr. Liverpool to Va, in *Gildart*, arr. Port North Potomac Md 5 Aug 1747. (P.2.168)(PRO.T1.328)

1638. Duff, Thomas, Jacobite, tr. 7 May 1716, fr. Liverpool to S.C., in *Susannah*. (SPC.1716.309)(CTB31.206)

1639. Duffus, Andrew, horsethief, res. Burghead Morayshire, tr. May 1775. (AJ1432)

1640. Duffus, Daniel, Jacobite, tr. 30 Mar 1716, fr. Liverpool to Antigua, in *Scipio*. (SPC.1716.310)

1641. Dugall, Alexander, b. 1753, farmer, res. Duffus Morayshire, sh. July 1775, fr. Stornaway to Philadelphia, in *Clementina*. (PRO.T47.12)

1642. Dun, James, b. 1746, farmer, res. Breadalbane Perthshire, sh. June 1775, fr. Greenock to N.Y., in *Commerce*, m. Katherine ... (PRO.T47.12)

1643. Dun, James, b. 1747, fiddler, res. Glencoe Argyllshire, sh. Feb 1775, fr. Greenock to N.Y., in *Commerce*, m. Mary Crerar, ch. John. (PRO.T47.12)

1644. Dun, John, b. 1749, fiddler, res. Breadalbane Perthshire, sh. June 1775, fr. Greenock to N.Y., in *Commerce*. (PRO.T47.12)

1645. Dunbar, Captain, sh. 1699, to Darien, d. 1700 Nevis. (DP335)

1646. Dunbar, Charles, res. Dumfriesshire, pre 1770, sett. Antigua. (SRO.RS 20.211)

1647. Dunbar, David, b. 1762, res. Wick Caithness, sh. June 1775, fr. Leith to Philadelphia, in *Friendship*. (PRO.T47.12)

1648. Dunbar, Elizabeth, infanticide, res. Banff, tr. Mar 1751, fr. Aberdeen to Va & West Indies, in *Adventure of Aberdeen*. (AJ142\170)

1649. Dunbar, George, merchant, res. Edinburgh, pre 1782, sett. N.Y. (SRO.RD2.235.17)

1650. Dunbar, George, gentleman, res. Invernessshire, 1735, sett. Ga. (PRO.CO5.670.219)

1651. Dunbar, Hancock, clergyman, sh. 1725, to Va. (EMA25)

1652. Dunbar, James, assault, tr. July 1668. (PC.2.491)
1653. Dunbar, James, pre 1717, sett. R.I. (SRO.GD298)
1654. Dunbar, James, b. 1730, laborer, Jacobite, res. Morayshire, tr. 5 May
       1747, fr. Liverpool to Leeward Islands, in *Veteran*, arr. Martinique
       June 1747. (P.2.170)(PRO.SP36.102)
1655. Dunbar, Jeremy, farmer, Jacobite, res. Cushnie Aberdeenshire, tr. 24 May
       1716, fr. Liverpool to Va, in *Friendship*, arr. Md Aug 1716.
       (SPC.1716.311)(JAB.1.151)(HM386)
1656. Dunbar, John, merchant, Jacobite, tr. 29 June 1716, fr. Liverpool to Va,
       in *Elizabeth & Anne*, arr. Sandy Point James River Va, sett.
       Newport R.I.
       (SRO.GD298)(SPC.1716.310)(CTB31.208)(SRO.GD103)(VSP.1.
       185)
1657. Dunbar, John, pts. George Dunbar of Leuchold, d. 19 June 1768 Sunbury
       Ga. (SM.30.973)
1658. Dunbar, Simon, mariner, pts. John Dunbar of Burgie, sh. pre 1748, sett.
       Newport R.I. & Charleston S.C. (SRO.GD199.99)
1659. Dunbar, Stephen, res. Forres Morayshire, pts. Walter Dunbar, d. Sept
       1780 Jamaica. (SM.42.617)
1660. Dunbar, William, barber & wigmaker, res. Edinburgh, tr. Aug 1763, m.
       (1)Penelope McEwan (2)Katherine Burnet. (SRO.RH2.4.255)
1661. Dunbar, William, res. Machriemore, sh. pre 1765, sett. Antigua.
       (SRO.CS.GMB51)
1662. Duncan, Alexander, Jacobite, tr. 26 Apr 1716, fr. Liverpool to Jamaica,
       in *Two Brothers*, arr. Montserrat June 1716.
       (SPC.1716.313)(CTB31.205)(CTP.CC.43)
1663. Duncan, Alexander, merchant, res. Edinburgh, pts. Charles Duncan, sh.
       pre 1758. (REB.1758.60)
1664. Duncan, Alexander, clergyman edu. St Andrews Uni 1712, sh. 1716, to
       Carolina. (EMA25)
1665. Duncan, Ann, b. 1744, res. Strathspey, sh. Mar 1774, fr. Greenock to
       N.Y., in *George*. (PRO.T47.12)
1666. Duncan, Christian, infanticide, res. St Ninian's Stirlingshire, tr. Sept
       1765. (AJ923)
1667. Duncan, Christian, tr. July 1751. (AJ187)
1668. Duncan, George, sh. Apr 1737, fr. Inverness to Ga, in *Two Brothers*, arr.
       Savannah Ga 16 Nov 1737. (PRO.CO5.690.169)(SPC.44.153)
1669. Duncan, Grizel, thief, res. Causeyside Perth, tr. Sept 1751, fr. Montrose
       Angus(?), m. Benjamin Davidson. (SRO.B59.26.11.5.20)(AJ145)
1670. Duncan, Grizell, forger, res. Kirkness, tr. Dec 1743, m. George Gray.
       (SRO.HCR.I.70)
1671. Duncan, Isobel, b. 1745, res. Strathspey, sh. May 1774, fr. Greenock to
       N.Y., in *George*. (PRO.T47.12)
1672. Duncan, James, Covenanter, res. Grange, tr. Aug 1670. (PC.3.206)

1673. Duncan, James, thief, res. Balquhan Stirlingshire, tr. May 1721. (SRO.JC13.6)
1674. Duncan, James, shoemaker, cattlethief, res. Cairngressie Kincardineshire, tr. Sept 1763. (AJ819) (alias 1455)
1675. Duncan, James, thief & housebreaker, res. Aberdeenshire, tr. Sept 1770. (SRO.RH2.4.255)(AJ1190)
1676. Duncan, James, b. 1747, farmer, res. Moudlein Farr Sutherland, sh. Apr 1774, to Wilmington N.C., in *Bachelor of Leith*. (PRO.T47.12)
1677. Duncan, James, b. 1759, storekeeper, res. Hawthorndean Midlothian, sh. May 1775, fr. Leith to Philadelphia, in *Friendship*. (PRO.T47.12)
1678. Duncan, James, b. 1760, laborer, res. Falkirk Stirlingshire, sh. Apr 1775, fr. Greenock to N.Y., in *Lilly*. (PRO.T47.12)
1679. Duncan, James, b. 1772, res. Strathspey, sh. May 1774, fr. Greenock to N.Y., in *George*. (PRO.T47.12)
1680. Duncan, Janet, infanticide, res. Glenisla Angus, tr. Sept 1755. (AJ400)
1681. Duncan, Jean, b. 1757, res. Strathspey, sh. May 1774, fr. Greenock to N.Y., in *George*. (PRO.T47.12)
1682. Duncan, John, Jacobite, tr. 26 Apr 1716, fr. Liverpool to Jamaica, in *Two Brothers*, arr. Montserrat June 1716. (SPC.1716.313)(CTP.CC.43)(CTB31.205)
1683. Duncan, John, servant, Jacobite, res. Perthshire, tr. 1747. (P.2.170)(MR99)
1684. Duncan, John, Jacobite, tr. 24 Feb 1747, fr. Liverpool to Va, in *Gildart*, arr. Port North Potomac Md 5 Aug 1747. (PRO.T1.328)
1685. Duncan, John, Jacobite, tr. 30 Mar 1716, fr. Liverpool to St Kitts, in *Scipio*. (SPC.1716.310)(CTB31.204)
1686. Duncan, John, b. 1705, fisherman, Jacobite, res. Montrose Angus, tr. 1747. (P.2.170)(MR93)
1687. Duncan, John, b. 1730, farmer, res. Strathspey, sh. May 1774, fr. Greenock to N.Y., in *George*. (PRO.T47.12)
1688. Duncan, John, b. 1733, carpenter, Jacobite, res. Dundee Angus, tr. 1747. (P.2.172)(MR99)
1689. Duncan, Katherine, b. 1769, res. Strathspey, sh. May 1774, fr. Greenock to N.Y., in *George*. (PRO.T47.12)
1690. Duncan, Owr, thief, res. Linlithgow West Lothian, tr. Mar 1754. (SRO.JC3.29.500) (alias 4932)
1691. Duncan, Peter, b. 1715, laborer, Jacobite, res. Dundee Angus, tr. 24 Feb 1747, fr. Liverpool to Va, in *Gildart*, arr. Port North Potomac Md 5 Aug 1747. (P.2.172)(MR99)(PRO.T1.328)
1692. Duncan, Robert, Jacobite, tr. 29 June 1716, fr. Liverpool to Jamaica or Va, in *Elizabeth & Anne*, arr. Va. (SPC.1716.310)(CTB31.208)(VSP.1.186)
1693. Duncan, Walter, skipper, res. Bo'ness West Lothian, sh. 169, to Darien, in *Duke of Hamilton*, m. Helen Hill, Edin pr 1707 CC8.8.83

81

1694. Duncan, William, b. 1732, gardener, Jacobite, res. Edinburgh, tr. 1747. (P.2.172)
1695. Duncan, William, b. 1753, clerk & book-keeper, sh. Dec 1774, fr. London to Va, in *Carolina*. (PRO.T47.9\11)
1696. Duncan, William, b. 1773, res. Strathspey, sh. May 1774, fr. Greenock to N.Y., in *George*. (PRO.T47.12)
1697. Duncanson, Hugh, b. 1756, carpenter, sh. Feb 1774, fr. London to St Vincent, in *Friendship*. (PRO.T47.9\11)
1698. Dundas, .., sh. 29 Nov 1773, fr. Greenock to Jamaica, in *Mary of Glasgow*. (SRO.CE60.1.7)
1699. Dundas, Alexander, factor, sh. pre 1721, sett. Barbados. (SRO.CS.GMB25\946)
1700. Dundas, Charles, merchant, pts. Lord Arniston, sh. pre 1718, sett. Barbados. (BGBG344)
1701. Dundas, James, merchant, sh. Aug 1685, fr. Leith to N.J., in *Henry of Newcastle*. (SRO.E72.15.32)
1702. Dundas, John, clergyman, sh. 1773, to S.C. (EMA25)
1703. Dundas, Walter, soldier, res. Harbiston, pts. Robert Dundas, sh. 1699, d. Darien, Edin pr 1707 CC8.8.83
1704. Dunlop, Alexander, merchant, pts. John Dunlop, pre 1751, sett. Va. (SRO.RD4.177.480)
1705. Dunlop, Archibald, merchant, res. Glasgow, sh. 1762, sett. Cabin Point James River Va. (SRA.CFI)(SRO.CS.GMB51)
1706. Dunlop, James, merchant, res. Glasgow, sh. 1774. (SRO.AC.GMB.404)
1707. Dunlop, James, Jacobite, tr. 21 Apr 1716, fr. Liverpool to S.C., in *Wakefield*. (SPC.1716.309)(CTB31.204)
1708. Dunlop, James, b. 1754, merchant, res. Garnkirk Lanarkshire, pts. James Dunlop, d. America. (SRA.CFI)
1709. Dunlop, Janet, tr. 1771, fr. Port Glasgow, in *Polly*, arr. Port Oxford Md 16 Sept 1771. (SRO.JC27.10.3)
1710. Dunlop, John, clergyman, res. Dolphinton Lanarkshire, sh. 1774, sett. Cambridge. (Dolphinton Gs)
1711. Dunlop, John, merchant, res. Glasgow, sett. Va, ch. Alexander, d. pre 1751. (SRO.RD4.177.480)
1712. Dunlop, William, merchant, sh. June 1684, fr. Port Glasgow to Carolina, in *Pelican of Glasgow*. (SRO.E72.19.9)
1713. Dunlop, William, b. 1654, clergyman, res. Paisley Renfrewshire, pts. Rev Alexander Dunlop, sh. 1684, fr. Glasgow to Carolina, in *Pelican*, m. Sarah Carstairs, ch. Alexander & William, d. 8 Mar 1700 Scotland. (F.7.396)
1714. Dunmore, John, b. 1763, res. Glasgow, sh. Apr 1775, fr. Greenock to Salem, in *Glasgow Packet*. (PRO.T47.12)
1715. Dunmore, Mary, b. 1748, res. Glasgow, sh. Apr 1775, fr. Greenock to Salem, in *Glasgow Packet*. (PRO.T47.12)

1716. Dunmore, Nelly, b. 1748, spinner, res. Paisley Renfrewshire, sh. Feb 1774, fr. Greenock to N.Y., in *Commerce*. (PRO.T47.12)
1717. Dunn, James, b. 1754, res. Aberdeen, sh. Sept 1774, fr. Greenock to Jamaica, in *Jamaica*. (PRO.T47.12)
1718. Dunn, Quentin, Covenanter, tr. 11 Aug 1685, fr. Leith to Jamaica. (PC.11.329)(ETR369)
1719. Dunn, William, Jacobite, tr. 29 June 1716, fr. Liverpool to Jamaica or Va, in *Elizabeth & Anne*, arr. Va. (SPC.1716.310)(CTB31.208)(VSP.1.185)
1720. Dunn, William, clergyman, sh. 1705, to Carolina. (EMA25)
1721. Dunsmuir, Hugh, b. 1734, weaver, res. Paisley Renfrewshire, sh. Feb 1774, fr. Greenock to N.Y., in *Commerce*. (PRO.T47.12)
1722. Durham, Mary, b. 1754, housekeeper, sh. June 1775, fr. London to Baltimore, in *Baltimore*. (PRO.T47.9\11)
1723. Durie, Isobel, Covenanter, tr. Aug 1685, fr. Leith to East N.J., in *Henry & Francis*. (PC.11.154)
1724. Durno, John, b. 20 Sept 1741, Kemnay Aberdeenshire, advocate edu. Marischal Col, pts. John Durno of Cattie & Lilias Gilchrist, m. Jane Byres, ch. Jane, d. 6 Dec 1816 Jamaica. (SAA167)
1725. Durrar, William, b. 1717, servant, Jacobite, res. Ashdale Aberdeen, tr. 20 Mar 1747, fr. Tilbury. (P.2.174)(JAB.2.424)(MR202)
1726. Dury, Margaret, Covenanter, res. Edinburgh, tr. July 1668, m. James Kello. (PC.2.500)
1727. Dutt, Alexander, Jacobite, tr. 30 Mar 1716, fr. Liverpool, in *Scipio*. (SPC.1716.310)
1728. Duys, Donald MacWilliam, cattlethief, res. Inverness-shire, tr. Sept 1752. (SM.14.461)
1729. Duys, Kenneth MacWilliam, cattlethief, res. Inverness-shire, tr. Sept 1752. (SM.14.461)
1730. Dyer, Mary, vagrant & thief, res. Dumfries-shire, tr. Apr 1751, m. Alexander McKenzie. (AJ175)
1731. Dykes, Andrew, Covenanter, res. St Bride's Chapel, tr. Oct 1684. (PC.10.275)
1732. Dykes, James, cabinetmaker, thief, res. Anderston Glasgow, tr. Apr 1774. (AJ1374)
1733. Dykes, Margaret, b. 1725, Jacobite, res. Linlithgow West Lothian, tr. 5 May 1747, fr. Liverpool to Leeward Islands, in *Veteran*, arr. Martinique June 1747. (P.2.154)(PRO.SP36.102)
1734. Dysart, George, Jacobite, tr. 21 Apr 1716, fr. Liverpool to S.C., in *Wakefield*. (SPC.1716.309)(CTB31.205)
1735. Eagleton, Archibald, sailor, res. Fisherrow Edinburgh, sh. 14 July 1698, fr. Leith to Darien, in *Unicorn*, Edin pr 1707 CC8.8.83
1736. Earle, Ann, infanticide, res. Ayrshire, tr. Sept 1753. (SM.15.468)

1737. Eason, John, b. 1717, gardener, res. Blairgowrie Perthshire, sh. 1741, to Md. (SRO.RH9.17.308)
1738. Easton, David, b. 1756, merchant, res. Ross-shire, sh. July 1775, fr. Greenock to Jamaica, in *Isabella*. (PRO.T47.12)
1739. Easton, Thomas, b. 1700, baker, res. Canongate Edinburgh, sh. Dec 1719, fr. London to Md. (CLRO\AIA)
1740. Eastoun, Agnes, res. Edinburgh, tr. 1696, fr. Newhaven to Va. (SRO.RH15.14.58)
1741. Eaton, Robina, b. 1750, sh. Apr 1775, fr. Greenock to N.Y., in *Lilly*. (PRO.T47.12)
1742. Eaton, Thomas, b. 1746, chapman, res. Edinburgh, sh. Aug 1774, fr. Greenock to Philadelphia, in *Magdalene*. (SRO.T47.12)
1743. Eccles, William, b. 1735, shoemaker, res. Inch, sh. May 1775, fr. Stranraer to N.C., in *Jackie*, m. Martha McKenzie, ch. John. (PRO.T47.12)
1744. Edmonstone, William, res. Stirling, sh. pre 1774, sett. Jamaica. (SRO.CS.GMB334)
1745. Edward, Andrew, b. 25 Apr 1722, Kirriemuir Angus, servant, Jacobite, res. Angus, pts. Alexander Edward, tr. 5 May 1747, fr. Liverpool to Leeward Islands, in *Veteran*, arr. Martinique June 1747. (P.2.176)(MR99)(PRO.SP36.102)
1746. Edward, James, Covenanter, res. Greenock Renfrewshire, tr. Aug 1684, fr. Leith to Carolina. (PC.9.28)(ETR221)
1747. Edward, John, Covenanter, res. Dalgaine, tr. June 1684, fr. Glasgow to Carolina, in *Pelican of Glasgow*. (PC.9.208)
1748. Edward, Robert, Covenanter, res. Cumnock Ayrshire, tr. Aug 1685, fr. Leith to Jamaica. (PC.11.136)
1749. Edwards, Charles, thief, res. Huntly Aberdeenshire, tr. Feb 1766. (AJ947)
1750. Edwards, James, Jacobite, res. Lintrathen Angus, tr. 1747. (P.2.176)(MR71)
1751. Eggoe, John, Jacobite, tr. 7 May 1716, fr. Liverpool to S.C., in *Susannah*. (SPC.1716.309)(CTB31.206)
1752. Eggoe, William, Jacobite, tr. 7 May 1716, fr. Liverpool to S.C., in *Susannah*. (SPC.1716.309)(CTB31.206)
1753. Eglinton, William, rioter, res. Glasgow, tr. 1751, fr. Glasgow. (AJ172)
1754. Elder, Daniel, b. 1753, book-keeper, sh. Jan 1774, fr. London to Barbados, in *Assistance*. (PRO.T47.9\11)
1755. Elder, Donald, shipwreck looter, res. Ifauld Reay Caithness, pts. William Elder, tr. 1772, fr. Glasgow to Va, in *Donald*, arr. Port James Upper District Va 13 Mar 1773. (SRO.JC27)(AJ1292)
1756. Elder, John, b. 26 Jan 1706, clergyman edu. Edinburgh Uni, pts. Robert & Eleanor Elder, sh. 1736, sett. Paxton & Pennsburg Pa, d. 17 July 1792 Swatara Pa. (F.7.663)

1757. Elder, John, b. 1752, smith, res. Glasgow, sh. May 1775, fr. Greenock to N.Y., in *Lilly*. (PRO.T47.12)
1758. Elder, William, farmer, shipwreck looter, res. Ifauld Reay Caithness, tr. 1772, fr. Glasgow to Va, in *Donald*, arr. Port James Upper District Va 30 Mar 1773. (SRO.JC27.10.3)(AJ1292)
1759. Elder, William, soldier, robber, tr. Mar 1747. (SRO.JC27)
1760. Elder, William, b. 1729, servant, Jacobite, res. Kilcoy Ross-shire, tr. 31 Mar 1747, fr. London to Barbados, in *Frere*. (P.2.178)(MR81)
1761. Elder, William, b. 1753, book-keeper, sh. Jan 1774, fr. London to Barbados, in *Assistance*. (PRO.T47.9\11)
1762. Elgin, James, b. 1751, clerk & book-keeper, sh. Nov 1774, fr. London to Va, in *Active*. (PRO.T47.9\11)
1763. Ell, John, b. 1734, laborer, res. Cavin, sh. May 1774, fr. Stranraer to N.Y., in *Gale*. (PRO.T47.12)
1764. Ellice, George, sett. Philadelphia, d. pre 1753, PCC pr 1753
1765. Ellice, Robert, sh. 16 Dec 1773, fr. Greenock to Jamaica, in *Ross*. (SRO.CE60.1.7)
1766. Elliot, Charles, attorney general, pts. Sir Gilbert Elliot of Stobs, sett. N.C., d. 2 Oct 1756 Newham N.C. (SM.18.627)
1767. Elliot, James, b. 1739, husbandman, sh. Aug 1774, fr. Whitby to Savanna Ga, in *Marlborough*. (PRO.T47.9\11)
1768. Elliot, John, Governor, d. June 1769 W Fla, PCC pr1769. (SM.21.391)
1769. Elliot, John, Covenanter, res. Teviotdale, tr. Aug 1685, fr. Leith to Jamaica, arr. Port Royal Jamaica 1685. (PC.11.329)(LJ44)
1770. Elliot, Robert, thief, res. Earlside Roxburghshire, tr. 1726. (SRO.JC12.4)
1771. Emiry, James, b. 1754, weaver, res. Paisley Renfrewshire, sh. Feb 1774, fr. Greenock to N.Y., in *Commerce*. (PRO.T47.12)
1772. Erskine, George, clergyman edu. St Andrews Uni 1704, sh. 1711, to Jamaica. (EMA26)
1773. Erwinn, Charles, Jacobite, tr. 30 Mar 1716, fr. Liverpool to Antigua, in *Scipio*. (CTB31.204)(SPC.1716.310)
1774. Esplin, John, soldier, sh. 14 July 1698, fr. Leith to Darien, in *Unicorn*, d. 1 July 1700 Darien. (DP352)
1775. Etburn, William, b. 1754, schoolmaster, sh. May 1774, fr. Whitehaven to Va, in *Molly*. (PRO.T47.9\11)
1776. Eunson, George, b. 1757, shoemaker, res. Kirkwall Orkney Islands, sh. Sept 1774, fr. Kirkwall to Savanna Ga, in *Marlborough*, sett. Richmond Co Ga. (PRO.T47.12)
1777. Ewan, John, thief, res. Waterside of Montrose Angus, tr. Sept 1773. (SM.35.557)
1778. Ewart, Jean, coal-bearer, infanticide, res. Edinburgh, tr. March 1771, fr. Port Glasgow, in *Crawford*, arr. Port Oxford Md 23 July 1771. (SRO.JC27.10.3)

1779. Ewart, William, shoemaker, rioter, res. Dumfries, tr. 1760. (SRO.JC27)(SM.22.668)

1780. Ewing, George, b. 1754, carpenter, res. Edinburgh, sh. Dec 1773, fr. London Dominica to GREYHOUND. (PRO.T47.9\11)

1781. Faa, Mary, gypsy, res. Jedburgh Roxburghshire, tr. 1 Jan 1715, fr. Glasgow to Va. (GR530)

1782. Faa, Peter, gypsy, res. Jedburgh Roxburghshire, tr. 1 Jan 1715, fr. Glasgow to Va. (GR530)

1783. Fairbairn, John, Covenanter, res. Kirkliston West Lothian, tr. 12 Dec 1678, fr. Leith to West Indies, in *St Michael of Scarborough*. (PC.6.76)

1784. Fairfax, Lord Thomas, b. 1693, d. 1782 Va. (GM.52.149)

1785. Fairholm, Thomas, pts. Thomas Fairholm & Eleanora Pringle, sh. pre 1783, sett. Tobago. (SRO.RD2.236.66)

1786. Fala, John, shoemaker, Covenanter, res. Kelso Roxburghshire, tr. Oct 1684. (PC.9.449)

1787. Falconer, James, clergyman, res. Morayshire, sh. 1718, to Va, York Va pr1728. (EMA27)

1788. Falconer, James, rioter, res. Glasgow, tr. Jan 1726, to Barbados. (PRO.T53.33.293)

1789. Falconer, Patrick, clergyman edu. Edinburgh Uni 1669(?), sh. 1710. (EMA27)

1790. Falconer, Patrick, sh. 1684, sett. Elizabethtown N.J. (Insh245)

1791. Falconer, Robert, smith, thief, res. Elgin Morayshire, tr. Jan 1767. (SRO.JC27)(SM.29.54)

1792. Farquhar, Alexander, b. 1713, res. Edinburgh, sh. Aug 1728, fr. London to Pa. (CLRO\AIA)

1793. Farquhar, David, merchant, sett. Kingston Jamaica, d. 1758 Jamaica, Edin pr1763 CC8.8.119

1794. Farquhar, George, sh. 29 Nov 1773, fr. Greenock to Jamaica, in *Mary of Glasgow*. (SRO.CE60.1.7)

1795. Farquhar, John, writer & merchant, res. Edinburgh, sett. Spanish Town Jamaica, d. pre 1767 Jamaica, Edin pr1767 CC8.8.120

1796. Farquharson, Alexander, clergyman edu. King's Col Aberdeen 1705, sh. 1717, to N.J. (EMA27)

1797. Farquharson, Alexander, Jacobite, tr. 31 Mar 1747, fr. London to Barbados, in *Frere*. (P.2.182)(MR202)

1798. Farquharson, Alexander, b. 1707, farmer, Jacobite, res. Auchenriachen Glenmoriston Inverness-shire, tr. 31 Mar 1747, fr. London to Barbados, in *Frere*. (P.2.182)(MR151)

1799. Farquharson, Donald, b. 1699, farmer, Jacobite, res. Balquhidder Perthshire, tr. 31 Mar 1747, fr. London to Barbados, in *Frere*. (P.2.182)(MR71)

1800. Farquharson, Donald, b. 1715, Jacobite, res. Auchnagoren Glenmoriston
Inverness-shire, tr. 31 Mar 1747, fr. London to Barbados, in *Frere*.
(P.2.182)(MR151)
1801. Farquharson, Duncan, b. 1724, Jacobite, res. Glenmoriston Inverness-
shire, tr. 31 Mar 1747, fr. London to Barbados, in *Frere*.
(P.2.182)(MR202)
1802. Farquharson, Elizabeth, res. Aberdeenshire, d. pre 1776 Kingston Jamaica.
(APB.4.83)
1803. Farquharson, George, Inveraven Banffshire, thief, tr. May 1773, fr.
Glasgow. (AJ1322\8)
1804. Farquharson, Harry, soldier, Jacobite, res. Cults Glengairn Aberdeenshire,
pts. Arthur Farquharson of Cults, tr. 1716, fr. Liverpool to Va, m.
Elizabeth Morgan. (JAB.1.72)
1805. Farquharson, Harry, merchant, res. Aberdeenshire, pts. Harry Farquharson
of Whitetoun, sett. Jamaica, d. 1755 Jamaica. (APB.3.183)
1806. Farquharson, Hugh William, Jacobite, tr. 1747, fr. Tilbury. (P.2.184)
1807. Farquharson, James, clergyman, sh. 1712, to Pa. (EMA27)
1808. Farquharson, Lawrence, Jacobite, res. Cobletown of Tulloch
Aberdeenshire, pts. Donald Farquharson & Helen Garden, tr. 28
July 1716, fr. Liverpool to Va, in *Godspeed*, arr. Md Oct 1716.
(SPC.1716.309)(JAB.1.73)(HM389)
1809. Farquharson, Mary, vagrant, res. Jedburgh Roxburghshire, tr. Sept 1753.
(SM.15.468)
1810. Farquharson, Peter, b. 1707, Jacobite, res. Auchnagoren Glenmoriston
Inverness-shire, tr. 31 Mar 1747, fr. London to Barbados, in *Frere*.
(P.2.186)(MR151)
1811. Farquharson, Robert, gentleman, Jacobite, res. Allanaquoich
Aberdeenshire, pts. Donald Farquharson & Helen Garden, tr. 31
July 1716, fr. Liverpool to Va, in *Anne*, m. Mary Gordon.
(SPC.1716.310)(CTB31.209)(JAB.1.73)
1812. Farquharson, Thomas, attorney, res. Perth, pts. Paul Farquharson, sh. pre
1774, sett. Kingston Jamaica. (SRO.RD2.216.923)
1813. Farquharson, William, farmer, Jacobite, res. Tarland Aberdeenshire, tr. 31
Mar 1747, fr. London to Barbados, in *Frere*. (P.2.186)(MR201)
1814. Farquharson, William, Jacobite, res. Achnagoneen, tr. 5 May 1746.
(MR151)
1815. Faw, Alexander, vagabond & robber, res. Annandale Dumfries-shire, tr.
1671(?). (PC.3.428)
1816. Faw, Henry, vagabond & robber, res. Annandale Dumfries-shire, tr.
1671(?). (PC.3.428)
1817. Faw, Ninian, vagabond & robber, res. Annandale Dumfries-shire, tr.
1671(?). (PC.3.428)
1818. Faw, Robert, vagabond & robber, res. Annandale Dumfries-shire, tr.
1671(?). (PC.3.428)

1819. Faw, Thomas, vagabond & robber, res. Annandale Dumfries-shire, tr. 1671(?). (PC.3.428)
1820. Faw, William, vagabond & robber, res. Annandale Dumfries-shire, tr. 1671(?). (PC.3.428)
1821. Fenton, Alexander, b. 1719, surgeon, res. Dundee Angus, sh. Sept 1738, fr. London to Antigua. (CLRO\AIA)
1822. Fenton, Richard, b. 1746, canvas weaver, sh. Aug 1774, fr. Whitby to Savannah Ga, in *Marlborough*. (PRO.T47.9\11)
1823. Fenwick, Barbara, tr. May 1672, fr. Leith, in *Ewe & Lamb*. (PC.3.523)
1824. Fenwick, James, Covenanter, tr. Aug 1685, fr. Leith to East N.J., in *Henry & Francis*. (PC.11.154)
1825. Fenwick, John, gypsy, res. Jedburgh Roxburghshire, tr. 1 Jan 1715, fr. Glasgow to Va. (GR530)
1826. Fergus, James, b. 1750, weaver, res. Glasgow, sh. May 1774, fr. Greenock to N.Y., in *Matty*. (PRO.T47.12)
1827. Ferguson, Agnes, tr. Aug 1685, fr. Leith to Jamaica, arr. Port Royal Jamaica Nov 1685. (PC.11.136)(LJ18)
1828. Ferguson, Alexander, soldier, res. Maybole Ayrshire, d. 1699 Darien, Edin pr 1707 CC8.8.83
1829. Ferguson, Alexander, forger, tr. Feb 1670, fr. Leith to Va, in *Ewe & Lamb*. (PC.3.650)
1830. Ferguson, Alexander, Jacobite, tr. 29 June 1716, fr. Liverpool to Va, in *Elizabeth & Anne*, arr. Va. (SPC.1716.310)(CTB31.208)(VSP.1.186)
1831. Ferguson, Alexander, b. 1717, farmer, Jacobite, res. Glenmoriston Inverness-shire, tr. 1747, fr. Tilbury. (P.2.186)(MR151)
1832. Ferguson, Angus, tr. Aug 1685, fr. Leith to Jamaica. (PC.11.149)
1833. Ferguson, David, Covenanter, res. Bridgend Glasgow, tr. 12 Dec 1678, fr. Leith to West Indies, in *St Michael of Scarborough*. (PC.6.76)
1834. Ferguson, David, merchant, sh. Mar 1683, fr. Ayr to Caribee Islands, in *James of Ayr*. (SRO.E72.3.12)
1835. Ferguson, Donald, Covenanter, res. Ruchoard, tr. Aug 1685, fr. Leith to Jamaica. (PC.11.136)
1836. Ferguson, Donald, Jacobite, tr. 29 June 1716, fr. Liverpool to Va or Jamaica, in *Elizabeth & Anne*. (SPC.1716.310)(CTB31.208)
1837. Ferguson, Donald, servant, Jacobite, res. Gartmore Skye Inverness-shire, tr. 1747, fr. Tilbury. (P.2.188)(MR68)
1838. Ferguson, Donald, b. 1754, farmer, res. Stirling, sh. May 1774, fr. Greenock to N.Y., in *Matty*. (PRO.T47.12)
1839. Ferguson, Duncan, Jacobite, tr. 22 Apr 1747, fr. Liverpool to Va, in *Johnson*, arr. Port Oxford Md 5 Aug 1747. (PRO.T1.328)
1840. Ferguson, Duncan, farmer, res. Polmaise St Ninian's Stirlingshire, tr. Aug 1685, fr. Leith to Jamaica. (PC.11.136)(ETR373)

1841. Ferguson, Duncan, Covenanter, tr. 5 Aug 1684, fr. Leith to Jamaica.
(PC.9.95)
1842. Ferguson, Duncan, Jacobite, tr. 28 July 1716, fr. Liverpool to Va, in
Godspeed, arr. Md Oct 1716.
(SPC.1716.310)(CTB31.209)(HM388)
1843. Ferguson, Duncan, b. 1713, farmer, Jacobite, res. Perthshire, tr. 22 Apr
1747, fr. Liverpool to Va, in Johnson, arr. Port Oxford Md 5 Aug
1747. (P.2.188)(MR71)(PRO.T1.328)
1844. Ferguson, Duncan, b. 1739, farmer, res. Falkirk Stirlingshire, sh. May
1775, fr. Greenock to N.Y. or Ga, in Christy. (PRO.T47.12)
1845. Ferguson, Elizabeth, b. 1747, spinner, res. Paisley Renfrewshire, sh. Feb
1774, fr. Greenock to N.Y., in Commerce. (PRO.T47.12)
1846. Ferguson, Elspeth, Covenanter, tr. Aug 1685, fr. Leith to East N.J., in
Henry & Francis. (PC.1.155)
1847. Ferguson, Finlay, Jacobite, tr. 21 May 1716, fr. Liverpool to S.C., in
Wakefield. (SPC.1716.309)(CTB31.205)
1848. Ferguson, Francis, farmer, Jacobite, res. Cushnie Aberdeenshire, tr. 30
Mar 1716, fr. Liverpool, in Scipio.
(SPC.1716.310)(CTB31.204)(JAB.1.151)
1849. Ferguson, Gilbert, Covenanter, tr. Aug 1685, fr. Leith to Jamaica.
(PC.11.329)
1850. Ferguson, H, b. 1753, planter, res. Aberdeen, sh. Dec 1773, fr. London to
Jamaica, in Esther. (PRO.T47.9\11)
1851. Ferguson, Halbert, res. Edinburgh, tr. June 1673, to Va. (SRO.JC2.13)
1852. Ferguson, Henry, Jacobite, tr. 24 May 1716, fr. Liverpool, in Friendship,
arr. Md Aug 1716. (SPC.1716.311)(HM387)
1853. Ferguson, James, mariner, res. Fife, sh. 14 July 1698, fr. Leith to
Darien, in Caledonia, m. Anna Abercromby, Edin pr 1707
CC8.8.83
1854. Ferguson, James, Jacobite, tr. 29 June 1716, fr. Liverpool to Jamaica or
Va, in Elizabeth & Anne, arr. Va.
(SPC.1716.310)(CTB31.208)(VSP.1.186)
1855. Ferguson, James, b. 1743, wright, res. Breadalbane Perthshire, sh. June
1775, fr. Greenock to N.Y., in Commerce, m. Jean McGregor, ch.
Mary Robert Helen Ann. (PRO.T47.12)
1856. Ferguson, James, b. 1754, farmer, res. Stirling, sh. May 1774, fr.
Greenock to N.Y., in Matty. (PRO.T47.12)
1857. Ferguson, James, b. 1755, farmer, res. Blair Atholl Perthshire, sh. May
1775, fr. Greenock to N.Y., in Monimia. (PRO.T47.12)
1858. Ferguson, Janet, Covenanter, tr. Aug 1685, fr. Leith to East N.J., in
Henry & Francis. (PC.11.155)
1859. Ferguson, Janet, b. 1743, res. Paisley Renfrewshire, sh. Apr 1775, fr.
Greenock to N.Y., in Lilly. (PRO.T47.12)

1860. Ferguson, John, b. 1747, weaver, res. Paisley Renfrewshire, sh. May 1774, fr. Greenock to N.Y. (PRO.T47.12)
1861. Ferguson, John, b. 1750, farmer, res. Doune Perthshire, sh. July 1775, fr. Greenock to Ga, in *Georgia*, m. Janet ... (PRO.T47.12)
1862. Ferguson, John, b. 1755, workman, res. Kintyre Argyll, sh. Aug 1774, fr. Greenock to Wilmington N.C., in *Ulysses*. (PRO.T47.12)
1863. Ferguson, Lawrence, Jacobite, tr. 29 June 1716, fr. Liverpool to Jamaica or Va, in *Elizabeth & Anne*, arr. Va. (SPC.1716.310)(CTB31.208)(VSP.1.186)
1864. Ferguson, N, attorney, sett. Jamaica, m. Elizabeth Johnston, d. pre 1765. (SRO.SH.28.6.1765)
1865. Ferguson, Patrick, Jacobite, tr. 29 June 1716, fr. Liverpool to Jamaica or Va, in *Elizabeth & Anne*, arr. Va. (SPC.1716.310)(CTB31.208)(VSP.1.185)
1866. Ferguson, Patrick, Jacobite, res. Perthshire, tr. 22 Apr 1747, fr. Liverpool to Va, in *Johnson*, arr. Port Oxford Md 5 Aug 1747. (PRO.T1.328)
1867. Ferguson, Peter, Jacobite, tr. 26 Apr 1716, fr. Liverpool to Jamaica, in *Two Brothers*, arr. Montserrat June 1716. (SPC.1716.313)(CTP.CC.43)(CTB31.206)
1868. Ferguson, Robert, Jacobite, tr. 31 July 1716, fr. Liverpool to Va, in *Anne*. (SPC.1716.310)
1869. Ferguson, William, weaver, Covenanter, res. Lanark, tr. Sept 1668, fr. Leith to Va, in *Convertin*. (PC.2.470)
1870. Ferguson, William, Jacobite, tr. 28 July 1716, fr. Liverpool to Va, in *Godspeed*, arr. Md Oct 1716. (SPC.1716.310)(CTB31.209)(HM389)
1871. Ferguson, William, rioter, res. Ballantrae Ayrshire, tr. Sept 1752. (AJ246)
1872. Ferguson, William, b. 1692, farmer, Jacobite, res. Glenmoriston Inverness-shire, tr. 1747, fr. Tilbury. (P.2.190)
1873. Fergusson, James, res. Kilkerran Dailly Ayrshire, pts. Sir James Fergusson, d. Dec 1777 Tobago. (SM.40.53)
1874. Ferrody, Joseph, soldier, shopbreaker, tr. May 1774. (AJ1376)
1875. Fiddes, David, b. 1729, Jacobite, res. Farnell Angus, tr. 31 Mar 1747, fr. London to Barbados, in *Frere*. (P.2.192)(MR100)
1876. Fife, Alexander, b. 1750, husbandman, sh. Feb 1774, fr. London to Jamaica, in *Royal Charlotte*. (PRO.T47.9\11)
1877. Fife, Isobel, b. 1748, res. Paisley Renfrewshire, sh. May 1775, fr. Greenock to N.Y., in *Lilly*. (PRO.T47.12)
1878. Fife, James, b. 1739, merchant, res. Renfrewshire, sh. Oct 1774, fr. Greenock to Charleston S.C., in *Countess*. (PRO.T47.12)
1879. Fife, Margaret, b. 1753, spinner, res. Edinburgh, sh. Oct 1774, fr. Kirkcaldy to Antigua, in *Jamaica Packet*. (PRO.T47.12)

1880. Fimister, Alexander, b. 1759, servant, res. Morayshire, sh. July 1775, fr. Stornaway to Philadelphia, in *Clementina*. (PRO.T47.12)
1881. Fimister, Elspia, b. 1761, servant, res. Morayshire, sh. July 1775, fr. Stornaway to Philadelphia, in *Clementina*. (PRO.T47.12)
1882. Fimister, John, b. 1765, servant, res. Avis, sh. July 1775, fr. Stornaway to Philadelphia, in *Clementina*. (PRO.T47.12)
1883. Fimister, Margaret, b. 1763, servant, res. Morayshire, sh. July 1775, fr. Stornaway to Philadelphia, in *Clementina*. (PRO.T47.12)
1884. Fimister, William, b. 1729, farmer, res. Avis, sh. July 1775, fr. Stornaway to Philadelphia, in *Clementina*, m. Elizabeth .. (PRO.T47.12)
1885. Findlater, John, clergyman edu. Marischal Col Aberdeen 1763-1767, sh. 1771, to Grenades. (EMA27)
1886. Findlay, Alexander, seaman, res. Queensferry West Lothian, pts. Elspeth Reid or Findlay, sh. 18 Aug 1699, fr. Clyde to Darien, Edin pr 1707 CC8.8.83
1887. Findlay, Alexander, res. Perth, tr. Sept 1757. (SRO.B59.26.11.2.27)
1888. Findlay, Alexander, clergyman, sh. 1770, to Ga. (EMA27)
1889. Findlay, Alexander, fireraiser, res. Forfar Angus, tr. Sept 1757. (AJ505)
1890. Findlay, Alexander, Covenanter, res. Buchlyvie Stirlingshire, tr. 12 Dec 1678, fr. Leith to West Indies, in *St Michael of Scarborough*. (PC.6.76)
1891. Findlay, Helen, res. Balkirsty Fife, pts. Thomas Findlay, sh. pre 1765, sett. St Michael's Barbados. (SRO.SH.31.10.1765)
1892. Findlay, Margaret, res. Balkirsty Fife, pts. Thomas Findlay, sh. pre 1765, sett. Barbados, m. W Forbes. (SRO.SH.31.10.1765)
1893. Findlay, Thomas, writer & attorney, res. Balchristie Colinsburgh Fife, pts. James Findlay, sh. pre 1741, sett. Barbados, ch. Thomas Isabella Margaret Helen, d. June 1760 Barbados. (SRO.SH.19.1.1741)(SRO.RD3.224.9)
1894. Finlay, Jean, thief, res. Aberdeenshire, tr. May 1753. (SM.15.260)
1895. Finlay, Robert, res. Glasgow, pts. Rev Robert Finlay, sh. pre 1772, sett. Md. (SRA.B10.15.7553)
1896. Finlay, William, Jacobite, tr. 29 June 1716, fr. Liverpool to Jamaica or Va, in *Elizabeth & Anne*, arr. Va. (SPC.1716.310)(CTB31.208)(VSP.1.186)
1897. Finlayson, Alexander, b. 1717, servant, Jacobite, res. Lochcarron Ross-shire, tr. 20 Mar 1747, fr. Tilbury. (P.2.192)(MR81)
1898. Finlayson, Finlay, thief, res. Ross-shire, tr. Sept 1751. (AJ194)
1899. Finlayson, John, b. 1723, servant, Jacobite, res. Ballygower Skye Inverness-shire, tr. 20 Mar 1747, fr. Tilbury. (P.2.192)(MR81)
1900. Finlayson, Peter, b. 1703, bricklayer, res. Edinburgh, sh. Oct 1723, fr. London to Jamaica. (CLRO\AIA)

1901. Finlayson, William, res. Stirling, sh. pre 1707, d. pre 1707 America, Edin pr 1707 CC8.8.83
1902. Finnelston, John, b. 1741, wright, res. Paisley Renfrewshire, sh. Oct 1774, fr. Greenock to Philadelphia, in *Sally*. (PRO.T47.12)
1903. Finney, Alexander, clergyman, res. Aberdeen, pts. William Finney, sh. 1724, to Va, sett. Brandon Va. (SRO.SH.1.2.1755)(EMA27)(OD16)
1904. Finney, Jean, infanticide, res. Paisley Renfrewshire, tr. 1758. (SM.20.328)
1905. Finney, Robert, Jacobite, tr. 29 June 1716, fr. Liverpool to Jamaica or Va, in *Elizabeth & Anne*, arr. York Va. (SPC.1716.310)(VSP.1.185)
1906. Finney, William, clergyman edu. Glasgow Uni, res. Glasgow, sh. pre 1714, sett. Henrico Va, d. 1727 Va. (SCHR.14.149)(OD15)
1907. Finnie, Alexander, clergyman edu. Marischal Col Aberdeen 1714, res. Aberdeen, pts. William Finnie, sh. 1724, to Va. (EMA27)
1908. Finnie, John, farmer, Jacobite, res. Cushnie Aberdeenshire, tr. 1716, fr. Liverpool to Va. (JAB.1.151)(CTB31.208)
1909. Finnison, John, Covenanter, tr. Aug 1685, fr. Leith to Jamaica. (PC.11.329)
1910. Finnison, Peter, Covenanter, tr. Oct 1684, fr. Glasgow. (PC.2.251)
1911. Fisher, Archibald, b. 1740, farmer, res. Breadalbane Perthshire, sh. May 1775, fr. Greenock to N.Y., in *Lilly*. (PRO.T47.12)
1912. Fisher, Donald, b. 1749, farmer, res. Breadalbane Perthshire, sh. May 1775, fr. Greenock to N.Y., in *Lilly*. (PRO.T47.12)
1913. Fisher, Finlay, b. 1751, farmer, res. Breadalbane Perthshire, sh. May 1775, fr. LILLY. (PRO.T47.12)
1914. Fisher, James, weaver, Covenanter, res. Bridgend Glasgow, tr. June 1678, to West Indies. (PC.5.474)
1915. Fisher, John, b. 1730, farmer, res. Breadalbane Perthshire, sh. May 1775, fr. Greenock to N.Y., in *Lilly*. (PRO.T47.12)
1916. Fisher, Margaret, whore & thief, res. Edinburgh, tr. 28 Nov 1704, fr. Leith to Md. (SRO.PC2.28.307)
1917. Fisher, Patrick, thief, res. Stirling, tr. 1752. (SM.14.212)
1918. Flanagan, James, b. 1753, husbandman, sh. Sept 1774, fr. London to Jamaica, in *Standlinch*. (PRO.T47.9\11)
1919. Fleming, Alexander, sailor, res. Dysart Fife, sh. 14 July 1698, fr. Leith to Darien, in *St Andrew*, Edin pr1707 CC8.8.83
1920. Fleming, Alexander, b. 1727, horsehirer, Jacobite, res. Aberdeen, tr. 24 Feb 1747, fr. Liverpool to Va, in *Gildart*, arr. Port North Potomac Md 5 Aug 1747. (P.2.197)(JAB.2.425)(MR129)(PRO.T1.328)
1921. Fleming, George, foremastman, res. Edinburgh, pts. George Fleming, sh. 14 July 1698, fr. Leith to Darien, in *Caledonia*, d. 1699 Darien, Edin pr 1707 CC8.8.83

1922. Fleming, John, Covenanter, res. Stenhouse Stirlingshire, tr. Aug 1684,
fr. Leith to Carolina. (PC.9.28)

1923. Fleming, John, commissary general, d. 8 Mar 1765 Grenada.
(SM.27.279)

1924. Fleming, Sir Collingwood, res. Farme Rutherglen Lanarkshire, d. 1764
Va. (SM.26.290)

1925. Fleming, Thomas, clergyman, pts. Rev James Fleming & Magdalene
Way, sh. 1730, to Leeward Islands, sett. St John Jamaica, d. 2 Dec
1741. (SP.8)(EMA27)

1926. Fleming, William, b. 1758, weaver, res. Glasgow, sh. Feb 1774, fr.
Greenock to N.Y., in *Commerce*. (PRO.T47.12)

1927. Fletcher, Alexander, soldier, sh. pre 1783, d. Sept 1793 St John's Island.
(GM.63.1149)

1928. Fletcher, Angus, b. 1728, farmer, res. Glen Orchy Argyll, sh. Aug 1774,
fr. Greenock to Wilmington N.C., in *Ulysses*, m. Katherine
McIntyre, ch. Euphame Mary Nancy. (PRO.T47.12)

1929. Fletcher, Duncan, Covenanter, tr. Aug 1685, fr. Leith to Jamaica.
(PC.11.136)

1930. Fletcher, John, Covenanter, res. Rumcadle Kintyre Argyll, tr. Aug 1685,
fr. Leith to Jamaica. (PC.11.329)

1931. Fletcher, John, d. 11 Nov 1698 Darien. (NLS.RY2b8\19)

1932. Flett, Elizabeth, res. Gruthay Orkney, pts. John Flett, sh. pre 1772, sett.
N.E., m. Alexander Ross. (SRO.SH.10.12.1772)

1933. Flint, James, Jacobite, tr. 21 May 1716, fr. Liverpool to S.C., in
Wakefield. (SPC.1716.309)(CTB31.205)

1934. Flood, Daniel, sailor, rioter, res. Greenock Renfrewshire, tr. May 1773,
fr. Glasgow. (AJ1325)

1935. Fogo, David, merchant, sh. pre 1749, sett. Antigua.
(SRO.SH.20.1.1749)

1936. Fogo, James, merchant, res. Glasgow, pts. James Fogo, sh. pre 1771,
sett. Clarendon Jamaica. (SRA.B10.15.7435)

1937. Foord, William, sailor, res. Burntisland Fife, sh. 14 July 1698, fr. Leith
to Darien, in *Caledonia*, m. Euphan Robertson, Edin pr 1707
CC8.8.83

1938. Forbes, Alexander, clergyman edu. King's Col Aberdeen 1706, sh. 1709,
to Va. (EMA27)

1939. Forbes, Alexander, b. 27 July 1689, Edinburgh, res. Edinburgh, pts. Sir
David Forbes of Newhall, sett. Jamaica, d. 13 Nov 1729 Jamaica,
bd. St Catherine's Spanish Town Jamaica. (MIBWI.4)

1940. Forbes, Alexander, b. 1727, servant, Jacobite, res. Wemyss Fife, tr. 31
Mar 1747, fr. London to Jamaica , in *St George or Carteret*, arr.
Jamaica 1747. (P.2.200)(MR71)(PRO.CO137.58)

1941. Forbes, Arthur, merchant, sh. Aug 1683, fr. Aberdeen to N.J., in
Exchange of Stockton. (SRO.E72.1.10)

1942. Forbes, Captain, soldier, sh. 14 July 1698, fr. Leith to Darien, in *Unicorn*, d. 25 July 1699 Bay of Matanzas Cuba. (DP196)

1943. Forbes, Charles, sh. 29 Nov 1773, fr. Greenock to Jamaica, in *Mary of Glasgow*. (SRO.CE60.1.7)

1944. Forbes, Donald, b. 1704, farmer, Jacobite, res. Strathnairn, tr. 20 Mar 1747, fr. London to Jamaica , in *St George or Carteret*, arr. Jamaica 1747. (P.2.200)(MR174)(PRO.CO137.58)

1945. Forbes, Donald, b. 1746, servant, res. Inverness, sh. July 1775, fr. Stornaway to Philadelphia, in *Clementina*. (PRO.T47.12)

1946. Forbes, George, res. Aberdeenshire, pre 1781, sett. St Anne Jamaica. (APB.4.96)

1947. Forbes, George, res. Deer Aberdeenshire, pts. Thomas & Margaret Forbes, sh. 1711, sett. Md, d. 1739, PCC pr1742. (APB.3.95)

1948. Forbes, George, merchant & planter, res. Aberdeen, sh. 1753, sett. St Thomas Jamaica, m. Elizabeth Gordon of Beldorny, d. pre 1766. (APB.2.5)

1949. Forbes, George, planter, res. Aberdeen, sett. St Anne Jamaica, d. June 1781 Charleston S.C. (APB.4.96)

1950. Forbes, George, Jacobite, tr. 7 May 1716, fr. Liverpool to S.C., in *Susannah*. (SPC.1716.309)(CTB31.206)

1951. Forbes, Janet, b. 1757, servant, res. Inverness, sh. July 1775, fr. Stornaway to Philadelphia, in *Clementina*. (PRO.T47.12)

1952. Forbes, Jean, res. Aberdeenshire, m. Ludovick Grant of Culnakyle, d. June 1781 Charleston S.C. (APB.4.96)

1953. Forbes, John, res. Barnla Aberdeenshire, sh. 1684, to East N.J., sett. Perth Amboy N.J. (Insh263)

1954. Forbes, John, b. 1740s, clergyman, res. Aberdeenshire, pts. Archibald Forbes of Deskrie, sh. 1764, sett. St Augustine E Fla, m. Dorothy Murray, ch. James John Ralph, d. 1783 England. (EMA28)(BLG2688)(HF384)

1955. Forbes, John, b. 1749, blacksmith, sh. Sept 1774, fr. London to Jamaica, in *Standlinch*. (PRO.T479\11)

1956. Forbes, Margaret, whore, res. Edinburgh, tr. 19 Mar 1695. (SRO.PC2.25.216)

1957. Forbes, Margaret, infanticide, res. Kirkton of Tough Aberdeenshire, tr. June 1755, fr. Aberdeen to Va, in *Hope*. (SM.17.266)(AJ388)

1958. Forbes, Robert, clergyman, sh. 1707, to Carolina. (EMA27)

1959. Forbes, Thomas, farmer, Jacobite, res. Cushnie Aberdeenshire, tr. 24 May 1716, fr. Liverpool to Va, in *Friendship*, arr. Md Aug 1716. (SPC.1716.311)(JAB.1.151)(HM387)

1960. Forbes, William, shoemaker, res. Aberdeen, sh. 1767, sett. Quebec, d. Apr 1776 Quebec. (APB.4.89)

1961. Forbes, William, merchant, res. Nether Whidlemont, sett. Jamaica, d. pre 1783. (SRO.SH.19.7.1783)

1962. Forbes, William, attorney, sh. pre 1764, sett. St Michael's Barbados, m. Margaret Finlay. (SRO.RD3.224.9)(SRO.RD4.248.891)
1963. Forbes, William, b. 1727, husbandman, Jacobite, res. Fochabers Morayshire, tr. 20 Mar 1747, fr. Tilbury. (P.2.202)(JAB.2.426)(MR127)
1964. Ford, John, Covenanter, tr. Aug 1685, fr. Leith to East N.J., in *Henry & Francis*. (PC.11.154)
1965. Fordyce, John, clergyman, sh. 1730, to Jamaica, sett. Prince Frederick Co S.C., d. 1751 S.C. (EMA28)
1966. Forfar, Margaret, b. 1756, servant, res. Perthshire, sh. May 1775, fr. Leith to Philadelphia, in *Friendship*. (PRO.T47.12)
1967. Forman, John, Covenanter, tr. Aug 1685, fr. Leith to East N.J., in *Henry & Francis*. (PC.11.154)
1968. Forrest, George, seaman, sh. Apr 1683, to Hudson Bay. (HBRS.9.92)
1969. Forrest, James, Covenanter, res. Cambusnethan, pts. James & Marion Forrest, tr. Aug 1685, fr. Leith to Jamaica, arr. Port Royal Jamaica Nov 1685. (PC.11.329)(LJ17)
1970. Forrest, Margaret, Covenanter, res. Cambusnethan, pts. Marion Forrest, tr. Aug 1685, fr. Leith to East N.J., in *Henry & Francis*. (PC.11.155)
1971. Forrester, John, forger, tr. Nov 1751. (AJ203)
1972. Forster, Thomas, b. 1739, shoemaker, res. Perthshire, sh. May 1775, fr. Greenock to N.Y., in *Monimia*, m. Janet Tasie. (PRO.T47.12)
1973. Forsyth, Archibald, b. 1753, farmer, res. Duffus Morayshire, sh. July 1775, fr. Stornaway to Philadelphia, in *Clementina*. (PRO.T47.12)
1974. Forsyth, Bezabeer, b. 1752, gentleman, sh. Oct 1774, fr. London to Carolina, in *James*. (PRO.T47.9\11)
1975. Forsyth, Hugh, Jacobite, tr. 30 Mar 1716, fr. Liverpool to Antigua, in *Scipio*. (SPC.1716.310)(CTB31.204)
1976. Forsyth, James, Covenanter, res. Annandale Dumfries-shire, tr. Aug 1685, fr. Leith to East N.J., in *Henry & Francis*. (PC.11.154)
1977. Fortune, William, b. 1745, saddler, res. Edinburgh, sh. May 1775, fr. Greenock to N.Y., in *Monimia*. (PRO.T47.12)
1978. Foster, George, sh. 1737, fr. Inverness to Savanna Ga, in *Two Brothers*, sett. Fredericia Ga. (SPC.43.161)
1979. Foster, John, b. 1677, husbandman, Jacobite, tr. 24 Apr 1747, fr. Liverpool to Va, in *Johnson*, arr. Port Oxford Md 5 Aug 1747. (P.2.204)(PRO.T1.328)
1980. Foster, Thomas, Jacobite, tr. 29 June 1716, fr. Liverpool to Jamaica or Va, in *Elizabeth & Anne*, arr. Va. (SPC.1716.310)(CTB31.208)(VSP.1.185)
1981. Fotheringham, John, Jacobite, tr. 7 May 1716, fr. Liverpool to S.C., in *Susannah*. (SPC.1716.309)(CTB31.206)

1982. Fotheringham, Thomas, res. Powrie Angus, pts. Thomas Fotheringham-Ogilvy, d. 16 Apr 1768 Jamaica. (SM.30.389)
1983. Fotheringham, William, clergyman, sh. 1762, to Newfoundland, arr. Trinity Bay Ferryland Newfoundland 22 Nov 1762, d. pre July 1763 St John's Newfoundland. (EMA28)
1984. Foulis, James, clergyman edu. Glasgow Uni 1734, res. Glasgow, pts. Andrew Foulis, sh. 1750, to Va, d. America. (MAGU13)(EMA28)
1985. Fouller, Thomas, sailor, res. Greenock Renfrewshire, sh. 12 Oct 1698, to Darien, in *Speedy Return*, m. Janet Bannatyne, Edin pr 1708 CC8.8.84
1986. Fowler, John, tr. 1775, fr. Greenock, in *Rainbow*, arr. Port Hampton Va 3 May 1775. (SRO.JC27.10.3)
1987. Fox, George, b. 1650, res. Teviotdale, pts. James Fox, sh. Jan 1685, fr. London to Jamaica. (CLRO\AIA)
1988. Foyer, Janet, servant, thief, res. Drymen Stirlingshire, tr. May 1754. (SM.16.258)
1989. Fraser, Alexander, soldier, d. 1699 Darien, Edin pr 1708 CC8.8.84
1990. Fraser, Alexander, sailor, res. Newhaven Midlothian, sh. 14 July 1698, fr. Leith to Darien, in *Unicorn*, m. Margaret Simpson, Edin pr 1708 CC8.8.84
1991. Fraser, Alexander, soldier, sh. pre 1773, sett. N.Y. (PCCol.1773.597)
1992. Fraser, Alexander, cattle thief, res. Stronarnat Kirkmichael Perthshire, tr. May 1774. (AJ1377)
1993. Fraser, Alexander, thief, res. Perthshire, tr. 18 Dec 1720, fr. Leith. (SRO.HH.11) (alias 353)
1994. Fraser, Alexander, miller, hamesucken, tr. Sept 1750. (SM.12.451)
1995. Fraser, Alexander, soldier, res. Dalcataig Inverness-shire, d. pre 1783 Savannah Ga, PCC pr1783
1996. Fraser, Alexander, merchant, d. Feb 1773 Jamaica. (SM.36.166)
1997. Fraser, Alexander, b. 1725, weaver, Jacobite, res. Inverness, tr. 31 Mar 1747, fr. London to Barbados, in *Frere*. (P.2.208)(MR117)
1998. Fraser, Alexander, b. 1725, Jacobite, res. Morayshire, tr. 20 Mar 1747, fr. London to Barbados, in *Frere*. (P.2.208)(MR71)
1999. Fraser, Allan, tr. Dec 1685, fr. Leith. (ETR390)
2000. Fraser, Anne, infanticide, res. Inverness-shire, tr. Sept 1750. (SM.12.451)
2001. Fraser, Anne, res. Freuchie Fife, sh. pre 1776, sett. Northampton Co Va, m. Kendall Harmonson, ch. John. (SRO.RD2.220.1267)
2002. Fraser, Christian, b. 1749, servant, res. Stornaway Isle of Lewis, sh. May 1774, fr. Stornaway to Philadelphia, in *Friendship*. (PRO.T47.12)
2003. Fraser, David, b. 1720, servant, Jacobite, res. Inverness, tr. 31 Mar 1747, fr. London to Barbados, in *Frere*. (P.2.208)(MR116)
2004. Fraser, David, b. 1725, fiddler, Jacobite, tr. 31 Mar 1747, fr. Tilbury. (P.2.210)(MR81)

2005. Fraser, David, b. 1725, Jacobite, res. Balagelken Glen Urquhart Inverness-shire, tr. 20 Mar 1747, fr. London to Barbados, in *Frere*. (P.2.210)(MR117)
2006. Fraser, Donald, res. Edinburgh, tr. 8 May 1663, fr. Leith to Barbados, in *Mary*. (EBR.186.13.4)
2007. Fraser, Donald, b. 1725, husbandman, Jacobite, res. Fort Augustus Inverness-shire, tr. 20 Mar 1747, fr. London to Jamaica, in *St George or Carteret*, arr. Jamaica 1747. (P.2.210)(MR117)(PRO.CO137.58)
2008. Fraser, Donald, b. 1728, tailor, Jacobite, res. Logie Ross-shire, tr. 31 Mar 1747, fr. London to Jamaica, in *St George or Carteret*, arr. Jamaica 1747. (P.2.210)(MR81)(PRO.CO137.58)
2009. Fraser, Donald, b. 1760, servant, res. Dunbalich, sh. July 1775, fr. Stornaway to Philadelphia, in *Clementina*. (PRO.T47.12)
2010. Fraser, Donald sr, thief, res. Inverness-shire, tr. Oct 1749. (AJ95)
2011. Fraser, Elizabeth, b. 1755, servant, res. Ross-shire, sh. May 1775, fr. Leith to Philadelphia, in *Friendship*. (PRO.T47.12)
2012. Fraser, Ewan, b. 1715, tailor, Jacobite, res. Colwoolen Inverness-shire, tr. 31 Mar 1747, fr. London to Barbados, in *Frere*. (P.2.212)(MR117) (alias 2017)
2013. Fraser, George, clergyman edu. Marischal Col 1728, sh. 1732, to Pa. (EMA28)
2014. Fraser, Helen, servant, infanticide, res. Ardgillian Scone Perthshire, tr. Oct 1760. (SRO.B59.26.11.6.43)
2015. Fraser, Helen, infanticide, res. Perthshire, tr. Sept 1763. (AJ815)
2016. Fraser, Hugh, sailor, sh. 14 July 1698, fr. Leith to Darien, in *Caledonia*, Edin pr1707 CC8.8.83
2017. Fraser, Hugh, b. 1715, tailor, Jacobite, res. Colwoolen Inverness-shire, tr. 31 Mar 1747, fr. London to Barbados, in *Frere*. (P.2.212)(MR117) (alias 2012)
2018. Fraser, Hugh, b. 1719, blacksmith, Jacobite, res. Montrose Angus, tr. 31 Mar 1747, fr. London to Jamaica, in *St George or Carteret*, arr. Jamaica 1747. (P.2.212)(MR101)(PRO.CO137.28)
2019. Fraser, Hugh, b. 1720, husbandman, Jacobite, res. Auchindach Inverness-shire, tr. 31 Mar 1747, fr. London to Jamaica, in *St George or Carteret*, arr. Jamaica 1747. (P.2.212)(MR62)(PRO.CO137.58)
2020. Fraser, Hugh, b. 1721, husbandman, Jacobite, res. Innermurie Inverness-shire, tr. 31 Mar 1747, fr. London to Jamaica, in *St George or Carteret*, arr. Jamaica 1747. (P.2.212)(MR117)(PRO.CO137.28)
2021. Fraser, Hugh, b. 1721, husbandman, Jacobite, res. Drumhardinich Inverness-shire, tr. 31 Mar 1747, fr. London to Jamaica, in *St George or Carteret*, arr. Jamaica 1747. (P.2.212)(MR117)(PRO.CO137.58)

97

2022. Fraser, Isobel, b. 1754, servant, sh. July 1775, fr. Stornaway to Philadelphia, in *Clementina*. (PRO.T47.12)
2023. Fraser, James, merchant, res. Inverness, sh. pre 1703, sett. Va. (SRO.CS96.3309)
2024. Fraser, James, b. 1679, laborer, Jacobite, res. Inverness, tr. 31 Mar 1747, fr. London to Barbados, in *Frere*. (P.2.212)(MR118)
2025. Fraser, Janet, b. 1757, servant, res. Inverness, sh. July 1775, fr. Stornaway to Philadelphia, in *Clementina*. (PRO.T47.12)
2026. Fraser, Jean, b. 1750, servant, res. Beauly Inverness-shire, sh. July 1775, fr. Stornaway to Philadelphia, in *Clementina*. (PRO.T47.12)
2027. Fraser, John, clergyman, sh. 1701, to Va, sett. Va & Md, d. Nov 1742 Piscataway Md. (EMA28)
2028. Fraser, John, clergyman edu. Edinburgh Uni, sh. 1769, to Va, sett. E Fla. (EMA28)(FPA308)
2029. Fraser, John, clergyman, Covenanter, tr. Aug 1685, fr. Leith to East N.J., in *Henry & Francis*, d. post 1691 Scotland. (PC.11.154)
2030. Fraser, John, Jacobite, tr. 30 Mar 1716, fr. Liverpool, in *Scipio*. (SPC.1716.310)(CTB31.204)
2031. Fraser, John, merchant & shipmaster, res. Aberdeen, sett. St Kitts, d. pre 1747. (APB.3.137)
2032. Fraser, John, Jacobite, tr. 21 May 1716, fr. Liverpool to S.C., in *Wakefield*. (SPC.1716.309)(CTB31.205)
2033. Fraser, John, b. 1658, clergyman, Covenanter, res. Pitcalzean, sh. pre 1684, sett. Woodsbury Ct, m. Jean Moffat, d. 7 Nov 1711 Alness Ross & Cromarty. (F.7.663)
2034. Fraser, John, b. 1697, farmer, Jacobite, res. Craigscory Inverness-shire, tr. 31 Mar 1747, fr. London to Barbados, in *Frere*. (P.2.214)(MR118)
2035. Fraser, John, b. 1707, Jacobite, res. Inverwick Glenmoriston Inverness-shire, tr. 20 Mar 1747, fr. Barbados to FRERE. (P.2.214)(MR152)
2036. Fraser, John, b. 1713, weaver, Jacobite, res. Inverness, tr. 31 Mar 1747, fr. London to Barbados, in *Frere*. (P.2.214)(MR118)
2037. Fraser, John, b. 27 Mar 1716, Aberdeen, shipmaster, res. Aberdeen, pts. Thomas Fraser & Isobel Gray, sh. 1741, sett. St Kitts, d. 1744. (APB.3.129)
2038. Fraser, John, b. 1717, farmer, Jacobite, res. Crochill Inverness-shire, tr. 31 Mar 1747, fr. London to Barbados, in *Frere*. (P.2.214)(MR118)
2039. Fraser, John, b. 1725, farmer, Jacobite, res. Delcaitack Glenmoriston Inverness-shire, tr. 31 Mar 1747, fr. London to Barbados, in *Frere*. (P.2.214)(MR151)
2040. Fraser, John, b. 1725, servant, Jacobite, res. Inverness, tr. 31 Mar 1747, fr. London to Barbados, in *Frere*. (P.2.214)(MR118)

2041. Fraser, John, b. 1735, farmer, res. Kinmily, sh. July 1775, fr. Stornaway to Philadelphia, in *Clementina*, m. Christian .., ch. Janet Margaret William Jean. (PRO.T47.12)
2042. Fraser, John, b. 1750, ship's carpenter, res. Ayrshire, sh. Mar 1775, fr. Glasgow to Quebec, in *Friendship*. (PRO.T47.12)
2043. Fraser, John, b. 1755, res. Inverness, sh. Sept 1774, fr. Greenock to Jamaica, in *Jamaica*. (PRO.T47.12)
2044. Fraser, Lauchlan, b. 1758, planter, res. Inverness, sh. July 1775, fr. Greenock to Jamaica, in *Isobella*. (PRO.T47.12)
2045. Fraser, Mary, b. 1757, servant, res. Park, sh. July 1775, fr. Stornaway to Philadelphia, in *Clementina*. (PRO.T47.12)
2046. Fraser, Mary, b. 1758, servant, res. Beauly Inverness-shire, sh. July 1775, fr. Stornaway to Philadelphia, in *Clementina*. (PRO.T47.12)
2047. Fraser, Owen, Jacobite, tr. 1747, fr. Tilbury. (P.2.216)
2048. Fraser, Peter, b. 1711, Jacobite, res. Inverness-shire, tr. 20 Mar 1747. (P.2.216)(MR118)
2049. Fraser, Roderick, b. 1719, farmer, Jacobite, res. Dingwall Ross & Cromarty, tr. 31 Mar 1747, fr. London to Barbados, in *Frere*. (P.2.216)(MR81)
2050. Fraser, Simon, soldier, res. Strathglass Inverness-shire, pts. William Fraser of Guisachan & Margaret McDonell, sh. pre 1773, sett. Bennington NY, m. Isabella Grant, ch. William Angus Simon, d. 177- Albany N.Y. (HOFL   )(PCCol.1773.597)
2051. Fraser, Simon, thief, res. Garthmore of Stratherick Inverness-shire, tr. June 1754. (SM.16.203)
2052. Fraser, Simon, b. 1727, Jacobite, res. Aird Inverness-shire, tr. 31 Mar 1747, fr. London to Jamaica , in *St George or Carteret*, arr. Jamaica 1747. (P.2.216)(MR118)(PRO.CO137.58)
2053. Fraser, Simon jr, merchant, res. Inverness, sh. Apr 1761, fr. Glasgow to North America. (SRO.SC29.55.10.266)
2054. Fraser, Thomas, physician, res. Inverness, sh. pre 1775, sett. Antigua, ch. Charles. (SRO.RS38.13.250\310)
2055. Fraser, Thomas, b. 1754, clerk, res. Ayr, sh. July 1775, fr. Greenock to Antigua, in *Chance*. (PRO.T47.12)
2056. Fraser, William, overseer, res. Inverness-shire, sh. 1698, ch. George, d. 1699 West Indies, Edin pr 1707 CC8.8.83
2057. Fraser, William, Jacobite, tr. 7 May 1716, fr. Liverpool to S.C., in *Susannah*. (SPC.1716.309)(CTB31.206)
2058. Fraser, William, thief, res. Perthshire, tr. 15 Dec 1720. (SRO.HH.11) (alias 5399)
2059. Fraser, William, b. 1721, husbandman, Jacobite, res. Kirkton Aird Inverness-shire, tr. 31 Mar 1747, fr. London to Jamaica, in *St George or Carteret*, arr. Jamaica 1747. (P.2.218)(MR118)(PRO.CO137.58)

2060. Fraser, William, b. 1743, clergyman edu. Marischal Col Aberdeen 1760-1764, sh. 1766, to N.J., d. 6 July 1795 Trenton N.J. (EMA28)
2061. Fraser, William, b. 1749, wright, res. Inverness, sh. July 1775, fr. Stornaway to Philadelphia, in *Clementina*, m. Anne .. (PRO.T47.12)
2062. Frazer, Duncan, Jacobite, tr. 7 May 1716, fr. Liverpool to S.C., in *Susannah*. (SPC.1716.309)(CTB31.206)
2063. Frazer, Hugh, Jacobite, tr. 7 May 1716, fr. Liverpool to S.C., in *Susannah*. (SPC.1716.309)(CTB31.206)
2064. Freebairn, John, physician, res. Hamilton Lanarkshire, pts. John Freebairn of Capplerig, sh. pre 1769, sett. Jamaica. (SRO.RS42.18.424)
2065. Freeman, James, b. 9 Dec 1711, Aberdeen, merchant & planter, res. Aberdeen, pts. James Freeman & Margaret Tennant, sh. Dec 1729, fr. London to Md, m. .. Wallace. (CLRO\AIA)(PerthMAGA)
2066. French, Andrew, Covenanter, tr. Dec 1685, fr. Leith to Barbados, in *John & Nicholas*. (ETR390)
2067. French, William, Covenanter, res. Cambusnethan, tr. Dec 1685, fr. Leith to Barbados, in *John & Nicholas*. (PC.11.232)(ETR389)
2068. Frew, John, sh. 29 Nov 1773, fr. Greenock to Jamaica, in *Mary of Glasgow*. (SRO.CE60.1.7)
2069. Frigg, Andrew, b. 20 Sept 1736, Kinloss Morayshire, shipmaster, pts. John Frigg & Helen Bremner, sett. Jamaica, d. 1769 Edinburgh, Edin pr1775 CC8.8.123
2070. Froud, John, b. 1702, res. Blackshaw Nithsdale Dumfries-shire, sh. Aug 1722, fr. London to Md. (CLRO\AIA)
2071. Fruid, James, pts. James Fruid, d. pre 1725 Md, PCC pr1725
2072. Fullarton, George, merchant, res. Ayrshire, sett. Charleston S.C., d. pre 1709 Charleston, PCC pr1709
2073. Fullarton, John, tradesman, res. Edinburgh, sh. 1683, to Hudson Bay, in *Diligence*, d. 1738 England. (HBRS.25.361)
2074. Fullarton, Robert, res. Kinaber Montrose Angus, sh. 1684, to East N.J., sett. New Caesarea N.J. (Insh250)
2075. Fullarton, Thomas, sea-captain, sh. 14 July 1698, fr. Leith to Darien, in *Dolphin*, d. 25 Dec 1698 Darien. (NLS.RY2b8\19)
2076. Fullerton, David, clergyman, sh. 1767, to Dominica. (EMA28)
2077. Fullerton, Robert, sh. June 1684, fr. Montrose to East N.J., in *Thomas & Benjamin*. (SRO.E72.16.13)
2078. Fullerton, Robert, merchant, sh. Feb 1681, fr. Ayr to West Indies, in *James of Ayr*. (SRO.E72.3.6)
2079. Fullerton, Robert, merchant, sh. Mar 1683, fr. Ayr to Caribee Islands, in *James of Ayr*. (SRO.E72.3.12)

2080. Fullerton, Thomas, seacaptain, sh. 14 July 1698, fr. Leith to Darien, in *Dolphin*, m. Isabel Hodgson, d. Dec 1699 Darien, Edin pr 1707 CC8.8.83
2081. Fulton, James, b. 1753, farmer, res. Inverness, sh. May 1774, fr. Greenock to N.Y., in *George*. (PRO.T47.12)
2082. Fulton, William, merchant & shipper, sh. pre 1699, sett. Bristol N.E. (SPC.1699.501)
2083. Fyfe, Alexander, weaver, assault, res. Wardend of Turfbegg Forfar Angus, tr. Sept 1726, fr. Glasgow to Jamaica. (SRO.JC11.6)(SRO.B59.26.11.1.36)
2084. Fyfe, William, clergyman, sh. 1729, to Va. (EMA29)
2085. Gaddie, George, thief, res. Aberdeenshire, tr. 1752. (SM.14.509)
2086. Gaft, John, thief, res. Loch Arkaig Lochaber Inverness-shire, tr. May 1755. (AJ386) (alias 3540)
2087. Gairdner, John, Covenanter, res. Monkland Lanarkshire, tr. 16 May 1684, to N.Y. (PC.8.516)
2088. Gairdner, John, servant, Covenanter, res. Wester Harieburn Lanarkshire, tr. 1 Aug 1684, fr. Leith to Carolina. (PC.9.28)(ETR271)
2089. Gairdner, William, sailor, res. Abbotshall Fife, pts. Agnes Davidson or Gairdner, sh. 14 July 1698, fr. Leith to Darien, in *Unicorn*, Edin pr1707 CC8.8.83
2090. Gairns, John, carpenter, res. Dundee Angus, sh. Nov 1752, fr. Leith to Cape Fear N.C., in *Grenadier*. (SRO.RD4.178.364)
2091. Galbraith, George, sh. pre 1752, sett. St Mary's Jamaica. (SRO.RD4.178.582)
2092. Galbraith, James, baker, res. Glasgow, pts. John Galbraith, sh. pre 1773, sett. Quebec. (SRO.AC.GMB.40)(SRO.CS.GMB.218)
2093. Galbraith, John, tr. Aug 1685. (PC.11.145)
2094. Galbraith, Thomas, merchant, res. Knockdaw Ayrshire, sh. pre 1776, sett. N.Y. (SRO.RD2.242.4)
2095. Galbraith, William, res. Stirlingshire, d. pre 1768 Jamaica, Edin pr1768 CC8.8.121
2096. Galbreath, Angus, b. 1744, workman, res. Glen Orchy Argyll, sh. Aug 1774, fr. Greenock to Wilmington N.C., in *Ulysses*, m. Katherine Brown. (PRO.T47.12)
2097. Galbreath, John, b. 1754, farmer, res. Stirling, sh. May 1774, fr. Greenock to N.Y., in *Matty*. (PRO.T47.12)
2098. Galbreath, Thomas, merchant, res. Glasgow, sh. pre 1777, to N.Y. (SRA.B10.12.4)
2099. Gall, Alexander, sheepstealer, res. Peterhead Aberdeenshire, tr. June 1755, fr. Aberdeen to Va, in *Hope*. (AJ383\8)
2100. Gall, Roger, merchant, sh. pre 1775, sett. Bay of Honduras. (SRO.RD4.228.1092)

101

2101. Galloway, Christine, adulteress & thief, res. Aberdeen, tr. 1668, fr. Aberdeen to Va, m. John Ord. (ABR.JCB.1.107)
2102. Galloway, John, bosun's mate, res. Culross Fife, pts. John Galloway, sh. 18 Aug 1699, fr. Clyde to Darien, in *Rising Sun*, Edin pr 1707 CC8.8.83
2103. Galloway, John, b. 1749, weaver, res. Paisley Renfrewshire, sh. Oct 1774, fr. Greenock to Philadelphia, in *Sally*. (PRO.T47.12)
2104. Galloway, John, b. 1752, joiner, res. Galloway, sh. May 1774, fr. Stranraer to N.Y., in *Gale*. (PRO.T47.12)
2105. Galloway, Robert, merchant edu. Glasgow Uni 1773, res. Glasgow, pts. Andrew Galloway, sett. Va, d. 1 Aug 1794 Fredericksburg Va. (MAGU.105)
2106. Galloway, Sarah, b. 1754, res. Galloway, sh. May 1774, fr. Stranraer to N.Y., in *Gale*. (PRO.T47.12)
2107. Galt, John, thatcher, Covenanter, res. Glasgow, tr. June 1684, fr. Clyde, in *Pelican*. (PC.9.208)
2108. Ganwoth, Elizabeth, b. 1749, res. Anwoth Kirkcudbrightshire, sh. May 1774, fr. GALE. (PRO.T47.12)
2109. Garden, Alexander, surgeon & physician edu. Marischal Col Aberdeen & Edinburgh Uni, res. Birse Aberdeenshire, pts. Rev Garden, sett. Charleston S.C. (MCA.2.117)
2110. Garden, Alexander, clergyman, sh. 1743, to S.C., d. 1783. (EMA29)
2111. Garden, Francis, physician edu. Edinburgh Uni 1768, sett. S.C., d. Oct 1770 Charleston S.C. (SA185)(SM.33.53)
2112. Garden, James, Crombie Banffshire, clergyman edu. Marischal Col Aberdeen 1743-1747, res. Kintore Aberdeenshire, pts. Alexander Garden, sh. 1754, to Va. (EMA29)(FPA307)
2113. Gardiner, Christine, infanticide, tr. Aug 1685, fr. Leith to Jamaica. (PC.11.330)(ETR369)
2114. Gardner, Archibald, Jacobite, tr. 5 May 1747, fr. Liverpool, in *Gildart*, arr. Port North Potomac Md 5 Aug 1747. (PRO.T1.328)
2115. Gardner, James, b. 1739, farmer, res. Stirling, sh. Apr 1775, fr. Greenock to N.Y., in *Lilly*. (PRO.T47.12)
2116. Gardner, Martin, b. 1655, husbandman, res. Edinburgh, sh. 1683, fr. London to Barbados, in *John & Elizabeth*. (CLRO\AIA)
2117. Gardner, Nicholas, b. 1720, Jacobite, res. Lancashire, tr. 1747. (P.2.222)
2118. Gardner, Patrick, Jacobite, tr. 25 June 1716, fr. Liverpool to S.C., in *Hockenhill*. (SPC.1716.312)(CTB31.207)
2119. Gardner, Peter, b. 1739, tailor, Jacobite, tr. 5 May 1747, fr. Liverpool, in *Johnson*, arr. Port North Potomac Md 5 Aug 1747. (P.2.222)(PRO.T1.328)
2120. Gardner, William, b. 1750, wright, res. Glasgow, sh. Oct 1774, fr. Greenock to Philadelphia, in *Sally*. (PRO.T47.12)

2121. Garge, William, res. Kirkwall Orkney Islands, sett. New Scotland Barbados, ch. Alexander, d. pre 1683. (SRO.SH.19.11.1683) (alias 5912)
2122. Garland, George, b. 1750, barber, res. Glasgow, sh. Apr 1775, fr. Greenock to N.Y., in *Lilly*. (PRO.T47.12)
2123. Garnock, George, shoplifter, res. Edinburgh, tr. Mar 1768. (AJ1056)
2124. Garson, Robert, b. 1725, farm servant, res. Sandwick Orkney Islands, sh. Sept 1775, fr. Kirkwall to Savanna Ga, in *Marlborough*, sett. Richmond Co Ga. (PRO.T47.12)
2125. Gartey, George, Jacobite, tr. 30 Mar 1716, fr. Liverpool to Antigua, in *Scipio*. (SPC.1716.310)
2126. Garvie, William, farmer, Jacobite, res. Inchrory Ross-shire, tr. 20 Mar 1747, fr. London to Barbados, in *Frere*. (P.2.222)(MR81)
2127. Gascoign, Francis, sailor, res. Newcastle upon Tyne, pts. Robert Gascoign & Isobel Smith, sh. 14 July 1698, fr. Leith to Darien, in *St Andrew*, Edin pr1707 CC8.8.83
2128. Gauldie, George, tr. 5 Feb 1752, fr. Aberdeen to Va, in *Planter*. (AJ265)
2129. Gauley, Jean, b. 1749, res. Dailly Ayrshire, sh. May 1774, fr. Stranraer to N.Y., in *Gale*. (PRO.T47.12)
2130. Gavin, John, tr. Aug 1685, fr. Leith to Jamaica. (PC.11.136)
2131. Gavine, James, Covenanter, res. Douglas Lanarkshire, tr. Aug 1685, fr. Leith to Jamaica, sett. Barbados, m. Helen Dickson, d. post 1695 Douglas. (PC.11.330)(ETR369)(Douglas gs.)
2132. Gay, Edward, Covenanter, res. Bridgend Glasgow, tr. 12 Dec 1678, fr. Leith to West Indies, in *St Michael of Scarborough*. (PC.6.76)
2133. Gay, William, merchant, sh. pre 1772, sett. Va. (SRO.SH.8.10.1772)
2134. Ged, William, merchant, res. Edinburgh, pts. William Ged, d. 4 Jan 1767 St James Jamaica. (SM.29.389)
2135. Gedd, James, printer, Jacobite, res. Edinburgh, pts. William Gedd, sett. Jamaica. (P.2.222)
2136. Geddes, Alexander, laborer, Jacobite, res. Sanston Aberdeenshire, tr. 5 May 1747, fr. Liverpool, in *Gildart*, arr. Port Nort Potomac Md 5 Aug 1747. (P.2.220)(JAB.2.427)(MR123)(PRO.T1.328)
2137. Geddes, Charles, watchmaker, res. Edinburgh, pts. James Geddes, sh. pre 1781, sett. N.Y. (SRO.RD2.232.86)
2138. Geddes, James, b. 1707, res. Morayshire, pts. Alexander Geddes & Margaret Innes, sh. 1737, to Ga. (SG.33.3.233)
2139. Geddes, John, sh. 1684, to East N.J. (Insh242)
2140. Geekie, Daniel, surgeon, pts. Alexander Geekie, d. pre 1740 S.C., PCC pr1740
2141. Geills, Andrew, tobacco merchant & shipmaster, res. Glasgow, sh. pre 1744. (SRA.B10.15.5959)

103

2142. Gellatly, Alexander, b. 1720, Perth, clergyman, sh. Apr 1753, sett. Octarara Pa, d. 12 Mar 1761 Warwick Pa. (SM.15.203)(AP278)(UPC654)
2143. Gellibrand, Andrew, clergyman, sh. 9 June 1690, to N.Y. (Rawl.MS.A306.142)
2144. Gemmill, Grissell, Covenanter, tr. Sept 1685, fr. Leith to East N.J., in *Henry & Francis*. (PC.11.154)
2145. Gemmill, John, Covenanter, tr. 17 Dec 1685, fr. Leith to Barbados, in *John & Nicholas*. (PC.11.255)(ETR389)
2146. Gentle, ..., carter, robber, res. Falkirk Stirlingshire, tr. Oct 1773. (AJ1347)
2147. Gentle, Robert, res. Crieff Perthshire, sh. Oct 1750, fr. London to Jamaica. (CLRO\AIA)
2148. George, James, b. 1752, laborer, res. Shetland Islands, sh. Oct 1774, fr. Kirkcaldy to Antigua, in *Jamaica Packet*. (PRO.T47.12)
2149. Gibb, Alexander, b. 1699, cordwainer, res. Linlithgow West Lothian, sh. Nov 1730, fr. London to Md. (CLRO\AIA)
2150. Gibb, James, sailor, res. Abercorn West Lothian, sh. 18 Aug 1699, fr. Clyde to Darien, in *Rising Sun*, Edin pr1707 CC8.8.83
2151. Gibb, John, foremastman, res. Bo'ness West Lothian, sh. 14 July 1698, fr. Leith to Darien, in *Caledonia*, Edin pr1707 CC8.8.83
2152. Gibb, John, tr. 16 May 1684, fr. Leith to N.Y. (PC.8.709)
2153. Gibb, John, tr. 30 July 1685, fr. Leith to East N.J. (PC.11.136)
2154. Gibb, John, Covenanter, tr. Aug 1685, fr. Leith to Jamaica. (PC.11.329)
2155. Gibb, Robert, merchant, sh. July 1681, fr. Leith to N.Y., in *Hope of Edinburgh*. (SRO.E72.15.32)
2156. Gibbon, Arthur, sheepstealer, res. Aberdeenshire, tr. 25 May 1749, fr. Aberdeen to Va, in *Dispatch of Newcastle*. (SM.11.252)(AJ68)
2157. Gibbon, Francis, Jacobite, tr. 1747, fr. Tilbury. (P.2.226)
2158. Gibbons, John, woolcomber, conspiracy, res. Aberdeen, tr. 1772, fr. Glasgow to Va, in *Brilliant*, arr. Port Hampton Va 7 Oct 1772. (SRO.JC27.10.3)
2159. Gibson, Adam, b. 1744, laborer, res. Kirkbean Galloway, sh. May 1775, fr. Dumfries to P.E.I., in *Lovely Nelly*. (PRO.T47.12)
2160. Gibson, Agnes, whore, res. Edinburgh, tr. 19 Mar 1695. (SRO.PC2.25.216)
2161. Gibson, Colin, b. 1749, tailor, res. Paisley Renfrewshire, sh. Feb 1774, fr. Greenock to N.Y., in *Commerce*, m. Janet ... (PRO.T47.12)
2162. Gibson, George, surgeon's mate, res. Edinburgh, pts. Thomas Gibson, sh. 18 Aug 1699, fr. Clyde to Darien, in *Rising Sun*, Edin pr1707 CC8.8.83
2163. Gibson, James, foremastman, res. Prestonpans East Lothian, sh. 14 July 1698, fr. Leith to Darien, in *Caledonia*, Edin pr1707 CC8.8.83

2164. Gibson, James, merchant, res. Dumfries-shire, sh. pre 1771, sett. Suffolk Va. (SRO.RS23.20.372.4)

2165. Gibson, James, merchant, res. Glasgow, sh. pre 1731, sett. Pungataigue Creek Accomack Co Va, m. Elizabeth Gray. (SRO.CS.GMB.36\328)

2166. Gibson, James, b. 1730, chapman, res. Kirkbean Galloway, sh. May 1775, fr. Dumfries to P.E.I., in *Lovely Nelly*. (PRO.T47.12)

2167. Gibson, John, Covenanter, res. Dalgain Ayrshire, tr. June 1684, fr. Clyde, in *Pelican*. (PC.9.208)

2168. Gibson, John, factor, res. Glasgow, sh. pre 1770, sett. Colchester Va. (SRA.779.21)

2169. Gibson, John, b. 1727, weaver, Jacobite, res. Dundee Angus, tr. 5 May 1747, fr. Liverpool to Va, in *Gildart*, arr. Port North Potomac Md 5 Aug 1747. (P.2.228)(PRO.T1.328)

2170. Gibson, John, b. 1755, farmer, res. Galloway, sh. May 1774, fr. Stranraer to N.Y., in *Gale*. (PRO.T47.12)

2171. Gibson, Malcolm, surgeon's mate, pts. Sir Alexander Gibson of Pentland, sh. 18 Aug 1699, fr. Clyde to Darien, in *Rising Sun*, Edin pr1707 CC8.8.83

2172. Gibson, Margaret, b. 1750, res. Galloway, sh. May 1774, fr. Stranraer to N.Y., in *Gale*. (PRO.T47.12)

2173. Gibson, Margaret, b. 1758, spinner, res. Paisley Renfrewshire, sh. Feb 1774, fr. Greenock to N.Y., in *Commerce*. (PRO.T47.12)

2174. Gibson, Robert, Covenanter, tr. Oct 1669, to Va. (PC.3.22)

2175. Gibson, William, b. 1748, weaver, res. Paisley Renfrewshire, sh. Apr 1775, fr. Greenock to N.Y., in *Lilly*. (PRO.T47.12)

2176. Gibson, William, b. 1755, weaver, res. Paisley Renfrewshire, sh. Feb 1774, fr. Greenock to N.Y., in *Commerce*. (PRO.T47.12)

2177. Giffard, John, schoolmaster edu. Edinburgh Uni 1702, sh. 1703, to Leeward Islands. (EMA29)

2178. Gilchrist, Andrew, merchant, res. Glasgow, pts. George Gilchrist & Agnes Gibson, sh. pre 1733, sett. Accomack Co Va, Glas pr17 CC9.7.62

2179. Gilchrist, Angus, b. 1749, res. Kintyre Argyll, sh. Aug 1774, fr. Greenock to Wilmington N.C., in *Ulysses*. (PRO.T47.12)

2180. Gilchrist, Bessie, Covenanter, res. Kilroy Dumfries-shire, tr. 1684. (PC.10.309)

2181. Gilchrist, Henry, seaman, res. Burntisland Fife, sh. 14 July 1698, fr. Leith to Darien, in *Caledonia*, Edin pr1707 CC8.8.83

2182. Gilchrist, Janet, whore & thief, res. Edinburgh, tr. 28 Apr 1704, fr. Leith to Md. (SRO.PC2.28.307)

2183. Gilchrist, John, merchant, res. Premnay Aberdeenshire, pts. Arthur Gilchrist & Lilias Barclay, d. 1762 Va. (APB.3.221)

105

2184. Gilchrist, John, b. 1749, cooper, res. Kintyre Argyll, sh. Aug 1774, fr. Greenock to Wilmington N.C., in *Ulysses*, m. Marion Taylor. (PRO.T47.12)
2185. Gilchrist, Robert, merchant, res. Duns Berwickshire, pts. John Gilchrist, sh. pre 1649, fr. Ayr, sett. Barbados, d. 1649 Barbados, Edin pr1653 CC8.8.67
2186. Gilchrist, Robert, Covenanter, res. Dalgarnock Nithsdale Dumfries-shire, tr. Sept 1685, fr. Leith to East N.J., in *Henry & Francis*. (PC.11.154)
2187. Gilchrist, Robert, merchant, res. Kilmarnock Ayrshire, pts. William Gilchrist & Grizel Paterson, sh. pre 1770, sett. Md. (SRO.RD3.246.375)
2188. Gilchrist, Thomas, res. Dumfries, pts. Thomas Gilchrist, sh. pre 1783, sett. Suffolk Va & Halifax N.C. (SRO.RD4.235.686)
2189. Gilchrist, William, blacksmith, rioter, res. Edinburgh, tr. Mar 1741. (SM.3.143)
2190. Gildart, Richard, b. 1744, dyer, sh. June 1774, fr. Whitehaven to N.Y., in *Golden Rule*. (PRO.T47.9\11)
2191. Gilfillan, John, Covenanter, tr. Sept 1685, fr. Leith to East N.J., in *Henry & Francis*. (PC.11.154)
2192. Gilhagie, Ninian, passenger, sh. Feb 1681, fr. Ayr to West Indies, in *James of Ayr*. (SRO.E72.3.6)
2193. Gilkerson, Gavin, Covenanter, res. Monkland Lanarkshire, tr. 16 May 1684, fr. Leith to N.Y. (PC.8.516)
2194. Gill, Henry, Jacobite, tr. 7 May 1716, fr. Liverpool to S.C., in *Susannah*. (SPC.1716.309)(CTB31.206)
2195. Gillespie, George, merchant, res. Tynwald Dumfries-shire, sett. St Mary's Md, d. pre 1724 St Mary's Md, PCC pr1724
2196. Gillespie, George, b. 1683, Glasgow, clergyman edu. Glasgow Uni 1700-1704, sh. 1712, to N.E. & N.J., sett. White Clay Creek Del, d. 2 Jan 1760. (AP171)(SA102)(F.7.663)
2197. Gillespie, John, b. 1750, farmer, res. Doune Perthshire, sh. July 1775, fr. Greenock to Ga, in *Georgia*. (PRO.T47.12)
2198. Gillespie, Thomas, b. 1755, farmer, res. Doune Perthshire, sh. July 1775, fr. Greenock to Ga, in *Georgia*. (PRO.T47.12)
2199. Gillies, McLaurin, b. 1 Aug 1754, Glasgow, merchant edu. Glasgow Uni 1766, res. Glasgow, pts. Rev John Gillies & Elizabeth McLaurin, sett. Jamaica. (MAGU80)
2200. Gilliland, John, Covenanter, tr. July 1685, fr. Leith to East N.J. (PC.11.329)
2201. Gillispie, William, b. 1754, farmer, res. Stirling, sh. May 1774, fr. Greenock to N.Y., in *Matty*. (PRO.T.47.12)
2202. Gilmour, Alexander, b. 1729, weaver, res. Glasgow, sh. Aug 1774, fr. Greenock to Philadelphia, in *Magdalene*. (PRO.T47.12)

2203. Gilmour, John, foremastman, sh. 14 July 1698, fr. Leith to Darien, in *Caledonia*, d. post July 1699, Edin pr1707 CC8.8.83

2204. Gilmour, Robert, wright, res. Kirkintilloch Dunbartonshire, sh. Mar 1763, fr. Glasgow to Jamaica. (SRO.SC36.63.7.371)

2205. Gilmour, Robert, merchant, res. Netherton Kilmarnock Ayrshire, sh. pre 1779, sett. Va, ch. John & Robert, Williamsburg pr1782. (SRO.RS42.21.92)

2206. Girvan, Catherine, Covenanter, tr. Aug 1685, fr. Leith to East N.J., in *Henry & Francis*. (PC.11.154)

2207. Givein, Robert, sailor, res. Leith Midlothian, sh. 14 July 1698, fr. Leith to Darien, in *Unicorn*, Edin pr1707 CC8.8.83

2208. Glance, David, b. 1705, groom, res. Edinburgh, sh. Mar 1724, fr. London to Jamaica. (CLRO\AIA)

2209. Glandy, John, Jacobite, tr. 24 May 1716, fr. Liverpool, in *Friendship*, arr. Md Aug 1716. (SPC.1716.311)(HM386)

2210. Glasgow, John, clergyman, sh. 1707, to Antigua. (EMA30)

2211. Glasgow, Robert, surgeon, sh. pre 1777, sett. St Vincent. (SRO.RD2.281.430)

2212. Glass, John, Jacobite, tr. 30 Mar 1716, fr. Liverpool to Antigua, in *Scipio*. (SPC.1716.310)(CTB31.204)

2213. Glass, John, b. 1707, brogmaker, Jacobite, res. Milton of Redcastle Ross-shire, tr. 31 Mar 1747, fr. London to Jamaica or Barbados. (P.2.230)(MRT81)

2214. Glass, William, b. 1758, servant, res. Stornaway Isle of Lewis, sh. May 1774, fr. Stornaway to Philadelphia, in *Friendship*. (PRO.T47.12)

2215. Glassford, James, merchant, res. Glasgow, sh. 1760, to Quebec, sett. Boston Mass & Norfolk Va. (SRA.CFI)

2216. Glassford, Robert, merchant, res. Glasgow, sh. pre 1764, sett. St Kitts & Grenada. (SRA.T-MJ)

2217. Glen, Alexander, b. 1738, weaver, res. Paisley Renfrewshire, sh. Feb 1774, fr. Greenock to N.Y., in *Commerce*, m. Ann ... (PRO.T47.12)

2218. Glen, Duncan, steward, res. Edinburgh, sh. 14 July 1698, fr. Leith to Darien, in *Unicorn*, Edin pr1707 CC8.8.83

2219. Glen, Henry, foremastman, res. Edinburgh, sh. 14 July 1698, fr. Leith to Darien, in *Unicorn*, Edin pr1707 CC8.8.83

2220. Glen, Robert, rioter, res. Ayrshire, tr. May 1726. (SRO.JC13.6)

2221. Glen, William, clergyman, sh. 1707, to Md. (EMA30)

2222. Glendinning, Agnes, res. Edinburgh, tr. 8 May 1663, fr. Leith to Barbados, in *Mary*. (EBR.186.13.4)

2223. Glessen, John, Jacobite, tr. 30 Mar 1716, fr. Liverpool to Antigua, in *Scipio*. (SPC.1716.310)

2224. Glessen, John, Jacobite, tr. 5 May 1747, fr. Liverpool to Va, in *Gildart*, arr. Port North Potomac Md 5 Aug 1747. (P.2.232)(PRO.T1.328)

2225. Glindenning, John, Jacobite, tr. 29 June 1716, fr. Liverpool to Jamaica or Va, in *Elizabeth & Anne*, arr. Va. (SPC.1716.310)(CTB31.208)(VSP.1.185)
2226. Glover, James, merchant, sh. 2 Dec 1682, fr. Port Glasgow to Va, in *Supply of Chester*. (SRO.E72.19.8)
2227. Goff, John, Jacobite, res. Ireland, tr. 1747. (MR137)
2228. Goldie, James, b. 1750, ship's carpenter, res. Ayrshire, sh. Mar 1775, fr. Glasgow to Quebec, in *Friendship*. (PRO.T47.12)
2229. Goldie, William, d. 1736 Carolina, PCC pr1736
2230. Goldie, William, b. 1736, husbandman, sh. Dec 1774, fr. London to Va, in *Carolina*. (PRO.T47.9\11)
2231. Gollan, Donald, Jacobite, res. Avoch Ross-shire, tr. 1747. (P.2.232)
2232. Goodbrand, Alexander, b. 1717, carpenter, Jacobite, res. Banff, tr. 5 May 1747, fr. Liverpool to Leeward Islands, in *Veteran*, arr. Martinique June 1747. (P.2.232)(JAB.2.428)(PRO.SP36.102)
2233. Goodwilly, David, res. Cupar Fife, tr. Apr 1752. (SRO.B59.26.11.5.13)
2234. Goodwin, Robert, Covenanter, res. Glasgow, tr. Sept 1685, fr. Leith to East N.J., in *Henry & Francis*. (PC.11.155)
2235. Gordon, ..., res. Highlands, sh. 1734, sett. S.C. (SPC.41.320)
2236. Gordon, Adam, b. 1738, laborer, res. Barwhinnoch Twynholm Kirkcudbrightshire, sh. May 1774, fr. Kirkcudbright to N.Y., in *Adventure*, m. Ann Bryce, ch. Hugh Agnes Mary. (PRO.T47.12)
2237. Gordon, Adam, b. 1757, farmer, res. Aberdeen, sh. May 1775, fr. Leith to Philadelphia, in *Friendship*. (PRO.T47.12)
2238. Gordon, Agnes, res. Edinburgh, tr. 8 May 1663, fr. Leith to Barbados, in *Mary*. (EBR.186.13.4)
2239. Gordon, Agnes, b. 1754, res. Queenshill, sh. May 1774, fr. Stranraer to N.Y., in *Gale*. (PRO.T47.12)
2240. Gordon, Alexander, farmer, Jacobite, res. Cushnie Aberdeenshire, tr. 24 May 1716, fr. Liverpool to Va or Md, in *Friendship*, arr. Md Aug 1716. (SPC.1716.311)(JAB.1.151)(HM386)
2241. Gordon, Alexander, thief, res. Kirkton of Cabrach Aberdeenshire, tr. July 1768, fr. Glasgow. (AJ1061\72)
2242. Gordon, Alexander, merchant, sh. 1754, sett. Boston Mass. (SRO.AC.GMB.46\101)
2243. Gordon, Alexander, planter, res. Methil Fife, pts. John & Jean Gordon, sh. pre 1780, sett. Jamaica, ch. Lewis, d. 1782 Jamaica, Edin pr1783 CC8.8.126. (SRO.RD2.234.1086)
2244. Gordon, Alexander, surgeon edu. Marischal Col Aberdeen 1749, sett. West Indies. (MCA.2.117)
2245. Gordon, Alexander, sh. 29 Nov 1773, fr. Greenock to Jamaica, in *Mary of Glasgow*. (SRO.CE60.1.7)
2246. Gordon, Alexander, b. 1692, edu. Marischal Col Aberdeen, d. 1754 S.C. (VI.113)

2247. Gordon, Alexander, b. 1738, customs collector, res. King's Grange Dumfries-shire, sh. pre 1773, sett. Montserrat, d. 16 June 1790, bd. St Anthony Montserrat. (MWI43)(SRO.RS .21.406)

2248. Gordon, Annabell, Covenanter, tr. Sept 1685, fr. Leith to East N.J., in *Henry & Francis*. (PC.11.154)

2249. Gordon, Anthony, planter, sh. pre 1772, sett. Dominica. (SRO.RD3.231.898)

2250. Gordon, Arthur, saddler, res. Fochabers Morayshire, pts. Robert Gordon, sh. pre 1771, sett. Matthew Brae St James Jamaica. (SRO.RS29.8.179)

2251. Gordon, Bessie, Covenanter, tr. Sept 1685, fr. Leith to East N.J., in *Henry & Francis*. (PC.11.164)

2252. Gordon, Charles, res. Straloch Aberdeenshire, sh. 1684, sett. Woodbridge N.J. (Insh255)

2253. Gordon, Charles, merchant, d. 1755 Jamaica. (SM.17.514)

2254. Gordon, Charles, b. 30 Aug 1719, Aberdeen, merchant, res. Aberdeen, pts. Charles Gordon & Jean Udny, sett. Jamaica. (SAA203)

2255. Gordon, Charles, b. 1730, Jacobite, res. Binhall Aberdeenshire, pts. Patrick Gordon, tr. 1747, to Md. (P.2.234)

2256. Gordon, Christian, vagrant & thief, res. Banff, tr. June 1773, fr. Glasgow. (AJ1322\3\8)

2257. Gordon, Elizabeth, whore & thief, res. Edinburgh, tr. 28 Nov 1704, fr. Leith to Md. (SRO.PC2.28.307)

2258. Gordon, Francis, merchant, res. Earlston Kirkcudbrightshire, pts. Sir Thomas Gordon, sett. Yeocomico Va, d. pre 1770 Va, Edin pr1770 CC8.8.121

2259. Gordon, George, physician, Jacobite, res. Glenbucket Aberdeenshire, pts. John Gordon, sett. Jamaica, d. Jamaica. (JAB.2.220)

2260. Gordon, George, forger, res. Aberdeenshire, tr. 5 Feb 1752, fr. Aberdeen to Va, in *Planter*. (SM.14.509)(AJ265)

2261. Gordon, George, merchant & planter, res. Ashkirk Roxburghshire, pts. Rev Charles Gordon, sett. Md, d. pre 1748 Md. (APB.3.139)

2262. Gordon, George, res. Auchanachy Cairnie Aberdeenshire, sh. pre 1772, sett. Jamaica, ch. Elizabeth. (SRO.SH.15.8.1772)

2263. Gordon, George, res. Knockspock Clatt Aberdeenshire, pts. George Gordon & Jean Leith, sett. Hanover Jamaica, ch. Mary, d. pre 1781 Jamaica, Edin pr1781 CC8.8.125

2264. Gordon, George, housebreaker, res. New Deer Aberdeenshire, tr. May 1766, fr. Aberdeen. (AJ958\964) (alias 7022)

2265. Gordon, George, merchant, sh. Aug 1685, fr. Leith to N.J., in *America*. (SRO.E72.15.32)

2266. Gordon, Gilbert, b. 1652, gentleman, sh. 1 Feb 1682, fr. London to Barbados, in *Hopewell*. (CLRO\AIA)

2267. Gordon, Hugh, b. 1753, yeoman, sh. Sept 1775, fr. Newcastle to Ga, in *Georgia Packet*, sett. Friendsborough Ga. (PRO.T47.9\11)
2268. Gordon, James, quartermaster, sh. 14 July 1698, fr. Leith to Darien, in *St Andrew*, Edin pr1707 CC8.8.83
2269. Gordon, James, sailor, sh. 14 July 1698, fr. Leith to Darien, in *Unicorn*, Edin pr1707 CC8.8.83
2270. Gordon, James, horsethief, res. Ordrettan Aberdeenshire, tr. May 1769. (AJ1115)
2271. Gordon, James, soldier, thief, tr. Oct 1764. (AJ878) (alias 2414)
2272. Gordon, James, merchant, d. 1770 St Kitts. (Clatt Gs)
2273. Gordon, James, res. Carnousie Banffshire, pts. Arthur Gordon, sh. pre 1744, sett. King & Queen Co Va. (SRO.RH15)
2274. Gordon, James, judge, res. Aberdeenshire, sh. pre 1768, sett. Grenada. (SRO.SH.7.3.1770) (alias 540)
2275. Gordon, James, b. 1719, Jacobite, res. Birkenbush Cullen Banffshire, tr. 1747, fr. London. (P.2.236)(MR132)
2276. Gordon, James jr, b. 1732, mahogony cutter, Jacobite, res. Terpersie Aberdeenshire, pts. James Gordon, sh. 1748, sett. Jamaica. (JAB.2.219)
2277. Gordon, Jean, thief, res. Jedburgh Roxburghshire, tr. May 1732. (SRO.JC12.4)
2278. Gordon, Joan, res. Edinburgh, tr. 1696, fr. Newhaven to Va. (SRO.RH15.14.58)
2279. Gordon, John, merchant, sh. pre 1771, sett. Va & N.C. (SRA.B10.15.8270)
2280. Gordon, John, horsethief, res. Aberdeen, tr. Sept 1767. (SM.29.498)(SRO.RH2.4.255)
2281. Gordon, John, tailor, rioter, res. Dumfries, tr. Dec 1760. (SRO.JC27)
2282. Gordon, John, res. Aberdeen, pts. George Gordon, sh. pre 1772, sett. Portland Surrey Jamaica. (SRO.SH.18.6.1772)
2283. Gordon, John, physician, sh. pre 1776, sett. Greencastle Jamaica, ch. Robert. (SRO.SH.23.8.1776)
2284. Gordon, John, clergyman, res. Aberdeenshire, sh. pre 1705, sett. Wilmington James City Va. (SCM.5.366)
2285. Gordon, John, b. 1706, gardener, res. Raise of Huntly Aberdeenshire, sh. Feb 1730, fr. London to Jamaica. (CLRO\AIA)
2286. Gordon, John, b. 1710, barber & periwig-maker, sh. Mar 1727, fr. London to Jamaica. (CLRO\AIA)
2287. Gordon, John, b. 1728, weaver, Jacobite, res. Loynavere Elgin Morayshire, tr. 5 May 1747, fr. Liverpool to Leeward Islands, in *Veteran*, arr. Martinique June 1747. (P.2.238)(MR123)(PRO.SP36.102)
2288. Gordon, Margaret, Covenanter, res. Arioland Wigtonshire, tr. Oct 1684. (PC.10.612)

110

2289. Gordon, Margaret, b. 1747, spinner, res. Edinburgh, sh. Oct 1774, fr. Kirkcaldy to Antigua, in *Jamaica Packet*. (PRO.T47.12)
2290. Gordon, Patrick, clergyman edu. Marischal Col Aberdeen 1658, res. Coull Aberdeenshire, pts. Patrick Alexander Gordon, sh. 28 Apr 1702, fr. Cowes to N.Y., d. July 1703 Jamaica Long Island N.Y. (SCHR.14.145)(EMA30)(SNQ.2.60)
2291. Gordon, Robert, sh. 1684, fr. Leith to Carolina. (PC.9.95)
2292. Gordon, Robert, sh. 1684, sett. Elizabethtown N.J. (Insh251)
2293. Gordon, Roderick, surgeon, res. Carnousie Banffshire, sh. 1728, to Va. (SRO.GD24)
2294. Gordon, Thomas, sh. 1684, to East N.J., sett. Perth Amboy & Elizabethtown N.J. (Insh264)
2295. Gordon, Thomas, judge, sett. Port Royal Jamaica, d. 3 Aug 1771 Kingston Jamaica. (SM.33.558)
2296. Gordon, Thomas, watchmaker, res. Garmouth Morayshire, pts. James Gordon, sh. pre 1770, sett. N.Y. (SRO.SH.18.5.1770)
2297. Gordon, Thomas, b. 1689, farmer, Jacobite, res. Strathbogie Aberdeenshire, tr. 31 Mar 1747, fr. London to Jamaica or Barbados. (P.2.242)(MR127)
2298. Gordon, Thomas, b. 1751, bleacher, res. Edinburgh, sh. Mar 1774, fr. London to Md, in *Speedwell*. (PRO.T47.9\11)
2299. Gordon, Thomas, b. 1756, book-keeper, res. Aberdeen, sh. Dec 1773, fr. London to Jamaica, in *Charming Nancy*. (PRO.T47.9\11)
2300. Gordon, Walter, overseer, res. Kirkcudbrightshire, sett. Airy Castle Plantation Jamaica, d. 1782 at sea, Edin pr1785 CC8.8.126
2301. Gordon, William, clergyman, sh. 1699, to Barbados. (EMA30)
2302. Gordon, William, clergyman, sh. 1767, to W Fla, sett. Va & Exuma Bahamas. (EMA30)
2303. Gordon, William, thief, res. Aberdeenshire, tr. May 1765. (AJ905)
2304. Gordon, William, thief, res. Aberdeenshire, tr. 5 Oct 1753, fr. Aberdeen to Va, in *Fanny & Betty*. (AJ300\23)
2305. Gordon, William, res. Aberdeenshire, tr. 12 Mar 1754, fr. Aberdeen, in *Fanny & Betty*. (ABR.Deeds.1754)
2306. Gordon, William, d. June 1766 Montego Bay Jamaica. (SM.28.446)
2307. Gordon, William, res. Peterhead Aberdeenshire, pts. Dr Thomas Gordon, d. pre 1783 Jamaica, Edin pr1783 CC8.8.126
2308. Gordon, William, b. 1714, farmer, res. Wynmore Clyne Sutherland, sh. Apr 1774, to Wilmington N.C., in *Bachelor of Leith*, ch. John & Alexander. (PRO.T47.12)
2309. Gordon, William, b. 1750, merchant, res. Aberdeen, sh. July 1775, fr. Greenock to Ga, in *Georgia*. (PRO.T47.12)
2310. Gordon, William, b. 1752, laborer, res. Twynholm Kirkcudbrightshire, sh. May 1774, fr. Kirkcudbright to N.Y., in *Adventure*. (PRO.T47.12)

2311. Gortie, George, Jacobite, tr. 30 Mar 1716, fr. Liverpool to Antigua, in *Scipio*. (CTB31.204)
2312. Gouk, David, b. 16 June 1723, Farnell Angus, servant, Jacobite, res. Montrose Angus, pts. John Gouk & Margaret Comb, tr. 31 Mar 1747, fr. London to Barbados, in *Frere*. (P.2.232)(MR101)
2313. Gourdon, John, schoolmaster, sh. 1700, to Barbados. (EMA30)
2314. Gourlay, James, clergyman edu. Glasgow Uni 1746-1754, res. St Ninians Stirlingshire, pts. Archibald Gourlay of Birkhill, sh. 1773. (MAGU34)
2315. Gousse, Capraise, servant, assault, res. Nelfield Edinburgh, tr. Dec 1765. (SRO.HCR.I.97)
2316. Govan, Christian, res. Glasgow, sh. pre 1777, sett. Charleston S.C., m. James Grindlay, ch. John, d. pre 1777, Glas pr1777 CC9.7.70 (alias 2532)
2317. Govan, John, tr. Nov 1679, fr. Leith. (ETR162)
2318. Govan, Thomas, servant, Covenanter, res. Craigprie, tr. 12 Dec 1678, fr. Leith to West Indies, in *St Michael of Scarborough*. (PC.6.76)
2319. Govan, William, servant, Covenanter, res. Puncheonlaw, tr. 12 Dec 1678, fr. Leith to West Indies, in *St Michael of Scarborough*. (PC.6.76)
2320. Gow, Donald, sheepstealer, tr. May 1753. (SM.15.261)
2321. Gowan, Donald, b. 1707, farmer, Jacobite, res. Aich Ross-shire, tr. 31 Mar 1747, fr. London to Barbados, in *Frere*. (P.2.244)(MR81)
2322. Gower, George, workman, Jacobite, res. Alyth Perthshire, tr. 1747. (P.2.244)
2323. Graeme, Janet, res. Aberfoyle Perthshire, tr. May 1770, fr. Port Glasgow, in *Crawford*, arr. Port Oxford Md 23 July 1771. (SRO.JC27.10.3)(AJ1170) (alias 5381)
2324. Graeme, Thomas, soldier, sh. pre 1765, sett. N.Y. (PCCol.4.818)
2325. Graeme, William, attorney, d. 29 July 1770 Savannah Ga. (SM.32.458)
2326. Graham, Alexander, Covenanter, tr. Aug 1685, fr. Leith to East N.J. (PC.11.136)
2327. Graham, Andrew, factor, sh. pre1770, sett. New Severn Hudson Bay, m. Patricia Shearer. (SRO.RD2.216.766)
2328. Graham, Charles, Jacobite, res. Tain Ross & Cromarty, tr. 31 Mar 1747. (P.2.246)
2329. Graham, Charles, b. 1725, Jacobite, res. Airth Stirlingshire, pts. John Graham, tr. 20 Mar 1747. (P.2.246)(MR152)
2330. Graham, David, Jacobite, tr. 28 July 1716, fr. Liverpool to Va, in *Godspeed*, arr. Md Oct 1716. (SPC.1716.310)(CTB31.209)(HM388)
2331. Graham, Duncan, merchant, res. Perthshire, sh. pre 1764, sett. Caroline Co Va. (SRO.RD2.197.470)

2332. Graham, Fergus, Jacobite, tr. 29 June 1716, fr. Liverpool to Jamaica or Va, in *Elizabeth & Anne*, arr. York Va. (SPC.1716.310)(CTB31.208)(VSP.1.185)
2333. Graham, Henry, b. 1749, yeoman, sh. Sept 1775, fr. Newcastle to Ga, in *Georgia Packet*. (PRO.T47.9\11)
2334. Graham, Hugh, res. Westhall Dunsyre Lanarkshire, pts. Anne Graham, sh. pre 1727, sett. Philadelphia, PCC pr1727
2335. Graham, Ivor, Covenanter, res. Innerneil Argyll, tr. Aug 1685, fr. Leith to Jamaica. (PC.11.329)
2336. Graham, James, midshipman, res. Edinburgh, pts. Patrick Graham, sh. 14 July 1698, fr. Leith to Darien, in *St Andrew*, Edin pr1707 CC8.8.83
2337. Graham, James, Jacobite, tr. 31 July 1716, fr. Liverpool to Va, in *Anne*. (SPC.1716.310)((CTB31.209)
2338. Graham, James, merchant & Indian trader, sett. Savannah Ga, m. Sally Stuart 1767. (SM.29.557)
2339. Graham, John, mariner, res. Burntisland Fife, pts. Euphan Watson or Graham, sh. 14 July 1698, fr. Leith to Darien, in *Endeavour*, Edin pr1707 CC8.8.83
2340. Graham, John, tailor, res. Glasgow, pts. Jean Luke or Graham, sh. pre 1756, sett. Albemarle Co Va. (SRA.B10.15.6950)
2341. Graham, John, merchant, res. Whitekirk Dunbar East Lothian, pts. Alexander Pyot or Graham, sh. pre 1756, sett. Savannah Ga. (SRO.GD105)
2342. Graham, John, tailor, res. Glasgow, pts. Robert Graham & Jean Luke, sh. pre 1765, sett. Albemarle Co Va. (SRA.CFI)
2343. Graham, John, b. 1749, farmer, res. Stirling, sh. May 1774, fr. Greenock to N.Y., in *Matty*. (PRO.T47.12)
2344. Graham, John, b. 1752, tailor, res. Glasgow, sh. Apr 1775, fr. Greenock to N.Y., in *Lilly*. (PRO.T47.12)
2345. Graham, John jr, res. Ledlevan, tr. 12 Dec 1678, fr. Leith to West Indies, in *St Michael of Scarborough*. (PC.6.76)
2346. Graham, Patrick, apothecary, res. Crieff Perthshire, sh. pre 1736, to Ga. (PRO.CO5.670.284)
2347. Graham, Peggy, b. 1754, servant, res. Caithness, sh. May 1775, fr. Leith to Philadelphia, in *Friendship*. (PRO.T47.12)
2348. Graham, Rev, clergyman, sh. 1773, to Md. (EMA30)
2349. Graham, Robert, res. Argyll, d. Nov 1780 Dominica, Edin pr1808 CC8.8.137
2350. Graham, Robert, b. 1730, res. Fintry Stirlingshire, sh. Mar 1750, fr. London to Md. (CLRO\AIA)
2351. Graham, Samuel, tr. Aug 1685. (PC.11.126)(ETR368)
2352. Graham, Thomas, Covenanter, res. Skirling Peebles-shire, tr. Sept 1685, fr. Leith to East N.J., in *Henry & Francis*. (PC.11.173)

113

2353. Graham, William, Covenanter, res. Linlithgow West Lothian, tr. 2 May 1684, fr. Glasgow. (PC.8

2354. Graham, William, tr. Dec 1685, fr. Leith to Barbados, in *John & Nicholas.* (ETR390)

2355. Graham, William, b. 1750, laborer, res. Drysdale Dumfries-shire, sh. May 1775, fr. Dumfries to P.E.I., in *Lovely Nelly.* (PRO.T47.12)

2356. Grahame, George, thief, res. Blackserk Edinburgh, tr. 1670, in *Merchant of Glasgow.* (PC.3.679)

2357. Grahame, Harry, res. Breckness, sh. 1668, sett. Va. (SRO.GD217)

2358. Grahame, Isabel, b. 1757, servant, res. Stornaway Isle of Lewis, sh. Nov 1774, fr. Stornaway to N.Y., in *Peace & Plenty.* (PRO.T47.12)

2359. Grahame, James, sh. 1668, sett. Va. (SRO.GD217)

2360. Grahame, James, b. 1728, housewright, pts. Rev Andrew Grahame & Christian Flett, sett. Boston Mass. (F.7.236)

2361. Grahame, John, planter, res. Islay Argyll, sh. pre 1776, sett. Caymanas Jamaica. (SRO.RS10.11.223)

2362. Grahame, Margaret, b. 1756, servant, res. Stornaway Isle of Lewis, sh. Nov 1774, fr. Stornaway to N.Y., in *Peace & Plenty.* (PRO.T47.12)

2363. Grahame, Peter, overseer, res. Stirlingshire, d. Sept 1755 Windsor Plantation Jamaica, Edin pr1776 CC8.8.123)

2364. Grainger, James, physician edu. Edinburgh Uni, sh. pre 1763, sett. St Kitts. (SRO.NRAS726.6)

2365. Grainger, Margaret, tr. 1771, fr. Port Glasgow, in *Polly,* arr. Port Oxford Md 16 Sept 1771. (SRO.JC27.10.3)

2366. Grant, Alexander, clergyman, sh. 1748, to Antigua. (EMA30)

2367. Grant, Alexander, b. 1690, farmer, Jacobite, res. Dalcataig Glenmoriston Inverness-shire, tr. 20 Mar 1747, fr. London to Barbados, in *Frere.* (P.2.250)(MR152)

2368. Grant, Alexander, b. 1692, farmer, Jacobite, res. Wester Innerwick Glenmoriston Inverness-shire, tr. 31 Mar 1747, fr. London to Barbados, in *Frere.* (P.2.248)(MR152)

2369. Grant, Alexander, b. 1699, boatman, Jacobite, res. West Innerwick Glenmoriston Inverness-shire, tr. 29 Mar 1747, fr. London to Barbados, in *Frere.* (P.2.248)(MR152)

2370. Grant, Alexander, b. 1712, Jacobite, res. Glenmoriston Inverness-shire, tr. 31 Mar 1747, fr. London to Barbados, in *Frere.* (P.2.250)(MR152)

2371. Grant, Alexander, b. 1716, farmer, Jacobite, res. Glenmoriston Inverness-shire, tr. 31 Mar 1747, fr. London to Barbados, in *Frere.* (P.2.250)(MR152)

2372. Grant, Alexander, b. 1722, carpenter, Jacobite, res. Aberdeen, tr. 5 May 1747, fr. Liverpool to Leeward Islands, in *Veteran,* arr. Martinique June 1747. (P.2.250)(JAB.2.429)(MR127)(PRO.SP36.102)

2373. Grant, Alexander, b. 1733, Glenmoriston Inverness-shire, soldier, res. Glenmoriston, pts. Patrick Grant, sh. 1754, sett. Charlotte Co N.Y., m. Therese Barthe, d. 18 Nov 1813 Gross Point Detroit. (EA.5197.13)(MAA

2374. Grant, Alexander, b. 1745, farmer, res. Strathspey, sh. May 1774, fr. Greenock to N.Y., in *George*. (PRO.T47.12)

2375. Grant, Alexander, b. 1749, farmer, res. Strathspey, sh. May 1774, fr. Greenock to N.Y., in *George*. (PRO.T47.12)

2376. Grant, Alexander, b. 1752, cooper, res. Stirling, sh. Oct 1774, fr. Greenock to Philadelphia, in *Sally*. (PRO.T47.12)

2377. Grant, Alexander, b. 1755, piper, res. Latheron Caithness, sh. Sept 1774, fr. Kirkwall to Savannah Ga, in *Marlborough*, sett. Richmond Co Ga. (PRO.Y47.12)

2378. Grant, Allan, b. 1687, laborer, Jacobite, res. Strathspey, tr. 5 May 1747, fr. Liverpool, in *Johnson*, arr. Port Oxford Md 5 Aug 1747. (P.2.250)(MR206)(PRO.T1.328)

2379. Grant, Allan, b. 1752, farmer, res. Strathspey, sh. May 1774, fr. Greenock to N.Y., in *George*. (PRO.T47.12)

2380. Grant, Andrew, merchant, res. Edinburgh, sh. 1733, sett. Ogychee Ga. (PRO.CO5.670.108)(SRO.RD2.171.33)

2381. Grant, Andrew, res. Elchies Craigellachie Morayshire, pts. Patrick Grant, d. 27 Nov 1779 Grenada. (SM.42.109)

2382. Grant, Angus, b. 1693, farmer, Jacobite, res. Wester Dundreggan Glenmoriston Inverness-shire, tr. 31 Mar 1747, fr. Tilbury. (P.2.250)

2383. Grant, Angus, b. 1697, farmer, Jacobite, res. Glenmoriston Inverness-shire, tr. 31 Mar 1747, fr. London to Barbados, in *Frere*. (P.2.250)

2384. Grant, Angus, b. 1716, farmer, Jacobite, res. Glenmoriston Inverness-shire, tr. 30 Mar 1747, fr. London to Barbados, in *Frere*. (P.2.250)

2385. Grant, Angus, b. 1725, laborer, Jacobite, res. Glengarry Inverness-shire, tr. 5 May 1747, fr. Liverpool to Va, in *Johnson*, arr. Port Oxford Md 5 Aug 1747. (P.2.250)(MR152)(PRO.T1.328)

2386. Grant, Ann, b. 1756, res. Strathspey, sh. May 1774, fr. Greenock to N.Y., in *George*. (PRO.T47.12)

2387. Grant, Archibald, b. 1707, farmer, Jacobite, res. Glen Urquhart Inverness-shire, tr. 31 Mar 1747, fr. London to Barbados, in *Frere*. (P.2.250)(MR72)

2388. Grant, Betty, tr. Mar 1751, fr. Aberdeen to Va or West Indies, in *Adventure of Aberdeen*. (AJ170)

2389. Grant, Charles, land laborer, thief & housebreaker, tr. 1773, fr. Port Glasgow, in *Phoenix*, arr. Port Accomack Va 20 Dec 1773. (SRO.JC27.10.3)

115

2390. Grant, Charles, b. 1728, miller, Jacobite, res. Abernethy Inverness-shire, tr. 5 May 1747, fr. Liverpool to Leeward Islands, in *Veteran*, arr. Martinique June 1747. (P.2.252)(MR206)(PRO.SP36.102)
2391. Grant, Daniel, Jacobite, tr. 28 July 1716, fr. Liverpool to Va, in *Godspeed*, arr. Md Oct 1716. (SPC.1716.310)(CTB31.209)(HM389)
2392. Grant, David, b. 1728, farmer, res. Strathspey, sh. May 1774, fr. Greenock to N.Y., in *George*. (PRO.T47.12)
2393. Grant, Donald, b. 1685, farmer, Jacobite, res. Glenmoriston Inverness-shire, tr. 20 Mar 1747, fr. Tilbury. (P.2.252)(MR152)
2394. Grant, Donald, b. 1687, Jacobite, res. Blairy Glenmoriston Inverness-shire, tr. 19 Mar 1747, fr. Tilbury to Barbados, in *Frere*. (P.2.252)(MR152)
2395. Grant, Donald, b. 1689, farmer, Jacobite, res. Glenmoriston Inverness-shire, tr. 31 Mar 1747, fr. London to Barbados, in *Frere*. (P.2.254)(MR152)
2396. Grant, Donald, b. 1707, farmer, Jacobite, res. Glenmoriston Inverness-shire, tr. 31 Mar 1747, fr. Tilbury. (P.2.254)
2397. Grant, Donald, b. 1707, farmer, Jacobite, res. Wester Dundreggan Glenmoriston Inverness-shire, tr. 31 Mar 1747, fr. London to Barbados, in *Frere*. (P.2.254)(MR152)
2398. Grant, Donald, b. 1711, farmer, Jacobite, res. Balnagarn Glenmoriston Inverness-shire, tr. 31 Mar 1747, fr. London to Barbados, in *Frere*. (P.2.252)(MR152)
2399. Grant, Donald, b. 1715, farmer, Jacobite, res. Ballintombuy Glenmoriston Inverness-shire, tr. 31 Mar 1747, fr. London to Barbados, in *Frere*. (P.2.254)(MR152)
2400. Grant, Dugal, b. 1697, farmer, Jacobite, res. Glenmoriston Inverness-shire, tr. 31 Mar 1747, fr. London to Barbados, in *Frere*. (P.2.254)(MR154)
2401. Grant, Duncan, b. 1702, farmer, Jacobite, res. Wester Dundreggan Glenmoriston Inverness-shire, tr. 20 Mar 1747, fr. Tilbury. (P.2.254)(MR152)
2402. Grant, Elizabeth, b. 1727, seamstress, Jacobite, res. Banff, tr. 20 Mar 1747. (P.2.254)
2403. Grant, Elspet, sheepstealer, res. Aberdeenshire, tr. 1751, m. William McDonald. (AJ175)
2404. Grant, Farquhar, Jacobite, tr. 31 Mar 1747. (P.2.254)(MR153)
2405. Grant, Farquhar, b. 1704, farmer, Jacobite, res. Glenmoriston Inverness-shire, tr. 20 Mar 1747. (P.2.254)(MR152)
2406. Grant, George, sailor, res. Prestonpans East Lothian, sh. 14 July 1698, fr. Leith to Darien, in *Union*, d. 1699 Darien, Edin pr1707 CC8.8.83

116

2407. Grant, George, b. 1707, farmer, Jacobite, res. Glenmoriston Inverness-shire, tr. 31 Mar 1747, fr. London to Barbados, in *Frere*. (P.2.256)(MR152)
2408. Grant, George, b. 1750, farmer, res. Strathspey, sh. May 1774, fr. Greenock to N.Y., in *George*. (PRO.T47.12)
2409. Grant, George, b. 1754, farmer, res. Aschog Kildonan Sutherland, sh. Apr 1774, to Wilmington N.C., in *Bachelor of Leith*. (PRO.T47.12)
2410. Grant, Gregor Rory, sheepstealer, res. Aberdeenshire, tr. Sept 1755. (AJ403) (alias 3867)
2411. Grant, Hugh, b. 1697, farmer, Jacobite, res. Glenmoriston Inverness-shire, tr. 31 Mar 1747, fr. London to Barbados, in *Frere*. (P.2.256)
2412. Grant, Humphrey, pts. James Grant of Milntown, d. Oct 1771 Jamaica. (SM.34.50)
2413. Grant, James, Governor, res. Ballinvalloch, sh. pre 1771, sett. E Fla. (SRO.RD4.210.541)
2414. Grant, James, soldier, thief, tr. Oct 1764. (AJ878) (alias 2271)
2415. Grant, James, b. 1686, farmer, Jacobite, res. Wester Innerwick Glenmoriston Inverness-shire, tr. 1747, fr. Tilbury. (P.2.258)(MR153)
2416. Grant, James, b. 1697, farmer, Jacobite, res. Blairy Glenmoriston Inverness-shire, tr. 31 Mar 1747, fr. London to Barbados, in *Frere*. (P.2.258)(MR153)
2417. Grant, James, b. 1727, farmer, res. Strathspey, sh. May 1774, fr. Greenock to N.Y., in *George*, m. Ann ..., ch. Janet Ann James Sally Margery Peter. (PRO.T47.12)
2418. Grant, James, b. 1727, farmer, res. Strathspey, sh. May 1774, fr. Greenock to N.Y., in *George*, ch. Swithin Betty Mary Francis. (PRO.T47.12)
2419. Grant, James, b. 1747, farmer, res. Strathspey, sh. May 1774, fr. Greenock to N.Y., in *George*. (PRO.T47.12)
2420. Grant, James, b. 1751, farmer, res. Strathspey, sh. May 1774, fr. Greenock to N.Y., in *George*. (PRO.T47.12)
2421. Grant, Jean, b. 1757, res. Strathspey, sh. May 1774, fr. Greenock to N.Y., in *George*. (PRO.T47.12)
2422. Grant, John, sett. E Fla 1767. (PRO.CO5.542)
2423. Grant, John, Jacobite, res. Glenmoriston Inverness-shire, tr. 1747. (P.2.262)(MR153)
2424. Grant, John, res. Forfar Angus, tr. Aug 1752, fr. Aberdeen to Va, in *St Andrew*. (AJ241)
2425. Grant, John, housebreaker, res. Inverness-shire, tr. Sept 1756. (AJ453) (alias 413)
2426. Grant, John, horsethief, res. Rictian Inverness-shire, tr. May 1768. (AJ1064\1080) (alias 526)

117

2427. Grant, John, merchant & planter, res. Aberdeen, sett. Grenada, d. Dec 1768 Grenada. (APB.4.31)
2428. Grant, John, thief, res. Aberdeenshire, tr. May 1751. (AJ175) (alias 3957)
2429. Grant, John, b. 1692, farmer, Jacobite, res. Glen Urquhart Inverness-shire, tr. 31 Mar 1747, fr. London to Barbados, in *Frere*. (P.2.260)(MR153)
2430. Grant, John, b. 1697, farmer, Jacobite, res. Glenmoriston Inverness-shire, tr. 31 Mar 1747, fr. London to Barbados, in *Frere*. (P.2.260)(MR153)
2431. Grant, John, b. 1702, farmer, Jacobite, res. Glenmoriston Inverness-shire, tr. 31 Mar 1747, fr. London to Barbados, in *Frere*. (P.2.260)(MR153)
2432. Grant, John, b. 1702, farmer, Jacobite, res. Balnagarn Glenmoriston Inverness-shire, tr. 31 Mar 1747, fr. London to Barbados, in *Frere*. (P.2.260)(MR153)
2433. Grant, John, b. 1706, farmer, Jacobite, res. East Achlein Glenmoriston Inverness-shire, tr. 31 Mar 1747, fr. London to Barbados, in *Frere*. (P.2.260)(MR153)
2434. Grant, John, b. 1707, farmer, Jacobite, res. Craskie Glenmoriston Inverness-shire, tr. 31 Mar 1747, fr. London to Barbados , in *Frere*. (P.2.258)(MR153)
2435. Grant, John, b. 1707, farmer, Jacobite, res. Glenmoriston Inverness-shire, tr. 31 Mar 1747, fr. London to Barbados, in *Frere*. (P.2.260)(MR153)
2436. Grant, John, b. 1707, farmer, Jacobite, res. Glenmoriston Inverness-shire, tr. 31 Mar 1747, fr. London to Barbados, in *Frere*. (P.2.260)(MR153)
2437. Grant, John, b. 1707, laborer, Jacobite, res. Badenoch or Lochaber Inverness-shire, tr. 5 May 1747, fr. Liverpool to Leeward Islands, in *Veteran*, arr. Martinique June 1747. (P.2.260)(MR35)(PRP.SP36.102)
2438. Grant, John, b. 1709, farmer, Jacobite, res. Inverwick Glenmoriston Inverness-shire, tr. 31 Mar 1747, fr. London to Barbados, in *Frere*. (P.2.260)(MR153)
2439. Grant, John, b. 1713, weaver, Jacobite, res. Banff, tr. 5 May 1747, fr. Liverpool to Va, in *Johnson*, arr. Port Oxford Md 5 Aug 1747. (P.2.262)(MR206)(PRO.T1.328)
2440. Grant, John, b. 1717, farmer, Jacobite, res. Glenmoriston Inverness-shire, tr. 31 Mar 1747, fr. London to Barbados, in *Frere*. (P.2.260)(MR153)
2441. Grant, John, b. 1721, farmer, Jacobite, res. Glenmoriston Inverness-shire, tr. 31 Mar 1747, fr. London to Barbados, in *Frere*. (P.2.262)(MR153)

2442. Grant, John, b. 1722, farmer, Jacobite, res. Glenmoriston Inverness-shire, tr. 31 Mar 1747, fr. London to Barbados, in *Frere*. (P.2.260)(MR153)
2443. Grant, John, b. 1724, Jacobite, res. Glenmoriston Inverness-shire, tr. 1747, fr. Tilbury. (P.2.262)
2444. Grant, John, b. 1725, Jacobite, res. Glenmoriston Inverness-shire, tr. 31 Mar 1747, fr. London to Barbados, in *Frere*. (P.2.262)(MR153)
2445. Grant, John, b. 1732, farmer, res. Strathspey, sh. May 1774, fr. Greenock to N.Y., in *George*, m. Margery ..., ch. Peter Donald Elizabeth Elspa Nelly Alexander Janet. (PRO.T47.12)
2446. Grant, John, b. 1737, laborer, sh. Feb 1774, fr. London to Ga, in *Mary*. (PRO.T47.9\11)
2447. Grant, John, b. 1755, farmer, res. Strathspey, sh. May 1774, fr. Greenock to N.Y., in *George*. (PRO.T47.12)
2448. Grant, John Dow, horsethief, res. Perthshire, tr. Nov 1764, fr. Greenock to N.J. (SRO.B59.26.11.6.39) (alias 3865)
2449. Grant, Joshua, planter, res. Inverness, pts. Duncan & Anne Grant, sh. pre 1766, sett. Basseterre St Kitts. (SRO.SC29.55.11.33)
2450. Grant, Lewis, b. 1742, farmer, res. Strathspey, sh. May 1774, fr. Greenock to N.Y., in *George*. (PRO.T47.12)
2451. Grant, Margaret, tr. Aug 1756, fr. Aberdeen to Va, in *St Andrew*. (AJ451)
2452. Grant, Margaret, fireraiser, tr. Mar 1758, fr. Aberdeen to Va, in *Leathly*. (AJ507\533)
2453. Grant, Margaret, b. 1760, servant, res. Holm Isle of Lewis, sh. May 1774, fr. Stornaway to Philadelphia, in *Friendship*. (PRO.T47.12)
2454. Grant, Mary, b. 1762, res. Strathspey, sh. May 1774, fr. Greenock to N.Y., in *George*. (PRO.T47.12)
2455. Grant, Mungo, coppersmith, res. Inverness-shire, sh. May 1753, fr. London to Md. (CLRO\AIA)
2456. Grant, Patrick, physician, d. 26 Dec 1770 Antigua. (SM.33.331)
2457. Grant, Patrick, b. 1717, farmer, Jacobite, res. Glenmoriston Inverness-shire, tr. 1747, fr. Tilbury. (P.2.262)(MR153)
2458. Grant, Patrick, b. 1733, book-keeper, res. Edinburgh, sh. Dec 1750, fr. London to Jamaica. (CLRO\AIA)
2459. Grant, Patrick, b. 1745, farmer, res. Strathspey, sh. May 1774, fr. Greenock to N.Y., in *George*. (PRO.T47.12)
2460. Grant, Peter, b. 1697, farmer, Jacobite, res. Tullocherchait Mor Glenmoriston Inverness-shire, tr. 31 Mar 1747, fr. London to Barbados, in *Frere*. (P.2.262)(MR153)
2461. Grant, Peter, b. 1701, Jacobite, res. East Achlein Glenmoriston Inverness-shire, tr. 20 Mar 1747, fr. Tilbury. (P.2.264)(MR153)
2462. Grant, Peter, b. 1723, fiddler, Jacobite, res. Glen Urquhart Inverness-shire, tr. 31 Mar 1747, fr. London to Jamaica , in *St George or Carteret*, arr. Jamaica 1747. (P.2.264)(PRO.CO137.58)

119

2463. Grant, Richard, res. Edinburgh, sh. c1660, fr. Bristol to St Kitts. (BRO.04220)
2464. Grant, Robert, farmer, Jacobite, res. Cushnie Aberdeenshire, tr. 29 June 1716, fr. Liverpool to Jamaica or Va, in *Elizabeth & Anne*, arr. Va. (SPC.1716.310)(JAB.1.151)(CTB31.208)(VSP.186)
2465. Grant, Robert, res. Auchindoir Aberdeenshire, pts. Gregor Grant & Agnes Durward, sh. 1715, to Va, d. pre 1735 Va. (APB.3.39)
2466. Grant, Robert, b. 1727, farmer, res. Strathspey, sh. May 1774, fr. Greenock to N.Y., in *George*, m. Mary ..., ch. Margaret Ellen Alexander Elizabeth Peter Katherine Donald Margaret Elle. (PRO.T47.12)
2467. Grant, Robert, b. 1745, farmer, res. Strathspey, sh. May 1774, fr. Greenock to N.Y., in *George*. (PRO.T47.12)
2468. Grant, Thomas, flesher, res. Edinburgh, sh. 18 Aug 1699, fr. Clyde to Darien, in *Rising Sun*, Edin pr1707 CC8.8.83
2469. Grant, Violet, res. Kilmalcolm Renfrewshire, sh. Oct 1774, fr. Greenock to Philadelphia, in *Sally*. (PRO.T47.12)
2470. Grant, Walter, physician & surgeon edu. Marischal Col Aberdeen 1738, sett. Jamaica. (MCA.2.315)
2471. Grant, Walter, b. 1707, Teviotdale, barber, Jacobite, res. Edinburgh, tr. 20 Mar 1747, fr. London to Jamaica , in *St George or Carteret*, arr. Jamaica 1747. (P.2.264)(MR44)(PRO.CO137.58)
2472. Grant, William, Jacobite, res. Carnach Argyll, tr. 1747. (MR153)
2473. Grant, William, farmer, res. Urquhart Inverness-shire, sh. July 1774, fr. Mull to N.Y., in *Moore of Greenock*. (SM.36.445)
2474. Grant, William, dyer, rioter, res. Waulkmill of Tolabeg Aberdeenshire, tr. May 1767. (SM.29.325)
2475. Grant, William, Jacobite, tr. 24 May 1716, fr. Liverpool, in *Friendship*, arr. Md Aug 1716. (SPC.1716.311)(HM386)
2476. Grant, William, schoolmaster, forger, res. Buckie Banffshire, tr. Mar 1758. (SRO.HCR.I.90) (alias 3814)
2477. Grant, William, b. 1699, linen weaver, Jacobite, res. Aberdeen, tr. 5 May 1747, fr. Liverpool to Va, in *Gildart*, arr. Port North Potomac Md 5 Aug 1747. (P.2.264)(MR127)(PRO.T1.328)
2478. Grant, William, b. 1702, Jacobite, res. Inverness, tr. 1747. (MR206)(P.2.264)
2479. Grant, William, b. 1722, farmer, res. Strathspey, sh. May 1774, fr. Greenock to N.Y., in *George*, m. Ann ..., ch. Barbara William Peter Peter Ann Margery Janet John Robert. (PRO.T47.12)
2480. Grant, William, b. 1750, groom, sh. Mar 1774, fr. London to Va, in *Brilliant*. (PRO.T47.9\11)
2481. Grapes, Henry, trumpeter, d. 5 Nov 1698 Darien. (NLS.RY.2b8\19)
2482. Gray, Daniel, b. 1743, farmer, res. Breadalbane Perthshire, sh. May 1775, fr. Greenock to N.Y., in *Lilly*. (PRO.T47.12)

2483. Gray, George, tailor, forger, res. Kirkness Kinross-shire, tr. 1743.
(SRO.HCR.I.70)
2484. Gray, Isabel, b. 1749, farm servant, res. Coiduch, sh. Nov 1774, fr.
Stornaway to N.Y., in *Peace & Plenty*. (PRO.T47.12)
2485. Gray, James, merchant, res. Aberdeen, sh. Feb 1748, fr. Aberdeen to Va.
(AJ.2)
2486. Gray, James, tr. 7 Dec 1665, fr. Leith to Barbados. (ETR104)
2487. Gray, James, tr. Nov 1679, fr. Leith. (ETR162)
2488. Gray, James, Covenanter, tr. Aug 1685, fr. Leith to Jamaica, arr. Port
Royal Jamaica Nov 1685. (PC.11.330)(ETR369)(LJ17)
2489. Gray, James, res. Leith Midlothian, tr. July 1737. (SRO.JC27)
2490. Gray, James, res. Aberdeen, pts. James Gray, d. 1769 Grenada.
(APB.4.45)
2491. Gray, James, b. 1753, blacksmith, res. Argyll, sh. Aug 1774, fr.
Greenock to Philadelphia, in *Magdalene*. (PRO.T47.12)
2492. Gray, Janet, whore, res. Edinburgh, tr. Mar 1695. (SRO.PC2.25.216)
2493. Gray, John, merchant edu. Glasgow Uni 1736, res. Glasgow, pts. John
Gray, sh. 1748, sett. Port Royal Caroline Co Va, d. 3 May 1787
Port Royal Va. (MAGU17)(PRO.AO13.30.398\424)
2494. Gray, John, Jacobite, res. Keith Banffshire, tr. 5 May 1747, fr. Liverpool
to Va, in *Gildart*, arr. Port North Potomac Md 5 Aug 1747.
(P.2.266)(JAB.2.430)(MR123)(PRO.T1.328)
2495. Gray, John, vagabond & robber, res. Annandale Dumfries-shire, tr.
1671(?). (PC.3.428)
2496. Gray, John, soldier, res. Creich Fife, sh. pre 1770, sett. Ga, PCC pr1770
2497. Gray, John, b. 1701, clerk & writer, res. Edinburgh, sh. Aug 1728, fr.
London to Antigua. (CLRO\AIA)
2498. Gray, John, b. 1725, weaver, Jacobite, res. Liff Angus, tr. 5 May 1747,
fr. Liverpool, in *Johnson*, arr. Port Oxford Md 5 Aug 1747.
(P.2.266)(MR102)(PRO.T1.328)
2499. Gray, Mary, whore & thief, res. Edinburgh, tr. 28 Nov 1704, fr. Leith to
Md. (SRO.PC2.28.307)
2500. Gray, Robert, res. Helmsdale Sutherland, pts. Hugh Gray, sh. pre 1772,
sett. Jamaica. (SRO.SH.9.12.1772)
2501. Gray, Thomas, tr. July 1751. (AJ187)
2502. Gray, Thomas, merchant, res. Glasgow, sh. pre 1766, sett. Boston Mass.
(SRA.B10.15.7234)
2503. Gray, William, attorney, res. Easter Larg Inverness-shire, pts. Patrick
Gray, sh. pre 1769, sett. Kingston Jamaica. (SRO.RS38.12.269)
2504. Gray, William, provost marshal, res. Caithness, sh. pre 1776, sett. Iter
Boreale Jamaica. (SRO.RS21.3.436)(SRO.RD4.233.1221)
2505. Gray, William, soldier, thief & housebraker, tr. 1772, fr. Port Glasgow,
in *Phoenix*, arr. Port Accomack Va 20 Dec 1772.
(AJ1293)(SRO.JC27.10.3)

2506. Gray, William, res. Edinburgh, tr. 1696, fr. Newhaven to Va. (SRO.RH15.14.58)
2507. Greenhill, William, gardener, Jacobite, res. Lethendy Perthshire, tr. 1747. (P.2.268)(MR102)
2508. Greenlees, John, b. 1749, farmer, res. Kintyre Argyll, sh. Aug 1774, fr. Greenock to Wilmington N.C., in *Ulysses*, m. Mary Howie. (PRO.T47.12)
2509. Greenlees, Peter, robber, tr. Apr 1754, fr. Leith to Va. (AJ326)
2510. Greg, Thomas, clergyman edu. St Andrews Uni, res. St Andrews Fife, pts. William Greg, sh. 1699, to Darien, d. West Indies, Edin pr1707 CC8.8.83
2511. Gregg, James, clergyman edu. King's Col Aberdeen 1697, sh. 1710, to St Kitts. (EMA31)
2512. Greig, Alexander, surgeon & physician, res. Perth, pts. Andrew Greig, d. pre 1778 Jamaica, Edin pr1778 CC8.8.124
2513. Greig, Jenny, b. 1751, res. Edinburgh, sh. May 1775, fr. Leith to Philadelphia, in *Friendship*. (PRO.T47.12)
2514. Greig, John, clergyman, sh. 1766(?), sett. Pa. (UPC655)
2515. Greig, Mary, cattlethief, res. Duns Berwickshire, tr. Sept 1768. (AJ1079)
2516. Greive, William, Covenanter, res. Linlithgow West Lothian, tr. June 1684, fr. Leith to Carolina. (PC.8.526)
2517. Grewer, George, laborer, Jacobite, res. GlenIsla Angus, tr. 22 Apr 1747, fr. Liverpool. (P.2.268)(MR102)
2518. Grier, Fergus, Covenanter, res. Dalry, tr. Sept 1685, fr. Leith to East N.J., in *Henry & Francis*. (PC.11.154)
2519. Grier, James, Covenanter, res. Dalry, tr. Sept 1685, fr. Leith, arr. Port Royal Jamaica Nov 1685. (PC.11.153)(LJ17)
2520. Grier, John, Covenanter, res. Brigmark Kirkcudbright, tr. Oct 1684. (PC.10.258)
2521. Grier, Robert, Covenanter, res. Lochenkitt, tr. Sept 1668, fr. Leith to Va, in *Convertin*. (PC.2.534)
2522. Grier, Thomas, Covenanter, res. Cormilligan Closburn Dumfries-shire, tr. Oct 1684. (PC.10.587)
2523. Grierson, James, sh. pre 1773, sett. Augusta Ga, ch. James Thomas David Katherine George, d. Ga, PCC pr1789
2524. Grierson, William, b. post 1712, res. Tingwall Shetland Islands, pts. Rev James Grierson & Elizabeth McPherson, d. 1765 West Indies. (F.7.291)
2525. Grierson, William, b. 1751, smith, res. Galloway, sh. May 1775, fr. Greenock to Philadelphia, in *Sally*. (PRO.T47.12)
2526. Grieve, Ann, b. 1758, res. Edinburgh, sh. Apr 1775, fr. Greenock to N.Y., in *Lilly*. (PRO.T47.12)
2527. Grieve, David, planter, res. Dundee Angus, sh. pre 1766, sett. New Pera St Thomas in the East Jamaica. (TRA.DRD.28.274)

2528. Grieve, Joseph, b. 1739, weaver, res. New Abbey Kirkcudbrightshire, sh. May 1775, fr. Dumfries to P.E.I., in *Lovely Nelly*, m. Marion Buckley, ch. John Robert Mary. (PRO.T47.12)

2529. Grieve, Walter, thief, res. Jedburgh Roxburghshire, tr. May 1726. (SRO.JC27.12.4)

2530. Grieve, William, sailor, res. Leith Midlothian, sh. 18 Aug 1699, fr. Clyde to Darien, in *Rising Sun*, d. Darien, Edin pr1707 CC8.8.83

2531. Grigorson, Dugald, b. 1743, farmer, res. Perthshire, sh. May 1775, fr. Greenock to N.Y., in *Monimia*, m. Jane Blue. (PRO.T47.12)

2532. Grindlay, Christian, res. Glasgow, sh. pre 1777, sett. Charleston S.C., m. James Grindlay, ch. John, d. pre 1777, Glas pr1777 CC9.7.70 (alias 2316)

2533. Grindlay, William, tr. Nov 1679, fr. Leith. (ETR162)

2534. Grintoun, Alexander jr, sailor, res. Bo'ness West Lothian, sh. 18 Aug 1699, fr. Clyde to Darien, in *Rising Sun*, Edin pr1700 CC8.8.81

2535. Groat, Daniel, seaman, res. Burntisland Fife, pts. William Groat, sh. 14 July 1698, fr. Leith to Darien, in *Unicorn*, Edin pr 1707 CC8.8.83

2536. Grosvenor, Robert, Jacobite, res. Lancashire, tr. 1747. (P.2.260)(MR62)

2537. Groves, William, soldier, rapist, tr. May 1775. (SM.37.406)

2538. Guild, Thomas, Jacobite, tr. 7 May 1716, fr. Liverpool to S.C., in *Susannah*. (SPC.1716.309)(CTB31.206)

2539. Guin, Christian, b. 1761, servant, res. Galsik Isle of Lewis, sh. May 1775, fr. Stornaway to Philadelphia, in *Friendship*. (PRO.T47.12)

2540. Guin, John, b. 1771, res. Galsik Isle of Lewis, sh. May 1774, fr. Stornaway to Philadelphia, in *Friendship*. (PRO.T47.12)

2541. Gunn, Angus, b. 1727, husbandman, Jacobite, res. Lairn Caithness, tr. 20 Mar 1747, fr. London to Jamaica or Barbados, arr. Jamaica 1747. (P.2.270)(MR82)(PRO.CO137.28)

2542. Gunn, Daniel, soldier, Jacobite, res. Caithness, tr. 31 Mar 1747. (P.2.270)(MR82)

2543. Gunn, Donald, b. 1707, husbandman, Jacobite, res. Dunbeath Caithness, tr. 31 Mar 1747, fr. London to Jamaica or Barbados, arr. Jamaica 1747. (P.2.272)(MR82)(PRO.CO137.58)

2544. Gunn, Donald, b. 1717, soldier, Jacobite, res. Caithness, tr. 31 Mar 1747, fr. London to Jamaica or Barbados. (P.2.270)

2545. Gunn, Donald, b. 1741, tailor, res. Achinnaris Halkirk Caithness, sh. Apr 1774, to Wilmington N.C., in *Bachelor of Leith*. (PRO.T47.12)

2546. Gunn, John, tr. 12 Mar 1754, fr. Aberden to Va, in *Fanny & Betty*, m. Agnes Taylor, ch. Sarah. (AJ323)

2547. Gunn, John, vagabond, res. Aberdeenshire, tr. May 1721. (SRO.JC27)

2548. Guthrie, James, mariner, res. Largo Fife, sh. 18 Aug 1699, fr. Clyde to Darien, in *Rising Sun*, d. Darien, Edin pr 1707 CC8.8.83

2549. Guthrie, John, Jacobite, tr. 7 May 1716, fr. Liverpool to S.C., in *Susannah*. (SPC.1716.309)(CTB31.206)

123

2550. Guthrie, John, Jacobite, tr. 21 May 1716, fr. Liverpool to S.C., in *Wakefield*. (CTB31.205)
2551. Guthrie, Robert, Jacobite, tr. 21 Apr 1716, fr. Liverpool to S.C., in *Wakefield*. (SPC.1716.309)(CTB31.205)
2552. Guthrie, Thomas, b. 1732, farmer, res. Stromness Orkney Islands, sh. Sept 1774, fr. Kirkwall to Savanna Ga, in *Marlborough*, sett. Richmond Co Ga, m. Jean ..., ch. Margaret Helen Adam Thomas John Jean Janet. (PRO.T47.12)
2553. Guthrie, William, clergyman edu. St Andrews Uni 1699-1701, sh. 1709, to Jamaica. (EMA31)(SPG.2.10)
2554. Guthrie, William, res. Edinburgh, pts. Rev Harry Guthrie & Rachel Milne, sh. pre 1774, sett. St Elizabeth Jamaica. (SRO.RD3.733.387)
2555. Hackstone, William, tailor, Covenanter, res. Edinburgh, tr. 12 Dec 1678, fr. Leith to West Indies, in *St Michael of Scarborough*. (PC.6.76)
2556. Hadden, ..., tr. Feb 1667, to Barbados or Va. (PC.2.263)
2557. Haddoway, Archibald, Covenanter, res. Glasgow, tr. 12 Dec 1678, fr. Leith to West Indies, in *St Michael of Scarborough*. (PC.6.76)
2558. Hagar, Katharine, whore & thief, res. Edinburgh, tr. 28 Nov 1704, fr. Leith to Md. (SRO.PC2.28.307)
2559. Haggart, Donald, b. 1714, farmer, res. Glen Coe Argyll, sh. Feb 1775, fr. Greenock to N.Y., in *Commerce*, m. Katherine Kippen. (PRO.T47.12)
2560. Haggart, Donald, b. 1749, tailor, res. Glen Coe Argyll, sh. Feb 1775, fr. Greenock to N.Y., in *Commerce*. (PRO.T47.12)
2561. Haggart, Duncan, b. 1743, smith, res. Glen Coe Argyll, sh. Feb 1775, fr. Greenock to N.Y., in *Commerce*. (PRO.T47.12)
2562. Haggart, James, b. 1754, weaver, res. Glen Coe Argyll, sh. Feb 1775, fr. Greenock to N.Y., in *Commerce*. (PRO.T47.12)
2563. Haggart, John, b. 1751, smith, res. Glen Coe Argyll, sh. Feb 1775, fr. Greenock to N.Y., in *Commerce*, sett. Kingsborough Patent N.Y. & Charlottenburg Ontario. (PRO.T47.12)
2564. Haggart, Katherine, b. 1759, servant, res. Glen Coe Argyll, sh. Feb 1775, fr. Greenock to N.Y., in *Commerce*. (PRO.T47.12)
2565. Haggins, Jonathan, merchant, sh. June 1684, fr. Port Glasgow to Carolina, in *Charles of Glasgow*. (SRO.E72.19.9)
2566. Hague, Ralph, b. 1749, painter, res. Edinburgh, sh. Oct 1774, fr. London to Md, in *Sophia*. (PRO.T47.9\11)
2567. Halcro, Magnus, b. 5 Nov 1729, Orphir Orkney Islands, servant, res. Orphir, pts. Robert Halcro & Katherine Seater, sh. Sept 1774, fr. Kirkwall to Savannah Ga, in *Marlborough*, sett. Richmond Co Ga, m. Elizabeth ..., ch. Hugh. (PRO.T47.12)
2568. Haldane, David, soldier, sh. pre 1765, sett. N.Y. (PCCol.1765.818)

2569. Haldane, George, governor, res. Gleneagles Perthshire, pts. Patrick Haldane & Margaret Forrester, d. 26 July 1759 Jamaica. (SP.4)(SM.20.501)

2570. Haldane, James, merchant, thief, res. Jedburgh Roxburghshire, tr. June 1722, fr. Glasgow to N.E. (SRO.JC.12.3)

2571. Haliburton, Elizabeth, whore & thief, res. Edinburgh, tr. 28 Nov 1704, fr. Leith to Md. (SRO.PC2.28.307)

2572. Haliday, Robert, soldier, bigamist, res. Dumfries-shire, tr. Sept 1770. (AJ1185)

2573. Halket, Charles, b. 1727, laborer, Jacobite, res. Aberdeen, tr. 5 May 1747, fr. Liverpool to Leeward Islands, in *Veteran*, arr. Martinique June 1747. (P.2.272)(JAB.2.430)(MR9)(PRO.SP36.102)

2574. Halkett, John, sailor, sh. May 1699, to Darien, in *Olive Branch*, Edin pr1707 CC8.8.83

2575. Hall, James, farmer, Covenanter, res. Kintyre Argyll, tr. Aug 1685, fr. Leith to Jamaica. (PC.11.136)

2576. Hall, John, b. 1729, farmer, res. Inchinnan Renfrewshire, sh. Apr 1775, fr. Greenock to Salem, in *Glasgow Packet*, m. Jean Allison, ch. William John Janet Robert James. (PRO.T47.12)

2577. Hall, William, coachbuilder, Jacobite, res. Perth, tr. 1747. (P.2.272)

2578. Hall, William, Jacobite, tr. 30 Mar 1716, fr. Liverpool to Antigua, in *Scipio*. (SPC.1716.310)(CTB31.204)

2579. Halliday, Thomas, clergyman edu. Edinburgh Uni 1702, sh. 1710, to East N.J., sett. N.J. & Del, d. pre May 1722. (EMA31)

2580. Hallyburton, William, soldier, sh. 1699, m. Janet Allan, d. Darien, Edin pr1707 CC8.8.83

2581. Halton, John, Jacobite, tr. 5 May 1747, fr. Liverpool to Va, in *Gildart*, arr. Port North Potomac Md 5 Aug 1747. (P.2.272)(PRO.T1.328)

2582. Halyburton, William, clergyman, sh. 1766, to Va, sett. N.Y. (EMA32)(PCCol.4.819)

2583. Hamigar, James, b. 1739, sailor, res. Evie Orkney Islands, sh. Sept 1774, fr. Kirkwall to Savannah Ga, in *Marlborough*, sett. Richmond Co Ga, m. Jean ... (PRO.T47.12)

2584. Hamilton of Bargeny, James, sh. 1765, sett. E Fla. (PCCol.4.814)

2585. Hamilton, ..., schoolmaster, sh. 1700, sett. Leeward Islands. (EMA32)

2586. Hamilton, Alexander, sh. pre 1700, sett. Nevis. (DP308)

2587. Hamilton, Alexander, mate, res. Bo'ness West Lothian, sh. 14 July 1699, to Darien, in *Dolphin*, Edin pr1707 CC8.8.83

2588. Hamilton, Alexander, councillor, res. Bo'ness West Lothian, d. 1699 Darien, Edin pr1707 CC8.8.83

2589. Hamilton, Alexander, midshipman, res. Inveresk Midlothian, pts. George Hamilton, sh. 14 July 1698, fr. Leith to Darien, in *Caledonia*, Edin pr1707 CC8.8.83

125

2590. Hamilton, Alexander, physician, res. Cramond Midlothian, pts. Prof
William Hamilton & Mary Hamilton, sh. 1739, sett. Annapolis
Md, d. May 1756. (NLS.6506)(MHS1265)
2591. Hamilton, Alexander, res. Lamlash Isle of Arran, tr. July 1754.
(SRO.JC3.29.591)
2592. Hamilton, Alexander, smuggler , res. Isle Of Arran, tr. July 1754.
(SM.16.307)
2593. Hamilton, Alexander, factor, res. Glasgow, sh. pre 1766, sett. Piscataway
Va. (SRA.CFI)
2594. Hamilton, Andrew, passenger, sh. Feb 1681, fr. Ayr to West Indies, in
James of Ayr. (SRO.E72.3.6)
2595. Hamilton, Andrew, res. Edinburgh, sh. 7 Oct 1698, fr. Liverpool to Va,
in Submission. (LRO.HQ325.2FRE)
2596. Hamilton, Andrew, d. May 1767 Mass. (SM.29.614)
2597. Hamilton, Andrew, midshipman, d. 22 Nov 1698 Darien.
(NLS.RY2b8\19)
2598. Hamilton, Archibald, sailor, res. Carriden West Lothian, sh. 14 July
1699, to Darien, in Dolphin, Edin pr1707 CC8.8.83
2599. Hamilton, Archibald, soldier, sh. pre 1765, sett. N.Y. (PCCol.1765.818)
2600. Hamilton, Archibald, merchant, res. Glasgow, sh. pre 1776, sett. Suffolk
Nansedmond Co N.C. (SRA.CFI)
2601. Hamilton, Beattie, whore, res. Edinburgh, tr. Mar 1695.
(SRO.PC2.25.216)
2602. Hamilton, Charles, midshipman, res. Edinburgh, pts. Frederick Hamilton,
sh. 14 July 1698, fr. Leith to Darien, in Union, Edin pr1707
CC8.8.83
2603. Hamilton, David, street caddy, assault, res. Edinburgh, tr. 1733.
(EBR.BC.2)
2604. Hamilton, Elizabeth, b. 1725, seamstress, Jacobite, res. Banff, tr. 5 May
1747, fr. Liverpool to Leeward Islands, in Veteran, arr. Martinique
June 1747, m. Edward Clavering.
(P.2.118)(JAB.2.422)(PRO.SP36.102) (alias 1142)
2605. Hamilton, Gavin, merchant, sh. Sept 1684, fr. Port Glasgow to N.E., in
Endeavour of Liverpool. (SRO.E72.19.9)
2606. Hamilton, Gavin, merchant, res. Glasgow, sh. pre1750, sett. Va.
(SRA.B10.15.6087)
2607. Hamilton, George, Covenanter, res. Brouncastle, tr. Dec 1684.
(PC.10.77)
2608. Hamilton, George, b. 1751, carver & guilder, sh. May 1774, fr.
Whitehaven to Va, in Molly. (PRO.T47.12)
2609. Hamilton, Isabel, b. 1697, knitter, Jacobite, res. Musselburgh
Midlothian, tr. 5 May 1747, fr. Liverpool to Leeward Islands, in
Veteran, arr. Martinique June 1747. (PRO.SP36.102)

2610. Hamilton, Isobel, res. Edinburgh, tr. Dec 1665, fr. Leith to Barbados. (ETR104)
2611. Hamilton, James, sailor, res. Edinburgh, pts. Frederick Hamilton, sh. 18 Aug 1699, fr. Clyde to Darien, in *Rising Sun*, Edin pr1707 CC8.8.83
2612. Hamilton, James, tanner, thief, res. Aberdeen, tr. Sept 1758. (AJ559)
2613. Hamilton, James, tr. Aug 1684, fr. Glasgow to Carolina. (PC.9.95)
2614. Hamilton, James, skinner, thief, res. Leith Midlothian, tr. Mar 1767. (SM.29.221)(SRO.JC27.D35)(AJ1001)
2615. Hamilton, James, b. 1733, farmer, res. Paisley Renfrewshire, sh. May 1774, fr. Greenock to N.Y., in *George*. (PRO.T47.12)
2616. Hamilton, John, res. Edinburgh, pts. Prof William & Mary Hamilton, sh. pre 1755, sett. Md. (NLS.6506)
2617. Hamilton, John, sh. pre 1765, sett. Nansedmond Va. (NRAS.0620)
2618. Hamilton, John, gypsy, tr. 21 Oct 1682, fr. Greenock to N.Y. (ETR221)
2619. Hamilton, John, merchant, res. Glasgow, sh. pre 1770, sett. Norfolk, Va & N.C. (SRA.T79.18)
2620. Hamilton, Margaret, servant, res. West Bow Edinburgh, tr. pre 1676, sett. Barbados. (PC.4.671)
2621. Hamilton, Matthew, husbandman, Covenanter, res. Kintyre Argyll, tr. Aug 1685, fr. Leith to Jamaica. (PC.11.329)(ETR369)
2622. Hamilton, Patrick, edu. Glasgow Uni 1775, res. Glasgow, pts. Rev John Hamilton, d. 15 Jan 1788 Jamaica. (MAGU113)
2623. Hamilton, Robert, gardener, Jacobite, res. Gorthie Perthshire, tr. 5 May 1747, fr. Liverpool to Va, in *Johnson*, arr. Port Oxford Md 5 Aug 1747. (P.2.274)(MR72)(PRO.T1.328)
2624. Hamilton, Thomas, overseer, res. Edinburgh, pts. Frederick Hamilton, sh. 1698, to Darien, Edin pr1707 CC8.8.83
2625. Hamilton, Thomas, overseer, res. Bathgate West Lothian, sh. 169, to Darien, Edinpr1707 CC8.8.83
2626. Hamilton, Thomas, smuggler, res. Lamlash Isle of Arran, tr. July 1754. (SRO.JC3.29.591)(SM.16.307)
2627. Hamilton, William, sailor, res. Crombie Fife, sh. 14 July 1698, fr. Leith to Darien, in *Unicorn*, Edin pr1707 CC8.8.83
2628. Hamilton, William, merchant, sh. June 1684, fr. Port Glasgow to Carolina, in *Pelican of Glasgow*. (SRO.E72.19.9)
2629. Hamilton, William, ensign, d. 3 Dec 1698 Darien. (NLS.RY2b8\19)
2630. Hamilton, William, b. 1717, cooper, res. Leith Midlothian, sh. Nov 1736, fr. London to Jamaica. (CLRO\AIA)
2631. Hamilton, William, b. 1745, farmer, res. Kilbride, sh. Oct 1774, fr. Greenock to Philadelphia, in *Sally*. (PRO.T47.12)
2632. Hamilton, William jr, highwayman, res. Upper Ctaigenputtock Dumfries-shire, tr. Oct 1749. (SM.11.509)

2633. Hammer, Martin, mariner, ch. Anne Catherine Beren Martin, d. pre 1704 Va, PCC pr.1704
2634. Hammond, George, Jacobite, tr. 7 May 1716, fr. Liverpool to S.C., in *Susannah*. (SPC.1716.309)(CTB31.206)
2635. Handiesyde, James, foremastman, res. Edinburgh, sh. 14 July 1698, fr. Leith to Darien, in *St Andrew*, Edin pr1707 CC8.8.83
2636. Handyside, Robert, Jacobite, tr. 26 Apr 1716, fr. Liverpool to Jamaica, in *Two Brothers*, arr. Montserrat June 1716. (SPC.1716.313)(CTB31.206)(CTP.CC.43)
2637. Hanna, William, clergyman edu. Glasgow Uni 1768, res. Galloway, pts. John Hanna, sh. 1772, to Va. (EMA32)(MAGU85)
2638. Hanna, William, Covenanter, res. Borders, tr. 5 Sept 1685, fr. Leith to East N.J., in *Henry & Francis*. (PC.11.94)
2639. Hannah, James, b. 1757, tailor, res. Gatehouse Kirkcudbrightshire, sh. May 1774, fr. Stranraer to N.Y., in *Gale*. (PRO.T47.12)
2640. Hannawinkle, Alexander, forger, tr. 1775. (SRO.HCR.I.112)
2641. Hannay, Andrew, b. 1733, Galloway, cooper, res. Gatehouse Kirkcudbrightshire, sh. 7 May 1774, fr. Stranraer to N.Y., in *Gale*, m. Catherine ..., ch. Elizabeth John James Andrew, d. 1808 Albany Co N.Y. (PRO.T47.12)(HS192)
2642. Hanton, James, thief, res. Brechin Angus, tr. Sept 1775. (AJ1446)
2643. Hardie, Alexander, res. Aberdeen, pts. Robert Hardie, sh. 1684, to East N.J. (Insh252)
2644. Hardie, Robert, merchant, res. Aberdeen, sh. 1684, sett. Elisabethtown East N.J., ch. William Alexander John Elspeth James Andrew. (Insh263)
2645. Hardie, William, res. Aberdeen, pts. Robert Hardie, sh. 1684, to East N.J., d. 1684. (Insh252)
2646. Hardwick, William, Jacobite, tr. 25 June 1716, fr. Liverpool to St Kitts, in *Hockenhill*. (SPC.1716.312)(CTB31.207)
2647. Hardy, James, sailor, res. Kinneil West Lothian, pts. Patrick & Agnes Hardy, sh. 18 Aug 1699, fr. Clyde to Darien, in *Rising Sun*, Edin pr1707 CC8.8.83
2648. Harkness, John, servant, Covenanter, res. Mitchellslacks Dumfries-shire, tr. Oct 1684. (PC.10.587)
2649. Harley, Adam, b. 1763, weaver, res. Glasgow, sh. Feb 1774, fr. Greenock to N.Y., in *Commerce*. (PRO.T47.12)
2650. Harley, James, b. 1754, weaver, res. Glasgow, sh. Feb 1774, fr. Greenock to N.Y., in *Commerce*. (PRO.T47.12)
2651. Harper, David, foremastman, res. Kirkcaldy Fife, pts. Bessie Salmond or Harper, sh. 14 July 1698, fr. Leith to Darien, in *Caledonia*, Edin pr1707 CC8.8.83
2652. Harper, John, Covenanter, res. Fenwick Ayrshire, tr. May 1684. (PC.8.516)

2653. Harper, Robert, Covenanter, tr. June 1669, to Va. (PC.3.22)
2654. Harris, David, chapman, thief, res. Angus, tr. May 1774. (AJ1376)
2655. Harris, David, chapman, res. Perthshire, tr. May 1774. (AJ1377)
2656. Harris, John, Jacobite, tr. 29 June 1716, fr. Liverpool to Jamaica or Va, in *Elizabeth & Anne*, arr. Va. (SPC.1716.310)(CTB31.208)(VSP.1.186)
2657. Harris, William, fraudster, tr. Aug 1751. (AJ189)
2658. Harrison, David, b. 1735, wheelwright, res. Ecclefechan Dumfries-shire, sh. 1775, fr. Dumfries to P.E.I., in *Lovely Nelly*, m. Janet Henderson, ch. Grizell Agnes Helen Janet Margaret. (PRO.T47.12)
2659. Harrison, James, seaman, res. Burntisland Fife, sh. Mar 1683, to Port Nelson Hudson Bay. (HBRS.9.90)
2660. Harroway, John, tr. 12 Dec 1678, fr. Leith to West Indies, in *St Michael of Scarborough*. (PC.6.76)
2661. Harrower, John, clerk & tutor, res. Lerwick Shetland Islands, sh. 7 Feb 1774, fr. London to Va, in *Planter*, arr. Fredericksburg Va 10 May 1774, sett. Belvidere Fredericksburg, m. Anne Graeme, ch. John Elizabeth George James, d. Apr 1777 Va. (PRO.T47.9\11)
2662. Hart, John, b. 1743, mason, res. Glasgow, sh. May 1775, fr. Greenock to N.Y., in *Monimia*. (PRO.T47.12)
2663. Harvey, Alexander, b. 1746, farmer, res. Gargunnock Stirlingshire, sh. May 1774, fr. Greenock to N.Y., in *Matty*, arr. N.Y. 22 July 1774, sett. Barnet N.H. (PRO.T47.12)
2664. Harvey, Daniel, b. 1744, gardener, sh. May 1774, fr. Liverpool to Philadelphia, in *Boston Packet*, m. Mary ... (PRO.T47.9\11)
2665. Harvie, ..., res. Stirling, pts. Patrick Harvie, sh. pre 1781, to West Indies. (SGB.135)
2666. Harvie, Barkie, b. 1758, servant, res. Kirkwall Orkney Islands, sh. Sept 1774, fr. Kirkwall to Savannah Ga, in *Marlborough*, sett. Richmond Co Ga. (PRO.T47.12)
2667. Harvie, John, Covenanter, res. Dalserf Lanarkshire, tr. 5 Sept 1685, fr. Leith to East N.J., in *Henry & Francis*, m. Marion Forrest. (PC.11.329)
2668. Harvie, Thomas, thief, res. Glasgow, pts. James Harvie, tr. 28 Nov 1704, fr. Leith to Md. (SRO.PC2.28.307)
2669. Hastie, Ann, infanticide, res. Dunbar East Lothian, pts. Robert Hastie, tr. Aug 1760. (SRO.HCR.I.92)
2670. Hastie, William, Covenanter, res. Carluke Lanarkshire, tr. July 1685, fr. Leith to Jamaica. (PC.11.136)
2671. Hay, Alexander, merchant, res. Morayshire, pts. Alexander Hay of Cairblie, sh. pre 1783, sett. Montreal. (SRO.RD4.239.760)
2672. Hay, Andrew, sailor, res. Dysart Fife, pts. Andrew Hay, sh. 14 July 1698, fr. Leith to Darien, in *St Andrew*, Edin pr1707 CC8.8.83
2673. Hay, Archibald, planter, sett. Barbados, d. pre 1652, PCC pr1652

2674. Hay, Edward, governor, res. Perthshire, sett. Barbados, m. Miss Barnwell, d. Nov 1779 Barbados. (SM.42.55)
2675. Hay, George, engineer & provost marshal, sh. pre 1705, sett. Barbados. (SPC.1705.409)
2676. Hay, Henry, b. 1739, joiner, res. Stirling, sh. May 1775, fr. Greenock to N.Y., in *Lilly*. (PRO.T47.12)
2677. Hay, Hugh, soldier, res. Nairn, sh. 1698, to Darien, Edin pr1707 CC8.8.83
2678. Hay, James, tailor, res. Aberdeenshire, pts. Alexander Hay of Raines, sett. Jamaica, d. pre 1748 Jamaica. (APB.3.147)
2679. Hay, James, b. 1754, accountant, sh. June 1775, fr. London to Baltimore, in *Nancy*. (PRO.T47.9\11)
2680. Hay, James, b. 1758, joiner, res. Edinburgh, sh. May 1775, fr. Leith to Philadelphia, in *Friendship*. (PRO.T47.12)
2681. Hay, John, soldier, sh. 1698, to Darien, Edin pr1707 CC8.8.83
2682. Hay, John, surgeon, res. Kirkintilloch Dunbartonshire, pts. Robert Hay, sh. pre 1755, sett. SurreyCo America. (SRO.RS10.8.462)
2683. Hay, John, Covenanter, tr. Aug 1685. (PC.11.130)(SRO.CH2.83.8)
2684. Hay, John, thief, res. Aberdeen, tr. 12 Mar 1754, fr. Aberdeen to Va, in *Fanny & Betty*. (AJ300\323)(ABR.EB.1754)
2685. Hay, John, Jacobite, tr. 24 May 1716, fr. Liverpool to Md, in *Friendship*, arr. Md Aug, sett. 1716. (SPC.1716.311)(HM386)
2686. Hay, John, merchant, res. Kilsyth Stirlingshire, pts. James Hay, sh. pre 1775, sett. Va. (SRO.RD2.220.10)
2687. Hay, Patrick, overseer, res. Edinburgh, sh. 1698, to Darien, Edin pr1707 CC8.8.83
2688. Hay, Robert, soldier, tr. Mar 1767. (SRO.RH2.4.255)
2689. Hay, Robert, cooper, res. Edinburgh, sh. 1737, fr. Cromarty to Savannah Ga, in *Two Brothers*. (SPC.43.513)(PRO.CO5.670.331)
2690. Hay, William, sh. pre 1645, to Barbados. (SRO.GD34.946)
2691. Hay, William, sailor, res. Edinburgh, sh. 18 Aug 1699, fr. Clyde to Darien, in *Rising Sun*, Edin pr1707 CC8.8.83
2692. Hay, William, tr. 12 Dec 1678, fr. Leith to West Indies, in *St Michael of Scarborough*. (PC.6.76)
2693. Hay, William, gardener, res. East Gordon Berwickshire, sh. Feb 1754, fr. London to Md. (CLRO\AIA)
2694. Hay, William, b. 10 Nov 1748, lawyer edu. Glasgow Uni 1766, res. Kilsyth Stirlingshire, pts. James Hay, sh. 18 July 1768, fr. Greenock to Va, d. 1823 Va. (MAGU79)(WMQ.15.85)
2695. Hay, William, b. 1750, clergyman edu. Scots Col Rome, res. Aberdeenshire, pts. James Hay & Joan Reafin, d. America. (RSC.1.141)
2696. Headrick, John, horsethief, res. Stirling, tr. Nov 1773. (SRO.RH2.4.255)

2697. Heastie, John, b. 1744, shoemaker, res. Perthshire, sh. Oct 1774, fr.
    Greenock to Charleston S.C., in *Countess*. (PRO.T47.12)
2698. Heathersgill, Robert, res. Jedburgh Roxburghshire, tr. 17 Apr 1666, fr.
    Leith to Barbados. (ETR106) (alias 206)
2699. Heckle, Robert, b. 1740, mason, res. Kirkcudbright, sh. May 1774, fr.
    Kirkcudbright to N.Y., in *Adventure*, m. Margaret McKitteich, ch.
    David William Thomas Robert. (PRO.T47.12)
2700. Hector, John, b. 30 Aug 1705, Aberdeen, salmon fisher, Jacobite, res.
    Cruives Old Machar Aberdeen, pts. James Hector & Margaret
    Clerk, tr. 5 May 1747, fr. Liverpool to Va, in *Johnson*, arr. Port
    Oxford Md 5 Aug 1747.
    (P.2.282)(MR211)(JAB.2.431)(PRO.T1.328)
2701. Hedderwick, John, b. 20 Sept 1679, Aberdeen, sailor, res. Aberdeen, pts.
    John Hedderwick & Elspet Hay, sh. 14 July 1698, fr. Leith to
    Darien, in *Caledonia*, Edin pr1708 CC8.8.84
2702. Hedderwick, William, surgeon's mate, res. Edinburgh, pts. Andrew
    Hedderwick, sh. 18 Aug 1699, to Darien, in *Duke of Hamilton*,
    Edin pr1707 CC8.8.83
2703. Heddle, Alexander, b. 1758, farm servant, res. Shapinsay Orkney Islands,
    sh. Sept 1774, fr. Kirkwall to Savannah Ga, in *Marlborough*, sett.
    Richmond Co Ga. (PRO.T47.12)
2704. Heidshoip, Anthony, res. Jedburgh Roxburghshire, tr. 17 Apr 1666, fr.
    Leith to Barbados. (ETR106) (alias 5556)
2705. Henderson, Alexander, b. 1737, merchant edu. Glagow Uni 1748, res.
    Blantyre Lanarkshire, pts. Rev Richard Henderson, sh. 1756, sett.
    Colchester & Dumfries Va, m. Sarah ..., d. 22 Nov 1815 Dumfries
    Va. (MAGU39)(SRA.T-MJ)
2706. Henderson, Alexander, b. 1751, tailor, res. Morayshire, sh. July 1775, fr.
    Stornaway to Philadelphia, in *Clementina*. (PRO.T47.12)
2707. Henderson, Charles, Jacobite, tr. 29 June 1716, fr. Liverpool to Jamaica
    or Va, in *Elizabeth & Anne*, arr. Va.
    (SPC.1716.310)(CTB31.208)(VSP.1.186)
2708. Henderson, Charles, servant, Jacobite, res. Rescobie Angus, tr. 1747.
    (MR102)
2709. Henderson, Colin, smith, thief, res. Torryburn Fife, tr. 1773, fr. Port
    Glasgow, in *Phoenix*, arr. Port Accomack Va 20 Dec 1773.
    (AJ1293)(SRO.JC27)
2710. Henderson, David, sailor, res. Burntisland Fife, sh. 14 July 1698, fr.
    Leith to Darien, in *Caledonia*, Edin pr1707 CC8.8.83
2711. Henderson, David, d. pre 1727 Bertie Co N.C. (SRO.SH.16.8.1737)
2712. Henderson, James, wright, res. Renfrewshire, sh. 25 Mar 1773, fr.
    Greenock to N.Y., in *Matty*, sett. Ryegate N.H. (PRO.T47.12)
2713. Henderson, James, chairman, assault, res. Edinburgh, tr. 1733.
    (EBR.BC.2)

131

2714. Henderson, James, surgeon & merchant, sett. Jamaica, d. 18 Apr 1755
Edinburgh, Edin pr1756 CC8.8.116
2715. Henderson, James, b. 1717, cook, Jacobite, res. Angus, tr. 5 May 1747,
fr. Liverpool to Leeward Islands, in *Veteran*, arr. Martinique June
1747. (P.2.282)(OR31)(PRO.SP36.102)
2716. Henderson, John, Covenanter, res. Ruchoard, tr. 5 Sept 1685, fr. Leith to
East N.J., in *Henry & Francis*. (PC.11.164)
2717. Henderson, John, saddler, res. Edinburgh, sh. pre1755, sett. Jamaica, Edin
pr1756 CC8.8.116
2718. Henderson, John, b. 1709, soldier, sh. pre 1762, sett. Fishkill N.Y., d.
13 Dec 1811 Fishkill. (SM.74.316)
2719. Henderson, Matthew, clergyman, sh. 1758, sett. Charteris Pa, d. 1795 Pa.
(UPC654)
2720. Henderson, Matthew, b. 25 Apr 1735, clergyman, res. Orwell Kinross-
shire, pts. Matthew Henderson, sh. pre 1782, sett. Pa & Del, d. 2
Oct 1795 Pittsburgh Washington Co Pa. (GM.65.1112)
2721. Henderson, Robert, farmer, Jacobite, res. Cushnie Aberdeenshire, tr. 24
May 1716, fr. Liverpool to Va, in *Friendship*, arr. Md Aug 1716.
(SPC.1716.311)(HM387)(JAB.1.151)(Md Arch.34.164)
2722. Henderson, Robert, b. 1749, gentleman, res. Lasswade Midlothian, sh.
May 1775, fr. Greenock to N.Y., in *Monimia*. (PRO.T47.12)
2723. Henderson, Thomas, b. 1743, joiner, res. Hoddom Dumfries-shire, sh.
May 1775, fr. Dumfries to P.E.I., in *Lovely Nelly*, m. Margery
Hogg, ch. Martha Hanny Thomas. (PRO.T47.12)
2724. Henderson, William, overseer, res. Edinburgh, sh. 1699, d. 1699 Darien,
Edin pr1707 CC8.8.83
2725. Henderson, William, planter, res. Newbigging, sh. pre 1743, sett.
Churchill's Plantation Rappahannock River Va.
(SRO.CH12.23.315\358)
2726. Henderson, William, Jacobite, tr. 25 June 1716, fr. Liverpool to St Kitts,
in *Hockenhill*. (SPC.1716.312)(CTB31.207)
2727. Henderson, William, Jacobite, tr. 21 Apr 1716, fr. Liverpool to S.C., in
Wakefield. (SPC.1716.309)(CTB31.205)
2728. Hendrie, George, merchant, sh. Aug 1685, fr. Leith to N.J., in *Henry of
Newcastle*. (SRO.E72.15.32)
2729. Hendry, Alexander, sailor, res. Linlithgow West Lothian, sh. 18 Aug
1699, fr. Clyde to Darien, in *Rising Sun*, Edin pr1707 CC8.8.83
2730. Hendry, Alexander, b. 1745, saddler, res. Edinburgh, sh. May 1775, fr.
Greenock to N.Y., in *Monimia*. (PRO.T47.12)
2731. Hendry, James, Jacobite, tr. 24 May 1716, fr. Liverpool to Md, in
Friendship, arr. Md Aug 1716. (SPC.1716.311)(HM386)
2732. Hendry, James, b. 1755, servant, res. Morayshire, sh. July 1775, fr.
Stornaway to Philadelphia, in *Clementina*. (PRO.T47.12)

2733. Hendry, Jean, b. 27 May 1733, Forfar, infanticide, res. Brechin Angus, pts. Thomas Hendry, tr. May 1757. (AJ490)(SRO.B59.26.11.3.2\28)
2734. Hendry, Neil, b. 1747, tailor, res. Kintyre Argyll, sh. Sept 1774, fr. Greenock to Wilmington N.C., in *Diana*. (PRO.T47.12)
2735. Hendry, Robert, b. 1752, tailor, res. Dundee Angus, sh. May 1774, fr. Greenock to N.Y., in *George*. (PRO.T47.12)
2736. Henning, Barbara, res. Galloway, sh. May 1775, fr. Dumfries to P.E.I., in *Lovely Nelly*. (PRO.T47.12)
2737. Henry, Alexander, tr. Dec 1685, fr. Leith to Barbados, in *John & Nicholas*. (ETR390)
2738. Henry, George, b. 1709, clergyman, sh. pre 1762, sett. Quebec, d. 6 July 1795. (F.7.637)
2739. Henry, John, clergyman edu. Edinburgh Uni, sh. 1710, fr. Dublin to Philadelphia, sett. Rehobeth Va. (AP164)
2740. Henry, Patrick, Aberdeenshire, clergyman, res. Aberdeenshire, pts. Alexander Henry & Jean Robertson, sh. 1732, sett. Hanover Co Va. (EMA33)
2741. Henshaw, William, b. 12 Sept 1643, Glasgow, merchant, Covenanter, res. Glasgow, pts. James Henshaw & Janet Neill, tr. June 1678, to West Indies. (PC.5.474)
2742. Hepburn, Charles, merchant, res. Glasgow, sh. pre 1741, sett. Cape Fear N.C., d. July 1741 N.C., Edin pr1744 CC8.8.107
2743. Hepburn, James, sh. pre 1773, sett. Halifax Co N.C. (SRO.RD4.214.545)
2744. Hepburn, Janet, fireraiser, res. Dumfries, pts. Alexander Hepburn, tr. 1767, m. Alexander Walker. (SM.29.497)
2745. Hepburn, Mary, whore & thief, res. Edinburgh, tr. 28 Nov 1704, fr. Leith to Md. (SRO.PC2.28.307)
2746. Hercules, William, b. 1750, weaver, res. Paisley Renfrewshire, sh. Feb 1774, fr. Greenock to N.Y., in *Commerce*. (PRO.T47.12)
2747. Herd, John, Jacobite, tr. 7 May 1716, fr. Liverpool to S.C., in *Susannah*. (SPC.1716.309)(CTB31.206)
2748. Herd, Walter, foremastman, sh. 14 July 1698, fr. Leith to Darien, in *Unicorn*, Edin pr1707 CC8.8.83
2749. Herdman, James, b. 12 May 1746, Dunottar Kincardineshire, clergyman edu. King's Col Aberdeen 1763, pts. William Herdman, sh. 1770, sett. Henrico Co Va. (EMA33)(FPA309)
2750. Heriot, Alexander, Covenanter, tr. Aug 1684, fr. Leith to Carolina. (PC.9.95)
2751. Herman, Matthew, seaman, sh. 14 July 1698, fr. Leith to Darien, in *St Andrew*, Edin pr1707 CC8.8.83
2752. Heron, Alexander, soldier, sh. pre 1738, sett. Ga. (PRO.CO5.670.347)

133

2753. Herries, Robert, surgeon, Covenanter, res. Dunbarton, tr. Nov 1678, to West Indies. (PC.6.53)
2754. Herring, Janet, washerwoman, Jacobite, res. East Lothian, tr. 5 May 1747, fr. Liverpool to Va, in *Johnson*, arr. Port Oxford Md 5 Aug 1747. (P.2.286)(PRO.T1.328)
2755. Herriot, William, b. 1753, baker, res. Gorbals Glasgow, sh. May 1775, fr. Greenock to N.Y. or Ga, in *Christy*. (PRO.T47.12)
2756. Herron, James, b. 1734, mason, res. Gatehouse Kirkcudbrightshire, sh. May 1774, fr. Dumfries to N.Y., in *Gale*, ch. Samuel Robert James John. (PRO.T47.12)
2757. Herschell, David, b. 29 Oct 1699, Brechin, shoemaker, Jacobite, res. Brechin Angus, pts. David Herschell & Katherine Adam, tr. 31 Mar 1747, fr. London to Jamaica or Barbados. (P.2.282)(MR102)
2758. Heugh, Andrew, planter, res. Falkirk Stirlingshire, pts. Thomas Heugh, sh. pre 1771, sett. Montgomery Co Md, m. Sarah .., ch. Elizabeth Ann Jean John Sarah Mary Andrew Harriet Christian MarElizabeth An, d. 6 Jan 1771 Md, Edin pr1791 CC8.8.128
2759. Hewatt, Alexander, clergyman edu. Edinburgh Uni, sh. 1763, sett. Charleston S.C. (F.7.663)
2760. Hewett, James, b. 1723, Jacobite, res. Newcastle, tr. 20 Mar 1747. (P.2.286)(MR63)
2761. Heys, James, Jacobite, tr. 25 June 1716, fr. Liverpool to St Kitts, in *Hockenhill*. (SPC.1716.312)(CTB31.207)
2762. Higgins, George, Covenanter, res. Linlithgow West Lothian, tr. 29 May 1684, fr. Leith to Carolina. (PC.8.526)
2763. Hill, Alexander, thief, res. Boyndie Banffshire, tr. May 1771. (AJ1219)
2764. Hill, James, Jacobite, tr. 24 May 1716, fr. Liverpool to Md, in *Friendship*, arr. Md Aug 1716. (SPC.1716.311)(HM387)(Md Arch.34.164)
2765. Hill, Janet, rioter, res. Glasgow, tr. Jan 1726, to Barbados. (PRO.T53.33.293)
2766. Hill, Janet, res. Edinburgh, tr. 1696, fr. Newhaven to Va. (SRO.RH15.14.58)
2767. Hill, Samuel, soldier, robber, tr. Mar 1772. (SRO.HCR.I.107)
2768. Hill, Thomas, joiner, res. Dundee Angus, sh. June 1775, fr. Kirkcaldy to S.C., in *Jamaica Packet*. (PRO.T47.12)
2769. Hinchcliffe, Joseph, b. 1716, tallow chandler, Jacobite, res. York, tr. 8 May 1747, fr. Liverpool to Antigua. (P.2.288)
2770. Hislop, Janet, infanticide, res. Glasgow, tr. Oct 1777. (SM.39.620)
2771. Hodge, Archibald, pedlar, tr. 9 Feb 1721, fr. Leith to Va. ((SRO.HH.11)
2772. Hodge, John, armorer, Covenanter, res. Glasgow, pts. Robert Hodge, tr. 5 Sept 1685, fr. Leith to East N.J., in *Henry & Francis*. (PC.11.155)

2773. Hodgeon, Adam, Covenanter, res. Douglas Lanarkshire, tr. June 1684, fr. Clyde, in *Pelican*. (PC.9.208)
2774. Hodgson, David, Jacobite, tr. 20 Mar 1747. (P.2.288)
2775. Hodgson, Edward, b. 1726, England, Jacobite, tr. 31 Mar 1747. (P.2.288)
2776. Hodgson, George, Jacobite, tr. 28 July 1716, fr. Liverpool to Va, in *Godspeed*, arr. Md Oct, sett. 1716. (SPC.1716.310)(CTB31.209)(HM388)
2777. Hodgson, John, bookseller, res. Glasgow, pts. William Hodgson, sh. pre 1772. (SRO.SH.20.1.1772)
2778. Hogg, Andrew, gypsy, tr. 21 Oct 1682, fr. Greenock to N.Y. (ETR221)
2779. Hogg, James, butcher, cattlethief, res. Falkirk Stirlingshire, tr. Sept 1767. (AJ1030)
2780. Hogg, John, Covenanter, tr. Dec 1685, fr. Leith to Barbados, in *John & Nicholas*. (PC.11.255)(ETR389)
2781. Hogg, John, sh. pre 1781, sett. Kingston Jamaica. (SRO.RD2.231.699)
2782. Hogg, Mark, sailor, res. Bonhardpans, pts. John Hogg, sh. 18 Aug 1699, fr. Clyde to Darien, in *Rising Sun*, Edin pr1707 CC8.8.83. Hogg Patrick
2783. Hogg, Patrick, sailor, sh. 14 July 1698, fr. Leith to Darien, in *St Andrew*, Edin pr1707 CC8.8.83
2784. Hoggan, James, tobacco factor, res. Glasgow, sh. pre 1774, sett. Bladensburg Va. (SRA.CFI)
2785. Hogie, Janet, b. 1760, spinner, res. Paisley Renfrewshire, sh. Feb 1774, fr. Greenock to N.Y., in *Commerce*. (PRO.T47.12)
2786. Holland, Thomas, Jacobite, tr. 29 June 1716, fr. Liverpool to Jamaica or Va, in *Elizabeth & Anne*. (SPC.1716.310)(CTB31.208)
2787. Holland, William, sailor, res. Ayr, pts. Ralph Holland, sh. 18 Aug 1699, fr. Clyde to Darien, in *Rising Sun*, Edin pr1708 CC8.8.84
2788. Holm, Lady, Covenanter, res. Kirkcudbrightshire, tr. Oct 1684. (PC.10.258)
2789. Holmes, Margaret, tr. Aug 1685, fr. Leith to Jamaica. (PC.11.330)(ETR369)
2790. Home, Alexander, res. Berwickshire, sh. pre 1769, sett. St Kitts. (SRO.RS .5.371)
2791. Home, Francis, Jacobite, res. Wedderburn Duns Berwickshire, tr. 29 June 1716, fr. Liverpool to Jamaica or Va, in *Elizabeth & Anne*, arr. Va. (SPC.1716.310)(CTB31.208)(VSP.1.185)
2792. Home, George, b. 1698, Wedderburn Duns Berwickshire, surveyor, Jacobite, tr. 1721, sett. Culpepper Co Va, m. Elizabeth Proctor, d. 1760. (OT91)
2793. Home, George, b. 1717, writer, Jacobite, res. Edinburgh, pts. George Home of Whitefield Duns Berwickshire, tr. 5 May 1747, fr. Liverpool to Leeward Islands, in *Veteran*, arr. Martinique June 1747. (P.2.290)(PRO.SP36.102)

2794. Home, Jean, thief & fireraiser, res. Carrington Midlothian, pts. Thomas Home, tr. July 1769. (SRO.JC27.D35)
2795. Home, Sir George, res. Eccles Berwickshire, sh. 1630, sett. Port Royal N.S. (PC.3.543)
2796. Honeybull, Ann, b. 1741, spinner, res. Glasgow, sh. Feb 1774, fr. Greenock to N.Y., in *Commerce*. (PRO.T47.12)
2797. Honeyman, James, b. 1675, Kinneff Kincardineshire, clergyman edu. Marischal Col Aberdeen, res. Kinneff, pts. Rev James Honeyman, sh. Apr 1703, in *Portsmouth Galley*, arr. Boston Mass 16 Nov 1703, sett. N.Y. & R.I., m. (1)Elizabeth Carr (2)Elizabeth Brown, ch. James Elizabeth Francis, d. 2 July 1750 Newport R.I. (SNQ.i.169)(SPG.11.89)(SM.12.502)
2798. Honeyman, James, b. 4 Jan 1745, Kinneff Kincardineshire, clergyman edu. Marischal Col Aberdeen 1763, res. Kinneff, pts. Rev James Honeyman & Katherine Allerdyce, sett. Newport R.I., d. 5 Aug 1781 Kinneff. (F.5.474)(F.7.663)(KCA.2.331)
2799. Honeyman, Robert, clergyman, res. Kinneff Kincardineshire, pts. Rev James Honeyman, sh. 1702, sett. N.Y. (F.7.663)
2800. Honeyman, Robert, b. 13 Dec 1747, Kinneff Kincardineshire, physician edu. Marischal Col Aberdeen & Edinburgh Uni, res. Kinneff, pts. Rev James Honeyman & Katherine Allerdyce, sh. 1773, sett. Louisa & Hanover Cos Va, m. Mary Pottle, d. 1824. (OD48)(Kinneff Gs)
2801. Hood, Adam, Covenanter, tr. 5 Sept 1685, fr. Leith to East N.J., in *Henry & Francis*. (PC.11.154)
2802. Hood, Alexander, b. 1737, Glasgow, physician, pts. James Hood, sh. pre 1773, sett. Montserrat, m. Martha Iles, d. 17 Aug 1817, bd. St Anthony Montserrat. (MWI48)
2803. Hood, Andrew, b. 1727, apprentice, Jacobite, res. Tain Ross-shire, tr. 19 Mar 1747. (P.2.290)(MR82)
2804. Hood, George, b. 23 Sept 1721, Cromarty, Jacobite, res. Cromarty, pts. Donald Hood & Katherine Hossack, tr. 1747. (MR82)
2805. Hood, John, merchant, res. Glasgow, sh. 1760, to Va. (SRO.CS.GMB50)
2806. Hooper, William, clergyman, res. Ednam Berwickshire, sh. 7 July 1747, to N.E., sett. Boston Mass, d. 14 Apr 1767. (EMA34)(SO107)
2807. Hope, John, merchant, res. Glasgow, sh. pre 1776, sett. Osborne & Halifax Va. (SRA.T79.25)
2808. Hope, Robert, b. 1754, servant, thief, res. Roxburghshire, tr. May 1771. (SRO.RH2.4.255)
2809. Hope, Thomas, soldier, pts. Alexander Hope of Kerse, sh. 14 July 1698, fr. Leith to Darien, in *Unicorn*, d. Jamaica, Edin pr1707 CC8.8.83
2810. Horn, Alexander, res. Cowland Mill Forgue Aberdeenshire, pts. Alexander Horn, sh. 1763, d. 1777 S.C. (APB.4.101)

2811. Horn, Janet, b. 1755, servant, res. Wick Caithness, sh. Sept 1775, fr. Kirkwall to Savannah Ga, in *Marlborough*, sett. Richmond Co Ga. (PRO.T47.12)

2812. Horn, John, b. 1752, blacksmith, res. Banff, sh. July 1775, fr. Greenock to Jamaica, in *Isabella*. (PRO.T47.12)

2813. Horn, William, b. 23 June 1717, Glamis Angus, laborer, Jacobite, res. Angus, pts. George Horn, tr. 1747. (P.2.290)(MR102)

2814. Horne, William, tr. Dec 1685, fr. Leith to West Indies, in *John & Nicholas*. (ETR390)

2815. Horner, Barbara, Covenanter, res. Dindaff Dumfries-shire, tr. Oct 1684, m. Thomas Hunter. (PC.10.587)

2816. Horsbell, John, b. 1684, res. Edinburgh, sh. 1700, fr. Liverpool. (LRO.HQ325.2FRE)

2817. Horsburgh, Alexander, merchant, res. Glasgow, sh. pre 1776, sett. Brunswick & Petersburg Va. (SRA.T79.1)

2818. Horseburgh, William, physician, d. pre 1763 New Providence. (SRO.CS.GMB50)

2819. Hosie, William, woolcomber, conspirator, res. Aberdeen, tr. July 1772, fr. Glasgow to Va, in *Brilliant*, arr. Port Hampton Va 7 Oct 1772. (SRO.JC27.10.3)(AJ1278)

2820. Houstoun, James, merchant, res. Glasgow, sh. 1733, sett. Ga. (PRO.CO5.670.125)

2821. Houstoun, James, clergyman, sh. 1747, sett. Md. (EMA34)

2822. Houstoun, James, b. 1747, farmer, res. Strathspey, sh. May 1774, fr. Greenock to N.Y., in *George*. (PRO.T47.12)

2823. Houstoun, Janet, whore, res. Edinburgh, tr. Mar 1695. (SRO.PC2.25.216)

2824. Houstoun, Patrick, b. 1698, Paisley Renfrewshire, merchant edu. Glasgow Uni, res. Glasgow, pts. Patrick Houstoun, sh. 1734, sett. Savannah Ga, m. Priscilla Dunbar, d. 5 Feb 1762 Ga, bd. Bonadventure, Ga pr1762 A.83. (PRO.CO5.670.101)

2825. Houstoun, William, sailor, res. Inishowen Donegal, sh. 18 Aug 1699, fr. Clyde to Darien, in *Rising Sun*, Edin pr1708 CC8.8.84

2826. Houstoun, William, physician & surgeon edu. St Andrews Uni, sh. 1732, sett. Ga. (PRO.CO5.670.1\100)

2827. Howard, Richard, servant, sh. 1637, sett. Barbados. (SRO.GD34.925)

2828. Howard, William, Jacobite, tr. 30 Mar 1716, fr. Liverpool to Antigua, in *Scipio*. (SPC.1716.310)(CTB31.204)

2829. Howatson, James, Covenanter, res. Craigbuie Dumfries-shire, tr. Oct 1684. (PC.10.587)

2830. Howet, Mary, b. 1749, spinner, res. Glasgow, sh. Feb 1774, fr. Greenock to N.Y., in *Commerce*. (PRO.T47.12)

137

2831. Howie, Alexander, clergyman edu. Marischal Col Aberdeen 1719, res. Birse Aberdeenshire, pts. Rev John Howie, sh. 1730, sett. Pa. (EMA34)
2832. Howie, David, b. 1737, farmer, sh. May 1775, fr. Greenock to N.Y. or Ga, in *Christy*. (PRO.T47.12)
2833. Howie, John, tr. 22 Dec 1665, fr. Leith to Barbados. (ETR104)
2834. Howie, John, Covenanter, tr. Aug 1685, fr. Leith to Jamaica. (ETR369)
2835. Howie, Robert, b. 1756, workman, res. Glen Orchy Argyll, sh. Aug 1774, fr. Greenock to Wilmington N.C., in *Ulysses*. (PRO.T47.12)
2836. Howie, Samuel, Covenanter, tr. Aug 1685, fr. Leith to Jamaica. (ETR369)(PC.11.329)
2837. Hownam, James, weaver, rioter, res. Langholm Dumfries-shire, pts. Andrew Hownam, tr. May 1750. (SM.12.252)
2838. Howname, Walter, Covenanter, res. Teviotdale, tr. Aug 1685, fr. Leith to Jamaica, arr. Port Royal Jamaica 1685. (PC.11.330)(LJ
2839. Huddleston, Hugh, merchant, res. Canongate Edinburgh, sett. Jamaica, m. Christian Mantleman, d. pre 1763, Edin pr1763 CC8.8.119
2840. Hughes, John, Jacobite, tr. 1747. (P.2.292)
2841. Hughes, Mary, b. 1760, servant, res. Glasgow, sh. Apr 1775, fr. London to Md, in *Adventure*. (PRO.T47.12)
2842. Hume, Benjamin, d. 8 July 1773 Jamaica. (SM.35.559)
2843. Hume, John, farmer, sh. Sept 1775, to Ga, in *Georgia Packet*, sett. Friendsborough Ga. (PRO.T47.10)
2844. Hume, John, b. 1747, farmer, sh. Sept 1775, fr. Newcastle to Ga, in *Georgia Packet*. (PRO.T47.9\11)
2845. Hume, Thomas, Jacobite, tr. 28 July 1716, fr. Liverpool to Va, in *Godspeed*, arr. Md Oct 1716. (SPC.1716.310)(CTB31.209)(HM389)
2846. Hume, William, b. 1735, shipmaster, res. Glasgow, sh. July 1775, fr. Greenock to Ga, in *Christy*. (PRO.T47.12)
2847. Hunt, Edward, Jacobite, tr. 30 Mar 1716, fr. Liverpool to Antigua, in *Scipio*. (SPC.1716.310)(CTB31.204)
2848. Hunter, Abram, b. 1746, shipmaster, res. Greenock Renfrewshire, sh. Aug 1774, fr. Greenock to Wilmington N.C., in *Ulysses*. (PRO.T47.12)
2849. Hunter, David, merchant, res. Ayr, sh. pre 1769, sett. Va. (SRO.CS.GMB53)
2850. Hunter, David, b. 1751, shipmaster, res. Ayr, sh. Oct 1774, fr. Greenock to Philadelphia, in *Sally*. (PRO.T47.12)
2851. Hunter, George, surveyor general, d. 10 July 1755 Charleston S.C. (SM.17.316)
2852. Hunter, James, res. Duns Berwickshire, pts. James Hunter, sh. pre 1776, sett. King George Co Va. (SRO.RS19.17.39)

2853. Hunter, James, merchant, res. Duns Berwickshire, sh. pre 1756.
(SRO.SH.29.7.1756)

2854. Hunter, James, merchant, res. Edinburgh, pts. James Hunter, sh. pre
1773, sett. James River Va. (SRO.RD2.256.112)

2855. Hunter, James, b. 1746, housewright, res. Kirkmichael, sh. 31 May
1775, fr. Stranraer to N.Y., in *Jackie*, m. Janet McKinnel, ch.
John. (PRO.T47.12)

2856. Hunter, Jean, tailor's servant, thief, res. Edinburgh, tr. 1773, fr. Port
Glasgow to Va, in *Phoenix*, arr. Port Accomack Va 20 Dec 1773.
(SRO.JC27.10.3) (alias 6439)

2857. Hunter, John, Covenanter, tr. Dec 1685, fr. Leith to Barbados, in *John &
Nicholas*. (PC.11.166)(ETR389)

2858. Hunter, John, Jacobite, tr. 29 June 1716, fr. Liverpool to Jamaica or Va,
in *Elizabeth & Anne*. (SPC.1716.310)(CTB31.208)

2859. Hunter, John, merchant, sh. Feb 1681, fr. Ayr to West Indies, in *James
of Ayr*. (SRO.E72.3.6)

2860. Hunter, John, merchant, sh. Mar 1683, fr. Ayr to Caribee Islands, in
James of Ayr. (SRO.E72.3.12)

2861. Hunter, Patrick, Jacobite, tr. 24 May 1716, fr. Liverpool to Va, in
Friendship, arr. Md Aug 1716.
(SPC.1716.311)(CTB31.207)(HM387)

2862. Hunter, Patrick, carpenter, res. Leith Midlothian, sh. Oct 1752, fr. Leith
to Cape Fear N.C. (SRO.RD4.178.365)

2863. Hunter, Robert, baker, res. Perth, m. Marian Henderson, d. 1703 Darien,
Edin pr1708 CC8.8.84

2864. Hunter, Thomas sr, Covenanter, res. Dinduff Dumfries-shire, tr. Oct
1684, m. Barbara Horner. (PC.10.587)

2865. Hunter, William, b. 1730, physician, sett. R.I., d. 1777. (SA184)

2866. Hurry, John, b. 1738, farmer, res. Stenness Orkney Islands, sh. Sept
1774, fr. Kirkwall to Savannah Ga, in *Marlborough*, sett.
Richmond Co Ga, m. Jean ..., ch. William & Jean. (PRO.T47.12)

2867. Hussie, Michael, sailor, sh. 14 July 1698, fr. Leith to Darien, in
Unicorn, Edin pr1707 CC8.8.83

2868. Hutcheon, Alexander, b. 1750, wright, res. Stirling, sh. May 1775, fr.
Greenock to N.Y., in *Monimia*. (PRO.T47.12)

2869. Hutcheson, Alexander, clergyman edu. Glasgow Uni, sh. 1722, to
Philadelphia, sett. Bohemia Manor Md. (AP193)

2870. Hutcheson, Janet, whore, res. Edinburgh, tr. Mar 1695.
(SRO.PC2.25.216)

2871. Hutcheson, John, farmer, Covenanter, res. Hairlaw Dumfries-shire, tr. 5
Sept 1685, fr. Leith to East N.J., in *Henry & Francis*, m. Marion
Weir. (PC.11.155)

2872. Hutcheson, Robert, tr. Aug 1685, fr. Leith to Jamaica. (PC.11.136)

2873. Hutchin, Thomas, carpenter, sh. 1637, sett. Barbados. (SRO.GD34.925)

2874. Hutchison, Alexander, sailor, sh. 18 Aug 1699, fr. Clyde to Darien, in
    Rising Sun, Edin pr1707 CC8.8.83
2875. Hutchison, John, b. 1754, weaver, res. Paisley Renfrewshire, sh. Feb
    1774, fr. Greenock to N.Y., in *Commerce*. (PRO.T47.12)
2876. Hutchison, William, sh. pre1700, sett. Port Royal Jamaica. (DP352)
2877. Hutchison, William, b. 1744, baker, res. Nairn, sh. May 1774, fr.
    Stornaway to Philadelphia, in *Friendship*. (PRO.T47.12)
2878. Hutson, Jean, gypsy & thief, res. Dumfries-shire, tr. May 1739.
    (SRO.JC12.5)
2879. Hutton, Barbara, whore, res. Edinburgh, tr. Feb 1697. (SRO.PC2.26)
2880. Hutton, David, thief, res. Perthshire, tr. Oct 1778. (SM
2881. Hutton, James, sailor, res. Cleish Kinross-shire, pts. John Hutton, sh. 14
    July 1698, fr. Leith to Darien, in *St Andrew*, Edin pr1707
    CC.8.83
2882. Hutton, John, clergyman, res. Chapel Lauder Berwickshire, pts. James
    Seaton or Hutton, sh. 14 July 1698, fr. Leith to Darien, in
    Caledonia, Edin pr1707 CC8.8.83 (alias 6035)
2883. Hyndman, Andrew, b. 1728, farmer, res. Kintyre Argyll, sh. Aug 1774,
    fr. Greenock to Wilmington N.C., in *Ulysses*, m. Catherine
    Campbell, ch. Mary Margaret. (PRO.T47.12)
2884. Hyndman, William, merchant, res. Glasgow, sh. pre 1769, sett. St Kitts.
    (SRO.SC36.63.13)
2885. Imlay, Jean, thief, res. Aberdeenshire, tr. Aug 1753, fr. Aberdeen to Va,
    in *St Andrew*. (AJ281\294)
2886. Imrie, Duncan, b. 4 Apr 1754, ship's carpenter, res. Dundee Angus, pts.
    John Imrie & Barbara Geddie, sh. pre 1782, sett. Carolina & St
    Augustine E Fla, d. pre 1782 at sea, Edin pr1782 CC8.8.125
2887. Inglis, Alison, adulterer, res. Scone Perthshire, tr. 1753. (SM.15.469)
2888. Inglis, Charles, sailor, res. St Andrews Fife, pts. James Inglis, sh. 18
    Aug 1699, fr. Clyde to Darien, in *Rising Sun*, Edin pr1707
    CC8.8.83
2889. Inglis, Henry, sailor, res. Kinghorn Fife, sh. 14 July 1698, fr. Leith to
    Darien, in *St Andrew*, Edin pr1707 CC8.8.83
2890. Inglis, James, overseer, res. Calder Midlothian, d. 1699 Darien, Edin
    pr1707 CC8.8.83
2891. Inglis, Peter, servant, housebreaker, res. Edinburgh, tr. 1772, fr. Port
    Glasgow, in *Matty*, arr. Port Oxford Md 16 May 1772.
    (SRO.JC27.10.3)
2892. Inglis, Robert, sailor, res. St Andrews Fife, pts. James Inglis, sh. 18 Aug
    1699, fr. Clyde to Darien, in *Rising Sun*, Edin pr1707 CC8.8.83
2893. Inglis, William, res. Farr(?) Sutherland, sh. 5 May 1698, fr. Liverpool to
    Barbados. (LRO.HQ325.2.FRE)
2894. Inglis, William, mason, Covenanter, res. Glasgow, tr. June 1684, fr.
    Glasgow to Carolina, in *Pelican of Glasgow*. (PC.9.208)

2895. Ingram, Archibald, merchant, res. East Kilpatrick Dunbartonshire, pts. Archibald Ingram of Cloberhill, sh. pre 1769, sett. St Kitts. (SRA.CFI)
2896. Ingram, James, merchant, res. East Kilpatrick Dunbartonshire, pts. Archibald Ingram of Cloberhill, sh. pre 1769, sett. Va. (SRA.CFI)
2897. Inkster, Joseph, b. 7 Apr 1751, Alford Aberdeenshire, house carpenter, res. Bridgend Alford, pts. John Inkster, sh. 1776, to Dominica, d. May 1783. (APB.4.99)
2898. Innes, Alexander, gunner's boy, res. West Lothian, sh. 14 July 1698, fr. Leith to Darien, in St Andrew, Edin pr1707 CC8.8.83
2899. Innes, Alexander, clergyman & schoolmaster edu. Aberdeen Uni, res. Aberdeenshire, sh. 1693, to N.E., d. Aug 1713 Elisabethtown N.J. (APB.2.118)
2900. Innes, Alexander, provost marshal, res. Caithness, sh. pre 1746, sett. Jamaica. (SRO.RS .2.374)
2901. Innes, George, b. 27 July 1760, Aberdeen, res. Aberdeen, pts. Alexander Innes & Ann Ross, d. 9 Nov 1784 Jamaica, bd. Kingston Cathedral. (MIBWI
2902. Innes, James, Jacobite, tr. 15 July 1716, fr. Liverpool to Barbados, in Africa. (SPC.1716.312)(CTB31.209)
2903. Innes, Katherine, b. 1755, servant, res. Caithness, sh. May 1775, fr. Leith to Philadelphia, in Friendship. (PRO.T47.12)
2904. Innes, William, wigmaker, Jacobite, res. Fochabers Morayshire, tr. 31 Mar 1747, fr. London to Barbados, in Frere. (P.2.296)(MR127)
2905. Innes, William, b. 1721, fiddler, Jacobite, res. Buckie Banffshire, tr. 31 Mar 1747, fr. London to Jamaica, in St George or Carteret, arr. Jamaica 1747. (P.2.296)(PRO.CO137.58)(MR127)
2906. Ireland, James, housebreaker, res. Edinburgh, pts. James Ireland, tr. Aug 1764. (SRO.HCR.I.96)
2907. Ireland, John, Covenanter, tr. 11 Aug 1685, fr. Leith to Jamaica. (PC.11.114)(ETR369)
2908. Ironside, Christian, infanticide, res. New Deer Aberdeenshire, tr. Sept 1749. (AJ93)
2909. Irvine, Andrew, b. 1668, Shetland Islands, pts. Andrew Irvine, sh. Aug 1684, fr. London to Barbados. (CLRO\AIA)
2910. Irvine, David, b. 1738, laborer, res. St Mungo Dumfries-shire, sh. May 1775, fr. Dumfries to P.E.I., in Lovely Nelly, m. Margaret Graham, ch. William Jean James. (PRO.T47.12)
2911. Irvine, James, b. 1713, shoemaker, Jacobite, res. Gribton Nithsdale Dumfries-shire, tr. 22 Apr 1747, fr. Liverpool to Va, in Johnson, arr. Port Oxford Md 5 Aug 1747. (P.2.298)(PRO.T1.328)
2912. Irvine, James, b. 1752, planter, res. Dumfries, sh. 1774, fr. Greenock to Jamaica, in Isobella. (PRO.T47.12)

141

2913. Irvine, James, b. 1758, Evie, farm servant, res. Evie Orkney Islands, pts. Nicol Irvine, sh. Sept 1775, fr. Kirkwall to Savannah Ga, in *Marlborough*, sett. Richmond Co Ga. (PRO.T47.12)

2914. Irvine, John, b. 1748, weaver, res. Stromness Orkney Islands, sh. Sept 1774, fr. Kirkwall to Savannah Ga, in *Marlborough*, sett. Richmond Co Ga. (PRO.T47.12)

2915. Irvine, Laurence, b. 1715, cutler, res. Glasgow, sh. Sept 1735, fr. London to Jamaica. (CLRO\AIA)

2916. Irvine, Robert, merchant, res. Dumfries-shire, sh. pre 1729, sett. Antigua, ch. Elizabeth. (SRO.RS .10.480)

2917. Irving, William, farmer & merchant, sh. pre 1765, sett. Va. (SRA.T.MJ)

2918. Irwin, George, Jacobite, tr. 22 Apr 1747, fr. Liverpool to Va, in *Johnson*, arr. Port Oxford Md 5 Aug 1747. (PRO.T1.328)(P.2.298)

2919. Isaac, Alexander, sailor, res. Tulliallan Fife, sh. 14 July 1698, fr. Leith to Darien, in *Unicorn*, Edin pr1707 CC8.8.83

2920. Isbister, Hugh, b. Feb 1757, Firth Orkney Islands, boatman, res. Stromness Orkney Islands, pts. David Isbister & Janet Omand, sh. Sept 1775, fr. Kirkwall to Savannah Ga, in *Marlborough*, sett. Richmond Co Ga. (PRO.T47.12)

2921. Ivar, John, tr. Aug 1685, fr. Leith to Jamaica. (PC.11.136)

2922. Ivar, Malcolm, Covenanter, tr. July 1685. (PC.11.126)

2923. Jack, Alexander, gardener, res. Dumfries-shire, tr. May 1746. (SRO.JC27)

2924. Jack, Andrew, b. 1717, husbandman, Jacobite, res. Elgin Morayshire, tr. 1747, fr. Tilbury. (P.2.300)

2925. Jack, Andrew, b. 1717, Jacobite, res. Caithness, tr. 20 Mar 1747, fr. London to Jamaica or Barbados, in *St George or Carteret*, arr. Jamaica 1747. (P.2.298)(MR82)(PRO.CO137.58)

2926. Jack, Donald, b. 1689, beggar, Jacobite, res. Ross-shire, tr. 20 Mar 1747, fr. London to Jamaica or Barbados. (P.2.300) (alias 2927)

2927. Jack, Duncan, b. 1689, beggar, Jacobite, res. Ross-shire, tr. 20 Mar 1747, fr. London to Jamaica or Barbados. (P.2.300) (alias 2926)

2928. Jack, Isobel, b. 1761, servant, res. Kilsain, sh. July 1775, fr. Stornaway to Philadelphia, in *Clementina*. (PRO.T47.12)

2929. Jack, James, b. 1757, merchant, res. Aberdeen, sh. July 1775, fr. Greenock to Jamaica, in *Isabella*. (PRO.T47.12)

2930. Jack, Janet, b. 1752, servant, res. Morayshire, sh. July 1775, fr. Stornaway to Philadelphia, in *Clementina*. (PRO.T47.12)

2931. Jack, John, b. 1745, servant, res. Morayshire, sh. July 1775, fr. Stornaway to Philadelphia, in *Clementina*. (PRO.T47.12)

2932. Jack, William, blacksmith, res. Rayne Aberdeenshire, pts. Charles Jack, d. 1773 Trelawney Co Jamaica. (APB.4.75)

2933. Jack, William, thief, res. Perthshire, tr. Apr 1752. (AJ227)(SM.14.212)

2934. Jack, William, b. 1711, merchant & messenger, Jacobite, res. Elgin
Morayshire, tr. 31 Mar 1747, fr. Tilbury to Barbados.
(P.2.300)(MR53)
2935. Jack, William, b. 1749, smith, sh. Feb 1774, fr. London to Md, in
Speedwell. (PRO.T47.9\11)
2936. Jackson, Ann, forger, res. Fort Augustus Inverness-shire, tr. Sept 1754.
(AJ350)
2937. Jackson, Annabel, Covenanter, tr. 5 Sept 1685, fr. Leith to East N.J., in
Henry & Francis. (PC.11.154)
2938. Jackson, James, sailor, res. Edinburgh, pts. Charles Jackson, sh. May
1699, fr. Clyde to Darien, in Olive Branch, Edin pr1707 CC8.8.83
2939. Jackson, John, servant, Covenanter, res. Braestob Glasgow, tr. Aug 1685,
fr. Leith to Jamaica, arr. Port Royal Jamaica Nov 1685, sett.
Spanish Town Jamaica. (PC.11.329)(LJ81)
2940. Jackson, Margaret, b. 1754, res. Edinburgh, sh. Apr 1775, fr. Greenock
to N.Y., in Lilly. (PRO.T47.12)
2941. Jackson, Robert, b. 1755, carpenter, res. Ayr, sh. Jan 1774, fr. Greenock
to Jamaica, in Janet. (SRO.CE60.1.7)
2942. Jackson, Thomas, Covenanter, tr. 5 Sept 1685, fr. Leith to East N.J., in
Henry & Francis. (PC.11.159)
2943. Jackson, William, Covenanter, tr. 5 Sept 1685, fr. Leith to East N.J., in
Henry & Francis. (PC.11.159)(ETR376)
2944. Jackson, William, b. 1709, carpenter & joiner, res. Edinburgh, sh. Oct
1773, fr. London to Jamaica. (CLRO\AIA)
2945. Jackson, William, b. 1713, husbandman, res. Peebles, sh. Sept 1735, fr.
London to Md. (CLRO\AIA)
2946. Jackson, William, b. 28 Apr 1725, Kettins Angus, laborer, Jacobite, res.
Angus, pts. John Jackson & Elizabeth Fife, tr. 5 May 1747, fr.
Liverpool to Leeward Islands, in Veteran, arr. Martinique June
1747. (P.2.300)(MR103)(OR33)(PRO.SP36.102)
2947. Jaffray, Andrew, d. 6 Feb 1699 Darien. (DP86)
2948. James, McBain, thief, res. Aberdeenshire, tr. May 1769. (AJ1115) (alias
4472)
2949. Jamie, Robert, b. 8 July 1742, Logie-Pert Angus, thief, res. Montrose
Angus, pts. John Jamie & Anne Piper, tr. Sept 1775.
(SM.37.524)
2950. Jamieson, Alexander, servant, Covenanter, res. Mauchline Ayrshire, tr.
Aug 1685, fr. Leith to Jamaica. (PC.11.136)(ETR369)
2951. Jamieson, Anne, thief, res. Ayrshire, tr. Aug 1748. (SM.10.248)
2952. Jamieson, Archibald, tr. July 1685, fr. Leith to East N.J. (PC.11.131)
2953. Jamieson, David, Covenanter, tr. 19 May 1684, fr. Leith to N.Y.
(PC.8.516)
2954. Jamieson, David, Covenanter, res. Linlithgow West Lothian, tr. 29 May
1684, fr. Leith to Carolina. (PC.8.526)

2955. Jamieson, James, sailor, res. Burntisland Fife, pts. James Jackson, sh. 14 July 1698, fr. Leith to Darien, in *Unicorn*, Edin pr1707 CC8.8.83

2956. Jamieson, James, farmer & fisherman, res. Shetland Islands, sh. June 1775, fr. Kirkcaldy to Brunswick N.C., in *Jamaica Packet*. (PRO.T47.12)

2957. Jamieson, James, surgeon & merchant, res. Greenock Renfrewshire, sh. pre 1783, sett. Tobago, d. pre 1783 Tobago, Edin pr1783 CC8.8.126

2958. Jamieson, John, sh. Feb 1683, fr. Port Glasgow to West Indies, in *Walter of Glasgow*. (SRO.E72.19.8)

2959. Jamieson, Mary, b. 1750, spinner, res. Paisley Renfrewshire, sh. Feb 1774, fr. Greenock to N.Y., in *Commerce*. (PRO.T47.12)

2960. Jamieson, Philip, book-keeper, res. Edinburgh, sh. Dec 1730, fr. London to Md. (CLRO\AIA)

2961. Jamieson, Thomas, horsethief, res. Aberdeenshire, tr. Apr 1754. (AJ326)

2962. Janson, Peter, seaman, sh. 14 July 1698, fr. Leith to Darien, in *St Andrew*, Edin pr1707 CC8.8.83

2963. Japp, John, b. 1731, carpenter, Jacobite, res. Banff, tr. 5 May 1747, fr. Liverpool to Leeward Islands, in *Veteran*, arr. Martinique June 1747. (P.2.302)(JAB.2.431)(MR72)(PRO.SP36.102)

2964. Jardine, Andrew, Covenanter, tr. Aug 1685. (PC.11.329)

2965. Jeddes, William, res. Edinburgh, sh. 1684, fr. London to Barbados. (WCF.MS6679)

2966. Jeffrey, William, res. Perth, pts. James Jeffrey, sh. pre 1758, sett. Philadelphia, ch. Jean, d. 1758 Philadelphia. (SRO.SH.30.9.1758)

2967. Jervy, John, wright, res. Falkirk Stirlingshire, tr. 12 Dec 1678, fr. Leith to West Indies, in *St Michael of Scarborough*. (PC.6.76)

2968. Johnson, Gavin, b. 1753, schoolmaster, res. Bothwell Lanarkshire, sh. May 1775, fr. Dumfries to P.E.I., in *Lovely Nelly*. (PRO.T47.12)

2969. Johnson, George, b. 1758, gentleman, res. Edinburgh, sh. Dec 1773, fr. London to Kingston Jamaica, in *Augustus*. (PRO.T47.9\11)

2970. Johnson, Hugh, b. 1720, weaver, Jacobite, res. Walton, tr. 8 May 1747, fr. Liverpool to Antigua. (P.2.305)(MR197)

2971. Johnson, John, b. 1717, husbandman, Jacobite, res. Lancashire, tr. 5 May 1747, fr. Liverpool to Leeward Islands, in *Veteran*, arr. Martinique June 1747. (P.2.307)(MR197)(PRO.SP36.102)

2972. Johnson, Richard, comb-maker, Jacobite, res. Lancaster Lancashire, tr. 24 Feb 1747, fr. Liverpool to Va, in *Gildart*, arr. Port North Potomac Md 5 Aug 1747. (P.2.306)(MR197)(PRO.T1.328)

2973. Johnson, William, Jacobite, tr. 28 July 1716, fr. Liverpool to Va, in *Godspeed*, arr. Md Oct 1716. (SPC.1716.310)(CTB31.209)(HM388)

2974. Johnson, William, b. 1730, tailor, res. Dumfries, sh. Apr 1750, fr. London to Jamaica. (CLRO\AIA)

2975. Johnston, Alexander, soldier, d. 1699 Darien, Edin pr1707 CC8.8.83
2976. Johnston, Andrew, schoolmaster, sh. 1706, to Jamaica. (EMA37)
2977. Johnston, Andrew, Councillor, d. 24 June 1762 Amboy N.J.
        (SM.24.451)
2978. Johnston, Andrew, b. 1744, farmer, res. Dumfries-shire, sh. Oct 1774, fr.
        Greenock to Charleston S.C., in *Countess*. (PRO.T47.12)
2979. Johnston, Ann, b. 1755, farm servant, res. Stenness Orkney Islands, sh.
        Sept 1774, fr. Kirkwall to Savannah Ga, in *Marlborough*, sett.
        Richmond Co Ga. (PRO.T47.12)
2980. Johnston, Anne, thief, res. Edinburgh, tr. Dec 1743. (EBR.BC.3.74)
        (alias 1258, 3806)
2981. Johnston, Archibald, merchant, sh. pre 1694, sett. Barbados, ch.
        Archibald. (SRO.PC2.25.98)
2982. Johnston, Cecilia, infanticide, res. Wick Caithness, tr. Sept 1759.
        (SM.21.494)
2983. Johnston, Donald, Covenanter, tr. Aug 1685, fr. Leith to Jamaica.
        (PC.11.136)
2984. Johnston, Gabriel, Governor of N.C., sett. Edenhouse Edenton N.C., d.
        Sept 1752 N.C., PCC pr1795. (SM.14.510)
2985. Johnston, George, Covenanter, res. Midcalder Midlothian, tr. 5 Sept
        1685, fr. Leith to East N.J. (PC.11.154)
2986. Johnston, Gideon, clergyman, sh. 1707, to Carolina. (EMA37)
2987. Johnston, Helen, thief, tr. Feb 1775. (SRO.HCR.I.112)
2988. Johnston, James, foremastman, res. Queensferry West Lothian, sh. 14
        July 1698, fr. Leith to Darien, in *Caledonia*, Edin pr1707
        CC8.8.83
2989. Johnston, James, sailor, res. Leith Midlothian, sh. 14 July 1698, fr.
        Leith to Darien, in *Unicorn*, Edin pr1707 CC8.8.84
2990. Johnston, James, Jacobite, tr. 29 June 1716, fr. Liverpool to Jamaica or
        Va, in *Elizabeth & Anne*, arr. Va.
        (SPC.1716.310)(CTB31.208)(VSP.1.186)
2991. Johnston, James, merchant, res. Glasgow, sh. 1760, to Va.
        (SRO.CS.GMB50)
2992. Johnston, Janet, b. 1715, res. Dumfries, sh. May 1775, fr. Dumfries to
        P.E.I., in *Lovely Nelly*. (PRO.T47.12)
2993. Johnston, Janet, b. 1754, servant, res. Evie Orkney Islands, sh. Sept
        1775, fr. Kirkwall to Savannah Ga, in *Marlborough*.
        (PRO.T47.12)
2994. Johnston, Jean, thief, tr. Apr 1754, fr. Leith to Va. (AJ326)
2995. Johnston, John, weaver, sh. 12 Oct 1699, fr. Clyde to Darien, in *Speedy
        Return*, Edin pr1708 CC8.8.84
2996. Johnston, John, Jacobite, tr. 7 May 1716, fr. Liverpool to S.C., in
        Susannah. (CTB31.206)

145

2997. Johnston, John, Jacobite, tr. 29 June 1716, fr. Liverpool to Jamaica or Va, in *Elizabeth & Anne*, arr. Va. (SPC.1716.310)(CTB31.208)(VSP.1.186)

2998. Johnston, John, apothecary, res. Edinburgh, pts. William Johnston of Labroiblan, sh. 5 Sept 1685, fr. Leith to East N.J., in *Henry & Francis*. (Insh242)(SRO.RD4.67.97)

2999. Johnston, John, 'pittyaguerman', res. Aberdeen, pts. James Johnston & Jean Ogilvie, d. Mar 1744 S.C. (APB.3.122)

3000. Johnston, John, b. 11 Sept 1739, Marnoch Banffshire, Jacobite, res. Banff, pts. William Johnston, tr. 1747, fr. Tilbury. (P.2.304)(MR44)

3001. Johnston, John, b. 1749, cooper, res. Coupar Angus Perthshire, sh. Aug 1774, fr. Greenock to Philadelphia, in *Magdalene*. (PRO.T47.12)

3002. Johnston, Lewis, merchant, res. Edinburgh, pts. James Johnston, sh. pre 1756, sett. St Kitts & Ga, ch. Ann Elizabeth & Rachel, d. pre 1798 Ga, PCC pr1798. (SRO.SH.27.4.1756)

3003. Johnston, Nicol, b. 1747, farmer, res. Evie Orkney Islands, sh. Sept 1775, fr. Kirkwall to Savannah Ga, in *Marlborough*, sett. Richmond Co Ga, m. Isobel Flett, ch. Janet. (PRO.T47.12)

3004. Johnston, Robert, Jacobite, tr. 29 June 1716, fr. Liverpool to Jamaica or Va, in *Elizabeth & Anne*, arr. Va. (SPC.1716.310)(CTB31.208)(VSP.1.186)

3005. Johnston, Robert, b. 1701, laborer, Jacobite, res. Stonehaven Kincardineshire, tr. 31 Mar 1747, fr. Jamaica or Barbados. (P.2.306)(MR30)

3006. Johnston, Thomas, clergyman, sh. 1751, to Md. (EMA37)

3007. Johnston, Thomas, merchant, sh. Mar 1685, fr. Port Glasgow to Caribee Islands, in *Mayflower of Glasgow*. (SRO.E72.19.9)

3008. Johnston, Thomas, sh. Feb 1683, fr. Port Glasgow to West Indies, in *Walter of Glasgow*. (SRO.E72.19.8)

3009. Johnston, Walter, surgeon's mate, res. Edinburgh, pts. James Johnston of Corhead, d. 1699 Darien, Edin pr1707 CC8.8.83

3010. Johnston, Walter, rioter, tr. Aug 1771. (SRO.HCR.I.106)

3011. Johnstone, James, res. Spotswood Berwickshire, sh. 1684, to East N.J., sett. Pitscataway N.J. (Insh264)

3012. Johnstone, Robert, b. 1738, fisherman, res. Shetland Islands, sh. Oct 1774, fr. Kirkcaldy to Antigua, in *Jamaica Packet*, m. Mary ... (PRO.T47.12)

3013. Joiner, David, b. 1727, laborer, Jacobite, res. Aberdeen, tr. 5 May 1747, fr. Liverpool to Leeward Islands, in *Veteran*, arr. Martinique June 1747. (P.2.306)(JAB.2.431)(MR72)(PRO.SP36.102)

3014. Jones, Humphrey, servant, sh. 1637, to Barbados. (SRO.GD34.925)

3015. Joss, Margaret, infanticide, res. Banffshire, tr. Apr 1752, fr. Aberdeen to Va, in *Ann of Aberdeen*. (AJ194\224)

146

3016. Junkein, James, assault, res. Kilmalcolm Renfrewshire, tr. June 1670. (PC.3.178)

3017. Junor, William, robber, res. Aberdeenshire, tr. June 1763. (SRO.RH2.4.255)

3018. Kay, Alexander, b. 1749, piper, res. Breadalbane Perthshire, sh. June 1775, fr. Greenock to N.Y., in *Commerce*. (PRO.T47.12)

3019. Keelly, John, thief, res. Branshog Stirlingshire, tr. May 1729. (SRO.JC27) (alias 1526)

3020. Kein, Patrick, tr. Nov 1679, fr. Leith. (ETR162)

3021. Keir, Agnes, assault, res. Glasgow, tr. May 1766, fr. Glasgow, m. Alexander Colquhoun. (AJ958)

3022. Keir, Alexander, thief, tr. July 1761. (AJ708)

3023. Keir, Alexander, servant, thief, res. Farskane Rathen Banffshire, tr. May 1766, fr. Aberdeen. (AJ958\964)

3024. Keir, James, merchant, res. Stirling, sh. 1699, to Darien. (RBS91)

3025. Keir, Mrs, b. 1716, sh. 1761, sett. James Island S.C., m. Rev Patrick Keir, d. 1798 Nassau Bahamas. (GC1083)

3026. Keith, Alexander, clergyman, sh. 1745, to S.C. (EMA39)

3027. Keith, Alexander, tr. 21 Oct 1682, fr. Grenock to N.Y. (ETR221)

3028. Keith, Andrew, farmer, housebreaker, res. Gerth Caithness, tr. July 1769. (SRO.JC27.D35)(AJ1126)

3029. Keith, Duncan, b. 1745, carpenter, sh. June 1775, fr. London to Baltimore, in *Nancy*. (PRO.T47.9\11)

3030. Keith, George, b. 1584, clergyman, sh. 1612, to Bermuda, in *Plough*, sett. Elizabeth City Va. (F.7.660)(PRO.CO1.3.114\72)

3031. Keith, George, b. 1638, Peterhead Aberdeenshire, clergyman edu. Marischal Col Aberdeen 1658, sh. 1685, to Philadelphia, sett. Perth Amboy N.J. & Md, d. 1714 England. (Insh171)(SNQ.I.60)

3032. Keith, George, b. 12 Sept 1714, Old Machar Aberdeen, shoemaker, Jacobite, res. Aberdeen, pts. George Keith & Isobel Leys, tr. 5 May 1747, fr. Liverpool to Leeward Islands, in *Veteran*, arr. Martinique June 1747. (P.2.308)(JAB.2.432)(PRO.SP36.102)

3033. Keith, James, clergyman, sh. pre 1645, sett. Hamilton Fauquier Co Va, m. Mary Ishan Randolph. (OD16)

3034. Keith, James, b. 1644, Aberdeen, clergyman, sh. pre 1644, sett. Bridgewater Mass, m. Susanna Edson, ch. Josiah, d. 23 July 1719. (F.7.664)

3035. Keith, James, b. 1727, servant, Jacobite, res. Glenbervie Kincardineshire, tr. 24 Feb 1747, fr. Liverpool to Va, in *Gildart*, arr. Port North Potomac Md 5 Aug 1747. (P.2.310)(PRO.T1.328)

3036. Keith, Robert, mariner, sh. May 1699, fr. Clyde to Darien, Edin pr1707 CC8.8.83

3037. Keith, Sir Basil, Governor of Jamaica, d. 15 June 1777 Spanish Town Jamaica, bd. St Catherine's. (SM.39.455)

147

3038. Keith, William, thief & vagrant, tr. 1775, in *Aeolis*, arr. Port North Potomac Md 17 Oct 1775. (SRO.JC27.10.3)
3039. Kell, Neil, tr. 7 Aug 1685; fr. Leith to Jamaica. (PC.11.130)
3040. Kellie, John, Covenanter, res. Dunbar East Lothian, tr. 5 Sept 1685, fr. Leith to East N.J., in *Henry & Francis*. (PC.10.129)
3041. Kellie, Katherine, Covenanter, tr. 5 Sept 1685, fr. Leith to East N.J., in *Henry & Francis*. (PC.11.154)
3042. Kello, John, tr. Aug 1684, fr. Leith to Carolina. (PC.9.95)
3043. Kelly, Alexander, b. 1752, laborer, res. Galloway, sh. May 1774, fr. Stranraer to N.Y., in *Gale*. (PRO.T47.12)
3044. Kelly, Anne, b. 1760, servant, res. Contin Ross & Cromarty, sh. July 1775, fr. Stornaway to Philadelphia, in *Clementina*. (PRO.T47.12)
3045. Kelly, Peter, b. 1734, res. Glen Luce Wigtonshire, sh. May 1774, fr. Stranraer to N.Y., in *Gale*, m. Ann Adair, ch. Jean Elizabeth Alexander. (PRO.T47.12)
3046. Kelly, Robert, b. 1736, husbandman, res. Galloway, sh. May 1774, fr. Stranraer to N.Y., in *Gale*, m. Mary ..., ch. Margaret James Jean. (PRO.T47.12)
3047. Kelso, Archibald, sailor, res. Edinburgh, sh. 14 July 1698, fr. Leith to Darien, in *Dolphin*, Edin pr1707 CC8.8.83
3048. Kelso, William, b. 1652, surgeon & apothecary, Covenanter, res. Ayr, sh. Apr 1680, to Boston Mass, in *Anne & Hester*. (SPC1682.441)(UJA.2.1.274)
3049. Kelvie, William, b. 1714, husbandman, res. Kilabright, sh. May 1739, fr. London to Md. (CLRO\AIA)
3050. Kemlo, Joseph, blacksmith, Jacobite, res. Hardgate Old Machar Aberdeen, tr. 24 Feb 1747, fr. Liverpool to Va, in *Gildart*, arr. Port North Potomac Md 5 Aug 1747. (P.2.310)(JAB.2.432)(MR211)(PRO.T1.328)
3051. Kemp, William, b. 1757, servant, res. Morayshire, sh. July 1775, fr. Stornaway to Philadelphia, in *Clementina*. (PRO.T47.12)
3052. Kempie, John, b. 1707, servant, Jacobite, res. Gask Perthshire, tr. 1747. (P.2.312)(MR54)
3053. Kennan, William, res. Dumfries-shire, sh. pre 1765, sett. Richmond Co Va, d. pre 1765, PCC pr1765
3054. Kennedy, Adam, sett. Antigua, d. pre 1698, PCC pr1698
3055. Kennedy, Alexander, Jacobite, tr. 26 Apr 1716, fr. Liverpool to Jamaica, in *Two Brothers*, arr. Montserrat June 1716. (SPC.1716.313)(CTB31.205)(CTP.CC.43)
3056. Kennedy, Alexander, b. 1736, cooper, res. Edinburgh, pts. Alexander Kennedy, sh. 26 Jan 1774, fr. London to Hampton Va, in *Planter*, 28 Apr 1774, sett. Fredericksburg Va. (PRO.T47.9\11)(OD60)
3057. Kennedy, Alexander, b. 1762, servant, res. Wester Leys, sh. July 1775, fr. Stornaway to Philadelphia, in *Clementina*. (PRO.T47.12)

3058. Kennedy, Angus, b. 1734, Jacobite, res. Shian, tr. 1747. (MR154)
3059. Kennedy, Angus, b. 1749, farmer, res. Breadalbane Perthshire, sh. June
1775, fr. Greenock to N.Y., in *Commerce*. (PRO.T47.12)
3060. Kennedy, Angus Baan, piper, thief, tr. Mar 1755. (SM.17.159)
3061. Kennedy, Anne, b. 1735, res. Wester Leys, sh. July 1775, fr. Stornaway
to Philadelphia, in *Clementina*, ch. Margaret. (PRO.T47.12)
3062. Kennedy, Anne, b. 1764, servant, res. Wester Leys, sh. July 1775, fr.
Stornaway to Philadelphia, in *Clementina*. (PRO.T47.12)
3063. Kennedy, Archibald, b. 1685, Receiver General of Customs, res.
Kirkoswald Ayrshire, pts. Alexander Kennedy of Kilhenzie &
Helen Monteith, sett. Pavonia Second River Hoboken N.Y., m. (1)
... Massam(2)Maria Walter Schuyler, ch. James Robert Archibald
Thomas Catherine, d. 14 June 1763 N.Y. (SP.2.494)(SM.25.415)
3064. Kennedy, Bessie, Covenanter, res. Cockethill, tr. Oct 1684. (PC.10.587)
3065. Kennedy, Daniel, Jacobite, tr. 28 July 1716, fr. Liverpool to Va, in
Godspeed, arr. Md Oct 1716.
(SPC.1716.310)(CTB31.209)(HM389)
3066. Kennedy, Donald, b. 1755, servant, res. Wester Leys, sh. July 1775, fr.
Stornaway to Philadelphia, in *Clementina*. (PRO.T47.12)
3067. Kennedy, Duncan Dow, cattle thief, res. Kilinan Glengarry Inverness-
shire, tr. May 1764. (SM.26.287)
3068. Kennedy, Duncan McEan, cattlethief, res. Lochiel Inverness-shire, tr. May
1763. (AJ802)
3069. Kennedy, John, Covenanter, tr. Aug 1685, fr. Leith to Jamaica.
(PC.11.329)
3070. Kennedy, John, Jacobite, tr. 26 Apr 1716, fr. Liverpool to Jamaica, in
Two Brothers, arr. Montserrat June 1716.
(SPC.1716.313)(CTB31.205)(CTP.CC.43)
3071. Kennedy, John, Jacobite, tr. 30 Mar 1716, fr. Liverpool to Antigua, in
Scipio. (SPC.1716.310)(CTB31.204)
3072. Kennedy, John, Jacobite, tr. 29 June 1716, fr. Liverpool to Jamaica or
Va, in *Elizabeth & Anne*, arr. Va.
(SPC.1716.310)(CTB31.208)(VSP.1.185)
3073. Kennedy, John, b. 1693, Jacobite, res. Perthshire, tr. 31 Mar 1747, fr.
London to Jamaica, in *St George or Carteret*, arr. Jamaica 1747.
(P.2.316)(MR163)(PRO.CO137.58)
3074. Kennedy, John, b. 1715, laborer, Jacobite, res. Perthshire, tr. 5 May
1747, fr. Liverpool to Leeward Islands, in *Veteran*, arr. Martinique
June 1747. (P.2.314)(PRO.SP36.102)
3075. Kennedy, John, b. 1727, cowherd, Jacobite, res. Dougin Inverness-shire,
tr. 31 Mar 1747, fr. London to Barbados, in *Frere*.
(P.2.314)(MR154)

3076. Kennedy, John, b. 1 June 1748, Kingussie Inverness-shire, clergyman edu. Aberdeen Uni 1770, sh. 1777, to E Fla, sett. St Mark's E Fla. (FPA300)(EMA39)
3077. Kennedy, John, b. 1752, laborer, res. Galloway, sh. May 1774, fr. Stranraer to N.Y., in *Gale*. (PRO.T47.12)
3078. Kennedy, John, b. 1758, servant, res. Leys, sh. July 1775, fr. Stornaway to Philadelphia, in *Clementina*. (PRO.T47.12)
3079. Kennedy, John McEan Bain, farmer, cattle thief, res. Clunie Lochiel Inverness-shire, tr. Nov 1763. (AJ802)(SRO.RH2.4.255)
3080. Kennedy, Malcolm, Jacobite, tr. 21 Apr 1716, fr. Liverpool to S.C., in *Wakefield*. (SPC.1716.309)(CTB31.205)
3081. Kennedy, Mary, b. 1727, washerwoman, Jacobite, res. Glengarry Inverness-shire, tr. 5 May 1747, fr. Liverpool to Leeward Islands, in *Veteran*, arr. Martinique June 1747. (P.2.316)(PRO.SP36.102)
3082. Kennedy, Mary, b. 1753, spinner, sh. May 1774, fr. London to Md, in *Joseph & Mary*. (PRO.T47.9\11)
3083. Kennedy, Mary, b. 1765, servant, res. Wester Leys, sh. July 1775, fr. Stornaway to Philadelphia, in *Clementina*. (PRO.T47.12)
3084. Kennedy, Patrick, res. Ayrshire, pts. Robert Kennedy of Pinmore, d. 1 Oct 1780 Pemberton Valley Jamaica. (SM.53.48)
3085. Kennedy, Samuel, b. 1720, clergyman edu. Edinburgh Uni, sh. post 1740, sett. Basking Ridge N.J. (SA102)
3086. Kennedy, William, b. 1739, servant, res. Wester Leys, sh. July 1775, fr. Stornaway to Philadelphia, in *Clementina*. (PRO.T47.12)
3087. Kennedy, William, b. 1762, servant, res. Wester Leys, sh. July 1775, fr. Stornaway to Philadelphia, in *Clementina*. (PRO.T47.12)
3088. Kenniburgh, James, b. 1748, laborer, res. Glasgow, sh. May 1775, fr. Greenock to N.C., in *Ulysses*. (PRO.T47.12)
3089. Kenniburgh, John, b. 1751, laborer, res. Glasgow, sh. May 1775, fr. Greenock to N.C., in *Ulysses*. (PRO.T47.12)
3090. Kennough, Alexander, Jacobite, tr. 1747. (P.2.316)
3091. Kenny, John, Jacobite, tr. 28 July 1716, fr. Liverpool to Va, in *Godspeed*, arr. Md Oct 1716. (SPC.1716.310)(HM388) (alias 4093)
3092. Kent, Andrew, b. 1684, dyer, res. Galloway, sh. Sept 1722, fr. London. (CLRO\AIA)
3093. Ker, Archibald, physician, d. 1750 Jamaica. (SM.12.302)
3094. Kerr, Anna, res. Edinburgh, tr. 1696, fr. Newhaven to Va. (SRO.RH15.14.58)
3095. Kerr, Daniel, Covenanter, tr. 9 July 1685, fr. Leith to N.E. (PC.11.94)
3096. Kerr, David, b. 1726, lawyer, res. Edinburgh, pts. Prof John Kerr, sh. 1744, to Va, sett. Middlesex Co Md, m. .. Tucker, d. 10 July 1771 Urbanna Va. (SM.34.517)

3097. Kerr, Donald, b. 1712, farmer, Jacobite, res. Achnagaird Ross-shire, tr. 20
Mar 1747, fr. Tilbury. (P.2.318)(MR82)
3098. Kerr, John, edu. Glasgow Uni 1760, res. Carmunnock Lanarkshire, pts.
Rev John Kerr, sett. Jamaica. (MAGU62)
3099. Kerr, John, merchant, res. Beith Ayrshire, pts. Ninian Kerr, sh. pre 1776,
sett. Henrico Va, Glasgow pr1776 CC9.7.70
3100. Kerr, John, Jacobite, tr. 30 Mar 1716, fr. Liverpool to Antigua, in
Scipio. (SPC.1716.310)(CTB31.204)
3101. Kerr, John, Jacobite, tr. 29 June 1716, fr. Liverpool to Jamaica or Va, in
Elizabeth & Anne, arr. Va.
(SPC.1716.310)(CTB31.208)(VSP.1.185)
3102. Kerr, John, b. 1757, res. Inverness, sh. Sept 1774, fr. Greenock to
Jamaica, in *Jamaica*. (PRO.T47.12)
3103. Kerr, Robert, Jacobite, tr. 29 June 1716, fr. Liverpool to Va, in *Elizabeth
& Anne*, arr. Va. (SPC.1716.310)(CTB31.208)(VSP.1.186)
3104. Kerr, Thomas, engineer, sh. 1699, to Darien, d. West Indies, Edin pr1707
CC8.8.83
3105. Kerr, Walter, Covenanter, tr. 5 Sept 1685, fr. Leith to East N.J., in
Henry & Francis. (PC.11.173)
3106. Kerr, William, sh. 16 Dec 1773, fr. Greenock to Jamaica, in *Ross*.
(SRO.CE60.1.7)
3107. Kidd, Alexander, Jacobite, tr. 29 June 1716, fr. Liverpool to Jamaica or
Va, in *Elizabeth & Anne*, arr. Va.
(SPC.1716.310)(CTB31.208)(VSP.1.186)
3108. Kidd, David, weaver, res. Logie, tr. 12 Dec 1678, fr. Leith to West Indies,
in *St Michael of Scarborough*. (PC.6.76)
3109. Kidd, John, Covenanter, res. Livingstone West Lothian, tr. June 1684, fr.
Clyde to Carolina, in *Pelican*. (PC.9.208) (alias 1509)
3110. Kilgour, Alexander, sailor, res. Lochgelly Fife, sh. 14 July 1698, fr.
Leith to Darien, in *Caledonia*, Edin pr1709 CC8.8.84
3111. Kilgour, Peter, horsethief, res. Ardoch Banchory Kincardineshire, tr. May
1770. (AJ1168)
3112. Kilman, William, b. 1750, blacksmith, sh. Dec 1773, fr. London to Va,
in *Elizabeth*. (PRO.T47.9\11)
3113. Kilpatrick, Agnes, whore & thief, res. Edinburgh, tr. 28 Nov 1704, fr.
Leith to Md. (SRO.PC2.28.307)
3114. Kilpatrick, Robert, clergyman, sh. 1730, to Newfoundland, sett. Trinity
Bay NFD & New Windsor N.Y., d. Aug 1741 Trinity Bay.
(EMA39)(SPG.4.22)
3115. Kincaid, John, Covenanter, res. Chalcarrock, tr. 5 Sept 1685, fr. Leith to
East N.J., in *Henry & Francis*. (PC.11.154)
3116. Kinchley, Joseph, Jacobite, tr. 8 May 1747, fr. Liverpool to Antigua.
(P.2.320)(MR197)

3117. King, Christian, b. 1757, servant, res. Perth, sh. May 1775, fr. Leith to Philadelphia, in *Friendship*. (PRO.T47.12)
3118. King, George, physician, res. Newmiln, d. 10 Aug 1782 Kingston Jamaica. (SM.44.615)
3119. King, Hugh, millwright, res. Renfrewshire, d. 1740 Jamaica, Edin pr1744 CC8.8.108
3120. King, James, b. 1726, laborer, Jacobite, res. Darrow Aberdeenshire, tr. 22 Apr 1747, fr. Liverpool to Va, in *Johnson*, arr. Port Oxford Md 5 Aug 1747. (P.2.322)(PRO.T1.328)
3121. King, John, Covenanter, tr. 5 Sept 1685, fr. Leith to East N.J., in *Henry & Francis*. (PC.11.155)
3122. King, Patrick, b. 1750, wright, res. Edinburgh, sh. Apr 1775, fr. Greenock to N.Y., in *Lilly*. (PRO.T47.12)
3123. Kinloch, Alexander, merchant, sh. pre 1723, sett. Red Bank S.C. (SRO.GD237.10.132)
3124. Kinloch, Alexander, Fochabers Morayshire, merchant, Jacobite, res. Fochabers, pts. Sir John Kinloch of Kinloch & Elizabeth Nevay, tr. 14 Aug 1748. (OR10)
3125. Kinloch, Alexander, merchant, sh. pre 1724, sett. Berkeley Co S.C. (SRO.GD237.10.1.42)
3126. Kinloch, George Oliphant, sett. Blacklaws Westmoreland Jamaica, d. pre Nov 1770. (SRO.SH.1.11.1770)
3127. Kinloch, James, merchant, res. Edinburgh, pts. Mary Lesly or Kinloch, sh. pre 1728, sett. Charleston S.C. (SRO.GD345)
3128. Kinnaird, Sir Alexander, d. 1699 Darien. (TDD325)
3129. Kinnear, John, b. 1744, porter, res. Kirkcudbright, sh. May 1774, fr. Kirkcudbright to N.Y., in *Adventure*, m. Nichola ..., ch. Anthony Elizabeth Nicola. (PRO.T47.12)
3130. Kinneir, Alexander, sailor, res. Edinburgh, sh. 14 July 1698, fr. Leith to Darien, in *Caledonia*, Edin pr1708 CC8.8.84
3131. Kinnell, William, tailor, res. Grangepans West Lothian, sh. 14 July 1698, fr. Leith to Darien, in *St Andrew*, Edin pr1707 CC8.8.83
3132. Kinninburgh, John, wright, res. Glasgow, pts. James Kinninburgh, sh. pre 1751, sett. Va. (SRO.SH.8.6.1751)
3133. Kirby, Thomas Alexander, b. 1692, res. Edinburgh(?), sh. 1720, sett. Westmoreland Co Mass, m. Elizabeth de Gast, ch. Roger, d. 1765. (BLG2779)
3134. Kirk, John, tr. Nov 1679, fr. Leith. (ETR162)
3135. Kirk, Margaret, res. Edinburgh, tr. 1696, fr. Newhaven to Va. (SRO.RH15.14.58)
3136. Kirk, Robert, tr. Nov 1679, fr. Leith. (ETR162)
3137. Kirkpatrick, Henry Erskine, clergyman, sh. 1768, to Leeward Islands. (EMA39)
3138. Kirkpatrick, John, soldier, sh. 1699, to Darien, Edin pr1707 CC8.8.83

3139. Kirkwall, Elizabeth, tr. 7 Aug 1685, fr. Leith to Jamaica. (PC.11.329)
3140. Kirkwood, James, Covenanter, tr. 5 Sept 1685, fr. Leith to East N.J., in
     Henry & Francis. (PC.11.154)
3141. Kirkwood, John, sh. 1736, to Boston Mass. (SRO.GD110)
3142. Kirkwood, William, sh. 1736, to Bston Mass. (SRO.GD110)
3143. Kisaach, John, b. 16 Feb 1724, Alves Morayshire, shoemaker, Jacobite,
     res. Alves, pts. John Kisaach & Margaret Smith, tr. 19 Mar 1747,
     fr. Tilbury. (P.2.320)(MR127)
3144. Knolls, George, sailor, res. Bo'ness West Lothian, sh. 14 July 1698, fr.
     Leith to Darien, in *Caledonia*, Edin pr1707 CC8.8.83
3145. Knowles, William, b. 16 July 1713, salmon fisher, Jacobite, res. Nether
     Banchory Kincardineshire, pts. John Knowles & Barbara Malcolm,
     tr. 24 Feb 1747, fr. Liverpool to Va, in *Gildart*, arr. Port North
     Potomac Md 5 Aug 1747. (P.2.326)(PRO.T1.328)
3146. Knowlin, Thomas, Jacobite, tr. 20 Mar 1747, fr. Tilbury. (P.2.326)
3147. Knox, Hugh, clergyman edu. Marischal Col Aberdeen, sh. pre 1773, sett.
     St Croix. (MCA.2.85)
3148. Knox, Hugh, b. 1715, Tillicoutry Clackmannanshire, horsethief, res.
     Causewayside Edinburgh, tr. May 1751, m. Janet Drysdale.
     (SRO.B59.2611.15.27\19)
3149. Knox, Isobel, b. 1754, servant, res. Stirling, sh. May 1775, fr. Leith to
     Philadelphia, in *Friendship*. (PRO.T47.12)
3150. Knox, James, horsethief, res. Causewayside Edinburgh, pts. Hugh Knox,
     tr. 1751, fr. Montrose(?). (SRO.B59.26.11.15.11)
3151. Knox, James, clergyman, res. Bowden Roxburghshire, pts. Rev Henry
     Knox, sh. pre 1719, sett. St Kitts. (SRO.SH.30.7.1719)
3152. Knox, James, b. 1753, weaver, res. Paisley Renfrewshire, sh. Feb 1774,
     fr. Greenock to N.Y., in *Commerce*. (PRO.T47.12)
3153. Knox, Janet, thief, res. Glasgow, tr. 1758, fr. Glasgow. (SM.20.328)
3154. Knox, John, res. Edinburgh, pts. David Knox, sh. pre 1750, sett. N.Y.
     (SRO.SH.27.7.1750)
3155. Knox, Thomas, servant, thief, res. Cruden Aberdeenshire, tr. Oct 1774, fr.
     Greenock to Va, in *Rainbow*, arr. Port Hampton Va 3 May 1775.
     (SRO.JC27.10.3)(AJ1396)
3156. Kretts, Henrick, trumpeter, sh. 14 July 1698, fr. Leith to Darien, in *St
     Andrew*, Edin pr1707 CC8.8.83
3157. Kretts, Paul, trumpeter, sh. 14 July 1698, fr. Leith to Darien, in *St
     Andrew*, Edin pr1707 CC8.8.83
3158. Kyd, George, physician, res. Elie Fife, pts. Captain Kyd, d. Mar 1775 St
     Vincent. (SM.37.286)
3159. Kyle, Forbes, b. 1755, coach-wheeler, sh. May 1774, fr. London to Md,
     in *Union*. (PRO.T47.9\11)
3160. Kynah, Alexander, b. 1731, laborer, Jacobite, tr. 1747. (P.2.326)

3161. Lacky, James, b. 1731, weaver, Jacobite, res. Edinburgh, tr. 5 May 1747, fr. Liverpool to Leeward Islands, in *Veteran*, arr. Martinique June 1747. (P.2.328)(PRO.SP36.102)

3162. Ladley, Walter, b. 1710, res. Langholm Dumfries-shire, sh. Feb 1730, fr. London to Jamaica. (CLRO\AIA)

3163. Laing, Alexander, b. 1754, servant, res. Morayshire, sh. July 1775, fr. Stornaway to Philadelphia, in *Clementina*. (PRO.T47.12)

3164. Laing, James, wright, tr. 1 May 1674, fr. Leith to Barbados, in *St John of Leith*, d. 1676 Barbados. (PC.4.608\675)

3165. Laing, James, horse and sheep thief, res. Renfrew, tr. 1754. (SM.16.450)

3166. Laing, Jean, thief, res. Walnuik of Paisley Renfrewshire, tr. May 1764, m. Andrew Meiklehose. (AJ855)

3167. Laing, Robert, clergyman, sh. 1722, sett. Philadelphia. (AP193)(F.7.664)

3168. Laing, Thomas, leadmine worker, Jacobite, res. Aberdeen, tr. 24 Feb 1747, fr. Liverpool to Va, in *Gildart*, arr. Port North Potomac Md 5 Aug 1747. (P.2.328)(JAB.2.432)(MR206)(PRO.T1.328)

3169. Laing, William, farmer, Covenanter, res. Cavers Roxburghshire, tr. 12 Dec 1678, fr. Leith to West Indies, in *St Michael of Scarborough*. (PC.6.76)

3170. Laing, William, Covenanter, res. Hawick Roxburghshire, tr. 19 May 1684, fr. Leith to N.Y. (PC.8.216)

3171. Laing, William, clergyman, res. Aberdeenshire, sett. Freehold Monmouth Co N.J., d. pre 1739, Edin pr1739 CC8.8.101

3172. Laing, William, b. 1760, weaver, res. Paisley Renfrewshire, sh. May 1775, fr. Leith to Philadelphia, in *Friendship*. (PRO.T47.12)

3173. Laird, James, b. 1721, servant, Jacobite, res. Muirie Errol Perthshire, tr. 31 Mar 1747, fr. London to Barbados , in *Frere*. (P.2.330)(MR104)

3174. Laird, Katherine, whore & thief, res. Edinburgh, tr. May 1666, fr. Leith to Va, in *Phoenix of Leith*. (ETR107)

3175. Laird, Samuel, clergyman edu. Glasgow Uni 1751, res. Desartmartin Londonderry, pts. James Laird, sh. 1755, to N.C. (EMA40)(FPA.21.304)

3176. Lamb, James, b. 1722, watchmaker, Jacobite, res. Edinburgh, tr. 5 May 1747, fr. Liverpool to Leeward Islands, in *Veteran*, arr. Martinique June 1747. (P.2.330)(MR133)(PRO.SP36.102)

3177. Lamb, William, b. 1753, husbandman, sh. Sept 1774, fr. London to Jamaica, in *Standlinch*. (PRO.T47.9\11)

3178. Lambie, William, edu. Glasgow Uni 1771, res. Kilmartin Argyll, pts. Rev Archibald Lambie, d. 29 July 1794 Jamaica. (MAGU97)

3179. Lambie, William, planter, res. Argyll, sh. pre 1769, sett. St Thomas in the East Jamaica, d. pre 1769 Jamaica. (SRA.B10.15.7303)

3180. Lamond, Archibald, Covenanter, res. Kilbride Argyll, tr. Aug 1685, fr. Leith to Jamaica. (PC.11.307)(LC289)

3181. Lamond, John, sailor, res. Kincardine on Forth Fife, sh. 14 July 1698, fr. Leith to Darien, in *Endeavour*, Edin pr1707 CC8.8.83

3182. Lamond, John, b. 1721, groom, Jacobite, res. Aberdeen, tr. 24 Feb 1747, fr. Liverpool to Va, in *Gildart*, arr. Port North Potomac Md 5 Aug 1747. (P.2.330)(JAB.2.432)(MR8)(PRO.T1.328) (alias 3183)

3183. Lamond, Joseph, b. 1721, groom, Jacobite, res. Aberdeen, tr. 24 Feb 1747, fr. Liverpool to Va, in *Gildart*, arr. Port North Potomac Md 5 Aug 1747. (P.2.330)(JAB.2.432)(MR8)(PRO.T1.328) (alias 3182)

3184. Lamond, Sorley, Covenanter, res. Drum, tr. Aug 1685, fr. Leith to Jamaica. (PC.11.136)(LC289)

3185. Lamont, Janet, b. 1757, res. Edinburgh, sh. Apr 1775, fr. Greenock to N.Y., in *Lilly*. (PRO.T47.12)

3186. Lamont, John, Argyll, sh. 1764, sett. Bedford Co Va, d. 1823. (LC311)

3187. Lamont, Lauchlan, res. Auchagoyl Argyll, pts. James Lamont & Isobel McAllister, sh. 1765, sett. Norfolk Va, d. 30 Apr 1773 Norfolk Va. (LC469)

3188. Lamont, Walter, soldier, res. Evanachan Strachlachlan Argyll, pts. John Og Lamont, sh. 1699, to Darien, m. Elizabeth Hamilton, d. 1700 Darien. (LC263)

3189. Lampo, Samuel, Yorkshire, shipmaster, fraudster, res. Leith Midlothian, tr. Nov 1751. (SRO.E173.J2.3\1)(AJ204)(SRO.ACR3.82)

3190. Lander, John, b. 1755, husbandman, res. Edinburgh, sh. Oct 1774, fr. London to Philadelphia, in *Mary*. (PRO.T47.9\11)

3191. Lang, Alexander, b. 1753, weaver, res. Paisley Renfrewshire, sh. Jan 1774, fr. Greenock to Nevis, in *Aurora*. (SRO.CE60.1.7)

3192. Lang, John, thief, tr. July 1749. (SRO.HCR.I.79)

3193. Lang, John, merchant, res. Glasgow, d. pre 1761 Jamaica. (SRO.SH.14.8.1761)

3194. Lang, John, b. 1744, weaver, res. Paisley Renfrewshire, sh. Feb 1774, fr. Greenock to N.Y., in *Commerce*, m. Margaret ... (PRO.T47.12)

3195. Lauchlison, Marie, Covenanter, res. Burnhead Dumfries-shire, tr. Oct 1684. (PC.10.587)

3196. Lauder, David, Jacobite, tr. 28 July 1716, fr. Liverpool to Va, in *Godspeed*, arr. Md Oct 1716. (SPC.1716.310)(CTB31.209)(HM388)

3197. Lauder, Francis, b. 22 Oct 1729, Auldearn Nairnshire, schoolmaster & clergyman edu. Marischal Co Aberdeen 1751, res. Petty Auldearn Nairnshire, sh. 1761, to Md. (FPA301)

3198. Lauder, George, Jacobite, tr. 29 June 1716, fr. Liverpool to Jamaica or Va, in *Elizabeth & Anne*, arr. Va. (SPC.1716.310)(CTB31.208)(VSP.1.186)

3199. Lauder, William, thief, res. Ballykinrian Stirlingshire, tr. May 1729. (SRO.JC27)

3200. Laughton, Patrick, gunner's mate, res. Kirkwall Orkney Islands, sh. 14 July 1698, fr. Leith to Darien, in *St Andrew*, Edin pr1707 CC8.8.83

3201. Laurie, Andrew, rapist, tr. 1775. (SRO.HCR.I.115)

3202. Laurie, James, b. 1716, tailor, res. Selkirk, sh. Jan 1736, fr. London to Md. (CLRO\AIA)

3203. Laurie, Peter, horsethief, res. Ayrshire, tr. Oct 1775. (AJ1449)

3204. Lauson, William, soldier, res. Edinburgh, sh. 1699, d. 1699 Darien, Edin pr1707 CC8.8.83

3205. Law, David, Covenanter, tr. July 1685. (PC.11.114)

3206. Law, George, merchant, sh. pre 1751, sett. Barbados. (SRO.RD2.170.187)

3207. Law, James, Covenanter, res. Kirkliston West Lothian, tr. 12 Dec 1678, fr. Leith to West Indies, in *St Michael of Scarborough*. (PC.6.76)

3208. Law, John, thief, res. Easthill of Johnston Aberdeenshire, tr. Dec 1752. (AJ259)

3209. Law, William, foremastman, res. Kirkcaldy Fife, sh. 14 July 1698, fr. Leith to Darien, in *Caledonia*, Edin pr1707 CC8.8.83

3210. Lawrie, Gavin, Governor of East N.J., d. pre 1696 N.J., PCC pr1696 205 Pyne

3211. Lawrie, John, b. 1747, servant, res. Kinross, sh. May 1775, fr. Leith to Philadelphia, in *Friendship*. (PRO.T47.12)

3212. Lawrie, Robert, gentleman, res. Edinburgh, pts. Robert Lawrie, sett. St George St Vincent, m. Isabella ..., d. 1770, Edin pr1782 CC8.8.125

3213. Lawry, Alexander, laborer, res. Dumfries, sh. Sept 1658, fr. Bristol to Va(?). (BRO04220)

3214. Lawry, Peter, Ireland, horsethief, res. Ayrshire, tr. Sept 1775. (SM.37.689)

3215. Lawry, Thomas, Jacobite, tr. 24 May 1716, fr. Liverpool to Md, in *Friendship*, arr. Md Aug 1716. (SPC.1716.311)(HM386)

3216. Lawson, Gavin, merchant, res. Lanarkshire, sh. pre 1779, sett. Va. (SRO.RS42.21.92)

3217. Lawson, James, b. 1725, workman, Jacobite, res. Wester Coull Lintrathen Angus, tr. 5 May 1747, fr. Liverpool to Leeward Islands, in *Veteran*, arr. Martinique June 1747. (P.2.334)(MR104)(OR34)(PRO.SP36.102)

3218. Lawson, John, b. 1738, fisherman, res. Shetland Islands, sh. Oct 1774, fr. Kirkcaldy to Antigua, in *Jamaica Packet*, m. Catherine ... (PRO.T47.12)

3219. Lawson, Marion, res. Edinburgh, tr. 21 Oct 1682, fr. Greenock to N.Y. (ETR221)

3220. Lawson, Marion, Covenanter, tr. Aug 1685, fr. Leith to Jamaica. (PC.11.329)

3221. Lawson, Mary, infanticide, res. Monymusk Aberdeenshire, tr. May 1766, fr. Aberdeen. (AJ959\964)
3222. Lawson, Peter, weaver, thief, res. Torryburn Fife, tr. 1773, fr. Port Glasgow to Va, in *Phoenix*, arr. Port Accomack Va 20 Dec 1773. (SRO.JC27.10.3)(AJ1293)
3223. Lawson, Robert, clergyman edu. Edinburgh Uni 1693, res. Torthorwald Dumfries-shire, sh. pre 1712, sett. Monikinie & Wicomico Pa, d. Nov 1712. (F.7.664)
3224. Lawson, William, tr. Dec 1685, fr. Leith to Barbados, in *John & Nicholas*. (ETR390)
3225. Lawson, William, Jacobite, res. Durham, tr. 24 Feb 1747, fr. Liverpool to Va, in *Gildart*, arr. Port North Potomac Md 5 Aug 1747. (P.2.335)(PRO.T1.328)
3226. Lawton, Alexander, Jacobite, tr. 25 June 1716, fr. Liverpool to St Kitts, in *Hockenhill*. (SPC.1716.312)(CTB31.207)
3227. Leal, Anne, b. 1754, servant, res. Canisbay Caithness, sh. Sept 1775, fr. Kirkwall to Savannah Ga, in *Marlborough*, sett. Richmond Co Ga. (PRO.T47.12)
3228. Learmonth, B, b. 1754, servant, res. Ratho Midlothian, sh. May 1775, fr. Leith to Philadelphia, in *Friendship*. (PRO.T47.12)
3229. Learmonth, Charles, merchant, res. Edinburgh, pts. Robert Learmonth, sh. 18 Aug 1699, fr. Clyde to Darien, in *Rising Sun*, d. 1699, Edin pr1744 CC8.8.109
3230. Learmonth, Euphame, b. 1752, servant, res. Ratho Midlothian, sh. May 1775, fr. Leith to Philadelphia, in *Friendship*. (PRO.T47.12)
3231. Leatherbarrow, Richard, b. 1715, weaver, Jacobite, res. Widwick Lancashire, tr. 1747. (P.2.337)(MR197)
3232. Leckie, Andrew, b. 1756, laborer, res. Anderston Glasgow, sh. Apr 1775, fr. Greenock to N.Y., in *Lilly*. (PRO.T47.12)
3233. Leckie, Catherine, infanticide, tr. Aug 1685, fr. Leith to Jamaica. (PC.11.136)
3234. Leckie, William, merchant, Covenanter, res. Glasgow, tr. June 1678, to West Indies, m. Marie Duncan. (PC.5.474)
3235. Leek, John, pickpocket, res. Ayrshire, tr. Oct 1775. (AJ1449)
3236. Lees, John, tr. 1773, fr. Glasgow, in *Thomas of Glasgow*, arr. James River Va 3 July 1773. (SRO.JC27.10.3)
3237. Leg, John, res. Grange Banffshire, pts. John Leg, sett. Crosspath Jamaica, d. 1764. (APB.3.228)
3238. Legg, John, merchant, res. Aberdeenshire, sett. Savannah la Mar Jamaica, d. pre 1776, Edin pr1776 CC8.8.123
3239. Leighton, S, S, b. 1747, clerk, res. Edinburgh, sh. July 1775, fr. Greenock to Ga, in *Georgia*. (PRO.T47.12)
3240. Leitch, David, vagabond & robber, res. Annandale Dumfries-shire, tr. 1671(?). (PC.3.428)

157

3241. Leitch, Robert, b. 1746, farmer, res. Glasgow, sh. Feb 1774, fr.
Greenock to N.Y., in *Commerce*. (PRO.T47.12)
3242. Leith, Alexander, merchant, d. pre 1750 Philadelphia, Edin pr1750
CC8.8.113
3243. Lemon, John, Jacobite, tr. 7 May 1716, fr. Liverpool to S.C., in
Susannah. (SPC.1716.309)(CTB31.206)
3244. Lendrum, Thomas, sett. Port Royal Va, ch. Thomas-Keith, d. pre 1784.
(SRO.SH.3.1.1784)
3245. Lennox, James, merchant, sh. pre 1765, sett. Charleston S.C.
(SRO.RD3.224.627)
3246. Lesley, David, b. 1750, joiner, sh. July 1774, fr. Hull to N.Y., in
Adventure. (PRO.T47.9\11)
3247. Lesley, Robert, b. 1757, husbandman, sh. Feb 1774, fr. London to Ga, in
Mary. (PRO.T47.12)
3248. Leslie, Alexander, b. 1701, fencing master, Jacobite, tr. 1747. (P.2.322)
3249. Leslie, Andrew, clergyman edu. Edinburgh Uni 1722, sh. 1729, sett. St
Paul's S.C., d. 1740. (EMA40)
3250. Leslie, Andrew, merchant, d. 1765 Barbados. (SM.27.391)
3251. Leslie, John, b. 1760, servant, res. Sutherland, sh. May 1775, fr. Leith to
Philadelphia, in *Friendship*. (PRO.T47.12)
3252. Leslie, Margaret, Covenanter, tr. 5 Sept 1685, fr. Leith to East N.J., in
Henry & Francis. (PC.11.154)
3253. Leslie, William, clergyman, sh. 1718, to Antigua. (EMA40)
3254. Lesser, Hugh, Jacobite, tr. 1746. (SRO.GD103)
3255. Lester, Francis, b. 1756, hairdresser, res. Edinburgh, sh. Sept 1774, fr.
London to Md, in *Neptune*. (PRO.T47.9\11)
3256. Leven, Abraham, b. 1721, tailor, res. Linlithgow West Lothian, sh. May
1739, fr. London to Md. (CLRO\AIA)
3257. Lickprivick, James, Covenanter, res. Cathcart Glasgow, tr. 12 Dec 1678,
fr. Leith to West Indies, in *St Michael of Scarborough*. (PC.6.76)
3258. Liddell, Beattie, whore, res. Edinburgh, tr. Mar 1695. (SRO.PC2.25.216)
3259. Liddell, John, clerk, sh. May 1699, fr. Clyde to Darien, in *Olive Branch*,
Edin pr1708 CC8.8.84
3260. Liddle, George, b. 1760, yeoman, sh. Sept 1775, fr. Newcastle to Ga, in
Georgia Packet, sett. Friendsborough Ga. (PRO.T47.9\11)
3261. Lighton, Patrick, seaman, res. Burntisland Fife, pts. Robert Lighton &
Christian Hay, sh. 18 Aug 1699, fr. Clyde to Darien, in *Rising
Sun*, Edin pr1707 CC8.8.83
3262. Lilbourne, James, tr. Nov 1679, fr. Leith. (ETR162)
3263. Linay, John, b. 1743, farmer, res. Evie Orkney Islands, sh. Sept 1774, fr.
Kirkwall to Savannah Ga, in *Marlborough*, sett. Richmond Co Ga,
m. Isobel ..., ch. James Ann. (PRO.T47.12)

3264. Lindsay, Benjamin, woolcomber, conspirator, res. Aberdeen, tr. July 1772, fr. Glasgow to Va, in *Brilliant*, arr. Port Hampton Va 7 Oct 1772. (SRO.JC27.10.3)(AJ1272)

3265. Lindsay, Eliza, res. Edinburgh, pts. William Lindsay, sh. pre 1771, sett. Charleston S.C. (SRO.RD4.213.1490)

3266. Lindsay, Elizabeth, gypsy, res. Jedburgh Roxburghshire, tr. 1 Jan 1715, fr. Glasgow to Va. (GR530)

3267. Lindsay, James, Jacobite, tr. 29 June 1716, fr. Liverpool to Jamaica or Va, in *Elizabeth & Anne*, arr. Va. (SPC.1716.310)(CTB31.208)(VSP.1.186)

3268. Lindsay, John, Jacobite, tr. 30 Mar 1716, fr. Liverpool to Antigua, in *Scipio*. (SPC.1716.310)(CTB31.204)

3269. Lindsay, John, b. 2 July 1694, Crail Fife, merchant, res. Wormistoun Fife, pts. John Lindsay & Margaret Haliburton, sh. 1729, to Philadelphia, sett. N.Y., d. 12 Oct 1751 Albany N.Y. (SP.5.415)(SRO.GD203)

3270. Lindsay, John, b. 1751, mercer, sh. Sept 1775, fr. London to Jamaica, in *Standlinch*. (PRO.T47.9\11)

3271. Lindsay, William, clergyman edu. Glasgow Uni, sh. 1735, sett. Bristol Va. (SCHR.14.149)

3272. Lindsay, William, b. 1758, cabinetmaker, res. Boreland Colvend Kirkcudbrightshire, sh. May 1774, fr. Kirkcudbright to N.Y., in *Adventure*. (PRO.T47.12)

3273. Linn, George, sett. Charleston S.C., d. pre 1735, PCC pr1735

3274. Linn, William, b. 1753, laborer, res. Galloway, sh. May 1774, fr. Stranraer to N.Y., in *Gale*. (PRO.T47.12)

3275. Linning, Elizabeth, sh. 21 July 1684, fr. Gourock to Port Royal S.C., in *Carolina Merchant*. (TC.2.424)

3276. Linnon, William, b. 1756, tailor, sh. Sept 1775, fr. Newcastle to Ga, in *Georgia Packet*, sett. Friendsborough Ga. (PRO.T47.9\11)

3277. Linsay, Donald, res. Largybreck Jura Argyll, sh. 1754, to Cape Fear N.C. (SRO.GD64\5.21)

3278. Lintron, Janet, Covenanter, tr. 5 Sept 1685, fr. Leith to East N.J., in *Henry & Francis*. (PC.11.164)

3279. Lisk, Adam, mariner, res. Shetland Islands, sh. Oct 1774, fr. Kirkcaldy to Antigua, in *Jamaica Packet*, m. Marjory ... (PRO.T47.12)

3280. Litster, Hugh, sailor, res. Aberdour Fife, pts. Rev Thomas Litster, sh. 18 Aug 1699, fr. Clyde to Darien, in *Rising Sun*, Edin pr1708 CC8.8.84

3281. Little, Andrew, b. 1704, Canonby Dumfries-shire, sh. Nov 1724, fr. London to Antigua. (CLRO\AIA)

3282. Little, George, b. 1756, merchant, res. Dumfries, sh. July 1775, fr. Greenock to Jamaica, in *Isobella*. (PRO.T47.12)

3283. Little, John, b. 1744, husbandman, sh. Dec 1774, fr. London to Va, in *Carolina*. (PRO.T47.12)
3284. Little, Margaret, res. Edinburgh, tr. 1696, fr. Newhaven to Va. (SRO.RH15.14.58)
3285. Littlejohn, Duncan, b. 1737, wright, res. Breadalbane Perthshire, sh. June 1775, fr. Greenock to N.Y., in *Commerce*. (PRO.T47.12)
3286. Littlejohn, John, woolcomber, conspirator, res. Aberdeen, tr. May 1772. (AJ1272)
3287. Livesay, John, b. 1730, cordiner, Jacobite, res. Lancashire, tr. 1747. (P.2.347)(MR197)
3288. Livingston, Katherine, whore & thief, res. Edinburgh, tr. 28 Nov 1704, fr. Leith to Md. (SRO.PC2.28.307)
3289. Livingston, William, clergyman edu. Edinburgh Uni 1701, sh. pre 1706, sett. Charleston S.C., d. 1724. (F.7.664)(AP163)
3290. Livingstone, Alexander, murderer, res. Falkirk Stirlingshire, tr. Dec 1749. (SRO.JC27)(SRO.HCR.I.79)
3291. Livingstone, Douglas, Jacobite, tr. 1746. (SRO.GD103)
3292. Livingstone, William, assault, tr. 5 Sept 1685, fr. Leith to East N.J., in *Henry & Francis*. (PC.11.165)(ETR378)
3293. Liviston, George, b. 1752, mason, res. Gatehouse Kirkcudbrighthshire, sh. May 1774, fr. Stranraer to N.Y., in *Gale*. (PRO.T47.12)
3294. LLoyd, John, soldier, shopbreaker, tr. May 1774. (AJ1376)
3295. Loch, William, res. Edinburgh, pts. William Loch, sh. pre 1766, sett. Savannah la Mar Jamaica. (SRO.RD4.227.1187)
3296. Lochhead, Henry, b. 16 Aug 1741, Glasgow, merchant, res. Glasgow, pts. Henry Lochhead & Jean Park, sh. 1769, to Va, sett. Petersburg Va. (SRA.B10.12.4\B10.15.7488)
3297. Lochhead, Hugh, b. 1736, farmer, res. Perthshire, sh. May 1775, fr. Greenock to N.Y., in *Monimia*, m. Isobel Bruce. (PRO.T47.12)
3298. Lockhart, Betty, b. 1760, servant, res. Foubriggs, sh. May 1775, fr. Leith to Philadelphia, in *Friendship*. (PRO.T47.12)
3299. Lockhart, Gavin, Covenanter, tr. 5 Sept 1685, fr. Leith to East N.J., in *Henry & Francis*. (PC.11.162)
3300. Lockhart, George, sh. Feb 1683, fr. Port Glasgow to West Indies, in *Walter of Glasgow*. (SRO.E72.19.8)
3301. Lockhart, Janet, b. 1759, servant, res. Edinburgh, sh. May 1775, fr. Leith to Philadelphia, in *Friendship*. (PRO.T47.12)
3302. Lockhart, John, sailor, res. Prestonpans West Lothian, sh. 14 July 1698, fr. Leith to Darien, in *Unicorn*, ch. John, d. 1699 Darien, Edin pr1707 CC8.8.83
3303. Lockhart, Penelope, whore, res. Edinburgh, tr. Mar 1695. (SRO.PC2.25.216)
3304. Lockhart, Robert, b. 1753, farmer, res. Kilbarchan Renfrewshire, sh. Oct 1774, fr. Greenock to Philadelphia, in *Sally*. (PRO.T47.12)

3305. Logan, Catherine, thief, res. Glasston Galloway, pts. John Logan, tr. 1762. (EBR.BC.3.110) (alias 116)
3306. Logan, George, merchant, res. Glasgow, sh. pre 1746, sett. Kemp's Landing Princess Anne Co Va, d. 15 June 1781 Glasgow, PCC pr1781. (SRO.RD3.211.295)
3307. Logan, James, b. 1756, wright, res. Paisley Renfrewshire, sh. May 1775, fr. Greenock to N.Y., in *Lilly*. (PRO.T47.12)
3308. Long, Henry, laborer, res. Galloway, sh. May 1774, fr. Stranraer to N.Y., in *Gale*. (PRO.T47.12)
3309. Lorimer, Hugh, b. 1753, laborer, res. Ayr, sh. Apr 1775, fr. Greenock to N.Y., in *Lilly*. (PRO.T47.12)
3310. Lorne, Peter, cooper, res. Zealand Netherlands, sh. 14 July 1698, fr. Leith to Darien, in *Unicorn*, m. Margaret Robertson, Edin pr1707 CC8.8.83
3311. Lothian, Abraham, soldier, res. Renfrew, sh. 1699, d. 1699 Darien, Edin pr1707 CC8.8.83
3312. Louden, James, stocking weaver, Jacobite, res. Hampshire, tr. 1747. (P.2.349)(MR38)
3313. Louttit, Thomas, b. 1 Oct 1764, Stromness, beggar, res. Stromness Orkney Islands, pts. Robert Louttit & Katherine Irvine, sh. Sept 1774, fr. Kirkwall to Savannah Ga, in *Marlborough*, sett. Richmond Co Ga. (PRO.T47.12)
3314. Love, Allan, merchant, sh. pre 1771, sett. Va & N.C. (SRA.B10.15.8270)
3315. Love, Christopher, cooper, res. Ayr, sh. 18 Aug 1699, fr. Clyde to Darien, in *Rising Sun*, Edin pr1708 CC8.8.84
3316. Love, David, clergyman edu. Edinburgh Uni, sh. 1764, to Md. (FPA301)
3317. Love, Hugh, merchant, sh. pre 1771, sett. Va & N.C. (SRA.B10.15.8270)
3318. Low, Alexander, whitesmith, Jacobite, res. Lancashire, tr. 8 May 1747, to Antigua. (P.2.351)
3319. Low, Alexander, b. 1755, laborer, res. Kilbirnie Ayrshire, sh. Oct 1774, fr. Greenock to Philadelphia, in *Sally*. (PRO.T47.12)
3320. Low, James, b. 1750, weaver, res. Glasgow, sh. Oct 1774, fr. Greenock to N.Y., in *Christy*. (PRO.T47.12)
3321. Low, John, res. Kincardineshire, tr. 5 Feb 1752, fr. Aberdeen to Va, in *Planter*. (AJ265)
3322. Low, Roderick, servant, Jacobite, res. Tarbat House Ross-shire, tr. 30 Mar 1747, fr. London to Jamaica, in *St George or Carteret*, arr. Jamaica 1747. (P.2.352)(MR73)(PRO.CO137.58)
3323. Low, William, foremastman, res. Kirkcaldy Fife, sh. 14 July 1698, fr. Leith to Darien, in *Caledonia*, Edin pr1707 CC8.8.83

161

3324. Lowe, Abraham, Jacobite, tr. 24 May 1716, fr. Liverpool to Md, in *Friendship*, arr. Md Aug 1716. (SPC.1716.311)(HM386)(MdArch.34.164)
3325. Lowe, James, Jacobite, tr. 24 May 1716, fr. Liverpool to Md, in *Friendship*, arr. Md Aug 1716. (SPC.1716.311)(HM387)
3326. Lowrie, Alexander, b. 1751, laborer, res. Monkland Lanarkshire, sh. Oct 1774, fr. Greenock to Philadelphia, in *Sally*. (PRO.T47.12)
3327. Lucky, John, b. 20 Oct 1728, St Nicholas Aberdeen, servant, Jacobite, res. Aberdeen, pts. William Lucky & Helen Black, tr. 24 Feb 1747, fr. Liverpool to Va, in *Gildart*, arr. Port North Potomac Md 5 Aug 1747. (P.2.352)(MR211)(JAB.2.433)(PRO.T1.328)
3328. Lugton, Simon, tailor, Jacobite, res. Edinburgh, tr. Nov 1748. (P.2.354)
3329. Luke, William, merchant, sh. Apr 1684, fr. Port Glasgow to West Indies, in *Jean of Largs*. (SRO.E72.19.9)
3330. Lumsden, Alexander, edu. King's Col Aberdeen 1770, res. Aberdeen, pts. Prof John Lumsden & Jean Leslie, sett. Jamaica. (KCA133)
3331. Lumsden, David, merchant, res. Aberdeen, d. pre 1763 Kingston Jamaica. (SRO.SH.26.2.1763)
3332. Lumsden, Henry, Jacobite, tr. 24 May 1716, fr. Liverpool to Md, in *Friendship*, arr. Md Aug 1747. (SPC.1716.311)(HM387)
3333. Lumsden, James, b. 1752, baker, sh. Mar 1774, fr. London to Va, in *Brilliant*. (PRO.T47.9\11)
3334. Lumsden, John, merchant, res. Aberdeen, sett. Kingston Jamaica, d. Feb 1770. (APB.4.35)
3335. Lunan, Patrick, clergyman, sh. 1760, to Va. (EMA41)
3336. Lundie, Archibald, b. 1750, merchant, res. Edinburgh, sh. July 1775, fr. Greenock to N.Y., in *Georgia*. (PRO.T47.12)
3337. Lundie, James, clergyman edu. King's Col Aberdeen 1741, res. Buchan Aberdeenshire, sh. 1767, to Va. (EMA41)
3338. Lundy, Charles, Jacobite, tr. 30 Mar 1716, fr. Liverpool to Antigua, in *Scipio*. (SPC.1716.310)(CTB31.204)
3339. Luttons, Herman, foremastman, sh. 14 July 1698, fr. Leith to Darien, in *Caledonia*, Edin pr1707 CC8.8.83
3340. Lyle, David, b. 1746, laborer, res. Edinburgh, sh. Apr 1775, fr. Greenock to N.Y., in *Lilly*. (PRO.T47.12)
3341. Lyle, John, b. 1748, farmer, res. Caithness, sh. May 1775, fr. Greenock to N.Y., in *Lilly*. (PRO.T47.12)
3342. Lymburner, Adam, b. 1746, Kilmarnock Ayrshire, merchant edu. Glasgow Uni 1766, sett. Quebec, d. 1836 London. (MAGU82)
3343. Lyon, George, merchant, sh. June 1684, fr. Port Glasgow to Carolina, in *Pelican of Glasgow*. (SRO.E72.19.9)
3344. Lyon, Henry, sailor, res. Edinburgh, sh. 18 Aug 1699, fr. Clyde to Darien, in *Rising Sun*, Edin pr1707 CC8.8.83
3345. Lyon, James, wright, sett. Barbados, d. pre 1676. (PC.4.671)

3346. Lyon, John, res. Forfar Angus, tr. Aug 1752, fr. Aberdeen to Va, in *St Andrew*. (AJ241)
3347. Lyon, Matthew, b. 1726, weaver, res. Glasgow, sh. May 1775, fr. Greenock to N.C., in *Ulysses*, m. Mary ..., ch. James. (PRO.T47.12)
3348. Lyon, Michael, tailor, Jacobite, res. Dublin, tr. 1747. (P.2.355)(MR137)
3349. Lyon, Philip, Jacobite, tr. 21 Apr 1716, fr. Liverpool to S.C., in *Wakefield*. (SPC.1716.309)(CTB31.205)
3350. Lyon, William, Jacobite, tr. 29 June 1716, fr. Liverpool to Jamaica or Va, in *Elizabeth & Anne*, arr. Va. (SPC.1716.310)(CTB31.208)(VSP.1.186)
3351. McAdam, Archibald, Covenanter, tr. July 1685, fr. Leith to N.E. (PC.11.94)
3352. McAdam, Gilbert, Covenanter, res. Dalmellington Ayrshire, tr. June 1684, fr. Glasgow, in *Pelican*. (PC.9.208)
3353. McAdam, William, b. 1746, tailor, res. Boreland Balmaghie Kirkcudbrightshire, sh. May 1774, fr. Kirkcudbright to N.Y., in *Adventure*. (PRO.T47.12)
3354. McAlester, Coll, b. 1750, tailor, res. Kintyre Argyll, sh. Sept 1774, fr. Greenock to Wilmington N.C., in *Diana*. (PRO.T47.12)
3355. McAlester, John, b. 1745, coppersmith, res. Edinburgh, sh. May 1775, fr. Greenock to N.Y. or Ga, in *Christy*. (PRO.T47.12)
3356. McAlester, Mary, b. 1743, res. Kintyre Argyll, sh. Sept 1774, fr. Greenock to Wilmington N.C., in *Diana*. (PRO.T47.12)
3357. McAllan, John, b. 1735, farmer, res. Lorne Argyll, sh. May 1775, fr. Greenock to N.Y., in *Monimia*, m. Janet ..., ch. Janet Donald Anne Katherine. (PRO.T47.12)
3358. McAllaster, Thomas, b. 1754, shoemaker, res. Glasgow, sh. Feb 1774, fr. Greenock to N.Y., in *Commerce*. (PRO.T47.12)
3359. McAllister, Hugh, res. Argyll, sh. pre 1732, sett. Lancaster Co Pa, m. Miss Harbison, ch. Hugh, d. 1769. (BLG2800)
3360. McAllum, Duncan, b. 1752, shoemaker, res. Kintyre Argyll, sh. Aug 1774, fr. Greenock to Wilmington N.C., in *Ulysses*, m. Catherine McAlester. (PRO.T47.12)
3361. McAlpin, Peter, b. 1726, farmer, res. Inverness, sh. May 1774, fr. Greenock to N.Y., in *George*, m. Eliza. (PRO.T47.12)
3362. McAndrew, Alexander, b. 1757, yeoman, sh. Sept 1775, fr. Newcastle to Ga, in *Georgia Packet*. (PRO.T47.9\11)
3363. McAndrew, John, farmer, sheepstealer, res. Southdale Ross-shire, tr. 1755. (SM.17.266) (alias 3772)
3364. McArran, Janet, b. 1731, spinner, Jacobite, res. Perth, tr. 1747. (P.33.18) (alias 4305)
3365. MacArthur, Archibald, gentleman, res. Highlands, sh. March 1683, to Hudson Bay. (HBRS.9.88)

3366. McArthur, Donald, b. 1716, farmer, res. Breadalbane Perthshire, sh. June 1775, fr. Greenock to N.Y., in *Commerce*, m. Katherine McNaughton, ch. John Donald Katherine Archibald. (PRO.T47.12)
3367. McArthur, Duncan, workman, res. Inveraray Argyll, pts. Charles McArthur, tr. 1772, fr. Port Glasgow, in *Phoenix*, arr. Port Accomack Va 20 Dec 1772. (AJ1290)(SRO.JC27.10.3)
3368. McArthur, Duncan, res. Crackaig Jura Argyll, sh. 1754, to Cape Fear N.C. (SRO.GD64\5.21)
3369. McArthur, Duncan, b. 1723, farmer, res. Breadalbane Perthshire, sh. June 1775, fr. Greenock to N.Y., in *Commerce*, m. Eliza McEwan, ch. John Donald Peter John Donald. (PRO.T47.12)
3370. McArthur, Duncan, b. 1755, weaver, res. Breadalbane Perthshire, sh. June 1775, fr. Greenock to N.Y., in *Commerce*. (PRO.T47.12)
3371. McArthur, Gilbert, drover, Covenanter, res. Islay Argyll, tr. Aug 1685, fr. Leith to Jamaica. (PC.11.329)
3372. McArthur, Isobel, b. 1747, res. Crawfordyke Renfrewshire, sh. May 1774, fr. Greenock to N.Y., in *George*. (PRO.T47.12)
3373. McArthur, John, b. 1648, Deputy Governor, sh. pre 1700, sett. Figtree St Thomas Middle Island St Kitts, ch. Gillies, d. 4 Apr 1704 St Kitts, bd. St Thomas. (DP310)(MWI182)
3374. McArthur, John, b. 1727, farmer, res. Breadalbane Perthshire, sh. Feb 1775, fr. Greenock to N.Y., in *Commerce*, m. Mary Fletcher, ch. Christian. (PRO.T47.12)
3375. McArthur, Peter, b. 1716, farmer, res. Kintyre Argyll, sh. Aug 1774, fr. Greenock to Wilmington N.C., in *Ulysses*, m. Christian Bride, ch. John Ann Joan John. (PRO.T47.12)
3376. McArthur, Peter, b. 1757, weaver, res. Breadalbane Perthshire, sh. Feb 1775, fr. Greenock to N.Y., in *Commerce*. (PRO.T47.12)
3377. McAskell, Allan, d. pre 1702 Barbados. (SRO.SH.2.7.1702)
3378. MacAulay, Alexander, Glasgow, sett. Yorktown Va, m. Elizabeth Jerdone, d. 17 July 1798 Yorktown. (OD105)
3379. McAulay, James, Jacobite, tr. 1747. (P.3.18)(MR206)
3380. McAulay, Kenneth, b. 1757, servant, res. Bayble Isle of Lewis, sh. May 1774, fr. Stornaway to Philadelphia, in *Friendship*. (PRO.T47.12)
3381. McAulay, Malcolm, Covenanter, res. Argyll, tr. Aug 1685, fr. Leith to Jamaica. (PC.11.136)
3382. McAulay, Norman, b. 1746, farmer, res. Bayble Isle of Lewis, sh. May 1774, fr. Stornaway to Philadelphia, in *Friendship*, m. Isobell McLeod, ch. Ann. (PRO.T47.12)
3383. McAulay, Robert, servant, res. Glasgow, pts. Duncan & Agnes McAulay, sh. 18 Aug 1699, fr. Clyde to Darien, in *Rising Sun*, Edin pr1707 CC8.8.83
3384. McAulay, William, rioter, res. Glasgow, tr. 1749. (SM.11.252)

3385. McBain, Donald, b. 1717, husbandman, Jacobite, res. Inverness-shire, tr. 1747. (P.3.20)(MR174) (alias 3386)
3386. McBain, Duncan, b. 1717, husbandman, Jacobite, res. Inverness-shire, tr. 1747. (P.3.20)(MR174) (alias 3385)
3387. McBain, James, b. 1699, catechist, Jacobite, res. Petty Inverness-shire, tr. 20 March 1747, fr. Tilbury. (P.3.20)
3388. McBain, John, b. 1699, servant, Jacobite, res. Dunkeld Perthshire, tr. 1747, fr. Tilbury. (P.3.20)(MR174)
3389. McBain, John, b. 1729, Jacobite, tr. 20 Mar 1747, fr. Tilbury. (P.3.20)(MR174)
3390. McBean, Angus, Jacobite, tr. 31 July 1716, fr. Liverpool to Va, in *Anne*. (SPC.1716.310)(CTB31.209)
3391. McBean, Archibald, sh. Apr 1737, fr. Inverness to Ga, in *Two Brothers*. (SPC.1737.248)
3392. McBean, Daniel, Jacobite, tr. 7 May 1716, fr. Liverpool to Va, in *Anne*. (SPC.1716.310)(CTB31.209)
3393. MacBean, Donald, soldier, sh. pre 1773, sett. N.Y. (PCCol.5.597)
3394. McBean, Elias, Jacobite, tr. 7 May 1716, fr. Liverpool to S.C., in *Susannah*. (SPC.1716.309)(CTB31.206)
3395. McBean, Francis, Jacobite, tr. 28 July 1716, fr. Liverpool to Va, in *Godspeed*, arr. Md Oct 1716. (SPC.1716.310)(CTB31.209)(HM388)
3396. McBean, John, Jacobite, tr. 24 May 1716, fr. Liverpool to Md, in *Friendship*, arr. Md Aug 1716. (SPC.1716.311)(HM387)(Md Arch.34.164)
3397. McBean, John, Jacobite, tr. 29 June 1716, fr. Liverpool to Jamaica or Va, in *Elizabeth & Anne*. (SPC.1716.310)(CTB31.208)
3398. McBean, John, Jacobite, tr. 31 July 1716, fr. Liverpool to Va, in *Anne*. (CTB31.209)
3399. McBean, Lachlan, Jacobite, tr. 21 Apr 1716, fr. Liverpool to S.C., in *Wakefield*. (SPC.1716.309)(CTB31.205)
3400. McBean, Laughlin, planter, res. Inverness, sh. pre 1756, sett. Augusta Ga, ch. William John. (SPC.1737.6)
3401. McBean, Loughlin, Jacobite, tr. 21 Apr 1716, fr. Liverpool to S.C., in *Wakefield*. (CTB31.205)
3402. MacBean, Robert, b. 1720, barber, res. Inverness, sh. Nov 1736, fr. London to Jamaica. (CLRO\AIA)
3403. McBean, William, Jacobite, tr. 24 May 1716, fr. Liverpool to Va, in *Friendship*, arr. Md 20 Aug 1716. (SPC.1716.311)(HM386)
3404. McBeath, George, b. 1756, farm servant, res. Wick Caithness, sh. Sept 1775, fr. Kirkwall to Savannah Ga, in *Marlborough*, sett. Richmond Co Ga. (PRO.T47.12)

165

3405. McBeath, John, b. 1737, farmer & shoemaker, res. Mault Kildonan
Sutherland, sh. Apr 1774, fr. Lerwick to Wilmington N.C., in
Bachelor of Leith. (PRO.T47.12)
3406. McBeth, James, b. 1716, res. Edinburgh, sh. Oct 1731, fr. London to
Antigua. (CLRO\AIA)
3407. McBrayne, Lachlan, Jacobite, tr. 21 Apr 1716, fr. Liverpool to S.C., in
Wakefield. (SPC.1716.309)
3408. McBride, Alexander, b. 1753, laborer, res. New Luce Wigtonshire, sh.
May 1775, fr. Stranraer to N.C., in *Jackie.* (PRO.T47.12)
3409. McBride, Duncan, b. 1729, farmer, res. Stirling, sh. May 1775, fr.
Greenock to N.Y., in *Monimia*, m. Marion Donaldson.
(PRO.T47.12)
3410. McBride, James, b. 1737, farmer, res. New Luce Wigtonshire, sh. May
1775, fr. Stranraer to N.C., in *Jackie*, m. Janet McMiken, ch.
Archibald Elizabeth Jenny. (PRO.T47.12)
3411. McBride, John, Covenanter, res. Argyll, tr. 6 July 1685, fr. Leith to N.E.
(PC.11.119)
3412. McBryde, Hugh, merchant, res. Irvine Ayrshire, sh. pre 1775, sett.
Dorchester Co Md. (SRO.RD2.232.642)
3413. McBryde, William, merchant, res. Irvine Ayrshire, sh. pre 1775, sett.
Dorchester Co Md. (SRO.RD2.232.642)
3414. McBurnie, Robert, b. 1755, joiner, res. Fairgirth Colvend
Kirkcudbrightshire, sh. May 1775, fr. Dumfries to P.E.I., in
Lovely Nelly. (PRO.T47.12)
3415. McBurnie, William, b. 1749, joiner, res. Fairgirth Colvend
Kirkcudbrightshire, sh. May 1775, fr. Dumfries to P.E.I., in
Lovely Nelly. (PRO.T47.12)
3416. McCall, James, storekeeper, res. Glasgow, sh. pre 1765, sett. North
Glasgow Essex Co Va. (SRA.T79.41)
3417. McCall, Martin, tr. July 1685. (PC.11.129)
3418. McCall, William, Covenanter, tr. Aug 1685, fr. Leith to Jamaica.
(PC.11.136)
3419. McCallachy, Robert, b. 1746, watchmaker, res. Dundee Angus, sh. May
1775, fr. Greenock to N.Y., in *Christy.* (PRO.T47.12)
3420. McCallum, Archibald, Covenanter, res. Argyll, tr. Aug 1685, fr. Leith to
Jamaica. (PC.11.136)
3421. McCallum, Archibald, sh. 29 Nov 1773, fr. Greenock to Jamaica, in
Mary of Glasgow. (SRO.CE60.1.7)
3422. McCallum, Donald, Jacobite, tr. 7 May 1716, fr. Liverpool to S.C., in
Susannah. (SPC.1716.309)(CTB31.206)
3423. McCallum, Duncan, Covenanter, res. Argyll, tr. July 1685, fr. Leith to
N.E. (PC.9.94)
3424. McCallum, Duncan, farmer, Covenanter, res. Otter Argyll, tr. July 1685,
fr. Leith to N.E. (PC.11.136)

3425. McCallum, Duncan, Jacobite, tr. 7 May 1716, fr. Liverpool to S.C., in *Susannah*. (SPC.1716.309)(CTB31.206)

3426. McCallum, Duncan, b. 1745, laborer, res. Breadalbane Perthshire, sh. Sept 1775, to Wilmington N.C., in *Jupiter*. (PRO.T47.12)

3427. McCallum, Gilbert, Jacobite, tr. 22 Apr 1747, fr. Liverpool to Va, in *Johnson*, arr. Port Oxford Md 5 Aug 1747. (P.3.22)(PRO.T1.328)

3428. McCallum, Hugh, b. 1743, farmer, res. Angus, sh. May 1775, fr. Greenock to N.Y., in *Lilly*. (PRO.T47.12)

3429. McCallum, John, Jacobite, tr. 26 Apr 1716, fr. Liverpool to Jamaica, in *Two Brothers*, arr. Montserrat June 1716. (CTB31.205)(SPC.1716.313)(CTP.CC.43)

3430. McCallum, John, Covenanter, res. Argyll, tr. Aug 1685, fr. Leith to East N.J., in *Henry & Francis*. (PC.11.126)

3431. McCallum, John, Jacobite, tr. 7 May 1716, fr. Liverpool to S.C., in *Susannah*. (SPC.1716.309)

3432. McCallum, John, Jacobite, tr. 28 July 1716, fr. Liverpool to Va, in *Godspeed*, arr. Md Oct 1716. (SPC.1716.310)(HM389)

3433. McCallum, John, b. 1756, laborer, res. Stornaway Isle of Lewis, sh. Apr 1775, fr. Greenock to N.Y., in *Lilly*. (PRO.T47.12)

3434. McCallum, Malcolm, Jacobite, tr. 28 July 1716, fr. Liverpool to Va, in *Godspeed*, arr. Md Oct 1716. (SPC.1716.310)(CTb31.209)(HM388)

3435. McCallum, Neil, Covenanter, res. Argyll, tr. Aug 1685, fr. Leith to Jamaica. (PC.11.330)

3436. McCallum, Peter, b. 1748, farmer, res. Breadalbane Perthshire, sh. June 1775, fr. Greenock to N.Y., in *Commerce*. (PRO.T47.12)

3437. MacCally, James, b. 1720, res. Galloway, sh. Mar 1737, fr. London to Jamaica. (CLRO\AIA)

3438. McCalman, William, Covenanter, res. Culbrattoun, tr. 5 Sept 1685, fr. Leith to East N.J., in *Henry & Francis*. (PC.10.612)

3439. McCann, Edward, Jacobite, tr. 26 Apr 1716, fr. Liverpool to Jamaica, in *Two Brothers*, arr. Montserrat June 1716. (SPC.1716.313)(CTP.CC.43)

3440. McCann, William, b. 1739, weaver, res. Galloway, sh. May 1775, fr. Stranraer to N.Y., in *Gale*, m. Jean ..., ch. Sarah John Janet. (PRO.T47.12)

3441. McCartney, Agnes, b. 1729, Jacobite, res. Belfast, tr. 1747. (P.3.22)

3442. McCartney, William, b. 1754, husbandman, res. Queenshill, sh. May 1774, fr. Stranraer to N.Y., in *Gale*. (PRO.T47.12)

3443. McCaul, James, b. 1754, farmer, res. Inverness, sh. May 1774, fr. Greenock to N.Y., in *George*. (PRO.T47.12)

3444. McCeun, Captain, b. 1744, mariner, sh. Feb 1774, fr. London to N.Y., in *Earl Dunmore*. (PRO.T47.9\11)

3445. McCharlartie, John, Covenanter, res. Argyll, tr. Aug 1685, fr. Leith to Jamaica. (PC.11.136)
3446. McChisholm, John, Covenanter, res. Spittal, tr. 19 Oct 1684, fr. Leith to Carolina. (PC.9.15)
3447. McClaser, Alexander, Jacobite, tr. 26 Apr 1716, fr. Liverpool to Jamaica, in *Two Brothers*, arr. Montserrat June 1716. (SPC.1716.313)(CTB31.206)(CTP.CC.43)
3448. McCleikeraye, John, tr. 15 Nov 1679, fr. Leith. (ETR162)
3449. McClelland, Andrew, Covenanter, tr. 5 Sept 1685, fr. Leith to East N.J., in *Henry & Francis*. (PC.11.154)
3450. McClelland, Robert, Covenanter, tr. 5 Sept 1685, fr. Leith to East N.J., in *Henry & Francis*. (PC.11.155)
3451. McClement, John, clergyman edu. Edinburgh Uni, sh. 1718, fr. London to Philadelphia, sett. Rehobeth Va. (AP192)
3452. McClilan, Anthony, sh. May 1775, fr. Kirkcudbright to P.E.I., in *Lovely Nelly*. (PRO.T47.12)
3453. McClintock, James, merchant, Covenanter, res. Glasgow, tr. June 1684, fr. Glasgow, in *Pelican*, m. Margaret Boyd. (PC.9.208)
3454. McCloughton, Peter, Jacobite, tr. 22 Apr 1747, fr. Liverpool to Va, in *Johnson*, arr. Port Oxford Md 5 Aug 1747. (PRO.T1.328)
3455. McClouthen, Hugh, Jacobite, tr. 1747. (P.3.24)
3456. McClumpha, Thomas, b. 1748, farmer, res. Galloway, sh. May 1774, fr. Stranraer to N.Y., in *Gale*, m. Jean ..., ch. John. (PRO.T47.12)
3457. McClure, Elisabeth, Covenanter, res. Barlay Kirkcudbrightshire, tr. Oct 1684. (PC.10.257)
3458. McClure, Mary, Covenanter, res. Barlay Kirkcudbrightshire, tr. Oct 1684. (PC.10.257)
3459. McClure, William, b. 1747, merchant, res. Ayr, sh. Oct 1774, fr. Greenock to Philadelphia, in *Sally*. (PRO.T47.12)
3460. McClurg, Margaret, Covenanter, tr. Oct 1684, m. Alexander Milligan. (PC.10.612)
3461. McCole, David, b. 1745, laborer, res. Breadalbane Perthshire, sh. Sept 1775, to Wilmington N.C., in *Jupiter*. (PRO.T47.12)
3462. McCole, Donald, b. 1741, laborer, res. Breadalbane Perthshire, sh. Sept 1775, to Wilmington N.C., in *Jupiter*, m. Katherine ..., ch. Ewan. (PRO.T47.12)
3463. McCole, Dugal, b. 1737, laborer, res. Glen Orchy Argyll, sh. Sept 1775, to Wilmington N.C., in *Jupiter*, m. Ann ..., ch. Margaret Mary Sarah. (PRO.T47.12)
3464. McCole, Duncan, b. 1730, farmer, res. Breadalbane Perthshire, sh. Sept 1775, to Wilmington N.C., in *Jupiter*, m. Christian ..., ch. Duncan Mary Sarah Christian Mildred Ann. (PRO.T47.12)

3465. McCole, Duncan, b. 1740, farmer, res. Breadalbane Perthshire, sh. Sept 1775, to Wilmington N.C., in *Jupiter*, m. Christian ..., ch. Dugald Christian Katherine. (PRO.T47.12)
3466. McCole, John, b. 1726, laborer, res. Breadalbane Perthshire, sh. Sept 1775, to Wilmington N.C., in *Jupiter*, m. Mildred ..., ch. John Samuel Donald Douglas Alexander Katherine. (PRO.T47.12)
3467. McColl, John, res. Glasgow, sh. 1781, to N.Y., in *Ruby of Greenock*. (SRO.GD170)
3468. McCollum, John, Jacobite, tr. 14 July 1716, fr. Liverpool to Va, in *Godspeed*. (CTB31.209)
3469. McColm, Quintin, merchant, res. Maybole Ayrshire, pts. John McColm & Elizabeth Kennedy, sh. pre 1745, sett. N.E., d. 3 Aug 1746 N.E., Edin pr1752 CC8.8.114
3470. McComb, Alexander, b. 1753, husbandman, res. Glen Luce Wigtonshire, sh. May 1774, fr. Stranraer to N.Y., in *Gale*. (PRO.T47.12)
3471. McComb, Gilbert, Jacobite, res. Perth, tr. 1747. (P.3.26)(MR73)
3472. McConachie, William, clergyman, sh. 1710, d. 1742 Portobacco Md. (EMA43)
3473. McConachy, ..., thief, res. Argyll, tr. 1747, fr. Greenock. (SRO.GD14.10.1)
3474. McConnell, James, thief, res. Whitelargs of Stratoun Ayrshire, tr. May 1717. (SRO.JC26.10.1007)
3475. McConochie, Dugal, servant, Covenanter, res. Craiginterve Argyll, tr. Aug 1685. (PC.11.126)
3476. McConochie, John, Covenanter, res. Argyll, tr. Aug 1685, fr. Leith to Jamaica. (PC.11.136)
3477. McConochie, Neil, Covenanter, res. Argyll, tr. Aug 1685, fr. Leith to Jamaica. (PC.11.136)
3478. MacConochy, John Dow, thief, res. Killinaw Inverness-shire, tr. June 1754. (SM.16.203) (alias 3669)
3479. McCook, John, Jacobite, tr. 30 Mar 1716, fr. Liverpool to Antigua, in *Scipio*. (SPC.1716.310)(CTB31.204)
3480. McCorkadale, Archibald, Covenanter, res. Argyll, tr. Aug 1685, fr. Leith to Jamaica. (PC.11.136)
3481. McCormack, Mark, b. 1731, laborer, Jacobite, res. Moidart Inverness-shire, tr. 5 May 1747, fr. Liverpool to Leeward Islands, in *Veteran*, arr. Martinique June 1747. (P.3.28)(PRO.SP36.102)
3482. McCormack, Robert, b. 1707, farmer, Jacobite, res. Clathill Eigg Inverness-shire, tr. 31 Mar 1747, fr. London to Jamaica, in *St George or Carteret*, arr. Jamaica 1747. (P.3.28)(PRO.CO137.58)(MR141)
3483. McCoul, Agnes, infanticide, tr. Aug 1751. (AJ189) (alias 3715)
3484. McCoull, Agnes, infanticide, res. Perthshire, tr. 1752. (SRO.B59.26.11.1.29) (alias 3719)

3485. MacCourtuie, James, b. 1757, servant, thief, res. Kirkcudbright, tr. 1771, fr. Port Glasgow to Md, in *Crawford*, arr. Port Oxford Md 23 July 1771. (AJ1167)(SRO.JC27.10.3)
3486. McCowan, William, Jacobite, tr. 22 Apr 1747, fr. Liverpool to Va, in *Johnson*, arr. Port Oxford Md 5 Aug 1747. (P.3.30)(PRO.T1.328)
3487. McCoy, Daniel, Jacobite, tr. 30 Mar 1716, fr. Liverpool to Antigua, in *Scipio*. (SPC.1716.310)(CTB31.204)
3488. McCoy, Daniel, Jacobite, tr. 8 May 1747, to Antigua. (P.3.30)
3489. McCoy, Donald, Jacobite, tr. 7 May 1716, fr. Liverpool to S.C., in *Susannah*. (SPC.1716.309)(CTB31.206)
3490. McCoy, Donald, Jacobite, tr. 21 Apr 1716, fr. Liverpool to S.C., in *Wakefield*. (SPC.1716.309)(CTB31.205)
3491. McCoy, Donald, Jacobite, tr. 8 May 1747, to Antigua. (P.3.30)
3492. McCoy, Hugh, Jacobite, tr. 21 Apr 1716, fr. Liverpool to S.C., in *Wakefield*. (SPC.1716.309)(CTB31.205)
3493. McCoy, John, Jacobite, tr. 25 June 1716, fr. Liverpool to St Kitts, in *Hockenhill*. (SPC.1716.312)(CTB31.207)
3494. McCoy, John, Jacobite, tr. 21 Apr 1716, fr. Liverpool to S.C., in *Wakefield*. (CTB31.205)
3495. McCoy, John, Jacobite, tr. 26 Apr 1716, fr. Liverpool to Jamaica, in *Two Brothers*, arr. Montserrat June 1716. (SPC.1716.313)(CTB31.205)(CTP.CC.43)
3496. McCoy, Patrick, Jacobite, tr. 28 July 1716, fr. Liverpool to Va, in *Godspeed*, arr. Md Oct 1716. (SPC.1716.310)(CTB31.209)(HM389)
3497. McCoy, Paul, Jacobite, tr. 30 Mar 1716, fr. Liverpool to Antigua, in *Scipio*. (SPC.1716.310)(CTB31.204)
3498. McCoy, Peter, Jacobite, res. Bellie Banffshire, tr. 22 Apr 1747, fr. Liverpool to Va, in *Johnson*, arr. Port Oxford Md 5 Aug 1747. (PRO.T1.328)(JAB.2.434)
3499. McCoy, Tascal, Jacobite, tr. 1747, in *St George or Carteret*, arr. Jamaica 1747. (PRO.CO137.58)
3500. McCra, Anne, b. 1752, servant, res. Inverness, sh. July 1775, fr. Stornaway to Philadelphia, in *Clementina*. (PRO.T47.12)
3501. McCra, Donald, b. 1766, res. Kinmily, sh. July 1775, fr. Stornaway to Philadelphia, in *Clementina*. (PRO.T47.12)
3502. McCra, Hugh, b. 1764, servant, res. Kinmily, sh. July 1775, fr. Stornaway to Philadelphia, in *Clementina*. (PRO.T47.12)
3503. McCrackan, John, res. Old Glenluce Galloway, pts. Andrew McCrackan, d. pre 1769 Newhaven N.E., PCC pr1769
3504. McCracken, James, b. 1747, tailor, res. Stonykirk Wigtonshire, sh. May 1775, fr. Stranraer to N.Y., in *Jackie*. (PRO.T47.12)
3505. McCracken, John, b. 1752, res. Galloway, sh. May 1775, fr. Dumfries to P.E.I., in *Lovely Nelly*. (PRO.T47.12)

3506. McCrae, Thomas, b. 1747, res. Paisley Renfrewshire, sh. Feb 1774, fr.
Greenock to N.Y., in *Commerce*, m. Elizabeth ... (PRO.T47.12)
3507. McCraig, Angus, cattle thief, res. Inverness-shire, tr. Sept 1752. (AJ248)
(alias 4626)
3508. MacCraing, Peter Dow, cattle thief, res. Blacklet Glencoe Argyll, tr. Sept
1766. (AJ978)
3509. McCrainie, Archibald, res. Knockcrainie Jura Argyll, sh. 1754, to Cape
Fear N.C. (SRO.GD64\5.21)
3510. McCrainkein, John, servant, res. Arefernal Jura Argyll, sh. 1754, to Cape
Fear N.C. (SRO.GD64\5.21)
3511. McCran, Ann, b. 1747, servant, res. Loch Broom Ross-shire, sh. Nov
1774, fr. Stornaway to N.Y., in *Peace & Plenty*. (PRO.T47.12)
3512. McCran, Mary, b. 1749, servant, res. Loch Broom Ross-shire, sh. Nov
1774, fr. Stornaway to N.Y., in *Peace & Plenty*. (PRO.T47.12)
3513. McCrea, Hugh, laborer, res. Galloway, sh. May 1774, fr. Stranraer to
N.Y., in *Gale*. (PRO.T47.12)
3514. McCreath, John, servant, murderer, res. Aston Ayrshire, tr. Aug 1748.
(SRO.JC27)
3515. McCubbin, James, Covenanter, res. Marwhirn Kirkcudbrightshire, tr. Oct
1684. (PC.10.587)
3516. McCuean, Walter, Covenanter, tr. Aug 1685, fr. Leith. (PC.11.154)
3517. McCuillan, William, servant, housebreaker & thief, res. Borrowstoun
Caithness, tr. 1773, fr. Glasgow to Va, in *Donald*, arr. Port James
Upper District Va 13 Mar 1773. (SRO.JC27.10.3)
3518. McCullie, John, Covenanter, tr. July 1685. (PC.11.114)
3519. McCulloch, Alexander, sh. 1718. (SRO.GD10.1.46)
3520. McCulloch, Anthony, sett. Queen Anne Co Md, d. 1770, Edin pr1773
CC8.8.122
3521. McCulloch, James, b. 1727, laborer, res. Dumfries, sh. May 1775, fr.
Dumfries to P.E.I., in *Lovely Nelly*. (PRO.T47.12)
3522. McCulloch, John, sailor, res. Lochgair Argyll, sh. 14 July 1698, fr.
Leith to Darien, in *Caledonia*, m. Sarah McLauchlan, Edin pr1709
CC8.8.84
3523. McCulloch, John, b. 1753, weaver, res. Paisley Renfrewshire, sh. Feb
1774, fr. Greenock to N.Y., in *Commerce*. (PRO.T47.12)
3524. McCulloch, Margaret, infanticide, res. Carngren Kirkmarden Wigtonshire,
pts. Godfrey McCulloch, tr. May 1729. (SRO.JC13.6)
3525. McCulloch, Robert, Jacobite, tr. 26 Apr 1716, fr. Liverpool to Jamaica,
in *Two Brothers*, arr. Montserrat June 1716.
(SPC.1716.313)(CTB31.206)(CTP.CC.43)
3526. McCulloch, William, b. 1751, barber, sh. Sept 1775, fr. Newcastle to
Ga, in *Georgia Packet*, sett. Friendsborough Ga, m. Barbara ...
(PRO.T47.9\11)

171

3527. McCullock, Alexander, b. 1750, servant, res. Braen, sh. July 1775, fr. Stornaway to Philadelphia, in *Clementina*. (PRO.T47.12)
3528. McCullon, John, Jacobite, tr. 29 June 1716, fr. Liverpool to Jamaica or Va, in *Elizabeth & Anne*. (SPC.1716.310)(CTB31.208)
3529. McCumming, John, Covenanter, tr. July 1685. (PC.11.329)
3530. McCureith, Archibald, tr. Aug 1685, fr. Leith to Jamaica. (PC.11.330)
3531. McCurr, Daniel, b. 1724, res. Edinburgh, sh. Nov 1736, fr. London to Jamaica. (CLRO\AIA)
3532. McCurrie, Donald, Covenanter, res. Argyll, tr. Aug 1685, fr. Leith to Jamaica. (PC.11.136)
3533. McDanell, Daniel, Jacobite, tr. 30 Mar 1716, fr. Liverpool to Antigua, in *Scipio*. (SPC.1716.310)
3534. McDaniel, Angus, Jacobite, tr. 22 Apr 1747, fr. Liverpool to Va, in *Johnson*, arr. Port Oxford Md 5 Aug 1747. (PRO.T1.328)
3535. McDaniel, Daniel, Jacobite, res. Perthshire, tr. 1747. (MR24)
3536. McDaniel, Daniel, Jacobite, res. Perth, tr. 22 Apr 1747, fr. Liverpool to Va, in *Johnson*, arr. Port Oxford Md 5 Aug 1747. (P.3.32)(MR24)(PRO.T1.328)
3537. McDaniel, John, Jacobite, tr. 22 Apr 1747, fr. Liverpool to Va, in *Johnson*, arr. Port Oxford Md 5 Aug 1747. (PRO.T1.328)
3538. McDaniel, Mary, b. 1712, Jacobite, res. Inverness, tr. 22 Apr 1747, fr. Liverpool to Va, in *Johnson*, arr. Port Oxford Md 5 Aug 1747. (P.3.74)(PRO.T1.328)
3539. McDarran, Archibald, Jacobite, tr. 24 May 1716, fr. Liverpool to Md, in *Friendship*, arr. Md Aug 1716. (SPC.1716.311)(HM387)
3540. McDermot, John, thief, res. Loch Arkaig Lochaber Inverness-shire, tr. May 1755. (AJ386) (alias 2086)
3541. McDermott, Angus, Jacobite, tr. 26 Apr 1716, fr. Liverpool to Jamaica, in *Two Brothers*, arr. Montserrat June 1716. (SPC.1716.313)(CTB31.206)(CTP.CC.43)
3542. McDermott, Angus, Jacobite, tr. 26 Apr 1716, fr. Liverpool to Jamaica, in *Two Brothers*, arr. Montserrat June 1716. (SPC.1716.313)(CTB31.205)(CTP.CC.43)
3543. McDermott, Angus, Jacobite, tr. 28 July 1716, fr. Liverpool to Va, in *Godspeed*, arr. Md Oct 1716. (SPC.1716.310)(CTB31.209)(HM389)
3544. McDermott, John, Jacobite, tr. 30 Mar 1716, fr. Liverpool to Antigua, in *Scipio*. (SPC.1716.310)(CTB31.204)
3545. McDiarmid, Angus, b. 1727, farmer, res. Breadalbane Perthshire, sh. Feb 1775, fr. Greenock to N.Y., in *Commerce*, m. Katherine McMartin, ch. Betty. (PRO.T47.12)
3546. McDiarmid, Duncan, b. 1753, smith, res. Breadalbane Perthshire, pts. Angus McDiarmid & Katherine McMartin, sh. Feb 1775, fr. Greenock to N.Y., in *Commerce*. (PRO.T47.12)

3547. McDiarmid, Eliza, b. 1758, servant, res. Breadalbane Perthshire, sh. June 1775, fr. Greenock to N.Y., in *Commerce*. (PRO.T47.12)
3548. McDiarmid, Jean, b. 1772, res. Breadalbane Perthshire, sh. June 1775, fr. Greenock to N.Y., in *Commerce*. (PRO.T47.12)
3549. McDiarmid, John, housebreaker, res. Edinburgh, pts. Patrick McDiarmid, tr. Aug 1764. (SRO.HCR.I.96)
3550. McDiarmid, John, b. 1772, res. Breadalbane Perthshire, sh. June 1775, fr. Greenock to N.Y., in *Commerce*. (PRO.T47.12)
3551. McDiarmid, Katherine, b. 1761, res. Breadalbane Perthshire, sh. June 1775, fr. Greenock to N.Y., in *Commerce*. (PRO.T47.12)
3552. McDiarmid, Mary, b. 1754, servant, res. Breadalbane Perthshire, sh. June 1775, fr. Greenock to N.Y., in *Commerce*. (PRO.T47.12)
3553. McDichmaye, Walter, tr. Nov 1679, fr. Leith. (ETR162)
3554. McDonald, Agnes, rioter, res. Perth, tr. May 1773. (AJ1322)
3555. McDonald, Alexander, Jacobite, tr. 24 Feb 1747, fr. Liverpool to Va, in *Gildart*, arr. Port North Potomac Md 5 Aug 1747. (PRO.T1.328)
3556. McDonald, Alexander, shipwreck looter, res. Reay Caithness, tr. 1773, fr. Glasgow to Va, in *Donald*, arr. Port James Upper District Va 13 Mar 1773. (SRO.JC27.10.3)(AJ1091\8)
3557. McDonald, Alexander, tr. Jan 1750. (AJ106)
3558. MacDonald, Alexander, soldier, sh. 1737, fr. Gravesend to Ga, in *Mary Ann*, m. Mary ... (SPC.43.459)
3559. McDonald, Alexander, res. Knockcrainie Jura Argyll, sh. 1754, to Cape Fear N.C. (SRO.GD64\5.21)
3560. McDonald, Alexander, b. 1687, farmer, Jacobite, res. Glenmoriston Inverness-shire, tr. 1747. (P.3.40)(MR155)
3561. McDonald, Alexander, b. 1701, Jacobite, res. Glen Urquhart Inverness-shire, tr. 31 Mar 1747, fr. London to Jamaica, in *St George or Carteret*, arr. Jamaica 1747. (P.3.40)(MR155)(PRO.CO137.58)
3562. McDonald, Alexander, b. 1709, farmer, Jacobite, res. Glenmoriston Inverness-shire, tr. 31 Mar 1747, fr. London to Barbados , in *Frere*. (P.3.40)(MR154)
3563. McDonald, Alexander, b. 1717, cattleherd, Jacobite, res. Corrimony Inverness-shire, tr. 1747. (P.3.42)
3564. McDonald, Alexander, b. 1717, farmer, Jacobite, res. Glenmoriston Inverness-shire, tr. 31 Mar 1747, fr. London to Barbados , in *Frere*. (P.3.40)(MR154)
3565. McDonald, Alexander, b. 1717, farmer, Jacobite, res. Glenmoriston Inverness-shire, tr. 31 Mar 1747, fr. London to Jamaica, in *St George or Carteret*, arr. Jamaica 1747. (P.3.40)(MR155)(PRO.CO137.58)
3566. McDonald, Alexander, b. 1723, merchant, Jacobite, res. Mickle Strath Ross-shire, tr. 1747. (P.3.40)(MR82)

173

3567. McDonald, Alexander, b. 1751, servant, res. Duffus Morayshire, sh. July 1775, fr. Stornaway to Philadelphia, in *Clementina*. (PRO.T47.12)
3568. McDonald, Alexander, b. 1754, servant, res. Strathpeffer Ross & Cromarty, sh. July 1775, fr. Stornaway to Philadelphia, in *Clementina*. (PRO.T47.12)
3569. McDonald, Allan, ex soldier, rioter, res. Mylnefield Perthshire, tr. May 1773. (SRO.B59.26.11.6.33) (alias 3573)
3570. McDonald, Allan, sh. pre 1767, sett. Fort William Newfoundland. (SRO.GD24.1.392)
3571. McDonald, Allan, b. 1711, soldier, Jacobite, res. Inverness, tr. 31 Mar 1747, fr. London to Barbados, in *Frere*. (P.3.44)(MR82)
3572. MacDonald, Angus, Jacobite, tr. 24 Feb 1747, fr. Liverpool to Va, in *Gildart*, arr. Port North Potomac Md 5 Aug 1747. (PRO.T1.328)
3573. McDonald, Angus, ex soldier, rioter, res. Mylnefield Perthshire, tr. May 1773. (SRO.B59.26.11.6.33) (alias 3569)
3574. McDonald, Angus, tailor, Jacobite, res. Kirkton of Raasay Inverness-shire, tr. 1747, fr. Tilbury. (P.3.46)(MR185)
3575. McDonald, Angus, farmer, Jacobite, res. Guilen Eigg Inverness-shire, tr. 20 Mar 1747, fr. Tilbury. (P.3.44)(MR142)
3576. McDonald, Angus, laborer, Jacobite, res. Inverness-shire, tr. 8 May 1747, to Antigua. (P.3.46)(MR155)
3577. McDonald, Angus, Jacobite, tr. 24 Feb 1747, fr. Liverpool to Va, in *Gildart*, arr. Port North Potomac Md 5 Aug 1747. (PRO.T1.328)
3578. McDonald, Angus, tr. 1771, fr. Port Glasgow to Md, in *Matty*, arr. Port Oxford Md 17 Dec 1771. (SRO.JC27.10.3)
3579. McDonald, Angus, b. 1697, Jacobite, res. Inverness-shire, tr. 20 Mar 1747, fr. Tilbury to Jamaica, in *St George or Carteret*, arr. Jamaica 1747. (P.3.44)(PRO.CO137.58)(MR142)
3580. McDonald, Angus, b. 1697, Jacobite, res. Rannoch Perthshire, tr. 1747. (P.3.46)(MR164)
3581. McDonald, Angus, b. 1707, Jacobite, res. Inverness-shire, tr. 1747. (P.3.46)(MR155)
3582. McDonald, Angus, b. 1727, farmer, Jacobite, res. Cromeil South Uist, tr. 1747. (P.3.46)(MR185)
3583. MacDonald, Angus Roy, cattlethief, res. Strathmassey Badenoch Inverness-shire, tr. Nov 1773, fr. Glasgow. (AJ1349)
3584. McDonald, Ann, thief, res. Inverness, tr. 1772, fr. Glasgow to Va, in *Brilliant*, arr. Port Hampton Va 7 Oct 1772. (SRO.JC27.10.3)(AJ1274)
3585. McDonald, Ann, thief, res. Castle Grant Forres Morayshire, tr. May 1770, m. James McIntosh. (AJ1183)
3586. MacDonald, Anne, thief, res. Easter Delnies Nairn, tr. May 1775. (AJ1432)

174

3587. McDonald, Archibald, b. 1702, laborer, Jacobite, res. Inverness, tr. 1747. (P.3.48)(MR164)
3588. McDonald, Archibald, b. 1705, farmer, Jacobite, res. Glenmoriston Inverness-shire, tr. 22 Apr 1747, fr. Liverpool to Va, in *Johnson*, d. 4 June 1747 at sea. (P.3.48)(MR155)(PRO.T1.328)
3589. McDonald, Archibald, b. 1722, farm servant, Jacobite, res. Kilcreich Inverness-shire, tr. 20 Mar 1747, fr. Tilbury. (P.3.48)(MR181)
3590. McDonald, Archibald, b. 1757, servant, res. Beauly Inverness-shire, sh. July 1775, fr. Stornaway to Philadelphia, in *Clementina*. (PRO.T47.12)
3591. McDonald, Bathia, b. 1760, servant, res. Beauly Inverness-shire, sh. July 1775, fr. Stornaway to Philadelphia, in *Clementina*. (PRO.T47.12)
3592. McDonald, Catherine, b. 1757, servant, res. Inverness, sh. July 1775, fr. Stornaway to Phiadelphia, in *Clementina*. (PRO.T47.12)
3593. McDonald, Christian, b. 1757, servant, res. Beauly Inverness-shire, sh. July 1775, fr. Stornaway to Philadelphia, in *Clementina*. (PRO.T47.12)
3594. McDonald, Christy, b. 1750, seamstress, res. Breadalbane Perthshire, sh. Sept 1775, to Wilmington N.C., in *Jupiter*. (PRO.T47.12)
3595. McDonald, Coll, Jacobite, tr. 21 Apr 1716, fr. Liverpool to S.C., in *Wakefield*. (SPC.1716.309)(CTB31.205)
3596. McDonald, Daniel, b. 1728, laborer, Jacobite, res. Lettochbeag Kinloch Inverness-shire, tr. 5 May 1747, fr. Liverpool to Leeward Islands, in *Veteran*, arr. Martinique June 1747. (P.3.52)(PRO.SP36.102)
3597. McDonald, David, res. Lochbank, pts. David Donald or McDonald of Shangzie, sh. 1699, to Darien, Edin pr 1709 CC8.8.84 (alias 1543)
3598. McDonald, Denis, Jacobite, tr. 26 Apr 1716, fr. Liverpool to Jamaica, in *Two Brothers*, arr. Montserrat June 1716. (SPC.1716.313)(CTB31.205)(CTP.CC.43)
3599. McDonald, Donald, Jacobite, tr. 21 Apr 1716, fr. Liverpool to S.C., in *Wakefield*. (SPC.1716.309)(CTB31.205)
3600. McDonald, Donald, res. Buchlyvie Stirlingshire, tr. 12 Dec 1678, fr. Leith to West Indies, in *St Michael of Scarborough*. (PC.6.76)
3601. McDonald, Donald, Jacobite, tr. 30 Mar 1716, fr. Liverpool to Antigua, in *Scipio*. (CTB31.204)
3602. McDonald, Donald, farmer, Jacobite, res. Fivepenny Eigg Inverness-shire, tr. 19 Mar 1747, fr. London to Jamaica, in *St George or Carteret*, arr. Jamaica 1747. (P.3.56)(PRO.CO137.58)
3603. MacDonald, Donald, merchant, res. Edinburgh, d. Jan 1773 Cross Creek N.C. (SM.35.223)
3604. McDonald, Donald, Jacobite, tr. 21 Apr 1716, fr. Liverpool to S.C., in *Wakefield*. (SPC.1716.309)(CTB31.205)

3605. McDonald, Donald, b. 1689, servant, Jacobite, res. Edinburgh, tr. 5 May 1747, fr. Liverpool to Leeward Islands, in *Veteran*, arr. Martinique June 1747. (PRO.SP36.102)
3606. McDonald, Donald, b. 1691, farmer, Jacobite, res. Clatil Eigg Inverness-shire, tr. 31 Mar 1747, fr. London to Jamaica, in *St George or Carteret*, arr. Jamaica 1747. (P.3.56)(PRO.CO137.58)(MR141)
3607. McDonald, Donald, b. 1692, laborer, Jacobite, res. Camghouran Rannoch Perthshire, tr. 24 Feb 1747, fr. Liverpool to Va, in *Gildart*, arr. Port North Potomac Md 5 Aug 1747. (P.3.56)(MR156)(PRO.T1.328)
3608. McDonald, Donald, b. 1697, farmer, Jacobite, res. Glen Urquhart Inverness-shire, tr. 31 Mar 1747, fr. London to Jamaica, in *St George or Carteret*, arr. Jamaica 1747. (P.3.56)(MR155)(PRO.CO137.58)
3609. McDonald, Donald, b. 1717, laborer, res. Kinmily, sh. July 1775, fr. Stornaway to Philadelphia, in *Clementina*. (PRO.T47.12)
3610. McDonald, Donald, b. 1722, Jacobite, res. Glen Urquhart Inverness-shire, tr. 20 Mar 1747, fr. Tilbury to Jamaica, in *St George or Carteret*, arr. Jamaica 1747. (P.3.56)(MR155)(PRO.CO137.58)
3611. McDonald, Donald, b. 1725, Jacobite, res. Inverness, tr. 31 Mar 1747, fr. London to Barbados, in *Frere*. (P.3.56)(MR118)
3612. McDonald, Donald, b. 1725, laborer, Jacobite, res. Inverness, tr. 5 May 1747, fr. Liverpool to Leeward Islands, in *Veteran*, arr. Martinique June 1747. (P.3.56)(MR156)(PRO.SP36.102)
3613. McDonald, Donald, b. 1745, farmer & tailor, res. Reay Caithness, sh. Apr 1774, to Wilmington N.C., in *Bachelor of Leith*. (PRO.T47.12)
3614. McDonald, Donald, b. 1758, weaver, res. Paisley Renfrewshire, sh. Feb 1774, fr. Greenock to N.Y., in *Commerce*. (PRO.T47.12)
3615. McDonald, Donald, b. 1763, servant, res. Stornaway Isle of Lewis, sh. May 1774, fr. Stornaway to Philadelphia, in *Friendship*. (PRO.T47.12)
3616. McDonald, Duncan, horsethief, res. Connichan Glenmoriston Inverness-shire, tr. June 1767. (AJ1018)(SM.29.325)
3617. McDonald, Duncan, b. 1702, farmer, Jacobite, res. Glenmoriston Inverness-shire, tr. 31 Mar 1747, fr. London to Barbados , in *Frere*. (P.3.58)(MR156)
3618. McDonald, Duncan, b. 1725, farmer, res. Beauly Inverness-shire, sh. July 1775, fr. Stornaway to Philadelphia, in *Clementina*, m. Christian ... (PRO.T47.12)
3619. McDonald, Duncan, b. 1726, servant, Jacobite, res. Inverness, tr. 31 Mar 1747, fr. London to Barbados , in *Frere*. (P.3.58)(MR118)
3620. McDonald, Elizabeth, b. 1745, servant, res. Farr Sutherland, sh. Apr 1775, to Wilmington N.C., in *Bachelor of Leith*. (PRO.T47.12)

3621. McDonald, Elizabeth, b. 1754, servant, res. Loch Broom Ross-shire, sh. July 1775, fr. Stornaway to Philadelphia, in *Clementina*. (PRO.T47.12)
3622. McDonald, Elspia, b. 1759, servant, res. Kinmily, sh. July 1775, fr. Stornaway to Philadelphia, in *Clementina*. (PRO.T47.12)
3623. McDonald, Ewan, b. 1712, Jacobite, tr. 1747, fr. Tilbury. (P.3.58)(MR156)
3624. McDonald, George, cattlethief, res. Moulin Perthshire, tr. Feb 1772. (SRO.HCR.I.107) (alias 229)
3625. McDonald, Hector, b. 1699, farmer, res. Langwell Rogart Sutherland, sh. Apr 1774, to Wilmington N.C., in *Bachelor of Leith*, ch. John Alexander George. (PRO.T47.12)
3626. McDonald, Hugh, tr. Feb 1756. (SRO.HCR.1.89)
3627. McDonald, Hugh, b. 1717, Jacobite, res. Glenmoriston Inverness-shire, tr. 1747. (P.3.60)(MR156)
3628. McDonald, Hugh, b. 1734, Jacobite, res. Arisaig Inverness-shire, tr. 5 May 1747, fr. Liverpool to Leeward Islands, in *Veteran*, arr. Martinique June 1747. (P.3.62)(PRO.SP36.102)
3629. McDonald, Hugh, b. 1750, servant, res. Loch Broom Ross-shire, sh. July 1775, fr. Stornaway to Philadelphia, in *Clementina*. (PRO.T47.12)
3630. McDonald, Isobel, b. 1760, servant, res. Inverness, sh. July 1775, fr. Stornaway to Philadelphia, in *Clementina*. (PRO.T47.12)
3631. McDonald, James, Jacobite, res. Banff, tr. 20 Mar 1747. (P.3.62)(MR123)
3632. McDonald, James, Jacobite, tr. 7 May 1716, fr. Liverpool to S.C., in *Susannah*. (SPC.1716.309)(CTB31.206)
3633. McDonald, James, b. 1698, farmer, Jacobite, res. Glenmoriston Inverness-shire, tr. 20 Mar 1747, fr. Tilbury to Jamaica, in *St George or Carteret*, arr. Jamaica 1747. (P.3.64)(MR156)(PRO.CO137.58)
3634. McDonald, James, b. 1700, farmer, Jacobite, res. Guilen Eigg Inverness-shire, tr. 31 Mar 1747, fr. London to Jamaica, in *St George or Carteret*, arr. Jamaica 1747. (P.3.62)(MR142)(PRO.CO137.58)
3635. McDonald, James, b. 1765, servant, res. Beauly Inverness-shire, sh. July 1775, fr. Stornaway to Philadelphia, in *Clementina*. (PRO.T47.12)
3636. McDonald, Janet, b. 1757, servant, res. Beauly Inverness-shire, sh. July 1775, fr. Stornaway to Philadelphia, in *Clementina*. (PRO.T47.12)
3637. McDonald, Jean, tr. 1772, fr. Glasgow to Va, in *Brilliant*, arr. Port Hampton Va 7 Oct 1772. (SRO.JC27.10.3) (alias 242)
3638. McDonald, John, Jacobite, tr. 24 Feb 1747, fr. Liverpool to Va, in *Gildart*, arr. Port North Potomac Md 5 Aug 1747. (PRO.T1.328)
3639. McDonald, John, Jacobite, tr. 22 Apr 1747, fr. Liverpool to Va, in *Johnson*, arr. Port Oxford Md 5 Aug 1747. (PRO.T1.328)

3640. McDonald, John, Jacobite, tr. 7 May 1716, fr. Liverpool to S.C., in *Susannah*. (SPC.1716.309)(CTB31.206)
3641. McDonald, John, Jacobite, tr. 21 Apr 1716, fr. Liverpool to S.C., in *Wakefield*. (SPC.1716.309)(CTB31.205)
3642. McDonald, John, Jacobite, tr. 24 May 1716, fr. Liverpool to Md, in *Friendship*, arr. Md Aug 1716. (SPC.1716.311)(HM387)
3643. McDonald, John, Jacobite, tr. 24 May 1716, fr. Liverpool to Md, in *Friendship*. (SPC.1716.311)
3644. McDonald, John, vagrant & thief, res. Dumfries-shire, tr. Apr 1751. (AJ175)
3645. McDonald, John, Jacobite, tr. 19 Mar 1747. (P.3.68)
3646. McDonald, John, laborer, Jacobite, res. Badenoch Inverness-shire, tr. 19 Mar 1747. (P.3.68)(MR164)
3647. McDonald, John, Jacobite, tr. 24 Feb 1747, fr. Liverpool to Va, in *Gildart*, arr. Port North Potomac Md 5 Aug 1747. (PRO.T1.328)
3648. McDonald, John, clergyman edu. King's Col Aberdeen 1764, res. North Uist Inverness-shire, sett. Jamaica. (EMA42)
3649. McDonald, John, b. 1687, farmer, Jacobite, res. Glenmoriston Inverness-shire, tr. 31 Mar 1747, fr. London to Barbados, in *Frere*. (MR156)(P.3.70)
3650. McDonald, John, b. 1689, farmer, Jacobite, res. Fivepenny Eigg Inverness-shire, tr. 30 Mar 1747, fr. London to Barbados , in *Frere*. (P.3.66)(MR142)
3651. McDonald, John, b. 1691, Jacobite, res. Redorach Elgin Morayshire, tr. 20 Mar 1747, fr. Tilbury. (P.3.70)(MR157)
3652. McDonald, John, b. 1691, tailor, Jacobite, res. Skye Inverness-shire, tr. 31 Mar 1747, fr. London to Jamaica, in *St George or Carteret*, arr. Jamaica 1747. (P.3.70)(MR157)(PRO.CO137.58)
3653. McDonald, John, b. 1707, cowherd, Jacobite, res. Dongon Glengarry Inverness-shire, tr. 20 Mar 1747, fr. Tilbury to Jamaica, in *St George or Carteret*, arr. Jamaica 1747. (P.3.70)(MR156)(PRO.CO137.58)
3654. McDonald, John, b. 1707, laborer, Jacobite, res. Inverness, tr. 31 Mar 1747, fr. London to Jamaica, in *St George or Carteret*, arr. Jamaica 1747. (MR157)(PRO.CO137.58)
3655. McDonald, John, b. 1707, laborer, Jacobite, res. Perth, tr. 1747. (P.3.66)(MR24)
3656. McDonald, John, b. 1707, farmer, Jacobite, res. Galmistal Eigg Inverness-shire, tr. 20 Mar 1747. (P.3.66)(MR142)
3657. McDonald, John, b. 1711, farmer, Jacobite, res. Glenistill Eigg Inverness-shire, tr. 20 Mar 1747, fr. Tilbury. (P.3.66)(MR142)
3658. McDonald, John, b. 1711, farmer, Jacobite, res. Howlin Eigg Inverness-shire, tr. 20 Mar 1747, fr. Tilbury. (P.3.66)(MR142)

3659. McDonald, John, b. 1717, farmer, Jacobite, res. Glen Urquhart Inverness-shire, tr. 20 Mar 1747, fr. Tilbury to Jamaica, in *St George or Carteret*, arr. Jamaica 1747. (P.3.70)(MR156)(PRO.CO137.58)

3660. McDonald, John, b. 1723, Jacobite, res. Stradoun Banffshire, tr. 31 Mar 1747, fr. London to Barbados, in *Frere*. (P.3.70)

3661. MacDonald, John, b. 1726, res. Strathspey, sh. May 1774, fr. Greenock to N.Y., in *George*, m. Jean ..., ch. Henrietta Janet Alexander Elspa. (PRO.T47.12)

3662. McDonald, John, b. 1727, cattleherd, Jacobite, res. Doune Glengarry Inverness-shire, tr. 20 Mar 1747. (P.3.70)(MR156)

3663. McDonald, John, b. 1727, tailor, Jacobite, res. Inverness, tr. 31 Mar 1747, fr. London to Jamaica, in *St George or Carteret*, arr. Jamaica 1747. (P.3.70)(MR156)(PRO.CO137.58)

3664. McDonald, John, b. 1733, husbandman, Jacobite, res. Isle of Barra Argyll, tr. 20 Mar 1747. (P.3.70)(MR164) (alias 3713)

3665. McDonald, John, b. 1737, farmer, res. Stirling, sh. May 1775, fr. Greenock to N.Y., in *Monimia*, m. Margaret Grieve. (PRO.T47.12)

3666. McDonald, John, b. 1752, farmer, res. Strathspey, sh. May 1774, fr. Greenock to N.Y., in *George*, m. Margery ... (PRO.T47.12)

3667. McDonald, John, b. 1752, husbandman, sh. July 1774, fr. London to Md, in *Peggy Stewart*. (PRO.T47.9\11)

3668. McDonald, John, b. 1762, servant, res. Stornaway Isle of Lewis, sh. May 1774, fr. Stornaway to Philadelphia, in *Friendship*. (PRO.T47.12)

3669. MacDonald, John Dow, thief, res. Killinaw Inverness-shire, tr. June 1754. (SM.16.203) (alias 3478)

3670. McDonald, Joseph, b. 1720, weaver, Jacobite, res. Morayshire, tr. 5 May 1747, fr. Liverpool to Leeward Islands, in *Veteran*, arr. Martinique June 1747. (P.3.72)(PRO.SP36.102)

3671. McDonald, Joseph, b. 1748, laborer, res. Wigton, sh. May 1775, fr. Greenock to N.Y., in *Christy*. (PRO.T47.12)

3672. McDonald, Katherine, b. 1744, servant, res. Coriby, sh. May 1774, fr. Stornaway to Philadelphia, in *Friendship*. (PRO.T47.12)

3673. MacDonald, Kenneth, thief, res. Ross-shire, tr. Sept 1754. (SM.16.448) (alias 3739)

3674. McDonald, Margaret, vagrant & thief, tr. Sept 1754. (AJ352) (alias 7043)

3675. McDonald, Margaret, b. 1724, spinner, Jacobite, res. Perthshire, tr. 5 May 1747, fr. Liverpool to Leeward Islands, in *Veteran*, arr. Martinique June 1747. (PRO.SP36.102)

3676. McDonald, Margaret, b. 1726, Jacobite, res. Inverness, tr. 1747. (P.3.72)

3677. McDonald, Martha, b. 1757, servant, res. Beauly Inverness-shire, sh. July 1775, fr. Stornaway to Philadelphia, in *Clementina*. (PRO.T47.12)

3678. McDonald, Mary, infanticide, res. Inverness-shire, tr. Sept 1770. (AJ1183)

179

3679. McDonald, Mary, b. 1712, Jacobite, res. Inverness, tr. 1747. (P.3.74)
3680. McDonald, Mary, b. 1745, servant, res. Kinmily, sh. July 1775, fr.
    Stornaway to Philadelphia, in *Clementina*. (PRO.T47.12)
3681. McDonald, Mary, b. 1757, servant, res. Beauly Inverness-shire, sh. July
    1775, fr. Stornaway to Philadelphia, in *Clementina*. (PRO.T47.12)
3682. McDonald, Mary, b. 1758, servant, res. Perth, sh. May 1775, fr. Leith to
    Philadelphia, in *Friendship*. (PRO.T47.12)
3683. McDonald, Mary, b. 1760, servant, res. Perth, sh. May 1775, fr. Leith to
    Philadelphia, in *Friendship*. (PRO.T47.12)
3684. McDonald, Owen, Jacobite, tr. 20 Mar 1747, fr. London to Barbados , in
    Frere. (P.3.74)(MR157)
3685. McDonald, Owen, b. 1707, farmer, Jacobite, res. Glen Urquhart
    Inverness-shire, tr. 31 Mar 1747, fr. London to Barbados , in *Frere*.
    (P.3.74)(MR157)
3686. MacDonald, Ranald, Jacobite, tr. 1747. (P.3.76)
3687. McDonald, Ranald, farmer, Jacobite, res. Grinlin Eigg Inverness-shire, tr.
    31 Mar 1747. (P.3.76)(MR143)
3688. MacDonald, Rob Roy, thief, res. Glen Garry Inverness-shire, tr. June
    1754. (SM.16.203))AJ328) (alias 3847)
3689. McDonald, Roderick, farmer, Jacobite, res. Kirkton Eigg Inverness-shire,
    tr. 31 Mar 1747, fr. London to Barbados , in *Frere*.
    (P.3.78)(MR143)
3690. McDonald, Roderick, b. 1725, husbandman, Jacobite, res. Sandvegg Eigg
    Inverness-shire, tr. 31 Mar 1747, fr. London to Jamaica, in *St
    George or Carteret*, arr. Jamaica 1747.
    (P.3.78)(MR143)(PRO.CO137.58)
3691. McDonald, Ronald, Jacobite, tr. 1747, in *St George or Carteret*, arr.
    Jamaica 1747. (PRO.CO137.58)
3692. McDonald, Ronald, city guardsman, Jacobite, res. Edinburgh, tr. 24 Feb
    1747, fr. Liverpool to Va, in *Gildart*, arr. Port North Potomac Md
    5 Aug 1747. (P.3.76)(PRO.T1.328)
3693. MacDonald, Ronald, mercenary soldier, res. Inverness-shire, pts.
    Archibald MacDonald of Barrisdale, tr. June 1755, fr. Leith.
    (SM.17.308)
3694. McDonald, Rory, Jacobite, tr. 7 May 1716, fr. Liverpool to S.C., in
    Susannah. (SPC.1716.309)(CTB31.206)
3695. MacDonald, Rory Dow, thief, res. Loddie of Slisgarne Glengarry
    Inverness-shire, tr. Sept 1753. (SM.15.468)
3696. McDonald, Sween, b. 1729, beggar, Jacobite, res. Inverness, tr. 31 Mar
    1747, fr. London to Barbados , in *Frere*. (P.3.78)(MR118)
3697. McDonald, William, arsonist, res. Reay Caithness, tr. Sept 1772.
    (AJ1292)
3698. McDonald, William, sheepstealer, res. Aberdeenshire, tr. May 1751.
    (AJ175)

3699. McDonald, William, Jacobite, tr. 26 Apr 1716, fr. Liverpool to Jamaica, in *Two Brothers*, arr. Montserrat June 1716. (SPC.1716.313)(CTB31.206)(CTP.CC.43)
3700. McDonald, William, Jacobite, tr. 7 May 1716, fr. Liverpool to S.C., in *Susannah*. (SPC.1716.309)(CTB31.206)
3701. McDonald, William, b. 1687, farmer, Jacobite, tr. 1747. (P.3.80)
3702. McDonald, William, b. 1692, farmer, Jacobite, res. Glenmoriston Inverness-shire, tr. 31 Mar 1747, fr. London to Barbados, in *Frere*. (P.3.78)(MR157)
3703. McDonald, William, b. 1697, farmer, Jacobite, res. Glenmoriston Inverness-shire, tr. 31 Mar 1747, fr. London to Jamaica, in *St George or Carteret*, arr. Jamaica 1747. (P.3.78)(MR157)(PRO.CO137.58)
3704. McDonald, William, b. 1703, farmer, res. Little Savall Lairg Sutherland, sh. Apr 1774, to Wilmington N.C., in *Bachelor of Leith*. (PRO.T47.12)
3705. McDonald, William, b. 1707, weaver, Jacobite, res. Drumnadeeven Inverness-shire, tr. 31 Mar 1747, fr. Barbados to FRERE. (P.3.80)(MR175)
3706. McDonald, William, b. 1712, farmer, Jacobite, res. Glenmoriston Inverness-shire, tr. 31 Mar 1747, fr. London to Barbados , in *Frere*. (P.3.78)(MR157)
3707. McDonald, William, b. 1734, farmer, sh. Sept 1774, fr. Greenock to Wilmington N.C., in *Diana*, m. Isobel Wright, ch. Mary Jessy. (PRO.T47.12)
3708. McDonald, William, b. 1759, servant, res. Beauly Inverness-shire, sh. July 1775, fr. Stornaway to Philadelphia, in *Clementina*. (PRO.T47.12)
3709. McDonall, Denis, Jacobite, tr. 26 Apr 1716, fr. Liverpool to Jamaica, in *Two Brothers*, arr. Montserrat June 1716. (SPC.1716.313)(CTP.CC.43)
3710. McDonell, John, b. 1680, sh. 1699, fr. Liverpool. (LRO.HQ325.2FRE)
3711. MacDonnell, John, soldier, sh. pre 1773, sett. N.Y. (PCCol.5.597)
3712. McDonnell, Kenneth, Jacobite, tr. 1747, in *St George or Carteret*, arr. Jamaica 1747. (PRO.CO137.58)
3713. McDonough, John, b. 1733, husbandman, Jacobite, res. Isle of Barra Argyll, tr. 20 Mar 1747. (P.3.70)(MR164) (alias 3664)
3714. MacDorton, Philip, Jacobite, tr. 26 Apr 1716, fr. Liverpool to Jamaica, in *Two Brothers*, arr. Montserrat June 1716. (SPC.1716.313)(CTB31.206)(CTP.CC.43)
3715. McDoual, Agnes, infanticide, tr. Aug 1751. (AJ189) (alias 3483)
3716. McDougal, John, b. 1721, tailor, Jacobite, res. Ballone Ross-shire, tr. 20 Mar 1747, fr. Tilbury. (P.3.82)(MR82)

181

3717. MacDougal, Miss, res. Caverton Kelso Roxburghshire, sh. pre 1767, sett. Jamaica, m. Andrew Herbert. (SM.29.669)
3718. MacDougald, William, merchant, res. Edinburgh, pts. William MacDougald, d. 8 July 1774 E Fla. (SM.36.562)
3719. McDougall, Agnes, infanticide, res. Perthshire, tr. 1752. (SRO.B59.26.11.1.29) (alias 3484)
3720. McDougall, Alexander, Jacobite, tr. 24 May 1716, fr. Liverpool to Md, in *Friendship*, arr. Md Aug 1716. (SPC.1716.311)(HM387)
3721. McDougall, Alexander, b. 1721, Jacobite, res. Inverness, tr. 31 Mar 1747, fr. London to Barbados, in *Frere*. (P.3.82)(MR118)
3722. McDougall, Alexander, b. 1753, gardener, res. Galloway, sh. May 1774, fr. Stranraer to N.Y., in *Gale*. (PRO.T47.12)
3723. McDougall, Allan, b. 1721, gardener, Jacobite, res. Strathlachlan Argyll, tr. 5 May 1747, fr. Liverpool to Leeward Islands, in *Veteran*, arr. Martinique June 1747. (P.3.80)(MR181)(PRO.SP36.102)
3724. McDougall, Charles, Covenanter, res. Kirkcudbrightshire, tr. Oct 1684. (PC.10.258)
3725. McDougall, Duncan, Covenanter, res. Argyll, tr. Aug 1685, fr. Leith to Jamaica. (PC.11.136)
3726. McDougall, John, pedlar, Jacobite, res. Galnashel Eigg Inverness-shire, tr. 31 Mar 1747, fr. London to Jamaica, in *St George or Carteret*, arr. Jamaica 1747. (P.3.84)(MR143)(PRO.CO137.58)
3727. MacDougall, William, planter, sh. 1766, sett. E Fla, d. 1774. (SRO.NRAS.0181)
3728. McDounie, John, Covenanter, tr. Aug 1685, fr. Leith to Jamaica. (PC.11.136)
3729. McDowall, Alexander, b. 1749, laborer, res. Galloway, sh. May 1774, fr. Stranraer to N.Y., in *Gale*. (PRO.T47.12)
3730. McDowall, Patrick, merchant, sh. pre 1758, sett. Onancocktown. (SRO.SH.22.2.1758)
3731. McDrummont, Mary, b. 1759, servant, res. Glen Coe Argyll, sh. Feb 1775, fr. Greenock to N.Y., in *Commerce*. (PRO.T47.12)
3732. McDuff, James, laborer, Jacobite, res. Ballincreughan Perthshire, tr. 22 Apr 1747, fr. Liverpool to Va, in *Johnson*, arr. Port Oxford Md 5 Aug 1747. (P.3.84)(PRO.T1.328)(MR207)
3733. McDuffie, John, horsethief, res. Suinart Argyll, tr. 1732. (JRA.2.451) (alias 821)
3734. McDugald, Alexander, res. Sannaig Jura Argyll, sh. 1754, to Cape Fear N.C. (SRO.GD64\5.21)
3735. McDugald, Allan, res. Brostile Jura Argyll, sh. 1754, to Cape Fear N.C. (SRO.GD64\5.21)
3736. McDugald, Neil, res. Jura Argyll, sh. 1754, to Cape Fear N.C., ch. Katherine. (SRO.GD64\5.21)

3737. McDugall, Hugh, Jacobite, tr. 28 July 1716, fr. Liverpool to Va, in *Godspeed*, arr. Md Oct 1716. (SPC.1716.310)(CTB31.209)(HM389)

3738. McEan, Alexander, cattlethief, res. Inverness-shire, tr. May 1765, fr. Glasgow. (AJ908) (alias 767)

3739. MacEanor, Kenneth, thief, res. Ross-shire, tr. Sept 1754. (SM.16.448) (alias 3673)

3740. McEwan, Andrew, thief, tr. 1775, in *Aeolis*, arr. Port North Potomac Md 17 Oct 1775. (SRO.JC27.10.3)

3741. McEwan, Archibald, Covenanter, res. Argyll, tr. Aug 1685, fr. Leith to Jamaica. (PC.11.136)

3742. McEwan, Donald, tr. Aug 1685, fr. Leith to Jamaica. (PC.11.136)(ETR373)

3743. McEwan, Duncan, Covenanter, tr. July 1685, fr. Leith to East N.J. (PC.11.131)

3744. McEwan, James, b. 1756, nailer, res. Stirling, sh. Apr 1775, fr. Greenock to N.Y., in *Lilly*. (PRO.T47.12)

3745. McEwan, John, Covenanter, tr. Aug 1685, fr. Leith to East N.J., in *Henry & Francis*. (PC.11.154)

3746. McEwan, John, Jacobite, tr. 28 July 1716, fr. Liverpool to Va, in *Godspeed*, arr. Md Oct 1716. (SPC.1716.310)(CTB31.209)(HM388)

3747. McEwan, Katherine, b. 1707, Jacobite, res. Fort William Inverness-shire, tr. 22 Apr 1747, fr. Liverpool to Va, in *Johnson*, arr. Port Oxford Md 5 Aug 1747. (P.3.174)(PRO.T1.328)

3748. MacEwen, William, pts. William McEwen, d. 1782 Jamaica. (SM.44.446)

3749. McEwer, Kenneth, b. 1751, laborer, res. Loch Broom Ross-shire, sh. July 1775, fr. Stornaway to Philadelphia, in *Clementina*. (PRO.T47.12)

3750. McFadine, James, b. 1758, joiner, res. Greenock Renfrewshire, sh. July 1775, fr. Greenock to Ga, in *Christy*. (PRO.T47.12)

3751. McFadine, John, b. 1739, joiner, res. Greenock Renfrewshire, sh. July 1775, fr. Greenock to Ga, in *Christy*. (PRO.T47.12)

3752. McFadyen, Daniel, lorimer, res. Glasgow, sh. pre 1781, sett. N.Y., m. Elizabeth ..., d. 1781, PCC pr1781

3753. McFadzean, Janet, Covenanter, res. Portrack Dumfries-shire, tr. Oct 1684, m. John Harper. (PC.10.590)

3754. McFaiden, Donald, b. 1733, farmer, res. Perthshire, sh. May 1775, fr. Greenock to N.Y., in *Monimia*. (PRO.T47.12)

3755. McFarlan, Ann, b. 1757, servant, res. Stornaway Isle of Lewis, sh. May 1774, fr. Stornaway to Philadelphia, in *Friendship*. (PRO.T47.12)

3756. McFarlan, John, b. 1758, servant, res. Lochs Isle of Lewis, sh. May 1774, fr. Stornaway to Philadelphia, in *Friendship*. (PRO.T47.12)

3757. McFarlan, Peter, b. 1755, servant, res. Galson Isle of Lewis, sh. May 1774, fr. Stornaway to Philadelphia, in *Friendship*. (PRO.T47.12)
3758. McFarlane, Alexander, judge & assemblyman, d. 23 Aug 1755 Kingston Jamaica. (SM.17.514)
3759. MacFarlane, Alexander, factor, res. Glasgow, sh. pre 1761, sett. Chaptico Md. (SRA.CFI)
3760. MacFarlane, Andrew, merchant, res. Blairnairns Dunbartonshire, sh. pre 1752, sett. N.Y. (SRO.RS .8.276)
3761. McFarlane, Andrew, res. Meikle Govan Glasgow , pts. Andrew McFarlane, sh. 1780, to Jamaica. (SRA.T.MJ369)
3762. McFarlane, Donald, b. 1748, farmer, res. Glen Orchy Argyll, sh. Aug 1774, fr. Greenock to Wilmington N.C., in *Ulysses*. (PRO.T47.12)
3763. McFarlane, Duncan, planter, sh. pre 1765, sett. St Thomas in the East, Jamaica. (SRO.RD2.198.163)
3764. McFarlane, Elizabeth, b. 1717, sewer, Jacobite, res. Perth, tr. 5 May 1747, fr. Liverpool to Leeward Islands, in *Veteran*, arr. Martinique June 1747. (P.3.88)(PRO.SP36.102)
3765. MacFarlane, George, sh. Apr 1756, fr. London to Md. (CLRO\AIA)
3766. MacFarlane, James, sh. 16 Dec 1773, fr. Greenock to Jamaica, in *Ross*. (SRO.CE60.1.7)
3767. McFarlane, Janet, servant, fireraiser, res. Perth, tr. Sept 1750. (AJ145)
3768. McFarlane, Janet, b. 1756, spinner, res. Glasgow, sh. May 1775, fr. Greenock to N.Y., in *Lilly*. (PRO.T47.12)
3769. McFarlane, John, counterfeiter, res. Stirlingshire, tr. June 1754. (SRO.JC3.29.574)(SRO.HCR.I.87)
3770. MacFarlane, John, housebreaker, res. Glasgow, tr. Nov 1772, fr. Glasgow. (SRO.RH2.4.255)
3771. McFarlane, John, Jacobite, tr. 26 Apr 1716, fr. Liverpool to Jamaica, in *Two Brothers*, arr. Montserrat June 1716. (SPC.1716.313)(CTB31.206)
3772. McFarlane, John, farmer, sheepstealer, res. Southdale Ross-shire, tr. 1755. (SM.17.266) (alias 3363)
3773. McFarlane, John, b. 1755, ropemaker, res. Glasgow, sh. Feb 1774, fr. Greenock to N.Y., in *Commerce*. (PRO.T47.12)
3774. McFarlane, John, b. 1757, hatter, res. Glasgow, sh. Feb 1774, fr. Greenock to N.Y., in *Commerce*. (PRO.T47.12)
3775. McFarlane, Katherine, b. 1758, servant, res. Edinburgh, sh. May 1775, fr. Leith to Philadelphia, in *Friendship*. (PRO.T47.12)
3776. McFarlane, R, b. 1747, wright, res. Kippen Stirlingshire, sh. July 1775, fr. Greenock to Ga, in *Georgia*, m. Janet ... (PRO.T47.12)
3777. McFarlane, Robert, tailor, Jacobite, res. Gartmore Perthshire, tr. 1747. (P.3.88) (alias 337)

3778. McFarlane, Robert, b. 1730, farmer, res. Caithness, sh. May 1775, fr. Greenock to N.Y. or Ga, in *Christy*. (PRO.T47.12)
3779. McFarlane, Walter, sailor, res. Tulliallan Fife, sh. 14 July 1698, fr. Leith to Darien, Edin pr1707 CC8.8.83
3780. McFarlane, Walter, b. 1755, merchant, sh. May 1775, fr. Greenock to N.C., in *Ajax*. (PRO.T47.12)
3781. McFarquhar, Colin, clergyman edu. King's Col Aberdeen 1753, sett. Applecross Pa. (KCA.2.320)
3782. McFarquhar, Kenneth, b. 1702, farmer, Jacobite, res. Newton of Redcastle Ross-shire, tr. 31 Mar 1747, fr. London to Barbados, in *Frere*. (P.3.90)(MR82)
3783. MacFarran, John, solicitor-general, sett. South Caribee Islands, d. 4 June 1770 Grenadines. (SM.32.458)
3784. MacFearghuis, Roderick, Jacobite, tr. 22 Apr 1747, fr. Liverpool to Nd, in *Johnson*, arr. Port Oxford Md 5 Aug 1747. (P.3.86)(PRO.T1.328)
3785. McFee, Archibald, b. 1745, shoemaker, res. Banff, sh. Aug 1774, fr. Greenock to Philadelphia, in *Magdalene*. (PRO.T47.12)
3786. McFee, Hugh, Jacobite, tr. 1747, in *St George or Carteret*, arr. Jamaica 1747. (PRO.CO137.58)
3787. McFee, Hugh, b. 1717, laborer, Jacobite, res. Inverness, tr. 5 May 1747, fr. Liverpool to Leeward Islands, in *Veteran*, arr. Martinique June 1747. (P.3.172)(PRO.SP36.102)
3788. McFie, John, piper & musician, res. Rothesay Isle of Bute, sh. 18 Aug 1699, fr. Clyde to Darien, in *Rising Sun*, sett. Janet McPherson, Edin pr1710 CC8.8.84
3789. MacGachan, Christian, vagrant, res. Kilwinning Ayrshire, tr. Sept 1754, fr. Glasgow, m. Alexander Banks. (SM.16.450)
3790. McGachin, James, Covenanter, res. Dalry, tr. Aug 1684, fr. Leith to Carolina. (PC.9.15)
3791. McGee, John, b. 1690, sh. 1705, fr. Liverpool. (LRO.HQ325.2FRE)
3792. McGeorge, John, b. 1751, res. Galloway, sh. May 1775, fr. Dumfries to P.E.I., in *Lovely Nelly*. (PRO.T47.12)
3793. McGhie, Hugh, highwayman, res. Ayrshire, tr. Oct 1750. (AJ148)
3794. McGibbon, Archibald, Covenanter, tr. Aug 1685, fr. Leith to Jamaica. (PC.11.329)
3795. McGibbon, Duncan, Jacobite, tr. 26 Apr 1716, fr. Liverpool to Jamaica, in *Two Brothers*, arr. Montserrat June 1716. (SPC.1716.313)(CTB31.206)
3796. McGibbon, Hector, Covenanter, tr. Aug 1685, fr. Leith to Jamaica. (PC.11.329)
3797. McGibbon, John, Covenanter, res. Glenowkeill Argyll, tr. Aug 1685, fr. Leith to Jamaica. (PC.11.329)

185

3798. McGibbon, Peter, b. 1748, tailor, res. Paisley Renfrewshire, sh. May 1775, fr. Greenock to N.Y. or Ga, in *Christy*. (PRO.T47.12)
3799. McGibbon, Robert, b. 1736, husbandman, res. Struan Perthshire, sh. July 1753, fr. London to Jamaica. (CLRO\AIA)
3800. McGichan, Christian, thief & vagrant, tr. Sept 1754. (AJ352)
3801. McGie, Jean, Covenanter, tr. 5 Sept 1685, fr. Leith to East N.J., in *Henry & Francis*. (PC.11.166)
3802. McGie, John, tr. 5 Sept 1685, fr. Leith to East N.J., in *Henry & Francis*. (PC.11.154)
3803. McGilchrist, William, clergyman, res. Inchinnan Renfrewshire, pts. James McGilchrist, sh. 2 Oct 1741, to S.C. (EMA42)
3804. McGill, Andrew, edu. Glasgow Uni 1765, res. Glasgow, pts. James McGill, d. 31 July 1805 Montreal. (GUMA77)
3805. McGill, Andrew, b. 1749, blacksmith, res. Edinburgh, sh. Aug 1774, fr. London to Va, in *Beith*. (PRO.T47.9\11)
3806. McGill, Anne, thief, res. Edinburgh, tr. Dec 1743. (EBR.BC.3.74) (alias 1258, 2980)
3807. McGill, Daniel, clergyman edu. Edinburgh Uni 1694, sh. 1712, fr. London to Philadelphia, sett. Patuxent, d. 10 Feb 1724. (F.7.664)(AP170)
3808. MacGill, James, clergyman, sh. 1727, sett. Queen Caroline Co Md, d. 26 Dec 1779 Md. (EMA42)
3809. McGill, James, b. 6 Oct 1744, Glasgow, fur trader edu. Glasgow Uni 1756, res. Glasgow, pts. James McGill, sh. pre 1776, to Canada, d. 19 Dec 1813 Montreal. (MAGU55)
3810. McGill, Janet, thief, res. Rackhead Kilmarnock Ayrshire, tr. 1772, fr. Glasgow to Va, in *Brilliant*, arr. Port Hampton Va 7 Oct 1772. (SRO.JC27.10.3)(AJ1270)
3811. McGill, Robert, tr. 15 Nov 1679, fr. Leith. (ETR162)
3812. McGilleverey, William, Jacobite, tr. 24 May 1716, fr. Liverpool to Md, in *Friendship*, arr. Md Aug 1716. (SPC.1716.311)(HM386)
3813. McGillevray, Farquhar, Jacobite, tr. 24 May 1716, fr. Liverpool to Md, in *Friendship*, arr. Md 20 Aug 1716. (SPC.1716.311)(HM386)
3814. McGillevray, William, schoolmaster, forger, res. Buckie Banffshire, tr. Mar 1758. (SRO.HCR.I.90) (alias 2476)
3815. McGillich, John, Covenanter, res. Argyll, tr. Aug 1685, fr. Leith to Jamaica. (PC.11.329)
3816. McGillies, Daniel, b. 1687, laborer, Jacobite, res. Arisaig Inverness-shire, tr. 8 May 1747, to Antigua. (P.3.90)(MR157)
3817. McGillies, Daniel, b. 1735, Jacobite, res. Arisaig Inverness-shire, pts. Daniel McGillies, tr. 5 May 1747, fr. Liverpool to Leeward Islands, in *Veteran*, arr. Martinique June 1747. (P.3.90)(MR158)(PRO.SP36.102)

3818. McGillis, Daniel, Jacobite, tr. 22 Apr 1747, fr. Liverpool to Va, in
    Johnson, arr. Port Oxford Md 5 Aug 1747. (PRO.T1.328)
3819. McGillis, Donald, b. 1729, laborer, Jacobite, res. Inverness, tr. 5 May
    1747, fr. Liverpool to Leeward Islands, in *Veteran*, arr. Martinique
    June 1747. (P.3.90)(MR158)(PRO.SP36.102)
3820. McGillis, Hector, b. 1731, herd, Jacobite, res. Inverness, tr. 5 May 1747,
    fr. Liverpool to Leeward Islands, in *Veteran*, arr. Martinique June
    1747. (P.3.90)(MR158)(PRO.SP36.102)
3821. McGillivary, Alexander, thief, res. Aberdeen, tr. May 1726. (SRO.JC27)
    (alias 4632)
3822. MacGillivray, Alexander, Drumnaglass Inverness-shire, Creek Chief, sett.
    Creek Territory, d. 1792. (SM.54.310)
3823. McGillivray, Alexander, Jacobite, tr. 21 Apr 1716, fr. Liverpool to S.C.,
    in *Wakefield*. (SPC.1716.309)(CTB31.205)
3824. McGillivray, Daniel, Jacobite, tr. 29 June 1716, fr. Liverpool to Jamaica
    or Va, in *Elizabeth & Anne*, arr. Va.
    (SPC.1716.310)(CTB31.208)(VSP.1.186)
3825. McGillivray, Donald, Jacobite, tr. 7 May 1716, fr. Liverpool to S.C., in
    Susannah. (SPC.1716.309)(CTB31.206)
3826. McGillivray, Fergus, Jacobite, tr. 7 May 1716, fr. Liverpool to S.C., in
    Susannah. (SPC.1716.309)(CTB31.206)
3827. McGillivray, James, Jacobite, tr. 21 Apr 1716, fr. Liverpool to S.C., in
    Wakefield. (SPC.1716.309)(CTB31.205)
3828. McGillivray, James, Jacobite, tr. 21 Apr 1716, fr. Liverpool to S.C., in
    Wakefield. (SPC.1716.309)(CTB31.206)
3829. McGillivray, John, Jacobite, tr. 21 Apr 1716, fr. Liverpool to S.C., in
    Wakefield. (SPC.1716.309)(CTB31.205)
3830. McGillivray, John, Jacobite, tr. 21 Apr 1716, fr. Liverpool to S.C., in
    Wakefield. (SPC.1716.309)(CTB31.205)
3831. McGillivray, Lauchlan, planter, sh. pre 1781, sett. Vale Royal Savannah
    Ga. (SRO.RD2.239.129)
3832. McGillivray, Lauchlin, Jacobite, res. Inverness-shire, pts. Daniel
    McGillivray, tr. 21 Apr 1716, fr. Liverpool to S.C., in *Wakefield*,
    d. 1736 S.C., S.C. pr1737.
    (SRO.SC29.55.6)(SPC.1716.309)(CTB31.205)
3833. McGillivray, Loughlan, Jacobite, tr. 21 Apr 1716, fr. Liverpool to S.C.,
    in *Wakefield*. (SPC.1716.309)(CTB31.205)
3834. McGillivray, Owen, Jacobite, tr. 21 Apr 1716, fr. Liverpool to S.C., in
    Wakefield. (SPC.1716.309)(CTB31.205)
3835. McGillivray, William, Jacobite, tr. 24 May 1716, fr. Liverpool to Md, in
    Friendship, arr. Md Aug 1716. (SPC.1716.311)(HM387)
3836. McGillivray, William, Jacobite, tr. 29 June 1716, fr. Liverpool to
    Jamaica or Va, in *Elizabeth & Anne*, arr. Va.
    (SPC.1716.310)(CTB31.208)(VSP.1.185)

3837. McGillivray, William, Jacobite, tr. 21 Apr 1716, fr. Liverpool to S.C., in *Wakefield*. (SPC.1716.309)(CTB31.205)
3838. McGillvray, Alexander, res. Petty Inverness-shire, sh. pre 1737, sett. Charleston S.C. (SRO.SC29.55.6)
3839. McGilreach, Hugh, servant, res. Knockcronie Jura Argyll, sh. 1754, to Cape Fear N.C. (SRO.GD64\5.21)
3840. McGilriach, John, res. Knockcronie Jura Argyll, sh. 1754, to Cape Fear N.C. (SRO.GD64\5.21)
3841. McGilveray, John, Jacobite, tr. 30 Mar 1716, fr. Liverpool to Antigua, in *Scipio*. (SPC.1716.310)(CTB31.204)
3842. McGiven, Alexander, Jacobite, tr. 28 July 1716, fr. Liverpool to Va, in *Godspeed*, arr. Md Oct 1716. (SPC.1716.310)(CTB31.209)(HM389)
3843. McGlashan, Hugh, farmer, horsethief, res. Narrachan Argyll, tr. 1713. (JRA.2.300)
3844. McGlashan, John, res. Edinburgh, tr. 1696, fr. Newhaven to Va. (SRO.RH15.14.58)
3845. McGlashan, Margaret, res. Edinburgh, tr. 1696, fr. Newhaven to Va. (SRO.RH15.14.58)
3846. McGlashan, Robert, b. 1736, farmer, res. Stranraer Wigtonshire, sh. May 1775, fr. Greenock to N.Y. or Ga, in *Christy*, ch. Jean & Catherine. (PRO.T47.12)
3847. MacGory, Rob Roy, thief, res. Glen Garry Inverness-shire, tr. June 1754. (SM.16.203))AJ328) (alias 3688)
3848. McGoughtry, JOhn, b. 1734, farmer, res. Gatehouse Kirkcudbrighthsire, sh. May 1774, fr. Stranraer to N.Y., in *Gale*, ch. James John Agnes Alexander William. (PRO.T47.12)
3849. McGoughtry, Margaret, b. 1753, res. Girthon Kirkcudbrightshire, sh. May 1774, fr. Stranraer to N.Y., in *Gale*, ch. Jane. (PRO.T47.12)
3850. McGoughtry, Richard, b. 1706, farmer, res. Gatehopuse Kirkcudbrightshire, sh. May 1774, fr. Stranraer to N.Y., in *Gale*. (PRO.T47.12)
3851. McGowan, John, Covenanter, res. Argyll, tr. Aug 1685, fr. Leith to Jamaica. (PC.11.136)
3852. McGowan, Margaret, b. 1754, res. Stirling, sh. May 1774, fr. Greenock to N.Y., in *Matty*. (PRO.T47.12)
3853. McGown, James, b. 1749, farmer, res. Stirling, sh. May 1774, fr. Greenock to N.Y., in *Matty*. (PRO.T47.12)
3854. McGrath, Henry, b. 1712, husbandman, res. Edinburgh, sh. Oct 1734, fr. London to Va. (CLRO\AIA)
3855. McGraw, Donald, b. 1699, Jacobite, res. Perth, tr. 1747. (P.3.182)(MR25)
3856. McGraw, Donald, b. 1723, farmer, Jacobite, res. Clochgolore Ross-shire, tr. 20 Mar 1747, fr. London to Barbados, in *Frere*. (P.3.182)

3857. McGregor, Callum, thief, tr. 2 Aug 1680, fr. Leith to Barbados, in *Blossom*. (ETR170)
3858. McGregor, Captain Patrick, res. Perthshire, sh. 1684, to East N.J. (Insh236)
3859. McGregor, D, sh. 1684, sett. Perth-Amboy East N.J. (Insh245)
3860. McGregor, Daniel, sailor, res. Calton, sh. 18 Aug 1699, fr. Clyde to Darien, in *Rising Sun*, Edin pr1707 CC8.8.83
3861. McGregor, Donald, thief, res. Stirlingshire, tr. 1684, fr. Leith to East N.J. (PC.8.514)
3862. McGregor, Duncan, Jacobite, tr. 7 May 1716, fr. Liverpool to S.C., in *Susannah*. (SPC.1716.309)(CTB31.206)
3863. McGregor, Duncan, Jacobite, tr. 22 Apr 1747, fr. Liverpool to Va, in *Johnson*, arr. Port Oxford Md 5 Aug 1747. (PRO.T1.328)
3864. McGregor, Duncan, farmer, Jacobite, res. Tarland Aberdeenshire, tr. 24 Feb 1747, fr. Liverpool to Va, in *Gildart*, arr. Port North Potomac Md 5 Aug 1747. (P.3.92)(JAB.2.434)(MR202)(PRO.T1.328)
3865. McGregor, Duncan, horsethief, res. Perthshire, tr. Nov 1764, fr. Greenock to N.J. (SRO.B59.26.11.6.39) (alias 2448)
3866. McGregor, Gregor, Jacobite, tr. 31 July 1716, fr. Liverpool to Va, in *Anne*. (SPC.1716.310)(CTB31.209)
3867. McGregor, Gregor Rory, sheepstealer, res. Aberdeenshire, tr. Sept 1755. (AJ403) (alias 2410)
3868. McGregor, Hugh, b. 1733, farmer, res. Breadalbane Perthshire, sh. June 1775, fr. Greenock to N.Y., in *Commerce*, m. Jean McNaughton, ch. Donald & Katherine. (PRO.T47.12)
3869. McGregor, Isabel, sheepstealer, res. Kirkmichael Banffshire, tr. May 1768. (AJ1062)
3870. McGregor, James, piper, Jacobite, res. Crieff Perthshire, tr. 21 Nov 1748. (P.2.94)(MR167) (alias 917)
3871. McGregor, John, Jacobite, res. Balnacuik Balquhidder Perthshire, tr. 1747. (P.2.164)(MR167) (alias 1615)
3872. McGregor, John, Jacobite, tr. 28 July 1716, fr. Liverpool to Va, in *Godspeed*, arr. Md Oct 1716. (SPC.1716.310)(CTB31.209)(HM388)
3873. McGregor, John, laborer, Jacobite, res. Perthshire, tr. 22 Apr 1747, fr. Liverpool to Md, in *Johnson*, arr. Port Oxford Md 5 Aug 1747. (P.3.94)(MR74)(PRO.T1.328)
3874. McGregor, John, laborer, Jacobite, res. Dundurn Perthshire, tr. 22 Apr 1747, fr. Liverpool to Va, in *Johnson*, arr. Port Oxford Md 5 Aug 1747. (P.3.94)(MR73)(PRO.T1.328)
3875. McGregor, Malcolm, Jacobite, tr. 7 May 1716, fr. Liverpool to S.C., in *Susannah*. (SPC.1716.309)(CTB31.206)

3876. McGregor, Mark, b. 1723, cook, Jacobite, res. Balnagowan Perthshire, tr. 24 Feb 1747, fr. Liverpool to Va, in *Gildart*, arr. Port North Potomac Md 5 Aug 1747. (P.3.96)(MR40)(PRO.T1.328)
3877. McGregor, Patrick, farmer, Jacobite, res. Perthshire, tr. 22 Apr 1747, fr. Liverpool to Va, in *Johnson*, arr. Port Oxford Md 5 Aug 1747. (P.3.220)(PRO.T1.328) (alias 5288)
3878. McGrigor, Duncan, b. 1736, piper, res. Glen Coe Argyll, sh. Feb 1775, fr. Greenock to N.Y., in *Commerce*, m. Katherine Duncan, ch. May Hugh. (PRO.T47.12)
3879. McGruther, William, Jacobite, tr. 29 June 1716, fr. Liverpool to Jamaica or Va, in *Elizabeth & Anne*, arr. Va. (SPC.1716.310)(CTB31.208)(VSP.1.186)
3880. McGuffog, Grizzel, infanticide, res. Banffshire, tr. Dec 1746. (SRO.HCR.I.73)
3881. McGuile, Duncan, res. Sroine Jura Argyll, sh. 1754, to Cape Fear N.C. (SRO.GD64\5.21)
3882. McGuire, John, Jacobite, tr. 1747, in *St George or Carteret*, arr. Jamaica 1747. (PRO.CO137.58)
3883. McGuire, Lauchlane McQuary, shipmaster, res. Campbelltown Argyll, sett. N.Y., m. Katherine ..., d. Jan 1783, Edin pr1785 CC8.8.126
3884. McGumri, Angus, b. 1755, res. Branahuie Isle of Lewis, sh. May 1774, fr. Stornaway to Philadelphia, in *Friendship*. (PRO.T47.12)
3885. McHaffie, John, Covenanter, res. Gargarie, tr. Oct 1684. (PC.10.612)
3886. McHaig, John, b. 1738, farmer, res. Galloway, sh. May 1774, fr. Stranraer to N.Y., in *Gale*, m. Grizzel ..., ch. Margaret & Ann. (PRO.T47.12)
3887. Machane, Matthew, res. Eaglesham Renfrewshire, tr. June 1684, fr. Clyde, in *Pelican*. (PC.9.208)
3888. MacHardy, John, Jacobite, tr. 28 July 1716, fr. Liverpool to Va, in *Godspeed*. (SPC.1716.310)(CTB31.209)
3889. McHatton, Neil, Covenanter, res. Argyll, tr. July 1685, fr. Leith to N.E. (PC.11.94)
3890. McHutchison, Hugh, b. 1751, ship's carpenter, res. Ayrshire, sh. Mar 1775, fr. Glasgow to Quebec, in *Friendship*. (PRO.T47.12)
3891. McIchan, John, Covenanter, res. Baranazare Lorne Argyll, tr. Aug 1685, fr. Leith to Jamaica. (PC.11.329)
3892. McIlbryde, Duncan, Covenanter, res. Argyll, tr. Aug 1685, fr. Leith to Jamaica. (PC.11.136)
3893. McIlbryde, Neil, farmer, Covenanter, res. Craigintervie Argyll, tr. Aug 1685, fr. Leith to Jamaica. (PC.11.136)
3894. McIlchallum, John, tr. Aug 1685, fr. Leith to Jamaica. (PC.11.136)
3895. McIlchallum, John Dow, horsethief, res. Achlauchrick Kilmaveonaig Blair Atholl Perthshire, tr. May 1756. (SRO.B59.26.11.4.21) (alias 6555)

190

3896. McIlmoon, Donald, Covenanter, res. Argyll, tr. Aug 1685, fr. Leith to Jamaica. (PC.11.329)
3897. McIlpherson, James, vagabond & robber, res. Annandale Dumfries-shire, tr. 1671(?). (PC.3.428)
3898. McIlriach, Angus jr, farmer, res. Brostile Jura Argyll, sh. 1754, to Cape Fear N.C. (SRO.GD64\5.21)
3899. McIlriach, Archibald, res. Corantural Jura Argyll, sh. 1754, to Cape Fear N.C. (SRO.GD64\5.21)
3900. McIlriach, Archibald, res. Knocksbreck Jura Argyll, sh. 1754, to Cape Fear N.C. (SRO.GD64\5.21)
3901. McIlriach, Gilbert, res. Jura Argyll, sh. 1754, to Cape Fear N.C. (SRO.GD64\5.21)
3902. McIlroy, Gilbert, Covenanter, tr. Aug 1685, fr. Leith to Jamaica. (ETR369)
3903. McIlroy, John, b. 1713, husbandman, res. Inch Wigtonshire, sh. Aug 1731, fr. London to Jamaica. (CLRO\AIA)
3904. McIlroy, William, tr. July 1685, fr. Leith to Jamaica. (PC.11.329)
3905. McIlshallum, John, tr. Aug 1685, fr. Leith to Jamaica. (PC.11.330)
3906. McIlvain, ..., thief, res. Argyll, tr. 1727, fr. Greenock. (SRO.GD14.10.1)
3907. McIlvain, Archibald, Covenanter, res. Glendaruel Argyll, tr. Aug 1685, fr. Leith to Jamaica. (PC.11.329)
3908. McIlvay, Duncan, tr. Aug 1684, fr. Leith to Carolina. (PC.9.95)
3909. McIlverran, Donald, Covenanter, res. Argyll, tr. Aug 1685, fr. Leith to Jamaica. (PC.11.136)
3910. MacIlvone, William, thief, res. Rieneclash Ross-shire, tr. 1755. (SM.17.266) (alias 354)
3911. McIlvory, Duncan, Covenanter, res. Argyll, tr. Aug 1685, fr. Leith to Jamaica. (PC.11.136)
3912. McIlvory, John, Covenanter, res. Cragintyrie Argyll, tr. Aug 1685. (PC.11.126)
3913. McInlay, Elizabeth, infanticide, res. Ayrshire, tr. Sept 1750. (SM.12.452)
3914. McInlay, Neil, tr. Aug 1685, fr. Leith to Jamaica. (PC.11.136)
3915. McInlier, Duncan, Jacobite, tr. 26 Apr 1716, fr. Liverpool to Jamaica, in Two Brothers, arr. Montserrat June 1716. (SPC.1716.313)
3916. McInnes, Andrew, b. 1720, grazier, Jacobite, res. Tray Morar Inverness-shire, tr. 30 Mar 1747. (P.3.100)(MR143)
3917. McInnes, John, Jacobite, tr. 7 May 1716, fr. Liverpool to S.C., in Susannah. (SPC.1716.309)(CTB31.206)
3918. MacInnes, John, tailor, thief, res. Maryburgh Inverness-shire, tr. May 1775. (AJ1432)
3919. McInnes, Malcolm, b. 1735, laborer, res. Breadalbane Perthshire, sh. Sept 1775, to Wilmington N.C., in Jupiter, m. Janet ..., ch. John Ann Catherine Donald Archibald. (PRO.T47.12)

3920. McInnis, Archibald, Jacobite, tr. 22 Apr 1747, fr. Liverpool to Va, in *Johnson*, arr. Port Oxford Md 5 Aug 1747. (PRO.T1.328)
3921. McInny, Alexander, Jacobite, tr. 24 Feb 1747, fr. Liverpool to Va, in *Gildart*, arr. Port North Potomac Md 5 Aug 1747. (PRO.T1.328)
3922. McIntaggart, John, servant, Covenanter, res. Argyll, tr. Aug 1685, fr. Leith to Jamaica. (PC.11.136)
3923. McIntaggart, Patrick, Jacobite, tr. 22 Apr 1747, fr. Liverpool to Va, in *Johnson*, arr. Port Oxford Md 5 Aug 1747. (P.3.100)(PRO.T1.328)
3924. McIntosh, Alexander, Jacobite, tr. 28 July 1716, fr. Liverpool to Va, in *Godspeed*, arr. Md Oct 1716. (SPC.1716.310)(CTB31.209)(HM388)
3925. McIntosh, Alexander, Jacobite, tr. 21 Apr 1716, fr. Liverpool to S.C., in *Wakefield*. (SPC.1716.309)(CTB31.205)
3926. McIntosh, Alexander, b. 1678, laborer, Jacobite, res. Balnabrough Perthshire, tr. 24 Feb 1747, fr. Liverpool to Va, in *Gildart*, arr. Port North Potomac Md 5 Aug 1747. (P.3.100)(PRO.T1.328)(MR74)
3927. McIntosh, Alexander, b. 1727, servant, Jacobite, res. Morayshire, tr. 31 Mar 1747, fr. London to Barbados , in *Frere*. (P.3.100)(MR176)
3928. McIntosh, Alexander, b. 1754, servant, res. Balnacoter, sh. July 1775, fr. Stornaway to Philadelphia, in *Clementina*. (PRO.T47.12)
3929. McIntosh, Andrew, b. 1748, laborer, res. Elgin Morayshire, sh. July 1775, fr. Stornaway to Philadelphia, in *Clementina*. (PRO.T47.12)
3930. McIntosh, Angus, Jacobite, tr. 26 Apr 1716, fr. Liverpool to Jamaica, in *Two Brothers*, arr. Montserrat June 1716. (SPC.1716.313)(CTB31.206)
3931. McIntosh, Angus, b. 1721, laborer, Jacobite, res. Inverness-shire, tr. 5 May 1747, fr. Liverpool to Leeward Islands, in *Veteran*, arr. Martinique June 1747. (P.3.100)(PRO.SP36.102)
3932. McIntosh, Ann, b. 1727, spinner, Jacobite, tr. 8 May 1747, to Antigua. (P.3.102)
3933. McIntosh, Ann, b. 1727, knitter, Jacobite, res. Inverness, tr. 5 May 1747, fr. Liverpool to Leeward Islands, in *Veteran*, arr. Martinique June 1747. (P.3.102)(PRO.SP36.102) (alias 3954)
3934. McIntosh, David, b. 1752, farmer, res. Perth, sh. May 1775, fr. Greenock to N.Y., in *Lilly*. (PRO.T47.12)
3935. McIntosh, Donald, Jacobite, tr. 21 Apr 1716, fr. Liverpool to S.C., in *Wakefield*. (SPC.1716.309)(CTB31.205)
3936. McIntosh, Donald, thief, res. Stirling, tr. 1684, fr. Leith to East N.J. (PC.8.514)
3937. McIntosh, Donald, Jacobite, tr. 21 Apr 1716, fr. Liverpool to S.C., in *Wakefield*. (SPC.1716.309)(CTB31.205)

3938. McIntosh, Duncan, Jacobite, tr. 21 Apr 1716, fr. Liverpool to S.C., in *Wakefield*. (SPC.1716.309)(CTB31.205)
3939. McIntosh, Duncan, Jacobite, tr. 7 May 1716, fr. Liverpool to S.C., in *Susannah*. (SPC.1716.309)(CTB31.206)
3940. McIntosh, Duncan, merchant, res. Edinburgh, sett. Jamaica, m. Margaret Dallas, d. pre 1744, Edin pr1744 CC8.8.108
3941. McIntosh, Duncan, b. 1687, carpenter, Jacobite, res. Inverness, tr. 22 Apr 1747, fr. Liverpool to Va, in *Johnson*, arr. Port Oxford Md 5 Aug 1747. (P.3.102)(MR74)(PRO.T1.328)
3942. McIntosh, Duncan, b. 1728, husbandman, Jacobite, res. Dyke Morayshire, tr. 20 Mar 1747, fr. London to Jamaica, in *St George or Carteret*, arr. Jamaica 1747. (P.3.102)(PRO.CO137.58)
3943. McIntosh, Elisabeth, pts. Lachlan McIntosh of Borlum, sh. pre 1773, sett. N.E., m. Isaac Ryall. (SRO.CS.GMB8\73)
3944. McIntosh, Ewan, Jacobite, tr. 7 May 1716, fr. Liverpool to S.C., in *Susannah*. (SPC.1716.309)(CTB31.206)
3945. McIntosh, Isabel, Petty Inverness-shire, servant, infanticide, res. Edinburgh, pts. John McIntosh, tr. Mar 1763. (SRO.HCR.I.94)
3946. MacIntosh, James, clergyman edu. Aberdeen Uni 1751, res. Nairn, pts. Donald Mackintosh, sh. Dec 1770, to Dominica. (FPA319)(EMAS42)(CPD624)
3947. McIntosh, James, Jacobite, tr. 21 Apr 1716, fr. Liverpool to S.C., in *Wakefield*. (SPC.1716.309)(CTB31.205)
3948. McIntosh, James, Jacobite, tr. 7 May 1716, fr. Liverpool to S.C., in *Susannah*. (SPC.1716.309)(CTB31.206)
3949. McIntosh, James, Jacobite, tr. 28 July 1716, fr. Liverpool to Va, in *Godspeed*, arr. Md Oct 1716. (SPC.1716.310)(CTB31.209)(HM389)
3950. McIntosh, James, Jacobite, tr. 29 June 1716, fr. Liverpool to Jamaica or Va, in *Elizabeth & Anne*, arr. Va. (SPC.1716.310)(CTB31.208)(VSP.1.186)
3951. McIntosh, James, Jacobite, tr. 29 June 1716, fr. Liverpool to Jamaica or Va, in *Elizabeth & Anne*, arr. Va. (SPC.1716.310)(CTB31.208)(VSP.1.185)
3952. McIntosh, James, dyer, housebreaker, res. Newmill Keith Banffshire, tr. Sept 1765, fr. Glasgow. (AJ924\7)
3953. McIntosh, James, Jacobite, tr. 28 July 1716, fr. Liverpool to Va, in *Godspeed*, arr. Md Oct 1716. (SPC.1716.310)(CTB31.209)(HM388)
3954. McIntosh, Jane, b. 1727, knitter, Jacobite, res. Inverness, tr. 5 May 1747, fr. Liverpool to Leeward Islands, in *Veteran*, arr. Martinique June 1747. (P.3.102)(PRO.SP36.102) (alias 3933)
3955. McIntosh, John, Jacobite, tr. 21 Apr 1716, fr. Liverpool to S.C., in *Wakefield*. (CTB31.205)

3956. McIntosh, John, Jacobite, tr. 22 Apr 1747, fr. Liverpool to Va, in *Johnson*, arr. Port Oxford Md 5 Aug 1747. (PRO.T1.328)
3957. McIntosh, John, thief, res. Aberdeenshire, tr. May 1751. (AJ175) (alias 2428)
3958. McIntosh, John, Jacobite, tr. 7 May 1716, fr. Liverpool to S.C., in *Susannah*. (SPC.1716.309)(CTB31.206)
3959. McIntosh, John, Jacobite, tr. 29 June 1716, fr. Liverpool to Jamaica or Va, in *Elizabeth & Anne*, arr. York Va. (SPC.1716.310)(CTB31.208)(VSP.1.185)
3960. McIntosh, John, Jacobite, tr. 29 June 1716, fr. Liverpool to Jamaica or Va, in *Elizabeth & Anne*, arr. Va. (SPC.1716.310)(CTB31.208)(VSP.1.185)
3961. McIntosh, John, Jacobite, tr. 21 Apr 1716, fr. Liverpool to S.C., in *Wakefield*. (SPC.1716.309)(CTB31.205)
3962. McIntosh, John, Jacobite, tr. 7 May 1716, fr. Liverpool to S.C., in *Susannah*. (SPC.1716.309)(CTB31.206)
3963. McIntosh, John, Jacobite, tr. 7 May 1716, fr. Liverpool to S.C., in *Susannah*. (SPC.1716.309)(CTB31.206)
3964. McIntosh, John, sailor, thief, res. Leith, tr. July 1764. (SRO.HCR.I.95)
3965. MacIntosh, John, sh. 1737, sett. Leniwilg Altamaha River Ga. (SPC.1737.454)
3966. McIntosh, John, Jacobite, tr. 21 Apr 1716, fr. Liverpool to S.C., in *Wakefield*. (SPC.1716.309)(CTB31.205)
3967. McIntosh, John, b. 1696, fiddler, Jacobite, res. Inverness, tr. 5 May 1747, fr. Liverpool to Leeward Islands, in *Veteran*, arr. Martinique June 1747. (P.3.102)(PRO.SP36.102)(MR74)
3968. McIntosh, John, b. 1743, ropemaker, sh. Sept 1775, fr. Newcastle to Ga, in *Georgia Packet*, sett. Friendsborough Ga. (PRO.T47.9\11)
3969. McIntosh, Lachlan, Jacobite, tr. 28 July 1716, fr. Liverpool to Va, in *Godspeed*, arr. Md Oct 1716. (SPC.1716.310)(CTB31.209)(HM388)
3970. McIntosh, Lachlan, Jacobite, tr. 30 Mar 1716, fr. Liverpool to Antigua, in *Scipio*. (SPC.1716.310)(CTB31.204)
3971. McIntosh, Lachlan, b. 1725, merchant tailor, Jacobite, res. Inverness, tr. 31 Mar 1747, fr. London to Barbados , in *Frere*. (P.3.100)
3972. McIntosh, Malcolm, Jacobite, tr. 30 Mar 1716, fr. Liverpool to Antigua, in *Scipio*. (SPC.1716.310)(CTB31.204)
3973. McIntosh, Mary, pts. Lachlan McIntosh of Borlum, sh. pre 1773, sett. N.E., m. ...Palmer. (SRO.CS.GMB8\73)
3974. MacIntosh, Myles, Indian trader, res. Kellochie Delarish Inverness-shire, sh. pre 1728, sett. Charleston S.C., m. Margaret McBean, ch. Katherine, d. 1728 Charleston, S.C. pr1729. (SRO.SC29.55.6.257)(SRO.SC29.55.6.215)
3975. McIntosh, Nicholas, merchant, d. pre 1770 Jamaica. (SRO.SH.3.1770)

3976. McIntosh, Peter, b. 1713, laborer, Jacobite, res. Inverness, tr. 5 May 1747, fr. Liverpool to Leeward Islands, in *Veteran*, arr. Martinique June 1747. (P.3.100)(MR74)(PRO.SP36.102)

3977. MacIntosh, Peter, b. 1747, wright, res. Glasgow, sh. May 1775, fr. Greenock to N.Y., in *Monimia*. (PRO.T47.12)

3978. McIntosh, Thomas, soldier, res. Kellochie Inverness-shire, d. Darien 1699, Edin pr1709 CC8.8.84

3979. McIntosh, Thomas, Jacobite, tr. 29 June 1716, fr. Liverpool to Jamaica or Va, in *Elizabeth & Anne*. (SPC.1716.310)(CTB31.208)

3980. McIntosh, William, Jacobite, tr. 21 Apr 1716, fr. Liverpool to S.C., in *Wakefield*. (SPC.1716.309)

3981. McIntosh, William, Jacobite, tr. 7 May 1716, fr. Liverpool to S.C., in *Susannah*. (SPC.1716.309)(CTB31.206)

3982. McIntosh, William, Jacobite, tr. 21 Apr 1716, fr. Liverpool to S.C., in *Wakefield*. (SPC.1716.309)(CTB31.205)

3983. McIntosh, William, Jacobite, tr. 30 Mar 1716, fr. Liverpool to Antigua, in *Scipio*. (SPC.1716.310)(CTB31.204)

3984. McIntosh, William, Jacobite, tr. 30 Mar 1716, fr. Liverpool to Antigua, in *Scipio*. (SPC.1716.310)(CTB31.204)

3985. McIntosh, William, Jacobite, tr. 31 July 1716, fr. Liverpool to Va, in *Anne*. (SPC.1716.310)(CTB31.209)

3986. McIntyre, Ann, b. 1715, spinner, res. Glen Orchy Argyll, sh. Sept 1775, to Wilmington N.C., in *Jupiter*. (PRO.T47.12)

3987. McIntyre, Ann, b. 1727, Jacobite, res. Argyll, tr. 8 May 1747, to Antigua. (P.3.104)

3988. McIntyre, Archibald, Covenanter, res. Glendaruel Argyll, tr. Aug 1685, fr. Leith to Jamaica. (PC.11.329)

3989. McIntyre, Archibald, b. 1697, leadminer, Jacobite, res. Argyll, tr. 22 Apr 1747, fr. Liverpool to Va, in *Johnson*, arr. Port Oxford Md 5 Aug 1747. (P.3.104)(PRO.T1.328)

3990. McIntyre, Charles, b. 1761, servant, res. Kilsyth Stirlingshire, sh. May 1775, fr. Leith to Philadelphia, in *Friendship*. (PRO.T47.12)

3991. McIntyre, Denis, Jacobite, tr. 26 Apr 1716, fr. Liverpool to Jamaica, in *Two Brothers*, arr. Montserrat June 1716. (SPC.1716.313)(CTB31.205)

3992. McIntyre, Donald, b. 1691, 'quack doctor', Jacobite, res. Argyll, tr. 22 Apr 1747, fr. Liverpool to Va, in *Johnson*, arr. Port Oxford Md 5 Aug 1747. (P.3.104)(PRO.T1.328)

3993. MacIntyre, Donald, b. 1721, laborer, res. Glen Orchy Argyll, sh. Sept 1775, to Wilmington N.C., in *Jupiter*, m. Katherine ..., ch. Mary Margaret John Duncan. (PRO.T47.12)

3994. McIntyre, Donald, b. 1732, schoolmaster, res. Breadalbane Perthshire, sh. June 1775, fr. Greenock to N.Y., in *Commerce*, m. Ann Walker, ch. Katherine Ann Archibald. (PRO.T47.12)

3995. McIntyre, Donald, b. 1746, farmer, res. Glen Orchy Argyll, sh. Aug 1774, fr. Greenock to Wilmington N.C., in *Ulysses*, m. Mary ... (PRO.T47.12)
3996. McIntyre, Duncan, ex soldier, horsethief, res. Killici Argyll, tr. 1773. (SM.35.334)
3997. McIntyre, Duncan, b. 1705, brewer, Jacobite, res. Lochielhead Invernessshire, tr. 20 Mar 1747. (P.3.104)(MR14)
3998. McIntyre, Duncan, b. 1720, laborer, res. Breadalbane Perthshire, sh. Sept 1775, to Wilmington N.C., in *Jupiter*, m. Katherine ..., ch. Mary Katherine Elizabeth. (PRO.T47.12)
3999. McIntyre, Duncan, b. 1733, mason, res. Perthshire, sh. May 1775, fr. Greenock to N.Y., in *Monimia*. (PRO.T47.12)
4000. McIntyre, Duncan, b. 1734, farmer, res. Glen Orchy Argyll, sh. Aug 1774, fr. Greenock to Wilmington N.C., in *Ulysses*, m. Katherine ... (PRO.T47.12)
4001. McIntyre, Finlay, Jacobite, tr. 28 July 1716, fr. Liverpool to Va, in *Godspeed*, arr. Md Oct 1716. (SPC.1716.310)(CTB31.209)(HM389)
4002. McIntyre, Gilbert, b. 1741, tailor, res. Breadalbane Perthshire, sh. Sept 1775, to Wilmington N.C., in *Jupiter*, m. Ann ..., ch. Charles Malcolm Margaret Ewan. (PRO.T47.12)
4003. McIntyre, Hugh, Jacobite, tr. 28 July 1716, fr. Liverpool to Va, in *Godspeed*, arr. Md Oct 1716. (SPC.1716.310)(CTB31.209)(HM389)
4004. McIntyre, John, Jacobite, tr. 26 Apr 1716, fr. Liverpool to Jamaica, in *Two Brothers*, arr. Montserrat June 1716. (SPC.1716.313)(CTP.CC.43)(CTB31.205)
4005. MacIntyre, John, Jacobite, tr. 24 May 1716, fr. Liverpool to Va, in *Friendship*, arr. Md Aug 1716. (HM387)
4006. McIntyre, John, soldier, thief, tr. Sept 1763. (SM.26)
4007. McIntyre, John, b. 1729, farmer, res. Glen Orchy Argyll, sh. Aug 1774, fr. Greenock to Wilmington N.C., in *Ulysses*, m. Mary Downie, ch. Nancy Christy John. (PRO.T47.12)
4008. McIntyre, John, b. 1739, farmer, res. Glen Orchy Argyll, sh. Aug 1774, fr. Greenock to Wilmington N.C., in *Ulysses*, m. Margaret ... (PRO.T47.12)
4009. McIntyre, John, b. 1740, laborer, res. Glen Orchy Argyll, sh. Sept 1775, to Wilmington N.C., in *Jupiter*, m. Ann ..., ch. Margaret Archibald John. (PRO.T47.12)
4010. McIntyre, John, b. 1743, tailor, res. Breadalbane Perthshire, sh. Sept 1775, to Wilmington N.C., in *Jupiter*, m. Katherine ..., ch. Donald & John. (PRO.T47.12)
4011. McIntyre, Mary, Jacobite, tr. 8 May 1747, to Antigua. (P.3.106)

4012. McIsaac, Malcolm, b. 1746, smith, res. Breadalbane Perthshire, pts. Archibald McIsaac, sh. June 1775, fr. Greenock to N.Y., in *Commerce*, d. pre 1781 N.Y., PCC pr1781. (PRO.T47.12)
4013. McIsaak, Murdoch, Covenanter, res. Machrimore Kintyre Argyll, tr. July 1685, fr. Leith to N.E. (PC.11.94)
4014. McIvar, Angus, Covenanter, res. Glassary Argyll, tr. 9 July 1685, fr. Leith to N.E. (PC.11.94)
4015. McIvar, Donald, Covenanter, res. Argyll, tr. Aug 1685, fr. Leith to Jamaica. (PC.11.136)
4016. McIvar, Duncan, Covenanter, res. Argyll, tr. Aug 1685, fr. Leith to Jamaica. (PC.11.136)
4017. McIvar, John, Covenanter, res. Tulloch Argyll, tr. Aug 1685, fr. Leith to Jamaica. (PC.11.136)
4018. McIvar, Malcolm, Covenanter, res. Glassary Argyll, tr. Aug 1685, fr. Leith to Jamaica. (PC.11.136)
4019. McIver, Alexander, b. 1753, merchant, res. Glasgow, sh. May 1774, fr. Greenock to N.Y., in *Matty*. (PRO.T47.12)
4020. McIver, Angus, b. 1757, servant, res. Back Isle of Lewis, sh. May 1774, fr. Stornaway to Philadelphia, in *Friendship*. (PRO.T47.12)
4021. McIver, Angus, b. 1761, servant, res. Uig Isle of Lewis, sh. May 1774, fr. Stornaway to Philadelphia, in *Friendship*. (PRO.T47.12)
4022. McIver, Annabel, b. 1746, res. Stornaway Isle of Lewis, sh. May 1774, fr. Stornaway to Philadelphia, in *Friendship*. (PRO.T47.12)
4023. McIver, Donald, thief, res. Upper Rudill Argyll, pts. Charles Dow Campbell or McIver, tr. Apr 1729. (JRA.2.403) (alias 883)
4024. McIver, Duncan, b. 1746, farmer, res. Coll Isle of Lewis, sh. May 1774, fr. Stornaway to Philadelphia, in *Friendship*, m. Margaret ... (PRO.T47.12)
4025. McIver, Duncan Dow, thief, res. Perthshire, tr. May 1776. (SRO.B59.26.16.10) (alias 5747)
4026. McIver, John, b. 1765, res. Sheshader Isle of Lewis, sh. May 1774, fr. Stornaway to Philadelphia, in *Friendship*. (PRO.T47.12)
4027. McIver, Katherine, b. 1761, servant, res. Sheshader Isle of Lewis, sh. May 1774, fr. Stornaway to Philadelphia, in *Friendship*. (PRO.T47.12)
4028. McIver, Mary, b. 1769, res. Sheshader Isle of Lewis, sh. May 1774, fr. Stornaway to Philadelphia, in *Friendship*. (PRO.T47.12)
4029. McIver, Peter, b. 1759, servant, res. Bragar Isle of Lewis, sh. May 1774, fr. Stornaway to Philadelphia, in *Friendship*. (PRO.T47.12)
4030. Mack, James, Covenanter, tr. Dec 1685, fr. Leith to Barbados, in *John & Nicholas*. (PC.11.386)(ETR389)
4031. McKackey, John, b. 1749, smith, res. Galloway, sh. May 1774, fr. Stranraer to N.Y., in *Gale*. (PRO.T47.12)

4032. McKairick, James, b. 1740, farmer, res. Morayshire, sh. July 1775, fr. Stornaway to Philadelphia, in *Clementina*, m. Mary ..., ch. John Alexander William Elizabeth. (PRO.T47.12)
4033. McKairne, Neil, Covenanter, res. Argyll, tr. Aug 1685, fr. Leith to Jamaica. (PC.11.136)
4034. McKandy, Jean, servant, infanticide, res. Cushnie Aberdeenshire, tr. Sept 1766, fr. Aberdeen to Grenada, in *Christie*. (SM.28.500)(AJ974\95)
4035. Mackay, Aeneas, merchant, res. Inverness, sh. pre 1745, sett. Boston Mass. (SRO.RD4.178.566\553)(NEHGS\SCS)
4036. MacKay, Aeneas, b. 1754, teacher & clerk, res. Tongue Sutherland, sh. Apr 1774, to Wilmington N.C., in *Bachelor of Leith*. (PRO.T47.12)
4037. McKay, Alexander, b. 1748, laborer, res. Beauly Inverness-shire, sh. July 1775, fr. Stornaway to Philadelphia, in *Clementina*, m. Anne ..., ch. Jean. (PRO.T47.12)
4038. MacKay, Andrew, Jacobite, tr. 22 Apr 1747, fr. Liverpool to Va, in *Johnson*, d. 15 June 1747 at sea. (PRO.T1.328)
4039. Mackay, Charles, soldier, sh. 1735, sett. Darien & Fredericia Ga. (PCCol.6.498)
4040. Mackay, Donald, weaver, thief, res. Edraboll Kildonan Sutherland, tr. May 1773. (AJ1325)
4041. McKay, Donald, vintner's servant, embezzler, res. South Queensferry West Lothian, tr. Mar 1751. (AJ167)
4042. McKay, Donald, weaver, thief, res. Edraboll Kildonan Sutherland, tr. June 1773, fr. Glasgow. (AJ1323\8)
4043. McKay, Donald, planter, Jacobite, res. Achmonie Glen Urquhart Inverness-shire, tr. 1747, to Barbados, sett. Jamaica. (P.3.108)(MR150)
4044. McKay, Donald, b. 1754, tailor, res. Kintyre Argyll, sh. Aug 1774, to Wilmington N.C., in *Ulysses*. (PRO.T47.12)
4045. McKay, Duncan, Covenanter, res. Skipnish Kintyre Argyll, tr. July 1685. (PC.11.153)
4046. McKay, Duncan, Inverness-shire, laborer, Jacobite, res. Castle Doune Perthshire, tr. 1747. (P.3.108)(MR105)
4047. McKay, George, b. 1734, farmer & tailor, res. Strathullie Kildonan Sutherland, sh. Apr 1774, to Wilmington N.C., in *Bachelor of Leith*. (PRO.T47.12)
4048. McKay, George, b. 1759, farmer, res. Sutherland, sh. July 1775, fr. Greenock to Jamaica, in *Isobella*. (PRO.T47.12)
4049. McKay, Isobel, b. 1752, servant, res. Ross-shire, sh. May 1775, fr. Leith to Philadelphia, in *Friendship*. (PRO.T47.12)
4050. McKay, Ivar, res. Crackaig Jura Argyll, sh. 1754, to Cape Fear N.C. (SRO.GD64/5.21)

4051. McKay, James, b. 1714, shoemaker, res. Strathnaver Sutherland, sh. Apr 1774, to Wilmington N.C., in *Bachelor of Leith*. (PRO.T47.12)
4052. MacKay, James, b. 1759, res. Edinburgh, sh. May 1775, fr. Leith to Philadelphia, in *Friendship*. (PRO.T47.12)
4053. McKay, John, Jacobite, tr. 29 June 1716, fr. Liverpool to Jamaica or Va, in *Elizabeth & Anne*. (CTB31.208)
4054. McKay, John, b. 1756, farmer, res. Strathspey, sh. May 1774, fr. Greenock to N.Y., in *George*. (PRO.T47.12)
4055. MacKay, John, b. 1759, husbandman, res. Inverness, sh. Jan 1774, fr. London to Philadelphia, in *Amelia*. (PRO.T47.9\11)
4056. McKay, John, b. 1759, servant, res. Beauly Inverness-shire, sh. July 1775, fr. Stornaway to Philadelphia, in *Clementina*. (PRO.T47.12)
4057. McKay, John, b. 1760, ballad-seller, res. Rogart Sutherland, sh. May 1775, fr. Leith to Philadelphia, in *Friendship*. (PRO.T47.12)
4058. McKay, Martin, tr. Aug 1685, fr. Leith to Jamaica. (PC.11.136)
4059. MacKay, Murdoch, b. 1755, piper, res. Bowar Caithness, sh. Sept 1775, fr. Kirkwall to Savannah Ga, in *Marlborough*, sett. Friendsborough Ga. (PRO.T47.12)
4060. Mackay, Patrick, sh. 1737, sett. Josephstown Ga. (PRO.CO5.640.45)
4061. McKay, Peter, Jacobite, tr. 1747. (P.3.110)(MR158)
4062. MacKay, Robert, soldier, res. Rothesay Isle of Bute, pts. Jean Mackay, d. pre 1772 Va, PCC pr1772
4063. McKay, Robert, merchant, res. Glasgow, sh. pre 1761, sett. Va. (SRA.B10.15.6729)
4064. McKay, Robert, b. 1721, Jacobite, res. Nether Clashmore Elgin Morayshire, tr. 20 Mar 1747, fr. Tilbury. (P.3.110)(MR80)
4065. McKay, Robert, b. 1725, Sutherland, cooper, Jacobite, res. Fochabers Morayshire, tr. 1747. (P.3.110)(MR128)
4066. McKay, Robert, b. 1727, Jacobite , res. Dornoch Sutherland, tr. 1747, fr. Tilbury. (P.3.110)(MR128)
4067. McKay, Taskel, b. 1681, soldier, Jacobite, res. Inverness-shire, tr. 1747. (MR83)
4068. McKay, Thomas, b. 1700, Banff, woodturner, Jacobite, res. Glenmoriston Inverness-shire, tr. 20 Mar 1747. (P.3.110)(MR158)
4069. McKay, William, forger, tr. Sept 1741. (SRO.HCR.I.69)
4070. McKay, William, b. 1737, farmer, res. Strathaledale Reay Caithness, sh. Apr 1774, to Wilmington N.C., in *Bachelor of Leith*. (PRO.T47.12)
4071. McKay, William, b. 1741, farmer, res. Dundee Angus, sh. Apr 1775, fr. Greenock to Salem, in *Glasgow Packet*, m. Helen Boyd, ch. Helen. (PRO.T47.12)
4072. McKay, William, b. 1744, farmer, res. Farr Strathnaver Sutherland, sh. Apr 1774, to Wilmington N.C., in *Bachelor of Leith*. (PRO.T47.12)

4073. McKay, William, b. 1748, farmer, res. Craigie Reay Caithness, sh. Apr 1774, to Wilmington N.C., in *Bachelor of Leith*. (PRO.T47.12)
4074. McKay, William, b. 1751, farmer, res. Inverness, sh. May 1774, fr. Greenock to N.Y., in *George*. (PRO.T47.12)
4075. McKay, William, b. 1751, servant, res. Duffus Morayshire, sh. July 1775, fr. Stornaway to Philadelphia, in *Clementina*. (PRO.T47.12)
4076. McKechan, Walter, res. Shirgarton, tr. 12 Dec 1678, fr. Leith to West Indies, in *St Michael of Scarborough*. (PC.6.76)
4077. McKechney, Alexander, res. Little Batturich Dunbartonshire, sh. pre 1769, sett. St Kitts & St Croix. (SRO.RS10.10.187)
4078. McKeels, Daniel, Jacobite, tr. 7 May 1716, fr. Liverpool to S.C., in *Susannah*. (SPC.1716.309)(CTB31.206)
4079. McKeichan, Neil, Covenanter, res. Baranazare Lorne Argyll, tr. Aug 1685, fr. Leith to Jamaica. (PC.11.136)
4080. McKellar, Angus, Covenanter, res. Argyll, tr. July 1685, fr. Leith to N.E. (PC.11.94)
4081. McKello, Donald, Covenanter, res. Argyll, tr. Aug 1685, fr. Leith to Jamaica. (PC.11.136)
4082. McKello, Dugald, Covenanter, res. Argyll, tr. Aug 1685, fr. Leith to Jamaica. (PC.11.136)
4083. McKello, John, Covenanter, res. Argyll, tr. Aug 1685, fr. Leith to Jamaica. (PC.11.136)
4084. McKello, Martin, Covenanter, res. Argyll, tr. Aug 1685. (PC.11.126)
4085. MacKenley, William, clergyman edu. King's Col Aberdeen 1772, sh. 1772, sett. Nevis. (EMA42)(FPA317)
4086. McKenn, Edward, Jacobite, tr. 26 Apr 1716, fr. Liverpool to Jamaica, in *Two Brothers*. (CTB31.205)
4087. McKennot, James, b. 1756, coppersmith, res. Glasgow, sh. Feb 1774, fr. Greenock to N.Y., in *Commerce*. (PRO.T47.12)
4088. MacKenny, ..., b. 1704, res. Argyll, sh. Feb 1724, fr. London to Md. (CLRO\AIA)
4089. McKenny, Alexander, Jacobite, tr. 29 June 1716, fr. Liverpool to Jamaica or Va, in *Elizabeth & Anne*, arr. Va. (SPC.1716.310)(CTB31.208)(VSP.1.185)
4090. McKenny, Colin, Jacobite, tr. 30 Mar 1716, fr. Liverpool to Antigua, in *Scipio*. (SPC.1716.310)(CTB31.204)
4091. McKenny, James, carpenter, res. Carsedyke Renfrewshire, sh. 1699, fr. Clyde to Darien, in *Speedy Return*, m. Janet Christie, d. Apr 1700, Edin pr1707 CC8.8.83
4092. MacKenny, James, b. 1714, res. Atholl Perthshire, sh. Sept 1733, fr. London to Pa. (CLRO\AIA)
4093. McKenny, John, Jacobite, tr. 28 July 1716, fr. Liverpool to Va, in *Godspeed*, arr. Md Oct 1716. (SPC.1716.310)(HM388) (alias 3091)

200

4094. McKenny, John, Jacobite, tr. 14 July 1716, fr. Liverpool to Va, in *Godspeed*. (CTB31.209)

4095. McKenzie of Corry, Alexander, b. 1707, factor, Jacobite, res. Thurso Caithness, tr. 31 Mar 1747, fr. London to Barbados, in *Frere*. (P.3.110)(MR79)

4096. MacKenzie, ..., res. Argyll, sh. 4 Feb 1724, fr. London to Md. (CLRO\AIA)

4097. MacKenzie, Aeneas, b. 1675, clergyman edu. Aberdeen & Edinburgh Unis 1692, sh. 1705, sett. N.J. & N.Y. (EMA42)

4098. MacKenzie, Agnes, thief, res. Paisley Renfrewshire, tr. May 1775, fr. Glasgow. (AJ1427)

4099. McKenzie, Agnes, thief, res. Glasgow, pts. Agnes McDonald, tr. May 1775, fr. Glasgow. (SM.37.405)

4100. McKenzie, Alexander, soldier, sh. 1699, to Darien, d. 1699 West Indies, Edin pr1707 CC8.8.83

4101. McKenzie, Alexander, res. Garmouth Morayshire, pts. John McKenzie, sh. pre 1780, sett. Morant Bay Jamaica. (SRO.RS29.8.474)

4102. McKenzie, Alexander, wright, housebreaker, res. Loist Sutherland, tr. Sept 1765. (AJ923)

4103. McKenzie, Alexander, vagrant & thief, res. Dumfries-shire, tr. Apr 1751. (AJ175)

4104. MacKenzie, Alexander, physician, d. 18 Aug 1780 Kingston Jamaica. (SM.42.617)

4105. McKenzie, Alexander, res. Garmouth Morayshire, pts. John McKenzie, sh. pre 1780, sett. Morant Bay Jamaica. (SRO.RS29.8.474)

4106. McKenzie, Alexander, b. 1697, farmer, Jacobite, res. Achendrein Ross-shire, tr. 31 Mar 1747, fr. London to Barbados, in *Frere*. (P.3.112)(MR83)

4107. McKenzie, Alexander, b. 1707, Jacobite, res. Cromarty, tr. 31 Mar 1747, fr. London to Jamaica, in *St George or Carteret*, arr. Jamaica 1747. (P.3.112)(MR83)(PRO.CO137.58)

4108. McKenzie, Alexander, b. 1715, Jacobite, res. Cromarty, tr. 31 Mar 1747, fr. London to Jamaica, in *St George or Carteret*, arr. Jamaica 1747. (P.3.114)(MR83)(PRO.CO137.58)

4109. McKenzie, Alexander, b. 1717, Jacobite, res. Cromarty, tr. 31 Mar 1747, fr. London to Jamaica, in *St George or Carteret*, arr. Jamaica 1747. (P.3.114)(MR83)(PRO.CO137.58)

4110. McKenzie, Alexander, b. 1719, snuffseller, Jacobite, res. Logie Ross-shire, tr. 31 Mar 1747, fr. London to Jamaica, in *St George or Carteret*, arr. Jamaica 1747. (P.3.114)(MR83)(PRO.CO137.58)

4111. McKenzie, Alexander, b. 1719, grieve, Jacobite, res. Coull Coutrie Ross-shire, tr. 31 Mar 1747, fr. London to Jamaica, in *St George or Carteret*, arr. Jamaica 1747. (P.3.112)(MR83)

4112. McKenzie, Alexander, b. 1722, husbandman, Jacobite, res. Drumhardinich Inverness-shire, tr. 1747. (P.3.114)(MR119)
4113. McKenzie, Alexander, b. 1723, Jacobite, tr. 31 Mar 1747, fr. Tilbury. (P.3.114)
4114. McKenzie, Alexander, b. 1723, Jacobite, res. Ross-shire, tr. 31 Mar 1747, fr. London to Barbados, in *Frere*. (P.3.112)(MR83)
4115. McKenzie, Alexander, b. 1724, servant, Jacobite, res. Ross-shire, tr. 31 Mar 1747, fr. London to Barbados, in *Frere*. (P.3.112)(MR83)
4116. McKenzie, Alexander, b. 1725, servant, Jacobite, res. Ballachriche Ross-shire, tr. 31 Mar 1747, fr. London to Barbados, in *Frere*. (P.3.112)(MR83)
4117. McKenzie, Alexander, b. 1729, tailor, Jacobite, res. Argyll, tr. 31 Mar 1747, fr. London to Barbados , in *Frere*. (P.3.112)(MR83)
4118. McKenzie, Alexander, b. 1733, weaver, res. Inverness, sh. July 1775, fr. Stornaway to Philadelphia, in *Clementina*, m. Isobel ..., ch. Anne Catherine Alexander Isobel. (PRO.T47.12)
4119. McKenzie, Alexander, b. 1755, servant, res. Fairburn Ross-shire, sh. July 1775, fr. Stornaway to Philadelphia, in *Clementina*. (PRO.T47.12)
4120. McKenzie, Alexander, b. 1762, res. Stornaway Isle of Lewis, sh. Nov 1774, fr. Stornaway to N.Y., in *Peace & Plenty*. (PRO.T47.12)
4121. McKenzie, Angus, b. 1757, spinner, res. Paisley Renfrewshire, sh. Feb 1774, fr. Greenock to N.Y., in *Commerce*. (PRO.T47.12)
4122. McKenzie, Ann, b. 1687, knitter, Jacobite, res. Glen Garry Inverness-shire, tr. 22 Apr 1747, fr. Liverpool to Va, in *Johnson*, arr. Port Oxford Md 5 Aug 1747. (P.3.114)(PRO.T1.328)
4123. McKenzie, Ann, b. 1756, servant, res. Coigach Ross-shire, sh. Nov 1774, fr. Stornaway to N.Y., in *Peace & Plenty*. (PRO.T47.12)
4124. McKenzie, Anne, pts. George, Earl of Cromartie, sh. pre 1761, sett. Charleston S.C., m. (1)Edmond Atkin (2)John Murray, d. 18 Jan 1768 Charleston. (SM.30.165)
4125. McKenzie, Anne, b. 1750, servant, res. Beauly Inverness-shire, sh. July 1775, fr. Stornaway to Philadelphia, in *Clementina*. (PRO.T47.12)
4126. McKenzie, Archibald, b. 1729, herd, Jacobite, tr. 1747. (P.3.114)(MR158)
4127. McKenzie, Catherine, b. 1746, servant, res. Beauly Inverness-shire, sh. July 1775, fr. Stornaway to Philadelphia, in *Clementina*. (PRO.T47.12)
4128. McKenzie, Christian, b. 1763, servant, res. Wester Leys Isle of Lewis, sh. July 1775, fr. Stornaway to Philadelphia, in *Clementina*. (PRO.T47.12)
4129. McKenzie, Christine, b. 1771, res. Stornaway Isle of Lewis, sh. May 1774, fr. Stornaway to Philadelphia, in *Friendship*. (PRO.T47.12)
4130. MacKenzie, Colin, res. Inverness, sh. Mar 1754, fr. London to Antigua. (CLRO\AIA)

4131. McKenzie, Colin, merchant, res. Dingwall Ross & Cromarty, d. pre 1783
Jamaica. (SRO.RD4.235.344)
4132. McKenzie, Daniel, Jacobite, res. Perth, tr. 1747. (P.3.116)(MR74)
4133. McKenzie, Daniel, b. 1714, servant, Jacobite, res. Curmigh Inverness-
shire, tr. 1747, fr. Tilbury. (P.3.116)(MR158)
4134. McKenzie, Daniel, b. 1746, farmer, res. Dundee Angus, sh. Apr 1775, fr.
Greenock to Salem, in Glasgow Packet. (PRO.T47.12)
4135. McKenzie, David, res. Auldearn Nairnshire, sh. Aug 1754, fr. London to
N.Y. (CLRO\AIA)
4136. McKenzie, Donald, farmer, Jacobite, res. Ivahanny Ross & Cromarty, tr.
1747. (P.3.116)(MR79)
4137. McKenzie, Donald, b. 1690, Jacobite, tr. 31 Mar 1747, fr. Tilbury.
(P.3.118)
4138. McKenzie, Donald, b. 1707, farmer, Jacobite, res. Ballevloide Ross-shire,
tr. 31 Mar 1747, fr. London to Barbados, in Frere.
(P.3.118)(MR83)
4139. McKenzie, Donald, b. 1707, farmer, Jacobite, res. Badrallach Ross &
Cromarty, tr. 31 Mar 1747, fr. London to Jamaica, in St George or
Carteret, arr. Jamaica 1747. (P.3.118)(MR83)(PRO.CO137.58)
4140. McKenzie, Donald, b. 1709, Jacobite, tr. 21 July 1748. (P.3.116)
4141. McKenzie, Donald, b. 1711, Jacobite, tr. 31 Mar 1747, fr. London to
Barbados, in Frere. (P.3.118)(MR83)
4142. McKenzie, Donald, b. 1712, husbandman, Jacobite, res. Letanochglass
Ross-shire, tr. 19 Mar 1747, fr. Tilbury. (P.3.118)(MR83)
4143. McKenzie, Donald, b. 1717, Jacobite, tr. 20 Mar 1747.
(P.3.118)(MR158)
4144. McKenzie, Donald, b. 1722, Jacobite, res. Inverness, tr. 20 Mar 1747.
(P.3.118)(MR119)
4145. McKenzie, Donald, b. 1722, Jacobite, res. Castleleod Ross & Cromarty,
tr. 31 Mar 1747, fr. London to Jamaica, in St George or Carteret,
arr. Jamaica 1747. (P.3.118)(MR83)(PRO.CO137.58)
4146. McKenzie, Donald, b. 1727, husbandman, Jacobite, res. Ballene Ross-
shire, tr. 20 Mar 1747. (P.3.118)(MR83)
4147. McKenzie, Donald, b. 1727, Jacobite , res. Ross-shire, tr. 31 Mar 1747,
fr. London to Barbados, in Frere. (P.3.118)(MR83)
4148. McKenzie, Donald, b. 1762, servant, res. Wester Leys Isle of Lewis, sh.
July 1775, fr. Stornaway to Philadelphia, in Clementina.
(PRO.T47.12)
4149. McKenzie, Duncan, tailor, Jacobite, res. Ferryhouse Locheil Inverness-
shire, tr. 1747. (P.3.118)(MR35)
4150. McKenzie, Duncan, b. 1707, farmer, Jacobite, res. Braemore Ross-shire,
tr. 20 Mar 1747, fr. Tilbury. (P.3.120)(MR83)

4151. McKenzie, Duncan, b. 1720, husbandman, Jacobite, res. Ballone Ross-shire, tr. 31 Mar 1747, fr. London to Jamaica, in *St George or Carteret*, arr. Jamaica 1747. (P.3.120)(MR83)(PRO.T1.328)
4152. McKenzie, Duncan, b. 1721, Jacobite, res. Cromarty, tr. 1747. (P.3.120)(MR83)
4153. McKenzie, Duncan, b. 1727, Jacobite, res. Ross-shire, tr. 1747. (P.3.120)(MR83)
4154. McKenzie, Duncan, b. 1729, Jacobite, res. Ross-shire, tr. 1747. (P.3.120)
4155. MacKenzie, Duncan, b. 1752, farmer, res. Strathspey, sh. May 1774, fr. Greenock to N.Y., in *George*. (PRO.T47.12)
4156. MacKenzie, Duncan, b. 1758, servant, res. Coll Isle of Lewis, sh. May 1774, fr. Stornaway to Philadelphia, in *Friendship*. (PRO.T47.12)
4157. McKenzie, Elizabeth, fireraiser, res. Inverness-shire, tr. May 1750. (AJ125)
4158. McKenzie, Elizabeth, murderer, res. Inverness-shire, tr. Oct 1749, m. ... Murchison. (SM.11.509)
4159. McKenzie, Elizabeth, b. 1763, servant, res. Wester Leys Isle of Lewis, sh. July 1775, fr. Stornaway to Philadelphia, in *Clementina*. (PRO.T47.12)
4160. MacKenzie, Eneas, b. 1675, clergyman edu. Edinburgh & Aberdeen Unis, sh. 1705, to Staten Island, sett. Va. (SCHR.14.149)(SPG.11.105)
4161. MacKenzie, Ewan Buy, thief, res. Inverness-shire, tr. May 1753. (SM.15.260)
4162. McKenzie, Finlay, b. 1702, cooper, res. Stornaway Isle of Lewis, sh. May 1774, fr. Stornaway to Philadelphia, in *Friendship*, m. Mary ..., ch. John Donald. (PRO.T47.12)
4163. McKenzie, Finlay, b. 1729, cooper, res. Stornaway Isle of Lewis, sh. May 1774, fr. Stornaway to Philadelphia, in *Friendship*, m. Mary .., ch. John. (PRO.T47.12)
4164. McKenzie, Francis, b. 1746, laborer, res. Islay Argyll, sh. Apr 1775, fr. Greenock to N.Y., in *Lilly*. (PRO.T47.12)
4165. McKenzie, George, merchant, res. Edinburgh, pts. John McKenzie, sh. pre 1698, sett. Bridgetown Barbados, d. 1711 Barbados, Barbados pr1711. (SRO.SH.25.10.1698)
4166. Mackenzie, George, merchant, res. Edinburgh, pts. Sir John MacKenzie, sh. 1684, to East N.J., sett. Elizabethtown N.J. (Insh237)
4167. McKenzie, George, merchant, res. Edinburgh, pts. George McKenzie & Bethia Law, sh. pre 1704, sett. Barbados, d. pre 1733, Edin pr1733 CC8.8.95. (SRO.SH.20.4.1704)
4168. McKenzie, George, b. 1715, Jacobite, res. Ross-shire, tr. 31 Mar 1747, fr. London to Barbados , in *Frere*. (P.3.122)(MR84)
4169. McKenzie, George, b. 1715, farmer, Jacobite, res. Coigach Ross-shire, tr. 1747. (P.3.122)(MR84)

4170. McKenzie, George, b. 1726, servant, Jacobite, res. Glasslaw Ross-shire, tr. 20 Mar 1747, fr. Tilbury. (P.3.122)(MR84)
4171. McKenzie, George, b. 1752, gentleman, sh. Dec 1774, fr. London to Jamaica, in *Woodley*. (PRO.T47.9\11)
4172. McKenzie, Gilbert, b. 1740, farmer, res. Kintyre Argyll, sh. Sept 1774, fr. Greenock to Wilmington N.C., in *Diana*, m. Margaret ... (PRO.T47.12)
4173. McKenzie, Hector, surgeon, sh. 14 July 1698, fr. Leith to Darien, in *Unicorn*, d. 12 Aug 1699 Cape St Antonio America, Edin pr1707 CC8.8.83. (DP196)
4174. McKenzie, Hector, b. 1703, forester, Jacobite, res. Loch Broom Ross-shire, tr. Oct 1748. (P.3.122)
4175. McKenzie, Isabel, b. 1756, servant, res. Stornaway Isle of Lewis, sh. Nov 1774, fr. Stornaway to N.Y., in *Peace & Plenty*. (PRO.T47.12)
4176. McKenzie, Isabel, b. 1757, servant, res. Coigach Ross-shire, sh. Nov 1774, fr. Stornaway to N.Y., in *Peace & Plenty*. (PRO.T47.12)
4177. McKenzie, Isabel, b. 1758, servant, res. Ross-shire, sh. May 1775, fr. Leith to Philadelphia, in *Friendship*. (PRO.T47.12)
4178. McKenzie, Isobel, b. 1735, res. Inverness, sh. July 1775, fr. Stornaway to Philadelphia, in *Clementina*, ch. Anne John. (PRO.T47.12)
4179. McKenzie, Isobel, b. 1747, servant, res. Braen, sh. July 1775, fr. Stornaway to Philadelphia, in *Clementina*. (PRO.T47.12)
4180. McKenzie, Isobel, b. 1762, servant, res. Wester Leys Isle of Lewis, sh. July 1775, fr. Stornaway to Philadelphia, in *Clementina*. (PRO.T47.12)
4181. MacKenzie, James, pickpocket, tr. Jan 1774. (SM.36.107)
4182. McKenzie, James, b. 1725, tailor, Jacobite, res. Oolder Hooste Inverness, tr. 31 Mar 1747, fr. London to Barbados , in *Frere*. (P.3.122)(MR84)
4183. McKenzie, James, b. 1727, Jacobite, res. Inverness, tr. 20 Mar 1747. (P.3.122)(MR84)
4184. McKenzie, Jane, b. 1728, sewer, Jacobite, res. Inverness, tr. 5 May 1747, fr. Liverpool to Leeward Islands, in *Veteran*, arr. Martinique June 1747. (P.3.124)(PRO.SP36.102)
4185. McKenzie, Jean, b. 1754, servant, res. Stornaway Isle of Lewis, sh. May 1774, fr. Stornaway to Philadelphia, in *Friendship*. (PRO.T47.12)
4186. McKenzie, John, gunner, sh. 14 July 1698, fr. Leith to Darien, in *Caledonia*, Edin pr1707 CC8.8.83
4187. MacKenzie, John, attorney, pts. Alexander MacKenzie of Inchcoulter, d. Dec 1780 Jamaica. (SM.43.166)
4188. McKenzie, John, b. 1691, farmer, Jacobite, res. Dormie Ross-shire, tr. 31 Mar 1747, fr. London to Jamaica, in *St George or Carteret*, arr. Jamaica 1747. (P.3.124)(MR84)(PRO.CO137.58)

4189. McKenzie, John, b. 1697, husbandman, Jacobite, res. Dingwall Ross & Cromarty, tr. 31 Mar 1747, fr. London to Barbados, in *Frere*. (P.3.124)

4190. McKenzie, John, b. 1702, farmer, Jacobite, res. Auchterdonald Ross-shire, tr. 20 Mar 1747. (P.3.126)

4191. McKenzie, John, b. 1707, farmer, Jacobite, res. Dornoch Sutherland, tr. 31 Mar 1747, fr. London to Barbados, in *Frere*. (P.3.124)(MR84)

4192. McKenzie, John, b. 1707, farmer, Jacobite, res. Logie Ross-shire, tr. 20 Mar 1747. (P.3.126)(MR84)

4193. McKenzie, John, b. 1709, servant, Jacobite, res. Ross-shire, tr. 31 Mar 1747, fr. Barbados to FRERE. (P.3.124)(MR84)

4194. McKenzie, John, b. 1711, farmer, Jacobite, res. Ashlet, pts. Ross-shire, tr. 20 Mar 1747. (P.3.124)(MR84)

4195. McKenzie, John, b. 1715, gentleman, Jacobite, res. Ardloch Assynt Sutherland, tr. 5 May 1747, fr. Liverpool to Leeward Islands, in *Veteran*, arr. Martinique June 1747. (P.3.124)(MR79)(PRO.SP36.102)

4196. McKenzie, John, b. 1719, Jacobite, res. Achtermead Ross-shire, tr. 31 Mar 1747, fr. London to Jamaica, in *St George or Carteret*, arr. Jamaica 1747. (P.3.124)(MR84)(PRO.CO137.58)

4197. McKenzie, John, b. 1720, Jacobite, res. Cromarty, tr. 1747. (P.3.126)(MR84)

4198. McKenzie, John, b. 1727, weaver, Jacobite, res. Achnashiel Ross-shire, tr. 31 Mar 1747, fr. London to Barbados, in *Frere*. (P.3.124)(MR84)

4199. McKenzie, John, b. 1727, servant, Jacobite, res. Strathpeffer Ross-shire, tr. 31 Mar 1747, fr. London to Barbados, in *Frere*. (P.3.124)(MR84)

4200. McKenzie, John, b. 1729, servant, Jacobite, res. Logie Ross-shire, tr. 20 Mar 1747. (P.3.126)(MR84)

4201. McKenzie, John, b. 1736, laborer, res. Beaauly Inverness-shire, sh. July 1775, fr. Stornaway to Philadelphia, in *Clementina*, m. Anne ..., ch. James Donald. (PRO.T47.12)

4202. McKenzie, John, b. 1744, tailor, res. Loch Broom Ross-shire, sh. Nov 1774, fr. Stornaway to N.Y., in *Peace & Plenty*. (PRO.T47.12)

4203. MacKenzie, John, b. 1749, farmer, res. Strathspey, sh. May 1774, fr. Greenock to N.Y., in *George*. (PRO.T47.12)

4204. McKenzie, John, b. 1754, servant, res. Stornaway Isle of Lewis, sh. Nov 1774, fr. Stornaway to N.Y., in *Peace & Plenty*. (PRO.T47.12)

4205. McKenzie, John, b. 1756, servant, res. Ness Isle of Lewis, sh. May 1774, fr. Stornaway to Philadelphia, in *Friendship*. (PRO.T47.12)

4206. McKenzie, John, b. 1757, servant, res. Poolewe Ross-shire, sh. Nov 1774, fr. Stornaway to N.Y., in *Peace & Plenty*. (PRO.T47.12)

4207. McKenzie, John, b. 1757, servant, res. Inverness, sh. July 1775, fr. Stornaway to Philadelphia, in *Clementina*. (PRO.T47.12)
4208. McKenzie, John, b. 1764, servant, res. Beauly Inverness-shire, sh. July 1775, fr. Stornaway to Philadelphia, in *Clementina*. (PRO.T47.12)
4209. McKenzie, Katherine, b. 1765, res. Stornaway Isle of Lewis, sh. May 1774, fr. Stornaway to Philadelphia, in *Friendship*. (PRO.T47.12)
4210. MacKenzie, Kenneth, clergyman, sh. 1712, in *Severn*, sett. St James Lawn Creek Va. (EMA43)(SRO.NRAS.0040)
4211. McKenzie, Kenneth, b. 1692, farmer, Jacobite, res. Invervaigh Lochbroom Ross-shire, tr. 19 Mar 1747, fr. Tilbury to Jamaica, in *St George or Carteret*, arr. Jamaica 1747. (P.3.128)(MR84)(PRO.CO137.58)
4212. McKenzie, Kenneth, b. 1709, servant, Jacobite, res. Ross-shire, tr. 31 Mar 1747, fr. London to Jamaica, in *St George or Carteret*, arr. Jamaica 1747. (P.3.128)(MR85)(PRO.CO137.58)
4213. McKenzie, Kenneth, b. 1715, farmer, Jacobite, res. Ballone Ross-shire, tr. 31 Mar 1747, fr. London to Barbados, in *Frere*. (P.3.128)(MR84)
4214. McKenzie, Kenneth, b. 1717, farmer, Jacobite, res. Aschellach Ross-shire, tr. 20 Mar 1747. (P.3.128)(MR84)
4215. McKenzie, Kenneth, b. 1717, husbandman, Jacobite, res. Ballone Ross-shire, tr. 31 Mar 1747, fr. London to Jamaica, in *St George or Carteret*, arr. Jamaica 1747. (P.3.128)(PRO.CO137.58)
4216. McKenzie, Kenneth, b. 1721, Jacobite, res. Loch Broom Ross-shire, tr. 31 Mar 1747, fr. London to Barbados, in *Frere*. (P.3.128)(MR84)
4217. McKenzie, Kenneth, b. 1725, servant, Jacobite, res. Contin Ross-shire, tr. 31 Mar 1747, fr. London to Barbados, in *Frere*. (P.3.128)(MR158)
4218. McKenzie, Kenneth, b. 1726, Jacobite, res. Ross-shire, tr. 19 Mar 1747, fr. Tilbury. (P.3.128)(MR85)
4219. McKenzie, Kenneth, b. 1728, husbandman, Jacobite, res. Little Strath Ross-shire, tr. 31 Mar 1747, fr. London to Barbados, in *Frere*. (P.2.128)(MR84)
4220. McKenzie, Kenneth, b. 1728, husbandman, Jacobite, res. Lochmallin Ross-shire, tr. 19 Mar 1747. (P.3.130)(MR85)
4221. McKenzie, Kenneth, b. 1737, farmer, res. Fairburn Ross-shire, sh. July 1775, fr. Stornaway to Philadelphia, in *Clementina*, ch. Mary John. (PRO.T47.12)
4222. McKenzie, Kenneth, b. 1750, gardener, res. Edinburgh, sh. May 1775, fr. Leith to Philadelphia, in *Friendship*. (PRO.T47.12)
4223. McKenzie, Kenneth, b. 1761, servant, res. Beauly Inverness-shire, sh. July 1775, fr. Stornaway to Philadelphia, in *Clementina*. (PRO.T47.12)

207

4224. McKenzie, Kenneth jr, res. Kildin Isle of Lewis, sh. 1684, to East N.J. (Insh236)
4225. McKenzie, Lewis, b. 1726, joiner, Jacobite, res. Elgin Morayshire, tr. Apr 1747, fr. Tilbury to Jamaica, in *St George or Carteret*, arr. Jamaica 1747. (P.3.130)(MR85)(PRO.CO137.58)
4226. McKenzie, Malcolm Forbes, b. 1752, barber, res. Edinburgh, sh. May 1775, fr. Greenock to N.Y., in *Lilly*. (PRO.T47.12)
4227. McKenzie, Margaret, b. 1752, servant, res. Culduthel Inverness-shire, sh. July 1775, fr. Stornaway to Philadelphia, in *Clementina*. (PRO.T47.12)
4228. McKenzie, Margaret, b. 1753, servant, res. Inverness, sh. July 1775, fr. Stornaway to Philadelphia, in *Clementina*. (PRO.T47.12)
4229. McKenzie, Marjory, b. 1755, servant, res. Wester Leys Isle of Lewis, sh. July 1775, fr. Stornaway to Philadelphia, in *Clementina*. (PRO.T47.12)
4230. McKenzie, Mary, pts. Earl of Cromarty, sh. pre 1762, sett. Charleston S.C., m. (1)Thomas Drayton (2)John Ainslie. (GM.32.390)
4231. MacKenzie, Mary, b. 1714, spinner, res. Banff, sh. July 1736, fr. London to N.C. (CLRO\AIA)
4232. McKenzie, Mary, b. 1727, spinner, Jacobite, res. Lochaber Inverness-shire, tr. 5 May 1747, fr. Liverpool to Leeward Islands, in *Veteran*, arr. Martinique June 1747. (P.3.130)(PRO.SP36.102)
4233. McKenzie, Mary, b. 1749, servant, res. Stornaway Isle of Lewis, sh. Nov 1774, fr. Stornaway to Philadelphia, in *Peace & Plenty*. (PRO.T47.12)
4234. McKenzie, Mary, b. 1763, servant, res. Stornaway Isle of Lewis, sh. May 1774, fr. Stornaway to Philadelphia, in *Friendship*. (PRO.T47.12)
4235. McKenzie, Murdo, b. 1734, farmer, res. Bayble Isle of Lewis, sh. May 1774, fr. Stornaway to Philadelphia, in *Friendship*, m. Annabella McIver, ch. Mary Katherine Christian. (PRO.T47.12)
4236. McKenzie, Murdo, b. 1744, farmer, res. Bayble Isle of Lewis, sh. May 1774, fr. Stornaway to Philadelphia, in *Friendship*, ch. Donald. (PRO.T47.12)
4237. McKenzie, Murdoch, b. 1707, farmer, Jacobite, res. Strathnacalliach Ross-shire, tr. 31 Mar 1747, fr. London to Barbados, in *Frere*. (P.3.130)(MR85)
4238. McKenzie, Murdoch, b. 1725, servant, Jacobite, res. Ross-shire, tr. 31 Mar 1747, fr. London to Jamaica, in *St George or Carteret*, arr. Jamaica 1747. (P.3.130)(MR85)(PRO.CO137.58)
4239. McKenzie, Murdoch, b. 1727, herdsman, Jacobite, res. Tully Dingwall Sutherland, tr. 31 Mar 1747, fr. London to Barbados , in *Frere*. (P.3.130)(MR85)
4240. McKenzie, Murdoch, b. 1738, servant, res. Leys Isle of Lewis, sh. July 1775, fr. Stornaway to Philadelphia, in *Clementina*. (PRO.T47.12)

4241. McKenzie, Murdoch, b. 1747, servant, res. Blysarry Inverness-shire, sh. Nov 1774, fr. Stornaway to N.Y., in *Peace & Plenty*. (PRO.T47.12)

4242. McKenzie, Murdoch, b. 1757, servant, res. Stornaway Isle of Lewis, sh. Nov 1774, fr. Stornaway to N.Y., in *Peace & Plenty*. (PRO.T47.12)

4243. Mackenzie, Robert, b. 1626, sh. 14 Aug 1657, fr. London to Va, in *Conquer*. (PRO.CO1.13.29i)

4244. McKenzie, Roderick, b. 1691, husbandman, Jacobite, res. Logie Caithness, tr. 31 Mar 1747, fr. London to Jamaica, in *St George or Carteret*, arr. Jamaica 1747. (P.3.132)(PRO.CO137.58) (alias 4249)

4245. McKenzie, Roderick, b. 1707, farmer, Jacobite, res. Batrialliach Ross-shire, tr. 20 Mar 1747. (P.3.132)

4246. McKenzie, Roderick, b. 1711, farmer, Jacobite, res. Loch Broom Ross-shire, tr. 20 Mar 1747. (P.3.132)(MR85)

4247. McKenzie, Roderick, b. 1721, servant, Jacobite, res. Loch Broom Ross-shire, tr. 31 Mar 1747, fr. London to Jamaica, in *St George or Carteret*, arr. Jamaica 1747. (P.3.132)(MR85)(PRO.CO137.58) (alias 4250)

4248. McKenzie, Roderick, b. 1724, husbandman, Jacobite, res. Strathnacalliach Ross-shire, tr. 1747. (P.3.134)(MR85) (alias 4253)

4249. McKenzie, Roger, b. 1691, husbandman, Jacobite, res. Logie Caithness, tr. 31 Mar 1747, fr. London to Jamaica, in *St George or Carteret*, arr. Jamaica 1747. (P.3.132)(PRO.CO137.58) (alias 4244)

4250. McKenzie, Roger, b. 1721, servant, Jacobite, res. Loch Broom Ross-shire, tr. 31 Mar 1747, fr. London to Jamaica, in *St George or Carteret*, arr. Jamaica 1747. (P.3.132)(MR85)(PRO.CO137.58) (alias 4247)

4251. McKenzie, Rory, b. 1691, husbandman, Jacobite, res. Little Strath Ross-shire, tr. 20 Mar 1747. (P.3.132)(MR85)

4252. McKenzie, Rory, b. 1721, Jacobite, res. Ross-shire, tr. 1747. (P.3.134)(MR85)

4253. McKenzie, Rory, b. 1724, husbandman, Jacobite, res. Strathnacalliach Ross-shire, tr. 1747. (P.3.134)(MR85) (alias 4248)

4254. McKenzie, Rory, b. 1760, servant, res. Stornaway Isle of Lewis, sh. May 1774, fr. Stornaway to Philadelphia, in *Friendship*. (PRO.T47.12)

4255. MacKenzie, Simon, surgeon, res. Fortrose Ross & Cromarty, pts. John MacKenzie, sh. pre 1773, sett. Jamaica. (SRO.SH.22.10.1773)

4256. McKenzie, Simon, res. Fortrose Ross-shire, pts. Dr John McKenzie, sh. pre 1783, sett. St Andrew, Surry Co Jamaica. (SRO.RD4.237.901)

4257. McKenzie, Thomas, Jacobite, tr. 25 June 1716, fr. Liverpool to St Kitts, in *Hockenhill*. (SPC.1716.312)(CTB31.217)

4258. McKenzie, Thomas, b. 1753, servant, res. Beauly Inverness-shire, sh. July 1775, fr. Stornaway to Philadelphia, in *Clementina*. (PRO.T47.12)

4259. McKenzie, Thomas, b. 1755, periwigmaker, res. Edinburgh, sh. Jan 1774, fr. London to Md, in *Chance*. (PRO.T47.9\11)

4260. McKenzie, Thomas, b. 1757, servant, res. Fairburn Ross-shire, sh. July 1775, fr. Stornaway to Philadelphia, in *Clementina*. (PRO.T47.12)

4261. McKenzie, William, Jacobite, tr. 21 Apr 1716, fr. Liverpool to S.C., in *Wakefield*. (SPC.1716.309)(CTB31.205)

4262. MacKenzie, William, merchant, sett. Charleston S.C., d. pre 1739. (SM.1.44)

4263. McKenzie, William, b. 1711, husbandman, Jacobite, res. Banffshire, tr. 1747. (P.3.134)(MR85)

4264. McKenzie, William, b. 1726, Jacobite , res. Ross-shire, tr. 1747. (P.3.136)(MR85)

4265. McKenzie, William, b. 1729, farmer, res. Auchall Ross-shire, sh. Nov 1774, fr. Stornaway to N.Y., in *Peace & Plenty*, m. Mary ..., ch. Catherine Barbara Molly Ann Florence Thomas Murdoch Belle NellyC. (PRO.T47.12)

4266. MacKenzie, William, b. 1757, farmer, res. Strathspey, sh. May 1774, fr. Greenock to N.Y., in *George*. (PRO.T47.12)

4267. McKenzie, William, b. 1759, servant, res. Poolewe Ross-shire, sh. Nov 1774, fr. Stornaway to N.Y., in *Peace & Plenty*. (PRO.T47.12)

4268. McKethrick, John, rioter, res. Bridgend Dumfries, pts. William McKethrick or MacKitterick, tr. 1771, fr. Port Glasgow to Md, in *Matty*, arr. Port Oxford Md 17 Dec 1771. (SRO.JC27.10.3)(SM.33.497) (alias 4316)

4269. Mackey, William, sailor, res. Woodhaven, pts. Robert Mackey, d. pre 1781 Savannah Ga, PCC pr1781

4270. MacKie, Alexander, forger, res. Glasgow, tr. 1773. (SM.35.334)

4271. MacKie, Alexander, merchant, res. Glasgow, sh. pre 1748, sett. Va. (SRA.B10.5959.6653)

4272. Mackie, Andrew, dyer & merchant, res. Glasgow, pts. Andrew Mackie of Lerbor, sh. pre 1766. (SRA.B10.15.7019)

4273. MacKie, Daniel, b. 1729, laborer, Jacobite, res. Morayshire, tr. 5 May 1747, fr. Liverpool to Leeward Islands, in *Veteran*, arr. Martinique June 1747. (P.3.108)(PRO.T1.328)

4274. Mackie, George, sailor, res. Fife, pts. James Mackie & Katherine Lumsden, sh. 14 July 1698, fr. Leith to Darien, in *Caledonia*, Edin pr1707 CC8.8.83

4275. McKie, George, b. 1727, farmer, res. Inch Wigtonshire, sh. 31 May 1775, fr. Stranraer to N.Y., in *Jackie*, m. Jean McMiken, ch. Peter Thomas Janet David Jean Alexander. (PRO.T47.12)

4276. McKie, James, sailor, sh. 14 July 1698, fr. Leith to Darien, in *St Andrew*, Edin pr1707 CC8.8.83

4277. MacKie, Janet, res. Edinburgh, tr. 21 Oct 1682, fr. Greenock to N.Y. (ETR221)

4278. McKie, Jean, b. 1772, res. Galloway, sh. May 1774, fr. Stranraer to N.Y., in *Gale*. (PRO.T47.12)

4279. McKie, John, b. 1757, laborer, res. Water of Orr Colvend Kirkcudbrightshire, sh. May 1774, fr. Kirkcudbright to N.Y., in *Adventure*. (PRO.T47.12)

4280. McKie, Margaret, b. 1748, res. Galloway, sh. May 1774, fr. Stranraer to N.Y., in *Gale*. (PRO.T47.12)

4281. MacKie, Robert, ostler, Jacobite, res. Brechin Angus, tr. 20 Mar 1747, fr. Tilbury. (P.3.110)

4282. McKie, Samuel, b. 1748, weaver, res. Galloway, sh. May 1774, fr. Stranraer to N.Y., in *Gale*. (PRO.T47.12)

4283. McKie, Taskel, b. 1687, ex soldier, Jacobite, res. Inverness, tr. 31 Mar 1747, fr. London to Barbados , in *Frere*. (P.3.110)

4284. MacKie, Thomas, b. 9 Jan 1704, Forres, saddler, res. Forres Morayshire, pts. John MacKie & Jean Scott, sh. pre 1767, sett. Tonquier Va. (SRO.SH.31.1.1767)

4285. MacKie, William, Covenanter, tr. July 1685, fr. Leith to N.J. (PC.11.95)

4286. Mackie, William, b. 1712, res. Aberdeen, sh. Oct 1731, fr. London to Antigua. (CLRO\AIA)

4287. McKie, William, b. 1745, mason, res. Cassaend Kelton Kirkcudbrightshire, sh. 1775, fr. Kirkcudbright to P.E.I., in *Lovely Nelly*, m. Isabel .., ch. John Eliza Mary. (PRO.T47.12)

4288. McKiehan, Robert, b. 1742, farmer, res. Kintyre Argyll, sh. Aug 1774, fr. Greenock to Wilmington N.C., in *Ulysses*, m. Janet McKendrick, ch. Neil. (PRO.T47.12)

4289. MacKier, William, b. 1709, gardener, res. Carnock Fife, sh. Sept 1731, fr. London to Jamaica. (CLRO\AIA)

4290. MacKillivandick, Donald, murderer, res. Inverness-shire, tr. Sept 1755. (AJ402)

4291. McKillon, Donald, Covenanter, res. Glendaruel Argyll, tr. Aug 1685, fr. Leith to Jamaica. (PC.11.136)

4292. McKinlay, John, b. 1754, weaver, res. Paisley Renfrewshire, sh. May 1775, fr. Greenock to N.Y., in *Lilly*. (PRO.T47.12)

4293. McKinlay, John jr, miller, cattle thief, res. Moymore Glendaruell Argyll, tr. Nov 1705. (JRA.2.203)

4294. McKinlay, Neil, farmer, Covenanter, res. Argyll, tr. Aug 1685, fr. Leith to Jamaica. (PC.11.136)

4295. McKinlay, Peter, b. 1751, wright, res. Glasgow, sh. May 1775, fr. Greenock to N.Y., in *Monimia*. (PRO.T47.12)

211

4296. McKinlay, Robert, sh. 16 Dec 1773, fr. Greenock to Jamaica, in *Ross*. (SRO.CE60.1.7)
4297. McKinly, Jean, b. 1748, res. Galloway, sh. May 1774, fr. Stranraer to N.Y., in *Gale*. (PRO.T47.12)
4298. McKinly, Michael, b. 1734, farmer, res. Galloway, sh. May 1774, fr. Stranraer to N.Y., in *Gale*. (PRO.T47.12)
4299. McKinnel, Mary, b. 1750, res. Kirkmichael, sh. 31 May 1775, fr. Stranraer to N.Y., in *Jackie*. (PRO.T47.12)
4300. McKinney, Donald, Jacobite, tr. 24 Feb 1747, fr. Liverpool to Va, in *Gildart*, arr. Port North Potomac Md 5 Aug 1747. (PRO.T1.328)
4301. McKinnon, Alexander, pipemaker, slanderer, res. Glasgow, tr. 10 Aug 1680, fr. Leith to Barbados, in *The Blossom*. (PC.6.456)(ETR171)
4302. McKinnon, Archibald, b. 1735, farmer, res. Isle of Mull, sh. July 1775, fr. Greenock to Ga, in *Georgia*, m. Janet .. (PRO.T47.12)
4303. McKinnon, Donald, b. 1707, Jacobite, res. Skye Inverness-shire, tr. 31 Mar 1747, fr. London to Barbados, in *Frere*. (P.3.136)(MR143)
4304. McKinnon, Donald, b. 9 Sept 1743, Sleat Inverness-shire, clergyman edu. King's Col Aberdeen 1764, sh. 1767, sett. Westwood Prince William Co Va. (FPA.25.105\18)
4305. McKinnon, Janet, b. 1731, spinner, Jacobite, res. Perth, tr. 1747. (P.33.18) (alias 3364)
4306. McKinnon, John, Covenanter, res. Duppen of Kintyre Argyll, tr. Aug 1685, fr. Leith to Jamaica. (PC.11.136)
4307. McKinnon, John, b. 1747, farmer, res. Isle of Mull, sh. July 1775, fr. Greenock to Ga, in *Georgia*. (PRO.T47.12)
4308. McKinvine, Duncan, servant, adulterer, res. Beach in Ross Argyll, tr. 2 Aug 1733, to Va. (SRO.JC27)
4309. McKirchin, John, b. 1726, farmer, res. Glen Coe Argyll, sh. Feb 1775, fr. Greenock to N.Y., in *Commerce*, m. Ann McGreig, ch. Donald Margaret Donald Eliza. (PRO.T47.12)
4310. McKirdy, James, farmer, res. Largybegg Lamlash Isle of Arran, tr. July 1754. (SRO.JC3.29.591)
4311. McKirrech, Archibald, Covenanter, res. Argyll, tr. Aug 1685, fr. Leith to Jamaica. (PC.11.136)
4312. McKissack, Janet, b. 1718, res. Galloway, sh. May 1774, fr. Stranraer to N.Y., in *Gale*. (PRO.T47.12)
4313. McKissack, Thomas, b. 1748, farmer, res. Galloway, sh. May 1774, fr. Stranraer to N.Y., in *Gale*. (PRO.T47.12)
4314. McKissock, Duncan, b. 1687, Jacobite, tr. 20 Mar 1747, fr. Tilbury. (P.3.138)(MR143)
4315. McKisson, Thomas, b. 1753, shoemaker, res. Perth, sh. May 1775, fr. Greenock to Salem, in *Glasgow Packet*. (PRO.T47.12)
4316. MacKitterick, John, rioter, res. Bridgend Dumfries, pts. William McKethrick or MacKitterick, tr. 1771, fr. Port Glasgow to Md, in

Matty, arr. Port Oxford Md 17 Dec 1771.
(SRO.JC27.10.3)(SM.33.497) (alias 4268)

4317. McKorest, Mary, b. 1757, servant, res. Breadalbane Perthshire, sh. June
1775, fr. Greenock to N.Y., in *Commerce*. (PRO.T47.12)

4318. McKriach(?), Hugh, servant, res. Ardfearnach Jura Argyll, sh. 1754, to
Cape Fear N.C. (SRO.GD64\5.21)

4319. McKriach, Malcolm, res. Ardfernach Jura Argyll, sh. 1754, to Cape Fear
N.C. (SRO.GD64\5.21)

4320. Mackway, William, b. 1701, schoolmaster, res. Galloway, sh. Apr 1721,
fr. London to Md. (CLRO\AIA)

4321. Macky, Alexander, clergyman, res. New Machar Aberdeenshire, sett. St
David's Jamaica, d. 1765. (APB.4.12)

4322. McLachlan, Archibald, farmer, Covenanter, res. Craigintervie Argyll, tr.
Aug 1685. (PC.11.126)

4323. McLachlan, Charles, vagrant & thief, res. Argyll, pts. Dugald Buy
McLachlan, tr. Mar 1726. (JRA.2.383)

4324. McLachlan, Donald, Covenanter, res. Argyll, tr. Aug 1685, fr. Leith to
Jamaica. (PC.11.136)

4325. McLachlan, Dougal, b. 1688, husbandman, Jacobite, res. Argyll, tr.
1747. (P.3.140)(MR181)

4326. McLachlan, Hugh, merchant, res. Cameron Dunbartonshire, sh. pre 1756,
sett. Kingston Jamaica, ch. Margaret. (SRO.SH.10.9.1756)

4327. McLachlan, James, res. Strathlachlan Argyll, pts. Lachlan McLachlan,
sh. pre 1762. (SRO.GD64)

4328. McLachlan, James, b. 22 Jan 1727, Glasgow, tailor, res. Glasgow, pts.
John McLachlan & Elizabeth Luke, sh. 1756. (SRA.B10.15.6682)

4329. McLachlan, John Dow, Covenanter, res. Achahouse Argyll, tr. Aug
1685, fr. Leith to Jamaica. (PC.11.329)

4330. McLachlan, Lachlan, sh. 1737, to Ga. (SPC.43.189)

4331. McLachlan, Peter, b. 1707, weaver, Jacobite, res. Fochabers Morayshire,
tr. 22 Apr 1747, fr. Liverpool to Va, in *Johnson*, arr. Port Oxford
Md 5 Aug 1747. (P.3.142)(MR123)

4332. MacLagan, John, b. 1716, husbandman, res. Kirkoven Galloway, sh. Oct
1736, fr. London to Jamaica. (CLRO\AIA)

4333. MacLairin, Robert, clergyman, sh. 1750, to Va, sett. Southam Va.
(EMA43)(OD17)

4334. McLaren, Alexander, Jacobite, tr. 30 Mar 1716, fr. Liverpool to Antigua,
in *Scipio*. (SPC.1716.310)

4335. McLaren, Alexander, res. Edinburgh, tr. 1696, fr. Newhaven to Va.
(SRO.RH15.14.58)

4336. MacLaren, Alexander, b. 1707, cook & butcher, res. Muthill Perthshire,
sh. 7 Aug 1731, fr. London to Jamaica. (CLRO\AIA)

4337. McLaren, Daniel, Jacobite, tr. 30 Mar 1716, fr. Liverpool to Antigua, in
Scipio. (SPC.1716.310)(CTB31.204)

213

4338. McLaren, Donald, b. 1763, laborer, res. Breadalbane Perthshire, sh. Sept 1775, to Wilmington N.C., in *Jupiter*. (PRO.T47.12)
4339. McLaren, Duncan, Jacobite, res. Perthshire, tr. 1747. (P.3.142)(MR25)
4340. McLaren, Duncan, b. 1745, laborer, res. Breadalbane Perthshire, sh. Sept 1775, to Wilmington N.C., in *Jupiter*. (PRO.T47.12)
4341. McLaren, Hugh, b. 1741, farmer, res. Breadalbane Perthshire, sh. June 1775, fr. Greenock to N.Y., in *Commerce*. (PRO.T47.12)
4342. McLaren, James, Jacobite, tr. 28 July 1716, fr. Liverpool to Va, in *Godspeed*, arr. Md Oct 1716. (SPC.1716.310)(CTB31.209)(HM389)
4343. McLaren, Janet, adulterer, res. Stirlingshire, tr. Sept 1752. (SM.14.461)
4344. McLaren, John, Jacobite, tr. 30 Mar 1716, fr. Liverpool to Antigua, in *Scipio*. (SPC.1716.310)(CTB31.204)
4345. McLaren, John, Jacobite, tr. 30 Mar 1716, fr. Liverpool to Antigua, in *Scipio*. (SPC.1716.310)(CTB31.204)
4346. McLaren, John, Jacobite, tr. 7 May 1716, fr. Liverpool to S.C., in *Susannah*. (SPC.1716.309)(CTB31.206)
4347. McLaren, John, weaver, thief, res. Paisley Renfrewshire, tr. Mar 1765. (SRO.HCR.I.96) (alias 4429)
4348. McLaren, John, b. 1706, banker, res. Edinburgh, sh. Dec 1737, fr. London to Md. (CLRO\AIA)
4349. McLaren, John, b. 1754, wright, res. Edinburgh, sh. Apr 1775, fr. Greenock to N.Y., in *Lilly*. (PRO.T47.12)
4350. McLaren, Lachlan, b. 1750, laborer, res. Breadalbane Perthshire, sh. Sept 1775, to Wilmington N.C., in *Jupiter*. (PRO.T47.12)
4351. McLaren, Laurence, res. Perthshire, tr. Apr 1699. (SRO.B59.26.11.1.4)
4352. McLaren, Lawrence, b. 1755, joiner, res. Breadalbane Perthshire, sh. Sept 1775, to Wilmington N.C., in *Jupiter*. (PRO.T47.12)
4353. McLaren, Murdo, thief, res. Perthshire, tr. 30 Oct 1699. (SRO.B59.26.11.1.1\8)
4354. McLaren, Patrick, Jacobite, tr. 7 May 1716, fr. Liverpool to S.C., in *Susannah*. (SPC.1716.309)(CTB31.206)
4355. McLaren, Walter, Jacobite, tr. 25 June 1716, fr. Liverpool to St Kitts, in *Hockenhill*. (SPC.1716.312)(CTB31.207)
4356. McLaurence, David, b. 1752, barber, res. Edinburgh, sh. Apr 1775, fr. Greenock to N.Y., in *Lilly*. (PRO.T47.12)
4357. McLea, Dougal, b. 1731, Jacobite, tr. 1747, fr. Tilbury. (P.3.142)(MR177)
4358. McLea, John, flesher, thief, res. Glasgow, tr. Sept 1775, fr. Glasgow to West Indies. (SM.37.523)
4359. McLea, William, b. 1746, laborer, res. Islay Argyll, sh. Apr 1775, fr. Greenock to N.Y., in *Lilly*. (PRO.T47.12)
4360. McLean, Alexander, tr. Aug 1685, fr. Leith to Jamaica. (ETR369)

4361. McLean, Alexander, Jacobite, tr. 21 Apr 1716, fr. Liverpool to S.C., in *Wakefield*. (SPC.1716.309)(CTB31.205)
4362. McLean, Alexander, pedlar, Jacobite, res. Inverness, tr. 1747. (P.3.144)(MR25)
4363. McLean, Alexander, b. 1707, Jacobite, res. Ross-shire, tr. 20 Mar 1747, fr. Tilbury to Jamaica, in *St George or Carteret*, arr. Jamaica 1747. (P.3.144)(MR85)(PRO.CO137.58)
4364. McLean, Allan, Jacobite, tr. 24 May 1716, fr. Liverpool to Md, in *Friendship*, arr. Md Aug 1716. (SPC.1716.311)(HM386)
4365. MacLean, Allen, merchant, d. 1783 Kingston Jamaica. (SM.46.111)
4366. McLean, Andrew, Covenanter, res. Argyll, tr. Aug 1685, fr. Leith to Jamaica. (PC.11.330)
4367. McLean, Angus, Jacobite, tr. 1747, in *St George or Carteret*, arr. Jamaica 1747. (PRO.CO137.58)
4368. McLean, Angus, tr. 7 Dec 1665, fr. Leith to Barbados. (ETR104)
4369. McLean, Angus, b. 1704, farmer, Jacobite, res. Eigg Inverness-shire, tr. 31 Mar 1747, fr. London to Jamaica, in *St George or Carteret*, arr. Jamaica 1747. (P.3.144)(MR143)(PRO.CO137.58)
4370. McLean, Archibald, Mull Argyll, surgeon & physician, sett. Trelawney Jamaica, d. 16 Apr 1772 N.Y. (SRO.GD174.159)
4371. McLean, Chrispin, servant, res. Kiles Jura Argyll, sh. 1754, to Cape Fear N.C. (SRO.GD64\5.21)
4372. McLean, Daniel, Jacobite, tr. 26 Apr 1716, fr. Liverpool to Jamaica, in *Two Brothers*, arr. Montserrat June 1747. (SPC.1716.313)(CTB31.205)(CTP.CC.43)
4373. McLean, Donald, planter & merchant, res. Gerradh Ardgour Argyll, d. 1778 St Augustine E Fla, Edin pr1786 CC8.8.127
4374. McLean, Donald, b. 1749, tailor, res. Stirling, sh. Oct 1774, fr. Greenock to Philadelphia, in *Sally*. (PRO.T47.12)
4375. McLean, Dougal, b. 1731, laborer, Jacobite, res. Ross-shire, tr. 31 Mar 1747, fr. London to Barbados , in *Frere*. (P.3.146)(MR177)
4376. McLean, Duncan, Covenanter, res. Argyll, tr. Aug 1685. (PC.11.126)
4377. MacLean, Duncan, sailor, thief, res. Fort William Inverness-shire, tr. May 1775. (AJ1432)
4378. McLean, Duncan, b. 1705, farmer, Jacobite, res. Dormie Ross-shire, tr. 31 Mar 1747, fr. London to Barbados , in *Frere*. (P.3.146)(MR85)
4379. McLean, Duncan, b. 1744, laborer, res. Lochaber Inverness-shire, sh. May 1775, fr. Greenock to N.Y. or Ga, in *Christy*. (PRO.T47.12)
4380. McLean, Duncan, b. 1754, periwigmaker, res. Edinburgh, sh. Mar 1775, fr. London to Md, in *Nelly Frigate*. (PRO.T47.9\11)
4381. McLean, Ewan, weaver, Jacobite, res. Tullocjallan Strathearn Perthshire, tr. 1747. (MR123)

4382. McLean, Farquhar, Jacobite, res. Ross-shire, tr. 31 Mar 1747, fr. London to Jamaica, in *St George or Carteret*, arr. Jamaica 1747. (P.3.146)(MR85)(PRO.CO137.58)
4383. McLean, Hector, b. 1703, farmer, Jacobite, res. Langwell Ross-shire, tr. 31 Mar 1747, fr. London to Barbados, in *Frere*. (P.3.148)(MR85)
4384. McLean, Hector, b. 1707, Jacobite, res. Cromarty, tr. 20 Mar 1747, fr. Tilbury. (P.3.148)(MR85)
4385. McLean, Hugh, Jacobite, tr. 22 Apr 1716, fr. Liverpool to Va, in *Johnson*, arr. Port Oxford Md 5 Aug 1747. (PRO.T1.328)
4386. McLean, Hugh, Covenanter, res. Argyll, tr. Aug 1685, fr. Leith to Jamaica. (PC.11.330)
4387. McLean, Hugh, res. Knockcrainie Jura Argyll, sh. 1754, to Cape Fear N.C. (SRO.GD64\5.21)
4388. MacLean, James, burglar, res. Gateside East Lothian, tr. May 1774. (AJ1374)
4389. McLean, James, b. 1728, nailmaker, Jacobite, res. Stirling, tr. 5 May 1747, fr. Liverpool to Leeward Islands, in *Veteran*, arr. Martinique June 1747. (P.3.148)(MR74)(PRO.SP36.102)
4390. McLean, James, b. 1759, merchant, res. Ayr, sh. July 1775, fr. Greenock to Jamaica, in *Isabella*. (PRO.T47.12)
4391. McLean, John, gardener, Jacobite, res. Laig Eigg Argyll, tr. 1747. (MR144)
4392. McLean, John, Covenanter, tr. July 1685. (PC.11.136)
4393. McLean, John, Covenanter, res. Portindryan Argyll, tr. Aug 1685, fr. Leith to Jamaica. (PC.11.136)
4394. McLean, John, Jacobite, tr. 21 Apr 1716, fr. Liverpool to S.C., in *Wakefield*. (SPC.1716.309)(CTB31.205)
4395. MacLean, John, Jacobite, tr. 24 May 1716, fr. Liverpool to Md, in *Friendship*, arr. Md Aug 1716. (HM387)
4396. MacLean, John, gardener, Jacobite, res. Laig Eigg Argyll, tr. 1747, fr. Tilbury. (P.3.148)
4397. McLean, John, Jacobite, tr. 24 Feb 1747, fr. Liverpool to Va, in *Gildart*, arr. Port North Potomac Md 5 Aug 1747. (PRO.T1.328)
4398. McLean, John, sh. May 1775, fr. Kirkcudbright to P.E.I., in *Lovely Nelly*. (PRO.T47.12)
4399. McLean, John, merchant, sett. Kingston Jamaica, d. 27 Nov 1764. (SM.27.55)
4400. McLean, John, b. 1661, d. 1770 Orange Co N.Y. (SM.32.630)
4401. McLean, John, b. 1722, Jacobite, tr. 1747, fr. Tilbury. (P.3.148)(MR144)
4402. McLean, John, b. 1731, laborer, Jacobite, res. Argyll, tr. 31 Mar 1747, fr. London to Jamaica, in *St George or Carteret*, arr. Jamaica 1747. (P.3.148)(MR181)(PRO.CO137.58)

216

4403. McLean, John, b. 1740, laborer, res. Lochaber Inverness-shire, sh. May 1775, fr. Greenock to N.Y. or Ga, in *Christy*. (PRO.T47.12)
4404. McLean, John, b. 1754, servant, res. Loch Broom Ross-shire, sh. Nov 1774, fr. Stornaway to N.Y., in *Peace & Plenty*. (PRO.T47.12)
4405. McLean, Katherine, servant, res. Coranhouse Jura Argyll, sh. 1754, to Cape fear N.C. (SRO.GD64\5.21)
4406. McLean, Lauchlan, thief, res. Mull Argyll, pts. Angus McLean, tr. 28 Nov 1704, fr. Leith to Md. (SRO.PC2.28.307)
4407. McLean, Lauchlan, thief, res. Aberdeenshire, tr. 1773, in *Donald*, arr. Port James Upper District Va 13 Mar 1773. (AJ1292)(SRO.JC.27.10.3) (alias 6997)
4408. McLean, Malcolm, b. 1730, bricklayer, Jacobite, tr. 24 Feb 1747, fr. Liverpool to Md, in *Gildart*, arr. Port North Potomac Md 5 Aug 1747. (P.3.150)(PRO.T1.328)
4409. McLean, Malcolm, b. 1750, farmer, res. Barvas Isle of Lewis, sh. May 1774, fr. Stornaway to Philadelphia, in *Friendship*. (PRO.T47.12)
4410. McLean, Margaret, b. 1745, res. Paisley Renfrewshire, sh. Apr 1775, fr. Greenock to Salem, in *Glasgow Packet*. (PRO.T47.12)
4411. McLean, Mary, infanticide, res. Argyll, tr. Aug 1733, to Va, m. Archibald McGowan or McDonald. (JRA.2.464)
4412. MacLean, Neil, horsethief, res. Kilmichael, pts. Gillian Campbell, tr. 1775, fr. Greenock, in *Rainbow*, arr. Port Hampton Va 3 May 1775. (SRO.JC27.10.3) (alias 974)
4413. McLean, Owen, weaver, Jacobite, res. Tullochallan Strathearn Perthshire, tr. 1747. (P.3.150)
4414. McLean, Peggy, b. 1756, res. Edinburgh, sh. Apr 1775, fr. Greenock to N.Y., in *Lilly*. (PRO.T47.12)
4415. McLean, Peter, Jacobite, tr. 30 Mar 1716, fr. Liverpool to Antigua, in *Scipio*. (SPC.1716.310)(CTB31.204)
4416. McLean, Peter, b. 1719, soldier, Jacobite, tr. 1747. (P.3.152)(MR62)
4417. McLean, Thomas, b. 1722, servant, Jacobite, res. Auchterlintor Ross-shire, tr. 31 Mar 1747, fr. London to Barbados , in *Frere*. (P.3.152)(MR85)
4418. McLean, William, Covenanter, tr. July 1685. (PC.11.114)
4419. MacLean, William, b. 1712, cooper, res. Portsoy Banffshire, sh. Aug 1734, fr. London to Md or Va. (CLRO\AIA)
4420. McLean, William, b. 1715, laborer, Jacobite, res. Inverness, tr. 5 May 1747, fr. Liverpool to Leeward Islands, in *Veteran*, arr. Martinique June 1747. (P.3.152)(PRO.SP36.102)
4421. McLean, William, b. 1733, Jacobite, res. Loch Broom Ross-shire, tr. 1747, fr. Tilbury. (P.3.152)(MR86)
4422. McLean, William, b. 1744, farmer, res. Bayble Isle of Lewis, sh. May 1774, fr. Stornaway to Philadelphia, in *Friendship*, m. Hendrea Murray, ch. Donald John. (PRO.T47.12)

4423. McLeanan, Alexander, b. 1735, servant, res. Beauly Inverness-shire, sh. July 1775, fr. Stornaway to Philadelphia, in *Clementina*. (PRO.T47.12)
4424. McLeanan, Anne, b. 1755, servant, res. Ferintosh Ross & Cromarty, sh. July 1775, fr. Stornaway to Philadelphia, in *Clementina*. (PRO.T47.12)
4425. McLeanan, Anne, b. 1762, servant, res. Beauly Inverness-shire, sh. July 1775, fr. Stornaway to Philadelphia, in *Clementina*. (PRO.T47.12)
4426. McLeanan, Marion, b. 1757, servant, res. Inverness, sh. July 1775, fr. Stornaway to Philadelphia, in *Clementina*. (PRO.T47.12)
4427. McLear, Alexander, Jacobite, tr. 26 Apr 1716, fr. Liverpool to Jamaica, in *Two Brothers*, arr. Montserrat June 1716. (SPC.1716.313)(CTB31.205)(CTP.CC.43)
4428. McLearins, Alexander, Jacobite, tr. 30 Mar 1716, fr. Liverpool to Antigua, in *Scipio*. (SPC.1716.310)(CTB31.204)
4429. McLearn, John, weaver, thief, res. Paisley Renfrewshire, tr. Mar 1765. (SRO.HCR.I.96) (alias 4347)
4430. MacLehose, James, b. 1754, Glasgow, attorney edu. Glasgow Uni 1767, res. Glasgow, pts. William MacLehose, sh. Nov 1784, fr. London to Jamaica, sett. Kingston Jamaica, d. Mar 1812 Kingston. (GUMA84)(SRO.RD3.280.579)
4431. McLehose, John, merchant, res. Glasgow, d. 1782 Jamaica. (SRO.SH.23.12.1782)
4432. McLeish, Duncan, b. 1729, pedlar, Jacobite, res. Perthshire, tr. 5 May 1747, fr. Liverpool to Leeward Islands, in *Veteran*, arr. Martinique June 1747. (P.3.152)(MR74)(PRO.SP36.102)
4433. McLelan, Margaret, Covenanter, tr. Sept 1685, fr. Leith to East N.J., in *Henry & Francis*. (PC.11.154)
4434. McLellan, Hugh, b. 1757, weaver, res. Paisley Renfrewshire, sh. Feb 1774, fr. Greenock to N.Y., in *Commerce*. (PRO.T47.12)
4435. McLellan, John, b. 1748, laborer, res. Glasgow, sh. Apr 1775, fr. Greenock to N.Y., in *Lilly*. (PRO.T47.12)
4436. MacLellan, William, d. 11 Dec 1698 Darien. (NLS.RY2b819)
4437. McLenan, Kenneth, b. 1753, servant, res. Contin Ross-shire, sh. Nov 1774, fr. Stornaway to N.Y., in *Peace & Plenty*. (PRO.T47.12)
4438. McLennan, Angus, farmer, Jacobite, res. Morar Inverness-shire, tr. 20 Mar 1747, fr. Tilbury. (P.3.154)(MR158)
4439. McLennan, Angus, b. 1714, farmer, Jacobite, res. Burblach Morar Inverness-shire, tr. 31 Mar 1747, fr. London to Barbados , in *Frere*. (P.3.154)(MR158)
4440. McLennan, Donald, farmer, Jacobite, res. Burblach Morar Inverness-shire, tr. 31 Mar 1747, fr. London to Barbados, in *Frere*. (P.3.134)(MR159)

4441. McLennan, Donald, farmer, Jacobite, res. Kilconan Inverness-shire, tr. 20 Mar 1747, fr. Tilbury. (P.3.134)(MR159)
4442. McLennan, Duncan, b. 1704, dairyman, Jacobite, res. Ross-shire, tr. 20 Mar 1747, fr. London to Barbados, in *Frere*. (P.3.154)(MR86)
4443. McLennan, Farquhar, b. 1709, farmer, Jacobite, res. Burt Glen Garry Inverness-shire, tr. 1747, fr. Tilbury. (P.3.154)(MR159)
4444. McLennan, John, b. 1714, tailor, Jacobite, res. Inverness, tr. 31 Mar 1747, fr. London to Barbados, in *Frere*. (P.3.156)(MR159)
4445. McLennan, John, b. 1743, servant, res. Isle of Skye Inverness-shire, sh. July 1775, fr. Stornaway to Philadelphia, in *Clementina*. (PRO.T47.12)
4446. McLennan, Murdoch, b. 1765, servant, res. Beauly Inverness-shire, sh. July 1775, fr. Stornaway to Philadelphia, in *Clementina*. (PRO.T47.12)
4447. McLennan, Roderick, b. 1722, farmer, Jacobite, res. Achtascaild Ross-shire, tr. 31 Mar 1747, fr. London to Barbados , in *Frere*. (P.3.156)(MR86)
4448. MacLeod of Colvecks, John, planter, d. 12 May 1775 Jamaica. (SM.37.406)
4449. McLeod, Aeneas, b. 1714, farmer, res. Tongue Sutherland, sh. Apr 1774, to Wilmington N.C., in *Bachelor of Leith*. (PRO.T47.12)
4450. McLeod, Alexander, Jacobite, tr. 22 Apr 1747, fr. Liverpool to Va, in *Johnson*, arr. Port Oxford Md 5 Aug 1747. (PRO.T1.328)
4451. McLeod, Alexander, b. 1697, husbandman, Jacobite, res. Dingwall Sutherland, tr. 20 Mar 1747, fr. Tilbury. (P.3.156)(MR86)
4452. McLeod, Alexander, b. 1697, soldier, Jacobite, res. Nithsdale Dumfries-shire, tr. 1747. (P.3.156)
4453. McLeod, Alexander, b. 1707, ploughman, Jacobite, res. Loch Broom Ross-shire, tr. 1747, fr. Tilbury. (P.3.156)(MR86)
4454. McLeod, Alexander, b. 1717, Jacobite, res. Inverness, tr. 1747. (P.3.156)
4455. McLeod, Alexander, b. 1721, farmer, Jacobite, res. Kirogarreoch Loch Broom Ross-shire, tr. 31 Mar 1747, fr. London to Jamaica, in *St George or Carteret*, arr. Jamaica 1747. (P.3.156)(MR86)(PRO.CO137.58)
4456. McLeod, Alexander, b. 1728, laborer, Jacobite, res. Inverness, tr. 5 May 1747, fr. Liverpool to Leeward Islands, in *Veteran*, arr. Martinique June 1716. (P.3.156)(MR159)(PRO.SP36.102)
4457. McLeod, Angus, tr. 1775, fr. Greenock to Va, in *Rainbow*, arr. Port Hampton Va 3 May 1775. (SRO.JC27.10.3)
4458. McLeod, Angus, b. 1712, laborer, Jacobite, res. Inverness-shire, tr. 22 Apr 1747, fr. Liverpool to Va, in *Johnson*, arr. Port Oxford Md 5 Aug 1747. (P.3.156)(MR159)(PRO.T1.328)

219

4459. McLeod, Angus, b. 1744, weaver, res. Stornaway Isle of Lewis, sh. May 1774, fr. Stornaway to Philadelphia, in *Friendship*, m. Ann McDonald, ch. Ann. (PRO.T47.12)
4460. McLeod, Angus, b. 1759, servant, res. Brenish Isle of Lewis, sh. May 1774, fr. Stornaway to Philadelphia, in *Friendship*. (PRO.T47.12)
4461. McLeod, Ann, b. 1752, servant, res. Barvas Isle of Lewis, sh. May 1774, fr. Stornaway to Philadelphia, in *Friendship*. (PRO.T47.12)
4462. McLeod, Daniel, b. 1703, Jacobite, res. Ross-shire, tr. 31 Mar 1747, fr. London to Barbados, in *Frere*. (P.3.158)(MR86)
4463. McLeod, Donald, servant, housebreaker & thief, res. Borrowstoun Caithness, tr. 1772, fr. Glasgow. (AJ1292\8) (alias 253)
4464. McLeod, Donald, b. 1703, farmer, Jacobite, res. Coigach Ross-shire, tr. 20 Mar 1747, fr. London to Jamaica, in *St George or Carteret*, arr. Jamaica 1747. (P.3.158)(MR86)(PRO.CO137.58)
4465. McLeod, Donald, b. 1721, farmer, Jacobite, res. Crosshill Ross-shire, tr. 31 Mar 1747, fr. London to Jamaica, in *St George or Carteret*, arr. Jamaica 1747. (P.3.158)(MR119)(PRO.CO137.58)
4466. McLeod, Donald, b. 1725, servant, Jacobite, res. Coigach Ross-shire, tr. 31 Mar 1747, fr. London to Jamaica, in *St George or Carteret*, arr. Jamaica 1747. (P.3.158)(MR86)(PRO.CO137.58)
4467. McLeod, Duncan, soldier, Jacobite, res. Inverness-shire, tr. 31 Mar 1747, fr. Tilbury. (P.3.160)(MR86)
4468. McLeod, Duncan, b. 1723, Jacobite, res. Cromarty, tr. 20 Mar 1747. (P.3.160)(MR86)
4469. McLeod, Duncan, b. 1724, Jacobite, res. Ross-shire, tr. 20 Mar 1747. (P.3.160)
4470. McLeod, Emilia, b. 1757, servant, res. Inverness, sh. May 1775, fr. Leith to Philadelphia, in *Friendship*. (PRO.T47.12)
4471. McLeod, Henrietta, tr. 1775, fr. Greenock to Va, in *Rainbow*, arr. Port Hampton Va 3 May 1775, m. Angus McLeod. (SRO.JC27.10.3)
4472. McLeod, Hugh, thief, res. Aberdeenshire, tr. May 1769. (AJ1115) (alias 2948)
4473. McLeod, Jean, b. 1758, res. Bayble Isle of Lewis, sh. May 1774, fr. Stornaway to Philadelphia, in *Friendship*. (PRO.T47.12)
4474. McLeod, John, Jacobite, tr. 21 Apr 1716, fr. Liverpool to S.C., in *Wakefield*. (SPC.1716.309)(CTB31.205)
4475. McLeod, John, clergyman, sh. 1735, sett. Darien Ga & Edisto Island S.C. (F.7.664)
4476. McLeod, John, b. 1690, farmer, Jacobite, res. Ullapool Ross-shire, tr. 31 Mar 1747, fr. London to Barbados, in *Frere*. (P.3.162)(MR86)
4477. McLeod, John, b. 1706, farmer, Jacobite, res. Dormie Ross-shire, tr. 20 Mar 1747, fr. Tilbury. (P.3.162)(MR86)

4478. McLeod, John, b. 1707, cook, Jacobite, res. Glenelg Inverness-shire, tr. 31 Mar 1747, fr. London to Jamaica, in *St George or Carteret*, arr. Jamaica 1747. (P.3.162)(PRO.CO137.58)

4479. McLeod, John, b. 1722, laborer, Jacobite, tr. 5 May 1747, fr. Liverpool to Leeward Islands, in *Veteran*, arr. Martinique June 1747. (P.3.162)(MR86)(PRO.SP36.102)

4480. McLeod, John, b. 1726, servant, Jacobite, res. Langwell Loch Broom Ross-shire, tr. 31 Mar 1747, fr. London to Jamaica, in *St George or Carteret*, arr. Jamaica 1747. (P.3.162)(MR86)(PRO.CO137.58)

4481. McLeod, John, b. 1729, cattleherd, Jacobite, res. Ross-shire, tr. 31 Mar 1747, fr. London to Jamaica, in *St George or Carteret*, arr. Jamaica 1747. (P.3.162)(MR86)(PRO.CO137.58)

4482. McLeod, John, b. 1741, farmer, res. Carloway Isle of Lewis, sh. May 1774, fr. Stornaway to Philadelphia, in *Friendship*, m. Katherine McIver, ch. Margaret Ann John Malcolm. (PRO.T47.12)

4483. McLeod, John, b. 1759, servant, res. Galson Isle of Lewis, sh. May 1774, fr. Stornaway to Philadelphia, in *Friendship*. (PRO.T47.12)

4484. McLeod, John jr, b. 1760, tailor, res. Glasgow, sh. Feb 1774, fr. Greenock to N.Y., in *Commerce*. (PRO.T47.12)

4485. McLeod, John sr, b. 1739, tailor, res. Glasgow, sh. Feb 1774, fr. Greenock to N.Y., in *Commerce*. (PRO.T47.12)

4486. McLeod, Kenneth, Jacobite, tr. 24 Feb 1747, fr. Liverpool to Va, in *Gildart*, arr. Port North Potomac Md 5 Aug 1747. (P.3.164)(PRO.T1.328)

4487. McLeod, Malcolm, b. 1756, servant, res. Stornaway Isle of Lewis, sh. May 1774, fr. Stornaway to Philadelphia, in *Friendship*. (PRO.T47.12)

4488. McLeod, Malcolm, b. 1760, servant, res. Contin Ross-shire, sh. July 1775, fr. Stornaway to Philadelphia, in *Clementina*. (PRO.T47.12)

4489. McLeod, Mary, b. 1746, res. Paisley Renfrewshire, sh. Apr 1775, fr. Greenock to N.Y., in *Lilly*. (PRO.T47.12)

4490. McLeod, Mary, b. 1754, servant, sh. May 1774, fr. Stornaway to Philadelphia, in *Friendship*. (PRO.T47.12)

4491. McLeod, Murdoch, b. 1702, farmer, Jacobite, res. Isle of Skye, tr. 31 Mar 1747, fr. London to Barbados , in *Frere*. (P.3.166)(MR159)

4492. McLeod, Murdoch, b. 1726, servant, Jacobite, res. Ferintosh Ross-shire, tr. 31 Mar 1747, fr. London to Jamaica, in *St George or Carteret*, arr. Jamaica 1747. (P.3.164)(MR86)(PRO.CO137.58)

4493. McLeod, Murdoch, b. 1729, herdsman, Jacobite, res. Asson Ross-shire, tr. 31 Mar 1747, fr. London to Barbados , in *Frere*. (P.3.164)(MR86)

4494. McLeod, Murdoch, b. 1742, farmer, res. Coigach Ross-shire, sh. Nov 1774, fr. Stornaway to N.Y., in *Peace & Plenty*, m. Christian .., ch. Mary Isabel. (PRO.T47.12)

221

4495. McLeod, Murdoch, b. 1757, servant, res. Contin Ross-shire, sh. July 1775, fr. Stornaway to Philadelphia, in *Clementina*. (PRO.T47.12)
4496. McLeod, Neil, b. 1726, husbandman, Jacobite, res. Hillach Raasay Inverness-shire, tr. 20 Mar 1747, fr. London to Jamaica, in *St George or Carteret*, arr. Jamaica 1747. (P.3.166)(MR185)(PRO.CO137.58)
4497. McLeod, Neil, b. 1744, farmer, res. Melbost Isle of Lewis, sh. May 1774, fr. Stornaway to Philadelphia, in *Friendship*, m. Margaret Murray, ch. Christian Normand Margaret. (PRO.T47.12)
4498. McLeod, Neill, b. 1740, merchant, res. Stornaway Isle of Lewis, sh. Nov 1774, fr. Stornaway to N.Y., in *Peace & Plenty*, m. Margaret ..., ch. John Janet Allan. (PRO.T47.12)
4499. McLeod, Norman, b. 1760, servant, res. Bayble Isle of Lewis, sh. May 1774, fr. Stornaway to Philadelphia, in *Friendship*. (PRO.T47.12)
4500. McLeod, Peggy, b. 1754, servant, res. Stornaway Isle of Lewis, sh. May 1774, fr. Stornaway to Philadelphia, in *Friendship*. (PRO.T47.12)
4501. McLeod, Ranald, b. 1724, farmer, res. Coigach Ross-shire, sh. Nov 1774, fr. Stornaway to N.Y., in *Peace & Plenty*. (PRO.T47.12)
4502. McLeod, Roderick, b. 1727, Jacobite, res. Langwell Ross-shire, tr. 31 Mar 1747, fr. London to Jamaica, in *St George or Carteret*, arr. Jamaica 1747. (P.3.166)(MR86)(PRO.CO137.58)
4503. McLeod, Roderick, b. 1758, clerk, sh. Jan 1775, fr. London to Tobago, in *Nautilus*. (PRO.T47.9\11)
4504. McLeod, Saunders, b. 1692, Jacobite, tr. 31 Mar 1747. (P.3.166)(MR86)
4505. McLeod, William, b. 1758, farmer, res. Adrachoolish Sutherland, sh. Apr 1774, to Wilmington N.C., in *Bachelor of Leith*. (PRO.T47.12)
4506. McLine, Alexander, Covenanter, res. Argyll, tr. Aug 1685, fr. Leith to Jamaica. (PC.11.136)
4507. McLinzey, Murray, b. 1746, cartwright, sh. Aug 1774, fr. London to Pensacola, in *Success's Increase*. (PRO.T47.9\11)
4508. McLochlan, Archibald, b. 1746, farmer, res. Doune Perthshire, sh. July 1775, fr. Greenock to Ga, in *Georgia*. (PRO.T47.12)
4509. McLoughlan, John, Jacobite, tr. 24 May 1716, fr. Liverpool to Md or Va, in *Friendship*. (SPC.1716.311)
4510. McLoughlin, Archibald, Jacobite, tr. 29 June 1716, fr. Liverpool to Jamaica or Va, in *Elizabeth & Anne*. (SPC.1716.310)(CTB31.208)
4511. McLure, John, sh. pre 1685, sett. S.C. (ECJ134)
4512. McMartin, Angus, b. 1727, Jacobite, tr. 31 Mar 1747, fr. London to Barbados, in *Frere*. (P.3.168)(MR144)
4513. McMartin, Angus, b. 1729, cowherd, Jacobite, res. Kirkton Isle of Eigg, tr. 31 Mar 1747, fr. London to Jamaica, in *St George or Carteret*, arr. Jamaica 1747. (P.3.168)(MR144)(PRO.CO137.58)
4514. MacMartin, Donald Dow Oig, thief, res. Westermains Braes of Aird Inverness-shire, tr. June 1754. (SM.16.203) (alias 794)

4515. McMartin, Duncan, b. 1728, farmer, res. Glen Coe or Breadalbane, sh. Feb 1775, fr. Greenock to N.Y., in *Commerce*, sett. Kingsborough Patent N.Y., m. Isobel Robertson, ch. Eliza Katherine Janet John Isobel Mary. (PRO.T47.12)

4516. McMartine Donald, b. 1755, wright, res. Breadalbane Perthshire, pts. Duncan McMartine & Isobel McGregor, sh. June 1775, fr. Greenock to N.Y., in *Commerce*. (PRO.T47.12)

4517. McMartine, Duncan, b. 1712, farmer, res. Breadalbane Perthshire, sh. June 1775, fr. Greenock to N.Y., in *Commerce*, m. Isobel McGregor. (PRO.T47.12)

4518. McMartine, Hugh, b. 1754, servant, res. Breadalbane Perthshire, pts. Duncan McMartine & Isobel McGregor, sh. June 1775, fr. Greenock to N.Y., in *Commerce*. (PRO.T47.12)

4519. McMartine, John, b. 1750, tailor, res. Glasgow, sh. Apr 1775, fr. Greenock to N.Y., in *Lilly*. (PRO.T47.12)

4520. McMartine, Malcolm, b. 1746, cooper, res. Glasgow, sh. Apr 1775, fr. Greenock to N.Y., in *Lilly*. (PRO.T47.12)

4521. McMartine, Margaret, b. 1751, servant, res. Breadalbane Perthshire, pts. Duncan McMartine & Isobel McGregor, sh. June 1775, fr. Greenock to N.Y., in *Commerce*. (PRO.T47.12)

4522. McMartine, Mary, b. 1752, brushmaker, res. Glasgow, sh. Apr 1775, fr. Greenock to N.Y., in *Lilly*. (PRO.T47.12)

4523. McMartine, Peter, b. 1754, smith, res. Breadalbane Perthshire, sh. June 1775, fr. Greenock to N.Y., in *Commerce*. (PRO.T47.12)

4524. MacMaster, Elizabeth, b. 1753, res. Galloway, sh. May 1774, fr. Stranraer to N.Y., in *Gale*. (PRO.T47.12)

4525. McMaster, John, b. 1754, wright, res. Galloway, sh. May 1774, fr. Stranraer to N.Y., in *Gale*. (PRO.T47.12)

4526. McMaster, Malcolm, b. 1687, husbandman, Jacobite, res. Fort William Inverness-shire, tr. 31 Mar 1747, fr. London to Jamaica, in *St George or Carteret*, arr. Jamaica 1747. (P.3.168)(PRO.CO137.58)

4527. McMaster, Robert, b. 1750, merchant, res. Galloway, sh. May 1774, fr. Stranraer to N.Y., in *Gale*. (PRO.T47.12)

4528. McMichael, Duncan, Covenanter, res. Islay Argyll, tr. Aug 1685, fr. Leith to Jamaica. (PC.11.136)

4529. McMichael, Roger, Covenanter, res. Dalry Galloway, tr. Aug 1685, fr. Leith to Jamaica. (PC.11.316)

4530. McMicken, Eleanora, b. 1749, res. Galloway, sh. May 1774, fr. Stranraer to N.Y., in *Gale*. (PRO.T47.12)

4531. McMicken, James, b. 1770, res. Galloway, sh. May 1774, fr. Stranraer to N.Y., in *Gale*. (PRO.T47.12)

4532. McMicken, Janet, b. 1753, res. Galloway, sh. May 1774, fr. Stranraer to N.Y., in *Gale*. (PRO.T47.12)

4533. McMicken, William, b. 1749, laborer, res. Dailly, sh. May 1774, fr. Stranraer to N.Y., in *Gale*. (PRO.T47.12)
4534. McMicken, William, b. 1772, res. Galloway, sh. May 1774, fr. Stranraer to N.Y., in *Gale*. (PRO.T47.12)
4535. McMicking, John, b. 1753, farmer, res. Galloway, sh. May 1774, fr. Stranraer to N.Y., in *Gale*. (PRO.T47.12)
4536. McMicking, Thomas, b. 1750, farmer, res. Galloway, sh. May 1774, fr. Stranraer to N.Y., in *Gale*. (PRO.T47.12)
4537. McMiken, Alexander, b. 1755, laborer, res. Inch Wigtonshire, sh. 31 May 1775, fr. Stranraer to N.Y., in *Jackie*. (PRO.T47.12)
4538. McMiken, Gilbert, b. 1735, laborer, res. Inch Wigtonshire, sh. 31 May 1775, fr. Stranraer to N.Y., in *Jackie*, m. Jean McKinnel. (PRO.T47.12)
4539. McMiken, Hugh, merchant, sh. pre 1774, sett. Portsmouth Va. (OD132)(SRO.CC8.8.123)
4540. McMiken, Janet, b. 1739, res. New Luce Wigtonshire, sh. 31 May 1775, fr. Stranraer to N.Y., in *Jackie*. (PRO.T47.12)
4541. McMiken, Sarah, b. 1754, res. New Luce Wigtonshire, sh. 31 May 1775, fr. Stranraer to N.Y., in *Jackie*. (PRO.T47.12)
4542. McMikine, John, b. 1734, joiner, res. Galloway, sh. May 1774, fr. Stranraer to N.Y., in *Gale*, m. Rosina ..., ch. Rosina Agnes May Jean Nanny. (PRO.T47.12)
4543. McMiking, James, b. 1756, farmer, res. Galloway, sh. May 1774, fr. Stranraer to N.Y., in *Gale*. (PRO.T47.12)
4544. McMillan, Alexander, Covenanter, res. Galloway, tr. Dec 1685, fr. Leith to Barbados. (ETR389)(PC.11.386)
4545. McMillan, Archibald, farmer, res. Kintyre Argyll, sh. Sept 1774, fr. Greenock to Wilmington N.C., in *Diana*. (PRO.T47.12)
4546. McMillan, Archibald, b. 1716, farmer, res. Glen Orchy Argyll, sh. Aug 1774, fr. Greenock to Wilmington N.C., in *Ulysses*, m. Mary Taylor, ch. Barbara. (PRO.T47.12)
4547. McMillan, Donald, b. 1717, Jacobite, res. Sheuglie Glen Urquhart Inverness-shire, tr. 1747. (P.3.168)(MR159)
4548. McMillan, Duncan, Covenanter, res. Carradale Kintyre Argyll, tr. Aug 1685, fr. Leith to Jamaica. (PC.11.329)
4549. McMillan, John, Covenanter, res. Argyll, tr. July 1685, fr. Leith to N.E. (PC.11.94)
4550. McMillan, John, b. 1738, res. Balmaghie Kirkcudbrightshire, sh. May 1774, fr. Kirkcudbright to N.Y., in *Gale*, m. Elizabeth Carson, ch. James James Janet Agnes Elizabeth. (PRO.T47.12)
4551. McMillan, John, b. 1748, farmer, res. Kintyre Argyll, sh. Aug 1774, fr. Greenock to Wilmington N.C., in *Ulysses*, m. Jean Huie. (PRO.T47.12)

4552. McMillan, John, b. 1750, laborer, res. Wigton, sh. Apr 1775, fr. Greenock to N.Y., in *Lilly*. (PRO.T47.12)
4553. McMillan, John, b. 1755, servant, res. Poolewe Ross-shire, sh. May 1774, fr. Stornaway to Philadelphia, in *Friendship*. (PRO.T47.12)
4554. McMillan, Malcolm, b. 1716, farmer, res. Kintyre Argyll, sh. Aug 1774, fr. Greenock to Wilmington N.C., in *Ulysses*, m. Catherine MacAlester, ch. Daniel Archibald Gilbert. (PRO.T47.12)
4555. McMillan, Margaret, b. 1749, res. Galloway, sh. May 1774, fr. Stranraer to N.Y., in *Gale*. (PRO.T47.12)
4556. MacMillan, Martin, b. 1699, husbandman, res. Galloway, sh. Mar 1730, fr. London to Jamaica. (CLRO\AIA)
4557. McMillan, William, clergyman edu. Glasgow Uni 1720, sh. 1724, to Philadelphia. (AP193)(F.7.664)
4558. McMorran, Edward, b. 1749, merchant, res. Dumfries, sh. May 1774, fr. Dumfries to N.Y., in *Adventure*. (PRO.T47.12)
4559. McMurchie, Hugh, b. 1738, farmer, res. Kintyre Argyll, sh. Sept 1774, fr. Greenock to Wilmington N.C., in *Diana*, m. Elizabeth Kelso, ch. Archibald Patrick Mary Elizabeth Robert. (PRO.T47.12)
4560. McMurray, Alan, b. 1708, farmer, res. Galmistal Eigg Inverness-shire, tr. 31 Mar 1747, fr. London to Jamaica, in *St George or Carteret*, arr. Jamaica 1747. (P.3.168)(MR144)(PRO.CO137.58)
4561. McMurray, Alexander, b. 1748, husbandman, res. Queenshill, sh. May 1774, fr. Stranraer to N.Y., in *Gale*. (PRO.T47.12)
4562. MacMurtry, Elizabeth, infanticide, res. Paisley Renfrewshire, tr. Oct 1774, fr. Glasgow. (SM.36.720)
4563. McNab, Archibald, soldier, d. pre 1767 N.Y., PCC pr1767
4564. McNab, James, thief, tr. 30 July 1750. (SRO.HCR.I.81)
4565. McNab, John, b. 1680, laborer, Jacobite, tr. 22 Apr 1747, fr. Liverpool to Va, in *Johnson*, arr. Port Oxford Md 5 Aug 1747. (P.3.170)(MR25)(PRO.T1.328)
4566. McNab, Patrick, thief, res. Perthshire, tr. 30 Oct 1699. (SRO.B59.26.11.1\6-8)
4567. McNabb, Alexander, Jacobite, tr. 26 Apr 1716, fr. Liverpool to Jamaica, in *Two Brothers*, arr. Montserrat June 1716. (SPC.1716.313)(CTB31.206)(CTP.CC.43)
4568. McNabb, John, Jacobite, tr. 26 Apr 1716, fr. Liverpool to Jamaica, in *Two Brothers*, arr. Montserrat June 1716. (SPC.1716.313)(CTB31.206)(CTP.CC.43)
4569. McNabb, John, b. 1761, laborer, res. Argyll, sh. May 1775, fr. Greenock to Wilmington N.C., in *Ulysses*, m. Jean ... (PRO.T47.12)
4570. McNabb, Thomas, Jacobite, tr. 24 May 1716, fr. Liverpool to Md, in *Friendship*, arr. Md Aug 1716. (SPC.1716.311)(HM387)
4571. McNabb, Tibby, b. 1755, res. Argyll, sh. May 1775, fr. Greenock to Wilmington N.C., in *Ulysses*. (PRO.T47.12)

4572. McNair, Robert, cooper, res. Newark Glasgow, sh. 14 July 1698, fr. Leith to Darien, in *Caledonia*, m. Katherine Purdy, Edin pr1707 CC8.8.83
4573. McNamail, Dougald, res. Jura Argyll, sh. 1754, to Cape Fear N.C. (SRO.GD64\5.21)
4574. McNamaile, Dugald, shoemaker, res. Jura Argyll, sh. 1754, to Cape Fear N.C. (SRO.GD64\5.21)
4575. McNaught, Daniel, b. 1751, husbandman, res. Largs of Twynholm Kirkcudbrightshire, sh. May 1774, fr. Stranraer to N.Y., in *Gale*. (PRO.T47.12)
4576. McNaught, John, b. 1754, husbandman, res. Largs of Twynholm Kirkcudbrightshire, sh. May 1774, fr. Stranraer to N.Y., in *Gale*. (PRO.T47.12)
4577. McNaughton, Angus, b. 1746, farmer, res. Breadalbane Perthshire, sh. June 1775, fr. Greenock to N.Y., in *Commerce*, m. Katherine Robertson, ch. John Jean. (PRO.T47.12)
4578. McNaughton, Christian, b. 1755, servant, res. Breadalbane Perthshire, sh. June 1775, fr. Greenock to N.Y., in *Commerce*. (PRO.T47.12)
4579. McNaughton, Donald, b. 1745, farmer, res. Breadalbane Perthshire, sh. May 1775, fr. Greenock to N.Y., in *Lilly*. (PRO.T47.12)
4580. McNaughton, Donald, b. 1756, farmer, res. Breadalbane Perthshire, sh. June 1775, fr. Greenock to N.Y., in *Commerce*. (PRO.T47.12)
4581. McNaughton, Duncan, Jacobite, tr. 7 May 1716, fr. Liverpool to S.C., in *Susannah*. (SPC.1716.309)(CTB31.206)
4582. McNaughton, Janet, b. 1742, res. Breadalbane Perthshire, sh. June 1775, fr. Greenock to N.Y., in *Commerce*. (PRO.T47.12)
4583. McNaughton, John, horsethief, res. Fortingall Glen Lyon Perthshire, tr. May 1758. (SRO.B59.26.111.3\37)
4584. McNaughton, John, b. 1737, farmer, res. Breadalbane Perthshire, sh. June 1775, fr. Greenock to N.Y., in *Commerce*, m. Janet Anderson, ch. Christian Katherine Duncan Katherine John Elizabeth Daniel JaneChristian Kat. (PRO.T47.12)
4585. McNaughton, John, b. 1751, farmer, res. Breadalbane Perthshire, sh. June 1775, fr. Greenock to N.Y., in *Commerce*. (PRO.T47.12)
4586. McNaughton, Malcolm, Jacobite, tr. 29 June 1716, fr. Liverpool to Jamaica or Va, in *Elizabeth & Anne*, arr. Va. (SPC.1716.310)(CTB31.208)(VSP.1.185)
4587. McNeil, Archibald, Covenanter, res. Argyll, tr. Aug 1685, fr. Leith to Jamaica. (PC.11.136)
4588. McNeil, Archibald, b. 1751, weaver, res. Paisley Renfrewshire, sh. Feb 1774, fr. Greenock to N.Y., in *Commerce*. (PRO.T47.12)
4589. McNeil, Christian, b. 1754, spinner, res. Paisley Renfrewshire, sh. Feb 1774, fr. Greenock to N.Y., in *Commerce*. (PRO.T47.12)

4590. McNeil, Gilbert, b. 1753, merchant, res. Kilmarnock Ayrshire, sh. May 1774, fr. Greenock to N.Y., in *George*. (PRO.T47.12)
4591. McNeil, Hector, Covenanter, res. Argyll, tr. Aug 1685, fr. Leith to Jamaica. (PC.11.136)
4592. McNeil, Hugh, merchant, res. Auchinsoul, pts. William McNeil, sh. pre 1762, sett. Antigua, d. pre 1762 Auchearn Ballantrae Ayrshire, Glasgow pr1762 CC9.7.64. (SRO.SC6.60.17)
4593. McNeil, John, Covenanter, res. Argyll, tr. Aug 1685, fr. Leith to Jamaica. (PC.11.136)
4594. MacNeil, John, cattle thief, res. Argyll, tr. May 1764. (AJ856)
4595. McNeil, Neil, merchant & planter, res. Ardglanie Knapdale Argyll, sett. Hanover Jamaica, ch. John, d. 1749 Glasgow, Glasgow pr1785 CC9.7.60\73
4596. McNeil, Neil, merchant, sh. pre 1758, sett. St Kitts. (SRO.CS237.74.1)
4597. McNeil, Neil, b. 1710, farmer, res. Kintyre Argyll, sh. Aug 1774, fr. Greenock to Wilmington N.C., in *Ulysses*, m. Isobel Simpson, ch. Daniel Hector Peter Neil William Mary. (PRO.T47.12)
4598. McNeil, Richard, Jacobite, res. Lancashire, tr. 1747. (MR98)
4599. McNeil, Roger, b. 1719, servant, Jacobite, res. Vatersay Isle of Barra, tr. 1747, fr. Tilbury. (P.3.174)(MR144)
4600. McNeil, William, b. 1757, weaver, res. Paisley Renfrewshire, sh. Feb 1774, fr. Greenock to N.Y., in *Commerce*. (PRO.T47.12)
4601. McNeill, Archibald, tacksman, res. Garvart Colonsay Argyll, sh. 1739, sett. Princess Anne Co Va, m. Elizabeth ..., ch. Malcolm & Alexander, d. 1741 Va, Norfolk Va pr 1741. (SRO.SC54.2.53.3)
4602. McNeill, Neill, foremastman, sh. 18 Aug 1699, fr. Clyde to Darien, in *Rising Sun*, Edin pr1707 CC8.8.83
4603. McNicol, Angus, b. 1745, laborer, res. Glen Orchy Argyll, sh. Sept 1775, to Wilmington N.C., in *Jupiter*, m. Ann ... (PRO.T47.12)
4604. MacNicol, Donald, b. 1735, laborer, res. Glen Orchy Argyll, sh. Sept 1775, to Wilmington N.C., in *Jupiter*, m. Katherine .., ch. John Nicol Archibald Mary. (PRO.T47.12)
4605. MacNicol, John, cattle thief, res. Barlea Glencoe Argyll, tr. Sept 1766. (AJ978)
4606. McNicol, John, b. 1750, workman, res. Glen Orchy Argyll, sh. Aug 1774, fr. Greenock to Wilmington N.C., in *Ulysses*. (PRO.T47.12)
4607. McNicol, Robert, b. 1744, gentleman, res. Glen Orchy Argyll, sh. Aug 1774, fr. Greenock to Wilmington N.C., in *Ulysses*, m. Jean Campbell, ch. Annabel. (PRO.T47.12)
4608. McNicoll, Archibald, smith, cattlethief, res. Inveraray Argyll, tr. Apr 1730. (JRA.2.435)
4609. McNicoll, Donald, merchant & factor, res. Glasgow, sh. pre 1760, sett. Pittsylvania Va. (SRA.CFI)

227

4610. McNicoll, Donald Glass, pedlar, cattle thief, res. Strathfillan Perthshire, tr. Dec 1721. (JRA.2.364)
4611. MacNish, George, b. 1684, Glasgow, clergyman edu. Glasgow Uni, sh. 1705, to Philadelphia, sett. Jamaica, N.Y., d. 10 Mar 1722 N.Y. (F.7.664)(AP140)
4612. McNormer, Duncan, Jacobite, tr. 26 Apr 1716, fr. Liverpool to Jamaica, in *Two Brothers*, arr. Montserrat June 1716. (SPC.1716.313)(CTB31.206)(CTP.CC.43)
4613. McOwan, Agnes, b. 1751, res. Glen Luce Wigtonshire, sh. May 1774, fr. Stranraer to N.Y., in *Gale*. (PRO.T47.12)
4614. MacOwin, Catherine, Jacobite, tr. 1747. (P.3.30)
4615. McPhail, Alexander, b. 1763, servant, res. Wester Leys Isle of Lewis, sh. July 1775, fr. Stornaway to Philadelphia, in *Clementina*. (PRO.T47.12)
4616. McPhail, Donald, soldier, thief, res. Argyll, tr. May 1763. (SM.25.353)
4617. McPhail, Donald, b. 1766, res. Leys Isle of Lewis, sh. July 1775, fr. Stornaway to Philadelphia, in *Clementina*. (PRO.T47.12)
4618. McPhail, Duncan, Jacobite, tr. 29 June 1716, fr. Liverpool to Jamaica or Va, in *Elizabeth & Anne*, d. 1716 at sea. (SPC.1716.310)(CTB31.208)
4619. McPhail, Jean, b. 1739, res. Inverness, sh. July 1775, fr. Stornaway to Philadelphia, in *Clementina*, ch. Duncan Jean. (PRO.T47.12)
4620. McPhail, John, b. 1739, servant, res. Wester Leys Isle of Lewis, sh. July 1775, fr. Stornaway to Philadelphia, in *Clementina*. (PRO.T47.12)
4621. McPhail, John, b. 1760, servant, res. Wester Leys Isle of Lewis, sh. July 1775, fr. Stornaway to Philadelphia, in *Clementina*. (PRO.T47.12)
4622. McPhail, Malcolm, horsethief, tr. Sept 1775, to West Indies. (SM.37.523) (alias 956)
4623. McPhail, William, b. 1758, servant, res. Wester Leys Isle of Lewis, sh. July 1775, fr. Stornaway to Philadelphia, in *Clementina*. (PRO.T47.12)
4624. McPhaill, Donald Dow, res. Argyll, tr. 1773, fr. Port Glasgow to Md, in *Dolphin*, arr. Port Oxford Md 1 Feb 1773. (SRO.JC27.10.3)
4625. MacPhaillate, John Dow, thief, res. Gortuleg Stratherick Inverness-shire, tr. June 1754. (SM.16.203)
4626. McPhee, Angus, cattle thief, res. Inverness-shire, tr. Sept 1752. (AJ248) (alias 3507)
4627. McPhee, Daniel, b. 1754, joiner, res. Glasgow, sh. Apr 1775, fr. London to Md, in *Adventure*. (PRO.T47.9\11)
4628. McPhee, Ewan, b. 1719, servant, Jacobite, res. Loch Arkaig Inverness-shire, tr. 31 Mar 1747, fr. London to Barbados, in *Frere*. (P.3.174)(MR36)
4629. McPhee, Murdoch, b. 1704, Morven Argyll, farmer, Jacobite, res. Sandvegg Eigg inverness-shire, tr. 31 Mar 1747, fr. London to

Jamaica, in *St George or Carteret*, arr. Jamaica 1747.
(P.3.174)(PRO.CO137.58)(MR144)
4630. McPherson, Alexander, Jacobite, tr. 21 Apr 1716, fr. Liverpool to S.C.,
in *Wakefield*. (SPC.1716.309)(CTB31.205)
4631. McPherson, Alexander, Jacobite, tr. 26 Apr 1716, fr. Liverpool to
Jamaica, in *Two Brothers*, arr. Montserrat June 1716.
(SPC.1716.313)(CTB31.206)(CTP.CC.43)
4632. McPherson, Alexander, thief, res. Aberdeen, tr. May 1726. (SRO.JC27)
(alias 3821)
4633. McPherson, Alexander, b. 1717, farmer, res. Inverness, sh. July 1775, fr.
Stornaway to Philadelphia, in *Clementina*. (PRO.T47.12)
4634. McPherson, Angus, Jacobite, tr. 7 May 1716, fr. Liverpool to S.C., in
Susannah. (SPC.1716.309)(CTB31.206)
4635. McPherson, Archibald, b. 1731, cowherd, Jacobite, res. Isle of Skye, tr. 5
May 1747, fr. Liverpool to Leeward Islands, in *Veteran*, arr.
Martinique June 1747. (P.3.176)(MR144)(PRO.SP36.102)
4636. McPherson, Daniel, Jacobite, tr. 30 Mar 1716, fr. Liverpool to Antigua,
in *Scipio*. (SPC.1716.310)(CTB31.204)
4637. McPherson, Donald, Jacobite, tr. 7 May 1716, fr. Liverpool to S.C., in
Susannah. (SPC.1716.309)(CTB31.206)
4638. McPherson, Donald, apprentice writer, res. Inverness, pts. John
McPherson, sh. 1771, sett. Pensacola W Fla. (PRO.CO5.613.141)
4639. McPherson, Donald, Jacobite, tr. 25 June 1716, fr. Liverpool to St Kitts,
in *Hockenhill*. (SPC.1716.312)(CTB31.207)
4640. McPherson, Donald, Jacobite, tr. 21 Apr 1716, fr. Liverpool to S.C., in
Wakefield. (SPC.1716.309)(CTB31.205)
4641. McPherson, Donald, Jacobite, tr. 7 May 1716, fr. Liverpool to S.C., in
Susannah. (SPC.1716.309)(CTB31.206)
4642. McPherson, Donald, b. 1728, farmer, res. Perthshire, sh. May 1775, fr.
Greenock to N.Y., in *Monimia*, m. Mary McFee. (PRO.T47.12)
4643. McPherson, Donald, b. 1743, farmer, res. Stirling, sh. May 1775, fr.
Greenock to N.Y., in *Monimia*, m. Janet McTaggart.
(PRO.T47.12)
4644. McPherson, Duncan, farmer, cattle thief, res. Inverawe Argyll, tr. Oct
1722. (JRA.2.382)
4645. McPherson, Duncan, Jacobite, tr. 7 May 1716, fr. Liverpool to S.C., in
Susannah. (SPC.1716.309)(CTB31.206)
4646. McPherson, Duncan, b. 1711, laborer, Jacobite, res. Inverness, tr. 5 May
1747, fr. Liverpool to Leeward Islands, in *Veteran*, arr. Martinique
June 1747. (P.3.176)(MR123)(PRO.SP36.102)
4647. McPherson, Duncan, b. 1743, farmer, res. Stirling, sh. May 1775, fr.
Greenock to N.Y., in *Monimia*, m. Jane McBride. (PRO.T47.12)
4648. McPherson, Isobel, b. 1754, servant, res. Inverness, sh. July 1775, fr.
Stornaway to Philadelphia, in *Clementina*. (PRO.T47.12)

4649. McPherson, James, b. 1708, printer, res. Kingussie Inverness-shire, sh. Sept 1727, fr. London to Jamaica. (CLRO\AIA)
4650. McPherson, James, b. 1725, laborer, Jacobite, res. Aberdeen, tr. 5 May 1747, fr. Liverpool to Leeward Islands, in *Veteran*, arr. Martinique June 1747. (P.3.176)(MR177)(PRO.SP36.102)
4651. McPherson, Janet, b. 1757, servant, res. Inverness, sh. July 1775, fr. Stornaway to Philadelphia, in *Clementina*. (PRO.T47.12)
4652. McPherson, Janet, b. 1763, servant, res. Inverness, sh. July 1775, fr. Stornaway to Philadelphia, in *Clementina*. (PRO.T47.12)
4653. McPherson, Jean, infanticide, res. Inverness-shire, tr. Oct 1749, fr. Glasgow. (SM.11.509)
4654. McPherson, Jean, b. 1755, servant, res. Wester Leys Isle of Lewis, sh. July 1775, fr. Stornaway to Philadelphia, in *Clementina*. (PRO.T47.12)
4655. McPherson, John, Jacobite, tr. 7 May 1716, fr. Liverpool to S.C., in *Susannah*. (SPC.1716.309)(CTB31.206)
4656. McPherson, John, b. 1704, servant, Jacobite, res. Inverness, tr. 31 Mar 1747, fr. London to Barbados , in *Frere*. (P.3.176)(MR177)
4657. McPherson, John, b. 1732, Jacobite, res. Glen Garry Inverness-shire, tr. 24 Feb 1747, fr. Liverpool to Va, in *Gildart*, arr. Port North Potomac Md 5 Aug 1747. (P.3.178)(MR159)(PRO.T1.328)
4658. McPherson, John, b. 1732, shipmaster, res. Greenock, sh. May 1774, fr. Greenock to N.Y., in *George*. (PRO.T47.12)
4659. McPherson, John, b. 1754, servant, res. Inverness, sh. July 1775, fr. Stornaway to Philadelphia, in *Clementina*. (PRO.T47.12)
4660. McPherson, Katherine, res. Strathmashie Inverness-shire, sh. pre 1780, sett. Quebec. (SRO.GD214.356)
4661. McPherson, Katherine, b. 1753, servant, res. Inverness, sh. May 1775, fr. Leith to Philadelphia, in *Friendship*. (PRO.T47.12)
4662. McPherson, Malcolm, b. 1734, farmer, res. Glen Orchy Argyll, sh. Aug 1774, fr. Greenock to Wilmington N.C., in *Ulysses*, m. Christian Downie, ch. Janet William. (PRO.T47.12)
4663. McPherson, Margaret, b. 1754, servant, res. Inverness, sh. July 1775, fr. Stornaway to Philadelphia, in *Clementina*. (PRO.T47.12)
4664. McPherson, Mary, thief, tr. May 1765, fr. Glasgow. (AJ908)
4665. McPherson, Owen, Jacobite, tr. 29 June 1716, fr. Liverpool to Jamaica or Va, in *Elizabeth & Anne*. (SPC.1716.310)(CTB31.208)
4666. McPherson, Owen, Jacobite, tr. 29 June 1716, fr. Liverpool to Jamaica or Va, in *Elizabeth & Anne*, arr. York Va. (SPC.1716.310)(CTB31.208)(VSP.1.185)
4667. McPherson, Peggy, b. 1758, res. Aberdeen, sh. May 1775, fr. Leith to Philadelphia, in *Friendship*. (PRO.T47.12)

4668. McPherson, William, Jacobite, tr. 28 July 1716, fr. Liverpool to Va, in *Godspeed*, arr. Md Oct 1716. (SPC.1716.310)(CTB31.209)(HM388)

4669. McPhie, Peter, murderer, res. Inverness-shire, tr. 1773. (CalHOpp.847)

4670. McPhie, Peter, servant, murderer, res. Waterstyne Isle of Skye, tr. June 1773. (SRO.RH2.4.255)(CalHPpp.847)

4671. McQuarry, Alexander, b. 1710, Morven, farmer, Jacobite, res. Fivepenny Isle of Eigg Inverness-shire, tr. 20 Mar 1747, fr. Tilbury. (P.3.178)(MR144)

4672. McQuarry, Donald, Jacobite, res. Isle of Eigg Inverness-shire, tr. 31 Mar 1747, fr. London to Barbados, in *Frere*. (P.3.178)(MR144)

4673. McQuarry, John, Jacobite, res. Isle of Eigg Inverness-shire, tr. 1747. (P.3.178)

4674. McQuarry, John, farmer, Jacobite, res. Galmistal Isle of Eigg Inverness-shire, tr. 31 Mar 1747, fr. London to Barbados , in *Frere*. (P.3.178)(MR144)

4675. McQuarry, John, b. 1707, Jacobite, res. Isle of Eigg Inverness-shire, tr. 1747. (P.3.178)(MR144)

4676. McQueen, Alexander, Jacobite, tr. 21 Apr 1716, fr. Liverpool to S.C., in *Wakefield*. (SPC.1716.309)(CTB31.205)

4677. McQueen, Alexander, Jacobite, tr. 21 Apr 1716, fr. Liverpool to S.C., in *Wakefield*. (SPC.1716.309)(CTB31.205)

4678. McQueen, Alexander, Jacobite, tr. 24 May 1716, fr. Liverpool to Md, in *Friendship*, arr. Md Aug 1716. (SPC.1716.311)(HM387)

4679. MacQueen, Alexander, b. 1705, barber, res. Banff, sh. Mar 1722, fr. London to Jamaica. (CLRO\AIA)

4680. McQueen, Angus, servant, Jacobite, res. Skye Inverness-shire, tr. 20 Mar 1747. (P.3.180)(MR185)

4681. McQueen, Daniel, Jacobite, tr. 30 Mar 1716, fr. Liverpool to Antigua, in *Scipio*. (CTB31.204)

4682. McQueen, David, Jacobite, tr. 21 Apr 1716, fr. Liverpool to S.C., in *Wakefield*. (SPC.1716.309)(CTB31.205)

4683. McQueen, David, Jacobite, tr. 24 May 1716, fr. Liverpool to Md, in *Friendship*, arr. Md Aug 1716. (SPC.1716.311)(HM387)

4684. McQueen, Dugall, Jacobite, tr. 24 May 1716, fr. Liverpool to Md, in *Friendship*, arr. Md Aug 1716. (SPC.1716.311)(HM386)

4685. McQueen, Duncan, Covenanter, res. Argyll, tr. Aug 1685, fr. Leith to Jamaica. (PC.11.136)

4686. McQueen, Duncan, Jacobite, tr. 21 Apr 1716, fr. Liverpool to S.C., in *Wakefield*. (SPC.1716.309)(CTB31.205)

4687. McQueen, Duncan, b. 1761, res. Braen Isle of Lewis, sh. July 1775, fr. Stornaway to Philadelphia, in *Clementina*. (PRO.T47.12)

4688. McQueen, George, clergyman, sh. pre 1703, sett. Va. (SCHR.14.149)

4689. McQueen, Hector, Jacobite, tr. 24 May 1716, fr. Liverpool to Md, in *Friendship*, arr. Md Aug 1716. (SPC.1716.311)(HM387)
4690. McQueen, Hugh, Covenanter, res. Argyll, tr. Aug 1685, fr. Leith to Jamaica. (PC.11.136)
4691. McQueen, Isobel, b. 1765, res. Braen Isle of Lewis, sh. July 1775, fr. Stornaway to Philadelphia, in *Clementina*. (PRO.T47.12)
4692. McQueen, Janet, Covenanter, tr. Aug 1685, fr. Leith to Jamaica. (PC.11.329)
4693. McQueen, John, Jacobite, tr. 21 Apr 1716, fr. Liverpool to S.C., in *Wakefield*. (SPC.1716.309)(CTB31.205)
4694. McQueen, Margaret, b. 1756, spinner, res. Paisley Renfrewshire, sh. Feb 1774, fr. Greenock to N.Y., in *Commerce*. (PRO.T47.12)
4695. McQueen, Margaret, b. 1759, servant, res. Braen Isle of Lewis, sh. July 1775, fr. Stornaway to Philadelphia, in *Clementina*. (PRO.T47.12)
4696. McQueen, Robert, Covenanter, res. Nithsdale Dumfries-shire, tr. 5 Sept 1685, fr. Leith to East N.J., in *Henry & Francis*. (PC.11.154)
4697. McQueen, Walter, tr. 5 Sept 1685, fr. Leith to East N.J., in *Henry & Francis*. (PC.11.154)
4698. McQueen, William, b. 1749, husbandman, res. Glen Luce Wigtonshire, sh. May 1774, fr. Stranraer to N.Y., in *Gale*. (PRO.T47.12)
4699. McQueeston, Anthony, b. 1756, baker, res. Galloway, sh. May 1774, fr. Stranraer to N.Y., in *Gale*. (PRO.T47.12)
4700. McQuerrist, John, Jacobite, tr. 22 Apr 1747, fr. Liverpool to Va, in *Johnson*, arr. Port Oxford Md 5 Aug 1747. (P.3.180)(PRO.T1.328)
4701. McQuerrist, Roderick, Jacobite, tr. 24 Apr 1747, fr. Liverpool to Va, in *Johnson*, arr. Port Oxford Md 5 Aug 1747. (P.3.180)(PRO.T1.328)
4702. McQuin, Alexander, Jacobite, tr. 21 Apr 1716, fr. Liverpool to S.C., in *Wakefield*. (SPC.1716.309)(CTB31.205)
4703. McQuin, Daniel, Jacobite, tr. 29 June 1716, fr. Liverpool to Jamaica or Va, in *Elizabeth & Anne*, arr. Va. (SPC.1716.310)(CTB31.208)(VSP.1.185) (alias 4704)
4704. McQuin, Duncan, Jacobite, tr. 29 June 1716, fr. Liverpool to Jamaica or Va, in *Elizabeth & Anne*, arr. Va. (SPC.1716.310)(CTB31.208)(VSP.1.185) (alias 4703)
4705. McQuin, Flora, b. 1737, Jacobite, res. Highlands, tr. 22 Apr 1747, fr. Liverpool to Va, in *Johnson*, arr. Port Oxford Md 5 Aug 1747. (P.3.180)(PRO.T1.328)
4706. McQuin, John, Jacobite, tr. 7 May 1716, fr. Liverpool to S.C., in *Susannah*. (SPC.1716.309)(CTB31.206)
4707. McQuinn, Daniel, Jacobite, tr. 30 Mar 1716, fr. Liverpool to Antigua, in *Scipio*. (SPC.1716.310)

4708. McQuire, Anne, b. 1763, servant, res. Braen Isle of Lewis, sh. July 1775, fr. Stornaway to Philadelphia, in *Clementina*. (PRO.T47.12)
4709. McQuiston, John, b. 1729, laborer, res. Inch Wigtonshire, sh. 31 May 1775, fr. Stranraer to Wilmington N.C., in *Jackie*. (PRO.T47.12)
4710. McRae, Christopher, b. 1733, Urquhart Inverness-shire, clergyman edu. Marischal Col 1753, pts. Christopher McRae, sh. 1766, sett. Surrey Co & Littleton Cumberland Co Va, d. 22 Dec 1808 Powhallen Co Va. (EMA43)(OD18)
4711. McRae, Donald, Jacobite , res. Loch Broom Ross-shire, tr. 1747, fr. Tilbury to Jamaica, in *St George or Carteret*, arr. Jamaica 1747. (P.3.182)(MR159)(PRO.CO137.58)
4712. MacRae, Duncan, res. Glenelcheat Kintail Ross-shire, pts. Findlay MacRae, sh. 1731, fr. London to Jamaica, d. 28 Sept 1734 Jamaica. (APB.
4713. McRae, John, servant, thief, res. Inchmartine Perthshire, tr. Mar 1767. (SRO.JC27.10.3)
4714. McRae, Margaret, b. 1756, servant, res. Edinburegh, sh. May 1775, fr. Leith to Philadelphia, in *Friendship*. (PRO.T47.12)
4715. McRanald, Donald, b. 1687, Jacobite, tr. 1747, fr. Tilbury. (P.3.182)(MR144)
4716. McRaw, Rory, b. 1723, farmer, Jacobite, res. Clochgowrie Ross-shire, tr. 1747. (MR87)
4717. McReady, John, Covenanter, res. Ratho Midlothian, tr. Aug 1678, fr. Leith to West Indies. (PC.5.488)
4718. MacReath, John, servant, murderer, res. Ayrshire, tr. Oct 1748. (SM.10.248)
4719. McRitchie, John, b. 1677, herd, Jacobite, res. Inverness-shire, tr. 1747. (P.3.184)(MR119)
4720. McRob, Duncan, b. 1758, tailor, res. Kintyre Argyll, sh. Sept 1774, fr. Greenock to Wilmington N.C., in *Diana*. (PRO.T47.12)
4721. McRobert, Peter, b. 1736, farmer, res. Drumlanrig Dumfries-shire, sh. May 1774, fr. Kirkcudbright to N.Y., in *Adventure*. (PRO.T47.12)
4722. McRoberts, Archibald, clergyman, sh. 1761, to Va. (EMA43)
4723. McRoss, Donald, b. 1723, Jacobite, res. Sutherland, tr. 1747. (P.3.184)(MR187)
4724. McSlipheder, John, res. Kiles Jura Argyll, sh. 1754, to Cape Fear N.C. (SRO.GD64\5.21)
4725. McSparran, James, clergyman edu. Glasgow & Oxford Unis , sh. 1720, to N.E., sett. Narragansett. (SCHR.14.145)(EMA43)
4726. McTaggart, James, b. 1754, laborer, res. Galloway, sh. May 1774, fr. Stranraer to N.Y., in *Gale*. (PRO.T47.12)
4727. McTaillior, Donald, Covenanter, res. Fordie Perthshire, tr. Aug 1685, fr. Leith to Jamaica. (PC.11.329)
4728. McTavish, Donald, murderer, res. Inverness-shire, tr. Sept 1755. (AJ402)

4729. McUrich, Archibald, herd, Covenanter, res. Argyll, tr. July 1685, fr. Leith to N.E. (PC.11.330)
4730. McVane, John, Jacobite, tr. 7 May 1716, fr. Liverpool to S.C., in *Susannah*. (SPC.1716.309)(CTB31.206)
4731. McVane, Katherine, b. 1745, spinner, res. Glen Orchy Argyll, sh. Sept 1775, to Wilmington N.C., in *Jupiter*, ch. Mary Joseph. (PRO.T47.12) (alias 1609)
4732. McVane, Malcolm, Jacobite, tr. 7 May 1716, fr. Liverpool to S.C., in *Susannah*. (SPC.1716.309)(CTB31.206)
4733. McVerran, Donald, tr. Aug 1685, fr. Leith to Jamaica. (PC.11.136)
4734. McVey, Donald, Covenanter, tr. 1685. (PC.11.289)
4735. McVey, Douglas, b. 1745, laborer, res. Argyll, sh. May 1775, fr. Greenock to Wilmington N.C., in *Ulysses*. (PRO.T47.12)
4736. McVian, Donald, b. 1736, farmer, res. Breadalbane Perthshire, sh. June 1775, fr. Greenock to N.Y., in *Commerce*, ch. Duncan. (PRO.T47.12)
4737. McVian, John, b. 1754, wright, res. Breadalbane Perthshire, sh. June 1775, fr. Greenock to N.Y., in *Commerce*. (PRO.T47.12)
4738. McVian, Mary, b. 1754, servant, res. Breadalbane Perthshire, sh. June 1775, fr. Greenock to N.Y., in *Commerce*. (PRO.T47.12)
4739. McVian, Sarah, b. 1758, servant, res. Breadalbane Perthshire, sh. June 1775, fr. Greenock to N.Y., in *Commerce*. (PRO.T47.12)
4740. McVicar, Archibald, b. 1747, farmer, res. Stirling, sh. May 1775, fr. Greenock to N.Y., in *Lilly*. (PRO.T47.12)
4741. McVicar, Donald, Covenanter, res. Inveraray Argyll, tr. July 1685, fr. Leith to N.E. (PC.11.94)
4742. McVicar, Duncan, b. 1668, Covenanter, res. Campbelltown Argyll, pts. Baillie McVicar, tr. July 1685, fr. Leith to N.E. (PC.11.94)
4743. McVicar, Duncan, b. 4 Aug 1741, Glasgow, merchant, res. Glasgow, pts. Archibald McVicar & Florence McVicar, sh. pre 1758, sett. Charleston S.C. & N.Y. (SRA.T-MJ427.140)
4744. McVicar, James, res. Stranraer Wigtonshire, pts. Robert McVicar & Mary Affleck, sh. pre 1771, sett. St Thomas in the East Jamaica. (SRO.RD4.210.550)
4745. McVicar, John, b. 1738, tailor, res. Glasgow, sh. Sept 1774, fr. Greenock to Wilmington N.C., in *Diana*. (PRO.T47.12)
4746. McVig, Duncan, Covenanter, res. Argyll, tr. Aug 1685, fr. Leith to Jamaica. (PC.11.329)
4747. McVorich, Malcolm, thief, res. Stirlingshire, tr. 1684, fr. Leith to East N.J. (PC.8.514)
4748. McVurah, Peter, b. 1756, founder, res. Breadalbane Perthshire, sh. June 1775, fr. Greenock to N.Y., in *Commerce*. (PRO.T47.12)
4749. McWarish, John, b. 1719, laborer, Jacobite, tr. 1747. (P.3.186)
4750. McWarish, Robert, b. 1705, laborer, Jacobite, tr. 1747. (P.3.186)

4751. McWhae, Robert, b. 1745, millwright, res. Genoch Balmaghie Kirkcudbrightshire, sh. May 1775, fr. Kirkcudbright to N.Y., in *Adventure*. (PRO.T47.12)
4752. McWhiddie, Allan, Covenanter, res. Argyll, tr. Aug 1685, fr. Leith to Jamaica. (PC.11.136)
4753. McWilliam, George, b. 1749, husbandman, res. Galloway, sh. May 1774, fr. Stranraer to N.Y., in *Gale*. (PRO.T47.12)
4754. McWilliam, James, b. 1750, mason, res. Galloway, sh. May 1774, fr. Stranraer to N.Y., in *Gale*. (PRO.T47.12)
4755. McWilliam, James, b. 1751, farmer, res. Galloway, sh. May 1774, fr. Stranraer to N.Y., in *Gale*. (PRO.T47.12)
4756. McWilliam, Janet, b. 1715, res. Kirkmichael, sh. May 1775, fr. Stranraer to N.Y., in *Jackie*. (PRO.T47.12)
4757. McWilliam, Janet, b. 1747, res. Galloway, sh. May 1774, fr. Stranraer to N.Y., in *Gale*. (PRO.T47.12)
4758. McWilliam, John, b. 1749, farmer, res. Galloway, sh. May 1774, fr. Stranraer to N.Y., in *Gale*. (PRO.T47.12)
4759. McWilliam, William, servant, housebreaker, res. Borrowstoun Caithness, tr. Sept 1772. (AJ1292)
4760. McWilliam, William, surgeon apothecary, sett. Md, ch. Janet, d. pre 1764. (SRO.RH9.7.173)
4761. McWillie, John, Covenanter, tr. Aug 1685, fr. Leith to Jamaica. (PC.11.329)(ETR369)
4762. Maddock, Samuel, apothecary, Jacobite, tr. 1747. (MR195)
4763. Maiden, William, b. 8 July 1733, Mains Dundee, res. Dundee, pts. John Maiden & Elspet Pattullo, d. pre 1756 Philadelphia, PCC pr1756
4764. Main, James, shoplifter, tr. Apr 1768. (AJ1056)
4765. Main, Joan, whore, res. Edinburgh, tr. 2 Feb 1697. (SRO.PC2.26)
4766. Main, John, b. 1725, fisherman, Jacobite, res. Footdee Aberdeen, tr. 22 Apr 1747, fr. Liverpool to Va, in *Johnson*, arr. Port Oxford Md 5 Aug 1747. (P.3.4)(MR129)(PRO.T1.328)
4767. Main, John, b. 1739, laborer, res. Glenluce Wigtonshire, sh. 31 May 1775, fr. Stranraer to N.Y., in *Jackie*, m. Margaret Thorborn, ch. Anne & John. (PRO.T47.12)
4768. Mair, Daniel, b. 1739, weaver, res. Glasgow, sh. Feb 1774, fr. Greenock to N.Y., in *Commerce*. (PRO.T47.12)
4769. Maitland, James, planter, d. Sept 1773 Jamaica. (SM.35.559)
4770. Maitland, John, clergyman edu. Edinburgh Uni 1695, sh. 1707, to Carolina. (EMA43)
4771. Maitland, John, tr. May 1684. (PC.8.710)
4772. Maitland, John, b. 1717, gardener, Jacobite, res. Armagh, tr. 1747. (P.3.6)

4773. Maitland, William, sailor, res. Linlithgow West Lothian, pts. Patrick Maitland, sh. 14 July 1698, fr. Leith to Darien, in *Caledonia*, Edin pr1707 CC8.8.83
4774. Maitland, William, sailor, res. Craigmill Logie Stirlingshire, pts. John Maitland, sh. 14 July 1698, fr. Leith to Darien , in *Union*, Edin pr1707 CC8.8.83
4775. Malcolm, Alexander, clergyman, sh. 1739, sett. Marblehead Mass & Annapolis Md. (EMA43)(SPG.3.20)
4776. Malcolm, Isobel, b. 1754, sh. Apr 1775, fr. Greenock to N.Y., in *Lilly*. (PRO.T47.12)
4777. Malcolm, James, Jacobite, tr. 29 June 1716, fr. Liverpool to Jamaica or Va, in *Elizabeth & Anne*, arr. York Va. (SPC.1716.310)(CTB31.208)(VSP.1.186)
4778. Malcolm, James, merchant, d. pre 1756 Jamaica. (CPD448)
4779. Malcolm, Neil, merchant, res. Argyll, sh. pre 1773, sett. Jamaica. (CC.2.131)
4780. Malloch, John, sea captain, res. Kirkcaldy Fife, sh. July 1698 Leith, tr. July 1698 Leith, fr. Darien to ENDEAVOUR, Edin pr1709 CC8.8.84
4781. Mallone, James, Jacobite, tr. 28 July 1716, fr. Liverpool to Va, in *Godspeed*, arr. Md Oct 1716. (SPC.1716.310)(CTB31.209)(HM388)
4782. Man, James, b. 1707, res. Dunkeld Perthshire, sh. Oct 1725, fr. London to Jamaica. (CLRO\AIA)
4783. Man, Robert, tr. June 1745. (SRO.HCR.I.72)
4784. Mann, Alexander, b. 1714, butcher, Jacobite, tr. 1747. (P.3.6)
4785. Mann, Isaac, clergyman, sh. 1774, sett. Dominica. (EMA43)
4786. Mann, James, b. 1727, baker, Jacobite, res. Dunkeld Perthshire, tr. 5 May 1747, fr. Liverpool to Leeward Islands, in *Veteran*, arr. Martinique June 1747. (P.3.6)(MR205)(PRO.SP36.102)
4787. Mann, William, Jacobite, tr. 24 May 1716, fr. Liverpool to Md, in *Friendship*, arr. Md Aug 1716. (SPC.1716.311)(HM387)
4788. Mann, William, woolcomber, conspirator, res. Aberdeen, tr. Aug 1772, fr. Glasgow to Va, in *Brilliant*, arr. Port Hampton Va 7 Oct 1772. (SRO.JC27.10.3)(AJ1272)
4789. Manson, Alexander, tr. Aug 1685, fr. Leith to Jamaica. (PC.11.329)(ETR369)
4790. Manson, Barbara, housebreaker, res. Halkirk Caithness, tr. May 1773, m. Alexander McLeod. (AJ1325)
4791. Manson, Barbara, b. 1752, spinner, sh. Sept 1775, fr. Newcastle to Ga, in *Georgia Merchant*, sett. Friendsborough Ga. (PRO.T47.9\11)
4792. Manson, Elizabeth, b. 20 Dec 1748, Kirkwall Orkney Islands, spinner, pts. William Manson & Marion Blaw, sh. Sept 1775, fr.

Newcastle to Ga, in *Georgia Merchant*, sett. Friendsborough Ga.
(PRO.T47.9\11)
4793. Manson, Elizabeth, b. 1766, sh. Sept 1775, fr. Newcastle to Ga, in
Georgia Merchant, sett. Friendsborough Ga. (PRO.T47.9\11)
4794. Manson, James, b. 1738, res. Gatehouse Kirkcudbrightshire, sh. May
1774, fr. Stranraer to N.Y., in *Gale*. (PRO.T47.12)
4795. Manson, Janet, b. 1756, servant, res. Dunnet Caithness, sh. Sept 1775,
fr. Kirkwall to Savannah Ga, in *Marlborough*, sett. Richmond Co
Ga. (PRO.T47.12)
4796. Manson, Margaret, b. 24 July 1751, Kirkwall Orkney Islands, spinner,
pts. William Manson & Marion Blaw, sh. Sept 1775, fr.
Newcastle to Ga, in *Georgia Merchant*, sett. Richmond Co Ga.
(PRO.T47.9\11)
4797. Manson, Thomas, b. 3 May 1759, Kirkwall Orkney Islands, yeoman, pts.
William Manson & Marion Blaw, sh. Sept 1775, fr. Newcastle to
Ga, in *Georgia Packet*, sett. Richmond Co Ga. (PRO.T47.9\11)
4798. Manson, William, b. 1744, laborer, res. Ferrytown Wigtonshire, sh. May
1774, fr. Stranraer to N.Y., in *Gale*. (PRO.T47.12)
4799. Manson, William, b. 24 July 1751, Kirkwall Orkney Islands, weaver, res.
Dunnet Caithness, sh. Sept 1775, fr. Kirkwall to Savannah Ga, in
Marlborough, sett. Richmond Co Ga, m. Elizabeth Sinclair.
(PRO.T47.12)
4800. Mant, Thomas, soldier, sh. pre 1766, sett. N.Y. (PCCol.4.820)
4801. Manuel, James, maltman, Covenanter, res. Glasgow, tr. June 1678, to
West Indies, m. ... Russell. (PC.5.474)
4802. Marjoribanks, Joseph, sailor, res. Edinburgh, pts. Joseph Marjoribanks of
Lauchrie & Margaret Brown, sh. 14 July 1698, fr. Leith to Darien,
in *St Andrew*, Edin pr1707 CC8.8.83)
4803. Marjorybanks, George, Jacobite, tr. 29 June 1716, fr. Liverpool to
Jamaica or Va, in *Elizabeth & Anne*, arr. York Va.
(SPC.1716.310)(CTB31.208)(VSP.1.185)
4804. Marjorybanks, James, forger, res. Dumfries, tr. 1753. (SM.15.204)
4805. Marjorybanks, Thomas, b. 1749, baker, res. Glasgow, sh. Oct 1774, fr.
Greenock to Philadelphia, in *Sally*. (PRO.T47.12)
4806. Marnoch, Alexander, b. 1 May 1720, St Nicholas, shoemaker, Jacobite,
res. Aberdeen, pts. John Marnoch & Janet Barnet, tr. 5 May 1747,
fr. Liverpool to Leeward Islands, in *Veteran*, arr. Martinique June
1747. (P.3.8)(JAB.2.436)(PRO.SP36.102)
4807. Marnock, Gilbert, chapman, Covenanter, tr. Aug 1678, fr. Leith to West
Indies, in *St Michael of Scarborough*. (PC.6.76)
4808. Marr, Alexander, Jacobite, tr. 22 Apr 1747, fr. Liverpool to Va, in
Johnson, arr. Port Oxford Md 5 Aug 1747.
(P.3.8)(MR123)(PRO.T1.328)
4809. Marr, Alexander, b. 1714, butcher, Jacobite, tr. 1747. (MR206)

4810. Marr, Ann, tr. 1764, in *Boyd*, arr. Norfolk Va 24 Aug 1764. (SRO.JC27.10.3)
4811. Marshall, Agnes, whore, res. Edinburgh, tr. Mar 1695. (SRO.PC2.25.216)
4812. Marshall, Agnes, servant, infanticide, res. Darnest Paisley Renfrewshire, tr. May 1770. (SM.32.337)
4813. Marshall, Andrew, horsethief, tr. Dec 1752, fr. Glasgow to Antigua. (AJ260)
4814. Marshall, Archibald, tr. July 1685. (PC.11.112)
4815. Marshall, David, b. 1750, clerk, sh. Feb 1774, fr. London to N.C., in *Margaret & Mary*. (PRO.T47.9\11)
4816. Marshall, James, innkeeper & merchant, res. Aberdeen, sett. St Phillip's Charleston S.C., d. 1765, PCC pr1767. (APB.4.9)
4817. Marshall, Janet, thief, res. Cowgate Edinburgh, tr. Jan 1767. (SRO.JC27)(SM.29.221)
4818. Marshall, John, pts. John Marshall of Starrieshaw, sh. 1684, to Carolina, d. pre 1699. (SRO.SH.15.7.1699)
4819. Marshall, John, smith, Covenanter, res. Glasgow, tr. June 1678, to West Indies. (PC.5.474)
4820. Marshall, John, Covenanter, res. Shotts Lanarkshire, tr. June 1684, fr. Glasgow, in *Pelican*. (PC.9.208)
4821. Marshall, John, cooper, res. Leith Midlothian, sh. June 1775, fr. Kirkcaldy to Brunswick N.C., in *Jamaica Packet*. (PRO.T47.12)
4822. Marshall, John, tr. 5 Sept 1685, fr. Leith to East N.J., in *Henry & Francis*. (PC.11.167)
4823. Marshall, Michael, res. Strathaven Lanarkshire, tr. 5 Sept 1685, fr. Leith to East N.J., in *Henry & Francis*. (PC.11.159)
4824. Marshall, Mungo, clergyman, sh. 1744, to Va. (EMA44)
4825. Marshall, Robert, bigamist, tr. Dec 1752, fr. Glasgow to Antigua. (AJ260)
4826. Marshall, Robert, b. 1742, weaver, res. Farquhar Galloway, sh. May 1775, fr. Dumfries to P.E.I., in *Lovely Nelly*, m. Elizabeth ..., ch. John Andrew & James. (PRO.T47.12)
4827. Marshall, Robert, b. 1746, wright, res. Glasgow, sh. Apr 1775, fr. Greenock to N.Y., in *Lilly*. (PRO.T47.12)
4828. Marshall, Thomas, Covenanter, res. Shotts Lanarkshire, tr. June 1684, fr. Glasgow, in *Pelican*. (PC.9.208)
4829. Marshall, William, tr. Aug 1685, fr. Leith to Jamaica, arr. Port Royal Jamaica Nov 1685. (PC.11.329)(LJ157)
4830. Marshall, William, clergyman, res. Abernethy, sh. 1764, sett. Deprun Forks of Delaware. (UPC655)
4831. Marshall, William, b. 1748, laborer, res. Renfrew, sh. Apr 1775, fr. Greenock to N.Y., in *Lilly*. (PRO.T47.12)

4832. Martin, Alexander, thief, res. Aberdeenshire, tr. Aug 1753, fr. Aberdeen to Va, in *St Andrew*. (SM.15.260)(AJ294)
4833. Martin, Alexander, b. 1717, res. Inverness, sh. Aug 1733, fr. London to Jamaica. (CLRO\AIA)
4834. Martin, Colin, soldier, vagrant, tr. Sept 1754. (SM.16.750)
4835. Martin, David, sheriff & schoolmaster, res. Banchory Kincardineshire, pts. Hugh Martin, sh. pre 1750, sett. Philadelphia. (APB.3.175)
4836. Martin, Grizel, res. Mill of Aries Glasgow, sett. Janefield N.Y.(?), m. William McCandlish, ch. Patrick John & Grizel, d. 1770, Edin pr1777 CC8.8.124
4837. Martin, James, sailor, res. Linlithgow West Lothian, sh. 18 Aug 1699, fr. Clyde to Darien, in *Hope*, Edin pr1707 CC8.8.83
4838. Martin, James, clergyman, sh. 1777. (UPC654)
4839. Martin, Jean, whore, res. Edinburgh, tr. 19 Mar 1695. (SRO.PC2.25.216)
4840. Martin, John, Covenanter, res. Kirkmichael Kintyre Argyll, tr. Aug 1685, fr. Leith to Jamaica. (PC.11.136)
4841. Martin, John, rioter, res. Cupar Fife, tr. June 1773. (SRO.B59.26.11.1.6.18)(AJ1322)
4842. Martin, John, res. Dumfries, sh. Mar 1684, fr. London to Jamaica. (CLRO\AIA)
4843. Martin, John, b. 1705, stocking weaver, Jacobite, res. Stonehaven Kincardineshire, tr. 31 Mar 1747, fr. London to Jamaica, in *St George or Carteret*, arr. Jamaica 1747. (P.3.8)(MR63)(PRO.CO137.58)
4844. Martin, John, b. 1732, farm servant, res. Achall Ross-shire, sh. Nov 1774, fr. Stornaway to N.Y., in *Peace & Plenty*. (PRO.T47.12)
4845. Martin, John jr, tr. May 1684, fr. Leith. (PC.8.710)
4846. Martin, John sr, tr. May 1684, fr. Leith. (PC.8.710)
4847. Martin, Mary, b. 1759, servant, res. Edinburgh, sh. May 1775, fr. Leith to Philadelphia, in *Friendship*. (PRO.T47.12)
4848. Martin, Murdoch, b. 1734, sheriff's officer, res. Stornaway Isle of Lewis, sh. Nov 1774, fr. Stornaway to N.Y., in *Peace & Plenty*, ch. John. (PRO.T47.12)
4849. Martin, Murdoch, b. 1759, servant, res. Barvas Isle of Lewis, sh. May 1774, fr. Stornaway to Philadelphia, in *Friendship*. (PRO.T47.12)
4850. Martin, Peter, b. 1739, linen weaver, sh. Dec 1774, fr. London to Va, in *William*. (PRO.T47.9\11)
4851. Martin, Robert, b. 1749, yeoman, sh. Sept 1775, fr. Newcastle to Ga, in *Georgia Merchant*, sett. Friendsborough Ga. (PRO.T47.9\11)
4852. Martin, William, tr. Nov 1750, fr. Aberdeen to Va or West Indies, in *Adventure*. (AJ152\170)

4853. Martin, William, Jacobite, tr. 29 June 1716, fr. Liverpool to Jamaica or Va, in *Elizabeth & Anne*, arr. York Va. (SPC.1716.310)(CTB31.208)(VSP.1.185)
4854. Martin, William, tr. 1764, to Va, in *Boyd*, arr. Norfolk Va 24 Aug 1764. (SRO.JC27.10.3)
4855. Martison, John, Jacobite, tr. 24 May 1716, fr. Liverpool to Md, in *Friendship*, arr. Md Aug 1716. (SPC.1716.311)(HM387)
4856. Mason, James, Jacobite, res. Morayshire, tr. 20 Mar 1747, fr. London to Jamaica, in *St George or Carteret*, arr. Jamaica 1747. (P.3.10)(MR128)(PRO.CO137.58)
4857. Mason, Janet, tr. 1696, fr. Newhaven to Va. (SRO.RH15.14.58)
4858. Mason, John, quartier, res. Burntisland Fife, sh. 14 July 1698, fr. Leith to Darien, in *Unicorn*, Edin pr1707 CC8.8.83
4859. Mason, John, clergyman, res. Craigmailen, sh. pre 1765, sett. N.Y. (UPC654)
4860. Mason, John, b. 1699, wright, Jacobite, res. Aberdeen, tr. 20 Mar 1747, fr. Tilbury. (P.3.10)(MR129)(JAB.2.436)
4861. Mason, John, b. 29 June 1727, Old Machar Aberdeenshire, barber, Jacobite, res. Aberdeen, pts. William Mason & Helen Mouat, tr. 5 May 1747, fr. Liverpool to Leeward Islands, in *Veteran*, arr. Martinique June 1747. (PRO.SP36.102)(JAB.2.436)
4862. Massie, Lawrence, tr. 1696, fr. Newhaven to Va. (SRO.RH15.14.58)
4863. Masterton, Alexander, bosun, res. Linlithgow West Lothian, pts. Alexander Masterton, sh. 14 July 1698, fr. Leith to Darien, in *Caledonia*, Edin pr1723 CC8.8.89
4864. Masterton, Christian, whore, res. Edinburgh, tr. Mar 1695. (SRO.PC2.25.216)
4865. Mather, David sr, Covenanter, res. Bridgeness West Lothian, tr. Aug 1670. (PC.3.206)
4866. Matheson, Alexander, b. 1747, husbandman, sh. May 1774, fr. London to Philadelphia, in *Sally*. (PRO.T47.9\11)
4867. Matheson, Hugh, b. 1742, farmer, res. Rumsdale Kildonan Sutherland, sh. Apr 1774, to Wilmington N.C., in *Bachelor of Leith*. (PRO.T47.12)
4868. Matheson, James, b. 1737, laborer, res. New Luce Wigtonshire, sh. 31 May 1775, fr. Stranraer to N.C., in *Jackie*, m. Jean McQuiston, ch. Margaret. (PRO.T47.12)
4869. Matheson, Katherine, b. 1758, res. Rumsdale Kildonan Sutherland, sh. Apr 1774, to Wilmington N.C., in *Bachelor of Leith*. (PRO.T47.12)
4870. Mathew, John, b. 1750, shoemaker, res. Ayr, sh. May 1774, fr. Greenock to N.Y., in *Matty*. (PRO.T47.12)
4871. Mathew, William, b. 1749, shoemaker, res. Ayr, sh. May 1774, fr. Greenock to N.Y., in *Matty*. (PRO.T47.12)

4872. Mathie, John jr, blacksmith, counterfeiter, res. Dunbarton, tr. Aug 1753. (SM.15.420)(SRO.JC3.29.263)
4873. Mathie, Thomas, sailor, sh. 18 Aug 1699, fr. Clyde to Darien, in *Rising Sun*, Edin pr1707 CC8.8.83
4874. Mathieson, E, b. 1758, res. Edinburgh, sh. Apr 1775, fr. Greenock to N.Y., in *Lilly*. (PRO.T47.12)
4875. Mathieson, Kenneth, b. 1721, servant, Jacobite, res. Strathpeffer Ross-shire, tr. 31 Mar 1747, fr. London to Barbados , in *Frere*. (P.3.12)(MR82)
4876. Mathieson, Murdoch, thief, res. Perth, tr. Sep 1699. (SRO.B59.26.11.1.16)
4877. Mathieson, Robert, b. 1752, laborer, res. Elgin Morayshire, sh. Apr 1775, fr. Greenock to N.Y., in *Lilly*. (PRO.T47.12)
4878. Mathieson, Walter, servant, housebreaker, tr. 1772, fr. Port Glasgow, in *Matty*, arr. Port Oxford Md 16 May 1772. (SRO.JC27.10.3)
4879. Mathison, Janet, b. 1763, servant, res. Ness Isle of Lewis, sh. May 1775, fr. Stornaway to Philadelphia, in *Friendship*. (PRO.T47.12)
4880. Matlock, Isobel, b. 1757, servant, res. Breadalbane Perthshire, sh. June 1775, fr. Greenock to N.Y., in *Commerce*. (PRO.T47.12)
4881. Matthew, Andrew, b. 14 Jan 1693, Auchterhouse Angus, Jacobite, res. Angus, tr. 8 May 1747. (P.3.12)(MR105)
4882. Matthew, Andrew, b. 1715, maltster, Jacobite, res. Perthshire, tr. 5 May 1747, fr. Liverpool to Leeward Islands, in *Veteran*, arr. Martinique June 1747. (P.3.12)(MR73)(PRO.SP36.102)
4883. Matthews, Matthew, weaver, Jacobite, res. Naas Co Kildare, tr. 21 July 1748. (P.3.14)(MR198)
4884. Matthewson, John, Jacobite, tr. 7 May 1716, fr. Liverpool to S.C., in *Susannah*. (SPC.1716.309)(CTB31.206)
4885. Matthewson, Roderick, b. 1756, res. Inverness, sh. Sept 1774, fr. Greenock to Jamaica, in *Jamaica*. (PRO.T47.12)
4886. Matthieson, Glashan, servant, thief, res. Leith Mid Lothian, tr. Aug 1680. (ETR170)
4887. Matthieson, John, Covenanter, res. Closeburn Dumfries-shire, tr. June 1684, fr. Leith to Carolina. (PC.9.15)
4888. Maule, Robert, clergyman, sh. 1706. (EMA44)
4889. Maull, James, clergyman, d. pre 1697 Antigua. (SRO.SH.8.5.1697)
4890. Mavor, Alexander, Covenanter, res. Urquhart Inverness-shire, tr. 1685. (PC.10.165)
4891. Mavor, Mark, Covenanter, res. Urquhart Inverness-shire, pts. Alexander Mavor, tr. 1685. (PC.10.165)
4892. Maxton, James, clerk, forger, res. Edinburgh, tr. Jan 1767. (SRO.HCR.I.99)
4893. Maxwell, Adam, b. 1730, laborer, Jacobite, tr. 22 Apr 1747. (P.3.14)(MR206)

4894. Maxwell, Charles, Covenanter, res. Netherkeir Nithsdale Dumfries-shire, tr. Oct 1684. (PC.10.587)
4895. Maxwell, David, b. 1740, tailor, res. Galloway, sh. May 1774, fr. Stranraer to N.Y., in *Gale*, m. Jean McGarvin, ch. Marion. (PRO.T47.12)
4896. Maxwell, James, Covenanter, res. Cathcart Glasgow, tr. 12 Dec 1678, fr. Leith to West Indies, in *St Michael of Scarborough*. (PC.6.76)
4897. Maxwell, James jr, Covenanter, res. Cathcart Glasgow, tr. 12 Dec 1678, fr. Leith to West Indies, in *St Michael of Scarborough*. (PC.6.76)
4898. Maxwell, Jean, b. 1742, res. Galloway, sh. May 1774, fr. Stranraer to N.Y., in *Gale*, ch. John. (PRO.T47.12)
4899. Maxwell, John, physician & clergyman edu. Edinburgh Uni 1658, res. Glasgow, sh. pre 1662, sett. Port Royal Jamaica, m. Mary ..., ch. John, d. 1673, Jamaica pr1673 LOS\f74. (SRA.TPM.113.562)
4900. Maxwell, Robert, Covenanter, res. Cathcart Glasgow, tr. 12 Dec 1678, fr. Leith to West Indies, in *St Michael of Scarborough*. (PC.6.76)
4901. Maxwell, Robert, b. 1725, weaver, res. Inch Wigtonshire, sh. 31 May 1775, fr. Stranraer to N.Y., in *Jackie*, m. Martha Carnochan, ch. Margaret Janet Sarah Martha. (PRO.T47.12)
4902. Maxwell, Robert, b. 1756, clerk, sh. Oct 1774, fr. London to Carolina, in *James*. (PRO.T47.9\11)
4903. Maxwell, William, clergyman, res. Glasgow, sh. 1726, sett. Edisto Island & Barnsted Downs S.C. (F.7.664)
4904. Maxwell, William, Jacobite, tr. 29 June 1716, fr. Liverpool to Jamaica or Va, in *Elizabeth & Anne*, arr. York Va. (SPC.1716.310)(CTB31.208)(VSP.1.186)
4905. Maxwell, William, assault, res. Glasgow, tr. May 1725. (SRO.JC27)
4906. Maxwell, William, b. 1742, yeoman, sh. Sept 1775, fr. Newcastle to Ga, in *Georgia Packet*, sett. Friendsborough Ga. (PRO.T47.10)
4907. Mean, John, Jacobite, res. Lancashire, tr. 31 Mar 1747. (P.3.186)(MR198)
4908. Mean, William, b. 1753, tailor, res. Ayr, sh. May 1774, fr. Stranraer to N.Y., in *Gale*. (PRO.T47.12)
4909. Mearns, Elizabeth, thief, res. Aberdeen, tr. Oct 1773, m. George Tod. (AJ1343)
4910. Mearson, John, b. 1744, wright, res. Stirling, sh. May 1775, fr. Greenock to N.Y., in *Christy*. (PRO.T47.12)
4911. Mechlane, Elizabeth, Covenanter, tr. Oct 1684. (PC.10.251)
4912. Meiblo, James, sailor, res. Dysart Fife, sh. 14 July 1698, fr. Leith to Darien, in *St Andrew*, ch. Elspeth, Edin pr1707 CC8.8.83
4913. Meik, William, sailor, res. Bo'ness West Lothian, sh. 18 Aug 1699, fr. Clyde to Darien, in *Rising Sun*, Edin pr1707 CC8.8.83
4914. Meikle, Robert, clergyman, Covenanter, tr. 12 Dec 1678, fr. Leith to West Indies, in *St Michael of Scarborough*. (PC.6.76)

4915. Meikle, Robert, thief, res. Paisley Renfrewshire, tr. 1771, fr. Port Glasgow to Md, in *Polly*, arr. Port Oxford Md 16 Sept 1771. (SRO.JC27.10.3)(AJ1175)

4916. Meikle, Robert, tr. 1772, fr. Port Glasgow to Md, in *Matty*, arr. Port Oxford Md 16 May 1772. (SRO.JC27.10.3)

4917. Meiklejohn, John, b. 1716, soldier, Jacobite, tr. 31 Mar 1747, fr. London to Barbados , in *Frere*. (P.3.186)

4918. Meiklejohn, Thomas, cook, res. Queensferry West Lothian, sh. 18 Aug 1699, fr. Clyde to Darien, in *Duke of Hamilton*, d. 1700 Darien, Edin pr1712 CC8.8.85

4919. Mein, Alexander, Covenanter, res. Kirkcudbright, tr. Oct 1684. (PC.10.257)

4920. Mein, John, bookseller, res. Edinburgh, pts. John Mein, sh. 1765, sett. Boston Mass. (NEHGS\SCS)(REB.1765.138)

4921. Mein, Patrick, merchant, sh. pre 1701, sett. Barbados. (SPC.1699.559)

4922. Meldrum, George, clergyman, res. Crombie Arberchirdor Banffshire, tr. Feb 1685. (PC.10.165)

4923. Meldrum, George, Jacobite, tr. 30 Mar 1716, fr. Liverpool to Antigua, in *Scipio*. (SPC.1716.310)

4924. Meldrum, William, clergyman, sh. 1756, to Va. (EMA45)

4925. Melville, David, merchant, res. Glasgow, sh. 1690s, sett. Boston Mass. (SO44)(BGBG.1717.330)

4926. Melville, John, sailor, res. Kinghorn Fife, sh. 18 Aug 1699, fr. Greenock to Darien, in *Rising Sun*, Edin pr1707 CC8.8.83

4927. Melville, John, smith, vagrant & thief, res. Perthshire, tr. Oct 1772, m. Mary Wilson. (SRO.JC27.10.3)(SRO.B59.26.11.16)(AJ1293)

4928. Melville, William, miner, Jacobite, res. Aberdeen, tr. 22 Apr 1747, fr. Liverpool to Md, in *Johnson*, arr. Port Oxford Md 5 Aug 1747. (P.3.188)(JAB.2.436)(MR211)(PRO.T1.328)

4929. Menzies of Cammo, John, b. 1650, advocate & judge, res. Cultermains, pts. Alexander Menzies, sett. Boston Mass, m. (1)Rachel Wilkie(2)Janet Bruce(3)Isabel Winram. (FAS417)

4930. Menzies, Adam, clergyman, sh. 1750, to Va. (EMA45)

4931. Menzies, Archibald, Jacobite, tr. 29 June 1716, fr. Liverpool to Jamaica or Va, in *Elizabeth & Anne*, arr. York Va. (SPC.1716.310)(CTB31.208)(VSP.1.185)

4932. Menzies, Donald, thief, res. Linlithgow West Lothian, tr. Mar 1754. (SRO.JC3.29.500) (alias 1690)

4933. Menzies, Donald, thief, tr. Apr 1754, fr. Leith to Va. (AJ324\6)

4934. Menzies, Gilbert, res. Aberdeen, sett. St Michael's Barbados, d. Sept 1764. (APB.4.55)

4935. Menzies, John, schoolmaster, res. Edinburgh, sh. pre 1676, sett. Barbados. (PC.4.671)

4936. Menzies, John, merchant, res. Edinburgh, d. 1768 Jamaica, Edin pr1769 CC8.8.121
4937. Menzies, Mary, b. 1750, lady, sh. May 1775, fr. Greenock to N.C., in *Ajax*. (PRO.T47.12)
4938. Menzies, Ninian, merchant, res. Glasgow, sh. pre 1775, sett. Richmond Va & St Eustatia, d. 18 Feb 1781 St Eustatia West Indies, Edin pr1799 CC8.8.131. (SM.43.223)
4939. Menzies, Robert, Jacobite, tr. 29 June 1716, fr. Liverpool to Jamaica or Va, in *Elizabeth & Anne*, arr. York Va. (SPC.1716.310)(CTB31.208)(VSP.1.186)
4940. Menzies, Walter, b. 1729, flaxdresser, Jacobite, res. Atholl Perthshire, tr. 5 May 1747, fr. Liverpool to Leeward Islands, in *Veteran*, arr. Martinique June 1747. (P.3.188)(MR106)(PRO.SP36.102)
4941. Menzies, William, goldsmith, res. Aberdeen, sett. Barbados, d. 30 June 1755. (APB.3.186)
4942. Mercer, Hugh, b. 17 Jan 1726, New Pisligo Aberdeenshire , planter & physician edu. King's Col Aberdeen 1744, res. Aberdeenshire, pts. Rev William Mercer & Anne Munro, sh. 1746, fr. Leith to Philadelphia, sett. Mercerburg & Fredericksburg King George Co Va, m. Isabella Gordon, ch. William John Ann Gordon, d. 12 Jan 1777 Princeton N.J., Spotsylvania pr1777 E169. (KCA.2.315)(OD43)(SA188)
4943. Mercer, James Francis, soldier, res. Perth, d. pre 1760 Oswego, PCC pr1760
4944. Mercer, Mary, res. Dumfries, pts. Charles Mercer, sh. pre 1772, sett. Jamaica, m. James Morine. (SRO.RS.21.15)
4945. Mercer, Robert, merchant, res. Pittendreich, sh. pre 1770, sett. N.Y. (SRO.GD1)
4946. Mercer, Robert, b. 1656, baker, res. Loudoun Ayrshire, sh. 1683, fr. London to Jamaica, in *Richard & Sarah*. (CLRO\AIA)
4947. Merchiston, Robert, surgeon's mate, res. Fife, sh. 14 July 1698, fr. Leith to Darien, in *St Andrew*, Edin pr1707 CC8.8.83
4948. Merston, John, soldier, m. Margaret Colville, d. 1699 Darien, Edin pr1707 CC8.8.83
4949. Michey, John, Jacobite, tr. 29 June 1716, fr. Liverpool to Jamaica or Va, in *Elizabeth & Anne*, arr. York Va. (SPC.1716.310)(VSP.1.186)
4950. Middlemiss, James jr, farmer, res. Southcoat Roxburghshire, tr. May 1726. (SRO.JC12.4)
4951. Middlemiss, James sr, farmer, res. Southcoat Roxburghshire, tr. May 1726. (SRO.JC12.4)
4952. Middleton, Alexander, b. 1706, servant, Jacobite, res. Edinburgh or Aberdeen, tr. 5 May 1747, fr. Liverpool to Leeward Islands, in *Veteran*, arr. Martinique June 1747. (P.3.190)(MR74)(PRO.SP36.102)

4953. Middleton, George, b. 1706, res. Aberdeen, sh. Apr 1724, fr. London to Jamaica. (CLRO\AIA)
4954. Middleton, James, thief, res. Aberdeenshire, tr. Aug 1753, fr. Aberdeen to Va, in *St Andrew*. (AJ281\294)
4955. Middleton, John, b. 1756, clerk, res. Stonehaven Kincardineshire, sh. July 1775, fr. Greenock to Jamaica, in *Isabella*. (PRO.T47.12)
4956. Middleton, John, b. 1760, res. Edinburgh, sh. May 1775, fr. Leith to Philadelphia, in *Friendship*. (PRO.T47.12)
4957. Middleton, Peter, physician edu. Edinburgh & St Andrews Unis 1750, sett. N.Y., d. 1752 N.Y. (SA181)(SRO.RD2.235.730)
4958. Middleton, William, b. 1751, carpenter, sh. Sept 1774, fr. London to Jamaica, in *Standlinch*. (PRO.T47.9\11)
4959. Miggleston, Thomas, sailor, res. Inverkeithing Fife, sh. 18 Aug 1699, fr. Clyde to Darien, in *Rising Sun*, m. Janet Ferguson, Edin pr1707 CC8.8.83
4960. Milburn, Elizabeth, b. 1755, spinner, sh. Sept 1775, to Ga, in *Georgia Packet*, sett. Friendsborough Ga. (PRO.T47.10)
4961. Mildrain, George, Jacobite, tr. 30 Mar 1716, fr. Liverpool to Antigua, in *Scipio*. (CTB31.204)
4962. Miles, George, servant, Jacobite, tr. Sept 1748. (P.3.192)
4963. Mill, Andrew, thief, res. Aberdeenshire, tr. 1752. (SM.14.509)
4964. Mill, Andrew, b. 1730, tailor, Jacobite, res. Banffshire, tr. 5 May 1747, fr. Liverpool to Leeward Islands, in *Veteran*, arr. Martinique June 1747. (P.2.196)(MR74)(JAB.2.437)(PRO.SP36.102)
4965. Mill, David, Jacobite, tr. 24 May 1716, fr. Liverpool to Md, in *Friendship*, arr. Md Aug 1716. (SPC.1716.311)(HM386)
4966. Mill, James, Jacobite, tr. 22 Apr 1747, fr. Liverpool to Va, in *Johnson*, arr. Port Oxford Md 5 Aug 1747. (PRO.T1.328)
4967. Mill, John, surgeon, res. Aberlady East Lothian, d. 1699 Darien, Edin pr1708 CC8.8.84
4968. Mill, William, midshipman, res. Haddington East Lothian, sh. 14 July 1698, fr. Leith to Darien, in *Unicorn*, Edin pr1707 CC8.8.83
4969. Mill, William, thief, res. Perthshire, tr. May 1775. (SM.37.405)
4970. Millen, Robert, b. 1755, spinner, sh. Sept 1775, fr. Newcastle to Ga, in *Georgia Packet*. (PRO.T47.9\11)
4971. Miller, Alexander, b. 1755, book-keeper, sh. Jan 1774, fr. London to Barbados, in *Assistance*. (PRO.T47.9\11)
4972. Miller, Andrew, tr. 21 Oct 1682, fr. Greenock to N.Y. (ETR221)
4973. Miller, Anne, thief, res. Ayr, tr. May 1749. (SM.11.252)
4974. Miller, David, sailor, res. Kirkcaldy Fife, sh. 14 July 1698, fr. Leith to Darien, in *Dolphin*, Edin pr1707 CC8.8.83
4975. Miller, David, tinker, thief, res. Perthshire, tr. Apr 1752. (AJ227)
4976. Miller, David, surgeon, sh. pre 1768, to Jamaica. (SRO.SH.8.11.1768)
4977. Miller, David, planter, d. 6 Dec 1698 Darien. (NLS.RY2b8\19)

4978. Miller, David, surgeon, res. Dundee Angus, sh. pre 1748, sett. Westmoreland Co Jamaica. (SRO.RD4.176.142)
4979. Miller, Elizabeth, b. 1747, servant, res. Bower Caithness, sh. Sept 1775, fr. Kirkwall to Savannah Ga, in *Marlborough*. (PRO.T47.12) (alias 6625)
4980. Miller, Elizabeth, b. 1752, servant, res. Perth, sh. May 1775, fr. Leith to Philadelphia, in *Friendship*. (PRO.T47.12)
4981. Miller, Farquhar, b. 1697, gardener, Jacobite, res. Edinburgh, tr. 24 Feb 1747, fr. Liverpool to Va, in *Gildart*, arr. Port North Potomac Md 5 Aug 1747. (P.3.194)(MR74)(PRO.T1.328)
4982. Miller, Gavin, b. 1738, farmer, sh. Apr 1775, fr. Greenock to N.Y., in *Lilly*. (PRO.T47.12)
4983. Miller, Hugh, res. Galloway, sh. pre 1777, sett. Mecklenburg Co Va. (SRO.RD2.224.234)
4984. Miller, James, Covenanter, res. Kirkcaldy Fife, tr. 12 Dec 1678, fr. Leith to West Indies, in *St Michael of Scarborough*. (PC.6.76)
4985. Miller, James, b. 1753, weaver, res. Paisley Renfrewshire, sh. Feb 1774, fr. Greenock to N.Y., in *Commerce*. (PRO.T47.12)
4986. Miller, John, thief, res. Shurrive Caithnesss, tr. June 1767. (AJ1018) (alias 259)
4987. Miller, John, sailor, res. Auchtertool Fife, pts. John Miller, sh. 14 July 1698, fr. Leith to Darien, in *Dolphin*, Edin pr1707 CC8.8.83
4988. Miller, John, b. 1710, res. Edinburgh, sh. July 1728, fr. London to N.Y. or Pa. (CLRO\AIA)
4989. Miller, Katherine, vintner's servant, res. Perth, tr. 1767. (SM.29.497)
4990. Miller, Malcolm, sailor, sh. 14 July 1698, fr. Leith to Darien, in *Caledonia*, Edin pr1707 CC8.8.83
4991. Miller, Margaret, Covenanter, tr. 5 Sept 1685, fr. Leith to East N.J., in *Henry & Francis*. (PC.11.154)
4992. Miller, Peter, clergyman edu. Glasgow Uni, sh. 1777, to Jamaica. (FPA316)
4993. Miller, Robert, thief, tr. 1653, fr. Ayr to Barbados. (SRO.JC27.10.3)
4994. Miller, Robert, tr. 15 Nov 1679, fr. Leith. (ETR162)
4995. Miller, Thomas, soldier, thief, tr. 27 Feb 1668, to Barbados. (PC.2.415)
4996. Miller, Thomas, tr. 15 Nov 1679, fr. Leith. (ETR162)
4997. Miller, Thomas, b. 1748, farmer, res. Kilbarchan Renfrewshire, sh. Apr 1775, fr. Greenock to N.Y., in *Lilly*. (PRO.T47.12)
4998. Miller, William, thief & vagabond, res. Roxburghshire, tr. May 1731. (SRO.JC12.4)
4999. Miller, William, b. 1736, farmer, res. Evie Orkney Islands, sh. Sept 1775, fr. Kirkwall to Savannah Ga, in *Marlborough*, sett. Richmond Co Ga, m. Margaret Irvine, ch. Isobel Hugh William John. (PRO.T47.12)

5000. Miller, William, b. 1751, weaver, res. Paisley Renfrewshire, sh. Feb 1774, fr. Greenock to N.Y., in *Commerce*. (PRO.T47.12)
5001. Milligan, Agnes, b. 1743, res. Gatehouse Kirkcudbrightshire, sh. May 1774, fr. Stranraer to N.Y., in *Gale*. (PRO.T47.12)
5002. Milligan, James, merchant, res. St John's Clachan Dalry Kirkcudbright, pts. Quintin Milligan, sh. pre 1772, sett. Philadelphia. (SRO.RS23.20.461)
5003. Milligan, Lilian, merchant's servant, infanticide, res. Dumfries, tr. 1775, fr. Greenock to Va, in *Rainbow*, arr. Port Hampton Va 3 May 1775. (SRO.JC27.10.3)
5004. Milligan, Margaret, Covenanter, res. Dumfries-shire, tr. Oct 1684, m. William Milligan. (PC.10.587)
5005. Milligan, Mary, b. 1740, res. Gatehouse Kirkcudbrightshire, sh. May 1774, fr. Stranraer to N.Y., in *Gale*. (PRO.T47.12)
5006. Milligan, William, weaver, rioter, res. Dumfries, tr. 1771, fr. Port Glasgow to Md, in *Matty*, arr. Port Oxford Md 17 Dec 1771. (SRO.JC27.10.3)(AJ1232)
5007. Milliken, Mr, sh. pre 1700, sett. Nevis. (DP332)
5008. Milliken, Thomas, merchant, sh. Mar 1683, fr. Ayr to Caribee Islands, in *James of Ayr*. (SRO.E72.3.12)
5009. Millroy, John, b. 1734, farmer, res. Galloway, sh. May 1774, fr. Stranraer to N.Y., in *Gale*, m. Eliza ..., ch. Mary Janet Eliza Anthony John Agnes. (PRO.T47.12)
5010. Millroy, John, b. 1744, shoemaker, res. Galloway, sh. May 1774, fr. Stranraer to N.Y., in *Gale*, m. Sarah ... (PRO.T47.12)
5011. Mills, Elizabeth, res. Dundee Angus, sh. June 1775, fr. Kirkcaldy to S.C., in *Jamaica Packet*. (PRO.T47.12)
5012. Mills, John, joiner, res. Dundee Angus, sh. June 1775, fr. Kirkcaldy to S.C., in *Jamaica Packet*. (PRO.T47.12)
5013. Mills, John, b. 1751, merchant, res. Aberdeen, sh. July 1775, fr. Greenock to Jamaica, in *Isabella*. (PRO.T47.12)
5014. Mills, William, Jacobite, tr. 1747. (MR198)
5015. Mills, William, b. 1725, servant, Jacobite, res. Aberdeen, tr. 5 May 1747, fr. Liverpool to Leeward Islands, in *Veteran*, arr. Martinique June 1747. (P.2.196)(PRO.SP36.102)
5016. Millwane, Mary, b. 1748, res. Galloway, sh. May 1774, fr. Stranraer to N.Y., in *Gale*. (PRO.T47.12)
5017. Millwane, Thomas, b. 1757, farmer, res. Galloway, sh. May 1774, fr. Stranraer to N.Y., in *Gale*. (PRO.T47.12)
5018. Milne, Andrew, tr. 5 Feb 1753, fr. Aberdeen to Va, in *Planter*. (AJ265)
5019. Milne, Andrew, b. 1730, tailor, Jacobite, res. Banff, tr. 8 May 1747, to Antigua. (P.3.196)
5020. Milne, Card James, adulterer, res. Strathbogie Aberdeenshire, tr. 1669, to Va. (RSM139)

5021. Milne, David, res. Carnoustie Angus, pts. James Milne, sh. pre 1776, sett. St George Tobago. (SRO.RD2.232.613)
5022. Milne, David, tr. 21 Oct 1682, fr. Greenock to N.Y. (ETR221)
5023. Milne, James, aleseller, res. Kirriemuir Angus, tr. May 1771. (SRO.B59.26.11.6.27)
5024. Milne, James, servant, thief, res. Alderston Muir Lothian, tr. Mar 1758. (SRO.JC27)
5025. Milne, James jr, merchant, assault, res. Dundee Angus, tr. Sept 1753. (SM.15.469)
5026. Milne, Robert, mariner, res. Auchlie Aberdeenshire, pts. Thomas Milne, sh. 1698, sett. Curacao, d. 29 Jan 1714. (APB.2.124)
5027. Milne, William, b. 1755, laborer, res. Sutherland, sh. Oct 1774, fr. Greenock to Philadelphia, in *Sally*. (PRO.T47.12)
5028. Milner, James, res. Mains of Carse Aberdeenshire, pts. James Milner & Margaret Ingram, sh. 1759, d. 1771 N.C. (APB.4.57)
5029. Milroy, Anthony, laborer, res. Galloway, sh. May 1774, fr. Stranraer to N.Y., in *Gale*. (PRO.T47.12)
5030. Miltoun, Mary, tr. 1696, fr. Newhaven to Va. (SRO.RH15.14.58)
5031. Milwain, Janet, b. 1717, res. New Luce Wigtonshire, sh. 31 May 1775, fr. Stranraer to N.Y., in *Jackie*. (PRO.T47.12)
5032. Mitchell, Agnes, infanticide, res. Linlithgow West Lothian, pts. William Mitchell, tr. Aug 1738. (SRO.JC27)
5033. Mitchell, Alexander, servant, thief, res. Arniston Cockpen Midlothian, tr. 20 Dec 1765. (SRO.HCR.I.97)
5034. Mitchell, Alexander, b. 1719, servant, Jacobite, tr. 31 Mar 1747, fr. London to Barbados , in *Frere*. (P.3.198)(JAB.2.437)(MR128)
5035. Mitchell, David, Jacobite, tr. 29 June 1716, fr. Liverpool to Jamaica or Va, in *Elizabeth & Anne*, arr. York Va. (SPC.1716.310)(CTB31.208)(VSP.1.185)
5036. Mitchell, George, Jacobite, tr. 21 Apr 1716, fr. Liverpool to S.C., in *Wakefield*. (SPC.1716.309)(CTB31.205)
5037. Mitchell, George, Jacobite, tr. 21 Apr 1716, fr. Liverpool to St Kitts, in *Hockenhill*. (CTB31.208)
5038. Mitchell, George, Jacobite, res. Old Machar Aberdeen, tr. 24 Feb 1747, fr. Liverpool to Va, in *Gildart*, arr. Port North Potomac Md 5 Aug 1747. (P.3.198)(JAB.2.437)(PRO.T1.328)(MR106)
5039. Mitchell, George, b. 1747, joiner, res. Glasgow, sh. May 1775, fr. Leith to Philadelphia, in *Friendship*. (PRO.T47.12)
5040. Mitchell, Gilbert, b. 1753, ropemaker, res. Glasgow, sh. May 1774, fr. Greenock to N.Y., in *Matty*. (PRO.T47.12)
5041. Mitchell, Henry, merchant, res. Glasgow, sh. pre 1770, sett. Fredericksburg Va. (SRA.CFI)
5042. Mitchell, James, mariner, res. Bo'ness West Lothian, pts. John Mitchell, sh. 18 Aug 1699, fr. Clyde to Darien, Edin pr1707 CC8.8.83

5043. Mitchell, James, Jacobite, tr. 24 May 1716, fr. Liverpool to Md, in *Friendship*, arr. Md Aug 1716. (SPC.1716.311)(HM387)

5044. Mitchell, James, res. Alford Aberdeenshire, pts. Alexander Mitchell, d. May 1767 Morant Town Jamaica. (APB.4.28)

5045. Mitchell, James, gunner, res. Montrose Angus, pts. Elizabeth Mitchell, d. pre 1781 R.I., PCC pr1781

5046. Mitchell, James, merchant, res. Glasgow(?), sh. pre 1761, sett. Va. (SRA.B10.15.7118)

5047. Mitchell, James, b. 1705, Glasgow, sh. 1730, to N.E., sett. Weathersfield Ct. (NNQ.7.89)(SRO.RD4.178.198)

5048. Mitchell, James, b. 1751, weaver, res. Paisley Renfrewshire, sh. Oct 1774, fr. Greenock to Philadelphia, in *Sally*. (PRO.T47.12)

5049. Mitchell, James, b. 1752, farmer, res. Strathspey, sh. May 1774, fr. Greenock to N.Y., in *George*, m. Mary ..., ch. John. (PRO.T47.12)

5050. Mitchell, John, tr. Aug 1685, fr. Leith to Jamaica. (PC.11.136)

5051. Mitchell, John, gardener, thief, res. Colonsay Argyll, tr. Dec 1718. (JRA.1.351)

5052. Mitchell, John, tobacco factor, res. Glasgow, sh. pre 1776, sett. Fredericksburg & Culpepper Co Va. (SRA.T79.32)

5053. Mitchell, John, b. 1699, alehouse-keeper, Jacobite, res. Edinburgh, tr. 20 Mar 1747. (P.3.200)(MR159)

5054. Mitchell, John, b. 1749, farmer, res. Glasgow, sh. May 1774, fr. Greenock to N.Y., in *Matty*. (PRO.T47.12)

5055. Mitchell, John, b. 1751, servant, res. Rothiemay Banffshire, sh. July 1775, fr. Stornaway to Philadelphia, in *Clementina*. (PRO.T47.12)

5056. Mitchell, Robert, b. 1704, schoolmaster, res. Edinburgh, sh. Nov 1723, fr. London to Md. (CLRO\AIA)

5057. Mitchell, Robert, b. 1748, tailor, res. Kintyre Argyll, sh. Aug 1774, fr. Greenock to Wilmington N.C., in *Ulysses*, m. Ann Campbell. (PRO.T47.12)

5058. Mitchell, Thomas, b. 1750, blacksmith, res. Edinburgh, sh. Dec 1773, fr. London to Dominica, in *Greyhound*. (PRO.T47.9\11)

5059. Mitchell, Walter, sailor, res. Alloway Ayrshire, sh. 18 Aug 1699, fr. Clyde to Darien, in *Hope*, Edin pr1707 CC8.8.83

5060. Mitchell, Walter, b. 1728, student edu. Aberdeen Uni, Jacobite, res. King Edward Aberdeenshire, tr. Sept 1748. (P.3.202)(JAB.2.354)

5061. Mitchell, William, farmer & fisherman, res. Shetland Islands, sh. June 1775, fr. Kirkcaldy to Brunswick N.C., in *Jamaica Packet*. (PRO.T47.12)

5062. Mitchell, William, res. Blairgetts, sh. pre 1764, to Jamaica. (SRO.SH.2.3.1764)

5063. Mitchell, William, b. 1742, res. Fife, sh. July 1775, fr. Stornaway to Philadelphia, in *Clementina*. (PRO.T47.12)

249

5064. Mitchell, William, b. 1743, laborer, res. Paisley Renfrewshire, sh. Apr 1775, fr. Greenock to N.Y., in *Lilly*. (PRO.T47.12)
5065. Mitchell, William, b. 1745, husbandman, sh. Dec 1773, fr. London to Md, in *Etty*. (PRO.T47.9\11)
5066. Moat, Alexander, b. 1757, house carpenter, res. Kirkwall Orkney Islands, sh. Sept 1775, fr. Kirkwall to Savannah Ga, in *Marlborough*. (PRO.T47.12)
5067. Mochline, William, planter, res. Rutherglen Glasgow, sh. pre 1749, sett. St Andrew's Brunswick Co Va. (SRO.RD2.168.10)
5068. Moffat, George, merchant, sh. 1699, to N.Y. (DP143)
5069. Moffat, James, sailor, res. Linlithgow West Lothian, sh. 18 Aug 1699, fr. Clyde to Darien, in *Rising Sun*, m. Elizabeth Grozart, Edin pr1707 CC8.8.83
5070. Moffat, James, tr. Aug 1684, to Carolina. (PC.9.95)
5071. Moffat, Jean, Covenanter, tr. 5 Sept 1685, fr. Leith to East N.J., in *Henry & Francis*. (PC.11.154)
5072. Moffat, John, clergyman & teacher, sh. 1751, sett. Wallkill Orange Co, d. 22 Apr 1788 Little Britain. (F.7.664)
5073. Moir, Alexander, physician edu. King's Col Aberdeen, res. Mortlich Banffshire, d. 1766 St Croix. (FAB207)(SM.28.615)
5074. Moir, Henry, sh. pre 1775, sett. Tortula. (SRO.RD2.236.499)
5075. Moir, Henry, surgeon, Jacobite, res. Kelso Roxburghshire, tr. Sept 1748. (P.3.202)(MR48)
5076. Moir, James, clergyman, res. Fife, sh. 1739, d. 31 Dec 1766 Edgecombe Co N.C. (SPG.3.20)(SM.28.615)
5077. Moir, John, res. Netherpark of Drim Aberdeenshire, pts. Thomas Moir & Christian Ross, sh. 1700, sett. Curacao. (APB.2.104)
5078. Moir, Malcolm, res. Perthshire, tr. 14 July 1698, fr. Leith to Darien, in *St Andrew*. (SRO.B59.26.11.3) (alias 5654)
5079. Moir, Robert, Jacobite, res. Kelso Roxburghshire, tr. Sept 1748. (P.2.204)(MR49)
5080. Moir, Stephen, merchant, sh. pre 1763, sett. Quebec. (REB.1763.117)
5081. Molison, Thomas, b. 1709, clerk or writer, res. Brechin Angus, sh. Mar 1730, fr. London to Md. (CLRO\AIA)
5082. Moncrieff, David, soldier, sh. 1699, to Darien, Edin pr1707 CC8.8.83
5083. Moncrieff, George, carpenter, sh. 18 Aug 1699, fr. Clyde to Darien, in *Rising Sun*, Edin pr1707 CC8.8.83
5084. Moncrieff, Robert, clergyman, sh. 1748, to Antigua. (EMA46)
5085. Mondell, John, Jacobite, tr. 29 June 1716, fr. Liverpool to Jamaica or Va, in *Elizabeth & Anne*, arr. York Va. (SPC.1716.310)(CTB31.208)(VSP.1.185)
5086. Monke, William, soldier, sh. 1659, to Jamaica, in *Grantham*. (SPC.1659.126)

5087. Monorgan, Gilbert, Covenanter, tr. 5 Sept 1685, fr. Leith to East N.J., in *Henry & Francis.* (PC.11.162)

5088. Monras, George, sh. 29 Nov 1773, fr. Greenock to Jamaica, in *Mary of Glasgow.* (SRO.CE60.1.7)

5089. Monro, Allan, b. 1719, farmer, Jacobite, res. Glenmoriston Inverness-shire, tr. 31 Mar 1747, fr. London to Barbados, in *Frere.* (P.3.204)(MR159)

5090. Monro, Duncan, b. 1728, laborer, Jacobite, res. Inverness, tr. 5 May 1747, fr. Liverpool to Leeward Islands, in *Veteran,* arr. Martinique June 1747. (P.3.204)(MR124)(PRO.SP36.102)

5091. Monro, Hector, b. 1716, drummer, Jacobite, tr. 31 Mar 1747, fr. London to Jamaica, in *St George or Carteret,* arr. Jamaica 1747. (P.3.206)(PRO.CO137.58)

5092. Monro, Hugh, overseer, sh. 1698, to Darien, Edin pr1707 CC8.8.83

5093. Monro, Hugh, b. 1748, shoemaker, res. Tongue Sutherland, sh. Apr 1774, to Wilmington N.C., in *Bachelor of Leith.* (PRO.T47.12)

5094. Monro, Janet, thief, res. Edinburgh, tr. May 1770, fr. Glasgow. (SM.32.337)

5095. Monro, William, b. 1740, shoemaker, res. Borgiemore Tongue Sutherland, sh. Apr 1774, to Wilmington N.C., in *Bachelor of Leith.* (PRO.T47.12)

5096. Montain, Joannes, sailor, res. Leith Midlothian, sh. 14 July 1698, fr. Leith to Darien, in *Unicorn,* Edin pr1707 CC8.8.83

5097. Monteath, .., b. 1759, merchant, res. Glasgow, sh. Jan 1774, fr. Greenock to Jamaica, in *Janet.* (SRO.CE60.1.7)

5098. Monteath, William, b. 1747, farmer, res. Caithness, sh. May 1775, fr. Greenock to N.Y., in *Lilly.* (PRO.T47.12)

5099. Monteith, Alexander, tr. May 1684, fr. Leith to N.Y. (PC.8.709)

5100. Monteith, Alexander, sh. pre 1749, sett. Kingston Jamaica. (SRO.GD30)

5101. Monteith, Robert, sailor, pts. Jane Monteith, sh. pre 1680, to Hudson Bay, in *John & Alexander,* d. 1680 Hudson Bay. (HBRS.8.44)

5102. Monteith, William, merchant, pts. Walter Monteith of Kepp & Jean Douglas, sh. pre 1777, sett. Green Island Jamaica. (SRO.RD4.237.607)

5103. Montgomery, ..., res. Crevock, sh. 21 July 1684, fr. Gourock to Port Royal S.C., in *Carolina Merchant.* (ECJ72)

5104. Montgomery, Alexander, Covenanter, res. Linlithgow West Lothian, tr. June 1684, fr. Leith to Carolina. (PC.8.524)

5105. Montgomery, Archibald, soldier, sh. pre 1764, sett. N.S. (PCCol.4.816)

5106. Montgomery, Hew, merchant, sh. Oct 1685, fr. Port Glasgow to Va, in *Boston.* (SRO.E72.19.8)

5107. Montgomery, James, planter, d. 29 Nov 1698 Darien. (NLS.RY2b8\19)

5108. Montgomery, James, merchant, sh. Mar 1683, fr. Ayr to Caribee Islands, in *James of Ayr.* (SRO.E72.3.12)

251

5109. Montgomery, Mary, b. 1756, servant, res. Inverness, sh. July 1775, fr. Stornaway to Philadelphia, in *Clementina*. (PRO.T47.12)

5110. Montgomery, Nicholas, Jacobite, tr. 29 June 1716, fr. Liverpool to Jamaica or Va, in *Elizabeth & Anne*. (SPC.1716.310)(CTB31.208)

5111. Montgomery, Sir Robert, res. Skermorlie Ayrshire, sh. 1717, sett. Ga. (SPC.1717.178)

5112. Montgomery, William, Covenanter, sett. S.C., d. pre Apr 1690. (LJ95)

5113. Moodie, Elisabeth, vagabond, res. Aberdeenshire, tr. May 1717. (SRO.JC.11.4)

5114. Moodie, John, b. 1757, servant, res. Perth, sh. May 1775, fr. Leith to Philadelphia, in *Friendship*. (PRO.T47.12)

5115. Moody, George, Jacobite, tr. 26 Apr 1716, fr. Liverpool to Jamaica, in *Two Brothers*, arr. Montserrat June 1716. (SPC.1716.313)(CTB31.205)(CTP.CC.43)

5116. Moor, Miles, Jacobite, tr. 21 Apr 1716, fr. Liverpool to S.C., in *Wakefield*. (SPC.1716.309)(CTB31.205)

5117. Moor, Robert, carpenter, res. Aberdeen, sett. Barbados & Antigua, m. Elizabeth Farquhar, d. 1760. (APB.4.7)

5118. Moor, William, res. Stirling, tr. Mar 1685. (PC.10.206)

5119. Moore, Colin, Jacobite, res. Beddyvaughan, tr. 1747. (P.3.206)

5120. Moore, Donald, Covenanter, res. Argyll, tr. Aug 1685, fr. Leith to Jamaica. (PC.11.136)

5121. Moore, Donald, Covenanter, tr. July 1685, fr. Leith to East N.J. (PC.11.136)

5122. Moore, George, Covenanter, tr. 5 Sept 1685, fr. Leith to East N.J., in *Henry & Francis*. (PC.11.154)

5123. Moore, Robert, res. Carluke Lanarkshire, tr. Aug 1685, fr. Leith to Jamaica, arr. Port Royal Jamaica Nov 1685. (PC.11.136)(LJ169)

5124. Moore, Samuel, merchant, sh. Feb 1681, fr. Ayr to West Indies, in *James of Ayr*. (SRO.E72.3.6)

5125. More, Alexander, b. 13 Apr 1756, Kirkwall, housecarpenter, res. Orkney Islands, pts. Alexander More & Isobel Spence, sh. Sept 1775, fr. Kirkwall to Ga, in *Marlborough*, sett. Richmond Co Ga. (PRO.T47.12)

5126. More, Peter, b. 1744, mason, res. Perthshire, sh. May 1775, fr. Greenock to N.Y., in *Monimia*. (PRO.T47.12)

5127. Morgan, Allan, b. 1722, Jacobite, tr. 31 Mar 1747, fr. London to Barbados , in *Frere*. (P.3.208)(MR185)

5128. Morgan, Charles, b. 1729, barber, Jacobite, res. Elgin Morayshire, tr. 5 May 1747, fr. Liverpool to Leeward Islands, in *Veteran*, arr. Martinique June 1747. (P.3.208)(MR124)(PRO.SP36.102)

5129. Morgan, George, b. 1737, farmer, res. Chabster Reay Caithness, sh. Apr 1774, to Wilmington N.C., in *Bachelor of Leith*. (PRO.T47.12)

5130. Morgan, John, sailor, res. Leven Fife, sh. 14 July 1698, fr. Leith to
        Darien, in *St Andrew*, Edin pr1707 CC8.8.83
5131. Morgan, John, sailor, Jacobite, res. Longford Ireland, tr. 31 Mar 1747.
        (P.3.210)(MR62)
5132. Morgan, Patrick, Jacobite, res. Foginell Aberdeenshire, tr. 22 Apr 1747,
        fr. Liverpool to Va, in *Johnson*, arr. Port Oxford Md 5 Aug 1747.
        (P.3.210)(JAB.2.438)(MR207)(PRO.T1.328) (alias 5133)
5133. Morgan, Peter, Jacobite, res. Foginell Aberdeenshire, tr. 22 Apr 1747, fr.
        Liverpool to Va, in *Johnson*, arr. Port Oxford Md 5 Aug 1747.
        (P.3.210)(JAB.2.438)(MR207)(PRO.T1.328) (alias 5132)
5134. Morgan, William, clergyman edu. Aberdeen Uni, pts. George Morgan, sh.
        1773, to Jamaica, sett. Kingston Jamaica, m. Martha Jopping, ch.
        James, d. 2 Sept 1788. (EMA46)(MCA47)(KCA103)
5135. Moriseite, John, sailor, res. Burntisland Fife, sh. 14 July 1698, fr. Leith
        to Darien, in *Unicorn*, m. Margaret Gray, Edin pr1707 CC8.8.83
5136. Morison, Alexander, b. 1714, farmer, res. Kinside Tongue Sutherland, sh.
        Apr 1774, to Wilmington N.C., in *Bachelor of Leith*.
        (PRO.T47.12)
5137. Morison, Alexander, b. 1742, mason, res. Aberdeen, sh. May 1774, fr.
        Greenock to N.Y., in *George*, m. Mary ... (PRO.T47.12)
5138. Morison, Ann, b. 1762, servant, res. Ness Isle of Lewis, sh. May 1774,
        fr. Stornaway to Philadelphia, in *Friendship*. (PRO.T47.12)
5139. Morison, Christian, b. 1750, res. Stirling, sh. May 1775, fr. Greenock to
        N.Y., in *Lilly*. (PRO.T47.12)
5140. Morison, David, b. 1749, wright, res. Glasgow, sh. May 1774, fr.
        Greenock to N.Y., in *Matty*. (PRO.T47.12)
5141. Morison, Dr, d. 24 Aug 1773 Kingston Jamaica. (SM.36.679)
5142. Morison, Duncan, b. 1747, farmer, res. Stirling, sh. May 1775, fr.
        Greenock to N.Y., in *Lilly*. (PRO.T47.12)
5143. Morison, George, b. 1760, servant, res. Beauly Inverness-shire, sh. July
        1775, fr. Stornaway to Philadelphia, in *Clementina*. (PRO.T47.12)
5144. Morison, Hugh, b. 1762, servant, res. Beauly Inverness-shire, sh. July
        1775, fr. Stornaway to Philadelphia, in *Clementina*. (PRO.T47.12)
5145. Morison, James, tr. 1696, fr. Newhaven to Va. (SRO.RH15.14.58)
5146. Morison, James, b. 1760, apprentice blacksmith, res. Stornaway Isle of
        Lewis, sh. Nov 1774, fr. Stornaway to N.Y., in *Peace & Plenty*.
        (PRO.T47.12)
5147. Morison, Janet, tr. 21 Oct 1682, fr. Greenock to N.Y. (ETR221)
5148. Morison, John, merchant, res. Aberdeenshire, sett. Antigua, d. pre 1770
        Dumfries, Dumfries pr1770 CC5.6.15
5149. Morison, John, clergyman, sh. 1699, to Va, sett. Nevis.
        (EMA46)(DP335)

5150. Morison, John, b. 1749, weaver, res. Beauly Inverness-shire, sh. July 1775, fr. Stornaway to Philadelphia, in *Clementina*, m. Isobel Fraser, ch. Alexander. (PRO.T47.12)

5151. Morison, Mary, b. 1753, servant, res. Inverness, sh. July 1775, fr. Stornaway to Philadelphia, in *Clementina*. (PRO.T47.12)

5152. Morison, Murdo, b. 1757, servant, res. Uig Isle of Lewis, sh. May 1774, fr. Stornaway to Philadelphia, in *Friendship*. (PRO.T47.12)

5153. Morison, Norman, b. 1724, farmer, res. Bragar Isle of Lewis, sh. May 1774, fr. Stornaway to Philadelphia, in *Friendship*. (PRO.T47.12)

5154. Morison, Peter, b. 1728, fisherman, res. Beauly Inverness-shire, sh. July 1775, fr. Stornaway to Philadelphia, in *Clementina*, m. Anne ..., ch. Betty. (PRO.T47.12)

5155. Morn, John, b. 1763, res. Birsay Orkney Islands, sh. Sept 1775, fr. Kirkwall to Savannah Ga, in *Marlborough*. (PRO.T47.12)

5156. Morrin, Charles, physician, res. Dumfries-shire, pts. James Morrin, sh. pre 1772, sett. Jamaica. (SRO.RS .21.15)

5157. Morris, Edward, b. 1725, Jacobite, res. London, tr. 1747. (MR137)

5158. Morrison, Alexander, robber, tr. 1773, fr. Glasgow to Va, in *Thomas of Glasgow*, arr. James River Va 3 July 1773. (SRO.JC27.10.3)

5159. Morrison, Alexander, b. 1697, Isle of Lewis, distiller, Jacobite, res. Mull Argyll, tr. 31 Mar 1747, fr. London to Barbados , in *Frere*. (P.3.210)(MR181)

5160. Morrison, Andrew, robber, tr. 1773, fr. Port Glasgow to Va, in *Thomas of Glasgow*, arr. Upper District James River Va 5 June 1773. (SRO.JC.27)

5161. Morrison, Ann, b. 1762, res. Ness Isle of Lewis, sh. May 1774, fr. Stornaway to Philadelphia, in *Friendship*. (PRO.T47.12)

5162. Morrison, Christopher, sailor, res. Greenock Renfrewshire, sh. 14 July 1698, fr. Leith to Darien, in *Dolphin*, d. 1699 Darien, Edin pr1707 CC8.8.83

5163. Morrison, Donald, Covenanter, res. Argyll, tr. Aug 1685, fr. Leith to Jamaica. (PC.11.136)

5164. Morrison, Donald, b. 1749, cooper, res. Stornaway Isle of Lewis, sh. May 1774, fr. Greenock to N.Y., in *George*. (PRO.T47.12)

5165. Morrison, James, Jacobite, tr. 30 Mar 1716, fr. Liverpool to Antigua, in *Scipio*. (SPC.1716.310)(CTB31.204)

5166. Morrison, James, res. Glasgow, pts. Marion Young, tr. pre 1654, sett. Barbados. (GR.1654.283)

5167. Morrison, John, thief, res. Turriff Aberdeenshire, tr. May 1767. (AJ1011)

5168. Morrison, John, Covenanter, res. Erickstane Dumfries-shire, tr. Oct 1684. (PC.10.275)

5169. Morrison, John, b. 1758, servant, res. Beauly Inverness-shire, sh. July 1775, fr. Stornaway to Philadelphia, in *Clementina*. (PRO.T47.12)

5170. Morrison, Philip, clergyman, sh. 1756, sett. Charleston S.C. (F.7.664)

5171. Morson, Arthur, merchant, res. Glasgow, sh. pre 1768, sett. Falmouth Va, ch. Alexander. (SRA.B10.15.7174)
5172. Morson, James, merchant, res. Greenock Renfrewshire, sh. pre 1755, sett. St Kitts. (SRA.CFI)
5173. Mortimer, Alexander, Jacobite, tr. 24 May 1716, fr. Liverpool to Md, in *Friendship*, arr. Md Aug 1716. (SPC.1716.311)(HM387)
5174. Mortimer, George, Jacobite, tr. 26 Apr 1716, fr. Liverpool to Jamaica, in *Two Brothers*, arr. Montserrat June 1716. (SPC.1716.313)(CTB31.206)(CTP.CC.43)
5175. Mortimer, Isabel, infanticide, res. Aberdeenshire, tr. June 1758. (AJ541)
5176. Morton, David, tr. 22 June 1671, fr. Leith. (PC.3.688)
5177. Morton, John, b. 1749, res. Calton, pts. John Morton & Eliza Crookshanks, d. 26 June 1785 Grenada. (Old Calton Gs)
5178. Morton, Robert, b. 1712, husbandman, res. Mauchline Ayrshire, sh. May 1731, fr. London to Jamaica. (CLRO\AIA)
5179. Morton, William, hamesucken, res. Craigieknow Gattonside Roxburghshire, tr. Sept 1763. (SM.25.579)
5180. Mossman of Mount, James, Covenanter, tr. 12 Dec 1678, fr. Leith to West Indies, in *St Michael of Scarborough*. (PC.6.76)
5181. Mossman, Archibald, d. 15 Nov 1698 Darien. (NLS.RY2b8\19)
5182. Moubray, Thomas, Covenanter, res. Kirkliston West Lothian, tr. 12 Dec 1678, fr. Leith to West Indies, in *St Michael of Scarborough*. (PC.6.76)
5183. Moubray, William, Jacobite, tr. 24 May 1716, fr. Liverpool to Md, in *Friendship*, arr. Md Aug 1716. (SPC.1716.311)(HM387)
5184. Moultrie, Walter, sailor, res. Markinch Fife, pts. George Moultrie, sh. 14 July 1698, fr. Leith to Darien, in *Union*, d. Darien, Edin pr1707 CC8.8.83
5185. Mount, George, tr. Feb 1674. (PC.4.134)
5186. Mowat, Alexander, housebreaker, res. Dunbeath Caithness, tr. June 1773, fr. Glasgow. (AJ1325\8)
5187. Mowat, Elizabeth, b. 1755, farm servant, res. Shetland Islands, sh. Sept 1774, fr. Kirkwall to Savannah Ga, in *Marlborough*, sett. Richmond Co Ga. (PRO.T47.12)
5188. Mowat, James, horsethief, res. Aberdeenshire, tr. Apr 1754. (AJ326)
5189. Mowat, James, b. 1761, farm servant, res. St Andrews Orkney Islands, sh. Sept 1774, fr. Kirkwall to Savannah Ga, in *Marlborough*, sett. Richmond Co Ga. (PRO.T47.12)
5190. Mowat, Janet, spinner, res. Sutherland, sh. Oct 1774, fr. Greenock to Philadelphia, in *Sally*. (PRO.T47.12)
5191. Mowat, John, b. 1758, farm servant, res. Deerness Orkney Islands, sh. Sept 1774, fr. Kirkwall to Savannah Ga, in *Marlborough*. (PRO.T47.12)

5192. Mowatt, John, res. Edinburgh, tr. 8 May 1663, fr. Leith to Barbados, in *Mary*. (EBR.186.13.4)

5193. Moyes, James, cooper, res. Kinghorn Fife, sh. 14 July 1698, fr. Leith to Darien, in *Dolphin*, m. Janet Spowart, Edin pr 1707 CC8.8.83

5194. Moyes, William, cooper, res. Burntisland Fife, sh. 14 July 1698, fr. Leith to Darien, in *Dolphin*, Edin pr1707 CC8.8.83

5195. Muckle, Robert, b. 1687, laborer, Jacobite, res. Duns Berwickshire, tr. 1747. (P.3.214)

5196. Mudie, David, res. Angus, sh. 1684, sett. New Perth East N.J. (Insh240)

5197. Mudie, James, cooper, res. Leith Midlothian, sh. Mar 1683, to Hudson Bay. (HBRS.9.86)

5198. Mudie, James, res. Angus, sh. 1684, sett. New Perth East N.J. (Insh260)

5199. Muir, Adam, Covenanter, tr. July 1685, fr. Leith. (PC.11.114)

5200. Muir, Alexander, sailor, res. Auchtermuchty Fife, sh. 18 Aug 1699, fr. Clyde to Darien, in *Rising Sun*, Edin pr1707 CC8.8.83

5201. Muir, Alexander, b. 1752, weaver, sh. Dec 1773, fr. London to Va, in *Virginia*. (PRO.T47.9\11)

5202. Muir, Ann, b. 1755, servant, res. Edinburgh, sh. May 1775, fr. Leith to Philadelphia, in *Friendship*. (PRO.T47.12)

5203. Muir, David, b. 1755, farmer, res. Kilsyth Stirlingshire, sh. May 1774, fr. Greenock to N.Y., in *George*. (PRO.T47.12)

5204. Muir, George, Covenanter, tr. Aug 1685, fr. Leith. (PC.11.154)

5205. Muir, Hugh, merchant, sh. Mar 1683, fr. Ayr to Caribee Islands, in *James of Ayr*. (SRO.E72.3.12)

5206. Muir, James, Covenanter, res. Lesmahagow Lanarkshire, tr. May 1684, fr. Leith to N.Y. (PC.8.516)

5207. Muir, James, tr. 1775, fr. Greenock to Va, in *Rainbow*, arr. Port Hampton Va 3 May 1775. (SRO.JC.27.10.3)

5208. Muir, James, b. 12 Apr 1757, Old Cumnock Ayrshire, clergyman edu. Glasgow Uni 1776, res. Paisley Renfrewshire, pts. George Muir, sh. 1781, to Bermuda, sett. Warwick Bermuda & Alexandria Va, m. Elizabeth Welman, d. 8 Aug 1820 Alexandria Va. (F.7.661)(MAGU97)

5209. Muir, Janet, b. 1746, servant, res. Edinburgh, sh. May 1775, fr. Leith to Philadelphia, in *Friendship*. (PRO.T47.12)

5210. Muir, John, b. 1751, shoemaker, res. Galloway, sh. Jan 1774, fr. Greenock to Jamaica, in *Janet*. (SRO.CE60.1.7)

5211. Muir, John, b. 1757, weaver, res. Paisley Renfrewshire, sh. Feb 1774, fr. Greenock to N.Y., in *Commerce*. (PRO.T47.12)

5212. Muir, Robert, thief, res. Stirling, tr. May 1731. (SRO.JC.13.6)

5213. Muir, Robert, b. 1744, weaver, res. Paisley Renfrewshire, sh. Feb 1774, fr. Greenock to N.Y., in *Commerce*, m. Jane ..., ch. Margaret Ann James. (PRO.T47.12)

5214. Muir, Robert, b. 1753, farmer, res. Perth, sh. Apr 1775, fr. Greenock to Salem, in *Glasgow Packet*. (PRO.T47.12)

5215. Muir, Robert, b. 1757, weaver, res. Paisley Renfrewshire, sh. Feb 1774, fr. Greenock to N.Y., in *Commerce*. (PRO.T47.12)

5216. Muir, Thomas, fireraiser, tr. Mar 1774. (SM.36.164)

5217. Muir, William, sailor, res. Portsburgh Edinburgh, sh. 14 July 1698, fr. Leith to Darien, in *St Andrew*, Edin pr1707 CC8.8.83

5218. Muir, William, res. Stirling, tr. 5 Sept 1685, fr. Leith to East N.J., in *Henry & Francis*. (PC.10.206)

5219. Muir, William, thief, res. Dumfries-shire, tr. 1753. (SM.15.204)

5220. Muir, William, b. 1757, weaver, res. Paisley Renfrewshire, sh. Feb 1774, fr. Greenock to N.Y., in *Commerce*. (PRO.T47.12)

5221. Muire, James, sett. Va, d. pre 1689, PCC pr1689

5222. Muirhead, Ebenezer, physician, res. Dumfries-shire, pts. William Muirhead of Crochmore & Janet Richardson, sh. pre 1754, sett. Providence R.I. (SRO.RS23.17.17)

5223. Muirhead, Gavin, Covenanter, res. Cambusnethan Lanarkshire, tr. May 1684, fr. Leith to N.Y. (PC.8.516)

5224. Muirhead, James, tr. Aug 1684, fr. Leith to Carolina. (PC.10.3)

5225. Muirhead, John, Covenanter, tr. 5 Sept 1685, fr. Leith to East N.J., in *Henry & Francis*. (PC.11.159(ETR376)

5226. Muirhead, John, merchant, sh. pre 1699, sett. Philadelphia. (SPC.1699.248)

5227. Muirhead, Margaret, tr. Aug 1684, fr. Leith to Carolina. (PC.9.95)

5228. Mun, Archibald, weaver, thief, res. Glasgow, tr. 1752. (SM.14.268)

5229. Munckland, Roger, d. 22 Nov 1698 Darien. (NLS.RY2b8\19)

5230. Mundill, John, Covenanter, tr. 5 Sept 1685, fr. Leith to East N.J., in *Henry & Francis*. (PC.11.330)(ETR369)

5231. Munro, Anne, b. 1757, servant, res. Balconie Ross & Cromarty, sh. July 1775, fr. Stornaway to Philadelphia, in *Clementina*. (PRO.T47.12)

5232. Munro, David, sh. 1699, fr. Darien to N.Y., in *Caledonia*. (SPC.1699.478)

5233. Munro, Donald, soldier, pts. Robert Munro & Christian Brown, tr. 1651, to Barbados. (MT16)

5234. Munro, Duncan, b. 1732, tailor, res. Perthshire, sh. May 1775, fr. Greenock to N.Y., in *Monimia*, m. Janet Brown. (PRO.T47.12)

5235. Munro, Florence, b. 1754, spinner, res. Glasgow, sh. Feb 1774, fr. Greenock to N.Y., in *Commerce*. (PRO.T47.12)

5236. Munro, George, b. 1745, wright, res. Glasgow, sh. May 1775, fr. Greenock to N.Y., in *Monimia*. (PRO.T47.12)

5237. Munro, Hugh, tr. Dec 1685, fr. Leith to Barbados, in *John & Nicholas*. (ETR390)

5238. Munro, Margaret, b. 1754, servant, res. Inverness, sh. July 1775, fr. Stornaway to Philadelphia, in *Clementina*. (PRO.T47.12)

5239. Munro, William, res. Birse Aberdeenshire, pts. William Munro, d. pre 1775 Grenada. (APB.4.71)
5240. Munroe, John, cattlethief, res. Inveraray Argyll, tr. May 1730. (JRA.2.435)
5241. Murchie, William, b. 1737, weaver, res. Paisley Renfrewshire, sh. Feb 1774, fr. Greenock to N.Y., in *Commerce*, m. Agnes ..., ch. William James John Gavin. (PRO.T47.12)
5242. Murchie, William jr, b. 1756, weaver, res. Paisley Renfrewshire, sh. Feb 1774, fr. Greenock to N.Y., in *Commerce*. (PRO.T47.12)
5243. Murdoch, Archibald, b. 1757, weaver, res. Paisley Renfrewshire, sh. Feb 1774, fr. Greenock to N.Y., in *Commerce*. (PRO.T47.12)
5244. Murdoch, David, sett. N.Y., m. Mary .., d. pre 1687, PCC pr1687
5245. Murdoch, George, res. Glasgow, pts. George Murdoch, d. 10 Dec 1771 Grenada. (SM.34.109)
5246. Murdoch, James, clergyman, sh. 1766, sett. N.S., d. 1767 River Misquoduboit. (UPC655)
5247. Murdoch, James, b. 1743, gardener, res. Glasgow, sh. Feb 1774, fr. Greenock to N.Y., in *Commerce*. (PRO.T47.12)
5248. Murdoch, John, merchant, sh. Mar 1683, fr. Ayr to Caribee Islands, in *James of Ayr*. (SRO.E72.3.12)
5249. Murdoch, John, b. 1749, farmer, res. Stirling, sh. May 1774, fr. Greenock to N.Y., in *Matty*. (PRO.T47.12)
5250. Murdoch, John, b. 1753, merchant, sh. June 1774, fr. Whitehaven to Va, in *Lonsdale*. (PRO.T47.9\11)
5251. Murdoch, John, b. 1757, res. Kilmarnock Ayrshire, sh. Sept 1774, fr. Greenock to Jamaica, in *Jamaica*. (PRO.T47.12)
5252. Murdoch, Patrick, res. Cumloden Minnigaff Galloway, pts. William Murdoch & Mary McDouall, sh. May 1774, m. Nicola Gibson, ch. John William Samuel Thomas, d. 1775 N.Y. (G.21.6.104)
5253. Murdoch, Samuel, b. 1755, merchant, sh. June 1774, fr. Whitehaven to Va, in *Lonsdale*. (PRO.T47.9\11)
5254. Murdoch, Thomas, b. 1757, merchant, sh. June 1774, fr. Whitehaven to Va, in *Lonsdale*. (PRO.T47.9\11)
5255. Murdoch, William, b. 1707, wool merchant, Jacobite, res. Callendar Perthshire, tr. 22 Apr 1747, fr. Liverpool to Va, in *Johnson*, arr. Port Oxford Md 5 Aug 1747. (P.3.216)(PRO.T1.328)
5256. Mure, ..., thief, res. Edinburgh, tr. 17 Feb 1714, fr. Leith to West Indies. (EBR.1714.263)
5257. Mure, Hutchison, merchant, sh. pre 1769, sett. King's Co P.E.I. (SRO.GD293.2.71)
5258. Murison, George, clergyman edu. King's Col Aberdeen 1701, sh. 1705, sett. Rye Ct, d. 1708. (SNQ.1.59)(SPG.11.86)

258

5259. Murray of McLeod, Margaret, b. 1749, sailor's wife, res. Stornaway Isle of Lewis, sh. May 1774, fr. Stornaway to Philadelphia, in *Friendship*, ch. George Malcolm Janet. (PRO.T47.12)
5260. Murray, Alexander, clergyman, tr. 1652, sett. Ware Va, d. pre 1703. (SPG.11.152)
5261. Murray, Alexander, Jacobite, tr. 31 July 1716, fr. Liverpool to Va, in *Anne*. (SPC.1716.310)(CTB31.209)
5262. Murray, Alexander, Jacobite, tr. 31 July 1716, fr. Liverpool to Va, in *Anne*. (SPC.1716.310)(CTB31.209)
5263. Murray, Alexander, merchant & naval officer, res. Lauderdale, pts. Charles Murray, sh. pre 1737, sett. Charleston S.C. (SRO.SH.17.12.1737)(SRO.RD3.210.491)
5264. Murray, Alexander, b. 1727, New Deer Aberdeenshire, clergyman & schoolmaster edu. King's Col Aberdeen 1746, res. Glenlivet Banffshire, sh. 1762, sett. Reading Pa, d. 14 Sept 1793 Philadelphia, bd. Christchurchyard, PCC pr1795. (F.6.341\664)(EMA47)(FAB209)(SNQ.2.10)
5265. Murray, Andrew, b. 1749, tailor, res. Paisley Renfrewshire, sh. Oct 1774, fr. Greenock to Philadelphia, in *Sally*. (PRO.T47.12)
5266. Murray, Ann, pts. Earl of Cromartie, d. 1768 Charleston S.C. (GM.38.142)
5267. Murray, Anna, infanticide, tr. Aug 1685, fr. Leith to Jamaica. (PC.11.330)(ETR369)
5268. Murray, David, horsethief, tr. Feb 1756. (SRO.HCR.I.89)
5269. Murray, David, pts. John Murray of Philiphaugh, sett. Christchurch Ga, m. Lucia ..., ch. Charles, d. 29 Apr 1771 Savannah Ga, Ga 1771. (AJ1226)
5270. Murray, David, Jacobite, tr. 31 July 1716, fr. Liverpool to Va, in *Anne*. (SPC.1716.310)(CTB31.209)
5271. Murray, David, b. 1755, housecarpenter, res. Kirkwall Orkney Islands, sh. Sept 1775, fr. Kirkwall to Savannah Ga, in *Marlborough*, sett. Richmond Co Ga. (PRO.T47.12)
5272. Murray, Henry, Jacobite, tr. 30 Mar 1716, fr. Liverpool to Antigua, in *Scipio*. (SPC.1716.310)(CTB31.204)
5273. Murray, Henry, Jacobite, tr. 24 May 1716, fr. Liverpool to Md, in *Friendship*, arr. Md Aug 1716. (SPC.1716.311)(HM387)
5274. Murray, James, Covenanter, res. Argyll, tr. 5 Sept 1685, fr. Leith to East N.J., in *Henry & Francis*. (PC.11.330)
5275. Murray, James, Jacobite, tr. 29 June 1716, fr. Liverpool to Jamaica or Va, in *Elizabeth & Anne*, arr. York Va. (SPC.1716.310)(CTB31.208)(VSP.1.186)
5276. Murray, James, 1754, laborer, res. Gatehouse Kirkcudbrightshire, sh. May 1774, fr. Stranraer to N.Y., in *Gale*. (PRO.T47.12)

5277. Murray, James, druggist, res. Edinburgh, pts. George Murray, d. Sept 1767 N.Y. (SM.29.557)
5278. Murray, James, res. Selkirkshire, pts. Gideon Murray of Sundhope, sh. pre 1766, sett. Airy Castle St Thomas in the East Jamaica. (SRO.RD2.236.634)
5279. Murray, Jean, res. Edinburgh, pts. William Murray & Janet Shaw, sh. pre 1778, sett. Dominica, m. Daniel Stewart. (SRO.RD4.223.624)
5280. Murray, John, thief, res. Perthshire, tr. Oct 1775. (AJ1449)
5281. Murray, John, res. Philiphaugh Selkirkshire, sh. pre 1769, sett. Queen's Co P.E.I. (SRO.GD293.2.72)
5282. Murray, John, murderer, res. Paisley Renfrewshire, tr. July 1767. (SRO.JC.27.D35)
5283. Murray, John, soldier, res. Edinburgh, d. pre 1759, PCC pr1759
5284. Murray, John, tobacco factor, res. Glasgow, sh. pre 1770, sett. Aquia Va. (SRA.779.21)
5285. Murray, John, b. 1717, weaver, Jacobite, res. Annandale Dumfries-shire, tr. 5 May 1747, fr. Liverpool to Leeward Islands, in *Veteran*, arr. Martinique June 1747. (PRO.SP36.102)(MR124)
5286. Murray, Katherine, b. 1753, servant, res. Stornaway Isle of Lewis, sh. May 1774, fr. Stornaway to Philadelphia, in *Friendship*. (PRO.T47.12)
5287. Murray, Patrick, Jacobite, tr. 25 June 1716, fr. Liverpool to St Kitts, in *Hockenhill*. (SPC.1716.312)(CTB31.207)
5288. Murray, Patrick, farmer, Jacobite, res. Perthshire, tr. 22 Apr 1747, fr. Liverpool to Va, in *Johnson*, arr. Port Oxford Md 5 Aug 1747. (P.3.220)(PRO.T1.328) (alias 3877)
5289. Murray, Walter, b. 1752, tailor, res. Banff, sh. Aug 1774, fr. Greenock to Philadelphia, in *Magdalene*. (PRO.T47.12)
5290. Murray, William, Jacobite, tr. 25 June 1716, fr. Liverpool to St Kitts, in *Hockenhill*. (SPC.1716.312)(CTB31.207)
5291. Murray, William, sh. Aug 1699, fr. Darien to N.Y., in *Caledonia*. (SPC.1699.478)
5292. Murray, William, b. 1715, res. Aberdeen, pts. Andrew Murray & Margery Milne, sh. 1732, sett. Jamaica, d. 1754. (APB.3.183)
5293. Murray, William, b. 1731, farmer, res. Breadalbane Perthshire, sh. June 1775, fr. Greenock to N.Y., in *Commerce*, m. Margaret McDougald, ch. John Alexander Archibald Christian Katherine James. (PRO.T47.12)
5294. Muschet, Robert, merchant, res. Dunbartonshire, sh. pre 1774, sett. Jamaica. (SRO.RD2.218.1162)
5295. Mushet, David, b. 1737, farmer, res. Stirling, sh. Apr 1775, fr. Greenock to N.Y., in *Lilly*. (PRO.T47.12)
5296. Mushet, Robert, res. Greenock Renfrewshire, pts. Robert Mushet, sh. pre 1773, sett. St Elizabeth Jamaica. (SRO.CS.GMB12\73)

5297. Nairn, James, b. 1755, smith, res. Paisley Renfrewshire, sh. Feb 1774, fr. Greenock to N.Y., in *Commerce*. (PRO.T47.12)
5298. Nairn, Janet, infanticide, res. Aberdeen, sh. July 1764, fr. Glasgow. (AJ802\861)
5299. Nairn, Thomas, b. 1712, chapman, Jacobite, res. Strathdon Aberdeenshire, tr. 19 Mar 1747, fr. London to Jamaica, in *St George or Carteret*, arr. Jamaica 1747. (P.3.224)(MR124)(PRO.CO137.58)
5300. Nairn, William, clergyman, sh. 1722, sett. Bermuda. (EMA47)
5301. Naismith, John, b. 22 Mar 1726, Dundee, woolweaver, Jacobite, res. Dundee Angus, pts. Robert Naismith & Jean Young, tr. 22 Apr 1747, fr. Liverpool to Va, in *Johnson*, arr. Port Oxford Md 5 Aug 1747. (P.3.224)(MR107)(PRO.T1.328)
5302. Naismith, William, sailor, res. Bo'ness West Lothian, sh. 14 July 1698, fr. Leith to Darien, in *Caledonia*, ch. Agnes, Edin pr1707 CC8.8.83
5303. Napier, Thomas, farmer, res. Monkland Lanarkshire, sh. Oct 1774, fr. Greenock to Philadelphia, in *Sally*. (PRO.T47.12)
5304. Napier, William, surgeon, res. Glasgow, pts. Peter Napier of Napierston, sett. Charleston S.C., d. pre 1735. (SRO.SH.30.5.1735)
5305. Nasmith, John, merchant, res. Edinburgh, pts. James Nasmith of Earlshaugh, d. 1747 Va, Edin pr1752 CC8.8.114
5306. Neal, Michael, b. 1713, laborer, Jacobite, tr. 1747. (P.3.224)
5307. Neave, Alexander, Jacobite, tr. 24 May 1716, fr. Liverpool to Md, in *Friendship*, arr. Md Aug 1716. (SPC.1716.311)(HM386)
5308. Neil, Henry, b. 1756, spinner, res. Paisley Renfrewshire, sh. Feb 1774, fr. Greenock to N.Y., in *Commerce*. (PRO.T47.12)
5309. Neilson, George, Jacobite, tr. 28 July 1716, fr. Liverpool to Va, in *Godspeed*, arr. Md Oct 1716. (SPC.1716.310)(CTB31.209)(HM388)
5310. Neilson, James, tr. 1696, fr. Newhaven to Va. (SRO.RH15.)
5311. Neilson, James, b. 1721, laborer, Jacobite, res. Aberdeen, tr. 5 May 1747, fr. Liverpool to Leeward Islands, in *Veteran*, arr. Martinique June 1747. (P.3.224)(PRO.SP36.102)
5312. Neilson, Thomas, captain's clerk, sh. 14 July 1698, fr. Leith to Darien, in *Unicorn*, Edin pr1707 CC8.8.83
5313. Neilson, William, horsethief, res. Rigg Gratany Dumfries-shire, tr. May 1766. (AJ958)
5314. Neilson, William, b. 1754, weaver, res. Paisley Renfrewshire, sh. Feb 1774, fr. Greenock to N.Y., in *Commerce*. (PRO.T47.12)
5315. Nelson, James, b. 1691, husbandman, res. Glasgow, sh. Feb 1722, fr. London to Antigua. (CLRO\AIA)
5316. Nevery, James, Jacobite, tr. 24 May 1716, fr. Liverpool to Md, in *Friendship*, arr. Md Aug 1716. (SPC.1716.311)(HM386)

5317. Newbigging, Andrew, tr. Nov 1679, fr. Leith. (ETR162)
5318. Newton, John, schoolmaster, fraudster, res. Haddington East Lothian, tr. Mar 1762. (SRO.HCR.I.94)
5319. Newton, John, b. 1731, weaver, Jacobite, res. Lancashire, tr. 22 Apr 1747, fr. Liverpool to Va, in *Johnson*, arr. Port Oxford Md 5 Aug 1747. (P.2.226)(MR198)(PRO.T1.328)
5320. Newton, Jonathan, Jacobite, tr. 7 May 1716, fr. Liverpool to S.C., in *Susannah*. (SPC.1716.309)(CTB31.206)
5321. Nicholl, George, b. 10 Sept 1721, Old Machar Aberdeen, weaver, Jacobite, res. Aberdeen, pts. Andrew Nicholl & Margaret Mitchell, tr. 5 May 1747, fr. Liverpool to Leeward Islands, in *Veteran*, arr. Martinique June 1747. (P.3.226)(PRO.SP36.102)
5322. Nicholl, James, b. 20 Jan 1723, Brechin Angus, ploughman, Jacobite, res. Brechin, pts. William Nicholl & Margaret Gourlay, tr. 20 Mar 1747, fr. London to Barbados , in *Frere*. (P.3.226)(MR107)
5323. Nicholl, John, Livingston Midlothian, physician edu. Edinburgh Uni, sh. pre 1712, sett. N.Y. (SRO.CH1.2.49.52)
5324. Nicholl, John, b. 1751, housecarpenter, sh. Jan 1774, fr. Greenock to Jamaica, in *Grandvale*. (SRO.CE60.1.7)
5325. Nicholson, John, carpenter, res. Kelso Roxburghshire, sh. pre 1775, sett. Tortula. (SRO.RD2.236.499)
5326. Nicholson, John, Jacobite, tr. 30 Mar 1716, fr. Liverpool to Antigua, in *Scipio*. (SPC.1716.204)(CTB31.204)
5327. Nicholson, John, Jacobite, tr. 21 Apr 1716, fr. Liverpool to S.C., in *Wakefield*. (SPC.1716.309)(CTB31.205)
5328. Nicholson, John, b. 1711, res. Anstruther Fife, sh. July 1729, fr. London to Jamaica. (CLRO\AIA)
5329. Nicholson, William, horsethief, res. Dyke Dumfries-shire, pts. John Nicholson, tr. Apr 1754. (SM.16.203)
5330. Nicol, Andrew, res. Aberdeen, d. 1742 N.Y. (APB.3.112)
5331. Nicol, Barbara, b. 29 Aug 1708, Old Machar Aberdeen, res. Bennyhillock Aberdeen, pts. Norman Nicol & Janet Smart, tr. May 1727. (SRO.HH.II)
5332. Nicol, George, res. Arthurstone Perthshire, sh. pre 1783, to Jamaica. (SRO.RD2.235.275)
5333. Nicol, Jean, housebreaker, res. Dunbeath Caithness, tr. June 1773, fr. Glasgow, m. Alexander Mowat. (AJ1325\8)
5334. Nicoll, John, thief, res. Bo'ness West Lothian, pts. John Nicoll, tr. 28 Nov 1704, fr. Leith to Md. (SRO.PC2.28.307)
5335. Nicoll, John, tr. Aug 1685, fr. Leith to Jamaica. (PC.11.136)
5336. Nicoll, Lewis, b. 1710, res. Edinburgh, sh. Aug 1730, fr. London to Jamaica. (CLRO\AIA)
5337. Nicolson, Finlow, b. 1758, servant, res. Bayble Isle of Lewis, sh. May 1774, fr. Stornaway to Philadelphia, in *Friendship*. (PRO.T47.12)

5338. Nicolson, Isabel, fireraiser & thief, tr. Aug 1711. (SRO.JC.3.3)
5339. Nicolson, John, adulterer, res. Bridgend Liberton Edinburgh, tr. May
      1684, fr. Leith to East N.J. (ETR257)
5340. Nicolson, Katherine, b. 1756, servant, res. Stornaway Isle of Lewis, sh.
      May 1774, fr. Stornaway to Philadelphia, in *Friendship*.
      (PRO.T47.12)
5341. Nimmo, Andrew, foremastman, res. Airth Stirlingshire, pts. James
      Nimmo, sh. 14 July 1698, fr. Leith to Darien, in *Caledonia*, Edin
      pr1707 CC8.8.83
5342. Nimmo, James, Jacobite, tr. 30 Mar 1716, fr. Liverpool to Antigua, in
      Scipio. (SPC.1716.310)(CTB31.204)
5343. Ninian, Grizel, infanticide, res. Largs Ayrshire, tr. 1772, fr. Glasgow to
      Va, in *Brilliant*, arr. Port Hampton Va 7 Oct 1772.
      (SRO.JC.27.10.3)(AJ1270)
5344. Nisbet of Dean, Sir Alexander, d. 7 Oct 1753 Charleston S.C.
      (SM.15.627)
5345. Nisbet, Alexander, merchant, sh. 1724, sett. Charleston S.C.
      (SRO.GD237.10.1.42)
5346. Nisbet, Archibald, b. 1747, farmer, res. Stirling, sh. May 1774, fr.
      Greenock to N.Y., in *Matty*. (PRO.T47.12)
5347. Nisbet, Giles, cattlethief, res. Duns Berwickshire, tr. Sept 1768.
      (AJ1079)
5348. Nisbet, James, Jacobite, tr. 29 Sept 1716, fr. Liverpool to Jamaica or Va,
      in *Elizabeth & Anne*, arr. Va.
      (SPC.1716.310)(CTB31.208)(VSP.1.185)
5349. Nisbet, Janet, cattlethief, res. Duns Berwickshire, tr. Sept 1768. (AJ1079)
5350. Nisbet, John, woolfiner, Covenanter, res. Glasgow, tr. 1684, fr. Clyde, in
      Pelican. (PC.9.208)
5351. Nisbet, John, b. 1726, tutor, Jacobite, res. Falkirk Stirlingshire, tr. 1747,
      fr. Tilbury. (P.3.224)(MR63)
5352. Nisbet, John, b. 1757, wright, res. Glasgow, sh. July 1775, fr. Greenock
      to Jamaica, in *Isabella*. (PRO.T47.12)
5353. Nisbet, Robert, apprentice merchant, sh. June 1721, sett. Charleston S.C.
      (SRO.GD237.10.1.29)
5354. Nisbet, Robert, merchant, sett. Nevis & St Kitts, d. pre 1743, Edin
      pr1743 CC8.8.108
5355. Nisbet, Robert, b. 19 Sept 1712, merchant, res. Carfin Lanarkshire, pts.
      Archibald Nisbet & Emilia Stewart, sett. Nevis & St Kitts, d. 29
      Sept 1740, bd. St James, Edin pr1743 CC8.8.108. (NC2)(MWI98)
5356. Nisbet, Walter, merchant, sh. pre 1724, sett. Berkeley Co S.C.
      (SRO.GD237.10.1.42)
5357. Nisbet, Walter, merchant, sh. pre 1743, sett. Nevis, Edin pr1743
      CC8.8.108

263

5358. Nisbet, Walter, b. 19 July 1706, pts. Archibald Nisbet of Carfin & Emilia Stuart, sh. pre 1743, sett. Nevis, ch. Walter Josiah James Ann Mary, d. 15 June 1765, bd. St James Montserrat, Nevis pr1765. (MWI97)

5359. Nisbet, William, b. 1721, Shapinsay Orkney Islands, clergyman, adulterer, res. Firth & Stenness Orkney Islands, pts. Alexander Nisbet, tr. June 1766, sett. Jamaica, m. Elizabeth Ritch. (F.7.236)(AJ961)

5360. Niven, William, res. Cathcart Glasgow, tr. 12 Dec 1678, fr. Leith to West Indies, in St Michael of Scarborough. (PC.6.76)

5361. Niven, William, laborer, pickpocket, res. Ayr, tr. May 1775. (SM.37.406)

5362. Niven, William, farmer, Covenanter, tr. 5 Sept 1685, fr. Leith to East N.J., in Henry & Francis. (PC.11.155)

5363. Noble, William, Jacobite, tr. 29 Sept 1716, fr. Liverpool to Jamaica or Va, in Elizabeth & Anne, arr. York Va. (SPC.1716.310)(CTB31.208)(VSP.1.186)

5364. Norie, Robert, sailor, res. Dalkeith Midlothian, sh. 14 July 1698, fr. Leith to Darien, in Unicorn, Edin pr1707 CC8.8.83

5365. Norn, John, b. 29 Nov 1761, Orphir Orkney Islands, res. Birsay Orkney Islands, pts. William Norn & Marjory Spence, sh. Sept 1775, fr. Kirkwall to Ga, in Marlborough, sett. Richmond Co Ga. (PRO.T47.10)

5366. Norvil, Adam, Jacobite, tr. 22 Apr 1747, fr. Liverpool to Va, in Johnson, arr. Port Oxford Md 5 Aug 1747. (P.3.230)(PRO.T1.328)

5367. Nowlan, Thopmas, b. 1717, smith, Jacobite, res. Carlow, tr. 1747. (P.3.230)

5368. Nutter, James, thief & housebreaker, res. Jedburgh Roxburghshire, tr. June 1771. (SRO.RH2.4.255)

5369. O'Brian, John, b. 1720, cook, Jacobite, res. Cork, tr. 1747. (P.3.232)

5370. Ochiltree, Daniel, pts. Margaret McGlashan, tr. 1696, fr. Newhaven to Va. (SRO.RH15.14.58)

5371. Ochiltree, David, Covenanter, tr. Aug 1685, fr. Leith to Jamaica. (PC.11.329)

5372. Ochiltree, Hugh, pts. Margaret McGlashan, tr. 1696, fr. Newhaven to Va. (SRO.RH15.14.58)

5373. Ockford, Janet, tr. 7 Dec 1665, fr. Leith to Barbados. (ETR104)

5374. Ockman, Mary, b. 1739, spinner, res. Stirling, sh. May 1775, fr. Greenock to N.Y., in Monimia, ch. Lisa Nelly Margaret. (PRO.T47.12)

5375. Ogden, Thomas, weaver, Jacobite, res. Manchester, tr. 1747. (MR198)

5376. Ogilvie, Alexander, bigamist, tr. Aug 1766. (SRO.HCR.I.98)

5377. Ogilvie, George, res. Banff, sett. St Mary Jamaica, d. post 1780. (SRO.RD4.249.742)

5378. Ogilvie, Isobel, infanticide, res. Banff, tr. 25 May 1749, fr. Aberdeen to Va, in *Dispatch of Newcastle*. (AJ68)
5379. Ogilvie, James, merchant, res. Aberdeen, pts. James Ogilvie of Auchyries & Mary Strachan, sh. 1744, sett. Charleston S.C., d. 1745. (APB.3.135)
5380. Ogilvie, James, b. 1747, res. Banff, pts. William Ogilvie & Helen Baird, d. 6 June 1774 Jamaica. (Banff Gs)(AOB.2.358)
5381. Ogilvie, Janet, res. Aberfoyle Perthshire, tr. May 1770, fr. Port Glasgow, in *Crawford*, arr. Port Oxford Md 23 July 1771. (SRO.JC27.10.3)(AJ1170) (alias 2323)
5382. Ogilvie, John, b. 1722, servant, Jacobite, tr. 24 Feb 1747, fr. Liverpool to Va, in *Gildart*, arr. Port North Potomac Md 5 Aug 1747. (P.3.238)(MR107)(PRO.T1.328)
5383. Ogilvie, John, b. 1728, physician, Jacobite, res. Aberdeenshire, pts. James Ogilvie of Auchiries, sett. St Eustatia. (JAB.2.368)
5384. Ogilvie, John, b. 1745, wright, res. Stirling, sh. May 1775, fr. Greenock to N.Y., in *Monimia*. (PRO.T47.12)
5385. Ogilvie, John, b. 1753, res. Banff, pts. William Ogilvie & Helen Baird, d. 30 Aug 1770 Antigua. (AOB.2.358)(Banff Gs)
5386. Ogilvie, Walter, clergyman, sh. 1709, to Jamaica. (EMA48)
5387. Ogilvie, William, physician, res. Shielhill Kirriemuir Angus, pts. William Ogilvie & Janet Webster, sh. pre 1713, sett. Va. (SRO.SH.27.4.1713)
5388. Ogilvie, William, b. 1728, Jacobite, res. Aberdeenshire, pts. James Ogilvie of Auchiries, d. 1750 Va. (JAB.2.369)
5389. Ogilvy, Henry, Jacobite, tr. 25 June 1716, fr. Liverpool to St Kitts, in *Hockenhill*. (SPC.1716.312)(CTB31.207)
5390. Ogilvy, Henry, shipmaster, pts. Henry Ogilvy of Templehall, sett. Charleston S.C., m. Hannah Meadows, ch. Harriet, d. 1779 Pensacola WFla, Edin pr1784 CC8.8.126 PCC pr1785
5391. Ogilvy, James, clergyman, res. Banff, sh. 1771, to Va. (EMA48)(AOB.2.427)
5392. Ogilvy, James, thief, tr. 4 May 1666, fr. Leith to Va, in *Phoenix of Leith*. (ETR107)
5393. Ogilvy, John, overseer, d. 1699 Darien, Edin pr1707 CC8.8.83
5394. Ogilvy, John, Jacobite, tr. 29 June 1716, fr. Liverpool to Jamaica or Va, in *Elizabeth & Anne*, arr. York Va. (SPC.1716.310)(CTB31.208)(VSP.1.186)
5395. Ogilvy, John, murderer, res. Quiech Angus, tr. Mar 1756. (AJ427)
5396. Oglebie, John, b. 1681, res. Edinburgh, sh. 1700, fr. Liverpool. (LRO.HQ325.2.FRE)
5397. Ogleby, Henry, Jacobite, tr. 25 June 1716, fr. Liverpool to St Kitts, in *Hockenhill*. (SPC.1716.312)

5398. Ogston, James, Jacobite, tr. 15 July 1716, fr. Liverpool to Va, in *Elizabeth & Anne.* (CTB31.209)

5399. Oig, William, thief, res. Perthshire, tr. 15 Dec 1720. (SRO.HH.11) (alias 2058)

5400. Oliphant, Calvin, seaman, res. Burntisland fife, sh. 28 Mar 1683, to Port Nelson, Hudson Bay. (HBRS.9.90)

5401. Oliphant, Charles, excise officer, Jacobite, res. Aberdeen or Inverness, tr. Sept 1748. (P.3.242)(JAB.2.374)

5402. Oliphant, David, physician, sh. pre 1772, sett. S.C. (SRO.RD3.235.265)

5403. Oliphant, James, b. 1741, yeoman, sh. Sept 1775, fr. Newcastle to Ga, in *Georgia Packet,* sett. Friendsborough Ga. (PRO.T47.9\11)

5404. Oliphant, John, foremastman, res. Kirkcaldy Fife, pts. James Oliphant & Isobel Wyse, sh. 14 July 1698, fr. Leith to Darien, in *Caledonia,* Edin pr1707 CC8.8.83

5405. Oliphant, Laurence, sailor, res. Williamstown, sh. 14 July 1698, fr. Leith to Darien, in *Caledonia,* Edin pr1708 CC8.8.84

5406. Oliphant, Lawrence, Jacobite, tr. 25 June 1716, fr. Liverpool to St Kitts, in *Hockenhill.* (SPC.1716.312)(CTB31.207)

5407. Oliphant, Thomas, sailor, res. Shetland Islands, pts. Patrick Oliphant, sh. 14 July 1698, fr. Leith to Darien, in *Unicorn,* Edin pr1708 CC8.8.84

5408. Oliphant, William, Covenanter, tr. 5 Sept 1685, fr. Leith to East N.J., in *Henry & Francis.* (PC.11.154)

5409. Oliver, James, Covenanter , res. Jedburgh Forest Roxburghshire, tr. Aug 1685, fr. Leith to Jamaica, arr. Port Royal Jamaica 1685. (PC.11.329)(LJ175)

5410. Oliver, James, b. 1752, ship's carpenter, res. Ayrshire, sh. Mar 1775, fr. Glasgow to Quebec, in *Friendship.* (PRO.T47.12)

5411. Oliver, John, tr. 16 Dec 1774. (SRO.HCR.I.112)

5412. Oliver, Thomas, b. 1745, blacksmith, sh. Aug 1774, fr. Whitby to Savannah Ga, in *Marlborough.* (PRO.T47.9\11)

5413. Oman, Daniel, b. 1760, servant, res. Leith Midlothian, sh. May 1775, fr. Leith to Philadelphia, in *Friendship.* (PRO.T47.12)

5414. Oman, Mary, b. 1754, milliner, res. Edinburgh, sh. May 1775, fr. Leith to Philadelphia, in *Friendship.* (PRO.T47.12)

5415. Ormiston, Thomas, merchant, res. Edinburgh, sh. 1736, sett. Savannah Ga. (SPC.143.148)(PRO.CO5.670.283\308)

5416. Ormond, John, b. 1759, laborer, res. Angus, sh. May 1775, fr. Leith to Philadelphia, in *Friendship.* (PRO.T47.12)

5417. Orr, Ann, b. 1756, spinner, res. Paisley Renfrewshire, sh. Feb 1774, fr. Greenock to N.Y., in *Commerce.* (PRO.T47.12)

5418. Orr, Duncan, b. 1706, laborer, Jacobite, res. Perthshire, tr. 5 May 1747, fr. Liverpool to Leeward Islands, in *Veteran,* arr. Martinique June, sett. 1747. (P.3.244)(PRO.SP36.102)

5419. Orr, Duncan, b. 1733, weaver, Jacobite, res. Perthshire, tr. 5 May 1747, fr. Liverpool to Leeward Islands, in *Veteran*, arr. Martinique June 1747. (P.3.244)(PRO.SP36.102)
5420. Orr, Isabella, b. 1754, spinner, res. Paisley Renfrewshire, sh. Feb 1774, fr. Greenock to N.Y., in *Commerce*. (PRO.T47.12)
5421. Orr, James, writer & merchant, res. Ayr, d. 1750 Jamaica, Edin pr1758 CC8.8.117
5422. Orr, Jean, b. 1747, spinner, res. Paisley Renfrewshire, sh. Feb 1774, fr. Greenock to N.Y., in *Commerce*, ch. John. (PRO.T47.12) (alias 1293)
5423. Orr, Matthew, merchant edu. Glasgow Uni 1761, res. Glasgow, pts. William Orr of Barrowfield, sh. Dec 1778, d. 1 Aug 1790 King's Bay Estate Tobago, PCC pr1790 Edin pr1791 CC8.8.128. (MAGU65)
5424. Orr, Robert, Covenanter, res. Milnbank, tr. 16 Aug 1670. (PC.3.320)
5425. Orr, William, clergyman edu. Glasgow Uni 1712, sh. 1730, to Philadelphia. (APC237)
5426. Orrock, Alexander, sailor, res. Fife, sh. 14 July 1698, fr. Leith to Darien, in *St Andrew*, m. Rachel Simpson, Edin pr1707 CC8.8.83
5427. Orrock, Alexander, Jacobite, tr. 28 July 1716, fr. Liverpool to Va, in *Godspeed*, arr. Md Oct 1716. (SPC.1716.310)(CTB31.209)(HM388)
5428. Orrock, John, sailor, res. Kinghorn Fife, pts. Isobel Steedman or Orrock, sh. 14 July 1698, fr. Leith to Darien, Edin pr1707 CC8.8.83
5429. Ostler, John, gentleman, Jacobite, res. Lincolnshire, tr. 8 May 1747, to Antigua. (P.3.232)
5430. Oswald, Henry, surgeon, res. Glasgow, sh. pre 1725, sett. Essex Co Va, m. Mary ..., ch. Ludovic John Mary Elizabeth, d. 1726 Va, Essex pr1726. (BGBG376)
5431. Oswald, John, thief, res. Aberdeen, pts. John Oswald, tr. Oct 1773. (AJ1343)
5432. Oswald, Joseph, Jacobite, tr. 30 Mar 1716, fr. Liverpool to Antigua, in *Scipio*. (SPC.1716.310)(CTB31.204)
5433. Ouchterlony, Patrick, res. Angus, sett. Calvert Co Md, m. Elizabeth ..., d. 18 May 1753 Md, Edin pr1758 CC8.8.17
5434. Owans, Thomas, sailor, res. Leith Midlothian, d. 1740 Jamaica, Edin pr1777 CC8.8.124
5435. Owens, Thomas, mariner, res. Leith Midlothian, sett. Jamaica, d. pre 1774. (SRO.CS.GMB366)
5436. Pader, Janet, b. 1754, spinner, res. Paisley Renfrewshire, sh. Feb 1774, fr. Greenock to N.Y., in *Commerce*. (PRO.T47.12)
5437. Paip, James, servant, res. Boghead Aberdeenshire, tr. Sept 1775. (AJ1446) (alias 128)

5438. Paisly, James, b. 1748, farmer, res. Dumfries-shire, sh. Oct 1774, fr. Greenock to Charleston S.C., in *Countess*. (PRO.T47.12)
5439. Paisly, John, b. 1751, weaver, res. Dumfries-shire, sh. Oct 1774, fr. Greenock to Charleston S.C., in *Countess*. (PRO.T47.12)
5440. Palmer, John, thief, res. Jedburgh Roxburghshire, tr. May 1726. (SRO.JC.12.4)
5441. Panton, Alexander, b. 1714, book-keeper, res. Aberdeenshire, sh. Sept 1733, fr. London to Jamaica. (CLRO\AIA)
5442. Panton, David, b. 1756, tailor, res. Rattray, sh. May 1775, fr. Leith to Philadelphia, in *Friendship*. (PRO.T47.12)
5443. Panton, George, clergyman & schoolmaster edu. Marischal Col Aberdeen 1772, res. Jedburgh, sh. 1772, sett. Trenton N.J. (SA107)
5444. Panton, Robert, res. Dalmeny West Lothian, tr. 12 Dec 1678, fr. Leith to West Indies, in *St Michael of Scarborough*. (PC.6.76)
5445. Park, Isobel, res. Edinburgh, tr. 8 May 1663, fr. Leith to Barbados, in *Mary*. (EBR.186.13.4)
5446. Park, John, weaver, Covenanter, res. Lanark, tr. Dec 1685, fr. Leith to Barbados, in *John & Nicholas*. (PC.11.254)(ETR389)
5447. Park, John, b. 1708, schoolmaster, res. Horndean Ladykirk Berwickshire, sh. Nov 1736, fr. London. (CLRO\AIA)
5448. Park, M, sh. 29 Nov 1773, fr. Greenock to Jamaica, in *Mary of Glasgow*. (SRO.CE60.1.7)
5449. Park, Patrick, merchant, res. Glasgow, sh. 14 July 1698, fr. Leith to Darien, in *Caledonia*, d. Darien, Edin pr1707 CC8.8.83
5450. Park, Robert, b. 1751, clerk, res. Greenock Renfrewshire, sh. July 1775, fr. Greenock to Ga, in *Christy*. (PRO.T47.12)
5451. Park, Thomas, Jacobite, tr. 24 May 1716, fr. Liverpool to Md, in *Friendship*, arr. Md Aug 1716. (SPC.1716.311)(HM388)
5452. Parker, James, merchant, res. Port Glasgow, pts. Patrick Parker, sh. pre 1754, sett. Jamaica. (SRO.SH.24.8.1754)
5453. Parker, William, soldier, forger, tr. June 1751, to Boston Mass. (AJ251)
5454. Paterson, Andrew, res. Hamilton Lanarkshire, tr. 5 Sept 1685, fr. Leith to East N.J., in *Henry & Francis*. (PC.11.154)
5455. Paterson, Andrew, b. 1744, sawyer, res. Glasgow, sh. Feb 1774, fr. Greenock to N.Y., in *Commerce*, m. Elizabeth ..., ch. John. (PRO.T47.12)
5456. Paterson, David, tr. 19 June 1754. (SRO.HCR.I.87)
5457. Paterson, David, Covenanter, res. Eaglesham Renfrewshire, tr. Dec 1685, fr. Leith to Barbados, in *John & Nicholas*. (PC.11.254)(ETR389)
5458. Paterson, George, b. 1753, farmer, res. Kilsyth Stirlingshire, sh. May 1774, fr. Greenock to N.Y., in *George*. (PRO.T47.12)
5459. Paterson, James, tr. Aug 1684, fr. Leith to Carolina. (PC.9.95)

5460. Paterson, Jean, stabler's servant, assault, res. Aberdeen, tr. July 1772, fr. Glasgow to Va, in *Brilliant*, arr. Port Hampton Va 7 Oct 1772. (SRO.JC27.10.3)(AJ1272)

5461. Paterson, John, merchant skipper, res. Glasgow, sh. pre 1690, sett. Boston Mass. (PC.15.307)

5462. Paterson, John, b. 1744, blacksmith, res. Stornaway Isle of Lewis, sh. Nov 1774, fr. Stornaway to N.Y., in *Peace & Plenty*, m. Margaret ..., ch. John. (PRO.T47.12)

5463. Paterson, Katherine, b. 1758, servant, res. Stornaway Isle of Lewis, sh. May 1774, fr. Stornaway to Philadelphia, in *Friendship*. (PRO.T47.12)

5464. Paterson, Margaret, whore, res. Edinburgh, tr. 19 Mar 1695. (SRO.PC2.25.216)

5465. Paterson, Margaret, res. Edinburgh, tr. 14 Nov 1694. (EBE.1694.163)

5466. Paterson, Mary, fireraiser, res. Dumfries, tr. 1767, m. William Ainsley. (SM.29.497)

5467. Paterson, Mrs, m. William Paterson, d. 14 Nov 1698 Darien. (NLS.RY2b8\19)

5468. Paterson, Ninian, tr. 21 Feb 1684, fr. Glasgow to East N.J. (PC.8.379)

5469. Paterson, Robert, Jacobite, res. Lancashire, tr. 8 May 1747, to Antigua. (P.3.246)(MR198)

5470. Paterson, Robert, b. 3 July 1728, Old Machar Aberdeen, hosier, Jacobite, res. Aberdeen, pts. Abraham Paterson & Elspet Shepherd, tr. 5 May 1747, fr. Liverpool to Leeward Islands, in *Veteran*, arr. Martinique June 1747. (P.2.248)(JAB.2.439)(PRO.SP36.102)

5471. Paterson, Stephen, clerk, forger, res. Carron Stirlingshire, tr. Feb 1765. (SRO.HCR.1.96)

5472. Paterson, Thomas, ropemaker, res. Leith Midlothian, sett. Baltimore Md, ch. William, d. pre 1780. (SRO.SH.24.2.1780)

5473. Paterson, William, rioter, res. Alloa Clackmannanshire, tr. Jan 1751. (AJ160)

5474. Paterson, William, attorney, res. Paisley Renfrewshire, pts. Robert Paterson & Barbara Montgomery, sh. pre 1778, sett. Jamaica. (SRO.SH.1.6.1778)

5475. Paterson, William, b. 1746, coppersmith, res. Glasgow, sh. Apr 1775, fr. Greenock to N.Y., in *Lilly*. (PRO.T47.12)

5476. Patillo, Henry, b. 1726, clergyman, sh. pre 1757, sett. Grassy Creek Nutbush, d. 1801. (F.7.665)

5477. Paton, Archibald, joiner, Jacobite, tr. 21 July 1748. (P.3.248)(MR198)

5478. Paton, George, b. 1727, brewer's servant, Jacobite, res. Dirleton East Lothian, tr. 1747. (P.3.248)

5479. Paton, John, res. Monkland Lanarkshire, tr. June 1684, fr. Clyde, in *Pelican*. (PC.9.208)

5480. Paton, John, Jacobite, tr. 24 Feb 1747, fr. Liverpool to Va, in *Gildart*, arr. Port North Potomac Md 5 Aug 1747. (PRO.T1.328)
5481. Paton, Joseph, b. 1705, res. East Mugland Lanark, sh. Mar 1735, fr. London to Jamaica. (CLRO\AIA)
5482. Paton, Joseph, b. 1745, farmer, res. Glasgow, sh. Feb 1774, fr. Greenock to N.Y., in *Commerce*. (PRO.T47.12)
5483. Paton, Robert, Covenanter, tr. 1669, to Va. (PC.3.22)
5484. Paton, Thomas, b. 1746, shoemaker, res. Edinburgh, sh. May 1775, fr. Greenock to N.Y. or Ga, in *Christy*. (PRO.T47.12)
5485. Paton, William, b. 1742, weaver, res. Paisley Renfrewshire, sh. Feb 1774, fr. Greenock to N.Y., in *Commerce*, m. Mary ..., ch. Janet Margaret Catherine. (PRO.T47.12)
5486. Patrick, James, Covenanter, res. Kilmarnock Ayrshire, tr. Dec 1685, fr. Leith to Barbados, in *John & Nicholas*. (PC.11.386)(ETR389)
5487. Patterson, Elizabeth, tr. 1696, fr. Newhaven to Va. (SRO.RH15.14.58)
5488. Patterson, James, Jacobite, tr. 29 June 1716, fr. Liverpool to Jamaica or Va, in *Elizabeth & Anne*, arr. York Va. (SPC.1716.310)(CTB31.208)(VSP.1.186)
5489. Patterson, John, b. 1751, gardener, res. Aberdeen, sh. Dec 1773, fr. London to Va, in *Elizabeth*. (PRO.T47.9\11)
5490. Patterson, Jonas, carpenter, res. Leith, sh. 18 Aug 1699, fr. Clyde to Darien, in *Hope*, Edin pr1707 CC8.8.83
5491. Patton, Henry, mate, res. Bo'ness West Lothian, sh. 14 July 1698, fr. Leith to Darien, Edin pr1707 CC8.8.83
5492. Patton, Robert, merchant & factor, res. Glasgow, sh. pre 1776, sett. Culpepper Co Va. (SRA.CFI)
5493. Pattullo, James, Jacobite, tr. 29 June 1716, fr. Liverpool to Jamaica or Va, in *Elizabeth & Anne*, arr. York Va. (SPC.1716.310)(CTB31.208)(VSP.1.185) (alias 5494)
5494. Pattullo, John, Jacobite, tr. 29 June 1716, fr. Liverpool to Jamaica or Va, in *Elizabeth & Anne*, arr. York Va. (SPC.1716.310)(CTB31.208)(VSP.1.185) (alias 5493)
5495. Paul, James, b. 1748, laborer, res. Ayr, sh. Apr 1775, fr. Greenock to N.Y., in *Lilly*. (PRO.T47.12)
5496. Paul, John, b. 1745, farmer, res. Glasgow, sh. May 1774, fr. Greenock to N.Y., in *Matty*, ch. Margaret. (PRO.T47.12)
5497. Paull, James, Aberdeenshire, clergyman, sh. 1720, sett. Warwick Bermuda, d. 1750. (F.7.661)
5498. Peacock, James, assault, res. Ayrshire, tr. Sept 1753. (SM.15.468)
5499. Pearson, Elspeth, rioter, res. Cupar Fife, tr. 1773, m. John Martin. (SRO.B59.26.1.6.18)(AJ1322)
5500. Pearson, John, res. Leith, sh. May 1684, sett. Hudson Bay. (HBRS.9.234)

5501. Pearson, Michael, sh. 14 July 1698, fr. Leith to Darien, 7 Oct 1698, sett. Crab Island West Indies. (DSP80)
5502. Pearson, Robert, d. 1 July 1700 Kingston Jamaica. (DP352)
5503. Pedden, James, sailor, res. Prestonpans East Lothian, sh. 18 Aug 1699, fr. Clyde to Darien, in *Rising Sun*, Edin pr1707 CC8.8.83
5504. Peddie, John, b. 6 July 1703, Arbroath Angus, merchant, Jacobite, res. Arbroath, pts. John Peddie & Jean Smith, tr. 24 Feb 1747, fr. Liverpool to Va, in *Gildart*, arr. Port North Potomac Md 5 Aug 1747. (P.2.250)(PRO.T1.328)
5505. Peddin, Alexander, tr. 12 Dec 1678, fr. Leith to West Indies, in *St Michael of Scarborough*. (PC.6.76)
5506. Peebles, Alexander, passenger, sh. Feb 1681, fr. Ayr to West Indies, in *James of Ayr*. (SRO.E72.3.6)
5507. Peebles, David, merchant, res. Edinburgh, sh. 1647, sett. Powell's Creek Va. (EBR129)(WM.2.13.132)
5508. Peirce, Lewis, sh. 1637, sett. Barbados. (SRO.GD34.925)
5509. Pendin, James, clergyman edu. Glasgow Uni, sh. pre 1732, sett. Va. (SCHR.14.148)
5510. Pendleton, John, b. 1732, weaver, Jacobite, res. Manchester, tr. 1747. (P.3.250)(MR198)
5511. Pendreick, Robert, sh. 14 July 1698, fr. Leith to Darien, d. 11 Dec 1698 Darien. (NLS.RY.2b.8\19)
5512. Penman, Edward, merchant, res. Edinburgh, pts. George Penman, sh. pre 1784, sett. Charleston S.C. (SRO.RD3.245.725)
5513. Perkle, James, b. 1752, printer, res. Edinburgh, sh. Sept 1774, fr. London to Md, in *Neptune*. (PRO.T47.9\11)
5514. Peter, Anne, infanticide, res. Kintore Aberdeenshire, tr. Sept 1776. (SM.38)
5515. Peter, James, Jacobite, tr. 29 June 1716, fr. Liverpool to Jamaica or Va, in *Elizabeth & Anne*, arr. York Va. (SPC.1716.310)(CTB31.208)(VSP.1.186)
5516. Peter, John, Jacobite, tr. 24 May 1716, fr. Liverpool to Md, in *Friendship*, arr. Md Aug 1716. (SPC.1716.311)(HM386)
5517. Peter, John, Jacobite, tr. 29 June 1716, fr. Liverpool to Jamaica or Va, in *Elizabeth & Anne*, arr. York Va. (SPC.1716.310)(CTB31.208)(VSP.1.185)
5518. Peters, Thomas, merchant, sh. 24 Oct 1685, fr. Port Glasgow to N.E., in *Boston Merchant*. (SRO.E72.19.8)
5519. Petrie, James, b. 1727, laborer, Jacobite, res. Angus, tr. 5 May 1747, fr. Liverpool to Leeward Islands, in *Veteran*, arr. Martinique June 1747. (P.3.250)(MRT108)(PRO.SP36.102)
5520. Petrie, Peter, b. 1764, farm servant, res. St Andrews Orkney Islands, sh. Sept 1774, fr. Kirkwall to Savannah Ga, in *Marlborough*, sett. Richmond Co Ga. (PRO.T47.12)

5521. Pettenreck, Robert, b. 1663, accountant, sh. Mar 1684, fr. London to Jamaica, in *George*. (CLRO\AIA)
5522. Petty, John, Covenanter, tr. July 1685. (PC.11.114)
5523. Phil, William, horsethief, res. Aberdeen, tr. May 1769. (SRO.RH2.4.255)
5524. Philip, Margaret, b. 1757, servant, res. Edinburgh, sh. May 1775, fr. Leith to Philadelphia, in *Friendship*. (PRO.T47.12)
5525. Philips, Robert, sailor, res. Leven Fife, sh. 18 Aug 1699, fr. Clyde to Darien, in *Rising Sun*, Edin pr1707 CC8.8.83
5526. Philp, George, physician, abortionist, res. Huntly Aberdeenshire, tr. 1772, to Va, in *Betsy*, arr. Port of James River Upper District Va 29 Apr 1772. (SRO.JC27.10.3)(AJ1238)
5527. Philp, William, farmer, horsethief, res. Stotfold of Skelmuir Aberdeenshire, tr. May 1769. (SM.31.333)
5528. Picken, William, b. 1742, farmer, res. Glen Orchy Argyll, sh. Aug 1774, fr. Greenock to Wilmington N.C., in *Ulysses*, m. Martha Huie. (PRO.T47.12)
5529. Piggott, Alexander, b. 1721, Jacobite, res. Bridgend Kingoldrum Angus, tr. 31 Mar 1747, fr. London to Jamaica, in *St George or Carteret*, arr. Jamaica 1747. (P.3.252)(MR108)(PRO.CO137.58)
5530. Pinkerton, Robert, sea captain, res. Liberton Edinburgh, sh. 14 July 1698, fr. Leith to Darien, in *Unicorn*, d. 1699, Edin pr1707 CC8.8.83
5531. Pinmurray, Janet, Jacobite, tr. 22 Apr 1747, fr. Liverpool to Va, in *Johnson*, arr. Port Oxford Md 5 Aug 1747. (P.3.254)(PRO.T1.328)
5532. Pirie, Joseph, pickpocket, res. Ayrshire, tr. Sept 1775. (AJ1449)
5533. Pirie, Margaret, infanticide, res. Banff, tr. 25 May 1749, fr. Aberdeen to Va, in *Dispatch of Newcastle*. (AJ68)
5534. Pitcairn, David, merchant, res. Dreghorn, pts. David Pitcairn & Mary Anderson, d. 1730 Jamaica, Edin pr1733 CC8.8.95
5535. Pitcairn, Robert, merchant, res. Pitblea, pts. Robert Pitcairn, sh. pre 1780, sett. St Catherine Middlesex Jamaica. (SRO.GD1.675.61)
5536. Pitcairn, Robert, tavernkeeper, res. Newburgh Fife, sh. pre 1780, sett. Spanish Town Jamaica. (SRO.GD1.675.113)
5537. Pitscottie, Colin, sailor, pts. John Pitscottie of Craigduchie, sh. 18 Aug 1699, fr. Clyde to Darien, in *Rising Sun*, Edin pr1707 CC8.8.83
5538. Pitterkin, Thomas, b. 1755, res. Fort Augustus Inverness-shire, sh. May 1775, fr. Leith to Philadelphia, in *Friendship*. (PRO.T47.12)
5539. Pittigrew, James, b. 1746, merchant, res. Glasgow, sh. Oct 1774, fr. Greenock to Charleston S.C., in *Countess*. (PRO.T47.12)
5540. Pollock, Catherine, whore, res. Edinburgh, tr. 19 Mar 1695. (SRO.PC2.25.216)

5541. Pollock, John, Covenanter, tr. 5 Sept 1685, fr. Leith to East N.J., in *Henry & Francis*. (PC.11.154)

5542. Pollock, William, clergyman edu. Edinburgh Uni 1699, sh. pre 1706, sett. James Island Carolina. (F.7.665)

5543. Pollock, William, horsehirer & brandy dealer, murderer, res. Glasgow, tr. Jan 1763. (SRO.HCR.I.94)

5544. Polson, Hugh, gentleman, res. Navidale Sutherland, pts. John Polson & Janet Mackay, sh. pre 1774, sett. St Andrews Jamaica. (BM295)(SRO.RD4.232.908)

5545. Porteous, Edward, merchant, Covenanter, res. Newbattle Midlothian, tr. 1685, to Va, sett. Petsworth Gloucester Co Va, m. Margaret ..., ch. Robert, d. 1700 Va, Gloucester pr1700 PCC pr1700. (SRO.GD297.114)

5546. Porteous, George, b. 1650, Leith, painter, rioter, res. Edinburgh, pts. John Porteous, tr. 13 Sept 1666, fr. Leith to Barbados. (PC.2.195)

5547. Porteous, John, Jacobite, tr. 29 June 1716, fr. Liverpool to Jamaica or Va, in *Elizabeth & Anne*. (SPC.1716.310)(CTB31.208)

5548. Porteous, Robert, servant, thief, res. Craigentinny Edinburgh, tr. Aug 1768. (SRO.JC27.D35)

5549. Porteous, Simon, b. 1726, mason, sh. Sept 1775, fr. Newcastle to Ga, in *Georgia Packet*, sett. Friendsborough Ga. (PRO.T47.9\11)

5550. Porteous, Steven, tailor, res. Canongate Edinburgh, tr. 12 Dec 1678, fr. Leith to West Indies, in *St Michael of Scarborough*. (PC.6.76)

5551. Porter, Abel, merchant, sh. Aug 1685, fr. Leith to N.J., in *America*. (SRO.E72.15.32)

5552. Porter, Francis, thief, res. Bridgend of Lunan Angus, tr. May 1755. (SM.17.265)

5553. Porter, William, pickpocket, res. Glasgow, pts. William Porter, tr. Aug 1766. (SRO.JC27)

5554. Porterfield, John, merchant skipper, sh. pre 1699, sett. Bristol N.E. (SPC.1700.195)

5555. Porterfield, William, edu. Glasgow Uni 1753, res. Hapland Ayrshire, sett. Pensacola W Fla, d. Mar 1767 at sea. (MAGU49)

5556. Pott, Anthony, res. Jedburgh Roxburghshire, tr. 17 Apr 1666, fr. Leith to Barbados. (ETR106) (alias 2704)

5557. Potts, Thomas, Jacobite, tr. 24 May 1716, fr. Liverpool to Md, in *Friendship*, arr. Md Aug 1716. (SPC.1716.311)(HM387)

5558. Pourie, Alexander, sailor, res. Edinburgh, pts. Andrew Pourie, sh. 14 July 1698, fr. Leith to Darien, in *St Andrew*, m. Elizabeth Smith, Edin pr1707 CC8.8.83

5559. Poustie, John, tailor, Jacobite, res. Edinburgh, tr. 9 Nov 1748, m. Elizabeth Yeaman. (P.3.256)(MR207)

5560. Power, Edward, seaman, sh. 14 July 1698, fr. Leith to Darien, in *St Andrew*, Edin pr1707 CC8.8.83

5561. Powrie, William, planter, res. Dawyck Peebleshire, pts. Richard Powrie, sh. pre 1630, sett. Barbados, d. 1648 Barbados, Barbados pr1649 RB3\532 PCC pr1651. (EBR.44.1912)(EBR25.1086)
5562. Pratt, Thomas, sailor, res. Bo'ness West Lothian, pts. Alexander Pratt, sh. 14 July 1698, fr. Leith to Darien, in *Dolphin*, Edin pr1708 CC8.8.84
5563. Price, Ralph, b. 1713, miller, Jacobite, tr. 24 Feb 1747, fr. Liverpool to Va, in *Gildart*, arr. Port North Potomac Md 5 Aug 1747. (P.2.258)(PRO.T1.328)
5564. Pride, David, b. 1757, shoemaker, res. Fife, sh. May 1775, fr. Leith to Philadelphia, in *Friendship*. (PRO.T47.12)
5565. Pringle, John, sh. pre 1769, sett. P.E.I. (SRO.GD293.2.74)
5566. Pringle, John, pickpocket, res. Edinburgh, tr. 15 Dec 1720. (SRO.HH11)
5567. Pringle, Robert, physician, pts. John Pringle of Haining, sett. Jamaica, d. 13 Oct 1775 Philadelphia. (SM.38.53)
5568. Pringle, Thomas, tr. Nov 1679, fr. Leith. (ETR162)
5569. Pringle, Walter, Governor of Dominica, d. 1768. (SM.30.279)
5570. Pringle, Walter, merchant, sett. St Kitts, ch. Thomas Eleanora Rebecca Ann Margaret, d. 1760 St Kitts, Edin pr1776 CC8.8.123
5571. Proctor, Joseph, Jacobite, tr. 30 Mar 1716, fr. Liverpool to Antigua, in *Scipio*. (SPC.1716.310)(CTB31.204)
5572. Proctor, Richard, b. 1727, Jacobite, res. Lancashire, tr. 8 May 1747, to Antigua. (P.3.258)(MR198)
5573. Proctor, William, Banff or Elgin, clergyman & schoolmaster edu. Aberdeen Uni 1733, res. Mortlach Banffshire, sh. 1737, sett. Nottoway Amelia Co Va, d. 1761. (AJ741)
5574. Proctor, William, b. 21 Sept 1736, Elgin Morayshire, wright, thief, res. Elgin, pts. Alexander Proctor & Isabel McKay, tr. Jan 1767. (SM.29.54)(SRO.JC.27)
5575. Prophet, Sylvester, Jacobite, tr. 29 June 1716, fr. Liverpool to Jamaica or Va, in *Elizabeth & Anne*, arr. York Va. (SPC.1716.310)(CTB31.208)(VSP.I.185)
5576. Proudfoot, James, clergyman, sh. 1754, sett. Recquec. (UPC654)
5577. Proudfoot, John, b. 1752, Edinburgh, hairdresser, sh. Nov 1774, fr. London to Va, in *Elizabeth*, sett. Va, m. Leanor Hitt, d. 1823, bd. Barbour Co WVa. (PRO.T47.9\11)
5578. Provan, Matthew, res. Dunbartonshire, sh. pre 1726, sett. Md, ch. William. (SRO.RS10.5.384.405)
5579. Provan, Robert, shopbreaker, tr. 1773, fr. Port Glasgow to Va, in *Thomas of Glasgow*, arr. James River Upper District Va 5 June 1773. (SRO.JC.27.10.3)
5580. Provost, John, b. 1732, farmer, res. Siddy, sh. July 1775, fr. Stornaway to Philadelphia, in *Clementina*, m. Isobel ..., ch. John Alexander. (PRO.T47.12)

5581. Provost, Paul, b. 1760, servant, res. Belmaduthy Ross & Cromarty, sh. July 1775, fr. Stornaway to Philadelphia, in *Clementina*. (PRO.T47.12)
5582. Provost, Rory, b. 1757, servant, res. Belmaduthy Ross & Cromarty, sh. July 1775, fr. Stornaway to Philadelphia, in *Clementina*. (PRO.T47.12)
5583. Pryde, James, weaver, Covenanter, res. Strathmiglo Fife, tr. 12 Dec 1678, fr. Leith to West Indies, in *St Michael of Scarborough*. (PC.6.76)
5584. Pullar, Charles, b. 1750, hairdresser, sh. June 1775, fr. London to Baltimore, in *Nancy*. (PRO.T47.9\11)
5585. Purdie, Robert, soldier, assault, tr. Oct 1749. (SM.11.509)
5586. Purdon, Gilbert, Jacobite, res. Ballyclogh Cork, tr. 1747. (P.3.258)
5587. Pye, John, thief, tr. May 1775. (SM.37.405)
5588. Pyper, Thomas, merchant, sh. July 1681, fr. Leith to N.Y., in *Hope of Edinburgh*. (SRO.E72.15.21)
5589. Queely, Mrs Dorothy, d. pre 1777 St Kitts, Edin pr1777 CC8.8.124
5590. Raddock, Samuel, apothecary, d. Apr 1769 Annapolis Royal Md. (SM.31.334)
5591. Rae, James, Covenanter, res. Uddingston Lanarkshire, tr. 12 Dec 1685, fr. Leith to Barbados, in *John & Nicholas*. (PC.11.254)(ETR389)
5592. Rae, James, farmer, res. Cushnie Aberdeenshire, tr. 29 June 1716, fr. Liverpool to Jamaica or Va, in *Elizabeth & Anne*, arr. York Va. (SPC.1716.310)(CTB31.208)(JAB.1.151)(VSP.1.186)
5593. Rae, James, merchant, res. Glasgow, d. 1764 Va. (SM.26.290)
5594. Rae, James, b. 19 Nov 1723, Govan, merchant edu. Glasgow Uni 1736, res. Glasgow, pts. Robert Rae & Elizabeth Dunlop, d. 1763 Va. (MAGU17)
5595. Rae, John, tailor, res. Falkirk Stirlingshire, tr. 12 Dec 1678, fr. Leith to West Indies, in *St Michael of Scarborough*. (PC.6.76)
5596. Rae, John, Jacobite, tr. 7 May 1716. fr. Liverpool to S.C., in *Susannah*. (SPC.1716.309)(CTB31.206)
5597. Rae, Margaret, cowthief, res. Echt Aberdeenshire, sh. June 1755, fr. Aberdeen to Va, in *Hope*, m. George Christie. (AJ350\388)
5598. Rae, William, weaver, res. Glasgow, tr. 12 Dec 1678, fr. Leith to West Indies, in *St Michael of Scarborough*. (PC.6.76)
5599. Rae, William, b. 1762, Dumfries, sh. 1782, sett. Jamaica, d. 7 May 1837 Kingston Jamaica, bd. Scots Cemetery. (MIBWI33)
5600. Rain, John, b. 1739, laborer, res. Kirkcudbright, sh. May 1774, fr. Kirkcudbright to N.Y., in *Adventure*, m. Elizabeth McWhinnie, ch. Thomas. (PRO.T47.12)
5601. Rait, John, b. 1653, res. Inverkeilor Angus, pts. John Rait, d. 1675 Nevis. (Inverkeilor Gs)

5602. Raitt, Margaret, b. 4 Sept 1677, Montrose Angus, res. Montrose, pts. Robert Raitt & Margaret Orrock, d. 1714 Va. (SRO.GD45.17.916)
5603. Ralston, David, merchant, res. Glasgow, sh. pre 1762, sett. Cabin Point James River Va. (SRA.CFI)
5604. Ralston, Marion, b. 1756, spinner, res. Paisley Renfrewshire, sh. Feb 1774, fr. Greenock to N.Y., in *Commerce*. (PRO.T47.12)
5605. Ramsay, Andrew, Jacobite, tr. 25 June 1716, fr. Liverpool to St Kitts, in *Hockenhill*. (SPC.1716.312)(CTB31.207)
5606. Ramsay, Cicella, res. Edinburgh, tr. 8 May 1663, fr. Leith to Barbados, in *Mary*. (EBR.186.13.4)
5607. Ramsay, Fanny, b. 1752, res. Edinburgh, sh. Apr 1775, fr. Greenock to N.Y., in *Lilly*. (PRO.T47.12)
5608. Ramsay, George, wheelwright & farmer, Jacobite, res. Strathbogie Aberdeenshire, tr. 21 July 1748, fr. London. (P.3.260)(MR68)
5609. Ramsay, George, pts. James Ramsay of Tullymurdoch, sett. Antigua & St Vincent, d. pre 1775, Edin pr1775 CC8.8.123
5610. Ramsay, Gilbert, clergyman edu. King's College Aberdeen 1673, sh. pre 1689, sett. St Paul's Antigua & Christ Church Barbados. (CAR.3.268)(KCA.2.243)
5611. Ramsay, James, b. 25 July 1733, Fraserburgh Aberdeenshire, clergyman & surgeon edu. King's Col Aberdeen 1747, res. Turriff Aberdeenshire, sh. 28 Nov 1761, to St Kitts, sett. Christchurch Nicola Town St Kitts. (MWI152)(EMA51)(FPA317)(KCA237)
5612. Ramsay, John, clergyman, sh. 1751, sett. Va. (EMA51)
5613. Ramsay, John, Jacobite, tr. 24 May 1716, fr. Liverpool to Md, in *Friendship*, arr. Md Aug 1716. (SPC.1716.311)(HM387)(Md Arch.34.164)
5614. Ramsay, John, b. 1701, res. Dalry Galloway, sh. Sept 1721, fr. London to Md. (CLRO\AIA)
5615. Ramsay, Margaret, res. Edinburgh, tr. 8 May 1663, fr. Leith to Barbados, in *Mary*. (EBR.186.13.4)
5616. Ramsay, Samuel, b. 1727, joiner, res. Gatehouse Kirkcudbrightshire, sh. May 1774, fr. Stranraer to N.Y., in *Gale*, ch. Jane John William George Jane Elizabeth Margaret. (PRO.T47.12)
5617. Ramsay, Thomas, b. 1756, gentleman planter, res. Edinburgh, sh. Dec 1773, fr. London to Jamaica, in *Eagle*. (PRO.T47.9\11)
5618. Ramsay, William, Jacobite, tr. 25 June 1716, fr. Liverpool to St Kitts, in *Hockenhill*. (SPC.1716.312)(CTB31.207)
5619. Ramsay, William, b. 1716, merchant, res. Dumfries-shire, sh. pre 1765, sett. Alexandria Va, m. Ann McCarty, ch. Dennis William, d. 1785 Alexandria. (SRO.SC15.55.2)(SRO.RS.19.376)(VG88)
5620. Ranald, Francis, b. 1731, herd, Jacobite, res. Strathbogie Aberdeenshire, tr. 31 Mar 1747, fr. London to Barbados, in *Frere*. (P.3.262)(MR128)

5621. Randal, Robert, b. 1753, printer & book-binder, res. Edinburgh, sh. July 1774, fr. London to Md, in *Russia Merchant*. (PRO.T47.9\11)
5622. Rankeiller, Thomas, sailor, res. Wemyss Fife, pts. James Rankeiller, sh. 18 Aug 1699, fr. Clyde to Darien, Edin pr1708 CC8.8.84
5623. Ranken, John, sailor, res. Ayr, sh. 18 Aug 1699, fr. Clyde to Darien, in *Rising Sun*, Edin pr1708 CC8.8.84
5624. Ranken, John, Jacobite, tr. 21 Apr 1716, fr. Liverpool to S.C., in *Wakefield*. (SPC.1716.309)(CTB31.205)
5625. Rankin, Daniel, b. 1756, laborer, res. Paisley Renfrewshire, sh. Feb 1774, fr. Greenock to N.Y., in *Commerce*. (PRO.T47.12)
5626. Rankin, Hugh, b. 1752, barber, res. Saltcoats Ayrshire, sh. Aug 1774, fr. Greenock to Philadelphia, in *Magdalene*. (PRO.T47.12)
5627. Rankin, John, Covenanter, res. Bonhardpans, tr. Aug 1670. (PC.3.206)
5628. Rankin, William, b. 1736, turner, res. Edinburgh, sh. Feb 1754, fr. London to Jamaica. (CLRO\AIA)
5629. Rankine, Hugh, sh. 29 Nov 1773, fr. Greenock to Jamaica, in *Mary of Glasgow*. (SRO.CE.60.1.7)
5630. Rannie, William, carter, thief, res. Herman St Termants, tr. Mar 1767. (SM.29.221)(SRO.JC27.D35)
5631. Rannoldson, James, b. 1722, weaver, Jacobite, res. Fettercairn Kincardineshire, tr. 31 Mar 1747, fr. London to Jamaica, in *St George or Carteret*, arr. Jamaica 1747. (P.3.270)(PRO.CO137.58)(MR30)
5632. Rarity, John, b. 1752, weaver, res. Paisley Renfrewshire, sh. Feb 1774, fr. Greenock to N.Y., in *Commerce*. (PRO.T47.12)
5633. Rash, James, Jacobite, tr. 21 Apr 1716, fr. Liverpool to S.C., in *Wakefield*. (SPC.1716.309)(CTB31.205)
5634. Rattray, Ann, murderer, res. Aberdeen, tr. 1728, fr. Glasgow to Md, in *Concord of Glasgow*, arr. Charles Co Md 24 May 1728. (SRO.JC11.6)(SRO.JC27.10.3)
5635. Rattray, James, b. 1713, res. Benathy Angus, sh. Aug 1728, fr. London to Antigua. (CLRO\AIA)
5636. Rattray, John, merchant, res. Glasgow, pts. Thomas Rattray & Janet Marshall, sh. 15 Nov 1763, sett. Jamaica. (SRA.B10.15.7056)
5637. Rattray, John, judge, d. 30 Sept 1761 Charleston S.C. (SM.13.671)
5638. Reach, Janet, b. 19 June 1757, Wick Caithness, servant, res. Wick, pts. John Reach & Janet Plewman, sh. Sept 1775, fr. Kirkwall to Ga, in *Marlborough*, sett. Richmond Co Ga. (PRO.T47.12)
5639. Reid, Alexander, Jacobite, res. Alford Aberdeenshire, tr. 24 May 1716, fr. Liverpool to Md, in *Friendship*, d. 14 Oct 1718 Md, Md pr1718 E18\6. (SPC.1716.311)
5640. Reid, Alexander, Jacobite, tr. 30 Mar 1716, fr. Liverpool to Antigua, in *Scipio*. (SPC.1716.310)(CTB31.204)

5641. Reid, Alexander, b. 1729, farmer, res. Brodie Morayshire, sh. May 1774, fr. Stornaway to Philadelphia, in *Friendship*, m. Katherine Hutchison, ch. Alexander Mary Isobel James George David Katherine Henry John. (PRO.T47.12)
5642. Reid, Andrew, Covenanter, res. Argyll, tr. Aug 1685, fr. Leith to Jamaica. (PC.11.328)(ETR369)
5643. Reid, David, workman, Jacobite, res. Myrend Kingoldrum Angus, tr. 1747. (P.3.266)(MR108)
5644. Reid, David, b. 1754, weaver, sh. Dec 1773, fr. London to Md, in *Etty*. (PRO.T47.9\11)
5645. Reid, George, b. 29 May 1716, Deskford Banffshire, laborer, Jacobite, res. Banff, pts. Walter Reid, tr. 5 May 1747, fr. Liverpool to Leeward Islands, in *Veteran*, arr. Martinique June 1747. (P.3.266)(MR75)(JAB.2.440)(PRO.SP36.102)
5646. Reid, Hugh, b. 1751, woolcomber, sh. Nov 1774, fr. London to Va, in *Elizabeth*. (PRO.T47.9\11)
5647. Reid, James, b. 1729, Aberdeen or Angus, laborer, Jacobite, tr. 5 May 1747, fr. Liverpool to Leeward Islands, in *Veteran*, arr. Martinique June 1747. (P.3.266)(MR108)(PRO.SP36.102)
5648. Reid, John, clergyman, sh. 1745, sett. N.C. (EMA52)
5649. Reid, John, thief, res. Culross Fife, pts. John Reid, tr. May 1763. (SRO.B59.26.11.6.41)
5650. Reid, John, b. 13 Feb 1655, Kirkliston West Lothian, gardener, sh. 1683, fr. Leith to East N.J., in *Henry & Francis*, sett. Perth Amboy N.J., m. Margaret Miller. (Insh240)
5651. Reid, John, b. 1663, groom, sh. Mar 1684, fr. London to Jamaica. (CLRO\AIA)
5652. Reid, John, b. 1749, farmer, res. Stirling, sh. May 1774, fr. Greenock to N.Y., in *Matty*. (PRO.T47.12)
5653. Reid, John, b. 1749, cooper, res. Glasgow, sh. May 1774, fr. Greenock to N.Y., in *Matty*. (PRO.T47.12)
5654. Reid, Malcolm, res. Perthshire, tr. 14 July 1698, fr. Leith to Darien, in *St Andrew*. (SRO.B59.26.11.3) (alias 5078)
5655. Reid, Malcolm, Jacobite, tr. 7 May 1716, fr. Liverpool to S.C., in *Susannah*. (SPC.1716.309)(CTB31.206)
5656. Reid, Margaret, oxen thief, res. Forfar Angus, tr. May 1753. (SM.15.260)
5657. Reid, Mary, b. 1758, servant, res. Edinburgh, sh. May 1775, fr. Leith to Philadelphia, in *Friendship*. (PRO.T47.12)
5658. Reid, Robert, robber, res. Glasgow, tr. Sept 1765. (AJ925)
5659. Reid, Robert, weaver, res. Langside Glasgow, tr. 12 Dec 1678, fr. Leith to West Indies, in *St Michael of Scarborough*. (PC.6.76)
5660. Reid, Robert, Cathcart Glasgow, tr. 12 Dec 1678, fr. Leith to West Indies, in *St Michael of Scarborough*. (PC.6.76)

5661. Reid, Robert, farmer, Jacobite, res. Mid Clova Aberdeenshire, tr. 29 June 1716, fr. Liverpool to Jamaica or Va, in *Elizabeth & Anne*. (SPC.1716.310)(CTB31.208)(JAB.1.151)

5662. Reid, Thomas, gunner, res. Edinburgh, sh. 14 July 1698, fr. Leith to Darien, in *Unicorn*, Edin pr1708 CC8.8.84

5663. Reid, Walter, b. 1759, wright, res. Dundee Angus, sh. Aug 1774, fr. Greenock to Philadelphia, in *Magdalene*. (PRO.T47.12)

5664. Reid, William, tr. 12 Dec 1685, fr. Leith to Barbados, in *John & Nicholas*. (ETR390)

5665. Reid, William, merchant & tobacco factor, res. Glasgow, sh. pre 1775, sett. Fredericksburg Va. (SRA.T79.1)

5666. Reid, William, b. 29 Oct 1744, Banff, physician & surgeon, sh. pre 1765, sett. Antigua, d. 14 Nov 1773 St John Antigua. (SM.36.111)

5667. Reid, William, b. 1746, barber, res. Paisley Renfrewshire, sh. May 1775, fr. Greenock to N.Y. or Ga, in *Christy*. (PRO.T47.12)

5668. Reidie, David, seaman, res. Burntisland Fife, sh. 28 Mar 1683, sett. Port Nelson Hudson Bay. (HBRS.9.90)

5669. Reirie, David, b. 1727, farmer, Jacobite, res. Latheron Caithness, tr. 1747. (MR87)

5670. Reith, Anne, fraudster, res. Pittenweem Fife, tr. Sept 1774, m. Alexander Morton. (SRO.B59.26.11.6.20)

5671. Renfrew, Janet, b. 1757, spinner, res. Paisley Renfrewshire, sh. Feb 1774, fr. Greenock to N.Y., in *Commerce*. (PRO.T47.12)

5672. Renney, Robert, clergyman edu. Glasgow & Aberdeen Unis 1755, sh. 1764, sett. Overwharton Va. (EMA52)(FPA308)

5673. Rennie, John, clergyman, sh. 1773, sett. Ga. (EMA52)

5674. Rennie, John, Covenanter, tr. 5 Sept 1685, fr. Leith to East N.J., in *Henry & Francis*. (PC.11.154)

5675. Rennie, Marion, Covenanter, tr. 5 Sept 1685, fr. Leith to East N.J., in *Henry & Francis*. (PC.11.154)

5676. Renny, James, merchant, res. Angus, sh. pre 1783, sett. Jamaica. (SRO.RD3.242.1202)

5677. Renta, James, b. 1747, laborer, res. Glasgow, sh. Feb 1774, fr. Greenock to N.Y., in *Commerce*. (PRO.T47.12)

5678. Renton, Alexander, Greenhill Lanarkshire, surveyor, res. Largs Ayrshire, sh. pre 1729, sett. Boston Mass, m. Mary Young, ch. Alexander Janet Jean John Mary William. (SRO.RS42.13\14)

5679. Renton, James, Jacobite, tr. 28 July 1716, fr. Liverpool to Va, in *Godspeed*, arr. Md Oct 1716. (SPC.1716.310)(CTB31.209)(HM389)(MdArch25.347)

5680. Renwick, John, Covenanter, res. Barsalloch Wigtonshire, tr. 1684. (PC.10.258)

5681. Reston, James, Covenanter, tr. 5 Sept 1685, fr. Leith to East N.J., in *Henry & Francis*. (PC.11.166)
5682. Reyley, David, farmer, Jacobite, res. Latheron Caithness, tr. 30 Mar 1747, fr. London to Jamaica, in *St George or Carteret*, arr. Jamaica 1747. (P.3.270)(PRO.CO137.58)
5683. Reynoldson, James, b. 1722, weaver, Jacobite, res. Fettercairn Kincardineshire, tr. 31 Mar 1747, fr. Tilbury. (P.3.270)
5684. Rhind, Alexander, Jacobite, tr. 24 May 1716, fr. Liverpool to Md, in *Friendship*, arr. Md Aug 1716. (SPC.1716.310)(HM387)(MdArch34.164)
5685. Rhind, David, schoolmaster, res. Aberdeen, sh. pre 1765, sett. Charleston S.C. (APB.4.9)
5686. Rhind, William, b. 1713, res. Prestonpans East Lothian, sh. July 1731, fr. London to Pa. (CLRO\AIA)
5687. Richard, Thomas, Covenanter, res. Greenock Mains, Muirkirk Ayrshire, tr. Aug 1685, fr. Leith to Jamaica. (PC.11.329)(ETR369)
5688. Richardson, John, Jacobite, tr. 21 Apr 1716, fr. Liverpool to S.C., in *Wakefield*. (SPC.1716.309)(CTB31.205)
5689. Richardson, Robert, Jacobite, tr. 21 Apr 1716, fr. Liverpool to S.C., in *Wakefield*. (SPC.1716.309)(CTB31.205)
5690. Richardson, William, tr. 17 Nov 1679. (PC.6.343)
5691. Richardson, William, b. 1752, printer, res. Edinburgh, sh. July 1774, fr. London to Md, in *Elizabeth*. (PRO.T47.9\11)
5692. Richmond, Helen, res. Edinburgh, tr. 1696, fr. Newhaven to Va. (SRO.RH15.14.58)
5693. Richmond, James, cattlethief, res. Glasgow, tr. Apr 1772. (SRO.RH2.4.255)
5694. Riddal, William, tr. June 1766, fr. Aberdeen. (AJ964)
5695. Riddel, George, physician, sett. Yorktown Va, d. 20 Jan 1779 Va. (SM.41.79)
5696. Riddell, Archibald, b. 1635, clergyman edu. Edinburgh Uni 1656, Covenanter, res. Kippen Stirlingshire, pts. Sir Walter Riddel & Janet Rigg, tr. 5 Sep 1685, fr. Leith to East N.J., in *Henry & Francis*, sett. Woodbridge N.J., m. Helen Aitkenhead, d. 17 Feb 1708 Scotland. (F.7.665)(PC.10.79)
5697. Riddell, George, physician, res. Kinglass West Lothian, pts. George Riddell & Christian Paterson, sh. 1751, sett. Yorktown & Williamsburg Va, d. Jan 1779. (OD40)(SM.41.167)
5698. Riddell, Helen, sh. 1684, sett. Perth Amboy N.J. (SRO.RH15)
5699. Riddell, Hugh, Covenanter, tr. 1683, fr. Leith to N.Y. (PC.8.253)
5700. Riddell, James, sailor, res. Sauchieglass St Ninian's Stirlingshire, pts. John Riddell, sh. 14 July 1698, fr. Leith to Darien, in *Unicorn*, Edin pr1707 CC8.8.83

5701. Riddell, John, merchant, res. Glasgow, sh. pre 1769, sett. Dumfries Prince William Co Va. (SRA.CFI)
5702. Riddell, Thomas, mate, res. Leith Midlothian, sh. 18 Aug 1699, fr. Clyde to Darien, in *Rising Sun*, Edin pr1707 CC8.8.83
5703. Riddle, Margaret, thief, tr. Feb 1775. (SRO.HCR.I.112)
5704. Riddoch, Alexander, merchant, sh. Aug 1685, fr. Leith to N.J., in *Henry of Newcastle*. (SRO.E72.15.32)
5705. Riddoch, Colin, physician, res. Perthshire, sh. pre 1774, sett. Newcastle Hanover Co Va, m. Jean ... (SRO.RD4.216.288)
5706. Riddoch, Dr Colin, physician, pre 1768, sett. Port Royal Caroline Co Va. (SRO.RD4.212.846)
5707. Riddoch, Peter, b. 1721, slater, Jacobite, res. Doune Stirlingshire, tr. 22 Apr 1747, fr. Liverpool to Va, in *Johnson*, arr. Port Oxford Md 5 Aug 1747. (P.3.272)(MR45)(PRO.T1.328)
5708. Riddock, John, b. 1748, laborer, res. Kilmalcolm Renfrewshire, sh. Apr 1775, fr. Greenock to N.Y., in *Lilly*. (PRO.T47.12)
5709. Riding, Richard, b. 1723, weaver, Jacobite, res. Lancashire, tr. 1747. (P.3.272)(MR198)
5710. Ridley, Alexander, Jacobite, tr. 30 Mar 1716, fr. Liverpool to Antigua, in *Scipio*. (SPC.1716.310)(CTB31.204)
5711. Ridley, John, Jacobite, tr. 30 Mar 1716, fr. Liverpool to Antigua, in *Scipio*. (SPC.1716.310)(CTB31.204)
5712. Ridley, John, Jacobite, tr. 25 June 1716, fr. Liverpool to St Kitts, in *Hockenhill*. (SPC.1716.312)(CTB31.207)
5713. Ridpath, John, tinker, adulterer, res. Edinburgh, tr. Dec 1662. (ETR80)
5714. Rish, John, b. 1736, gardener, res. Glasgow, sh. May 1774, fr. London to Philadelphia, in *Sally*. (PRO.T47.9\11)
5715. Ritchie, Alexander, Jacobite, res. Arbroath Angus, tr. 1747. (P.3.274)(MR108)
5716. Ritchie, Alexander, butcher, thief, res. Kirkcudbright, tr. May 1770. (AJ1167)
5717. Ritchie, John, soldier, Jacobite, res. Kirkcaldy Fife, tr. 1747. (P.3.274)
5718. Ritchie, John, b. 1755, thief, res. Kirkcudbright, pts. Alexander Ritchie, tr. 1771, fr. Port Glasgow to Md, in *Crawford*, arr. Port Oxford Md 23 July 1771. (SRO.JC.27.10.3)(AJ1167)
5719. Ritchie, Joseph, Jacobite, tr. 30 Mar 1716, fr. Liverpool to Antigua, in *Scipio*. (SPC.1716.310)(CTB31.204)
5720. Ritchie, William, b. 1729, Jacobite, res. Inverness-shire, tr. 30 Mar 1747, fr. London to Jamaica, in *St George or Carteret*, arr. Jamaica 1747. (P.3.274)(MR75)(PRO.CO137.58)
5721. Robb, Alexander, thief, res. Banff, tr. June 1766. (SM.23.388)
5722. Robb, Elizabeth, b. 1712, knitter, Jacobite, res. Aberdeen, tr. 5 May 1747, fr. Liverpool to Leeward Islands, in *Veteran*, arr. Martinique June 1747. (P.3.274)(JAB.2.441)(PRO.SP36.102)

5723. Robb, Hugh, b. 1735, tailor, res. Glasgow, sh. Feb 1774, fr. Greenock to N.Y., in *Commerce*. (PRO.T47.12)
5724. Robb, James, Jacobite, tr. 7 May 1716, fr. Liverpool to S.C., in *Susannah*. (SPC.1716.309)(CTB31.206)
5725. Robb, James, factor, res. Glasgow, pts. William Robb, sh. pre 1753, sett. Port Royal Va. (SRA.T-MJ)
5726. Robb, John, Jacobite, tr. 7 May 1716, fr. Liverpool to S.C., in *Susannah*. (SPC.1716.309)(CTB31.206)
5727. Robb, John, b. 1748, servant, res. Duffus Morayshire, sh. July 1775, fr. Stornaway to Philadelphia, in *Clementina*. (PRO.T47.12)
5728. Robb, Thomas, Jacobite, tr. 7 May 1716, fr. Liverpool to S.C., in *Susannah*. (SPC.1716.309)(CTB31.206)
5729. Roberts, John, b. 1745, merchant, sh. Mar 1775, fr. London to Ga, in *Diana*, m. Margaret ... (PRO.T47.9\11)
5730. Roberts, Margaret, b. 1749, res. Glasgow, sh. May 1774, fr. Greenock to N.Y., in *Matty*. (PRO.T47.12)
5731. Robertson, ..., thief, res. Stirling, tr. Oct 1773. (AJ1347) (alias 414)
5732. Robertson, Agnes, thief & whore, res. Edinburgh, tr. 28 Nov 1704, fr. Leith to Md. (SRO.PC2.28.307)
5733. Robertson, Alexander, sh. pre 1769, sett. Wicomico River Somerset Co Md. (SRO.NRAS.0247)
5734. Robertson, Alexander, clergyman, sh. 1775, sett. Jamaica. (EMA52)
5735. Robertson, Alexander, Jacobite, tr. 30 Mar 1716, fr. Liverpool to Antigua, in *Scipio*. (SPC.1716.310)
5736. Robertson, Alexander, Jacobite, tr. 30 Mar 1716, fr. Liverpool to Antigua, in *Scipio*. (SPC.1716.310)(CTB31.204)
5737. Robertson, Alexander, b. 1707, laborer, Jacobite, res. Struan Perthshire, tr. 5 May 1747, fr. Liverpool to Leeward Islands, in *Veteran*, arr. Martinique June 1747. (P.3.276)(MR26)(PRO.SP36.102)
5738. Robertson, Archibald, merchant, sh. pre 1750, sett. Md. (SRO.SC26.63.2)
5739. Robertson, Captain, planter, sh. pre 1700, sett. Northside Jamaica. (DP.305\13)
5740. Robertson, Daniel, Jacobite, tr. 30 Mar 1716, fr. Liverpool to Antigua, in *Scipio*. (SPC.1716.310)(CTB31.204)
5741. Robertson, Daniel, Jacobite, tr. 26 Apr 1716, fr. Liverpool to Jamaica, in *Two Brothers*, arr. Montserrat June 1716. (SPC.1716.313)(CTB31.205)(CTP.CC.43)
5742. Robertson, Daniel, b. 1757, weaver, res. Perth, sh. May 1775, fr. Leith to Philadelphia, in *Friendship*. (PRO.T47.12)
5743. Robertson, Donald, Jacobite, tr. 7 May 1716, fr. Liverpool to S.C., in *Susannah*. (SPC.1716.309)(CTB31.206)
5744. Robertson, Donald, Jacobite, tr. 24 May 1716, fr. Liverpool to Md, in *Friendship*, arr. Md Aug 1716. (SPC.1716.311)(HM387)

5745. Robertson, Duncan, Jacobite, tr. 30 Mar 1716, fr. Liverpool to Antigua, in *Scipio*. (SPC.1716.310)(CTB31.204)
5746. Robertson, Duncan, Jacobite, tr. 26 Apr 1716, fr. Liverpool to Jamaica, in *Two Brothers*, arr. Montserrat June 1716. (SPC.1716.313)(CTB31.205)(CTP.CC.43)
5747. Robertson, Duncan Dow, thief, res. Perthshire, tr. May 1776. (SRO.B59.26.16.10) (alias 4025)
5748. Robertson, Euphame, shopbreaker, res. Ayrshire, tr. Sept 1754. (SM.16.450) (alias 6708)
5749. Robertson, Francis, Jacobite, tr. 30 Mar 1716, fr. Liverpool to Antigua, in *Scipio*. (SPC.1716.310)
5750. Robertson, George, thief, res. Edinburgh, tr. Feb 1697. (SRO.PC2.26)
5751. Robertson, George, thief & forger, res. Dam of Careston Angus, tr. Sept 1756. (SRO.B59.26.114.19)
5752. Robertson, George, clergyman, sh. pre 1693, sett. Dinwiddie Co Va. (SCHR.14.142)(OD12)
5753. Robertson, George, b. 1726, apprentice weaver, Jacobite, res. Logginish Perthshire, tr. 31 Mar 1747, fr. London to Barbados , in *Frere*. (P.3.278)(MR27)
5754. Robertson, George, b. 1741, merchant, res. Aberdeen, sh. July 1775, fr. Greenock to Jamaica, in *Isabella*. (PRO.T47.12)
5755. Robertson, George, b. 1753, merchant, res. Inverness, sh. Jan 1774, fr. Greenock to Nevis, in *Aurora*. (SRO.CE.60.1.7)
5756. Robertson, Henry, laborer, res. Lothian, sh. Oct 1774, fr. Greenock to Philadelphia, in *Sally*. (PRO.T47.12)
5757. Robertson, Hugh, b. 1718, laborer, res. Inverness, sh. Jan 1736, fr. London to Md. (CLRO\AIA)
5758. Robertson, James, Jacobite, tr. 7 May 1716, fr. Liverpool to S.C., in *Susannah*. (CTB31.206)
5759. Robertson, James, clergyman, sh. 1717, sett. Va. (EMA52)
5760. Robertson, James, printer & publisher, sh. 1759, sett. Charleston, N.Y., Boston, & Halifax, N.S. (SRO.CS236.R12\3)
5761. Robertson, James, Jacobite, tr. 30 Mar 1716, fr. Liverpool to Antigua, in *Scipio*. (SPC.1716.310)
5762. Robertson, James, Jacobite, tr. 26 Apr 1716, fr. Liverpool to Jamaica, in *Two Brothers*, arr. Montserrat June 1716. (SPC.1716.313)(CTB31.206)(CTP.CC.43)
5763. Robertson, James, Jacobite, tr. 7 May 1716, fr. Liverpool to S.C., in *Susannah*. (SPC.1716.309)(CTB31.206)
5764. Robertson, James, Jacobite, tr. 24 May 1716, fr. Liverpool to Md, in *Friendship*, arr. Md Aug 1716. (SPC.1716.311)(HM387)
5765. Robertson, James, b. 1739, farm servant, res. Evie Orkney Islands, sh. Sept 1775, fr. Kirkwall to Savannah Ga, in *Marlborough*, sett. Richmond Co Ga, m. Christian Linay. (PRO.T47.12)

5766. Robertson, James, b. 1742, weaver, res. Paisley Renfrewshire, sh. Feb 1774, fr. Greenock to N.Y., in *Commerce*, m. Jean ..., ch. James Robert Jean. (PRO.T47.12)
5767. Robertson, Janet, thief & whore, res. Edinburgh, tr. 28 Nov 1704, fr. Leith to Md. (SRO.PC2.28.307)
5768. Robertson, Janet, infanticide, tr. Aug 1755. (SRO.HCR.I.89)
5769. Robertson, Jean, thief, res. Edinburgh, tr. Jan 1767, m. Angus Byers. (SRO.JC.27)(SM.29.221)
5770. Robertson, John, seaman, res. Burntisland Fife, sh. 14 July 1698, fr. Leith to Darien, in *St Andrew*, Edin pr1707 CC8.8.83
5771. Robertson, John, Jacobite, tr. 30 Mar 1716, fr. Liverpool to Antigua, in *Scipio*. (SPC.1716.310)(CTB31.204)
5772. Robertson, John, Jacobite, tr. 26 Apr 1716, fr. Liverpool to Jamaica, in *Two Brothers*, arr. Montserrat June 1716. (SPC.1716.313)(CTB31.206)(CTP.CC.43)
5773. Robertson, John, Jacobite, tr. 24 May 1716, fr. Liverpool to Md, in *Friendship*, arr. Md Aug 1716. (SPC.1716.311)(HM386)
5774. Robertson, John, Jacobite, res. Stratherrol Perthshire, tr. 1747. (P.3.278)(MR91)
5775. Robertson, John, postman, thief, res. Glasgow, tr. May 1776, to West Indies. (SRO.RH2.4.255)
5776. Robertson, John, vagabond & robber, res. Annandale Dumfries-shire, tr. 1671(?). (PC.3.428)
5777. Robertson, John, secretary, d. 21 Aug 1773 Spanish Town Jamaica. (SM.36.558)
5778. Robertson, John, b. 1728, laborer, Jacobite, res. Inverness, tr. 5 May 1747, fr. Liverpool to Leeward Islands, in *Veteran*, arr. Martinique June 1747. (P.3.278)(PRO.SP36.102)
5779. Robertson, John, b. 1728, sh. 1745, d. 30 Oct 1784 St Thomas in the East Jamaica. (SM.46.663)
5780. Robertson, John, b. 1750, gardener, sh. Feb 1774, fr. London to Md, in *Jenny*. (PRO.T47.9\11)
5781. Robertson, John, b. 1754, schoolmaster, sh. Apr 1775, fr. London to Md, in *Nancy*. (PRO.T47.9\11)
5782. Robertson, Leonard, Jacobite, tr. 24 May 1716, fr. Liverpool to Md, in *Friendship*, arr. Md Aug 1716. (SPC.1716.311)(HM386)(MdArch34.164)
5783. Robertson, Malcolm, Jacobite, tr. 22 Apr 1747, fr. Liverpool to Va, in *Johnson*, arr. Port Oxford Md 5 Aug 1747. (PRO.T1.328)
5784. Robertson, Margaret, gypsy, res. Jedburgh Roxburghshire, tr. 1 Jan 1715, fr. Glasgow to Va. (GR530)
5785. Robertson, Michael, b. 1755, farm servant, res. Harray Orkney Islands, sh. Sept 1775, fr. Kirkwall to Savannah Ga, in *Marlborough*, sett. Richmond Co Ga. (PRO.T47.12)

5786. Robertson, Neil, cordwainer, Jacobite, res. Logerait Perthshire, tr. 22 Apr 1747, fr. Liverpool to Va, in *Johnson*, arr. Port Oxford Md 5 Aug 1747. (P.3.278)(MR27)(PRO.T1.328)

5787. Robertson, Patrick, merchant, res. Edinburgh, pts. William Robertson & Agnes Fleming, sh. pre 1772, sett. New London N.E. (SRO.RD4.211.547)

5788. Robertson, Patrick, Jacobite, tr. 24 May 1716, fr. Liverpool to Md, in *Friendship*. (SPC.1716.311)

5789. Robertson, Richard, tr. 1773, fr. Port Glasgow to Va, in *Thomas of Glasgow*, arr. Upper District James River Va 5 June 1773. (SRO.JC.27.10.3)

5790. Robertson, Robert, journeyman wright, housebreaker, res. Edinburgh, tr. Dec 1774. (SRO.HCR.I.112)

5791. Robertson, Robert, b. 18 Mar 1681, Edinburgh, clergyman, sh. 1706, sett. St Paul's Charlestown Nevis, m. Mary Podgson, ch. Mary Elizabeth, bd. St Paul's. (EMA52)(CAR.1.9)

5792. Robertson, Robert, b. 1744, weaver, res. Glasgow, sh. May 1774, fr. Greenock to N.Y., in *Matty*. (PRO.T47.12)

5793. Robertson, Rowland, Jacobite, tr. 28 July 1716, fr. Liverpool to Va, in *Godspeed*, arr. Md Oct 1716. (SPC.1716.310)(CTB31.209)(HM389)

5794. Robertson, Thomas, sailor, sh. 14 July 1698, fr. Leith to Darien, in *Caledonia*, Edin pr1707 CC8.8.83

5795. Robertson, Thomas, farmer, Jacobite, res. Windyedge Aberdargie Perthshire, tr. 1747. (P.3.280)(MR19)

5796. Robertson, Walter, merchant, res. Glasgow, sh. pre 1765, sett. Petersburg Va. (SRA.T.MJ)

5797. Robertson, Walter, res. Old Meldrum Aberdeenshire, pts. Arthur Robertson & Katherine Stewart, sh. pre 1771, sett. Tobago. (SRO.RD3.238.23)

5798. Robertson, William, Jacobite, tr. 1747, in *St George or Carteret*, arr. Jamaica 1747. (P.3.280)(PRO.CO137.58)

5799. Robertson, William, shopkeeper, thief, res. Aberdeen, tr. May 1769. (AJ1115)

5800. Robertson, William, planter, sh. pre 1739, sett. N.J. (SRO.SH.27.1.1739)

5801. Robertson, William, res. Edinburgh, sh. pre 1750, sett. N.Y. (SRO.RD4.176.448)

5802. Robertson, William, b. 1727, weaver, Jacobite, res. Spynie Morayshire, tr. 5 May 1747, fr. Liverpool to Leeward Islands, in *Veteran*, arr. Martinique June 1747. (P.3.280)(MR128)(PRO.SP36.102)

5803. Robertson, William, b. 1730, laborer, Jacobite, res. Perth, tr. 5 May 1747, fr. Liverpool to Leeward Islands, in *Veteran*, arr. Martinique June 1747. (P.3.280)(MR75)(PRO.SP36.102)

5804. Robertson, William, b. 1761, pickpocket, res. Perth, tr. May 1775. (SM.37.405)
5805. Robeson, Thomas, b. 1735, farmer, res. Stirling, sh. May 1775, fr. Greenock to N.Y., in *Monimia*, m. Mary ..., ch. Mary Agnes Alexander James Betty. (PRO.T47.12)
5806. Robinson, Alexander, b. 1712, Jacobite, res. Angus, tr. 1747. (P.3.280)
5807. Robinson, Alexander, b. 1755, student, res. Loch Broom Ross-shire, sh. July 1775, fr. Stornaway to Philadelphia, in *Clementina*. (PRO.T47.12)
5808. Robinson, Christian, pickpocket, res. Perth, tr. May 1765. (AJ908)
5809. Robinson, Daniel, Jacobite, tr. 24 Feb 1747, fr. Liverpool to Va, in *Gildart*, arr. Port North Potomac Md 5 Aug 1747. (P.3.282)(PRO.T1.328) (alias 5813)
5810. Robinson, David, Jacobite, tr. 7 May 1716, fr. Liverpool to S.C., in *Susannah*. (CTB31.206)(SPC.1716.309)
5811. Robinson, David, b. 1677, laborer, Jacobite, tr. 1747. (P.3.282)
5812. Robinson, Donald, Jacobite, tr. 7 May 1716, fr. Liverpool to S.C., in *Susannah*. (SPC.1716.309)(CTB31.206)
5813. Robinson, Donald, Jacobite, tr. 24 Feb 1747, fr. Liverpool to Va, in *Gildart*, arr. Port North Potomac Md 5 Aug 1747. (P.3.282)(PRO.T1.328) (alias 5809)
5814. Robinson, Donald, b. 1743, farmer, res. Kilenbrie, sh. Apr 1775, fr. Greenock to N.Y., in *Lilly*. (PRO.T47.12)
5815. Robinson, Donian, b. 1738, farmer, res. Kilenbrie, sh. Apr 1775, fr. Greenock to N.Y., in *Lilly*. (PRO.T47.12)
5816. Robinson, Duncan, Jacobite, tr. 7 May 1716, fr. Liverpool to S.C., in *Susannah*. (SPC.1716.309)(CTB31.206)
5817. Robinson, James, Jacobite, tr. 7 May 1716, fr. Liverpool to S.C., in *Susannah*. (SPC.1716.309)(CTB31.206)
5818. Robinson, James, Jacobite, tr. 29 June 1716, fr. Liverpool to Jamaica or Va, in *Elizabeth & Anne*, arr. York Va. (SPC.1716.310)(CTB31.208)(VSP.1.185)
5819. Robinson, James, merchant , res. Glasgow, sh. 1767, sett. Falmouth Va. (SRA.CFI)
5820. Robinson, James, b. 1758, whitesmith, sh. Mar 1775, fr. London to Va, in *Betsey*. (PRO.T47.9\11)
5821. Robinson, John, Jacobite, tr. 25 June 1716, fr. Liverpool to St Kitts, in *Hockenhill*. (SPC.1716.312)(CTB31.207)
5822. Robinson, John, Jacobite, tr. 29 June 1716, fr. Liverpool to Jamaica or Va, in *Elizabeth & Anne*, arr. York Va. (SPC.1716.310)(CTB31.208)(VSP.1.186)
5823. Robinson, John, Jacobite, tr. 7 May 1716, fr. Liverpool to S.C., in *Susannah*. (SPC.1716.309)(CTB31.206)

5824. Robinson, John, b. 1708, res. Fordyce Banffshire, sh. Feb 1724, fr. London to Md. (CLRO\AIA)
5825. Robinson, Margaret, b. 1746, spinner, res. Paisley Renfrewshire, sh. Feb 1774, fr. Greenock to N.Y., in *Commerce*. (PRO.T47.12)
5826. Robinson, Robert, Jacobite, tr. 29 June 1716, fr. Liverpool to Jamaica or Va, in *Elizabeth & Anne*, arr. York Va. (SPC.1716.310)(CTB31.208)(VSP.1.186)
5827. Robinson, Thomas, Jacobite, tr. 1747. (P.3.282)
5828. Robinson, Thomas, b. 1760, res. Irvine Ayrshire, sh. Jan 1774, fr. Greenock to Jamaica, in *Janet*. (SRO.CE.60.1.7)
5829. Robinson, Walter, b. 1712, res. Edinburgh, sh. Sept 1730, fr. London to Jamaica. (CLRO\AIA)
5830. Robinson, William, physician, res. Burntisland Fife, sh. 1684, fr. Leith to East N.J. (Insh236)
5831. Robinson, William, b. 1688, res. Dumfries, pts. Thomas Robinson, sh. 17 Mar 1706, fr. Liverpool. (LRO.HQ325.2FRE)
5832. Robinson, William, b. 1701, carpenter, res. Edinburgh, sh. Jan 1721, fr. London to Jamaica. (CLRO\AIA)
5833. Robinson, William, b. 1750, smith, res. Paisley Renfrewshire, sh. Apr 1775, fr. Greenock to N.Y., in *Lilly*. (PRO.T47.12)
5834. Robison, Andrew, tr. Apr 1668, to N.E. (PC.2.428)
5835. Robison, James, clerk & factor, res. Dalry Ayrshire, pts. Andrew Robison, sh. Apr 1761, fr. Glasgow to Va, sett. Rappahannock River Va. (SRO.NRAS.1892)
5836. Robison, James, b. 1732, servant, res. Aberdeen, sh. Nov 1750, fr. London to Jamaica. (CLRO\AIA)
5837. Robison, John, thief, res. Dumfries-shire, tr. May 1728, to West Indies. (SRO.JC.12.4)
5838. Robson, George, b. 1726, tailor, res. Perthshire, sh. May 1775, fr. Greenock to N.Y., in *Monimia*, m. Marion Weir. (PRO.T47.12)
5839. Robson, Robert, b. 1747, yeoman, sh. Sept 1775, fr. Newcastle to Ga, in *Georgia Packet*, sett. Richmond Co Ga, m. Jane ..., ch. Eleanor James Mary. (PRO.T47.9\11)
5840. Rodan, Homer, sh. Dec 1698, fr. Liverpool to Va, in *Globe*. (LRO.HQ325.2FRE)
5841. Rodeak, William, b. 1739, farmer, res. Dumfries-shire, sh. Oct 1774, fr. Greenock to Charleston S.C., in *Countess*. (PRO.T47.12)
5842. Rodrie, Thomas, gunner, sh. 14 July 1698, fr. Leith to Darien, in *Unicorn*, m. Janet Beattie, d. 1699 Darien, Edin pr1707 CC8.8.83
5843. Roger, John, clergyman, res. Muckart Perthshire, sh. 1770, sett. Pa. (UPC656)
5844. Rogerson, Janet, b. 1750, res. Drysdale Dumfries-shire, sh. May 1775, fr. Dumfries to P.E.I., in *Lovely Nelly*. (PRO.T47.12)

5845. Roll, John, b. 1752, gardener, res. Aberdeen, sh. May 1774, fr. London to Md, in *Minerva*. (PRO.T47.9\11)
5846. Rolland, Henry, carpenter, res. Culross Fife, pts. James Rolland, sh. pre 1774, sett. Charleston S.C. (SRO.CS.GMB398)
5847. Rome, George, Covenanter, tr. 1684, fr. Leith to Carolina. (PC.9.95)
5848. Ronald, Alexander, clergyman, sh. 1760, sett. Va. (EMA52)
5849. Ronald, David, storekeeper, res. Aberdeen, sh. pre 1752, sett. Old Harbour Jamaica. (APB.3.187)
5850. Ronald, George, merchant, res. Glasgow, sh. pre 1741, sett. Cape Fear N.C. (SRO.CC8.8.107)
5851. Ronald, William jr, mariner, res. Grangepans West Lothian, pts. William Ronald, sh. 14 July 1698, fr. Leith to Darien, in *Dolphin*, d. 1699 Darien, Edin pr1707 CC8.8.83
5852. Ronald, William sr, mariner, res. Grangepans West Lothian, sh. 14 July 1698, fr. Leith to Darien, in *Dolphin*, ch. William Elizabeth, d. 1699 Darien, Edin pr1707 CC8.8.83
5853. Rose, Alexander, b. 1729, Jacobite, tr. 31 Mar 1747, fr. London to Barbados , in *Frere*. (P.3.284)(MR128)
5854. Rose, Alexander, b. 1738, merchant, res. Inverness, sh. pre 1755, sett. Va & N.C., m. Eunice Lea, d. 12 Apr 1807 Person Co N.C. (RSA137)
5855. Rose, Betty, b. 1758, res. Inverness, sh. July 1775, fr. Stornaway to Philadelphia, in *Clementina*. (PRO.T47.12)
5856. Rose, Charles, clergyman, res. Alves Morayshire, sh. 1731, to Barbados, sett. Cople Va, d. 1761. (OD16)(SA31)(EMA53)
5857. Rose, Charles, merchant, res. Tain Ross & Cromarty, sh. pre 1776, sett. Smithfield Va. (SRO.CS.GMB55)
5858. Rose, Duncan, merchant, res. Glasgow, sh. pre 1764, sett. Va. (SRA.B10.15.6969)
5859. Rose, James, exciseman, forger, res. Muthill Perthshire, tr. Feb 1757. (SRO.HH.11)
5860. Rose, John, res. Aberdeenshire, pts. Hugh Rose of Tulliesnaught, d. 1 Aug 1775 Jamaica, Edin pr1776 CC8.8.123
5861. Rose, John, b. 1709, pewterer, res. Inverness, sh. Oct 1730, fr. London to Jamaica. (CLRO\AIA)
5862. Rose, Patrick, clergyman, sh. 1727, to Barbados. (EMA53)
5863. Rose, Robert, b. 12 Feb 1704, Wester Alves Morayshire, clergyman, res. Morayshire, pts. John Rose & Mary Grant, sh. 1725, sett. Essex Co & Albemarle Co Va, m. (1)Mary Tarrant (2)Anne Fitzhugh, ch. John & Hugh, d. 30 June 1751 Va, bd. Richmond. (OD102)(SA31)(BLG3017)
5864. Ross, Aeneas, clergyman, sh. 1740, to Pa. (EMA53)
5865. Ross, Agnes, b. 1715, spinner, res. Kirkcaldy Fife, sh. July 1736, fr. London to N.C. (CLRO\AIA)

5866. Ross, Alexander, sheepstealer, res. Aberdeenshire, tr. June 1766, fr. Aberdeen. (AJ959\964)
5867. Ross, Alexander, b. 1697, farmer, Jacobite, res. Kirkton of Loch Broom Ross & Cromarty, tr. 31 Mar 1747, fr. London to Jamaica, in *St George or Carteret*, arr. Jamaica 1747. (P.3.286)(MR87)(PRO.CO137.58)
5868. Ross, Alexander, b. 1727, servant, Jacobite, res. Carrol Clyne Sutherland, tr. 1747. (P.3.286)(MR27)
5869. Ross, Alexander, b. 1729, Jacobite, res. Nairn, tr. 1747, fr. Tilbury to Jamaica, in *St George or Carteret*, arr. Jamaica 1747. (P.3.286)(PRO.CO137.58)(MR128)
5870. Ross, Alexander, b. 1742, carpenter, res. Galloway, sh. May 1774, fr. Stranraer to N.Y., in *Gale*, m. Jean ..., ch. Isabel Jean Margaret. (PRO.T47.12)
5871. Ross, Andrew, merchant edu. Glasgow Uni 1729, res. Glasgow, pts. Prof Andrew Ross, sett. Va, d. 9 June 1752. (MAGU3)
5872. Ross, Ann, b. 1754, res. Kilsyth Stirlingshire, sh. May 1774, fr. Greenock to N.Y., in *George*. (PRO.T47.12)
5873. Ross, Charles, Jacobite, tr. 21 Apr 1716, fr. Liverpool to S.C., in *Wakefield*. (SPC.1716.309)(CTB31.205)
5874. Ross, Charles, soldier, robber, tr. Mar 1747. (SRO.JC.27)
5875. Ross, Christine, thief, res. Rosekien Ross-shire, tr. Nov 1773, fr. Glasgow. (AJ1349)
5876. Ross, Daniel, b. 1707, servant, Jacobite, res. Ross-shire, tr. 5 May 1747, fr. Liverpool to Leeward Islands, in *Veteran*, arr. Martinique June 1747. (P.3.286)(PRO.SP36.102)
5877. Ross, David, b. 1709, distiller, res. Inverness, sh. Jan 1736, fr. London to Jamaica. (CLRO\AIA)
5878. Ross, Donald, b. 1691, Jacobite, tr. 31 Mar 1747, fr. London to Jamaica, in *St George or Carteret*, arr. Jamaica 1747. (P.3.288)(MR87)(PRO.CO137.58)
5879. Ross, Donald, b. 1723, servant, Jacobite, res. Inverness-shire, tr. 20 Mar 1747, fr. Tilbury. (P.3.288)(MR207)
5880. Ross, Donald, b. 1727, Jacobite, tr. 20 Mar 1747, fr. Tilbury. (P.3.288)(MR87)
5881. Ross, Duncan, b. 1717, farmer, Jacobite, res. Auchenarvier Ross-shire, tr. 31 Mar 1747, fr. London to Barbados, in *Frere*. (P.3.288)(MR87)
5882. Ross, Elizabeth, infanticide, res. Perthshire, tr. Apr 1752. (AJ227)
5883. Ross, George, cattlethief, res. Ross-shire, tr. Sept 1752. (AJ248)
5884. Ross, George, Ross-shire, clergyman edu. Edinburgh Uni, sh. 1705, to N.J., sett. Newcastle & Chester Del, ch. George. (SCHR.14.147)(EMA53)(AP307)
5885. Ross, Hugh, writer & secretary, d. pre 1708 N.E., Edin pr1708 CC8.8.84

5886. Ross, Hugh, Jacobite, tr. 30 Mar 1716, fr. Liverpool to Antigua, in *Scipio*. (SPC.1716.310)(CTB31.204)
5887. Ross, Hugh, b. 1757, farmer, res. Strathspey, sh. May 1774, fr. Greenock to N.Y., in *George*. (PRO.T47.12)
5888. Ross, Isabel, thief, res. Rosekien Ross-shire, tr. Nov 1773, fr. Glasgow. (AJ1349)
5889. Ross, James, thief, res. Edinburgh, tr. Feb 1697. (SRO.PC2.26)
5890. Ross, James, b. 1727, carpenter, Jacobite, res. Edinburgh, tr. 5 May 1747, fr. Liverpool to Leeward Islands, in *Veteran*, arr. Martinique June 1747. (P.3.288)(MR75)(PRO.SP36.102)
5891. Ross, James, b. 1744, farmer, res. Strathspey, sh. May 1774, fr. Greenock to N.Y., in *George*. (PRO.T47.12)
5892. Ross, Janet, thief & whore, res. Edinburgh, tr. 28 Nov 1704, fr. Leith to Md. (SRO.PC2.28.307)
5893. Ross, Jean, gypsy, res. Jedburgh Roxburghshire, tr. 1 Jan 1715, fr. Glasgow to Va. (GR530)
5894. Ross, John, forger, tr. Feb 1670, fr. Leith to Va, in *Ewe & Lamb*. (PC.3.650)
5895. Ross, John, Jacobite, tr. 24 May 1716, fr. Liverpool to Md, in *Friendship*, arr. Md Aug 1716. (SPC.1716.311)(HM387)
5896. Ross, John, res. Ellon Aberdeenshire, sh. Feb 1670, to Barbados. (EPR130)
5897. Ross, John, res. Leith, sh. pre 1768, sett. Fla, d. 1786 Dominica. (SRO.GD188)
5898. Ross, John, res. Bute, sh. pre 1663, fr. Bristol to Va. (BRO.04220)
5899. Ross, John, planter, pts. John Ross of Arnage, sh. pre 1775, sett. Indian Town Creek EFla. (SRO.GD186)
5900. Ross, John, b. 1727, farmer, res. Kabel Farr Sutherland, sh. Apr 1774, to Wilmington N.C., in *Bachelor of Leith*. (PRO.T47.12)
5901. Ross, John, b. 1730, miller, Jacobite, res. Forbloch Ross-shire, tr. 31 Mar 1747, fr. London to Jamaica, in *St George or Carteret*, arr. Jamaica 1747. (P.3.290)(MR159)(PRO.CO137.58)
5902. Ross, John, b. 1750, farmer, res. Strathspey, sh. May 1774, fr. Greenock to N.Y., in *George*. (PRO.T47.12)
5903. Ross, Lucy, b. 1754, servant, res. Caithness, sh. May 1775, fr. Leith to Philadelphia, in *Friendship*. (PRO.T47.12)
5904. Ross, Mrs, res. Edinburgh, sh. July 1775, fr. Greenock to Jamaica, in *Isabella*. (PRO.T47.12)
5905. Ross, Nelly, b. 1753, servant, res. Cullen Banffshire, sh. May 1775, fr. Leith to Philadelphia, in *Friendship*. (PRO.T47.12)
5906. Ross, Patrick, b. 1739, schoolmaster, res. Farr Sutherland, sh. Apr 1774, fr. Leith to Wilmington N.C., in *Bachelor of Leith*. (PRO.T47.12)
5907. Ross, Rachel, b. 1745, res. Paisley Renfrewshire, sh. May 1774, fr. Greenock to N.Y., in *George*. (PRO.T47.12)

5908. Ross, Ranald, b. 1729, husbandman, Jacobite, res. Milton of Ord Ross-shire, tr. 31 Mar 1747, fr. London to Jamaica, in *St George or Carteret*, arr. Jamaica 1747. (P.3.290)(MR87)(PRO.CO137.58)

5909. Ross, Robert, glover, forger, res. Perth, tr. Dec 1767. (SRO.JC.D35)

5910. Ross, Thomas, Jacobite, tr. 7 May 1716, fr. Liverpool to S.C., in *Susannah*. (SPC.1716.309)(CTB31.206)

5911. Ross, Thomas, b. 1683, laborer, Jacobite, res. Aberdeen, tr. 22 Apr 1747, fr. Liverpool to Md, in *Johnson*, arr. Port Oxford Md 5 Aug 1747. (P.3.290)(JAB.2.442)(PRO.T1.328)

5912. Ross, William, res. Kirkwall Orkney Islands, sett. New Scotland Barbados, ch. Alexander, d. pre 1683. (SRO.SH.19.11.1683) (alias 2121)

5913. Ross, William, tailor, res. Sandwick Orkney Islands, d. 1782 Hudson Bay, Edin pr1784 CC8.8.126

5914. Ross, William, b. 1711, sailor, Jacobite, res. Aberdeenshire, tr. 5 May 1747, fr. Liverpool to Leeward Islands, in *Veteran*, arr. Martinique June 1747. (P.3.290)(PRO.SP36.102)

5915. Ross, William, b. 1720, res. Cottleshin, sh. Nov 1738, fr. London to Jamaica. (CLRO\AIA)

5916. Ross, William, b. 1734, painter, res. Edinburgh, sh. May 1774, fr. London to Philadelphia, in *Sally*. (PRO.T47.9\11)

5917. Ross, William, b. 1760, farmer, res. Strathspey, sh. May 1774, fr. Greenock to N.Y., in *George*. (PRO.T47.12)

5918. Rosse, John, clergyman edu. Aberdeen uni, sh. 10 Oct 1754, sett. All Hallows Worcester Md. (EMA53)

5919. Rouan, Alexander, res. Greenhead Glasgow, sh. May 1763, fr. Glasgow to Jamaica. (SRO.SC36.637.405)

5920. Rouan, Thomas, res. Govan Glasgow, pts. Hugh Rouan, sh. Feb 1769. (SRO.SC36.63.11)

5921. Rowan, John, thief, res. Glasgow, tr. 1753. (SM.15.468)

5922. Rowan, William, cooper, sh. June 1684, fr. Port Glasgow to Carolina, in *Pelican of Glasgow*. (SRO.E72.19.9)

5923. Rowsay, John, goldsmith & jeweller, res. Orkney Islands, sh. pre 1773, sett. Va. (SRO.SH.1.6.1773)

5924. Roxburgh, James, b. 1758, husbandman, sh. Mar 1774, fr. Whitehaven to Va, in *Ann*. (PRO.T47.9\11)

5925. Roxburgh, Robert, b. 1757, laborer, res. Kippen Stirlingshire, sh. May 1775, fr. Greenock to N.Y., in *Lilly*. (PRO.T47.12)

5926. Roxburgh, William, merchant, res. Kilmarnock Ayrshire, pts. William Roxburgh, sh. pre 1783. (SRO.SH.16.12.1783)

5927. Roy, Donald, b. 1750, tailor, res. Glasgow, sh. May 1775, fr. Greenock to N.Y., in *Monimia*. (PRO.T47.12)

5928. Roy, James, shipmaster, res. Lanark, pts. James Roy, sh. pre 1777, sett. N.Y., m. Elizabeth Wishart. (SRO.RD4.773.618)

5929. Roy, William, cooper, rioter, res. Huntly Aberdeenshire, tr. May 1767. (SM.29.325)
5930. Rudderford, John, b. 1766, res. Tongland Kirkcudbrightshire, sh. May 1774, fr. Kirkcudbright to N.Y., in *Gale*. (PRO.T47.12)
5931. Ruddiman, Janet, b. 1755, res. Montrose Angus, sh. Apr 1775, fr. Greenock to N.Y., in *Lilly*. (PRO.T47.12)
5932. Rudiman, William, b. 5 Sept 1703, Turriff Aberdeenshire, baker, res. Aberdeen, d. Nov 1769 N.Y. (APB.4.91)
5933. Rugg, Donald, farmer, housebreaker & thief, res. Freswick Caithness, tr. Sept 1768. (AJ1080)
5934. Russel, David, b. 1749, cooper, sh. Feb 1774, fr. London to Boston Mass, in *Success*. (PRO.T47.9\11)
5935. Russell, Ann, res. Lanarkshire, sh. pre 1766, sett. Barbados, m. Thomas Clarkson. (SRO.RS42.18.33)
5936. Russell, David, b. 1727, glover, Jacobite, res. Aberdeen, tr. 22 Apr 1747, fr. Liverpool to Md, in *Johnson*, arr. Port Oxford Md 5 Aug 1747. (P.3.294)(PRO.T1.328)
5937. Russell, Gavin, Covenanter, tr. July 1685. (PC.11.114)
5938. Russell, George, sailor, sh. 14 July 1698, fr. Leith to Darien, in *Unicorn*, Edin pr1707 CC8.8.83
5939. Russell, George, cordwainer, Covenanter, res. Glasgow, pts. George Russell, tr. June 1678, to West Indies. (PC.5.474)
5940. Russell, George, b. 1757, farmer, res. Avis, sh. July 1775, fr. Stornaway to Philadelphia, in *Clementina*. (PRO.T47.12)
5941. Russell, James, res. Edinburgh, tr. 8 May 1663, fr. Leith to Barbados, in *Mary*. (EBR.186.13.4)
5942. Russell, James, sailor, res. Edinburgh, sh. 14 July 1698, fr. Leith to Darien, in *Caledonia*, d. 1699 Darien, Edin pr1707 CC8.8.83
5943. Russell, James, Covenanter, tr. Oct 1684. (PC.10.251)
5944. Russell, John, thief, res. Edinburgh, tr. Feb 1697. (SRO.PC2.26)
5945. Russell, John, Covenanter, tr. Oct 1684. (PC.10.251)
5946. Russell, John, b. 1723, sail weaver, Jacobite, res. Backmyre Barry Angus, tr. 24 Feb 1747, fr. Liverpool to Va, in *Gildart*, arr. Port North Potomac Md 5 Aug 1747. (P.3.294)(PRO.T1.328)
5947. Russell, John, b. 1758, weaver, res. Paisley Renfrewshire, sh. Feb 1774, fr. Greenock to N.Y., in *Commerce*. (PRO.T47.12)
5948. Russell, Peter, Covenanter, tr. 5 Sept 1685, fr. Leith to East N.J., in *Henry & Francis*. (PC.11.154)
5949. Russell, Robert, res. Stirling, sh. 1698, fr. Leith to Darien. (RBS343)
5950. Russell, Robert, tr. Nov 1679, fr. Leith. (ETR162)
5951. Russell, Thomas, Covenanter, tr. 5 Sept 1685, fr. Leith to East N.J., in *Henry & Francis*. (PC.11.164)
5952. Russell, Thomas, b. 1760, Slamannan Stirlingshire, clergyman edu. Glasgow Uni, sh. 1783, sett. Halifax N.S. (F.7.617)

5953. Russell, William, surgeon, res. Stirlingshire, d. pre 1766 Jamaica. (SRO.SH.17.10.1766)
5954. Russell, William, b. 1751, farmer, res. Cupar, sh. Apr 1775, fr. Greenock to Salem, in *Glasgow Packet.* (PRO.T47.12)
5955. Rutherford, Anne, res. Bowland, pts. James Rutherford & Isabella Simpson, sett. Wilmington N.C., m. R Shaw, d. 11 Jan 1767 Wilmington. (RTI.Ped)(SM.29.166)
5956. Rutherford, Barbara, res. Bowland, pts. James Rutherford & Isabella Simpson, sett. Wilmington N.C., m. Alexander Chapman, d. Nov 1763 Wilmington. (RTI.Ped)(SM.26.55)
5957. Rutherford, George, surgeon's mate, res. Jedburgh Roxburghshire, sh. 14 July 1698, fr. Leith to Darien, in *St Andrew*, Edin pr1709 CC8.8.84
5958. Rutherford, George, Jacobite, tr. 29 June 1716, fr. Liverpool to Jamaica or Va, in *Elizabeth & Anne.* (SPC.1716.310)(CTB31.208)
5959. Rutherford, James, Jacobite, tr. 28 July 1716, fr. Liverpool to Va, in *Godspeed*, arr. Md Oct 1716. (SPC.1716.310)(CTB31.209)(HM389)
5960. Rutherford, John, Jacobite, tr. 29 June 1716, fr. Liverpool to Jamaica or Va, in *Elizabeth & Anne*, arr. Va. (SPC.1716.310)(CTB31.208)(VSP.1.186)
5961. Rutherford, John, Jacobite, tr. 29 June 1716, fr. Liverpool to Jamaica or Va, in *Elizabeth & Anne*, arr. York Va. (SPC.1716.310)(CTB31.208)(VSP.1.186)
5962. Rutherford, John, res. Bowland, sh. pre 1752, sett. Wilmington N.C. (SRO.RD3.171.273)
5963. Rutherford, Thomas, planter, sh. pre 1770, sett. St James Cornwall Co Jamaica. (SRO.RD4.209.401)
5964. Rutherford, Thomas, b. 7 Jan 1766, Glasgow, merchant edu. Glasgow Uni 1778, res. Glasgow, pts. Thomas Rutherford & Janet McCallum, sh. 1783, fr. Dublin to Va, sett. Richmond Va, m. Sallie Winston, ch. John, d. 31 Jan 1852 Richmond. (MAGU123)(BLG2897)
5965. Rutherford, Walter, b. 29 Dec 1723, Edgerston Roxburghshire, soldier & merchant, pts. Sir John Rutherford & Elizabeth Cairncross, sh. pre 1758, sett. Hunterdon Co N.Y., m. Catherine Alexander, ch. John, d. 10 Jan 1804 N.Y. (SRO.RD2.210.911)(BLG2897)
5966. Saddler, William, merchant, sh. 1758, sett. St Kitts, d. pre 1781 St Kitts. (SRO.SH.21.2.1781)(SRO.CS.237.14.1)
5967. Salisbury, Charles, b. 1745, yeoman, sh. Sept 1775, fr. Newcastle to Ga, in *Georgia Packet*, sett. Friendsborough Ga. (PRO.T47.9\11)
5968. Salkeld, James, Jacobite, tr. 30 Mar 1716, fr. Liverpool to Antigua, in *Scipio.* (SPC.1716.310)(CTB31.204)

293

5969. Sample, William, surgeon & planter, res. Edinburgh, pts. Agnes Sample, sh. pre 1709, sett. Nevis, ch. John, d. 1712, St Kitts pr1713. (PRO.CO.243.4.f49)

5970. Samuel, George, b. 1729, bookbinder, Jacobite, res. Edinburgh, tr. 5 May 1747, fr. Liverpool to Leeward Islands, in *Veteran*, arr. Martinique June 1747. (P.3.298)(MR76)(PRO.SP.36.102)

5971. Sanderson, Beattie, whore, res. Edinburgh, tr. Mar 1695. (SRO.PC2.25.216)

5972. Sanderson, Daniel, servant, vagabond, res. Tyninghame East Lothian, tr. Sept 1668, fr. Leith to Va, in *Convertin*. (PC.2.534)

5973. Sanderson, William, ensign, res. Kinghorn Fife, d. 1699 Darien, Edin pr1707 CC8.8.83

5974. Sands, Alexander, b. 1758, chapman, res. Edinburgh, sh. May 1775, fr. Leith to Philadelphia, in *Friendship*. (PRO.T47.12)

5975. Sands, James, merchant, d. 3 Aug 1767 Charleston S.C. (SM.31.502)

5976. Sands, William, sailor, res. Dunfermline Fife, sh. 18 Aug 1699, fr. Greenock to Darien, in *Rising Sun*, Edin pr1707 CC8.8.83

5977. Sangster, Andrew, Jacobite, tr. 21 Apr 1716, fr. Liverpool to S.C., in *Wakefield*. (SPC.1716.309)

5978. Saunders, William, b. 1758, ploughman, res. Angus, sh. May 1775, fr. Leith to Philadelphia, in *Friendship*. (PRO.T47.12)

5979. Sayers, John, merchant, sh. Aug 1683, fr. Leith to Va, in *Ewe & Lamb*. (SRO.E72.15.12)

5980. Schaw, John, soldier, horsethief, tr. Mar 1747. (SRO.JC27)

5981. Schaw, William, b. 1754, laborer, res. Paisley Renfrewshire, sh. Feb 1774, fr. Greenock to N.Y., in *Commerce*. (PRO.T47.12)

5982. Schoalla, Robert, joiner, res. Papa Orkney Islands, pts. James Schoalla, sh. 14 July 1698, fr. Leith to Darien, in *Unicorn*, Edin pr1707 CC8.8.83

5983. Scholler, Barbara, b. 1659, res. Stronsay Orkney Islands, pts. Edward Scholler, sh. Aug 1685, fr. London to Va, m. ... Whitefield. (CLRO\AIA)

5984. Scotland, John, merchant, res. Edinburgh, sh. pre 1773, sett. Antigua. (SRO.RD3.232.432)

5985. Scotland, Lawrence, b. 1678, sh. Mar 1699, fr. Liverpool to N.E., in *Virginia Merchant*. (LRO.HQ.3252.FRE)

5986. Scott of Pitlochy, George, res. Fife, sh. 5 Sept 1685, fr. Leith to East N.J., in *Henry & Francis*, d. at sea, Edin pr1692 CC8.8.79

5987. Scott, Adam, clergyman edu. Edinburgh Uni 1691, res. Jedburgh Roxburghshire, sh. 14 July 1698, fr. Leith to Darien, d. 20 Nov 1698 Darien. (F.7.665)(NLS.RY2b8\19)

5988. Scott, Alexander, planter, sett. Grenada, m. Mary Scott, d. Feb 1773, Edin pr1775 CC8.8.123

5989. Scott, Alexander, merchant, res. Glasgow, sh. pre 1755, sett. Norfolk Va. (SRA.CFI)

5990. Scott, Alexander, b. 20 July 1686, Dipple Elgin Morayshire, clergyman, res. Dipple, pts. John Scott & Marjory Stuart, sh. 1710, to Va, sett. Stafford Co Va, m. Sarah Gibbs, d. 1 Apr 1738 Dipple Va, Edin pr1739 CC8.8.101. (EMA53)(OD14)(SNQ.2.24)

5991. Scott, Andrew, Covenanter, res. Teviotdale Roxburghshire, tr. July 1685, fr. Leith to Jamaica, arr. Port Royal Jamaica Nov 1685. (PC.11.329)(LJ195)

5992. Scott, Andrew, merchant, sh. Mar 1683, fr. Ayr to Caribee Islands, in James of Ayr. (SRO.E72.3.12)

5993. Scott, Archibald, b. 1748, tailor, res. Glasgow, sh. Feb 1774, fr. Greenock to N.Y., in Commerce. (PRO.T47.12)

5994. Scott, Christian, Covenanter, tr. 5 Sept 1685, fr. Leith to East N.J., in Henry & Francis. (PC.11.166)

5995. Scott, Christian, servant, infanticide, res. Kirkcaldy Fife, pts. James Scott, tr. Aug 1762. (SRO.HCR.I.94)

5996. Scott, David, tailor, Jacobite, res. Arbroath Angus, tr. 24 Feb 1747, fr. Liverpool to Va, in Gildart, arr. Port North Potomac Md 5 Aug 1747. (P.3.300)(PRO.T1.328)(MR109)

5997. Scott, David, merchant, res. Edinburgh, sh. pre 1779, sett. Antigua. (SRO.RD4.226.1004)

5998. Scott, Euphemia, pts. George Scott of Pitlochie, sh. 5 Sept 1685, fr. Leith to East N.J., in Henry & Francis, m. John Johnston. (Insh178)

5999. Scott, Hugh, ensign, res. Galashiels Selkirkshire, pts. Hugh Scott of Gala, d. 1699 Darien, Edin pr1708 CC8.8.84

6000. Scott, James, foremastman, res. Falkirk Stirlingshire, sh. 14 July 1698, fr. Leith to Darien, in Caledonia, Edin pr1707 CC8.8.83

6001. Scott, James, clergyman, res. Dipple Elgin Morayshire, pts. John Scott & Helen Grant, sh. pre 1719, sett. Prince William Co Va, m. Sarah Brown, d. 1782 Va. (SRO.RS29.5.228\7.216\8.172)(SA32)

6002. Scott, James, b. 1750, carpenter, sh. Sept 1775, fr. Newcastle to Ga, in Georgia Packet, sett. Friendsborough Ga. (PRO.T47.9\11)

6003. Scott, John, res. Berwickshire, pts. James Scott of Thirleston, d. Darien, Edin pr1707 CC8.8.83

6004. Scott, John, sailor, Jacobite, res. Aberdeen, pts. Robert Scott, tr. 8 May 1747, to Antigua. (P.3.302)

6005. Scott, John, tr. Nov 1679, fr. Leith. (ETR162)

6006. Scott, John, Jacobite, tr. 26 Apr 1716, fr. Liverpool to Jamaica, in Two Brothers, arr. Montserrat June 1716. (SPC.1716.313)(CTB31.206)(CTP.CC.43)

6007. Scott, John, b. 1730, herd, Jacobite, res. Atholl Perthshire, tr. 5 May 1747, fr. Liverpool to Leeward Islands, in *Veteran*, arr. Martinique June 1747. (PRO.SP.36.102)(MR209)
6008. Scott, John, b. 1745, yeoman, sh. Sept 1775, fr. Newcastle to Ga, in *Georgia Packet*, sett. Friendsborough Ga, m. Margaret ..., ch. William John Mary Agnes Margaret. (PRO.T47.9\11)
6009. Scott, Margaret, b. 1758, spinner, sh. Feb 1774, fr. London to N.C., in *Margaret & Mary*. (PRO.T47.9\11)
6010. Scott, Matthew, b. 1660, sh. Feb 1683, fr. London to Barbados, in *Barbados Merchant*. (CLRO\AIA)
6011. Scott, Mr, sh. 29 Nov 1773, fr. Greenock to Jamaica, in *Mary of Glasgow*. (SRO.CE.60.1.7)
6012. Scott, Robert, mariner, res. Linlithgow West Lothian, pts. John Scott, sh. 18 Aug 1699, fr. Clyde to Darien, in *Rising Sun*, Edin pr1707 CC8.8.83
6013. Scott, Robert, watchmaker, res. North Leith Midlothian, pts. George Scott, sh. pre 1779. (SRO.SH.21.5.1779)
6014. Scott, Robert, b. 1708, husbandman, res. Berwick, sh. 7 Jan 1736, fr. London to Md. (CLRO\AIA)
6015. Scott, Thomas, res. Selkirk, sh. Feb 1721, fr. London to Pa. (CLRO\AIA)
6016. Scott, Thomas, Barbados, tailor edu. Aberdeen 1732, pts. Robert Scott, sh. 1748, to Barbados. (APB.3.127)
6017. Scott, Walter, Jacobite, tr. 30 Mar 1716, fr. Liverpool to Antigua, in *Scipio*. (SPC.1716.310)(CTB31.204)
6018. Scott, William, tr. 22 Dec 1665, fr. Leith or Buckhaven to Barbados. (ETR104)
6019. Scott, William, b. 1737, clergyman edu. King's Col Aberdeen 1753, res. Banff, sh. 1767, sett. Nevis, d. 24 Sept 1789, bd. St Thomas Lowland Nevis. (MWI110)(FPA317)
6020. Scott, William, b. 1753, maltster, sh. Feb 1774, fr. London to N.C., in *Margaret & Mary*. (PRO.T47.9\11)
6021. Scott, William jr, b. 1749, weaver, res. Paisley Renfrewshire, sh. Feb 1774, fr. Greenock to N.Y., in *Commerce*, m. Margaret .. (PRO.T47.12)
6022. Scott, William sr, b. 1735, weaver, res. Paisley Renfrewshire, sh. Feb 1774, fr. Greenock to N.Y., in *Commerce*, m. Margaret .., ch. John. (PRO.T47.12)
6023. Scougal, James, clergyman, res. Paisley Renfrewshire, sh. pre 1743, sett. Ferry Worcester Co Md, d. 1746. (F.7.665)
6024. Scoure, William, b. 1753, merchant, res. Stirling, sh. July 1775, fr. Greenock to Antigua, in *Chance*. (PRO.T47.12)
6025. Scrimgeour, James, b. 1745, mariner, res. Greenock Renfrewshire, sh. May 1774, fr. Greenock to N.Y., in *George*. (PRO.T47.12)

6026. Scrimgeour, John, weaver, thief, res. North Leith Midlothian, tr. Aug 1753. (SM.15.420)(SRO.JC3.29.274)
6027. Scrimgeour, John, clergyman, sett. Nominie Westmoreland Co Va, d. pre 1693, PCC pr1693
6028. Scroggie, John, sh. pre 1776, sett. Jamaica, ch. John Alexander Elizabeth Murdoch. (SRO.RD4.220.1144)
6029. Scrogie, Alexander, sailor, sh. 18 Aug 1699, fr. Clyde to Darien, in *Rising Sun*, Edin pr1707 CC8.8.83
6030. Scrogie, Robert, sailor, sh. 14 July 1698, fr. Leith to Darien, in *St Andrew*, m. Helen Ferrier, Edin pr1707 CC8.8.83
6031. Scrymgeour, H Y, b. 1756, gentleman, sh. Jan 1774, fr. London to Jamaica, in *Henry*. (PRO.T47.9\11)
6032. Seaman, George, merchant, res. Leith Midlothian, pts. Alexander Seaman, d. 1769 Charleston S.C., PCC pr1769
6033. Seaton, Andrew, b. 1752, clerk, sh. Apr 1774, fr. London to Grenada, in *Industry*. (PRO.T47.9\11)
6034. Seaton, Daniel, Jacobite, tr. 30 Mar 1716, fr. Liverpool to Antigua, in *Scipio*. (SPC.1716.310)(CTB31.204)
6035. Seaton, John, clergyman, res. Chapel Lauder Berwickshire, pts. James Seaton or Hutton, sh. 14 July 1698, fr. Leith to Darien, in *Caledonia*, Edin pr1707 CC8.8.83 (alias 2882)
6036. Selbie, Thomas, Jacobite, tr. 30 Mar 1716, fr. Liverpool to Antigua, in *Scipio*. (SPC.1716.310)(CTB31.204)
6037. Selkeld, James, Jacobite, tr. 30 Mar 1716, fr. Liverpool to Antigua, in *Scipio*. (SPC.1716.310)
6038. Selkirk, James, b. 1752, tailor, res. Gatehouse Kirkcudbrightshire, sh. May 1774, fr. Stranraer to N.Y., in *Gale*. (PRO.T47.12)
6039. Semple, John, merchant, sh. pre 1757, sett. Portobacco Md. (SRO.CS230.19\21)
6040. Semple, John, merchant, res. Glasgow, sh. pre 1765, sett. Va Md. (SRA.B10.15.7082)
6041. Seranda, Joannes, sailor, sh. 14 July 1698, fr. Leith to Darien, in *Unicorn*, Edin pr1707 CC8.8.83
6042. Serjeant, Henry, Jacobite, tr. 7 May 1716, fr. Liverpool to S.C., in *Susannah*. (SPC.1716.309)(CTB31.206)
6043. Seton, Alexander, captain's clerk, sh. 14 July 1698, fr. Leith to Darien, in *St Andrew*, Edin pr1708 CC8.8.84
6044. Seton, George, sailor, res. Burntisland Fife, pts. John Seton, sh. 14 July 1698, fr. Leith to Darien, in *St Andrew*, Edin pr1707 CC8.8.83
6045. Seton, John, pts. William Seton, sh. pre 1777, sett. Jamaica. (SRO.RD2.227.237)
6046. Seton, Margaret, b. 1753, servant, res. Aberdeen, sh. May 1775, fr. Leith to Philadelphia, in *Friendship*. (PRO.T47.12)

6047. Seton, William, surgeon, res. Inverness, pts. William Seton, sh. pre
      1750, sett. Jamaica. (SRO.RS38.10.405)(SRO.SH.17.4.1781)
6048. Seymour, James, clergyman edu. King's Col Aberdeen 1766, sh. 1771,
      sett. Augusta Ga. (FPA300)
6049. Shade, William, b. 1723, laborer, Jacobite, tr. 1747. (P.3.306)
6050. Shadforth, Whitaker, b. 1754, watchmaker, sh. Sept 1775, fr. Newcastle
      to Ga, in *Georgia Merchant*, sett. Friendsborough Ga.
      (PRO.T47.9\11)
6051. Shaftoe, John, Jacobite, tr. 28 July 1716, fr. Liverpool to Va, in
      Godspeed, arr. Md. (SPC.1716.310)(CTB31.209)(MdArch.34.164)
6052. Shairp, Robert, ensign, pts. Thomas Shairp of Houstoun, d. 1699 Darien,
      Edin pr1707 CC8.8.83
6053. Shand, John, servant, res. Aberdeen, pts. Alexander Shand, sh. 1725, sett.
      Boston Mass, d. 1738 Boston. (APB.3.65)
6054. Shand, John, b. 22 July 1705, Old Machar Aberdeenshire, plantation
      overseer, res. Aberdeen, pts. Alexander Shand & Margaret Ritchie,
      sh. 1726, to Jamaica, d. pre 1740. (APB.3.77)
6055. Shannon, Henry, b. 1755, res. Galloway, sh. 1775, fr. Dumfries to
      P.E.I., in *Lovely Nelly*. (PRO.T47.12)
6056. Sharp, John, clergyman edu. King's Col Aberdeen, sh. 1699, to Va, sett.
      N.Y. (F.Ab.442)(EMA54)(KCA99)
6057. Sharp, Robert, Covenanter, tr. Aug 1685, fr. Leith to Jamaica.
      (PC.11.329)
6058. Sharp, William, rioter, res. Alloa Clackmannanshire, tr. Jan 1751.
      (AJ160)
6059. Sharp, William, b. 1729, laborer, Jacobite, res. Aberdeen, tr. 5 May
      1747, fr. Liverpool to Leeward Islands, in *Veteran*, arr. Martinique
      June 1747. (P.3.308)(JAB.2.442)(PRO.SP.36.102)(MR128)
6060. Sharroch, David, Jacobite, tr. 8 May 1747, to Antigua. (P.3.308)
6061. Shaw, Alexander, Jacobite, tr. 21 Apr 1716, fr. Liverpool to S.C., in
      Wakefield. (SPC.1716.309)(CTB31.205)
6062. Shaw, Alexander, Jacobite, tr. 7 May 1716, fr. Liverpool to S.C., in
      Susannah. (SPC.1716.309)(CTB31.206)
6063. Shaw, Alexander, cattlethief, res. Inverness-shire, tr. Sept 1763. (AJ820)
6064. Shaw, Alexander, b. 1755, servant, res. Daimie, sh. July 1775, fr.
      Stornaway to Philadelphia, in *Clementina*. (PRO.T47.12)
6065. Shaw, Angus, Jacobite, tr. 29 June 1716, fr. Liverpool to Jamaica or Va,
      in *Elizabeth & Anne*, arr. York Va.
      (SPC.1716.310)(CTB31.208)(VSP.1.185)
6066. Shaw, David, b. 1708, joiner & carpenter, res. Edinburgh, sh. May 1731,
      fr. London to Jamaica. (CLRO\AIA)
6067. Shaw, Donald, Jacobite, tr. 29 June 1716, fr. Liverpool to Jamaica or Va,
      in *Elizabeth & Anne*, arr. York Va.
      (SPC.1716.310)(CTB31.208)(VSP.1.185)

6068. Shaw, Donald, Jacobite, tr. 7 May 1716, fr. Liverpool to S.C., in *Susannah*. (SPC.1716.309)(CTB31.206)
6069. Shaw, Ewan, Jacobite, tr. 7 May 1716, fr. Liverpool to S.C., in *Susannah*. (SPC.1716.309)(CTB31.206)
6070. Shaw, James, Jacobite, tr. 24 May 1716, fr. Liverpool to Va, in *Friendship*, arr. Md. (SPC.1716.311)(HM387)
6071. Shaw, James, Jacobite, tr. 28 July 1716, fr. Liverpool to Va, in *Godspeed*, arr. Md Oct 1716. (SPC.1716.310)(CTB31.209)(HM389)
6072. Shaw, John, cabinetmaker, sh. 1772, sett. Annapolis Md. (SRA.CFI)
6073. Shaw, John, Jacobite, tr. 29 June 1716, fr. Liverpool to Jamaica or Va, in *Elizabeth & Anne*, arr. York Va. (SPC.1716.310)(CTB31.208)(VSP.1.186)
6074. Shaw, John, Jacobite, tr. 30 Mar 1716, fr. Liverpool to Antigua, in *Scipio*. (SPC.1716.310)(CTB31.204)
6075. Shaw, John, Jacobite, tr. 21 Apr 1716, fr. Liverpool to S.C., in *Wakefield*. (SPC.1716.309)(CTB31.205)
6076. Shaw, John, Jacobite, tr. 21 Apr 1716, fr. Liverpool to S.C., in *Wakefield*. (SPC.1716.309)(CTB31.205)
6077. Shaw, John, Jacobite, tr. 7 May 1716, fr. Liverpool to S.C., in *Susannah*. (SPC.1716.309)(CTB31.206)
6078. Shaw, John, cabinet maker, res. Glasgow, sh. 1775, sett. Annapolis Md. (SRA.CFI)
6079. Shaw, John, res. Knockantavile Jura Argyll, sh. 1754, to Cape Fear N.C. (SRO.GD64\5.21)
6080. Shaw, John, b. 1751, smith, res. Galloway, sh. May 1774, fr. Stranraer to N.Y., in *Gale*. (PRO.T47.12)
6081. Shaw, John, b. 1761, res. Fordardich, sh. July 1775, fr. Stornaway to Philadelphia, in *Clementina*. (PRO.T47.12)
6082. Shaw, Lachlan, soldier, m. Mary .., ch. Bridget Lachlan, d. 1761 S.C., Edin pr1762 CC8.8.119 PCC pr1765
6083. Shaw, Margaret, b. 1732, spinner, Jacobite, res. Perthshire, tr. 22 Apr 1747, fr. Liverpool to Va, in *Johnson*, arr. Port Oxford Md 5 Aug 1747. (P.3.308)(PRO.T1.328)
6084. Shaw, Mary, b. 1707, Jacobite, res. Inverness, tr. 22 Apr 1747, fr. Liverpool to Va, in *Johnson*, arr. Port Oxford Md 5 Aug 1747. (P.3.308)(PRO.T1.328)
6085. Shaw, Peter, Jacobite, tr. 7 May 1716, fr. Liverpool to S.C., in *Susannah*. (SPC.1716.309)(CTB31.206)
6086. Shaw, Robert, b. 1753, baker, sh. Apr 1774, fr. London to Md, in *Diana*. (PRO.T47.9\11)
6087. Shaw, Thomas, Jacobite, tr. 28 July 1716, fr. Liverpool to Va, in *Godspeed*, arr. Md Oct 1716. (SPC.1716.310)(CTB31.209)(HM388)

6088. Shaw, William, Jacobite, tr. 7 May 1716, fr. Liverpool to S.C., in *Susannah*. (SPC.1716.309)(CTB31.206)
6089. Shaw, William, Jacobite, tr. 28 July 1716, fr. Liverpool to Va, in *Godspeed*, arr. Md Oct 1716. (SPC.1716.310)(CTB31.209)(HM389)
6090. Shearer, James, barber, rapist, res. Ayrshire, tr. May 1764. (AJ855)
6091. Shearer, James, soldier, thief, res. Elgin Morayshire, tr. Jan 1767. (SRO.JC27)(SM.26.287)
6092. Shedden, Robert, chapman, pickpocket, tr. Sept 1775, fr. Glasgow to West Indies. (SM.37.523)
6093. Shedden, Robert, merchant, res. Beith Ayrshire, pts. William Shedden, sh. pre 1767, sett. Va. (SRO.SH.17.11.1767)
6094. Shedden, William Ralston, b. 23 Apr 1747, Beith Ayrshire, merchant, pts. John Shedden of Roughwood & Jean Ralston, sh. 1770, sett. Va Bermuda N.Y., ch. Jane, d. 1798 N.Y. (HAF.1.275)(SRO.SH.20.12.1771)
6095. Sheddon, Charles, b. 1677, coalgrieve, Jacobite, res. Ayr, tr. 1747. (P.3.304)(MR45)
6096. Sheils, Barbara, b. 1755, spinner, res. Glasgow, sh. Oct 1774, fr. Greenock to Philadelphia, in *Sally*. (PRO.T47.12)
6097. Shepherd, Andrew, b. 16 Aug 1759, St Nicholas Aberdeen, merchant edu. Marischal Col 1772, res. Aberdeen, pts. George Shepherd & Isabel Smith, sett. Va. (MCA.2.342)
6098. Shepherd, John, b. 1727, innservant, Jacobite, res. Ferryden Montrose Angus, tr. 24 Feb 1747, fr. Liverpool to Va, in *Gildart*, arr. Port North Potomac Md 5 Aug 1747. (P.3.310)(PRO.T1.328)(MR109)
6099. Sheridan, Thomas, soldier, thief, tr. 1772, fr. Port Glasgow to Md, in *Matty*, arr. Port Oxford Md 16 May 1772. (SRO.JC27.10.3)
6100. Sheriff, John, pts. Matthew Sheriff , sh. pre 1783, sett. St Thomas West Indies. (SRO.RD4.234.764)
6101. Shield, George, tr. 22 Dec 1665, fr. Leith or Buckhaven to Barbados. (ETR104)
6102. Shields, Alexander, clergyman, sh. 21 July 1699, fr. Greenock to Darien, d. 14 June 1700 Port Royal Jamaica. (F.7.665)
6103. Shields, James, tr. 24 Apr 1666, fr. Leith to Va, in *Phoenix of Leith*. (ETR107)
6104. Shields, John, Jacobite, tr. 30 Mar 1716, fr. Liverpool to Antigua, in *Scipio*. (SPC.1716.310)(CTB31.204)
6105. Shiels, John, gardener, sheepstealer, res. Edinburgh, tr. July 1769. (SRO.HCR.I.104) (alias 7034)
6106. Shileston, Thomas, Covenanter, res. Hillend Dunspurn, tr. 5 Sept 1685, fr. Leith to East N.J., in *Henry & Francis*. (PC.11.155)

6107. Shirar, Joseph, b. 1744, weaver, res. Paisley Renfrewshire, sh. Feb 1774, fr. Greenock to N.Y., in *Commerce*, m. Janet .., ch. Archibald. (PRO.T47.12)

6108. Shirmlaw, William, b. 1761, res. Glasgow, sh. May 1775, fr. Leith to Philadelphia, in *Friendship*. (PRO.T47.12)

6109. Shish, James, Covenanter, res. Bo'ness West Lothian, tr. Aug 1670. (PC.3.206)

6110. Shonger, Alexander, Jacobite, tr. 24 May 1716, fr. Liverpool to Va, in *Friendship*, arr. Md Aug 1716. (SPC.1716.311)(HM387) (alias 6605)

6111. Shorrock, David, b. 1728, weaver, Jacobite, res. Lancashire, tr. 1747. (P.3.312)(MR198)

6112. Shorrock, James, b. 1726, tailor, Jacobite, res. Preston Lancashire, tr. 1747. (P.3.312)(MR198)

6113. Short, George, cordiner, forger, res. Glasgow, tr. Mar 1766. (SRO.HCR.I.98)

6114. Shorter, Duncan, Jacobite, tr. 26 Apr 1716, fr. Liverpool to Jamaica, in *Two Brothers*, arr. Montserrat June 1716. (SPC.1716.313)(CTB31.206)(CTP.CC.43)

6115. Shungers, John, b. 1 June 1725, Glamis Angus, ploughman, Jacobite, res. Glen Ogilvy Angus, pts. John Shungers, tr. 1747. (MR110)

6116. Shuttard, Bernard, Jacobite, tr. 7 May 1716, fr. Liverpool to S.C., in *Susannah*. (SPC.1716.309)(CTB31.206)

6117. Sibbald, David, planter, res. Aberdeen, sh. pre 1772, sett. Trelawney Cornwall Co Jamaica. (SRO.RD2.232.795)

6118. Sibbet, Peter, res. Haddington East Lothian, d. pre 1678 Va, PCC pr1678

6119. Sillar, Hugh, b. 1719, farmer, res. Kintyre Argyll, sh. Sept 1774, fr. Greenock to Wilmington N.C., in *Diana*, m. Catherine Currie, ch. Mary Catherine. (PRO.T47.12)

6120. Silver, Andrew, thief, res. Aberdeenshire, tr. May 1750. (AJ124)

6121. Sim, John, vagrant & thief, res. Dumfries-shire, tr. Apr 1751. (AJ175)

6122. Sim, John, sailor, d. 16 Nov 1698 Darien. (NLS.RY2b8\19)

6123. Sim, John, b. 1758, weaver, res. Paisley Renfrewshire, sh. Feb 1774, fr. Greenock to N.Y., in *Commerce*. (PRO.T47.12)

6124. Sim, William, b. 1750, husbandman, sh. Feb 1774, fr. London to N.C., in *Margaret & Mary*, m. Jane .. (PRO.T46.9\11)

6125. Sime, Archibald, sailor, res. Bo'ness West Lothian, sh. 18 Aug 1699, fr. Clyde to Darien, in *Rising Sun*, Edin pr1707 CC8.8.83

6126. Simm, William, Jacobite, tr. 24 May 1716, fr. Liverpool to Va, in *Friendship*, arr. Md Aug 1716. (SPC.1716.311)(HM386)

6127. Simpson, Alexander, mariner, res. Dysart Fife, sh. 14 July 1698, fr. Leith to Darien, in *St Andrew*, ch. Elizabeth, Edin pr1707 CC8.8.83

6128. Simpson, David, clergyman edu. St Andrews Uni 1650, Covenanter, res. Kintyre Argyll, tr. 5 Sept 1685, fr. Leith to East N.J., in *Henry & Francis*, m. Jean Thomson, ch. David, d. pre Aug 1697 N.J. (F.4.66)
6129. Simpson, David, b. 1691, linen weaver, Jacobite, res. Auldbar Angus, tr. 1747. (P.3.314)(MR110)
6130. Simpson, Elizabeth, thief, res. Dumfries-shire, tr. May 1728. (SRO.JC12.4)
6131. Simpson, George, clerk, d. 1775 Grenada, Edin pr1779 CC8.8.124
6132. Simpson, George, b. 1732, book-keeper, res. Edinburgh, sh. Aug 1749, fr. London to Jamaica. (CLRO\AIA)
6133. Simpson, James, gentleman, res. Tibbers Dumfries-shire, sh. pre 1764, sett. Charleston S.C. (SRO.SC15.55.2)
6134. Simpson, James, b. 1727, shoemaker, Jacobite, res. Arbroath Angus, tr. 22 Apr 1747, fr. Liverpool to Va, in *Johnson*, arr. Port Oxford Md 5 Aug 1747. (P.3.314)(PRO.T1.328)(MR110)
6135. Simpson, Jean, b. 1755, servant, res. Dunbar East Lothian, sh. May 1775, fr. Leith to Philadelphia, in *Friendship*. (PRO.T47.12)
6136. Simpson, John, gentleman, res. Tibbers Dumfries-shire, sh. pre 1764, sett. Charleston S.C. (SRO.SC15.55.2)
6137. Simpson, John, merchant, sh. pre 1772, sett. S.C. (SRO.RD4.212.722)
6138. Simpson, John, Covenanter, res. Gariside Roxburghshire, tr. Aug 1685, fr. Leith to Jamaica, arr. Port Royal Jamaica Nov 1685. (PC.11.330)(ETR369)(LJ15)
6139. Simpson, John, b. 16 Apr 1728, merchant, res. Glasgow, pts. Matthew Simpson of Milncroft & Marion Prentice, sh. pre 1750, sett. St Vincent. (SRO.RS42.17.16)
6140. Simpson, Margaret, servant, Jacobite, res. Haddington East Lothian, tr. 1747. (P.3.314)
6141. Simpson, Margaret, b. 1752, servant, res. Dunfermline Fife, sh. May 1775, fr. Leith to Philadelphia, in *Friendship*. (PRO.T47.12)
6142. Simpson, Margaret, b. 1757, spinner, res. Crawforddykes Renfrewshire, sh. Oct 1774, fr. Greenock to Philadelphia, in *Sally*. (PRO.T47.12)
6143. Simpson, William, sailor, res. Edinburgh, sh. 18 Aug 1699, fr. Clyde to Darien, in *Rising Sun*, Edin pr1707 CC8.8.83
6144. Simpson, William, Jacobite, tr. 28 July 1716, fr. Liverpool to Ba, in *Godspeed*, arr. Md Oct 1716. (SPC.1716.310)(CTB31.209)(HM388)
6145. Simpson, William, b. 1744, laborer, res. Lochwinnoch Renfrewshire, sh. Apr 1775, fr. Greenock to N.Y., in *Lilly*. (PRO.T47.12)
6146. Simson, Dugald, clergyman edu. Glasgow Uni 1682, sh. 1685, sett. Brookhaven, m. Jean Hutchison, d. 1704 Scotland. (F.7.665)

6147. Simson, James, Jacobite, tr. 7 May 1716, fr. Liverpool to S.C., in *Susannah*. (SPC.1716.309)(CTB31.206)

6148. Simson, Thomas, res. Fife, pts. John Simson of Balchristie, d. 1699 Darien, Edin pr1708 CC8.8.84

6149. Sinclair, Alexander, res. Glasgow, sh. 19 Oct 1698, fr. Liverpool to Va, in *Loyalty*. (LRO.HQ325.2.FRE)

6150. Sinclair, Alexander, b. 1738, farmer, res. Dollochlagy Reay Caithness, sh. Apr 1774, to Wilmington N.C., in *Bachelor of Leith*. (PRO.T47.12)

6151. Sinclair, Ann, b. 1710, spinner, res. Glen Orchy Argyll, sh. Sept 1775, to Wilmington N.C., in *Jupiter*, ch. Margaret. (PRO.T47.12)

6152. Sinclair, Archibald, sh. 1737, sett. Frederica Ga. (SPC.1737.256)

6153. Sinclair, Archibald, res. Stempster Thurso Caithness, d. 1778 Jamaica. (SRO.SH.9.12.1778)

6154. Sinclair, Archibald, merchant, res. Greenock Renfrewshire, sh. pre 1781, sett. Kingston Jamaica. (SRO.RD2.235.39\RD2.236.651)

6155. Sinclair, David, mariner, pts. George Sinclair of Barrack, d. pre 1733 Jamaica, Edin pr1733 CC8.8.95

6156. Sinclair, Duncan, Covenanter, tr. Aug 1685, fr. Leith to Jamaica. (PC.11.136)

6157. Sinclair, Duncan, b. 1750, farmer, res. Glen Orchy Argyll, sh. Aug 1774, fr. Greenock to Wilmington N.C., in *Ulysses*, m. Isobel McIntyre. (PRO.T47.12)

6158. Sinclair, Duncan, b. 1765, servant, res. Inverness, sh. July 1775, fr. Stornaway to Philadelphia, in *Clementina*. (PRO.T47.12)

6159. Sinclair, James, seaman, res. Scourie Sutherland, sh. 16 Mar 1683, sett. Hudson Bay. (HBRS.9.86)

6160. Sinclair, James, Jacobite, tr. 28 July 1716, fr. Liverpool to Va, in *Godspeed*, arr. Md Oct 1716. (SPC.1716.310)(CTB31.209)(HM388)(MdArch34.164)

6161. Sinclair, James, sh. May 1725, fr. London to Antigua or Montserrat. (CLRO\AIA)

6162. Sinclair, James, b. 1728, husbandman, Jacobite, res. Dunbeath Caithness, tr. 31 Mar 1747, fr. London to Jamaica, in *St George or Carteret*, arr. Jamaica 1747. (P.3.316)(PRO.CO.137.58)(MR87)

6163. Sinclair, James, b. 1753, farmer, res. Forsenain Reay Caithness, sh. Apr 1774, to Wilmington N.C., in *Bachelor of Leith*. (PRO.T47.12)

6164. Sinclair, James, b. 1755, farm servant, res. Holm Orkney Islands, sh. Sept 1775, fr. Kirkwall to Savannah Ga, in *Marlborough*, sett. Richmond Co Ga. (PRO.T47.12)

6165. Sinclair, John, coxswain, res. Inverkip Renfrewshire, sh. 18 Aug 1699, fr. Clyde to Darien, in *Rising Sun*, Edin pr1707 CC8.8.83

6166. Sinclair, John, pts. Sir William Sinclair, sh. 1767, sett. E Fla. (PRO.CO5.542)

6167. Sinclair, John, res. Dunnet Caithness, pts. William Sinclair, tr. Aug 1680, fr. Leith, in *Blossom*. (ETR170)
6168. Sinclair, John, b. 1730, tailor, res. Inverness, sh. July 1775, fr. Stornaway to Philadelphia, in *Clementina*. (PRO.T47.12)
6169. Sinclair, John, b. 1742, farmer, res. Glen Orchy Argyll, sh. Aug 1774, fr. Greenock to Wilmington N.C., in *Ulysses*, m. Mary .. (PRO.T47.12)
6170. Sinclair, John, b. 1760, servant, res. Inverness, sh. July 1775, fr. Stornaway to Philadelphia, in *Clementina*. (PRO.T47.12)
6171. Sinclair, Margaret, res. Caithness, pts. Sir James Sinclair of Dunbeath, sh. pre 1778, sett. St Catherine Middlesex Co Jamaica. (SRO.RD4.232.906)
6172. Sinclair, Margaret, b. 1755, servant, res. Bower Caithness, sh. Sept 1775, fr. Kirkwall to Savannah Ga, in *Marlborough*. (PRO.T47.12)
6173. Sinclair, Patrick, Jacobite, tr. 21 Apr 1716, fr. Liverpool to S.C., in *Wakefield*. (SPC.1716.309)(CTB31.205)
6174. Sinclair, Robert, sh. pre 1772, sett. N.Y. (SRO.RD4.212.95)
6175. Sinclair, Robert, b. 1685, clergyman, sh. pre 1709, sett. Newcastle Del. (SCHR.14.148)(SPG.2.11)
6176. Sinclair, Sir William, sh. 1767, sett. E Fla. (PRO.CO5.542)
6177. Sinclair, William, Jacobite, tr. 31 July 1716, fr. Liverpool to Va, in *Anne*. (SPC.1716.310)(CTB31.209)
6178. Singleton, Robert, Jacobite, res. Lancashire, tr. 1747. (MR198)
6179. Sivewright, David, b. 1754, gentleman, sh. Jan 1774, fr. London to Jamaica, in *Henry*. (PRO.T47.9\11)
6180. Skene, A, secretary, sh. pre 1705, sett. Barbados. (SPC.1705.409)
6181. Skene, James, physician edu. Marischal Col Aberdeen, res. Aberdeen, pts. Prof Francis Skene, sh. pre 1766, sett. Charleston S.C. (MCA.2.123)
6182. Skene, John, governor edu. Marischal Col Aberdeen 1663, sett. N.J. (KCA.2.229)
6183. Skene, Robert, res. Dyce Aberdeenshire, pts. Alexander Skene, sh. 1700, sett. Md. (APB.3.101)
6184. Skene, Robert, res. Aberdeenshire, d. 1736 Md, Edin pr1741 CC8.8.105
6185. Skinner, Charles, b. 1746, husbandman, sh. June 1774, fr. London to Md, in *Industry*. (PRO.T47.9\11)
6186. Skinner, William, b. 1687, schoolmaster & clergyman, sh. 1718, sett. Philadelphia & N.J., d. 1758 Perth Amboy. (EMA55)(SCHR.14.145)
6187. Slater, James, b. 1734, chapman, res. Glasgow, sh. Feb 1774, fr. Greenock to N.Y., in *Commerce*. (PRO.T47.12)
6188. Sleiman, Gabriel, sailor, res. Paisley Renfrewshire, sh. 18 Aug 1699, fr. Clyde to Darien, in *Rising Sun*, Edin pr1707 CC8.8.83

6189. Sloan, John, b. 1735, weaver, res. Inch Wigtonshire, sh. May 1775, fr. Stranraer to N.Y., in *Jackie*, m. Eliza McCubbin, ch. Grizel Alexander John Jean. (PRO.T47.12)

6190. Sloss, Robert, Covenanter, res. Ayr, tr. Feb 1685. (PC.10.129)

6191. Slovewright, James, farm servant, thief, res. Coathill Lunan Angus, tr. Oct 1774. (SM.36)

6192. Slowan, George, res. Dumfries, tr. May 1726. (SRO.JC12.4)

6193. Small, James, Jacobite, tr. 24 May 1716, fr. Liverpool to Md, in *Friendship*, arr. Md Aug 1716. (SPC.1716.311)(HM387)

6194. Small, John, Jacobite, res. Dundee Angus, tr. 22 July 1748. (P.3.318)

6195. Small, Robert, b. 1759, barber, res. Perth, sh. May 1775, fr. Leith to Philadelphia, in *Friendship*. (PRO.T47.12)

6196. Small, Thomas, b. 1743, smith, res. Glasgow, sh. May 1775, fr. Greenock to N.Y., in *Christy*. (PRO.T47.12)

6197. Smart, David, founder, res. Strathmiglo Fife, sh. pre 1775, sett. N.Y. (SRO.SH.7.11.1775)

6198. Smart, John, vagrant & thief, res. Huntly Aberdeenshire, tr. Feb 1766. (AJ947)

6199. Smeall, Elizabeth, servant, infanticide, res. St Cuthbert's Edinburgh, tr. Mar 1768. (SRO.JC27.D35)

6200. Smellie, John, merchant, res. Glasgow, pts. John Smellie, sh. pre 1729, sett. Kingston Jamaica. (SRO.SH.2.5.1729)

6201. Smellie, Thomas, b. 1757, weaver, res. Paisley Renfrewshire, sh. Feb 1774, fr. Greenock to N.Y., in *Commerce*. (PRO.T47.12)

6202. Smewrey, Cornelius, b. 1662, weaver, res. Berwick, sh. 15 May 1686, fr. London to Barbados. (CLRO\AIA)

6203. Smith, Alexander, Jacobite, tr. 26 Apr 1716, fr. Liverpool to Jamaica, in *Two Brothers*, arr. Montserrat June 1716. (SPC.1716.313)(CTB31.205)(CTP.CC.43)

6204. Smith, Alexander, Jacobite, tr. 24 May 1716, fr. Liverpool to Md, in *Friendship*, arr. Md Aug 1716. (SPC.1716.311)(HM386)

6205. Smith, Alexander, b. 1719, Jacobite, tr. 1747, fr. Tilbury. (P.3.318)

6206. Smith, Alexander, b. 1727, Jacobite, tr. 22 Apr 1747, fr. Liverpool to Va, in *Johnson*, arr. Port Oxford Md 5 Aug 1747. (P.3.318)(PRO.T1.328)

6207. Smith, Andrew, b. 1716, husbandman, Jacobite, res. Meldrum Aberdeenshire, pts. Patrick Smith & Elizabeth Kerr, tr. 24 Feb 1747, fr. Liverpool to Va, in *Gildart*, arr. Port North Potomac Md 5 Aug 1747. (P.2.320)(JAB.2.443)(PRO.T1.328)

6208. Smith, Andrew, b. 1726, husbandman, Jacobite, res. Old Meldrum Aberdeenshire, tr. 31 Mar 1747, fr. London to Barbados , in *Frere*. (P.3.320)(MR129)(JAB.2.443)

6209. Smith, Andrew, b. 1729, weaver, Jacobite, res. Edinburgh, tr. 24 Feb 1747, fr. Liverpool to Va, in *Gildart*, arr. Port North Potomac Md 5 Aug 1747. (P.3.320)(MR207)(PRO.T1.328)

6210. Smith, Charles, student, res. Craignish Argyll, sh. 1738. (SRO.SC54.2.52.2)

6211. Smith, Charles, Jacobite, tr. 29 June 1716, fr. Liverpool to Jamaica or Va, in *Elizabeth & Anne*. (SPC.1716.310)(CTB31.208)

6212. Smith, Charles, drummer, robber, tr. Mar 1747. (SRO.JC27)

6213. Smith, Daniel, Jacobite, tr. 26 Apr 1716, fr. Liverpool to Jamaica, in *Two Brothers*, arr. Montserrat June 1716. (SPC.1716.313)(CTB31.205)(CTP.CC.43)

6214. Smith, David, weaver, thief, res. Dundee Angus, tr. May 1774. (AJ1377)

6215. Smith, David, Jacobite, tr. 7 May 1716, fr. Liverpool to S.C., in *Susannah*. (SPC.1716.309)(CTB31.206)

6216. Smith, David, b. 1753, clerk, sh. Nov 1774, fr. London to Jamaica, in *Davies*. (PRO.T47.9\11)

6217. Smith, Donald, Jacobite, tr. 29 Apr 1716, fr. Liverpool to S.C., in *Wakefield*. (SPC.1716.309)(CTB31.205)

6218. Smith, Donald, Jacobite, tr. 7 May 1716, fr. Liverpool to S.C., in *Susannah*. (SPC.1716.309)(CTB31.206)

6219. Smith, Donald, b. 1697, Jacobite, res. Glen Urquhart Inverness-shire, tr. 31 Mar 1747, fr. London to Barbados , in *Frere*. (P.3.320)

6220. Smith, Duncan, b. 1741, farmer, res. Paisley Renfrewshire, sh. Apr 1775, fr. Greenock to Salem, in *Glasgow Packet*. (PRO.T47.12)

6221. Smith, Elizabeth, tr. Aug 1756, fr. Aberdeen to Va, in *St Andrew*. (AJ451)

6222. Smith, Euphame, tr. 1696, fr. Newhaven to Va. (SRO.15.14.58)

6223. Smith, Frances, res. Linlithgow West Lothian, pts. William Smith & Mary Nimnah, sh. pre 1783, sett. N.Y., m. ... Smeal, ch. Mary. (SRO.RD5.33.98)

6224. Smith, George, Covenanter, res. Avondale Lanarkshire, tr. June 1684, fr. Glasgow, in *Pelican*. (PC.9.208)

6225. Smith, George, chapman, thief, res. Dundee Angus, tr. May 1774. (AJ1377)

6226. Smith, George, thief, tr. Sept 1775. (AJ1449)

6227. Smith, George, b. 1723, husbandman, Jacobite, res. Cairnbulg Aberdeenshire, tr. 31 Mar 1747, fr. London to Jamaica, in *St George or Carteret*, arr. Jamaica 1747. (P.3.322)(MR45)(PRO.CO137.58)

6228. Smith, Isobel, b. 1749, res. Crawforddykes Renfrewshire, sh. May 1774, fr. Greenock to N.Y., in *George*. (PRO.T47.12)

6229. Smith, James, Jacobite, res. Strathspey, tr. 24 Feb 1747, fr. Liverpool to Va, in *Gildart*, arr. Port North Potomac Md 5 Aug 1747. (P.3.322)(MR193)(PRO.T1.328)

6230. Smith, James, thief, res. Craigends Renfrewshire, tr. Sept 1752. (AJ246)
6231. Smith, James, weaver, res. Kininmonth Aberdeenshire, tr. 1772, fr.
Glasgow to Va, in *Brilliant*, arr. Port Hampton Va 7 Oct 1772.
(SRO.JC.27.10.3)(AJ1272)
6232. Smith, James, cattlethief, tr. Mar 1767. (SRO.RH2.4.255) (alias 6494)
6233. Smith, James, b. 1688, workman, Jacobite, res. Loanhead Old Machar
Aberdeenshire, tr. 31 Mar 1747, fr. London to Jamaica, in *St
George or Carteret*, arr. Jamaica 1747.
(P.3.322)(JAB.2.443)(MR129)(PRO.CO137.58)
6234. Smith, James, b. 1712, res. Air, sh. Jan 1729, fr. London to Md.
(CLRO\AIA)
6235. Smith, Janet, b. 1742, res. Kirkcudbright, sh. May 1774, fr.
Kirkcudbright to N.Y., in *Adventure*. (PRO.T47.12)
6236. Smith, Jean, servant, res. Montrose Angus, tr. May 1760.
(SRO.B59.26.11.6.44)
6237. Smith, Jean, b. 1754, servant, res. Dunfermline Fife, sh. May 1775, fr.
Leith to Philadelphia, in *Friendship*. (PRO.T47.12)
6238. Smith, Jean, b. 1757, spinner, res. Paisley Renfrewshire, sh. Feb 1774,
fr. Greenock to N.Y., in *Commerce*. (PRO.T47.12)
6239. Smith, John, counterfeiter, tr. Aug 1749. (AJ86)
6240. Smith, John, res. Hamilton Lanarkshire, tr. 21 Mar 1684, fr. Leith to
Carolina. (PC.8.710)
6241. Smith, John, Covenanter, res. Kirkintilloch Dunbartonshire, tr. 5 Sept
1685, fr. Leith to East N.J., in *Henry & Francis*. (PC.11.167)
6242. Smith, John, tr. 1730, fr. Glasgow to S.C., in *John & Robert*, 22 July
1730. (SRO.JC27.10.3)
6243. Smith, John, weaver, rioter, res. Dumfries, tr. Dec 1760. (SRO.JC27)
6244. Smith, John, m. Jane .., d. pre 1689 Pa, PCC pr1689
6245. Smith, John, passenger, sh. Feb 1681, fr. Ayr to West Indies, in *James
of Ayr*. (SRO.E72.3.6)
6246. Smith, John, clergyman, sh. 1770. (UPC656)
6247. Smith, John, b. 1708, husbandman, res. Edinburgh, sh. May 1731, fr.
London to Jamaica. (CLRO\AIA)
6248. Smith, John, b. 1726, Derby, Jacobite, tr. 1747. (MR137)
6249. Smith, John, b. 1726, goldsmith, Jacobite, res. Aberdeen, tr. 5 May
1747, fr. Liverpool to Leeward Islands, in *Veteran*, arr. Martinique
June 1747. (P.3.322)(JAB.2.443)(PRO.SP36.102)
6250. Smith, John, b. 1729, mason, res. Preston Kirkbean Kirkcudbrightshire,
sh. 1775, fr. Kirkcudbright to P.E.I., in *Lovely Nelly*, m. Janet
Sturgeon, ch. Janet Mary Jean Agnes Isabel Nelly. (PRO.T47.12)
6251. Smith, John, b. 1741, blacksmith, res. Lochend Colvend Lockerbie
Dumfries-shire, sh. 1774, fr. Dumfries to P.E.I., in *Lovely Nelly*,
arr. Three Rivers, sett. Truro N.S., m. Margaret McVicar, ch.
William Mary. (PRO.T47.12)

6252. Smith, Lewis, b. 1751, silversmith, res. Aberdeen, sh. May 1775, fr. Leith to Philadelphia, in *Friendship*. (PRO.T47.12)
6253. Smith, Malcolm, b. 1710, farmer, res. Kintyre Argyll, sh. Aug 1774, fr. Greenock to Wilmington N.C., in *Ulysses*, m. Mary McAlester, ch. Peter Mary. (PRO.T47.12)
6254. Smith, Margaret, b. 1744, servant, res. Galson Isle of Lewis, sh. May 1774, fr. Stornaway to Philadelphia, in *Friendship*. (PRO.T47.12)
6255. Smith, Mary, b. 1750, res. Edinburgh, sh. Apr 1775, fr. Greenock to N.Y., in *Lilly*. (PRO.T47.12)
6256. Smith, Matthew, shipscarpenter, res. Irvine Ayrshire, sett. Pasquatank N.C., d. pre 1771 N.C., Edin pr1771 CC8.8.122
6257. Smith, Patrick, Jacobite, tr. 7 May 1716, fr. Liverpool to S.C., in *Susannah*. (SPC.1716.309)(CTB31.206)
6258. Smith, Patrick, Jacobite, tr. 27 July 1716, fr. Liverpool to Va, in *Godspeed*, arr. Md Oct 1716. (SPC.1716.310)(HM388)
6259. Smith, Patrick, b. 22 Mar 1747, Glasgow, merchant, res. Glasgow, pts. Patrick Smith & Janet Maxwell, sh. 1763, to Jamaica. (SRA.B10.15.7085)
6260. Smith, Robert, Jacobite, tr. 29 June 1716, fr. Liverpool to Jamaica or Va, in *Elizabeth & Anne*, arr. York Va. (SPC.1716.310)(CTB31.208)(VSP.1.185)
6261. Smith, Robert, b. 1754, husbandman, sh. Mar 1774, fr. Whitehaven to Va, in *Ann*. (PRO.T47.9\11)
6262. Smith, Robert Thomson, murderer, res. Aberlady East Lothian, tr. 1739. (SM.1.
6263. Smith, Roger, robber, tr. Dec 1752, fr. Glasgow to Antigua. (AJ260)
6264. Smith, Thomas, soldier, thief, tr. Sept 1662. (ETR77)
6265. Smith, Thomas, Jacobite, tr. 24 May 1716, fr. Liverpool to Md, in *Friendship*, arr. Md Aug 1716. (SPC.1716.311)(HM387)
6266. Smith, Thomas, b. 1757, weaver, res. Glasgow, sh. Feb 1774, fr. Greenock to N.Y., in *Commerce*. (PRO.T47.12)
6267. Smith, Thomas sr, housebreaker, res. Knock Banffshire, tr. Apr 1754. (SM.16.203)
6268. Smith, William, cattlethief, tr. Mar 1767. (CHOpp1767.285) (alias 6490)
6269. Smith, William, Covenanter, res. Carmunnock Lanarkshire, tr. June 1684, fr. Glasgow, in *Pelican*. (PC.9.208)
6270. Smith, William, Covenanter, res. Kimgatyhill Cambusnethan Lanarkshire, pts. John Smith, tr. Aug 1685, fr. Leith to Jamaica, d. at sea. (PC.11.329)(LJ203)
6271. Smith, William, Jacobite, tr. 24 Feb 1747, fr. Liverpool to Va, in *Gildart*, arr. Port North Potomac Md 5 Aug 1747. (PRO.T1.328)
6272. Smith, William, pts. William Smith, sh. July 1684, fr. London to Md. (CLRO\AIA)

6273. Smith, William, res. Dunbar East Lothian, m. Jane Bulcraig, d. pre 1738 Va, PCC pr1738
6274. Smith, William, b. 7 Sept 1727, Aberdeenshire, clergyman edu. Aberdeen Uni, sh. 1751, sett. Philadelphia, m. Rebecca Moore, d. 14 May 1803 Philadelphia. (EMA56)
6275. Smith, William, b. 1751, laborer, res. Corsack Colvend Dumfries-shire, sh. 1775, fr. Dumfries to P.E.I., in *Lovely Nelly*. (PRO.T47.12)
6276. Smyth, Henry, sh. 1761, sett. Charleston S.C. (SRO.NRAS.0387)
6277. Snodgrass, John, factor, res. Glasgow, sh. pre 1776, sett. Goochland Va. (SRA.B10.12.4)
6278. Snodgrass, Neil, merchant, res. Paisley Renfrewshire, sh. pre 1782, sett. Va, d. 1782 N.Y., Edin pr1788 CC8.8.127 PCC pr1785
6279. Snodgrass, William, factor, res. Glasgow, sh. 1766, sett. Va. (SRA.B10.15.8269)
6280. Snodgrass, William, merchant, res. Glasgow, sh. pre 1782, sett. Richmond Va. (SRO.CS.GMB58)
6281. Somerville, James, assistant armorer, res. Dalkeith Midlothian, sh. 14 July 1698, fr. Leith to Darien, in *Unicorn*, m. Agnes Scoon, Edin pr1707 CC8.8.83
6282. Somerville, James, clergyman, sh. 1768, sett. Antigua. (EMA56)
6283. Somerville, James, fermorer, Covenanter, res. Cambusnethan Lanarkshire, tr. Dec 1685, fr. Leith to Barbados, in *John & Nicholas*. (PC.11.254)(ETR389)
6284. Somerville, James, Jacobite, tr. 28 July 1716, fr. Liverpool to Va, in *Godspeed*, arr. Md Oct 1716. (SPC.1716.310)(CTB31.209)(HM389)
6285. Somerville, John, merchant, sh. pre 1763, sett. St Mary's Co Va. (SRO.RD4.208.430)
6286. Somerville, Patrick, tailor, Covenanter, res. Canongate Edinburgh, tr. 1678, fr. Leith to West Indies, in *St Michael of Scarborough*. (PC.6.76)
6287. Somerville, Peter, b. 1732, shoemaker, Jacobite, res. Angus or Lothian, tr. 5 May 1747, fr. Liverpool to Leeward Islands, in *Veteran*, arr. Martinique June 1747. (P.3.326)(MR94)(PRO.SP36.102)
6288. Somerville, William, sailor, res. Culross Fife, sh. 14 July 1698, fr. Leith to Darien, in *St Andrew*, m. Isobel Dalgleish, Edin pr1707 CC8.8.83
6289. Somerville, William, Covenanter, res. Cambusnethan Lanarkshire, tr. Dec 1685, fr. Leith to Barbados, in *John & Nicholas*. (PC.11.254)(ETR389)
6290. Songster, Andrew, Jacobite, tr. 21 Apr 1716, fr. Liverpool to S.C., in *Wakefield*. (CTB31.205)
6291. Soutar, Angus, b. 1758, spinner, res. Paisley Renfrewshire, sh. Feb 1774, fr. Greenock to N.Y., in *Commerce*. (PRO.T47.12)

6292. Soutar, Charles, b. 1743, weaver, res. Paisley Renfrewshire, sh. Feb 1774, fr. Greenock to N.Y., in *Commerce*. (PRO.T47.12)
6293. Soutar, James, b. 1739, weaver, res. Paisley Renfrewshire, sh. Feb 1774, fr. Greenock to N.Y., in *Commerce*. (PRO.T47.12)
6294. Soutar, James, b. 1759, weaver, res. Paisley renfrewshire, sh. Feb 1774, fr. Greenock to N.Y., in *Commerce*. (PRO.T47.12)
6295. Soutar, John, joiner, Jacobite, res. Ellon Aberdeenshire, tr. 22 Apr 1747, fr. Liverpool to Va, in *Johnson*, arr. Port Oxford Md 5 Aug 1747. (P.3.360)(MR133)(PRO.T1.328)
6296. Souter, William, oxen thief, res. Aberdeen, tr. July 1774, fr. Glasgow. (SRO.RH2.4.255)(AJ1384)
6297. Southland, Adam, Jacobite, tr. May 1747, fr. Liverpool. (P.3.326)
6298. Spalding, Alexander, Jacobite, tr. 24 May 1716, fr. Liverpool to Md, in *Friendship*, arr. Md Aug 1716. (SPC.1716.311)(HM386)
6299. Spalding, James, merchant, res. Bonnington Mills Edinburgh, pts. James Spalding, sh. pre 1772, sett. E Fla Ga. (SRO.GD174)(SRO.RD4.259.758)
6300. Spalsie, John, surgeon, res. Kirkcudbright, ch. Margaret, d. Darien, Edin pr 1708 CC8.8.84
6301. Spark, Alexander, b. 7 Jan 1752, Marykirk Kincardineshire, clergyman & schoolmaster edu. King's Col Aberdeen 1776, res. Marykirk, pts. John Spark & Margaret Low, sh. 1780, sett. Quebec, m. Mary Ross, d. 7 Mar 1819 Quebec. (KCA252)(F.7.652)
6302. Speed, William, Jacobite, tr. 24 Feb 1747, fr. Liverpool to Va, in *Gildart*, arr. Port North Potomac Md 5 Aug 1747. (PRO.T1.328)
6303. Speir, Alexander, b. 1755, clerk, res. Glasgow, sh. Sept 1774, fr. Greenock to Wilmington N.C., in *Diana*. (PRO.T47.12)
6304. Speirs, Alexander, b. 1714, Edinburgh, merchant planter, sh. 1740, sett. Elderslie Va, m. (1)Sarah Carey (2)Mary Buchanan, d. 1782 Glasgow. (SRA.B10.15.5943)
6305. Speirs, James, planter merchant, res. Glasgow, sh. pre 1754, sett. Va. (SRA.B10.15.6653)
6306. Speirs, Joseph, tailor's servant, sh. pre 1676, sett. Barbados. (PC.4.671)
6307. Spence, George, judge, d. 30 Sept 1780 Lucea Hanover Jamaica. (SM.53.48)
6308. Spence, Helen, tr. 1696, fr. Newhaven to Va. (SRO.RH15.14.58)
6309. Spence, James, clergyman schoolmaster, res. Inch Aberdeenshire, pts. George Spence Christian Thorn, sh. 1698, sett. St Mary's Jamaica, d. 1737. (APB.3.57)(EBR.162.6294)
6310. Spence, James, b. 30 Oct 1732, St Andrews Orkney Islands, farmer, res. St Andrews Orkney Islands, pts. John Spence Ann Petrie, sh. Sept 1774, fr. Kirkwall to Savannah Ga, in *Marlborough*, sett. Richmond Co Ga, m. Mary Gorne, ch. Barbara James Helen. (PRO.T47.12)

6311. Spence, James, b. 1749, cartwright, res. Paisley Renfrewshire, sh. Feb 1774, fr. Greenock to N.Y., in *Commerce*. (PRO.T47.12)
6312. Spence, John, b. 29 Dec 1728, Kirkwall Orkney Islands, sailor, res. Kirkwall, pts. Gilbert & Elizabeth Spence, sh. Sept 1774, fr. Kirkwall to Savannah Ga, in *Marlborough*, sett. Richmond Co Ga. (PRO.T47.12)
6313. Spence, John, b. 1745, weaver, res. Paisley Renfrewshire, sh. Feb 1774, fr. Greenock to N.Y., in *Commerce*, m. Margaret .. (PRO.T47.12)
6314. Spence, John jr, sailor, res. Leith Midlothian, pts. John Spence, sh. 18 Aug 1699, fr. Clyde to Darien, in *Rising Sun*, d. Darien, Edin pr1707 CC8.8.83
6315. Spence, John sr, sailor, res. Leith Midlothian, pts. John Spence, sh. 18 Aug 1699, fr. Clyde to Darien, in *Rising Sun*, Edin pr1707 CC8.8.83
6316. Spence, Peter, surgeon, res. Linlithgow West Lothian, pts. Peter Spence, sh. pre 1774, sett. Va. (SRO.CS.GMB301)
6317. Spence, Robert, merchant, forger, res. Kirkcaldy Fife, tr. July 1769. (SRO.HCR.I.104)
6318. Spence, Walter, b. 1750, merchant, res. Edinburgh, sh. July 1775, fr. Greenock to Ga, in *Georgia*. (PRO.T47.12)
6319. Spence, William, b. 1751, baker, sh. Apr 1774, fr. London to Md, in *Diana*. (PRO.T47.9\11)
6320. Spens, Alexander, pts. Thomas Spens of Lathallan, d. Dec 1755 Jamaica. (SM.18.198)
6321. Spittle, James, housebreaker, tr. Aug 1773. (SRO.HCR.I.110)
6322. Sproat, Hugh, b. 1747, farmer, res. Kirkcudbright, sh. May 1774, fr. Kirkcudbright to N.Y., in *Adventure*. (PRO.T47.12)
6323. Sproat, John, b. 1751, laborer, res. Miln of Borgue Kirkcudbrightshire, sh. May 1774, fr. Kirkcudbright to N.Y., in *Adventure*. (PRO.T47.12)
6324. Sproat, Thomas, b. 1738, joiner, res. Kirkcudbright, sh. May 1774, fr. Kirkcudbright to N.Y., in *Adventure*. (PRO.T47.12)
6325. Sprott, John, thief, tr. 1769. (SM.31.500)
6326. Sproule, Andrew, merchant, res. Milton, pts. John Sproule, sett. Gosport Norfolk Co Va, m. Annabella McNeill, d. Va, bd. Portsmouth, Edin pr1779 CC8.8.124 PCC pr1782
6327. Sprout, William, Covenanter, res. Clontarch, tr. 5 Sept 1685, fr. Leith to East N.J., in *Henry & Francis*. (PC.10.612)
6328. Squire, George, b. 1745, mason, res. Aberdeen, sh. May 1774, fr. Greenock to N.Y., in *George*. (PRO.T47.12)
6329. Stalker, Duncan Buie, cattlethief, res. Lubea Glencoe Argyll, tr. Sept 1766. (AJ978)
6330. Stark, Donald jr, housebreaker, res. Olrig Caithness, tr. July 1769. (SRO.HCR.I.104)(AJ126)

311

6331. Stark, John, thief, res. Stirlingshire, tr. May 1754. (SM.16.258)
6332. Steel, Alexander, forger, tr. Feb 1670, fr. Leith to Va, in *Ewe & Lamb*. (PC.3.650)
6333. Steel, Alexander, b. 1748, laborer, res. Glasgow, sh. May 1775, fr. Greenock to N.Y., in *Lilly*. (PRO.T47.12)
6334. Steel, Hugh, shipmaster, res. Saltcoats Ayrshire, sett. Philadelphia, d. 1757 Pa, Edin pr1759 CC8.8.118. (SRO.SH.23.6.1759)
6335. Steel, John, sailor, sh. 18 Aug 1699, fr. Clyde to Darien, in *Rising Sun*, Edin pr1708 CC8.8.84
6336. Steel, John, merchant, res. Glasgow, sh. pre 1782, sett. Savannah la Mar Jamaica. (SRA.B10.15.8403)
6337. Steel, John, apprentice tailor, murderer, res. Lanark, tr. 1767. (AJ1031)
6338. Steel, Mary, b. 1757, spinner, res. Paisley Renfrewshire, sh. Feb 1774, fr. Greenock to N.Y., in *Commerce*. (PRO.T47.12)
6339. Steel, Michael, laborer, Jacobite, res. Logie Almond Perthshire, tr. 22 Apr 1747, fr. Liverpool to Va, in *Johnson*, arr. Port North Potomac Md 5 Aug 1747. (P.3.332)(MR27)(PRO.T1.328)
6340. Steel, Ross, b. 1754, servant, res. Heriot Midlothian, sh. May 1775, fr. Leith to Philadelphia, in *Friendship*. (PRO.T47.12)
6341. Steel, Thomas, sh. 1684, fr. Gourock to S.C., in *Carolina Merchant*. (ECJ72) (alias 6732)
6342. Steel, William, b. 1744, laborer, res. Glasgow, sh. May 1774, fr. Greenock to N.Y., in *Matty*. (PRO.T47.12)
6343. Steele, James, clergyman edu. Edinburgh Uni, sh. 1782, sett. Jamaica. (FPA316)
6344. Steenson, Ann, b. 1756, servant, res. Dysart Fife, sh. May 1775, fr. Leith to Philadelphia, in *Friendship*. (PRO.T47.12)
6345. Stenhouse, George, sailor, res. Burntisland Fife, sh. 14 July 1698, fr. Leith to Darien, in *Caledonia*, Edin pr1707 CC8.8.83
6346. Stephen, George, tailor, res. Aberdeen, sh. Aug 1736, fr. London to Jamaica. (CLRO\AIA)
6347. Stephen, James, cooper, res. Peterculter Aberdeenshire, pts. David Stephen & Elspet Gavin, d. 1766 Charleston S.C. (APB.4.41)
6348. Stephen, James, b. 17 Nov 1721, Fordoun Kincardineshire, Jacobite, res. Kincardineshire, pts. Alexander Stephen, tr. 31 Mar 1747, fr. London to Jamaica, in *St George or Carteret*, arr. Jamaica 1747. (P.3.332)(MR30)(PRO.CO137.58)
6349. Stephen, John, b. 2 Sept 1740, Gaitly, clergyman, sh. 1764, sett. Tobago & Md, d. 1784 Md. (EMA57)(FPA318)
6350. Stephen, William, divinity student, fireraiser, res. Stirlingshire, tr. May 1764. (SM.26.287)
6351. Stephens, William, b. 1751, carpenter, sh. Aug 1774, fr. London to Pensacola W Fla, in *Success's Increase*. (PRO.T47.9\11)

312

6352. Steuart, Adam, res. Kilmarnock Ayrshire, sh. pre 1783, sett. Kingston Jamaica. (SRO.RD2.237.825)
6353. Steuart, Alexander, res. Shetland Islands, sh. 7 Feb 1774, fr. London to Va, in *Planter*, arr. Fredericksburg Va 10 May 1774. (PRO.T47.9\11)
6354. Steuart, John, clergyman, sh. 1770, sett. N.Y. (EMA57)
6355. Steven, Christian, b. 1752, res. Inch Wigtonshire, sh. 31 May 1775, fr. Stranraer to N.C., in *Jackie*. (PRO.T47.12)
6356. Steven, James, b. 1748, farmer, res. Inch Wigtonshire, sh. 31 May 1775, fr. Stranraer to N.C., in *Jackie*. (PRO.T47.12)
6357. Steven, Jean, tr. Aug 1756, fr. Aberdeen to Va, in *St Andrew*. (AJ451)
6358. Steven, Sarah, b. 1749, res. Inch Wigtonshire, sh. 31 May 1775, fr. Stranraer to N.C., in *Jackie*. (PRO.T47.12)
6359. Steven, Thomas, b. 1764, res. Inch Wigtonshire, sh. 31 May 1775, fr. Stranraer to N.C., in *Jackie*. (PRO.T47.12)
6360. Steven, William, Covenanter, res. Glasgow, tr. 12 Dec 1678, fr. Leith to West Indies, in *St Michael of Scarborough*. (PC.6.76)
6361. Steven, William, res. Aberdeenshire, d. pre 1740 Jamaica, Edin pr1740 CC8.8.103
6362. Stevens, David, b. 1756, servant, res. Inverness, sh. July 1775, fr. Stornaway to Philadelphia, in *Clementina*. (PRO.T47.12)
6363. Stevenson, James, sailor, sh. 14 July 1698, fr. Leith to Darien, in *St Andrew*, Edin pr1707 CC8.8.83
6364. Stevenson, Janet, b. 1755, servant, res. Aberdeen, sh. May 1775, fr. Leith to Philadelphia, in *Friendship*. (PRO.T47.12)
6365. Stevenson, John, quartermaster, res. Culross Fife, sh. 18 Aug 1699, fr. Clyde to Darien, in *Rising Sun*, Edin pr1708 CC8.8.84
6366. Stevenson, John, sh. pre 1783, sett. Kingston Jamaica. (SRO.RD2.234.1440)
6367. Stevenson, Marion, thief, res. Ayrshire, tr. Sept 1758. (AJ559)
6368. Stevenson, Robert, b. 1708, bookbinder, res. Edinburgh, sh. Aug 1728, fr. London to Antigua. (CLRO\AIA)
6369. Stevenson, William, forger, res. Dykes Ayrshire, tr. Sept 1750. (SM.12.452)
6370. Stewart of Kingarrochie, John, soldier, d. 1699 Darien, Edin pr1707 CC8.8.83
6371. Stewart, ..., physician, sh. pre 1700, sett. Port Morant Jamaica. (DP305)
6372. Stewart, ..., sh. 29 Nov 1773, fr. Greenock to Jamaica, in *Mary of Glasgow*. (SRO.CE60.1.7)
6373. Stewart, Agnes, res. Edinburgh, tr. 8 May 1663, fr. Leith to Barbados, in *Mary*. (EBR186.13.4)
6374. Stewart, Agnes, housebreaker, res. Hilltown Dundee, pts. William Stewart, tr. Apr 1773. (SRO.B59.26.11.16.18)

313

6375. Stewart, Alexander, tailor, res. Kincarrochie, sh. 14 July 1698, fr. Leith to Darien, in *St Andrew*, Edin pr1707 CC8.8.83
6376. Stewart, Alexander, Jacobite, tr. 29 June 1716, fr. Liverpool to Jamaica or Va, in *Elizabeth & Anne*. (SPC.1716.310)(CTB31.208)
6377. Stewart, Alexander, clergyman, sh. 1703, sett. N.Y. (EMA57)
6378. Stewart, Alexander, Covenanter, res. Kirkliston West Lothian, tr. 12 Dec 1678, fr. Leith to West Indies, in *St Michael of Scarborough*. (PC.6.76)
6379. Stewart, Alexander, shopbreaker, tr. July 1750. (AJ135)
6380. Stewart, Alexander, Jacobite, tr. 30 Mar 1716, fr. Liverpool to Antigua, in *Scipio*. (SPC.1716.310)(CTB31.204)
6381. Stewart, Alexander, Jacobite, tr. 7 May 1716, fr. Liverpool to S.C., in *Susannah*. (SPC.1716.309)(CTB31.206)
6382. Stewart, Alexander, Jacobite, tr. 29 June 1716, fr. Liverpool to Jamaica or Va, in *Elizabeth & Anne*, arr. York Va. (SPC.1716.310)(CTB31.208)(VSP.1.186)
6383. Stewart, Alexander, Jacobite, tr. 29 June 1716, fr. Liverpool to Jamaica or Va, in *Elizabeth & Anne*, arr. York Va. (SPC.1716.310)(CTB31.208)(VSP.1.186)
6384. Stewart, Alexander, soldier, sett. Fredericia Ga, d. pre 1748 Ga, PCC pr1748
6385. Stewart, Alexander, b. 1691, registrar, d. 18 May 1763 Charleston S.C. (SM.25.415)
6386. Stewart, Alexander, b. 1713, footman, Jacobite, res. Perthshire, tr. 14 May 1747, fr. Liverpool to Wicomica Md, arr. Port North Potomac Md 5 Aug 1747. (P.3.336)(MR8)(PRO.T1.328)
6387. Stewart, Alexander, b. 1724, mariner, Jacobite, tr. 24 Feb 1747, fr. Liverpool to Va, in *Gildart*, arr. Port North Potomac Md 5 Aug 1747. (P.3.334)(PRO.T1.328)
6388. Stewart, Alexander, b. 1740, farmer, res. Breadalbane Perthshire, sh. Sept 1775, to Wilmington N.C., in *Jupiter*, ch. Charles. (PRO.T47.12)
6389. Stewart, Allan, b. 1731, res. Breadalbane Perthshire, sh. Sept 1775, to Wilmington N.C., in *Jupiter*. (PRO.T47.12)
6390. Stewart, Andrew, res. Edinburgh, sh. 1763, sett. Massacre Rivulet Dominica. (PCCol.4.568)
6391. Stewart, Archibald, surgeon, sh. 1699, fr. London to N.Y. (DP175)
6392. Stewart, Archibald, b. 1745, shoemaker, res. Glen Orchy Argyll, sh. Sept 1775, to Wilmington N.C., in *Jupiter*. (PRO.T47.12)
6393. Stewart, Catherine, b. 1756, spinner, res. Paisley Renfrewshire, sh. Feb 1774, fr. Greenock to N.Y., in *Commerce*. (PRO.T47.12)
6394. Stewart, Charles, robber, tr. Dec 1752, fr. Glasgow to Antigua. (AJ260)
6395. Stewart, Charles, Jacobite, tr. 30 Mar 1716, fr. Liverpool to Antigua, in *Scipio*. (SPC.1716.310)(CTB31.204)

6396. Stewart, Charles, cattlethief, res. Cromdale Inverness-shire, tr. May 1768. (AJ1064)
6397. Stewart, Charles, housebreaker, res. Newton of Glamis Angus, pts. James Stewart, tr. Apr 1773. (AJ1322)
6398. Stewart, Daniel, sailor, res. West Lothian, sh. 14 July 1698, fr. Leith to Darien, in *Unicorn*, Edin pr1707 CC8.8.83
6399. Stewart, Daniel, tr. 1775, fr. Greenock to Va, in *Rainbow*, arr. Port Hampton Va 3 May 1775. (SRO.JC27.10.3)
6400. Stewart, Daniel, Jacobite, tr. 30 Mar 1716, fr. Liverpool to Antigua, in *Scipio*. (SPC.1716.310)(CTB31.204)
6401. Stewart, Daniel, Jacobite, tr. 30 Mar 1716, fr. Liverpool to Antigua, in *Scipio*. (SPC.1716.310)(CTB31.204)
6402. Stewart, Daniel, Jacobite, tr. 30 Mar 1716, fr. Liverpool to Antigua, in *Scipio*. (SPC.1716.310)(CTB31.204)
6403. Stewart, Daniel, Jacobite, tr. 28 July 1716, fr. Liverpool to Va, in *Godspeed*, arr. Md Oct 1716. (SPC.1716.310)(CTB31.209)(HM388)
6404. Stewart, Daniel, pts. Sir John Stewart of Castlemilk, d. 30 Nov 1770 Jamaica. (SM.33.53)
6405. Stewart, David, res. Inverkeillor Angus, d. pre 1698 Barbados. (SRO.PC2.27.109)
6406. Stewart, David, Jacobite, tr. 24 May 1716, fr. Liverpool to Md, in *Friendship*, arr. Md Aug 1716. (SPC.1716.311)(HM387)
6407. Stewart, David, b. 1707, Jacobite, res. Banff, tr. 1747. (P.3.340)(MR128)
6408. Stewart, Donald, oxenthief, res. Dallachie Mortlach Banffshire, tr. Oct 1774. (AJ1396)
6409. Stewart, Donald, Jacobite, tr. 21 Apr 1716, fr. Liverpool to S.C., in *Wakefield*. (SPC.1716.309)(CTB31.205)
6410. Stewart, Donald, Jacobite, tr. 29 June 1716, fr. Liverpool to Jamaica or Va, in *Elizabeth & Anne*, arr. York Va. (SPC.1716.310)(CTB31.208)(VSP.1.186)
6411. Stewart, Donald, horsethief, res. Strathie Aberdeenshire, tr. 1775, fr. Greenock to Va, in *Rainbow*, arr. Port Hampton Va 3 May 1775. (SRO.JC27)(AJ1321)
6412. Stewart, Donald, b. 1756, husbandman, sh. Feb 1774, fr. London to Ga, in *Mary*. (PRO.T47.9\11)
6413. Stewart, Dougald, b. 1735, laborer, res. Glen Orchy Argyll, sh. Sept 1775, to Wilmington N.C., in *Jupiter*, ch. John James Thomas Alexander. (PRO.T47.12)
6414. Stewart, Dougall, merchant, sett. Kingston Jamaica, d. pre 1777. (SRO.RD3.237.36)
6415. Stewart, Dr, physician, sh. pre 1699, sett. Port Morant Jamaica. (DP350)
6416. Stewart, Duncan, Jacobite, tr. 7 May 1716, fr. Liverpool to S.C., in *Susannah*. (SPC.1716.309)(CTB31.206)

6417. Stewart, Duncan, Jacobite, tr. 26 Apr 1716, fr. Liverpool to Jamaica, in
   Two Brothers, arr. Montserrat June 1716.
   (SPC.1716.313)(CTB31.206)(CTP.CC.43)
6418. Stewart, Duncan, b. 1726, cattleherd, Jacobite, res. Breadalbane
   Perthshire, tr. 1747. (P.3.340)
6419. Stewart, Duncan, b. 1726, Jacobite, res. Argyll, tr. 31 Mar 1747, fr.
   London to Jamaica, in *St George or Carteret*, arr. Jamaica 1747.
   (P.3.342)(PRO.CO137.58)
6420. Stewart, Francis, b. 1750, gentleman, res. Glasgow, sh. July 1775, fr.
   Greenock to Antigua, in *Chance*. (PRO.T47.12)
6421. Stewart, Gabriel, blacksmith, thief, res. Calton Edinburgh, tr. Jan 1767.
   (SRO.HCR.I.99)(SM.29.221) (alias 6423)
6422. Stewart, George, res. Wigtownshire, sh. 1774, sett. Newfoundland.
   (PCCol.5.368)
6423. Stewart, Gilbert, blacksmith, thief, res. Calton Edinburgh, tr. Jan 1767.
   (SRO.HCR.I.99)(SM.29.221) (alias 6421)
6424. Stewart, Grizel, infanticide, tr. Apr 1752. (AJ227)
6425. Stewart, Hugh, tinker, sheepstealer, res. East Wemyss Fife, tr. May
   1774. (AJ1376)
6426. Stewart, Hugh, Jacobite, tr. 7 May 1716, fr. Liverpool to S.C., in
   Susannah. (SPC.1716.309)(CTB31.206)
6427. Stewart, James, pts. Thomas Stewart of Kinnaird, sh. 1725, sett. Va.
   (SRO.GD38.3)
6428. Stewart, James, Covenanter, tr. 30 July 1685, fr. Leith to East N.J.
   (PC.11.329)
6429. Stewart, James, Jacobite, tr. 29 June 1716, fr. Liverpool to Jamaica or
   Va, in *Elizabeth & Anne*, arr. York Va.
   (SPC.1716.310)(CTB31.208)(VSP.1.186)
6430. Stewart, James, Jacobite, res. Ardsheal Argyll, tr. 1747.
   (P.3.344)(MR13)
6431. Stewart, James, shipwright, res. Dalguise Dunkeld Perthshire, pts. John
   Stewart, sh. 1749, fr. Gravesend to Charleston S.C., d. 1755
   Charleston, PCC pr1755. (SRO.GD38)(SA28)
6432. Stewart, James, clergyman, sh. 1760, sett. Pa. (UPC655)
6433. Stewart, James, b. 1743, farmer, res. Strathspey, sh. May 1774, fr.
   Greenock to N.Y., in *George*, ch. Mary George Henry Gilbert.
   (PRO.T47.12)
6434. Stewart, James, b. 1752, farmer, res. Strathspey, sh. May 1774, fr.
   Greenock to N.Y., in *George*. (PRO.T47.12)
6435. Stewart, James, b. 1752, clerk bookkeeper, res. Edinburgh, sh. Oct 1774,
   fr. London to Philadelphia, in *Two Friends*. (PRO.T47.9\11)
6436. Stewart, James, b. 1754, farmer, res. Blair Atholl Perthshire, sh. May
   1775, fr. Greenock to N.Y., in *Monimia*. (PRO.T47.12)

6437. Stewart, Janet, sewing mistress, infanticide, res. Corstorphine Midlothian, tr. 1771, fr. Port Glasgow to Md, in *Crawford*, arr. Port Oxford Md 23 July 1771. (SRO.JC27.10.3)

6438. Stewart, Janet, b. 1761, res. Southwick Kirkcudbrightshire, sh. 1775, fr. Kirkcudbright to P.E.I., in *Lovely Nelly*. (PRO.T47.12)

6439. Stewart, Jean, tailor's servant, thief, res. Edinburgh, tr. 1773, fr. Port Glasgow to Va, in *Phoenix*, arr. Port Accomack Va 20 Dec 1773. (SRO.JC27.10.3) (alias 2856)

6440. Stewart, Jean, b. 1753, sh. Apr 1775, fr. Greenock to N.Y., in *Lilly*. (PRO.T47.12)

6441. Stewart, John, thief, res. Atholl Perthshire, pts. Angus Stewart, tr. 28 Nov 1704, fr. Leith to Md. (SRO.PC2.28.307)

6442. Stewart, John, Jacobite, tr. 30 Mar 1716, fr. Liverpool to Antigua, in *Scipio*. (SPC.1716.310)

6443. Stewart, John, sh. pre 1690, sett. Wadboo S.C. & Va. (LJ34)

6444. Stewart, John, Jacobite, tr. 26 Apr 1716, fr. Liverpool to Jamaica, in *Two Brothers*. (CTB31.206)

6445. Stewart, John, Jacobite, tr. 30 Mar 1716, fr. Liverpool to Antigua, in *Scipio*. (SPC.1716.310)(CTB31.204)

6446. Stewart, John, Jacobite, tr. 30 Mar 1716, fr. Liverpool to Antigua, in *Scipio*. (SPC.1716.310)(CTB31.204)

6447. Stewart, John, Jacobite, tr. 29 June 1716, fr. Liverpool to Jamaica or Va, in *Elizabeth & Anne*, arr. York Va. (SPC.1716.310)(CTB31.208)(VSP.1.186)

6448. Stewart, John, Jacobite, tr. 26 Apr 1716, fr. Liverpool to Jamaica, in *Two Brothers*, arr. Montserrat June 1716. (SPC.1716.313)(CTB31.205)(CTP.CC.43)

6449. Stewart, John, Jacobite, tr. 29 June 1716, fr. Liverpool to Jamaica or Va, in *Elizabeth & Anne*, arr. York Va. (SPC.1716.310)(CTB31.208)(VSP.1.185)

6450. Stewart, John, Jacobite, tr. 29 June 1716, fr. Liverpool to Jamaica or Va, in *Elizabeth & Anne*, arr. York Va. (SPC.1716.310)(CTB31.208)(VSP.1.185)

6451. Stewart, John, Jacobite, tr. 29 June 1716, fr. Liverpool to Jamaica or Va, in *Elizabeth & Anne*, arr. York Va. (SPC.1716.310)(CTB31.208)(VSP.1.185)

6452. Stewart, John, Jacobite, tr. 26 Apr 1716, fr. Liverpool to Jamaica, in *Two Brothers*, arr. Montserrat June 1716. (SPC.1716.313)(CTB31.205)(CTP.CC.43)

6453. Stewart, John, Jacobite, tr. 7 May 1716, fr. Liverpool to S.C., in *Susannah*. (CTB31.206)

6454. Stewart, John, Jacobite, tr. 28 July 1716, fr. Liverpool to Va, in *Godspeed*, arr. Md Oct 1716. (SPC.1716.310)(CTB31.209)(HM388)

6455. Stewart, John, thief, res. Ayrshire, tr. Apr 1752. (AJ228)
6456. Stewart, John, sh. pre 1712, sett. Carolina. (SPC.1712.440)
6457. Stewart, John, b. 1705, res. New Church Argyll, sh. Sept 1723, fr.
London to Pa. (CLRO\AIA)
6458. Stewart, John, b. 1727, clothier, res. Glen Orchy Argyll, sh. Sept 1775,
to Wilmington N.C., in *Jupiter*, m. Elizabeth .., ch. John
Margaret Janet Patrick Elizabeth. (PRO.T47.12)
6459. Stewart, John, b. 1729, Jacobite, res. Perthshire, tr. 8 May 1747, to
Antigua. (P.3.346)
6460. Stewart, John, b. 1729, laborer, Jacobite, res. Aberdeen, tr. 5 May 1747,
fr. Liverpool to Leeward Islands, in *Veteran*, arr. Martinique June
1747. (P.3.346)(JAB.2.443)(MR124)(PRO.SP36.102)
6461. Stewart, John, b. 1730, laborer, Jacobite, res. Perthshire, tr. 5 May 1747,
fr. Liverpool to Leeward Islands, in *Veteran*, arr. Martinique June
1747. (P.3.346)(MR207)(PRO.SP36.102)
6462. Stewart, John, b. 1734, Jacobite, res. Fort Augustus Inverness-shire, tr.
31 Mar 1747, fr. London to Barbados , in *Frere*. (P.3.348)(MR160)
6463. Stewart, John, b. 1739, farmer, res. Strathspey, sh. May 1774, fr.
Greenock to Strathspey, in *George*. (PRO.T47.12)
6464. Stewart, John, b. 1751, farmer, res. Strathspey, sh. May 1774, fr.
Greenock to N.Y., in *George*. (PRO.T47.12)
6465. Stewart, John, b. 23 Dec 1753, Dundee Angus, wright, res. Dundee, pts.
Angus Stewart & Christian McFearson, sh. Aug 1774, fr.
Greenock to Philadelphia, in *Magdalene*. (PRO.T47.12)
6466. Stewart, Joseph, thief, res. Ayrshire, tr. Apr 1752. (AJ228)
6467. Stewart, Kenneth, b. 1735, shipmaster, res. Breadalbane Perthshire, sh.
Sept 1775, to Wilmington N.C., in *Jupiter*, m. Isobel .., ch.
Alexander John Banco Christian William. (PRO.T47.12)
6468. Stewart, Malcolm, Jacobite, tr. 29 June 1716, fr. Liverpool to Jamaica or
Va, in *Elizabeth & Anne*, arr. York Va.
(SPC.1716.310)(CTB31.208)(VSP.1.186)
6469. Stewart, Margaret, thief & pickpocket, res. Spittal Roxburghshire, tr.
Sept 1766, m. William Wilson. (AJ979)
6470. Stewart, Marjory, whore & thief, res. Edinburgh, tr. 28 Nov 1704, fr.
Leith to Md. (SRO.PC2.28.307)
6471. Stewart, Mrs, b. 1736, res. Glasgow, sh. May 1775, fr. Greenock to
N.Y., in *Lilly*. (PRO.T47.12)
6472. Stewart, Nathaniel, b. 26 Sept 1710, Forgue Aberdeenshire, horsethief,
res. Aberdeenshire, tr. May 1766. (AJ959)
6473. Stewart, Neil, Jacobite, tr. 7 May 1716, fr. Liverpool to S.C., in
Susannah. (SPC.1716.309)(CTB31.206)
6474. Stewart, Neil, Jacobite, tr. 7 May 1716, fr. Liverpool to S.C., in
Susannah. (SPC.1716.309)(CTB31.206)

6475. Stewart, Patrick, Covenanter, res. Argyll, tr. Aug 1685, fr. Leith to Jamaica. (PC.11.329)
6476. Stewart, Patrick, Jacobite, tr. 7 May 1716, fr. Liverpool to S.C., in *Susannah*. (SPC.1716.309)(CTB31.206)
6477. Stewart, Patrick, Jacobite, tr. 29 June 1716; fr. Liverpool to Jamaica or Va, in *Elizabeth & Anne*, arr. York Va. (SPC.1716.310)(CTB31.208)(VSP.1.186)
6478. Stewart, Peter, thief, res. Ayrshire, tr. Apr 1752. (AJ228)
6479. Stewart, Richard, b. 1754, baker, res. Edinburgh, sh. May 1774, fr. London to Md, in *Brothers*. (PRO.T47.12)
6480. Stewart, Robert, clerk, sh. pre 1705, sett. Barbados. (SPC.1705.409)
6481. Stewart, Robert, Jacobite, tr. 29 Apr 1716, fr. Liverpool to Va, in *Elizabeth & Anne*. (SPC.1716.310)(CTB31.208)
6482. Stewart, Robert, thief, res. Stirlingshire, tr. Apr 1774. (AJ1370)
6483. Stewart, Robert, Jacobite, tr. 29 June 1716, fr. Liverpool to Jamaica or Va, in *Elizabeth & Anne*, arr. York Va. (SPC.1716.310)(CTB31.208)(VSP.1.186)
6484. Stewart, Robert, b. 1756, smith, res. Glasgow, sh. Oct 1774, fr. Greenock to Philadelphia, in *Sally*. (PRO.T47.12)
6485. Stewart, Robert, b. 1757, laborer, res. Paisley Renfrewshire, sh. Feb 1774, fr. Greenock to N.Y., in *Commerce*. (PRO.T47.12)
6486. Stewart, Robert, b. 1759, laborer, res. Southwick Kirkcudbrightshire, sh. 1775, fr. Kirkcudbright to P.E.I., in *Lovely Nelly*. (PRO.T47.12)
6487. Stewart, Thomas, Jacobite, tr. 1747. (P.3.348)(MR76)
6488. Stewart, Walter, Jacobite, tr. 25 June 1716, fr. Liverpool to St Kitts, in *Hockenhill*. (SPC.1716.312)(CTB31.207)
6489. Stewart, William, clergyman edu. Glasgow Uni, sh. 1718, sett. Monokin & Wicomico. (APC.192)
6490. Stewart, William, cattlethief, tr. Mar 1767. (CHOpp1767.285) (alias 6268)
6491. Stewart, William, Jacobite, tr. 30 Mar 1716, fr. Liverpool to Antigua, in *Scipio*. (SPC.1716.310)(CTB31.204)
6492. Stewart, William, Jacobite, res. Ardsheal Argyll, tr. 22 Apr 1747, fr. Liverpool to Va, in *Johnson*, arr. Port Oxford Md 5 Aug 1747. (P.3.348)(PRO.T1.328)(MR12)
6493. Stewart, William, weaver, rioter, res. Paisley Renfrewshire, tr. 1752. (SM.14.268)
6494. Stewart, William, cattlethief, tr. Mar 1767. (SRO.RH2.4.255) (alias 6232)
6495. Stewart, William, soldier, housebreaker, res. Hilltown Dundee, tr. Apr 1773. (AJ1322)
6496. Stewart, William, res. Renfrewshire, sh. pre 1776, sett. Crawl River Clarendon Jamaica. (SRO.RD2.220.656)

6497. Stewart, William, b. 1750, merchant, res. Ayr, sh. July 1775, fr. Greenock to Jamaica, in *Isobella*. (PRO.T47.12)
6498. Stewart, William, b. 1751, mason, sh. Sept 1775, fr. Newcastle to Ga, in *Georgia Packet*, sett. Friendsborough Ga. (PRO.T47.9\11)
6499. Stewart, William, b. 1752, wright, res. Galloway, sh. May 1774, fr. Stranraer to N.Y., in *Gale*. (PRO.T47.12)
6500. Stirke, George, clergyman, sh. 1623, sett. Bermuda, d. 1637 Bermuda. (AP90)
6501. Stirling of Achyle, Alexander, soldier, res. Port of Menteith Perthshire, ch. Joan, d. 1699 Darien, Edin pr1710 CC8.8.84
6502. Stirling, Charles, planter, sh. pre 1765, sett. Jamaica. (SRO.GD24)
6503. Stirling, George, soldier, res. Edinburgh, pts. John Stirling, d. pre 1749 Ga, PCC pr1749
6504. Stirling, Hugh, merchant, res. Glasgow, sh. 1734, sett. Ogychee Ga. (PRO.CO5.670.127)
6505. Stirling, Hugh, sh. 1737, sett. Ogychee Ga. (PRO.CO5.640.45)
6506. Stirling, James, clergyman, sh. 1737, sett. Md. (EMA57)
6507. Stirling, Mabel, gypsy, res. Roxburghshire, tr. 1 Jan 1715, fr. Glasgow to Va. (GR530)
6508. Stirling, Patrick, res. Kippendavie Perthshire, d. 12 Dec 1775 Jamaica. (SM.38.163)
6509. Stirling, Robert, merchant, res. Glasgow, d. abroad(Darien?), Edin pr1707 CC8.8.83
6510. Stirling, William, merchant, res. Glasgow, sh. 1734, sett. Ogychee Ga. (PRO.CO5.670.128)
6511. Stirling, William, b. 1746, weaver, res. Glasgow, sh. May 1774, fr. Greenock to N.Y., in *Matty*, ch. John Mary. (PRO.T47.12)
6512. Stitt, Edward, Covenanter, res. Durisdeer Dumfries-shire, tr. Aug 1685, fr. Leith to Jamaica. (PC.11.145)(ETR372)
6513. Stiven, William, merchant, res. Aberdeen, pts. William Stiven & Barbara Wilkie, sh. 1715, sett. Gunaboa Jamaica, d. pre 1734. (APB.3.3)
6514. Stobie, Adam, Covenanter, res. Lascar, tr. 12 Dec 1678, fr. Leith to West Indies, in *St Michael of Scarborough*. (PC.6.76)
6515. Stobo, Archibald, b. 1674, clergyman edu. Edinburgh Uni, sh. 18 Aug 1699, fr. Clyde to Darien, in *Rising Sun*, sett. Charleston S.C., m. Elizabeth Jean Park, ch. Jean, d. 1741 S.C. (F.7.665)(SHR.1904.416)
6516. Stobo, Robert, merchant, res. Glasgow, sh. pre 1750, sett. Va. (SRO.SC36.63.2)
6517. Stoddart, Lawrence, b. 1750, laborer, res. Greenock Renfrewshire, sh. Aug 1774, fr. Greenock to Philadelphia, in *Magdalene*. (PRO.T47.12)
6518. Stonyer, William, soldier, thief, tr. Sept 1754. (SM.16.448)

6519. Storie, Francis, sailor, res. Linlithgow West Lothian, sh. 14 July 1698, fr. Leith to Darien, in *St Andrew*, d. 1699 West Indies, Edin pr1707 CC8.8.83

6520. Storie, James, tr. May 1684, fr. Glasgow to Carolina. (PC.8.710)

6521. Stormonth, James, res. Pitscandly Angus, d. pre 1761 St Kitts, Edin pr1761 CC8.8.118

6522. Stormonth, James, b. 2 Apr 1705, Jacobite, res. Kingoldrum Angus, pts. Thomas Stormonth of Kinclune & Isobel Hood, tr. 1747, sett. West Indies, m. Elizabeth Farquhar. (OR163)

6523. Strachan, Adam, schoolmaster, sh. 1700, to Leeward Islands. (EMA57)

6524. Strachan, Alexander, huckster, thief, res. Loanhead, tr. Oct 1773. (AJ1343)

6525. Strachan, Charles, Jacobite, tr. 21 Apr 1716, fr. Liverpool to S.C., in *Wakefield*. (SPC.1716.309)(CTB31.205)

6526. Strachan, David, clergyman, sh. 1715, to Va. (EMA57)

6527. Strachan, James, clergyman edu. Edinburgh Uni 1702, sh. 1713, to Jamaica. (EMA57)

6528. Strachan, James, tailor, res. Aberdeen, pts. Patrick Strachan & Jean Rait, sh. 1711, to Va, sett. Providence R.I., d. pre Sept 1723 Jamaica. (APB.2.153)

6529. Strachan, James, b. 1728, student edu. Aberdeen Uni, Jacobite, res. Kincardineshire, tr. 24 Feb 1747, fr. Liverpool to Va, in *Gildart*, arr. Port North Potomac Md 5 Aug 1747. (P.3.352)(JAB.2.444)(MR76)(PRO.T1.328)

6530. Strachan, James, b. 1756, laborer, sh. Nov 1774, fr. Bristol to Md, in *Sampson*. (PRO.T47.9\11)

6531. Strachan, John, sh. Dec 1698, fr. Liverpool to Va, *Globe*. (LRO.HQ325.2.FRE)

6532. Strachan, John, b. 1758, weaver, res. Paisley Renfrewshire, sh. Feb 1774, fr. Greenock to N.Y., in *Commerce*. (PRO.T47.12)

6533. Strachan, Margaret, thief, res. Aberdeen, tr. Nov 1667, fr. Aberdeen to Va. (ABR.ARC1667)

6534. Strachan, Margaret, tr. 1696, fr. Newhaven to Va. (SRO.RH15.14.58)

6535. Strang, Christopher, Covenanter, res. Kilbride, tr. 5 Sept 1685, fr. Leith to East N.J., in *Henry & Francis*. (PC.11.154)

6536. Strange, David, clergyman, res. Cabrach Aberdeenshire, tr. Dec 1738. (SRO.JC27)

6537. Straton, Janet, tr. 1696, fr. Newhaven to Va. (SRO.RH15.14.58)

6538. Straton, Thomas, b. 25 July 1704, Dunnottar, res. Stonehaven Kincardineshire, pts. Alexander Straton & Christian Robertson, d. May 1777 Jamaica. (Dunnottar Gs)

6539. Stratton, James, b. 1672, mason, Jacobite, res. Morayshire, tr. 24 Apr 1747, fr. Liverpool to Va, in *Johnson*, arr. Port Oxford Md 5 Aug 1747. (P.3.356)(PRO.T1.328)

6540. Stretton, James, b. 1651, sh. May 1683, fr. London to Md, in *Elizabeth & Mary*. (CLRO\AIA)

6541. Stroak, William, Jacobite, tr. 29 June 1716, fr. Liverpool to Jamaica or Va, in *Elizabeth & Anne*, arr. York Va. (SPC.1716.310)(CTB31.208)(VSP.1.186)

6542. Strock, James, Jacobite, tr. 30 Mar 1716, fr. Liverpool to Antigua, in *Scipio*. (SPC.1716.310)(CTB31.204)

6543. Stuart, Alexander, b. 1712, soapboiler, res. Stranraer Wigtonshire, sh. Nov 1731, fr. London to Jamaica. (CLRO\AIA)

6544. Stuart, Angus, thief, tr. Mar 1758, fr. Aberdeen to Va, in *Leathly*. (AJ533)

6545. Stuart, Anthony, b. 1666, sh. 10 Apr 1700, fr. Liverpool. (LRO.HQ325.2.FRE)

6546. Stuart, Callum, servant, Jacobite, res. Milton of Redcastle Ross & Cromarty, tr. 1747. (MR87)(LP81)

6547. Stuart, Charles, merchant, res. North Leith Midlothian, pts. John Stuart & Henrietta Burnett, sh. pre 1718, sett. Carolina, Edin pr1718 CC8.8.87

6548. Stuart, David, b. 1697, Jacobite, res. Ross-shire, tr. 20 Mar 1747. (P.3.340)(MR212)

6549. Stuart, Hugh, b. 1688, gardener, Jacobite, res. Fort Augustus Inverness-shire, tr. 31 Mar 1747, fr. London to Barbados, in *Frere*. (P.3.342)(MR160)

6550. Stuart, James, clergyman, sh. 1766, to Va. (EMA57)

6551. Stuart, James, chairman, bigamist, res. Edinburgh, tr. Dec 1752, fr. Glasgow to Antigua. (AJ260)

6552. Stuart, John, merchant, res. North Leith Midlothian, sh. post 1680, sett. Carolina, m. Henrietta Burnett, ch. John Charles, d. pre 1718, Edin pr1718 CC8.8.87

6553. Stuart, John, merchant, res. North Leith Midlothian, pts. John Stuart & Henrietta Burnett, sh. pre 1718, sett. Carolina, Edin pr1718 CC8.8.87

6554. Stuart, John, b. 1747, laborer, res. Leswalt Wigtonshire, sh. 31 May 1775, fr. Stranraer to N.Y., in *Jackie*, m. Jean McWhinnie, ch. Mary Margaret. (PRO.T47.12)

6555. Stuart, John Dow, horsethief, res. Achlauchrick Kilmaveonaig Blair Atholl Perthshire, tr. May 1756. (SRO.B59.26.11.4.21) (alias 3895)

6556. Stuart, Lady Christian Elizabeth, res. Traquair Peebles-shire, pts. John Stuart & Christian Anstruther, sh. pre 1779, sett. Va, m. Cyrus Griffin. (SRO.RD3.239.683)

6557. Stuart, Robert, schoolmaster, sh. 3 Jan 1689, to Jamaica. (Rawl.A306.93)

6558. Stuart, Robert, Jacobite, tr. 29 June 1716, fr. Liverpool to Jamaica or Va, in *Elizabeth & Anne*, arr. York Va. (SPC.1716.310)(VSP.1.186)
6559. Stuart, William, sh. 1691, d. 25 Oct 1719 York Fort Hudson Bay. (HBRS.25.413)
6560. Stuart, William, clergyman, sh. 1747, to Pa. (EMA57)
6561. Stuart, William, sh. 1691, sett. Hudson Bay, d. 25 Oct 1719 York Fort. (HBRS.25.413)
6562. Stubbs, Robert, Jacobite, tr. 24 May 1716, fr. Liverpool to Md, in *Friendship*, arr. Md 20 Aug 1716. (SPC.1716.311)(HM387)
6563. Sullivan, Jeremy, b. 1727, Jacobite, res. Cork, tr. 1747. (MR63)
6564. Summers, Bartholemew, b. 1749, butcher, res. Elgin Morayshire, sh. May 1774, fr. Greenock to N.Y., in *George*. (PRO.T47.12)
6565. Summers, Janet, b. 1743, res. Glasgow, sh. May 1775, fr. Greenock to N.Y., in *Lilly*. (PRO.T47.12)
6566. Summers, Margaret, b. 1748, res. Paisley Renfrewshire, sh. Apr 1775, fr. Greenock to N.Y., in *Lilly*. (PRO.T47.12)
6567. Summers, Robert, b. 1747, joiner, res. Elgin Morayshire, sh. May 1774, fr. Greenock to N.Y., in *George*. (PRO.T47.12)
6568. Sushan, William, yeoman, res. Edinburgh, sh. 14 July 1698, fr. Leith to Darien, in *Caledonia*, Edin pr1707 CC8.8.83
6569. Suster, Margaret, b. 1756, spinner, res. Paisley Renfrewshire, sh. Feb 1774, fr. Greenock to N.Y., in *Commerce*. (PRO.T47.12)
6570. Sutherland, Adam, housebreaker, res. Grange Prestonpans East Lothian, tr. Aug 1745. (SRO.HCR.I.72)
6571. Sutherland, Adam, Jacobite, tr. 22 Apr 1747, fr. Liverpool to Va, in *Johnson*, arr. Port Oxford Md 5 Aug 1747. (PRO.T1.328)
6572. Sutherland, Adam, b. 1691, laborer, Jacobite, res. Sutherland, tr. 5 May 1747, fr. Liverpool to Leeward Islands, in *Veteran*, arr. Martinique June 1747. (P.3.358)(MR124)(PRO.SP36.102)
6573. Sutherland, Alan, b. 1728, Jacobite, tr. 1747, fr. Tilbury. (P.3.358)
6574. Sutherland, Alexander, housebreaker & thief, res. Inverness-shire, tr. Sept 1763. (SM.25.579)
6575. Sutherland, Alexander, b. 1713, cheeseseller, Jacobite, res. Caithness, tr. 30 Mar 1747, fr. London to Jamaica, in *St George or Carteret*, arr. Jamaica 1747. (P.3.358)(MR30)(PRO.CO137.58)
6576. Sutherland, Alexander, b. 1728, husbandman, Jacobite, res. Ballyhardrie Sutherland, tr. 31 Mar 1747, fr. London to Barbados , in *Frere*. (P.3.358)(MR88)
6577. Sutherland, Catherine, b. 1736, servant, res. Stornaway Isle of Lewis, sh. Nov 1774, fr. Stornaway to N.Y., in *Peace & Plenty*. (PRO.T47.12)
6578. Sutherland, Daniel, vagrant & pickpocket, res. Perthshire, tr. Oct 1772. (AJ1293)

6579. Sutherland, Daniel, pickpocket & vagrant, tr. 1773, fr. Glasgow to Va, in *Donald*, arr. Port James Upper District Va 13 Mar 1773. (SRO.B59.26.116.21)(SRO.JC27.10.3)(AJ1293)(SM.34.579)

6580. Sutherland, Donald, planter, res. Tain Ross & Cromarty, pts. Rev John & Ann Sutherland, sh. pre 1780, sett. St George Surry Co Jamaica. (SRO.RD2.228.652)

6581. Sutherland, Francis, b. 1756, weaver, res. Wick Caithness, sh. Sept 1775, fr. Kirkwall to Savannah Ga, in *Marlborough*, sett. Richmond Co Ga. (PRO.T47.12)

6582. Sutherland, George, b. 1746, farmer, res. Neilston Renfrewshire, sh. Oct 1774, fr. Greenock to Philadelphia, in *Sally*. (PRO.T47.12)

6583. Sutherland, Janet, thief, res. Aberdeen, tr. Feb 1766. (AJ947)

6584. Sutherland, John, Jacobite, tr. 30 Mar 1716, fr. Liverpool to Antigua, in *Scipio*. (SPC.1716.310)(CTB31.204)

6585. Sutherland, John, b. 1684, res. Elgin Morayshire, pts. James Sutherland, sh. 1699, fr. Liverpool. (LRO.HQ325.2.FRE)

6586. Sutherland, John, b. 1723, soldier, Jacobite, tr. 1747. (P.3.360)

6587. Sutherland, John, b. 1725, husbandman, Jacobite, res. Dunbeath Caithness, tr. 31 Mar 1747, fr. London to Jamaica, in *St George or Carteret*, arr. Jamaica 1747. (P.3.360)(MR88)(PRO.T1.328)

6588. Sutherland, John, b. 1753, servant, res. Duffus Morayshire, sh. July 1775, fr. Stornaway to Philadelphia, in *Clementina*. (PRO.T47.12)

6589. Sutherland, Katherine, b. 1747, servant, res. Stornaway Isle of Lewis, sh. May 1774, fr. Stornaway to Philadelphia, in *Friendship*. (PRO.T47.12)

6590. Sutherland, Neil, b. 1712, soldier, Jacobite, res. Caithness, tr. 31 Mar 1747, fr. London to Barbados , in *Frere*. (P.3.360)(MR88)

6591. Sutherland, William, b. 1717, husbandman, Jacobite, res. Dunbeath Caithness, tr. 31 Mar 1747, fr. London to Jamaica, in *St George or Carteret*, arr. Jamaica 1747. (P.3.360)(MR88)(PRO.CO137.58)

6592. Sutherland, William, b. 4 Jan 1734, Watten Caithness, Jacobite, res. Caithness, pts. Neil Sutherland & Christian Shearer, tr. 31 Mar 1747, fr. London to Barbados , in *Frere*. (P.3.360)

6593. Sutherland, William, b. 1734, farmer, res. Strathalidale Reay Caithness, sh. Apr 1774, to Wilmington N.C., in *Bachelor of Leith*. (PRO.T47.12)

6594. Sutherland, William, b. 1750, farmer, res. Latheron Caithness, sh. Apr 1774, to Wilmington N.C., in *Bachelor of Leith*. (PRO.T47.12)

6595. Sutherland, William, b. 1760, servant, res. Dunnet Caithness, sh. Sept 1775, fr. Kirkwall to Savannah Ga, in *Marlborough*, sett. Richmond Co Ga. (PRO.T47.12)

6596. Suttie, David, mariner, res. Kirkcaldy Fife, pts. James Suttie & Bessie Law, sh. 14 July 1698, fr. Leith to Darien, in *Caledonia*, Edin pr1707 CC8.8.83

6597. Sutton, Andrew, b. 1753, gentleman, sh. Feb 1774, fr. London to N.Y.,
in *Earl Dunmore*. (PRO.T47.12)
6598. Swan, David, thief, res. Dumfries-shire, tr. Apr 1752. (AJ227)
6599. Swan, James, res. Prestonpans East Lothian, sh. Feb 1684, to Hudson
Bay. (HBRS.9.203)
6600. Swan, John, Covenanter, tr. 30 July 1685, fr. Leith to East N.J.
(PC.11.329)
6601. Swan, Robert, b. 1753, laborer, res. Kilmacolm Renfrewshire, sh. Oct
1774, fr. Greenock to Philadelphia, in *Sally*. (PRO.T47.12)
6602. Swanston, Charles, servant, housebreaker, res. Thirdistoft, tr. July 1769.
(SRO.JC27.D35)(AJ1126)
6603. Swanston, John, army pensioner, housebreaker & thief, res. Caithness, tr.
Sept 1768. (AJ1080)
6604. Swanston, William, Covenanter, res. Loudoun Ayrshire, tr. 15 Nov
1679, fr. Leith. (SRO.JC27.10.3)
6605. Swinger, Alexander, Jacobite, tr. 24 May 1716, fr. Liverpool to Va, in
Friendship, arr. Md Aug 1716. (SPC.1716.311)(HM387) (alias
6110)
6606. Swinhoe, James, Jacobite, tr. 7 May 1716, fr. Liverpool to S.C., in
Susannah. (SPC.1716.309)(CTB31.206)
6607. Swinton, Alexander, ensign, res. Glasgow, pts. William Swinton & Jean
Wright, d. 6 Feb 1699 Darien, Edin pr1707 CC8.8.83. (DP86)
6608. Swinton, Douglas, Jacobite, tr. 1747, to Jamaica, in *St George or
Carteret*, arr. Jamaica 1747. (PRO.CO137.58)
6609. Swinton, John, Quaker, res. Teviotdale Roxburghshire, tr. 5 Sept 1685,
fr. Leith to East N.J., in *Henry & Francis*. (PC.11.154)
6610. Swinton, William, merchant, res. Stirling, sh. 18 Aug 1699, fr. Clyde to
Darien, in *Rising Sun*. (RSB.91)
6611. Sword, Humphrey, Jacobite, tr. 29 July 1716, fr. Liverpool to Va, in
Godspeed, arr. Md Oct 1716.
(SPC.1716.310)(CTB31.209)(HM389)
6612. Sword, John, Jacobite, tr. 25 June 1716, fr. Liverpool to St Kitts, in
Hockenhill. (SPC.1716.312)(CTB31.207)
6613. Sym, Robert, physician edu. Glasgow Uni 1771, res. Glasgow, pts. John
Sym, d. 7 Sept 1807 Montreal. (MAGU94)
6614. Syme, Hugh, Covenanter, res. Eaglesham Renfrewshire, tr. June 1684, fr.
Glasgow, in *Pelican*. (PC.9.208)
6615. Syme, John, Covenanter, res. Eaglesham Renfrewshire, tr. 1684, fr.
Glasgow, in *Pelican*. (PC.9.208)
6616. Syme, John, cook, res. Earlsferry Fife, sh. 18 Aug 1699, fr. Clyde to
Darien, in *Rising Sun*, m. Katherine Downie, Edin pr1707
CC8.8.83
6617. Syme, Patrick, tr. 7 Dec 1665, fr. Leith to Barbados. (ETR104)

6618. Syme, William, Covenanter, res. Eaglesham Renfrewshire, tr. June 1684, fr. Glasgow, in *Pelican*. (PC.9.208)

6619. Symes, William, b. 1753, saddler, sh. Feb 1774, fr. London to Va, in *Betsy*. (PRO.T47.9\11)

6620. Symmer, Alexander, merchant, res. Edinburgh, pts. Alexander Symmer, sh. pre 1756, to Md. (SM.18.524)

6621. Symmer, Andrew, merchant, res. Edinburgh, pts. Alexander Symmer, sh. pre 1756, to Md. (SM.18.524)

6622. Taggart, John, Covenanter, res. Roaderheuk Annandale Dumfries-shire, tr. 5 Sept 1685, fr. Leith to East N.J., in *Henry & Francis*. (PC.11.155)

6623. Tailfer, Patrick, physician, res. Edinburgh, sh. 1733, sett. River Neuse Ga. (PRO.CO5.670.106)

6624. Tailor, George, physician edu. Glasgow Uni, sh. pre 1771, sett. St Kitts. (SRO.NRAS726.8)

6625. Tait, Elizabeth, b. 1747, servant, res. Bower Caithness, sh. Sept 1775, fr. Kirkwall to Savannah Ga, in *Marlborough*. (PRO.T47.12) (alias 4979)

6626. Tait, James, seaman, res. Burntisland Fife, pts. William Tait & Bethea Hunter, sh. 14 July 1698, fr. Leith to Darien, in *Endeavour*, Edin pr1707 CC8.8.83

6627. Tait, John, Covenanter, res. Camphill Dumfriesshire, tr. Oct 1684. (PC.10.591)

6628. Tait, Mary, thief & gypsy, res. Dumfriesshire, tr. May 1739. (SRO.JC.12.5)

6629. Tait, Thomas, Jacobite, tr. 30 Mar 1716, fr. Liverpool to Antigua, in *Scipio*. (SPC.1716.310)(CTB31.204)

6630. Tait, William, thief & gypsy, res. Dumfries-shire, tr. May 1739. (SRO.JC.12.5)

6631. Tankard, Walter, Jacobite, tr. 29 June 1716, fr. Liverpool to Jamaica or Va, in *Elizabeth & Anne*, arr. York Va. (SPC.1716.310(CTB31.208)(VSP.1.185)

6632. Tannis, Agnes, Covenanter, tr. 5 Sept 1685, fr. Leith to East N.J., in *Henry & Francis*. (PC.11.154)

6633. Tanyhill, John, b. 1755, farmer, res. Glasgow, sh. Feb 1774, fr. Greenock to N.Y., in *Commerce*. (PRO.T47.12)

6634. Tanyhill, Robert, b. 1749, farmer, res. Glasgow, sh. Feb 1774, fr. Greenock to N.Y., in *Commerce*. (PRO.T47.12)

6635. Tassie, William, b. 1748, smith, res. Glasgow, sh. Apr 1775, fr. Greenock to Salem, in *Glasgow Packet*. (PRO.T47.12)

6636. Tate, John, b. 1749, carpenter, sh. Aug 1774, fr. Whitby to Savannah Ga, in *Marlborough*. (PRO.T47.9\11)

6637. Taylor, Agnes, thief, res. Aberdeen, tr. 13 Mar 1754, fr. Aberdeen, in *Fanny & Betty*, m. John Gunn. (SM.15.468)

6638. Taylor, Agnes, thief, res. Paisley Renfrewshire, tr. May 1770. (SM.32.337)
6639. Taylor, Agnes, tr. 13 Mar 1754, fr. Aberdeen, in *Fanny & Betty*. (ABR
6640. Taylor, Alexander, seaman, res. Burntisland Fife, sh. 14 July 1698, fr. Leith to Darien, in *St Andrew*, Edin pr1707 CC8.8.83
6641. Taylor, Alexander, mason, rioter, res. Aberdeen, tr. May 1767. (AJ1011)(SM.29.325)
6642. Taylor, Alexander, b. 1709, laborer, Jacobite, res. Edinburgh, tr. 22 Apr 1747, fr. Liverpool to Va, in *Johnson*, arr. Port Oxford Md 5 Aug 1747. (P.3.362)(PRO.T1.328)
6643. Taylor, Andrew, b. 1712, husbandman, res. Kilrenny Fife, sh. Mar 1730, fr. London to Jamaica. (CLRO\AIA)
6644. Taylor, Andrew, b. 1757, tailor, res. Irvine Ayrshire, sh. Jan 1774, fr. Greenock to Jamaica, in *Janet*. (SRO.CE60.1.7)
6645. Taylor, Anne, b. 1756, servant, res. Findhorn Morayshire, sh. July 1775, fr. Stornaway to Philadelphia, in *Clementina*. (PRO.T47.12)
6646. Taylor, Archibald, res. Glasgow, pts. James Taylor & Janet Marr, sett. Tobago, d. pre 1775 Tobago, Edin pr1775 CC8.8.123
6647. Taylor, Christopher, Jacobite, res. Wigan Lancashire, tr. 21 July 1748. (P.3.364)(MR195)
6648. Taylor, James, sailor, res. Greenock Renfrewshire, sh. 18 Aug 1699, fr. Clyde to Darien, in *Hope*, Edin pr1707 CC8.8.83
6649. Taylor, James, Jacobite, tr. 30 Mar 1716, fr. Liverpool to Antigua, in *Scipio*. (SPC.1716.310)(CTB31.204)
6650. Taylor, James, smith & nailer, housebreaker, res. The Folly Redheugh Cockpen Midlothian, tr. Aug 1775. (SRO.HCR.I.113)
6651. Taylor, James, res. Aberdeen, pts. Robert Taylor, sh. Sept 1667, to Va. (REA90)
6652. Taylor, James, b. 1750, wright, res. Galloway, sh. 1775, fr. Dumfries to P.E.I., in *Lovely Nelly*. (PRO.T47.12)
6653. Taylor, John, goldsmith, res. Greenock Renfrewshire, m. Elizabeth Morrison, d. St Eustatia March 1783, Edin pr1784 CC8.8.126
6654. Taylor, John, b. 1702, barber, res. Montrose Angus, sh. Feb 1720, fr. London to Barbados. (CLRO\AIA)
6655. Taylor, John, b. 1719, servant, Jacobite, res. Boharm Banffshire, tr. 22 Apr 1747, fr. Liverpool to Va, in *Johnson*, arr. Port Oxford Md 5 Aug 1747. (P.3.366)(MR128)(PRO.T1.328)
6656. Taylor, John, b. 1749, bricklayer, res. Argyll, sh. Aug 1774, fr. Greenock to Philadelphia, in *Magdalene*. (PRO.T47.12)
6657. Taylor, Joseph, horsethief, tr. Apr 1767. (SM.29.221)
6658. Taylor, Margaret, whore, res. Edinburgh, tr. 2 Feb 1697. (SRO.PC2.26)
6659. Taylor, Nathaniel, Fife(?), clergyman, sh. post 1703, sett. Marlborough Patuxent, d. 1710. (F.7.665)

6660. Taylor, Peter, carpenter, res. Gartmore Perthshire, tr. 28 Dec 1750, to Cape Fear N.C. (SRO.B59.26.11.15.28)
6661. Taylor, Robert, robber, tr. 1771, fr. Port Glasgow to Md, in *Crawford*, arr. Port Oxford Md 23 July 1771. (SRO.JC.27.10.3)
6662. Taylor, Thomas, res. Edinburgh, tr. 11 Aug 1753. (SRO.JC3.29.268)
6663. Taylor, William, forger, res. Halltree of Stow Midlothian, tr. Aug 1753. (SM.15.420)
6664. Telfer, Alexander, merchant, res. Kirkcudbright, pts. David Telfer, sh. pre 1779. (SRO.RD2.225.1299)
6665. Telfer, Peter, planter, d. 24 Dec 1698 Darien. (NLS.RY2b8\19)
6666. Telford, John, b. 1758, husbandman, sh. Mar 1774, fr. Whitehaven to Va, in *Ann*. (PRO.T47.9\11)
6667. Temple, William, res. Linton Roxburghshire, tr. 12 Dec 1678, fr. Leith to West Indies, in *St Michael of Scarborough*. (PC.6.76)
6668. Templeton, Isobel, thief, res. Sorn Ayrshire, pts. James Templeton, tr. 1772, fr. Glasgow to Va, in *Brilliant*, arr. Port Hampton Va 7 Oct 1772. (SRO.JC.27.10.3)(AJ1270)
6669. Templeton, William, b. 1747, weaver, res. Paisley Renfrewshire, sh. Feb 1774, fr. Greenock to N.Y., in *Commerce*, m. Margaret .. (PRO.T47.12)
6670. Tennant, James, Covenanter, tr. Aug 1684, fr. Leith to Carolina. (PC.9.95)
6671. Tenter, William, d. 11 Dec 1698 Darien. (NLS.RY2b8\19)
6672. Teviotdale, James, horsethief, res. Clatt Aberdeenshire, tr. Jan 1754. (AJ309)
6673. Thain, Daniel, b. 1721, St Nicholas Aberdeen, clergyman edu. Aberdeen Uni, res. Aberdeen, pts. Robert Thain & Jean Robertson, sh. 1750, sett. Connecticut Farms N.J., d. 1763. (F.7.666)
6674. Thare, .., council clerk, sh. pre 1705, sett. Barbados. (SPC.1705.410)
6675. Thom, John, thief, res. Glasgow, pts. James Thom, tr. 28 Nov 1704, fr. Leith to Md. (SRO.PC2.28.307)
6676. Thom, Robert, b. 1731, laborer, Jacobite, res. Angus, tr. 5 May 1747, fr. Liverpool to Leeward Islands, in *Veteran*, arr. Martinique June 1747. (P.3.370)(MR111)(PRO.SP36.102)
6677. Thomas, John, sh. 1637, to Barbados. (SRO.GD34.925)
6678. Thomas, John Edward, Jacobite, res. Shropshire, tr. 1747. (P.3.371)(MR137)
6679. Thomas, Robert, b. 1748, tailor, res. Paisley Renfrewshire, sh. Apr 1775, fr. Greenock to N.Y., in *Lilly*. (PRO.T47.12)
6680. Thompson, Alexander, merchant, d. 1770 N.Y. (SM.32.630)
6681. Thompson, Andrew, b. 1673, Stonehaven Kincardineshire, clergyman edu. Marischal Col Aberdeen 1691, sh. 1712, sett. Hampton Va, d. Sept 1719 Va. (OD15)((EMA58)

6682. Thompson, Daniel, Jacobite, tr. 29 June 1716, fr. Liverpool to Jamaica or Va, in *Elizabeth & Anne*, arr. York Va. (SPC.1716.310)(CTB31.208)(VSP.1.185)
6683. Thompson, George, Jacobite, tr. 24 May 1716, fr. Liverpool to Md, in *Friendship*, arr. Md Aug 1716. (SPC.1716.311)(HM387)(MdArch34.164)
6684. Thompson, James, b. 1680, sh. Mar 1699, fr. Liverpool to N.E., in *Virginia Merchant*. (LRO.HQ325.2FRE)
6685. Thompson, James, b. 1726, gardener, Jacobite, res. Fingask Kinnaird Perthshire, tr. 5 May 1747, fr. Liverpool to Leeward Islands, in *Veteran*, arr. Martinique 5 May 1747. (P.3.372)(MR69)(PRO.SP36.102)
6686. Thompson, James, b. 1726, gardener, Jacobite, res. Fingask Kinnaird Perthsire, tr. 5 May 1747, fr. Liverpool to Leeward Islands, in *Veteran*, arr. Martinique June 1747. (P.3.372)(MR69)(PRO.SP36.102)
6687. Thompson, James, b. 1732, Tain Ross-shire, soldier, sh. pre 1758, sett. Quebec, ch. James & John, d. 1830. (SRO.GD45.422)
6688. Thompson, John, b. 18 June 1730, Rathven Banffshire, Jacobite, res. Banff, pts. William Thompson & Margaret Innes, tr. 5 May 1747, fr. Liverpool to Leeward Islands, in *Veteran*, arr. Martinique June 1747. (P.3.372)(MR128)(JAB.2.446)(PRO.SP36.102)
6689. Thompson, John, b. 18 June 1730, Rathven Banffshire, Jacobite, res. Banff, pts. William Thompson & Margaret Innes, tr. 5 May 1747, fr. Liverpool to Leeward Islands, in *Veteran*, arr. Martinique June 1747. (P.3.372)(MR128)(JAB.2.446)(PRO.SP36.102)
6690. Thompson, Robert, Jacobite, res. Dublin, tr. 22 Apr 1747. (P.3.372)
6691. Thompson, Thomas, b. 1746, laborer, sh. Sept 1775, fr. Newcastle to Ga, in *Georgia Packet*. (PRO.T47.9\11)
6692. Thompson, William, b. 1707, laborer, Jacobite, res. Little Kenny Kingoldrum Angus, tr. 5 May 1747, fr. Liverpool to Leeward Islands, in *Veteran*, arr. Martinique June 1747. (P.3.372)(MR111)(PRO.SP36.102)
6693. Thompson, William, b. 1744, schoolmaster, sh. Aug 1774, fr. London to Va, in *Beith*. (PRO.T47.9\11)
6694. Thomson, Adam, physician edu. Edinburgh Uni, sh. pre 1755, sett. Upper Marlborough Prince George Co Md, d. 18 Sept 1767 N.Y. (AP339)(SA183)
6695. Thomson, Alexander, surgeon, sh. pre 1772, sett. St Thomas in the Vale Middlesex Co Jamaica. (SRO.RD2.771.170)
6696. Thomson, Alexander, b. 1727, farmer, res. Breadalbane Perthshire, sh. June 1775, fr. Greenock to N.Y., in *Commerce*, m. Janet Forest, ch. William Katherine Betty Henry. (PRO.T47.12)

6697. Thomson, Alexander, b. 1745, wright, res. Stirling, sh. May 1775, fr. Greenock to N.Y., in *Monimia*. (PRO.T47.12)
6698. Thomson, Alexander, b. 1752, wright, res. Stirling, sh. Apr 1775, fr. Greenock to N.Y., in *Lilly*. (PRO.T47.12)
6699. Thomson, Andrew, sailor, res. Leith Midlothian, sh. 14 July 1698, fr. Leith to Darien, in *Dolphin*, Edin pr1707 CC8.8.83
6700. Thomson, Andrew, clergyman, d. pre 1727 Va, Edin pr1727 CC8.8.91
6701. Thomson, Anne, servant, infanticide, res. Perthshire, tr. Nov 1764, fr. Greenock to N.J. (SRO.B59.26.11.639)
6702. Thomson, Archibald, sh. 29 Nov 1773, fr. Greenock to Jamaica, in *Mary of Glasgow*. (SRO.CE60.1.7)
6703. Thomson, Archibald, Covenanter, tr. Aug 1685, fr. Leith to Jamaica. (PC.11.329)
6704. Thomson, Daniel, b. 1761, res. Forfar Angus, sh. May 1775, fr. Leith to Philadelphia, in *Friendship*. (PRO.T47.12)
6705. Thomson, David, baillie, res. Inverkeithing Fife, sh. 14 July 1698, fr. Leith to Darien, in *Unicorn*, m. Janet .., Edin pr1707 CC8.8.83
6706. Thomson, Donald, Covenanter, res. Argyll, tr. July 1685, fr. Leith to N.E. (PC.11.94)
6707. Thomson, Duncan, Covenanter, res. Argyll, tr. Aug 1685, fr. Leith to Jamaica. (PC.11.130)
6708. Thomson, Elizabeth, shopbreaker, res. Ayrshire, tr. Sept 1754. (SM.16.450) (alias 5748)
6709. Thomson, Elizabeth, whore, res. Edinburgh, tr. 19 Mar 1695. (SRO.PC2.25.216)
6710. Thomson, Gabriel, merchant, Covenanter, res. Glasgow, tr. 12 Dec 1678, fr. Leith to West Indies, in *St Michael of Scarborough*. (PC.6.76)
6711. Thomson, George, b. 1734, farmer, res. Breadalbane Perthshire, sh. June 1775, fr. Greenock to N.Y., in *Commerce*, m. Janet Wilson, ch. Peter. (PRO.T47.12)
6712. Thomson, Henry, sailor, sh. 14 July 1698, fr. Leith to Darien, in *Unicorn*, Edin pr1707 CC8.8.83
6713. Thomson, Isobel, b. 1735, res. Burghead Morayshire, sh. July 1775, fr. Stornaway to Philadelphia, in *Clementina*, ch. John Isobel William George. (PRO.T47.12)
6714. Thomson, James, sailor, res. Aberdour Fife, sh. 18 Aug 1699, fr. Clyde to Darien, in *Rising Sun*, Edin pr1707 CC8.8.83
6715. Thomson, James, sailor, res. Edinburgh, sh. 14 July 1698, fr. Leith to Darien, in *St Andrew*, Edin pr1707 CC8.8.83
6716. Thomson, James, clergyman edu. Marischal Col Aberdeen 1748, res. Aberdeen, pts. James Thomson, sh. 1767, sett. Leeds Fauquier Co Va, d. 1812 Va. (EMA59)(OD19)
6717. Thomson, James, b. 1733, coal hewer, res. Glasgow, sh. Apr 1775, fr. Greenock to Salem, in *Glasgow Packet*. (PRO.T47.12)

6718. Thomson, James, b. 21 May 1750, Aberdour Aberdeenshire, surveyor, res. Tough Aberdeenshire, pts. Rev Patrick Thomson & Helen Copland, d. Sept 1774 St Vincent. (APB.4.73)

6719. Thomson, John, horsethief, res. Ardkinglass Argyll, pts. James Thomson, tr. Sept 1706. (JRA.2.204)

6720. Thomson, John, Covenanter, res. Argyll, tr. 6 July 1685, fr. Leith to N.E. (PC.11.94)

6721. Thomson, John, clergyman edu. Marischal Col Aberdeen 1715, sh. 1739, sett. St Mark's Culpepper Co Va, d. 1772 Va. (EMA58)(OD16)

6722. Thomson, John, Covenanter, res. Argyll, tr. 6 July 1685, fr. Leith to N.E. (PC.11.94)

6723. Thomson, John, b. 1742, servant, res. Burghead Morayshire, sh. July 1775, fr. Stornaway to Philadelphia, in *Clementina*. (PRO.T47.12)

6724. Thomson, Margaret, whore & thief, res. Edinburgh, tr. 28 Nov 1704, fr. Leith to Md. (SRO.PC2.28.307)

6725. Thomson, Mary, infanticide, res. Jedburgh Roxburghshire, tr. Sept 1773. (SM.35.557)

6726. Thomson, Neil, Covenanter, res. Argyll, tr. Aug 1685, fr. Leith to Jamaica. (PC.11.136)

6727. Thomson, Neil, b. 1751, farmer, res. Kintyre Argyll, sh. Aug 1774, fr. Greenock to Wilmington N.C., in *Ulysses*. (PRO.T47.12)

6728. Thomson, Patrick, shoemaker, Jacobite, res. Dundee Angus, tr. 8 May 1747, to Antigua. (P.3.372)(MR111)

6729. Thomson, Richard, b. 1713, surgeon, res. Falkirk Stirlingshire, sh. Aug 1734, fr. London to St Kitt's or Jamaica. (CLRO\AIA)

6730. Thomson, Robert, res. Edinburgh, tr. Jan 1740, to Jamaica. (SRO.JC3.23.163)

6731. Thomson, Thomas, soldier, rapist, tr. Mar 1754. (SRO.HCR.I.87)(SRO.JC3.29)

6732. Thomson, Thomas, sh. 1684, fr. Gourock to S.C., in *Carolina Merchant*. (ECJ72) (alias 6341)

6733. Thomson, Walter, sailor, res. Bo'ness West Lothian, sh. 18 Aug 1699, fr. Clyde to Darien, in *Duke of Hamilton*, ch. David, Edin pr1709 CC8.8.84

6734. Thomson, William, sailor, res. Hopetoun West Lothian, sh. 18 Aug 1699, fr. Clyde to Darien, in *Rising Sun*, Edin pr1707 CC8.8.83

6735. Thomson, William, sailor, res. Edinburgh, sh. 14 July 1698, fr. Leith to Darien, in *Caledonia*, Edin pr1707 CC8.8.83

6736. Thomson, William, merchant, res. Glasgow, sett. Kingston Jamaica, d. pre 1783 Jamaica, Edin pr1783 CC8.8.126

6737. Thomson, William, Covenanter, tr. 31 July 1685, fr. Leith to East N.J. (PC.11.131)

6738. Thomson, William, b. 1730, tailor, Jacobite, res. Glasgow, tr. 24 Feb 1747, fr. Liverpool to Va, in *Gildart*, arr. Port North Potomac Md 5 Aug 1747. (P.3.372)(PRO.T1.328)

6739. Thomson, William jr, sailor, res. Irvine Ayrshire, pts. John Thomson, sh. 18 Aug 1699, fr. Clyde to Darien, in *Rising Sun*, Edin pr1710 CC8.8.84

6740. Thorburn, William, Jacobite, tr. 30 Mar 1747, fr. Liverpool to Antigua, in *Scipio*. (SPC.1716.310)(CTB31.204)

6741. Thornson, Andrew, b. 1754, merchant, res. Glasgow, sh. Oct 1774, fr. Greenock to Charleston S.C., in *Countess*. (PRO.T47.12)

6742. Thornton, James, b. 1765, res. Paisley Renfrewshire, sh. Feb 1774, fr. Greenock to N.Y., in *Commerce*. (PRO.T47.12)

6743. Tickall, William, b. 1717, tailor, Jacobite, res. Lancashire, tr. 21 Feb 1747. (P.3.374)(MR198)

6744. Tillery, Andrew, b. 24 Sept 1710, Old Machar Aberdeenshire, horsehirer, Jacobite, res. Aberdeen, pts. Andrew Tillery & Margaret Brown, tr. 22 Apr 1747, fr. Liverpool to Va, in *Johnson*, arr. Port Oxford Md 5 Aug 1747. (P.3.374)(JAB.2.446)(PRO.T1.328)

6745. Tod, George, thief, res. Aberdeen, tr. Nov 1773, fr. Glasgow. (AJ1343\1351)

6746. Tod, George, res. Holm Orkney Islands, sh. pre 1765, sett. Carolina Co Va. (SRO.SH.23.1.1765)

6747. Tod, Quentin, goat-thief, res. Kirkcudbright, tr. Jan 1666, to Barbados. (PC.2.134)

6748. Tod, William, coachbuilder, res. Edinburgh, sh. pre 1775, sett. Philadelphia, ch. Alexander Helen. (SRO.RD4.718.858)

6749. Todd, Andrew, b. 1712, carpenter, res. Irvine Ayrshire, sh. Nov 1731, fr. London to Jamaica. (CLRO\AIA)

6750. Todd, George, surgeon, res. Westshore Holm Orkney Islands, pts. Charles Todd, sh. pre 1763, sett. Caroline Co Va. (SRO.NRAS.1246)

6751. Todd, John, Jacobite, tr. 30 Mar 1716, fr. Liverpool to Antigua, in *Scipio*. (SPC.1716.310)

6752. Todshall, John, tr. 22 Dec 1665, fr. Leith or Buckhaven to Barbados. (ETR104)

6753. Tolmie, Donald, b. 1757, servant, res. Downie Castle, sh. July 1775, fr. Stornaway to Philadelphia, in *Clementina*. (PRO.T47.12)

6754. Torburn, Andrew, b. 1767, res. Glenluce Wigtonshire, sh. May 1774, fr. Stranraer to N.Y., in *Gale*. (PRO.T47.12)

6755. Tosh, David, b. 27 Nov 1731, Tannadice Angus, chapman, horsethief, res. Easter Ordy Oathlaw Angus, pts. John Tosh, tr. Sept 1767. (SM.29.497)

6756. Toshach, David, res. Monivaird Perthshire, sh. 1684, fr. Leith to East N.J. (Insh236)

6757. Toshach, Katherine, infanticide, res. Perthshire, tr. May 1728. (SRO.B59.26.11.148)
6758. Toward, Henry, seaman, res. Bo'ness West Lothian, pts. John Toward, sh. 14 July 1698, fr. Leith to Darien, in *Unicorn*, Edin pr1707 CC8.8.83
6759. Toward, Janet, whore & thief, res. Edinburgh, tr. 28 Nov 1704, fr. Leith to Md. (SRO.PC2.28.307)
6760. Tower, James, b. 5 Apr 1760, St Nicholas Aberdeen, physician edu. Marischal Col Aberdeen 1775, res. Aberdeen, pts. John Tower & Margaret Scott, sett. St Thomas West Indies. (MCA.2.347)
6761. Trail, Dr, d. 5 Feb 1779 Ga. (SM.41.286)
6762. Trail, William, b. 28 Sept 1640, Edinburgh, clergyman edu. Edinburgh Uni 1658, res. Edinburgh, pts. Robert Trail & Jean Annand, sh. 1682, sett. Potomac Md, m. (1)Euphan Sword(2)Eleanor Trail, ch. Mary Sarah James William Robert Jean Margaret Eleanor Elizabeth, d. 3 May 1714 Borthwick Midlothian. (F.1.302)
6763. Traill, George, surgeon, res. Edinburgh, d. pre 1759 North America, PCC pr1759
6764. Traill, Janet, whore & thief, res. Edinburgh, tr. 28 Nov 1704, fr. Leith to Md. (SRO.PC2.28.307)
6765. Traill, Janet, b. 9 Nov 1756, Kirkwall Orkney Islands, servant, res. Kirkwall, pts. Peter Traill & Mary Reasson, sh. Sept 1775, fr. Kirkwall to Savannah Ga, in *Marlborough*, sett. Richmond Co Ga. (PRO.T47.12)
6766. Traill, William, b. 12 Aug 1759, Deerness Orkney Islands, farm servant, res. Deerness, pts. William Traill & Ursilla Cromerty, sh. Sept 1774, fr. Kirkwall to Savannah Ga, in *Marlborough*, sett. Richmond Co Ga. (PRO.T47.12)
6767. Tran, Hugh, b. 29 July 1730, Glasgow, merchant, res. Glasgow, pts. Arthur Tran & Elizabeth Warden, sh. pre 1768, sett. St Kitts. (SRO.SH.12.2.1768)(SRO.B10.15.714)
6768. Traquair, James, sailor, res. Torpichen West Lothian, sh. 14 July 1698, fr. Leith to Darien, in *Caledonia*, Edin pr1707 CC8.8.83
6769. Trent, Lawrence, merchant, res. Newbattle Midlothian, sh. pre 1689, sett. Barbados. (SRO.SH.28.7.1703)
6770. Troop, John, b. 1727, gardener, Jacobite, res. Stirling, tr. 5 May 1747, fr. Liverpool to Leeward Islands, in *Veteran*, arr. Martinique June 1747. (P.3.378)(MR132)(PRO.SP36.102)
6771. Troop, John, b. 1753, laborer, res. Kelton Kirkcudbrightshire, sh. 1775, fr. Dumfries to P.E.I., in *Lovely Nelly*. (PRO.T47.12)
6772. Troup, James, sailor, res. Edinburgh, sh. May 1699, fr. Clyde to Darien, in *Olive Branch*, Edin pr1707 CC8.8.83
6773. Troup, John, physician edu. Marischal Col Aberdeen 1770, sett. Jamaica. (MCA.2.125)

6774. Troup, Robert, sett. Morris Co N.Y., d. 28 Feb 1769. (SM.31.111)
6775. Trumball, Michael, Jacobite, tr. 26 Apr 1716, fr. Liverpool to Jamaica, in *Two Brothers*, arr. Montserrat June 1716. (SPC.1716.313)(CTB31.205)(CTP.CC.43)
6776. Trumbell, Thomas, res. Dumfries, sh. May 1775, fr. Douglas Isle of Man to P.E.I., in *Lovely Nelly*, m. Jean Mackay. (PRO.T47.12)
6777. Tullideph, Walter, physician, res. Tullideph Hall Angus, d. 16 Mar 1772 Antigua. (SM.34.276)
6778. Turnbull, Alexander, sh. June 1684, fr. Montrose to East N.J. (SRO.E72.16.13)
6779. Turnbull, Andrew, b. 1719, Annan Dumfries-shire, physician, d. 16 Mar 1792 Charleston S.C. (GM.62.673)
6780. Turnbull, Ann, b. 1751, farm servant, res. Evie Orkney Islands, sh. Sept 1774, fr. Kirkwall to Savannah Ga, in *Marlborough*, sett. Richmond Co Ga. (PRO.T47.12)
6781. Turnbull, David, b. 1757, surveyor, res. Glasgow, sh. July 1775, fr. Greenock to Jamaica, in *Isabella*. (PRO.T47.12)
6782. Turnbull, James, b. 1755, laborer, res. Glasgow, sh. Oct 1774, fr. Greenock to Philadelphia, in *Sally*. (PRO.T47.12)
6783. Turnbull, Thomas, Covenanter, res. Argyll, tr. Aug 1685, fr. Leith to Jamaica. (PC.11.330)(ETR369)
6784. Turnbull, Walter, schoolmaster, assault, res. Hawick Roxburghshire, tr. May 1751. (AJ178)
6785. Turnbull, William, bosun's mate, sh. 14 July 1698, fr. Leith to Darien, in *St Andrew*, m. Bessie Dempster, Edin pr1707 CC8.8.83
6786. Turnbull, William, tr. 12 Dec 1678, fr. Leith or Newhaven to West Indies, in *St Michael of Scarborough*. (PC.6.76)
6787. Turnbull, William, Covenanter, tr. 5 Sept 1685, fr. Leith to East N.J., in *Henry & Francis*. (PC.11.154)
6788. Turner, Charles, b. 1721, mason, res. Wigton, sh. Mar 1774, fr. London, in *John & Thomas*. (PRO.T47.9\11)
6789. Turner, Charles, b. 1752, mason, res. Wigton, pts. Charles Turner, sh. Mar 1774, fr. London, in *John & Thomas*. (PRO.T47.9\11)
6790. Turner, James, sailor, res. Alloway Ayrshire, sh. 18 Aug 1699, fr. Clyde to Darien, in *Rising Sun*, Edin pr1707 CC8.8.83
6791. Turner, John, thief, res. Glasgow, tr. Oct 1752. (AJ248)
6792. Turner, John, b. 1711, res. Dunoon Argyll, sh. Feb 1732, fr. London to Jamaica. (CLRO\AIA)
6793. Turner, John, b. 1757, mason, res. Wigton, pts. Charles Turner, sh. Mar 1774, fr. London, in *John & Thomas*. (PRO.T47.9\11)
6794. Turner, William, Jacobite, tr. 29 June 1716, fr. Liverpool to Jamaica or Va, in *Elizabeth & Anne*, arr. York Va. (SPC.1716.310)(CTB31.208)(VSP.1.185)

6795. Turpney, John, Covenanter, tr. 5 Sept 1685, fr. Leith to East N.J., in *Henry & Francis*. (PC.11.154)
6796. Tweedie, Janet, infanticide, res. Roxburghshire, tr. May 1764. (SM.26.287)
6797. Ure, Alexander, weaver, res. Cardross Dunbartonshire, sh. 21 July 1684, fr. Gourock to Port Royal S.C., in *Carolina Merchant*. (ECJ72)
6798. Urie, John, Covenanter, res. Blairgorts, tr. 12 Dec 1678, fr. Leith to West Indies, in *St Michael of Scarborough*. (PC.6.76)
6799. Urie, John, Covenanter, tr. 5 Sept 1685, fr. Leith to East N.J., in *Henry & Francis*. (PC.11.166)
6800. Urie, Patrick, Covenanter, tr. 5 Sept 1685, fr. Leith to East N.J., in *Henry & Francis*. (PC.11.155)
6801. Urie, Robert, weaver, Covenanter, res. Little Govan Glasgow, tr. Jun 1684, fr. Clyde, in *Pelican*. (PC.9.208)
6802. Urie, William, Covenanter, res. Cathcart Glasgow, tr. 12 Dec 1678, fr. Leith to West Indies, in *St Michael of Scarborough*. (PC.6.76)
6803. Urquhart, Alexander, res. Tannachie Forres Morayshire, sh. pre 1770, sett. St Mary's Md. (SRO.RS29.8.188)
6804. Urquhart, Andrew, b. 1755, servant, res. Duffus Morayshire, sh. July 1775, fr. Stornaway to Philadelphia, in *Clementina*. (PRO.T47.12)
6805. Urquhart, Ann, b. 1758, servant, res. Ross-shire, sh. May 1775, fr. Leith to Philadelphia, in *Friendship*. (PRO.T47.12)
6806. Urquhart, Donald, b. 1697, blacksmith, Jacobite, tr. 20 Mar 1747, fr. Tilbury. (P.3.382)(MR160)
6807. Urquhart, Hector, b. 1700, farmer, Jacobite, res. Achterneed Strathpeffer Ross & Cromarty, tr. 20 Mar 1747, fr. Tilbury. (P.3.382)(MR88)
6808. Urquhart, James, Covenanter, tr. 1685. (PC.10.165)
6809. Urquhart, James, Jacobite, tr. 29 June 1716, fr. Liverpool to Jamaica or Va, in *Elizabeth & Anne*, arr. York Va. (SPC.1716.310)(CTB31.208)(VSP.1.186)
6810. Urquhart, James, b. 1729, laborer, Jacobite, res. Aberdeenshire, tr. 5 May 1747, fr. Liverpool to Leeward Islands, in *Veteran*, arr. Martinique June 1747. (P.3.382)(JAB.2.446)(MR124)(PRO.SP36.102)
6811. Urquhart, John, clergyman, sh. 1732, to Md. (EMA61)
6812. Urquhart, William, lawyer, pts. Leonard Urquhart, d. 1783 Jamaica. (SM.45.279)
6813. Urquhart, William, clergyman, sh. 1702, sett. Long Island N.Y., d. 1709. (EMA61)(SNQ.1.59)
6814. Valentine, Andrew, b. 1762, ship's carpenter, res. Ayrshire, sh. Mar 1775, fr. Glasgow to Quebec, in *Friendship*. (PRO.T47.12)
6815. Vallance, Alexander, Covenanter, res. Ayr, tr. 1685. (PC.10.129)
6816. Vallance, Robert, tr. 1728, fr. Glasgow to Md, in *Concord of Glasgow*, arr. Charles Co Md 24 May 1728. (SRO.JC.27.10.3)

6817. Van, Heston Sophia, whore & thief, res. Edinburgh, tr. 28 Nov 1704, fr. Leith to Md. (SRO.PC2.28.307)
6818. Vass, Charles, sailor, res. Edinburgh, pts. Patrick Vass & Margaret Hamilton, sh. 14 July 1698, fr. Leith to Darien, in *Caledonia*, Edin pr1707 CC8.8.83
6819. Veatch, William, res. Dumfries, pts. Rev William Veatch, d. 1699 Darien, Edin pr1709 CC8.8.84
6820. Vernor, John, merchant, sh. Apr 1684, fr. Port Glasgow to Va, in *Margaret of Morfin*. (SRO.E72.19.9)
6821. Violent, David, lawyer, res. Edinburgh, sh. 1684, fr. Leith to East N.J. (Insh242)
6822. Volva, Edward, b. 1719, Jacobite, res. Dunkirk, tr. 1747. (P.3.382)(MR63)
6823. Waddell, James, tr. Nov 1679, fr. Leith. (ETR162)
6824. Waddell, Thomas, sailor, res. Prestonpans East Lothian, pts. William Waddell & Margaret Cuby, sh. 18 Aug 1699, fr. Clyde to Darien, in *Rising Sun*, d. 1699 Darien, Edin pr1707 CC8.8.83
6825. Wait, Hugh, b. 1748, farmer, res. Neilston Renfrewshire, sh. May 1775, fr. Greenock to N.Y. or Ga, in *Christy*. (PRO.T47.12)
6826. Wales, Margaret, b. 11 June 1651, Dundee Angus, res. Angus, pts. Alexander Wales, sh. Aug 1684, fr. London to Md. (CLRO\AIA)
6827. Walker, Adam, tailor, res. Edinburgh, pts. ... Walker & Janet Handiesyde, sh. 14 July 1698, fr. Leith to Darien, in *St Andrew*, Edin pr1707 CC8.8.82
6828. Walker, Agnes, infanticide, res. Crossmichael Kirkcudbrightshire, tr. Sept 1763. (SM.25.579)
6829. Walker, Alexander, b. 16 Aug 1723, Bervie Kincardineshire, servant, Jacobite, res. Bervie, pts. William Walker, tr. 22 Apr 1747, fr. Liverpool to Va, in *Johnson*, arr. Port Oxford Md 5 Aug 1747. (P.3.384)(PRO.T1.328)
6830. Walker, Catherine, res. New Luce Wigtonshire, sh. 31 May 1775, fr. Stranraer to N.Y., in *Jackie*. (PRO.T47.12)
6831. Walker, David, b. 1757, piper, res. Breadalbane Perthshire, sh. June 1775, fr. Greenock to N.Y., in *Commerce*. (PRO.T47.12)
6832. Walker, Donald, farmer, Covenanter, res. Otter Argyll, tr. Aug 1685, fr. Leith to Jamaica. (ETR373)
6833. Walker, Donald, b. 1762, tailor, res. Breadalbane Perthshire, sh. June 1775, fr. Greenock to N.Y., in *Commerce*. (PRO.T47.12)
6834. Walker, Duncan, Covenanter, res. Argyll, tr. Aug 1685, fr. Leith to Jamaica. (PC.11.136)
6835. Walker, Eliza, b. 1757, servant, res. Breadalbane Perthshire, sh. June 1775, fr. Greenock to N.Y., in *Commerce*. (PRO.T47.12)
6836. Walker, Elizabeth, whore, res. Edinburgh, tr. 19 Mar 1695. (SRO.PC2.25.216)

6837. Walker, George, flesher, res. Edinburgh, sh. 14 July 1698, fr. Leith to Darien, in *Caledonia*, Edin pr1707 CC8.8.83
6838. Walker, Isobel, murderer, res. Cluden Irongray Kirkcudbrightshire, tr. June 1738. (SRO.JC27)
6839. Walker, James, b. 1724, blacksmith, sh. Mar 1774, fr. London to Philadelphia, in *Bellar*, m. Ann.. (PRO.T47.9\11)
6840. Walker, John, b. 1750, shoemaker, res. Paisley Renfrewshire, sh. Apr 1775, fr. Greenock to N.Y., in *Lilly*. (PRO.T47.12)
6841. Walker, John, b. 1753, weaver, res. Glasgow, sh. May 1774, fr. Greenock to N.Y., in *Matty*. (PRO.T47.12)
6842. Walker, Joseph, b. 3 Mar 1706, Dunnottar Kincardineshire, res. Stonehaven Kincardineshire, pts. George Walker, sh. July 1728, fr. London to Pa. (CLRO\AIA)
6843. Walker, Joseph, b. 1744, blacksmith, sh. Mar 1774, fr. London to Philadelphia, in *Bellar*, m. Mary .. (PRO.T47.9\11)
6844. Walker, Patrick, Covenanter, tr. 5 Sept 1685, fr. Leith to East N.J., in *Henry & Francis*. (PC.11.155)
6845. Walker, Patrick, b. 1666, Covenanter, tr. July 1684, fr. Leith to Carolina. (PC.9.69)
6846. Walker, Simeon, cook, res. Burntisland Fife, sh. 14 July 1698, fr. Leith to Darien, in *Caledonia*, m. Janet Scott, Edin pr1707 CC8.8.83
6847. Walker, William, sailor, res. Coaltown of Durie Fife, pts. William Walker, sh. 14 July 1698, fr. Leith to Darien, in *Unicorn*, Edin pr1707 CC8.8.83
6848. Walker, William, tr. Aug 1685, fr. Leith to Jamaica. (PC.11.136)
6849. Walkingshaw, William, merchant, sh. Dec 1682, fr. Port Glasgow to Va, in *Supply of Chester*. (SRO.E72.19.8)
6850. Walkingshaw, William, merchant, sh. 9 Oct 1685, fr. Port Glasgow to Va, in *Supply of Chester*. (SRO.E72.19.8)
6851. Wallace, Andrew, tr. Nov 1679, fr. Leith. (ETR162)
6852. Wallace, Archibald, res. Ayrshire, pts. William Wallace of Cairnhill & Jean Campbell, d. 8 Nov 1779 Jamaica. (HCA.1.345)
6853. Wallace, David, res. Stonehaven Kincardineshire, pts. David Wallace & Margaret Hanton, sh. 1723, sett. Va, m. Mrs Hall, ch. David, d. pre 1741 Va. (APB.3.92)
6854. Wallace, George, b. 1731, fisherman, Jacobite, tr. 24 Feb 1747, fr. Liverpool to Va, in *Gildart*, arr. Port North Potomac Md 5 Aug 1747. (P.3.386)(PRO.T1.328)
6855. Wallace, Hugh, planter, pts. Thomas Wallace of Cairnhill & Lillias Cunningham, sh. pre 1772, sett. Jamaica. (SRO.RD2.211.805)
6856. Wallace, James, gentleman, sh. pre 1769, sett. Antigua. (SRO.RD4.209.637)
6857. Wallace, Janet, infanticide, tr. Aug 1685, fr. Leith to Jamaica. (PC.11.330)(ETR369)

6858. Wallace, John, engineer, res. Edinburgh, d. 1699 Darien, Edin pr1707 CC8.8.83
6859. Wallace, John, quartermaster, res. Musselburgh Midlothian, sh. 14 July 1698, fr. Leith to Darien, in *Unicorn*, m. Katherine Carmichael, Edin pr1707 CC8.8.83
6860. Wallace, John, b. 1749, weaver, res. Paisley Renfrewshire, sh. Feb 1774, fr. Greenock to N.Y., in *Commerce*. (PRO.T47.12)
6861. Wallace, Margaret, whore & thief, res. Edinburgh, tr. 28 Nov 1704, fr. Leith to Md. (SRO.PC2.28.307)
6862. Wallace, Mary, infanticide, res. Fife, tr. May 1753. (SM.15.260)
6863. Wallace, Robert, Jacobite, tr. 26 Apr 1716, fr. Liverpool to Jamaica, in *Two Brothers*, arr. Montserrat June 1716. (SPC.1716.313)(CTB31.206)(CTP.CC.43)
6864. Wallace, William, b. 1739, weaver, res. Paisley Renfrewshire, sh. Apr 1775, fr. Greenock to N.Y., in *Lilly*. (PRO.T47.12)
6865. Wallet, John, Covenanter, tr. May 1685, fr. Leith. (PC.11.289)
6866. Walls, Herbert, Covenanter, res. Lawriddings Dumfries-shire, tr. Oct 1684. (PC.10.206)
6867. Wanless, Alexander, res. Perth, tr. Sept 1758. (SRO.B59.26.11.6.46)(AJ557)
6868. Warden, Ebenezer, journeyman wright, housebreaker & thief, res. Leith Mills, pts. Henry Warden, tr. 1771, fr. Port Glasgow to Md, in *Matty*, arr. Port Oxford Md 17 Dec 1771. (SRO.JC.27.10.3)
6869. Warden, James, clergyman, sh. 1711, sett. James City Va. (SCHR.14.144)
6870. Warden, Samuel, clergyman, sh. 1712, to Va. (EMA64)
6871. Wardrobe, John, b. 1744, tailor, res. Glasgow, sh. Feb 1774, fr. Greenock to N.Y., in *Commerce*. (PRO.T47.12)
6872. Wardrop, James, b. 1749, mason, res. Haliaths Lochmaben Dumfries-shire, sh. 1775, fr. Dumfries to P.E.I., in *Lovely Nelly*. (PRO.T47.12)
6873. Wardrope, James, merchant, sh. Apr 1684, fr. Port Glasgow to West Indies, in *Jean of Largs*. (SRO.E72.19.9)
6874. Wardrope, James, passenger, sh. Feb 1681, fr. Ayr to West Indies, in *James of Ayr*. (SRO.E72.3.6)
6875. Wardrope, Joseph, housecarpenter, res. Edinburgh, pts. David Wardrope of Easter Quill, sh. 1733, sett. Ga. (PRO.CO5.670.128)
6876. Wark, John, b. 1745, millwright, sh. Sept 1775, fr. Newcastle to Ga, in *Georgia Packet*, sett. Friendsborough Ga. (PRO.T47.9\11)
6877. Wark, Robert, housebreaker, tr. Nov 1772, fr. Glasgow. (SRO.RH2.4.255)
6878. Warnock, Robert, tr. Oct 1684. (PC.10.251)

338

6879. Warrack, James, sailor, res. Canongate Edinburgh, sh. 18 Aug 1699, fr. Clyde to Darien, in *Rising Sun*, ch. Robert, Edin pr1707 CC8.8.83
6880. Warrand, James, b. 1750, farmer, res. Strathspey, sh. May 1774, fr. Greenock to N.Y., in *George*. (PRO.T47.12)
6881. Warren, John, carpenter, Jacobite, res. Clitheroe Lancashire, tr. 1747. (MR45)
6882. Warren, Robert, b. 1727, weaver, Jacobite, res. Aberdenshire or Banffshire, tr. 5 May 1747, fr. Liverpool to Leeward Islands, in *Veteran*, arr. Martinique June 1747. (P.3.390)(JAB.2.446)(MR124)(PRO.SP36.102)
6883. Warren, Thomas, b. 1716, attorney general, d. 2 June 1779 St John's Antigua. (SM.41.455)
6884. Warrender, William, foremastman, res. East Wemyss Fife, sh. 14 July 1698, fr. Leith to Darien, in *Caledonia*, Edin pr1707 CC8.8.83
6885. Warrior, John, Jacobite, res. England, tr. 22 Apr 1747, fr. Liverpool to Va, in *Johnson*, arr. Port Oxford Md 5 Aug 1747. (P.3.388)(PRO.T1.328)
6886. Watson, Alexander, b. 1739, farmer, res. Strathspey, sh. May 1774, fr. Greenock to N.Y., in *George*. (PRO.T47.12)
6887. Watson, Andrew, b. 1754, smith, sh. Sept 1775, fr. Newcastle to Ga, in *Georgia*. (PRO.T47.9\11)
6888. Watson, George, laborer, Jacobite, res. Banff, tr. 22 Apr 1747, fr. Liverpool to Va, in *Johnson*, arr. Port Oxford Md 5 Aug 1747. (P.3.390)(JAB.2.446)(PRO.T1.328)
6889. Watson, Gilbert, sh. 29 Nov 1773, fr. Greenock to Jamaica, in *Mary of Glasgow*. (SRO.CE60.1.7)
6890. Watson, James, merchant, sh. pre 1749, sett. Kingston Jamaica. (SRO.RD2.170.264\RD2.167.216)
6891. Watson, James, planter, res. Dalkeith Midlothian, sh. pre 1655, sett. Barbados. (BritMus.Add MS34015)
6892. Watson, James, sailor, res. Burntisland Fife, sh. 14 July 1698, fr. Leith to Darien, in *Caledonia*, Edin pr1707 CC8.8.83
6893. Watson, James, rioter, res. Kilmacolm Renfrewshire , tr. 16 June 1670. (PC.3.178)
6894. Watson, James, Jacobite, tr. 29 June 1716, fr. Liverpool to Jamaica or Va, in *Elizabeth & Anne*, arr. York Va. (SPC.1716.310)(CTB31.208)(VSP.1.186)
6895. Watson, James, Jacobite, tr. 29 June 1716, fr. Liverpool to Jamaica or Va, in *Elizabeth & Anne*, arr. York Va. (SPC.1716.310)(CTB31.208)(VSP.1.186)
6896. Watson, James, tr. 25 Jan 1728. (SRO.JC.27.10.3)
6897. Watson, James, b. 1744, farmer, res. Stirling, sh. May 1775, fr. Greenock to N.Y., in *Matty*. (PRO.T47.12)

6898. Watson, James, b. 1750, servant, res. Duffus Morayshire, sh. July 1775, fr. Stornaway to Philadelphia, in *Clementina*. (PRO.T47.12)
6899. Watson, Janet, whore, res. Edinburgh, tr. 19 Mar 1695. (SRO.PC2.25.216)
6900. Watson, John, innkeeper & brewer, Jacobite, res. Arbroath Angus, tr. 1747. (P.3.392)(MR77)
6901. Watson, John, thief, res. Parkstile of Tillyfour Aberdeenshire, tr. Oct 1749. (AJ93)
6902. Watson, John, res. Hamilton Lanarkshire, sh. 2 Oct 1684, fr. Bristol to Va, in *Bristol Merchant*. (BRO.04220)
6903. Watson, John, merchant, sh. Mar 1683, fr. Ayr to Caribee Islands, in *James of Ayr*. (SRO.E72.3.12)
6904. Watson, John, b. 1753, smith, res. Duffus Morayshire, sh. July 1775, fr. Stornaway to Philadelphia, in *Clementina*. (PRO.T47.12)
6905. Watson, John, b. 1755, cooper, res. Glasgow, sh. Apr 1775, fr. Greenock to Salem, in *Glasgow Packet*. (PRO.T47.12)
6906. Watson, John, b. 1756, servant, res. Bayble Isle of Lewis, sh. May 1774, fr. Stornaway to Philadelphia, in *Friendship*. (PRO.T47.12)
6907. Watson, John jr, merchant, res. Edinburgh, sh. pre 1756, sett. Charleston S.C., m. ... Blair, ch. Margaret, d. 1756 Charleston, Edin pr1756 CC8.8.116
6908. Watson, Katherine, infanticide, res. Cupar Fife, tr. May 1777. (SM.38.511)
6909. Watson, Peter, res. Selkirk, sh. 1683, fr. Leith to East N.J., sett. New Perth, ch. Richard. (Insh247)
6910. Watson, Peter, Jacobite, tr. 30 Mar 1716, fr. Liverpool to Antigua, in *Scipio*. (SPC.1716.310)(CTB31.204)
6911. Watson, Samuel, thief, res. Minnigaff Kirkcudbrightshire, pts. Alexander Watson, tr. May 1719, to West Indies. (SRO.JC.12.3)
6912. Watson, Thomas, merchant, Jacobite, res. Arbroath Angus, tr. 1746. (P.3.392)(MR92)
6913. Watson, Thomas, mason & bricklayer, res. Boghead of Kirkintulloch Dunbartonshire, sh. Apr 1763, fr. Glasgow to Jamaica. (SRO.SC36.63.7.370)
6914. Watson, William, res. Aberdeen, pts. Alexander Watson, sh. pre 1769, sett. Jamaica. (SRO.SH.1.7.1769)
6915. Watson, William, Covenanter, res. Islay Argyll, tr. Aug 1685, fr. Leith to Jamaica. (PC.11.136)
6916. Watson, William, Jacobite, tr. 30 Mar 1716, fr. Liverpool to Antigua, in *Scipio*. (SPC.1716.310)(CTB31.204)
6917. Watson, William, Jacobite, tr. 30 Mar 1716, fr. Liverpool to Antigua, in *Scipio*. (SPC.1716.310)(CTB31.204)

6918. Watt, Alexander, Jacobite, tr. 29 June 1716, fr. Liverpool to Jamaica or
Va, in *Elizabeth & Anne*, arr. York Va.
(SPC.1716.310)(CTB31.208)(VSP.1.185)

6919. Watt, Christine, res. Edinburgh, tr. 1696, fr. Newhaven to Va.
(SRO.RH15.14.58)

6920. Watt, James, b. 26 May 1740, Panbride Angus, merchant, res. Panbride,
pts. James Watt & Jean Clark, sh. pre 1775, sett. Va.
(SRO.SH.22.11.1775)

6921. Watt, John, armorer, res. Newcastle on Tyne, sh. 14 July 1698, fr. Leith
to Darien, in *Caledonia*, m. Elizabeth Smith, Edin pr1707
CC8.8.83

6922. Watt, John, tr. 5 Sept 1685, fr. Leith to East N.J., in *Henry & Francis*.
(PC.11.167)

6923. Watt, John, b. Feb 1724, Gamrie Banffshire, fisherman, Jacobite, res.
Gamrie, pts. John Watt, tr. 22 Apr 1747, fr. Liverpool to Va, in
Johnson, arr. Port Oxford Md 5 Aug 1747.
(P.3.392)(JAB.2.446)(PRO.T1.328)

6924. Watt, Robert, merchant, res. Edinburgh, pts. John Watt of Rosehill, sh.
pre 1717, sett. N.Y. (REB213)

6925. Watt, Thomas, foremastman, res. Cairsay Knowe Auchtervale Fife, sh.
14 July 1698, fr. Leith to Darien, in *Caledonia*, Edin pr1707
CC8.8.83

6926. Watt, William, b. 1745, Symington Lanarkshire, mason, sh. 1771, sett.
Tobago, d. 7 Jan 1795 Brest France. (Symington Gs)

6927. Wattie, John, farmer, murderer, res. Towie Aberdeenshire, tr. 18 Jan
1760, fr. Aberdeen to Va, in *Montrose of Aberdeen*. (AJ611\628)

6928. Watts, Thomas, b. 1753, baker, res. Ballantrae Ayrshire, sh. Oct 1774, fr.
Greenock to Philadelphia, in *Sally*. (PRO.T47.12)

6929. Wauchope, Elisabeth, whore, res. Edinburgh, tr. 19 Mar 1695.
(SRO.PC2.25.216)

6930. Waugh, Thomas, factor & surgeon, res. Jedburgh Roxburghshire, sh. pre
1778, sett. N.Y. (SRO.GD5)

6931. Waugh, Wellwood, b. 1742, joiner, res. Brownmoor Annan Dumfries-
shire, sh. 1775, fr. Dumfries to P.E.I., in *Lovely Nelly*, sett.
Pictou N.S. (PRO.T47.12)

6932. Weatherspoon, David, b. 1752, weaver, sh. Sept 1775, fr. Newcastle to
Ga, in *Georgia Packet*, sett. Friendsborough Ga. (PRO.T47.9\11)

6933. Weatherton, William, b. 1753, baker, sh. May 1774, fr. London to Md,
in *Union*. (PRO.T47.9\11)

6934. Webster, Charles, b. 1738, husbandman, sh. Aug 1774, fr. London to
Quebec, in *Mercury*, m. Jenna .. (PRO.T47.9\11)

6935. Webster, David, gunner, res. Pinkie Musselburgh Midlothian, d. pre 1767
Va, PCC pr1767

6936. Webster, Elizabeth, tr. 7 Dec 1665, fr. Leith to Barbados. (ETR104)

341

6937. Webster, George, Jacobite, tr. 1747. (P.3.396)
6938. Webster, James, merchant, res. Dundee Angus, sh. pre 1780, sett.
Richmond Vale Cornwall Co Jamaica. (TRA.TC.CC15.91)
6939. Webster, James, Jacobite, tr. 24 May 1716, fr. Liverpool to Va, in
Friendship, arr. Md Aug 1716. (SPC.1716.311)(HM386)
6940. Webster, Philip, res. Birse Aberdeenshire, pts. William Webster, sh.
1729, to N.Y., d. pre 1749. (APB.3.151)
6941. Webster, Thomas, b. 21 Apr 1716, Kincardine O'Neil Aberdeenshire, pts.
John Webster & Elspet Stiven, sh. 1730s, to Jamaica, d. May
1749 Burton Jamaica. (APB.3.162)
6942. Wedderburn, James, pts. Sir John Wedderburn of Blackness, sh. pre 1774,
sett. Jamaica, m. Isabella Blackburn. (SRO.RD2.286.408)
6943. Wedderburn, James, clerk, sh. pre 1734, sett. Charleston S.C.
(SRO.GD24.1.464)
6944. Wedderburn, Sir John, b. 1704, lawyer, Jacobite, res. Mains of Nevay
Newtyle Angus, sh. 1746. (MR91)
6945. Wedderston, John, surgeon, res. Galashiels, pts. John Wedderston, sh. pre
1773, sett. Kingston Jamaica. (SRO.CS.GMB7.73)
6946. Week, Alexander, b. 1758, husbandman, sh. Mar 1774, fr. Whitehaven to
Va, in *Ann*. (PRO.T47.9\11)
6947. Weems, James, d. 9 Nov 1698 Darien. (NLS.RY2b8\19)
6948. Weir, Elizabeth, infanticide, res. Ayrshire, tr. Sept 1749. (SM.11.462)
6949. Weir, Hugh, b. 1755, laborer, res. Gourock Renfrewshire, sh. Jan 1774,
fr. Greenock to Jamaica, in *Janet*. (SRO.CE60.1.7)
6950. Weir, John, gunner, res. Canongate Edinburgh, sh. 18 Aug 1699, fr.
Clyde to Darien, in *Rising Sun*, m. Mary Brown, ch. Thomas,
Edin pr1707 CC8.8.83
6951. Weir, John, Covenanter, tr. Aug 1685, fr. Leith to Jamaica. (PC.11.130)
6952. Weir, Mary, tr. 1 Feb 1670, fr. Leith to Va. (ETR129)
6953. Weir, Robert, painter, res. Edinburgh, pts. Walter Weir, d. 1761 Jamaica.
(SRO.SH.22.10.1761)
6954. Weir, Thomas, merchant, sett. Jamaica & London, d. June 1736, Edin
pr1740 CC8.8.103
6955. Weir, Thomas, Covenanter, res. Lesmahagow Lanarkshire, tr. Aug 1685,
fr. Leith to Jamaica, arr. Port Royal Jamaica Nov 1685.
(PC.11.329)(LJ225)
6956. Weir, William, merchant, res. Tarland Aberdeenshire, pts. Robert Weir &
Catherine Gillanders, sett. St James Co Jamaica, d. pre 1753.
(APB.3.182)
6957. Welsh, Archibald, weaver, cattle poisoner, res. Newburnfoot Dumfries-
shire, tr. Apr 1751. (AJ175)
6958. Wemyss, Alexander, sett. N.Y., m. Mary .., d. 1782.
(SRO.RD3.254.772)

6959. Wemyss, James, ensign, ch. Helen, d. 1699 Darien, Edin pr1707 CC8.8.83

6960. Wemyss, John, sailor, res. Canongate Edinburgh, pts. Alexander Wemyss & Bessie Innes, sh. 14 July 1698, fr. Leith to Darien, in *Caledonia*, Edin pr1707 CC8.8.83

6961. Weshelt, Margaret, b. 1756, sh. Aug 1774, fr. London to Quebec, in *Mercury*. (PRO.T47.9\11)

6962. Whair, William, b. 1755, farm servant, res. Wick Caithness, sh. Sept 1775, fr. Kirkwall to Savannah Ga, in *Marlborough*, sett. Richmond Co Ga. (PRO.T47.12)

6963. Wharry, James, Covenanter, tr. 11 Oct 1681, fr. Leith. (PC.7.219)

6964. White, Alexander, planter, d. 24 Dec 1698 Darien. (NLS.RY2b8\19)

6965. White, Alexander, Jacobite, tr. 29 June 1716, fr. Liverpool to Jamaica or Va, in *Elizabeth & Anne*, arr. York Va. (SPC.1716.310)(CTB31.208)(VSP.1.185)

6966. White, David, planter, d. Darien 11 Dec 1698. (NLS.RY2b8\19)

6967. White, Hector, Jacobite, tr. 28 July 1716, fr. Liverpool to Va, in *Godspeed*. (SPC.1716.3100(CTB31.209)

6968. White, James, clergyman, res. Maryculter Aberdeenshire, pts. Rev George White, sh. pre 1692, sett. Kingston Jamaica. (APB.2.188)

6969. White, James, Covenanter, res. Douglas Lanarkshire, tr. 1684, fr. Leith to N.Y. (PC.8.516)

6970. White, James, Jacobite, tr. 24 May 1716, fr. Liverpool to Md, in *Friendship*, arr. Md 20 Aug 1716. (SPC.1716.311)(HM387)

6971. White, John, Jacobite, tr. 29 June 1716, fr. Liverpool to Jamaica or Va, in *Elizabeth & Anne*, arr. York Va. (SPC.1716.310)(CTB31.208)(VSP.1.185)

6972. White, Patrick, merchant, res. Fraserburgh Aberdeenshire, pts. Patrick White, sh. pre 1749, d. 1754 Leeward Islands. (APB.3.177)

6973. White, Patrick, b. 1749, farmer, res. Coupar, sh. Apr 1775, fr. Greenock to Salem, in *Glasgow Packet*. (PRO.T47.12)

6974. White, Robert, surgeon, sh. pre 1760, sett. Va. (SRO.SH.6.1.1762)

6975. White, Robert, gardener, Jacobite, res. Linktown of Arnot Fife, tr. 1747. (P.3.400)(MR133)

6976. White, Robert, Jacobite, tr. 24 Feb 1747, fr. Liverpool to Va, in *Gildart*, arr. Port North Potomac Md 5 Aug 1747. (PRO.T1.328)

6977. White, Robert, b. 1692, sawyer, res. Falkirk Stirlingshire, sh. Dec 1722, fr. London to Jamaica. (CLRO\AIA)

6978. White, Robert, b. 23 Sept 1718, Glasgow, painter, Jacobite, res. Glasgow, pts. James White & Jane Selkrig, tr. 1747. (P.3.400)

6979. White, Robert, b. 1758, weaver, res. Glasgow, sh. Feb 1774, fr. Greenock to N.Y., in *Commerce*. (PRO.T47.12)

6980. White, William, thief, res. Roxburghshire, tr. Sept 1753. (SM.15.468)

6981. White, William, b. 1734, merchant, sh. Mar 1774, fr. London to
Jamaica, in *Jamaica Planter*. (PRO.T47.9\11)
6982. Whiteford, James, b. 1701, husbandman, res. Lanark, sh. Nov 1730, fr.
London to Md. (CLRO\AIA)
6983. Whitehead, James, b. 1756, cordiner, res. Edinburgh, sh. Dec 1773, fr.
London to Va, in *Elizabeth*. (PRO.T47.9\11)
6984. Whitelaw, Elizabeth, Covenanter, tr. 5 Sept 1685, fr. Leith to East N.J.,
in *Henry & Francis*. (PC.11.154)
6985. Whitelaw, Elpeth, res. Edinburgh, tr. 8 May 1663, fr. Leith to Barbados,
in *Mary*. (EBR.186.13.4)
6986. Whitelaw, James, b. 1749, farmer, res. Glasgow, sh. May 1774, fr.
Greenock to N.Y., in *Matty*. (PRO.T47.12)
6987. Whyte, Archibald, sailor, res. Clackmannan, sh. 18 Aug 1699, fr. Clyde
to Darien, in *Rising Sun*, Edin pr1708 CC8.8.84
6988. Whyte, Elizabeth, b. 1754, servant, res. Arnot Mill, sh. May 1775, fr.
Leith to Philadelphia, in *Friendship*. (PRO.T47.12)
6989. Whyte, John, tr. 5 Sept 1685, fr. Leith to East N.J., in *Henry & Francis*.
(ETR379)
6990. Whyte, Malcolm, Covenanter, res. Argyll, tr. Aug 1685, fr. Leith to
Jamaica. (PC.11.126)
6991. Whyte, Walter, sh. 1675, fr. Glasgow to Barbados. (GR195)
6992. Whyte, William, thief, res. Roxburghshire, tr. Sept 1753. (AJ298)
6993. Wighton, Henry, foremastman, res. Kirkcaldy Fife, pts. Henry Wighton
& Isobel Ogilvie, sh. 14 July 1698, fr. Leith to Darien, in
Caledonia, Edin pr1707 CC8.8.83
6994. Wildrige, James, b. 1757, farm servant, res. Holm Orkney Islands, sh.
Sept 1774, fr. Kirkwall to Savannah Ga, in *Marlborough*, sett.
Richmond Co Ga. (PRO.T47.12)
6995. Wilkie, Isobel, res. Haddington East Lothian, pts. Rev Patrick Wilkie,
sh. Apr 1773, fr. Deptford to Dominica. (SRO.RD3.733.208)
6996. Wilkie, James, Jacobite, tr. 21 Apr 1716, fr. Liverpool to S.C., in
Wakefield. (SPC.1716.309)(CTB31.205)
6997. Will, Lauchlan, thief, res. Aberdeenshire, tr. 1773, in *Donald*, arr. Port
James Upper District Va 13 Mar 1773. (AJ1292)(SRO.JC.27.10.3)
(alias 4407)
6998. Williams, George, b. 1755, baker, sh. Mar 1774, fr. Hull to Md, in
Shipwright. (PRO.T47.9\11)
6999. Williams, Thomas, bosun, res. Leith Midlothian, sh. 14 July 1698, fr.
Leith to Darien, in *Caledonia*, m. Margaret Tod, Edin pr1707
CC8.8.83
7000. Williamson, Alexander, Forres Morayshire, clergyman edu. King's Col
Aberdeen 1705, sh. 1710, sett. St Paul's Kent Co Md, m. Anne ..
(ANQ.1.73)(EMA63)

7001. Williamson, Alexander, b. 14 July 1730, Elgin Morayshire, glover, thief, res. Elgin, pts. James Williamson & Katherine Fraser, tr. Jan 1767. (SM.29.54)(SRO.JC27)
7002. Williamson, Andrew, fisherman & farmer, res. Shetland Islands, sh. June 1775, fr. Kirkcaldy to Brunswick N.C., in *Jamaica Packet.* (PRO.T47.12)
7003. Williamson, James, Forres Morayshire, clergyman edu. King's Col Aberdeen 1711, sh. 1712, sett. Shrewsbury Kent Co Md. (ANQ.1.73)(EMA63)
7004. Williamson, John, sailor, res. Cardenden Fife, pts. James Williamson, sh. 14 July 1698, fr. Leith to Darien, in *Unicorn,* Edin pr1707 CC8.8.83
7005. Williamson, John, b. 1730, laborer, Jacobite, res. Angus or Aberdeenshire, tr. 5 May 1747, fr. Liverpool to Leeward Islands, in *Veteran,* arr. Martinique June 1747. (P.3.402)(MR112)(PRO.SP36.102)
7006. Williamson, Thomas, tr. Nov 1679, fr. Leith. (ETR162)
7007. Williamson, Thomas, b. 1723, clerk, Jacobite, res. Edinburgh, tr. 31 Mar 1747, fr. London to Jamaica, in *St George or Carteret,* arr. Jamaica 1747. (MR9)(PRO.CO137.58)
7008. Williamson, Walter, surgeon, pts. Walter Williamson of Chapeltown, sh. pre 1761, sett. St Paul's Stafford Co Va, d. 1772 Va, Edin pr1776 CC8.8.123. (SRO.SH.14.8.1761)
7009. Willox, Alexander, surveyor, res. Duffus Morayshire, pts. Rev James Willox, sh. 1745, sett. Jamaica, d. 1760. (APB.3.209)
7010. Wilson, Alexander, b. 1750, mariner, res. Greenock Renfrewshire, sh. May 1774, fr. Greenock to N.Y., in *George.* (PRO.T47.12)
7011. Wilson, Alexander, b. 1758, weaver, res. Paisley Renfrewshire, sh. Feb 1774, fr. Greenock to N.Y., in *Commerce.* (PRO.T47.12)
7012. Wilson, Andrew, founder, thief, res. Aberfoyle Perthshire, tr. 1771, fr. Port Glasgow to Md, in *Crawford,* arr. Port Oxford Md 23 July 1771. (AJ1170)(SROJC27.10.3)
7013. Wilson, Andrew, tailor, rioter, res. Dumfries, tr. 1771, fr. Port Glasgow to Md, in *Matty,* arr. Port Oxford Md 17 Dec 1771. (AJ1232)(SRO.JC27)(SM.33.497)
7014. Wilson, Andrew, b. 1750, tailor, res. Aberdeen, sh. May 1774, fr. Greenock to N.Y., in *George.* (PRO.T47.12)
7015. Wilson, Anne, thief & pickpocket, res. Roxburghshire, tr. Sept 1766, m. David Douglas. (AJ979)
7016. Wilson, Anne, thief, res. Stirling, tr. Sept 1776. (SM.38.675)
7017. Wilson, Barbara, vagrant & thief, res. Banff, tr. June 1773, fr. Glasgow. (AJ1323\8)
7018. Wilson, Charles, mate, res. Coaltown of Balgonie Fife, sh. 1698, fr. Clyde to Darien, in *Olive Branch,* Edin pr1707 CC8.8.83

345

7019. Wilson, David, sailor, res. Wemyss Fife, sh. 14 July 1698, fr. Leith to Darien, in *Caledonia*, Edin pr1707 CC8.8.83
7020. Wilson, David, b. 1701, clerk, res. Edinburgh, sh. June 1721, fr. London to Va. (CLRO\AIA)
7021. Wilson, George, sailor, res. Dysart Fife, pts. James Wilson & Margaret McEwan, sh. 18 Aug 1699, fr. Clyde to Darien, in *Rising Sun*, d. 1699 Darien, Edin pr1707 CC8.8.83
7022. Wilson, George, housebreaker, res. New Deer Aberdeenshire, tr. May 1766, fr. Aberdeen. (AJ958\964) (alias 2264)
7023. Wilson, George, b. 1755, laborer, res. Paisley Renfrewshire, sh. Feb 1774, fr. Greenock to N.Y., in *Commerce*. (PRO.T47.12)
7024. Wilson, Grizel, forger, res. New Galloway Kirkcudbrightshire, tr. July 1754. (SRO.JC3.29.589)
7025. Wilson, Helen, infanticide, res. Didrigg Midcalder Midlothian, tr. Feb 1747. (SRO.JC27)(SRO.HCR.I.73)
7026. Wilson, Henry, Jacobite, tr. 24 May 1716, fr. Liverpool to Md, in *Friendship*, arr. Md Aug 1716. (SPC.1716.311)(HM386)
7027. Wilson, James, vagrant, res. Perth, tr. 13 Aug 1769. (SRO.B59.26.11.6.45)
7028. Wilson, James, Jacobite, tr. 21 Apr 1716, fr. Liverpool to S.C., in *Wakefield*. (SPC.1716.309)(CTB31.205)
7029. Wilson, James, vagrant & thief, res. Dumfries-shire, tr. Apr 1751. (AJ175)
7030. Wilson, James, b. 1712, husbandman, res. Dumfries, sh. Aug 1734, fr. London to Jamaica. (CLRO\AIA)
7031. Wilson, James, b. 1755, laborer, res. Paisley Renfrewshire, sh. Feb 1774, fr. Greenock to N.Y., in *Commerce*. (PRO.T47.12)
7032. Wilson, Jane, b. 1752, spinner, sh. Aug 1774, fr. Whitby to Savannah Ga, in *Marlborough*. (PRO.T47.9\11)
7033. Wilson, Jean, infanticide, res. Ayrshire, tr. May 1752. (AJ228)
7034. Wilson, John, gardener, sheepstealer, res. Edinburgh, tr. July 1769. (SRO.HCR.I.104) (alias 6105)
7035. Wilson, John, bosun, res. Coaltown of Balgonie Fife, sh. 1698, fr. Clyde to Darien, in *Dolphin*, Edin pr1708 CC8.8.84
7036. Wilson, John, b. 1739, farmer, res. Glamis Angus, sh. Apr 1775, fr. Greenock to Salem, in *Glasgow Packet*, ch. Peter. (PRO.T47.12)
7037. Wilson, John, b. 1742, weaver, res. Paisley Renfrewshire, sh. Feb 1774, fr. Greenock to N.Y., in *Commerce*, ch. William James. (PRO.T47.12)
7038. Wilson, John, b. 1754, laborer, res. Colvend Kirkcudbrightshire, sh. 1775, fr. Kirkcudbright to P.E.I., in *Lovely Nelly*. (PRO.T47.12)
7039. Wilson, Joseph, b. 1755, fruiterer, res. Glasgow, sh. Feb 1774, fr. Greenock to N.Y., in *Commerce*. (PRO.T47.12)
7040. Wilson, Maisie, whore, res. Edinburgh, tr. Feb 1697. (SRO.PC2.26)

7041. Wilson, Margaret, spinner, res. Sutherland, sh. Oct 1774, fr. Greenock to Philadelphia, in *Sally*. (PRO.T47.12)
7042. Wilson, Margaret, vagrant, res. Glasgow, pts. George Wilson, tr. Sept 1754, m. ..MacDonald. (SM.16.450)
7043. Wilson, Margaret, vagrant & thief, tr. Sept 1754. (AJ352) (alias 3674)
7044. Wilson, Margaret, b. 1751, res. Glasgow, sh. Apr 1775, fr. Greenock to Salem, in *Glasgow Packet*. (PRO.T47.12)
7045. Wilson, Mary, thief, res. Brechin Angus, tr. Oct 1772, fr. Port Glasgow to Va, in *Phoenix*, arr. Port Accomack Va 20 Dec 1772, m. Charles Stewart. (SRO.JC27.10.3)(AJ1293)
7046. Wilson, Mary, b. 1725, res. Galloway, sh. 1775, fr. Dumfries to P.E.I., in *Lovely Nelly*. (PRO.T47.12)
7047. Wilson, Patrick, writer, illegal marriage, res. Edinburgh, tr. 15 June 1671, fr. Leith, m. (1)Janet Cowle(2)Jean Carmichael. (PC.3.688)
7048. Wilson, Patrick, tr. Nov 1679, fr. Leith. (ETR162)
7049. Wilson, Peter, schoolmaster, clandestine marriage, res. Edinburgh, tr. Mar 1768. (SRO.JC27.10.3)
7050. Wilson, Philip, planter, res. Edinburgh, pts. William Wilson of Soonhope, sh. pre 1777, sett. St Kitts. (SRO.RD4.775.589\RD2.234.787)
7051. Wilson, Richard, judge, d. July 1759 Antigua. (SM.20.557)
7052. Wilson, Robert, res. Edinburgh, pts. William Wilson of Soonhope, d. 29 Aug 1771 St Kitts. (SM.33.614)
7053. Wilson, Robert, sailor, res. Linlithgow West Lothian, pts. James Wilson, sh. 14 July 1698, fr. Leith to Darien, in *St Andrew*, Edin pr1708 CC8.8.84
7054. Wilson, Robert, apothecary & surgeon, res. Burntisland Fife, sh. Sept 1753, fr. London to S.C. (CLRO\AIA)
7055. Wilson, William, tinker, pickpocket, res. Spittal Co Durham, tr. Sept 1766. (AJ979)
7056. Wilson, William, Covenanter, res. Galloway, tr. 5 Sept 1685, fr. Leith to East N.J., in *Henry & Francis*. (PC.11.154)
7057. Wilson, William, thief, res. Hattonslap Aberdeenshire, tr. Sept 1775. (AJ1446)
7058. Wilson, William, horsethief, res. Glasgow, tr. Sept 1775, to West Indies. (SM.37.523)
7059. Wilson, William, b. 1744, weaver, res. Paisley Renfrewshire, sh. Feb 1774, fr. Greenock to N.Y., in *Commerce*. (PRO.T47.12)
7060. Wilson, William, b. 1752, laborer, res. Colvend Kirkcudbrightshire, sh. 1775, fr. Kirkcudbright to P.E.I., in *Lovely Nelly*. (PRO.T47.12)
7061. Windram, Robert, foremastman, res. Leith Midlothian, sh. 14 July 1698, fr. Leith to Darien, in *Caledonia*, Edin pr1707 CC8.8.83
7062. Windwick, Janet, servant, infanticide, res. Grimness South Ronaldsay Orkney Islands, tr. May 1769. (SM.31.333)

7063. Wingate, John, b. 31 July 1741, Kincardine, clergyman edu. Glasgow Uni 1763, pts. Thomas Wingate, sh. 1771, sett. Dale Va. (FPA310)(MAGU71)(EMA64)

7064. Wingate, Joseph, clergyman, sh. 1763, to N.E. (EMA64)

7065. Winstanley, William, weaver, Jacobite, res. Wigan Lancashire, tr. 1747. (MR198)

7066. Winter, Edward, res. Edinburgh, tr. 17 Dec 1685, fr. Leith to Barbados, in *John & Nicholas*, m. Elizabeth McMath. (ETR390)

7067. Winton, David, mate, res. Edinburgh, sh. May 1699, fr. Clyde to Darien, in *Olive Branch*, Edin pr1707 CC8.8.83

7068. Wise, Ninian, b. 1714, laborer, Jacobite, tr. 22 Apr 1747, fr. Liverpool to Va, in *Johnson*, arr. Port Oxford Md 5 Aug 1747. (P.3.406)(PRO.T1.328)

7069. Wishart, Alexander, b. 29 Aug 1725, Montrose Angus, servant, Jacobite, res. Montrose, pts. John Wishart & Isabel Lawson, tr. 19 Mar 1747, fr. London to Jamaica, in *St George or Carteret*, arr. Jamaica 1747. (P.3.400)(PRO.CO137.58)(MR112)

7070. Wishart, Elizabeth, res. Bo'ness West Lothian, pts. George Wishart, sh. pre 1777, sett. N.Y., m. James Roy. (SRO.SH.21.11.1777)(SRO.RD4.773.618)

7071. Wishart, James, res. Mill of Kincardine Kincardineshire, pts. Alexander Wishart, d. pre 1755 Black River Jamaica. (APB.3.182)

7072. Wishart, John, clergyman, sh. 1764, to Va. (EMA64)

7073. Wishart, Margaret, b. 1756, spinner, sh. Aug 1774, fr. London to Quebec, in *Mercury*. (PRO.T47.9\11)

7074. Wishart, Robert, b. 1707, laborer, Jacobite, tr. 1747. (P.3.408)

7075. Wishart, William, Covenanter, tr. 1684, fr. Leith to Carolina. (PC.9.95)

7076. Withards, Michael, sailor, res. Edinburgh, sh. 14 July 1698, fr. Leith to Darien, in *Unicorn*, Edin pr1707 CC8.8.83

7077. Witherington, Richard, Jacobite, tr. 28 July 1716, fr. Liverpool to Va, in *Godspeed*, arr. Md Oct 1716. (SPC.1716.310)(HM389)(CTB.31.209)

7078. Witherspoon, John, b. 1670s, clergyman, res. Glasgow, pts. David Witherspoon, sh. Oct 1727, fr. Glasgow to S.C., sett. James Island & Williamsburg S.C., ch. James, d. 1737. (APC225)(BLG2981)

7079. Witherspoon, John, b. 5 Feb 1722, Gifford East Lothian, clergyman edu. Edinburgh Uni 1739, res. Paisley Renfrewshire, pts. Rev James Witherspoon, sh. pre 1768, sett. Princeton N.J., d. 1794 Princeton. (F.7.666)

7080. Witherspoon, Robert, clergyman edu. Glasgow Uni, sh. 1713, sett. Appoquinimy Pa, d. May 1718. (F.7.666)

7081. Woddrop, William, merchant, res. Edinburgh, pts. John Woddrop, sh. pre 1772, sett. Tappahannock Va. (SRO.SH.22.1.1772)

7082. Wood, Alexander, clergyman, sh. 1707, to Carolina. (EMA64)
7083. Wood, David, b. 1699, laborer, Jacobite, res. Kinneff Kincardineshire, tr. 24 Feb 1747, fr. Liverpool to Va, in *Gildart*, arr. Port North Potomac Md 5 Aug 1747. (P.3.408)(MR112)(PRO.T1.328)
7084. Wood, David, b. 1737, cordiner, sh. Apr 1774, fr. London to Md, in *Diana*. (PRO.T47.9\11)
7085. Wood, Isaac, court marshal, sh. pre 1705, sett. Barbados. (SPC.1705.410)
7086. Wood, James, Jacobite, tr. 29 June 1716, fr. Liverpool to Jamaica or Va, in *Elizabeth & Anne*, arr. York Va. (SPC.1716.310)(CTB31.208)(VSP.1.185)
7087. Wood, Janet, res. Edinburgh, tr. 8 May 1663, fr. Leith to Barbados, in *Mary*. (EBR186.13.4)
7088. Wood, John, res. Edinburgh, sh. pre 1775, sett. St Kitts. (SRO.RD4.227.789)
7089. Wood, John, tr. 7 Dec 1665, fr. Leith to Barbados. (ETR104)
7090. Wood, John, sea captain, res. Greenock Renfrewshire, sh. pre 1773. (SRO.CS.GMB12\73)
7091. Wood, John, b. 1711, tailor, res. Monson Annandale Dumfries-shire, sh. Sept 1731, fr. London to Jamaica. (CLRO\AIA)
7092. Woodrop, William, factor, res. Glasgow, sh. pre 1770, sett. Essex Co Va. (SRA.CFI)
7093. Woodrup, William, merchant & factor, sh. pre 1776, sett. Rappahannock Va. (SRA.CFI)
7094. Woodrup, William, merchant, res. Glasgow, pts. William Woodrup, sett. St Kitts, ch. Margaret Barbara William, d. 15 May 1687, bd. St Anne's Sandy Point St Kitts. (MWI154)
7095. Woods, Andrew, b. 1684, sh. 1724. (BLG2983) (alias 7096)
7096. Woods, Michael, b. 1684, sh. 1724. (BLG2983) (alias 7095)
7097. Woolfe, William, Jacobite, tr. 30 Mar 1716, fr. Liverpool to Antigua, in *Scipio*. (SPC.1716.310)(CTB31.204)
7098. Wotherspoon, Grizzell, Covenanter, tr. 5 Sept 1685, fr. Leith to East N.J., in *Henry & Francis*. (PC.11.155)
7099. Wright, Andrew, b. 1754, laborer, res. Glasgow, sh. Oct 1774, fr. Greenock to Philadelphia, in *Sally*. (PRO.T47.12)
7100. Wright, Archibald, d. 6 Nov 1698 Darien. (NLS.RY.2b8\19)
7101. Wright, Duncan, b. 1707, farmer, Jacobite, res. Appin Argyll, tr. 31 Mar 1747, fr. London to Jamaica, in *St George or Carteret*, arr. Jamaica 1747. (P.3.410)(PRO.CO137.58)(MR207)
7102. Wright, James, sailor, res. Carriden West Lothian, sh. 14 July 1698, fr. Leith to Darien, in *St Andrew*, Edin pr1708 CC8.8.84
7103. Wright, James, b. 1754, cooper, res. Dunbarton, sh. Jan 1774, fr. Greenock to Jamaica, in *Janet*. (SRO.CE60.1.7)

7104. Wright, John, sailor, res. Keith Banffshire, pts. George Wright & Agnes Grant, sh. 14 July 1698, fr. Leith to Darien, in *St Andrew*, Edin pr1733 CC8.8.95

7105. Wright, John, sailor, res. Edinburgh, sh. May 1699, fr. Clyde to Darien, in *Olive Branch*, Edin pr1707 CC8.8.83

7106. Wright, John, Covenanter, tr. Sept 1668, fr. Leith to Va, in *Convertin*. (PC.2.534)

7107. Wright, Robert, b. 1749, tinker, res. Edinburgh, sh. Oct 1774, fr. Greenock to Philadelphia, in *Sally*. (PRO.T47.12)

7108. Wright, William, Jacobite, tr. 29 June 1716, fr. Liverpool to Jamaica or Va, in *Elizabeth & Anne*, arr. York Va. (SPC.1716.310)(CTB31.208)(VSP.1.185)

7109. Wright, William, tr. 1775, in *Aeolis*, arr. Port North Potomac Md 17 Oct 1775. (SRO.JC.27.10.3)

7110. Wright, William, b. 1707, postillion, res. Glasgow, sh. May 1725, fr. London to Pa or Md. (CLRO\AIA)

7111. Wright, William, b. 1751, tinker, res. Edinburgh, sh. Oct 1774, fr. Greenock to Philadelphia, in *Sally*. (PRO.T47.12)

7112. Wyllie, Alexander, sailor, res. Grahamshall Orkney Islands, pts. Alexander Wyllie, sh. 14 July 1698, fr. Leith to Darien, in *Endeavour*, Edin pr1707 CC8.8.83

7113. Wyllie, Thomas, Covenanter, tr. Dec 1685, fr. Leith to Barbados, in *John & Nicholas*. (PC.11.254)(ETR389)

7114. Wyllie, Thomas, b. 1735, weaver, res. Dalry, sh. Aug 1774, fr. Greenock to Philadelphia, in *Magdalene*. (PRO.T47.12)

7115. Wyllie, William, clergyman, res. 'the Highlands', sh. pre 1740, sett. Albemarle Va. (SCHR.14.142)

7116. Yates, Francis, Jacobite, res. Fochabers Morayshire, tr. 24 Feb 1747, fr. Liverpool to Va, in *Gildart*, arr. Port North Potomac Md 5 Aug 1747. (P.3.412)(MR124)(PRO.T1.324)

7117. Yates, William, weaver, Jacobite, res. Clunybeg Banffshire, tr. 1747. (P.3.412)

7118. Yeaman, Francis, Jacobite, tr. 7 May 1716, fr. Liverpool to S.C., in *Susannah*. (SPC.1716.309)(CTB31.206)

7119. Yeaman, Isobel, whore, res. Edinburgh, tr. 19 Mar 1695. (SRO.PC2.25.216)

7120. Yeaman, James, b. 1759, barber, res. Dundee Angus, sh. May 1775, fr. Leith to Philadelphia, in *Friendship*. (PRO.T47.12)

7121. Yeaman, John, farmer, Covenanter, res. Edington Berwickshire, tr. 12 Dec 1678, fr. Leith to West Indies, in *St Michael of Scarborough*. (PC.6.76)

7122. Yeaman, William, farmer, Covenanter, res. Edington Berwickshire, tr. 12 Dec 1685, fr. Leith to West Indies, in *St Michael of Scarborough*. (PC.6.76)

7123. Yeates, Benjamin, b. 1702, Berwick, sh. 9 Apr 1720, fr. London to Va. (CLRO\AIA)
7124. Yeates, William, weaver, Jacobite, res. Clunybeggs Banffshire, tr. 22 Apr 1747, fr. Liverpool to Va, in *Johnson*, arr. POrt North Potomac Md 5 Aug 1747. (MR124)(JAB.2.447)(PRO.T1.328)
7125. Yorston, Mary, thief & vagabond, res. Roxburghshire, tr. May 1732. (SRO.JC.12.4) (alias 104)
7126. Yorstoun, Janet, gypsy, res. Roxburghshire, tr. 1 Jan 1715, fr. Glasgow to Va. (GR530)
7127. Young, Alexander, vagrant & thief, res. Banff, tr. June 1773, fr. Glasgow. (AJ1323\5)
7128. Young, Alexander, b. 1749, wright, res. Glasgow, sh. May 1774, fr. Greenock to N.Y., in *Matty*. (PRO.T47.12)
7129. Young, Alexander, b. 1755, tailor, res. Glasgow, sh. Oct 1774, fr. Greenock to Philadelphia, in *Sally*. (PRO.T47.12)
7130. Young, Andrew, b. 1735, farmer, res. Stirling, sh. May 1775, fr. Greenock to N.Y., in *Monimia*, m. Mary .., ch. James Katherine John William. (PRO.T47.12)
7131. Young, Betty, thief, res. Stirling, tr. Sept 1776. (SM.38.675)
7132. Young, Charles, res. Stirling, sh. 1698, to Darien. (RBS.343)
7133. Young, Charles, surgeon's mate, res. Kippen Stirlingshire, pts. Rev Robert Young & Margaret McFarlane, sh. 14 July 1698, fr. Leith to Darien, in *St Andrew*, Edin pr1707 C8.8.83
7134. Young, David, planter, sett. Grenada, d. pre 1783. (SRO.SH.2.4.1783)
7135. Young, Elizabeth, b. 1755, servant, res. Edinburgh, sh. May 1775, fr. Leith to Philadelphia, in *Friendship*. (PRO.T47.12)
7136. Young, George, res. Stonehaven Kincardineshire, tr. June 1767, fr. Greenock. (SRO.B59.26.11.6.32)
7137. Young, George, housebreaker, res. Stonehaven Kincardineshire, tr. May 1767. (AJ1011)
7138. Young, George, sorner, res. Aberdeen, tr. Mar 1751. (AJ169)
7139. Young, George, Covenanter, res. Teviotdale Roxburghshire, tr. Aug 1685, fr. Leith to Jamaica, arr. Port Royal Jamaica Nov 1685. (PC.11.329)(LJ17)
7140. Young, James, sailor, d. 27 Nov 1698 Darien. (NLS.RY2b8\19)
7141. Young, James, merchant, res. Glasgow, sh. pre 1745, sett. Va. (SRA.CFI)
7142. Young, James, Covenanter, res. Irvine Ayrshire, tr. 1679. (Irvine Gs)
7143. Young, James, foremastman, res. Abbotshall Fife, sh. 14 July 1698, fr. Leith to Darien, in *Caledonia*, Edin pr1707 CC8.8.83
7144. Young, James, counterfeiter, res. Stirling, tr. 19 June 1754. (SRO.JC3.29.574)(SRO.HCR.I.87)
7145. Young, James, vagrant & thief, res. Banff, tr. May 1773. (AJ1322)

7146. Young, James, tr. Mar 1751, fr. Aberdeen to Va or West Indies, in *Adventure of Aberdeen*. (AJ170)
7147. Young, James, farmer, fireraiser, res. Home Berwickshire, tr. Oct 1748. (SM.10.499)
7148. Young, James, Covenanter, res. Netherfield Avondale Lanarkshire, tr. Aug 1685, fr. Leith to Jamaica. (PC.11.129)(ETR373)
7149. Young, James, b. 1751, laborer, res. Glasgow, sh. Feb 1774, fr. Greenock to N.Y., in *Commerce*. (PRO.T47.12)
7150. Young, John, assault, tr. Mar 1751. (SRO.HCR.I.82)
7151. Young, John, thief, tr. 5 Aug 1668, fr. Leith. (PC.2.513)
7152. Young, John, Covenanter, res. Eaglesham Kirk Renfrewshire, tr. June 1684, fr. Clyde, in *Pelican*. (PC.9.208)
7153. Young, John, soldier, thief, res. Roxburghshire, tr. Oct 1749. (SM.11.509)
7154. Young, Magnus, b. 1692, Ross-shire, husbandman, Jacobite, res. Aberdeen, tr. 31 Mar 1747, fr. London to Jamaica, in *St George or Carteret*, arr. Jamaica 1747. (P.3.412)(PRO.CO137.58)
7155. Young, Margaret, thief, res. Roxburghshire, tr. Oct 1749, m. John Young. (SM.11.509)
7156. Young, Mark, Covenanter, res. Barnhills Roxburghshire, tr. Oct 1684. (PC.9.449)
7157. Young, Patrick, sailor, res. Edinburgh, sh. May 1699, fr. Clyde to Darien, in *Olive Branch*, Edin pr1707 CC8.8.83
7158. Young, Robert, physician, Jacobite, res. Tipparary, tr. 1747. (P.3.412)(MR136)
7159. Young, Robert, tr. Nov 1679, fr. Leith. (ETR162)
7160. Young, Robert, Covenanter, res. Goodsburn Avondale Lanarkshire, tr. 5 Sept 1685, fr. Leith to East N.J., in *Henry & Francis*. (PC.11.154)
7161. Young, Robert, Jacobite, tr. 21 Apr 1716, fr. Liverpool to S.C., in *Wakefield*. (SPC.1716.309)(CTB31.205)
7162. Young, Robert, vagabond & robber, res. Annandale Dumfries-shire, tr. 1671(?). (PC.3.428)
7163. Young, Robert, b. 1741, carpenter, res. Edinburgh, sh. Dec 1773, fr. London to Dominica, in *Greyhound*. (PRO.T47.9\11)
7164. Young, Thomas, customs officer, assault, res. Bo'ness West Lothian, tr. 1771, in *St Vincent Planter*, arr. St Vincent 4 Feb 1772. (SM.33.497)(SRO.JC27.10.3)
7165. Young, Thomas, b. 1725, Jacobite, res. Martin Loch Broom Ross-shire, tr. 31 Mar 1747, fr. London to Barbados, in *Frere*. (P.3.414)(MR88)
7166. Young, Thomas, b. 1753, surgeon, res. Glasgow, sh. Aug 1774, fr. Greenock to Wilmington N.C., in *Ulysses*. (PRO.T47.12)

7167. Young, William, planter, sh. pre 1766, sett. Carricou Grenada. (SRO.RD3.239.161)

7168. Young, William, res. Glasgow, pts. James Young, sh. pre 1749, sett. Northampton Va. (SRO.SH.22.5.1749)

7169. Young, William, sheepstealer, res. Kelty Fife, tr. May 1774. (AJ1377)

7170. Young, William, Jacobite, tr. 30 Mar 1716, fr. Liverpool to Antigua, in *Scipio*. (SPC.1716.310)(CTB31.204)

7171. Young, William, Jacobite, tr. 31 July 1716, fr. Liverpool to Va, in *Anne*. (SPC.1716.310)(CTB31.209)

7172. Younger, James, sailor, res. Bo'ness West Lothian, sh. 14 July 1698, fr. Leith to Darien, in *Caledonia*, ch. Janet, d. America, Edin pr1707 CC8.8.83

7173. Younger, John, thief, tr. 1653, fr. Ayr to Barbados. (SRO.JC27.10.3)

7174. Younger, William, tr. Nov 1679, fr. Leith. (ETR162)

7175. Younghusband, John, sh. 1737, fr. Inverness to Ga, in *Two Brothers*. (SPC.43.161)

7176. Yuill, Alexander, b. 1747, wright, res. Glasgow, sh. Feb 1774, fr. Greenock to N.Y., in *Commerce*. (PRO.T47.12)

7177. Yuill, Elspeth, res. Edinburgh, tr. 8 May 1663, fr. Leith to Barbados, in *Mary*. (EBR.186.13.4)

7178. Yuille, John, merchant, res. Glasgow, sh. pre 1745, sett. Va. (SRA.B10.15.5959)

7179. Yuille, John, b. 1719, merchant, res. Dunbartonshire, pts. Thomas Yuille of Darleith, d. 1746 Williamsburg Va. (SRA.CFI)

7180. Yule, James, merchant, res. Strathaven Lanarkshire, pts. Claud Yule, sh. pre 1773, sett. Boston Mass, m. Jean Baillie. (SRO.RS42.15.96)

Ships

Abraham of London 723
Active 1762
Adventure 1494, 2236,
2310, 2699, 2841,
3129, 3246, 3272,
3353, 4279, 4558,
4627, 4721, 4751,
4852, 5600, 6235,
6322, 6323, 6324
Adventure of Aberdeen
1648, 2388, 7146
Aeolis 3038, 3740,
7109
Africa 2902
Ajax 3780, 4937
Amelia 4055
America 2265, 5551
Amherst 649
Amity's Desire 743,
744
Ann 5924, 6261, 6666,
6946
Ann of Aberdeen 3015
Anne 520, 628, 629,
648, 1064, 1354,
1811, 1868, 2337,
3390, 3392, 3398,
3866, 3985, 5261,
5262, 5270, 6177,
7171
Anne & Hester 3048
Assistance 1754, 1761,
4971
Augustus 2969
Aurora 383, 873, 952,
1306, 3191, 5755
Bachelor of Leith 268,
851, 888, 908,

1051, 1676, 2308,
2409, 2545, 3405,
3613, 3620, 3625,
3704, 4036, 4047,
4051, 4070, 4072,
4073, 4449, 4505,
4867, 4869, 5093,
5095, 5129, 5136,
5900, 5906, 6150,
6163, 6593, 6594
Baltimore 492, 1722
Barbados Merchant
6010
Beith 3805, 6693
Bellar 6839, 6843
Betsey 5820
Betsy 4, 621, 5526,
6619
Blossom 1382, 3857,
4301, 6167
Boston 5106
Boston Merchant 5518
Boston Packet 2664
Boyd 1024, 4810, 4854
Brilliant 242, 1125,
1181, 2158, 2480,
2819, 3264, 3333,
3584, 3637, 3810,
4788, 5343, 5460,
6231, 6668
Bristol Merchant 6902
Britannia 379
Briton 1572
Brothers 6479
Brothers Adventure 542
Caledonia 14, 293,
303, 309, 393,
410, 442, 482,

702, 755, 756,
1021, 1147, 1209,
1250, 1507, 1510,
1602, 1853, 1921,
1937, 2016, 2151,
2163, 2181, 2203,
2589, 2651, 2701,
2710, 2882, 2988,
3110, 3130, 3144,
3209, 3323, 3339,
3522, 4186, 4274,
4572, 4773, 4863,
4990, 5232, 5291,
5302, 5341, 5404,
5405, 5449, 5794,
5942, 6000, 6035,
6345, 6568, 6596,
6735, 6768, 6818,
6837, 6846, 6884,
6892, 6921, 6925,
6960, 6993, 6999,
7019, 7061, 7143,
7172
Carolina 1695, 2230,
3283
Carolina Merchant 678,
1357, 3275, 5103,
6341, 6732, 6797
Catherine of Glasgow
1291
Chance 1187, 2055,
4259, 6024, 6420
Charles of Glasgow
1303, 2565
Charming Nancy 2299
Charming Peggy 1443,
1463
Christie 4034

Christy 73, 134, 137,
149, 153, 321,
327, 430, 673,
1247, 1405, 1515,
1539, 1844, 2755,
2832, 2846, 3320,
3355, 3419, 3671,
3750, 3751, 3778,
3798, 3846, 4379,
4403, 4910, 5450,
5484, 5667, 6196,
6825
Clementina 169, 217,
232, 574, 588,
781, 782, 790,
793, 813, 828,
833, 836, 903,
1085, 1127, 1155,
1641, 1880, 1881,
1882, 1883, 1884,
1945, 1951, 1973,
2009, 2022, 2025,
2026, 2041, 2045,
2046, 2061, 2706,
2732, 2928, 2930,
2931, 3044, 3051,
3057, 3061, 3062,
3066, 3078, 3083,
3086, 3087, 3163,
3500, 3501, 3502,
3527, 3567, 3568,
3590, 3591, 3592,
3593, 3609, 3618,
3621, 3622, 3629,
3630, 3635, 3636,
3677, 3680, 3681,
3708, 3749, 3928,
3929, 4032, 4037,
4056, 4075, 4118,
4119, 4125, 4127,
4128, 4148, 4159,
4178, 4179, 4180,
4201, 4207, 4208,
4221, 4223, 4227,
4228, 4229, 4240,
4258, 4260, 4423,
4424, 4425, 4426,
4445, 4446, 4488,

4495, 4615, 4617,
4619, 4620, 4621,
4623, 4633, 4648,
4651, 4652, 4654,
4659, 4663, 4687,
4691, 4695, 4708,
5055, 5063, 5109,
5143, 5144, 5150,
5151, 5154, 5169,
5231, 5238, 5580,
5581, 5582, 5727,
5807, 5855, 5940,
6064, 6081, 6158,
6168, 6170, 6362,
6588, 6645, 6713,
6723, 6753, 6804,
6898, 6904
Commerce 9, 24, 25,
26, 27, 49, 52, 56,
95, 103, 272, 334,
347, 384, 407,
440, 472, 484,
509, 555, 569,
664, 726, 749,
750, 778, 871,
955, 967, 983,
1138, 1199, 1200,
1211, 1274, 1293,
1297, 1331, 1332,
1394, 1564, 1568,
1620, 1642, 1643,
1644, 1716, 1721,
1771, 1845, 1855,
1926, 2161, 2173,
2176, 2217, 2559,
2560, 2561, 2562,
2563, 2564, 2649,
2650, 2746, 2785,
2796, 2830, 2875,
2959, 3018, 3059,
3152, 3194, 3241,
3285, 3358, 3366,
3369, 3370, 3374,
3376, 3436, 3506,
3523, 3545, 3546,
3547, 3548, 3550,
3551, 3552, 3614,
3731, 3773, 3774,

3868, 3878, 3994,
4012, 4087, 4121,
4309, 4317, 4341,
4434, 4484, 4485,
4515, 4516, 4517,
4518, 4521, 4523,
4577, 4578, 4580,
4582, 4584, 4585,
4588, 4589, 4600,
4694, 4736, 4737,
4738, 4739, 4748,
4768, 4880, 4985,
5000, 5211, 5213,
5215, 5220, 5235,
5241, 5242, 5243,
5247, 5293, 5297,
5308, 5314, 5417,
5420, 5422, 5436,
5455, 5482, 5485,
5604, 5625, 5632,
5671, 5677, 5723,
5766, 5825, 5947,
5981, 5993, 6021,
6022, 6107, 6123,
6187, 6201, 6238,
6266, 6291, 6292,
6293, 6294, 6311,
6313, 6338, 6393,
6485, 6532, 6569,
6633, 6634, 6669,
6696, 6711, 6742,
6831, 6833, 6835,
6860, 6871, 6979,
7011, 7023, 7031,
7037, 7039, 7059,
7149, 7176
Concord 455, 1183
Concord of Glasgow
5634, 6816
Conquer 4243
Convertin 20, 126,
436, 659, 1869,
2521, 5972, 7106
Countess 367, 445,
607, 882, 1031,
1056, 1220, 1878,
2697, 2978, 5438,
5439, 5539, 5841,

359

Henry & Francis
(continued) 6989,
7056, 7098, 7160
Henry of Newcastle
1701, 2728, 5704
Hockenhill 310, 359,
796, 799, 802,
1077, 1092, 1197,
1309, 1409, 1431,
2118, 2646, 2726,
2761, 3226, 3493,
4257, 4355, 4639,
5037, 5287, 5290,
5389, 5397, 5406,
5605, 5618, 5712,
5821, 6488, 6612
Hope 494, 1404, 1957,
2099, 4837, 5059,
5490, 5597, 6648
Hope & Rising Sun 918
Hope of Edinburgh
2155, 5588
Hopewell 2266
Hound 1441
Industry 6033, 6185
Isabella 65, 155, 962,
1308, 1348, 1429,
1738, 2812, 2929,
4390, 4955, 5013,
5352, 5754, 5904,
6781
Isobella 2044, 2912,
3282, 4048, 6497
Jackie 5, 1213, 1215,
1273, 1434, 1456,
1457, 1636, 1743,
2855, 3408, 3410,
3504, 4275, 4299,
4537, 4538, 4540,
4541, 4709, 4756,
4767, 4868, 4901,
5031, 6189, 6355,
6356, 6358, 6359,
6554, 6830
Jamaica 658, 676, 861,
890, 1074, 1717,
2043, 3102, 4885,
5251

Jamaica Packet 1501,
1585, 1616, 1879,
2148, 2289, 2768,
2956, 3012, 3218,
3279, 4821, 5011,
5012, 5061, 7002
Jamaica Planter 536,
6981
James 1423, 1974,
4902
James of Ayr 446,
1044, 1045, 1473,
1834, 2078, 2079,
2192, 2594, 2859,
2860, 5008, 5108,
5124, 5205, 5248,
5506, 5992, 6245,
6874, 6903
Janet 2941, 5097,
5210, 5828, 6644,
6949, 7103
Jean & Elizabeth of
Aberdeen 662
Jean of Largs 3329,
6873
Jenny 5780
John & Alexander 5101
John & Elizabeth 2116
John & Nicholas 143,
191, 1022, 1393,
2066, 2067, 2145,
2354, 2737, 2780,
2814, 2857, 3224,
4030, 5237, 5446,
5457, 5486, 5591,
5664, 6283, 6289,
7066, 7113
John & Robert 1502,
6242
John & Thomas 6788,
6789, 6793
Johnson 98, 195, 400,
401, 502, 669,
724, 784, 787,
797, 815, 819,
820, 841, 844,
968, 1017, 1065,
1072, 1106, 1201,

1263, 1279, 1367,
1453, 1476, 1635,
1839, 1843, 1866,
1979, 2119, 2378,
2385, 2439, 2498,
2623, 2700, 2754,
2911, 2918, 3120,
3427, 3454, 3486,
3498, 3534, 3536,
3537, 3538, 3588,
3639, 3732, 3747,
3784, 3818, 3863,
3873, 3874, 3877,
3920, 3923, 3941,
3956, 3989, 3992,
4038, 4122, 4331,
4385, 4450, 4458,
4565, 4700, 4701,
4705, 4766, 4808,
4928, 4966, 5132,
5133, 5255, 5288,
5301, 5319, 5366,
5531, 5707, 5783,
5786, 5911, 5936,
6083, 6084, 6134,
6206, 6295, 6339,
6492, 6539, 6571,
6642, 6655, 6744,
6829, 6885, 6888,
6923, 7068, 7124
Joseph & Mary 3082
Jupiter 420, 431, 433,
981, 1005, 1006,
1007, 1008, 1009,
1609, 1611, 3426,
3461, 3462, 3463,
3464, 3465, 3466,
3594, 3919, 3986,
3993, 3998, 4002,
4009, 4010, 4338,
4340, 4350, 4352,
4603, 4604, 4731,
6151, 6388, 6389,
6392, 6413, 6458,
6467
Katherine of London
1292
Leathly 2452, 6544

Monimia (continued)
1972, 1977, 2531,
2662, 2722, 2730,
2868, 3297, 3357,
3409, 3665, 3754,
3977, 3999, 4295,
4642, 4643, 4647,
5126, 5234, 5236,
5374, 5384, 5805,
5838, 5927, 6436,
6697, 7130
Montrose of Aberdeen
6927
Moore of Greenock
2473
Nancy 2679, 3029,
5584, 5781
Nautilus 4503
Nelly Frigate 4380
Neptune 3255, 5513
Olive Branch 317, 705,
2574, 2938, 3259,
6772, 7018, 7067,
7105, 7157
Peace & Plenty 262,
2358, 2362, 2484,
3511, 3512, 4120,
4123, 4175, 4176,
4202, 4204, 4206,
4233, 4241, 4242,
4265, 4267, 4404,
4437, 4494, 4498,
4501, 4844, 4848,
5146, 5462, 6577
Peace and Plenty 772,
834
Peggy 251
Peggy Stewart 3667
Pelican 70, 76, 423,
661, 686, 1383,
1509, 1713, 2107,
2167, 2773, 3109,
3352, 3453, 3887,
4820, 4828, 5350,
5479, 6224, 6269,
6614, 6615, 6618,
6801, 7152

Pelican of Glasgow
1712, 1747, 2628,
2894, 3343, 5922
Phoenix 2389, 2505,
2709, 2856, 3222,
3367, 6439, 7045
Phoenix of Leith 1452,
3174, 5392, 6103
Planter 714, 2128,
2260, 2661, 3056,
3321, 5018, 6353
Plough 3030
Polly 1709, 2365,
4915
Portsmouth Galley 2797
Providence 17
Rainbow 63, 582, 974,
1986, 3155, 4412,
4457, 4471, 5003,
5207, 6399, 6411
Richard & Sarah 4946
Rising Sun 34, 244,
266, 299, 329,
757, 845, 915,
972, 1129, 1144,
1192, 1245, 1288,
1295, 1542, 1567,
1626, 2102, 2150,
2162, 2171, 2468,
2530, 2534, 2548,
2611, 2647, 2691,
2729, 2782, 2787,
2825, 2874, 2888,
2892, 3229, 3261,
3280, 3315, 3344,
3383, 3788, 3860,
4602, 4873, 4913,
4926, 4959, 5069,
5083, 5200, 5503,
5525, 5537, 5623,
5702, 5976, 6012,
6029, 6125, 6143,
6165, 6188, 6314,
6315, 6335, 6365,
6515, 6610, 6616,
6714, 6734, 6739,
6790, 6824, 6879,
6950, 6987, 7021

Ross 474, 624, 1290,
1765, 3106, 3766,
4296
Royal Charlotte 1876
Ruby of Greenock 3467
Russia Merchant 5621
Sally 1081, 1103,
1321, 1624, 1902,
2103, 2120, 2376,
2469, 2525, 2631,
2850, 3304, 3319,
3326, 3459, 4374,
4805, 4866, 5027,
5048, 5190, 5265,
5303, 5714, 5756,
5916, 6096, 6142,
6484, 6582, 6601,
6782, 6928, 7041,
7099, 7107, 7111,
7129
Sampson 6530
Scipio 216, 219, 298,
300, 409, 457,
550, 551, 734,
916, 919, 992,
1251, 1265, 1355,
1356, 1497, 1562,
1628, 1640, 1685,
1727, 1773, 1848,
1975, 2030, 2125,
2212, 2223, 2311,
2578, 2828, 2847,
3071, 3100, 3268,
3338, 3479, 3487,
3497, 3533, 3544,
3601, 3841, 3970,
3972, 3983, 3984,
4090, 4334, 4337,
4344, 4345, 4415,
4428, 4636, 4681,
4707, 4923, 4961,
5165, 5272, 5326,
5342, 5432, 5571,
5640, 5710, 5711,
5719, 5735, 5736,
5740, 5745, 5749,
5761, 5771, 5886,
5968, 6017, 6034,

Spouses

369

Milligan, William 5004
Moffat, Jean 2033
Moore, Rebecca 6274
Morgan, Elizabeth 1804
Morine, James 4944
Morrison, Elizabeth
 6653
Morrison, Margaret 850
Morton, Alexander
 5670
Mowat, Alexander 5333
Murchison, ... 4158
Murray, Dorothy 1954
Murray, Hendrea 4422
Murray, John 4124
Murray, Margaret 4497
Napier, Margaret 1102
Neish, Janet 1583
Ord, John 2101
Orrock, Marion 755
Palmer, ... 3973
Park, Elizabeth jean
 6515
Paterson, William 5467
Peters, Thomas 691
Podgson, Mary 5791
Pottle, Mary 2800
Proctor, Elizabeth 2792
Purdy, Katherine 4572
Randolph, Mary Ishan
 3033
Rattoun, Christine 1166
Ritch, Elizabeth 5359
Robertson, Euphan
 1937
Robertson, Isobel 4515
Robertson, Katherine
 4577
Robertson, Margaret
 3310
Roddan, Agnes 750
Ross, Alexander 1932
Ross, Mary 6301
Roy, James 7070

Russell, ... 4801
Russell, Anne 1141
Ryall, Isaac 3943
Sands, Margaret 1101
Schuyler, Maria Walter
 3063
Scoon, Agnes 6281
Scott, Janet 6846
Scott, Mary 5988
Shaw, R 5955
Shearer, Patricia 2327
Simpson, Isobel 4597
Simpson, Margaret
 1990
Simpson, Rachel 5426
Sinclair, Elizabeth 4799
Smeal, ... 6223
Smith, Christian 403
Smith, Elizabeth 5558,
 6921
Spowart, Janet 5193
Stewart, Charles 7045
Stewart, Daniel 5279
Stuart, Sally 2338
Sturgeon, Janet 6250
Sword, Euphan 6762
Tarrant, Mary 5863
Tasie, Janet 1972
Taylor, Agnes 2546
Taylor, Marion 2184
Taylor, Mary 4546
Thomson, Jean 6128
Thorborn, Margaret
 4767
Tod, George 4909
Tod, Margaret 6999
Trail, Eleanor 6762
Tucker, ... 3096
Walker, Alexander 2744
Walker, Ann 3994
Wallace, ... 2065
Waterstone, Katherine
 1580
Watson, Margaret 725

Weir, Marion 2871,
 5838
Welman, Elizabeth
 5208
Whitefield, ... 5983
Wilkie, Ann 1130
Wilkie, Rachel 4929
Wilson, Janet 6711
Wilson, Margaret 1021
Wilson, Mary 4927
Wilson, William 6469
Winram, Isabel 4929
Winston, Sallie 5964
Wishart, Elizabeth 5928
Woodrop, Helen 1046
Wright, Isobel 3707
Yeaman, Elizabeth 5559
Young, John 7155
Young, Margaret 1322
Young, Mary 5678